Áquila Mazzinghy

# Beyond a Reasonable Doubt

# Religious Freedom Series (IIRF)

## Volume 7

Áquila Mazzinghy

# BEYOND A REASONABLE DOUBT

## Did the Islamic State commit genocide against Christians in Iraq?

Verlag für Kultur und Wissenschaft
Culture and Science Publ.
Dr. Thomas Schirrmacher
Bonn 2023

**Bibliographic information published by the Deutsche Nationalbibliothek**

The Deutsche Nationalbibliothek lists this publication in the Deutsche Nationalbibliografie; detailed bibliographic data are available on the Internet at http://dnb.d-nb.de

ISSN 1995-011X
ISBN 978-3-86269-267-5

Cover motif: Fernanda Leão

Printed in Germany

Cover design:
HCB Verlagsservice Beese, Hamburg

Production:
CPI Books / www.cpi-print.de

Complete directory for the book trade: www.vkwonline.com
Publishing distribution: info@vkwonline.com or Fax +49 / 228 / 9650389

Private customers: in any book store or at www.vkwonline.com

# Contents – Overview

# Contents – in Detail

# Abstract

The self-proclaimed Islamic State in Iraq and the Levant (ISIL/DAESH) occupied large parts of Iraq from 2014 to 2017. During this time, ISIL/DAESH members committed grave violations of International Criminal Law and International Humanitarian Law. In March 2015, an OHCHR (the Office of the United Nations High Commissioner for Human Rights) mission field investigation in Iraq reported on "reliable information about acts of violence perpetrated against civilians because of their affiliation or perceived affiliation to a religious group" (A/HRC/28/18). This book was particularly focused on the violations of international criminal law that ISIL/DAESH perpetrated against the religious group of Christians in Iraq.

This book's main goal was to determine the legal nature, typification of, and criminal responsibility for these violations. In this case study, the author attempted to determine whether the *actus reus* and the perpetrators *mens rea* behind this criminal conduct fall under the definition of genocide, as prescribed by the Rome Statute, or fall under the crime of persecution, as a crime against humanity, as defined in the Rome Statute – *the test of equal gravity.* To address these issues, the author explored a vast body of literature and provided the reader with a detailed, methodical, and scrutinized account of the major criminal acts that ISIL/DAESH perpetrated against civilians in Iraq, focusing on the violations against Christians.

The author also legally assessed the factual matrix of human rights and humanitarian law violations in the case-law from the Nuremberg, the ICTR, the ICTY, the SCSL, and ICC tribunals. In the Conclusion, the author presents the reader with possible judicial models to hold ISIL/DAESH fighters accountable for their violations of international criminal law. This research contributes to the current literature on genocide and persecution as a crime against humanity.

**KEY-WORDS:** Genocide; Crimes Against Humanity; Religious Persecution; ISIL; DAESH; Christians in Iraq.

To all the victims of the ISIL/DAESH:
May justice and healing shine upon them as the noonday sun.

# Dedication

This book is dedicated:

**To my dad, Lino, and to my mom, Maria,**

for their unconditional love, dedication, sacrifice, encouragement, reassuring words, constant prayers, and valuable advice throughout my entire life. Their lives have been a constant source of support during the research and writing of this book. For many times, many days, when life felt like a rollercoaster, they were always ready to embrace my sorrows and make me feel stronger. To them, my heartfelt gratitude and love.[1]

---

[1]     Ao meu pai, Lino, e à minha mãe, Maria, por seu amor incondicional, dedicação, sacrifícios, encorajamento, palavras de afirmação, constantes orações, e conselhos valiosos durante toda a minha vida. Vocês foram uma fonte constante de suporte durante todas as fases de escrita desta Tese de Doutorado. Muitas vezes, em muitos dias, quando minha vida na Turquia parecia estar numa montanha russa, vocês sempre estiveram prontos para abraçar minhas fraquezas e me fazer sentir forte, mesmo nesta distância oceânica do Brasil. Minha dedicação a vocês, minha fonte constante de gratidão, dívida, e amor.

# Acknowledgements

This book is the result of my Ph.D. Thesis, which was written from 2020 to 2021. So, first, I would like to thank Prof. Dr. Murat Önok for being my advisor during my Ph.D. studies at Koç University in Turkey. From our very first meeting preceding my enrolment in the doctoral program, he has been a source of inspiration and courage. In the face of my challenging personal health circumstances, he has patiently and generously assisted me throughout his classes, supported my long and arduous doctoral project, and encouraged me in my personal life. His immense knowledge, education, courtesy, and scholarship make him a brilliant and very tough professor at the same time. He has never lowered his academic threshold, but his confidence in me assured me that I could finish his very demanding disciplines with excellence and success. I am very grateful that he agreed to supervise this project. His scholarly contributions, insightful comments, stewardship, rigor, mentorship, patience, support, and trust guided every aspect of the writing and completion of this book, and is highly appreciated.

I also want to thank Professor Dr. Bertil Emrah Oder, Dean of Koç University Law School, for her helpful advice, time, support, and encouragement, provided when much needed. I am deeply thankful for the Koç family in Turkey for the doctoral scholarship and financial support I received throughout my doctorate, which made the writing of this book possible. I am also thankful to all my professors at Koç University, for the dedication, kindness, advice, encouragement, and shared knowledge. I heartfelt thank Professor Dr. Başak Çalı for her guidance and cooperation at each step of my Ph.D. journey.

I am immensely thankful for the administrative support that I received throughout my time at Koç University. In particular, I would like to thank Esra Özcan, Funda Mürekepçi, Melissa Abache, Mert Şanıvar, Nilüfer Akpınar, Seda Akçakoca, Semra Tiryaki, Tuğçe Şatana, and Zeynep Koçer, for offering their time, skills, experience, compassion, solutions, positive words, and personal friendship.

I would never have been able to finish this book without the tireless support of medical doctors and therapists who have been by my side throughout the serious health storms I have been facing in the last decade. I want to thank them for every miracle they brought to my life, their time, professionalism, their compassionate attention, and altruism. Thank you, Özge Kılıç, Gustavo Maia Marques, and Aurélio M. Péres.

Like all major and challenging accomplishments in my life, completing this book would not have been possible without the love, support, smiles, comfort, kindness, prayers, songs, and words of my closest friends, to whom I also dedicate this victory.

I would also like to thank my colleagues of the Ph.D. Program at the Koç Law School, for their friendship, generous support, conversations, laughs, for sharing their personal experiences, and the long time spent together in academic assignments. They touched and influenced my life in several ways. I am grateful for having learned from Irina Crivets's courage amidst hardship, Arina Kostina's resilience throughout the long Ph.D. journey, Hoitsimolimo Mutlokwa's contentment in all circumstances, Betul Durmus's passion for academic life, Ezgi Arik's willingness to help, Matteo Mastracci's simplicity, İlayda Eskitaşcioğlu's brilliant intelligence, Asylai Akisheva's poetic insight into simple facts of daily life, Esra Öğünç's love for her family, Ezel Buse's musicality, and Sevi Kayikchi's joy.

In addition, I want to thank my current and former students from different universities for their patience, friendship, and joy.

I especially want to thank my former professors in Brazil, Jamile Bergamaschine Mata Diz, Roberta Guerra, Wagner Inácio Freitas Dias, and Patrícia Aurélia Del Nero. For almost twenty years, their support, encouraging words, trust, and friendship have been fundamental to my personal and professional growth and helped me press on even when I thought I could not achieve my goals.

To the love of my life, my wife Maria, for her companionship, friendship, love, prayers, laughs and tears, for her ever-present support, and for being at my side throughout the writing and completion of this book.

Above all, I thank my God, my Lord, my father, my helper, my constant friend, the rock of my life, my strength, the one to whom I give all the glory and praise for this achievement, for his grace, sustenance, and love.

# Table of abbreviations, acronyms, and correspondences

| Term | Meaning |
|---|---|
| ACHR | American Convention on Human Rights |
| AFRC | Armed Forces Revolutionary Council |
| AP I | Additional Protocol I to the 1949 Geneva Conventions (1977) |
| AP II | Additional Protocol II to the 1949 Geneva Conventions (1977) |
| AP III | Additional Protocol III to the 1949 Geneva Conventions (2005) |
| Apr. | April |
| AU | African Union |
| Aug. | August |
| CA 3 | Common Article 3 to the Geneva Conventions |
| CAT | Convention Against Torture and Other Cruel, Inhuman or Degrading Treatment or Punishment |
| CCT | Counter-Terrorism Committee |
| CEDAW | Convention on the Elimination of all Forms of Discrimination Against Women |
| CEDAW Committee | United Nations Committee on the Elimination of Discrimination Against Women |
| CERD | United Nations Committee on the Elimination of Racial Discrimination |
| CoE | Council of Europe |
| Counter-ISIL Coalition | Global Coalition to Defeat ISIL |
| CRC | Convention on the Rights of the Child |
| CTED | Counter-Terrorism Committee Executive Directorate |
| CTITF | Counter-Terrorism Implementation Task Force |

| Daesh | ad-Dawlah al-Islāmiyah fı 'l-'Irāq wa-sh-Shām |
|---|---|
| Darfur Commission | International Commission of Inquiry on Darfur |
| Dec. | December |
| ECHR | European Convention on Human Rights (European Convention for the Protection of Human Rights and Fundamental Freedoms) |
| ECOMOG | The Economic Community of West African States Monitoring Group |
| EU | European Union |
| Eur. Ct. H.R. | European Court of Human Rights |
| Eur. Parl. | European Parliament |
| Feb. | February |
| FTF(s) | Foreign Terrorist Fighter(s) |
| G. A. Res. | United Nations General Assembly Resolution |
| GCs | Geneva Conventions |
| Genocide Convention | Convention for the Prevention and Punishment of the Crime of Genocide |
| H.R. | United States House of Representatives |
| H.R.Con.Res. | United States House of Representatives concurrent resolution |
| Ibidem | Exactly the same citation/reference |
| ICC | International Criminal Court |
| ICC Statute | Rome Statute of the International Criminal Court |
| ICCPR | International Covenant on Civil and Political Rights |
| ICERD | International Convention on the Elimination of all forms of Racial Discrimination |
| ICESCR | International Covenant on Economic Social and Cultural Rights |
| ICJ | International Court of Justice |
| ICRC | International Committee of the Red Cross |
| ICTR | International Criminal Tribunal for Rwanda |

| | |
|---|---|
| **ICTR Statute** | Statute of the International Criminal Tribunal for Rwanda |
| **ICTY** | International Tribunal for the Prosecution of Persons Responsible for Serious Violations of International Humanitarian Law Committed in the Territory of the Former Yugoslavia |
| **ICTY Statute** | Statute of the International Criminal Tribunal for the Former Yugoslavia |
| *Idem* | Same citation/reference, but different page or paragraph |
| **IDP(s)** | Internally Displaced Person(s) |
| **IED** | Improvised explosive device |
| **IHEC** | Independent High Electoral Commission in Iraq |
| **IKR** | Kurdish Autonomous Region |
| **IMT** | International Military Tribunal (Nuremberg Tribunal) |
| **IMTFE** | International Military Tribunal of the Far East |
| **Inter-Am. Ct. H.R.** | Inter-American Court of Human Rights |
| **IS** | Islamic State |
| **ISF** | Iraqi security forces |
| **ISIL** | Islamic State of Iraq and the Levant |
| **ISIS** | Islamic State of Iraq and Syria |
| **Jan.** | January |
| **Mar.** | March |
| **NATO** | The North Atlantic Treaty Organization |
| **NGO** | Non-Governmental Organization |
| **NMI** | North Atlantic Treaty Organization Mission in Iraq |
| **Nov.** | November |
| **OAS** | Organization of American States |
| **Oct.** | October |
| **OGPRP** | United Nations Office on Genocide Prevention and the Responsibility to Protect |

| OHCHR | Office of the United Nations High Commissioner for Human Rights |
|---|---|
| OPCAT | Optional Protocol to the Convention Against Torture |
| OSAPG | United Nations Office of the Special Adviser on the Prevention of Genocide |
| OSRSG-SVC | United Nations Special Representative of the Secretary-General on Sexual Violence in Conflict |
| p. | Page |
| para. or ¶ | Paragraph |
| paras. or ¶¶ | Paragraphs |
| pp. | Pages |
| R2P | Responsibility to Protect |
| Res. | Resolution |
| Residual Mechanism | United Nations International Residual Mechanism for Criminal Tribunals |
| RUF | Revolutionary United Front |
| S. | United States Senate |
| S.C. | United Nations Security Council |
| S.C. Res. | United Nations Security Council Resolution |
| S.C. Res. 2379 Team | United Nations Investigative Team to Promote Accountability for Crimes Committed by Da'esh/Islamic State in Iraq and the Levant |
| SASGRP | United Nations Special Adviser of the Secretary-General on the Responsibility to Protect |
| SCSL | Special Court for Sierra Leone |
| Sept. | September |
| SRSG | United Nations Special Representative of the Secretary-General on Violence Against Children |
| SRSG/CAAC | United Nations Special Representative of the Secretary-General for Children and Armed Conflict |
| SS | The Schutzstaffel |
| U.N. | United Nations |

| U.N. Charter | Charter of the United Nations |
|---|---|
| U.N. Doc. | United Nations Document |
| U.N.G.A. | United Nations General Assembly |
| U.N.H.C.H.R. | United Nations High Commissioner for Human Rights |
| U.N.H.R.C. | United Nations Human Rights Council |
| U.N.S.G. | United Nations Secretary-General |
| U.S. | The United States of America |
| U.S. Dep't of State | United States Department of State |
| UAM | Unaccompanied minor |
| UK | The United Kingdom |
| UNAMI | United Nations Assistance Mission for Iraq |
| UNAMID | United Nations-African Union Hybrid Mission in Darfur |
| UNAMIR | United Nations Assistance Mission in Rwanda |
| UNESCO | United Nations Educational, Scientific and Cultural Organization |
| UNHCR | Office of the United Nations High Commissioner for Refugees |
| UNICEF | United Nations Children's Fund |
| UNMIS | United Nations Mission in the Sudan |
| UNMISS | United Nations Mission in South Sudan |
| UNOCT | United Nations Office of Counter-Terrorism |
| UNODC | United Nations Office on Drugs and Crime |
| UNTS | United Nations Treaty Series |
| VCLT | Vienna Convention on the Law of Treaties |
| WASH | Water, Sanitation and Hygiene (cluster) |
| WG on OP to CRC | United Nations Working Group on an Optional Protocol to the Convention on the Rights of the Child |
| Workers Party | Nationalsozialistische Deutsche Arbeiterpartei (National Socialist German Workers Party) |

# Table of cases

## International Military Tribunal – Nuremberg

| # | Case Name (Chronological Order) | Case Number | Type of Decision | Date |
|---|---|---|---|---|
| 1 | 1 Trial of the Major War Criminals Before the International Military Tribunal | | | 1947 |
| 2 | United States of America v. Oswald Pohl, et al. Case 4 (*Pohl case*) | | | 1947 |
| 3 | 4 Trial of the Major War Criminals Before the International Military Tribunal | | | 1947 |
| 4 | 5 Trial of the Major War Criminals Before the International Military Tribunal | | | 1947 |
| 5 | United States of America vs. Friedrich Flick et al. | | | 1947 |
| 6 | United States of America v. Ulrich Greifelt, et al. (*RuSHA case*) | | | 1947 |
| 7 | United States of America v. Carl Krauch, et al. Volume 8 (*I.G. Farben case*) | | | 1947 |
| 8 | 11 Trial of the Major War Criminals Before the International Military Tribunal | | | 1947 |
| 9 | 30 Trial of the Major War Criminals Before the International Military Tribunal | | | 1948 |
| 10 | 36 Trial of the Major War Criminals Before the International Military Tribunal | | | 1948 |

# International Court of Justice – ICJ

| # | Case Name (Alphabetical Order) | Case Number | Type of Decision | Date |
|---|---|---|---|---|
| 1 | Application of the Convention on the Prevention and Punishment of the Crime of Genocide | 1996 1. C. J. 595 | Preliminary Objections, Judgement | July 11, 1996 |
| 2 | Bosnia and Herzegovina v. Serbia and Montenegro: Application of the Convention on the Prevention and Punishment of the Crime of Genocide | 2007, I.C.J. 43 | Judgement | Feb. 26, 2007 |
| 3 | Bosnia and Herzegovina v. Yugoslavia: Application for Revision of the Judgement of 11 July 1996 in the Case concerning Application of the Convention on the Prevention and Punishment of the Crime of Genocide | 2003, I.C.J. 7 | Preliminary Objections | Feb. 3, 2003 |
| 4 | Croatia v. Serbia: Application of the Convention on the Prevention and Punishment of the Crime of Genocide | 2008, I.C.J. 412 | Judgement | Nov. 18, 2008 |
| 5 | Croatia v. Serbia: Application of the Convention on the Prevention and Punishment of the Crime of Genocide | 2015 I.C.J. 3 | Judgement | Feb. 3, 2015 |
| 6 | Democratic Republic of the Congo v. Belgium: Arrest Warrant of 11 April 2000 | 2000, I.C.J. 3 | Judgement | Feb. 14, 2000 |
| 7 | Reservations to Convention on the Prevention and Punishment of the Crime of Genocide | 1951 I.C.J. 15 | Advisory Opinion | May 28, 1951 |

# International Criminal Tribunal for the former Yugoslavia – ICTY

| # | Case Name (Alphabetical Order) | Case Number | Type of Decision | Date |
|---|---|---|---|---|
| 1 | Prosecutor v. Ante Gotovina, Ivan Čermak, and Mladen Markač | IT-06-90-T | Judgement, vol. I | April 15, 2011 |
| | | | Judgement, vol. II | |
| 2 | Prosecutor v. Biljana Plavšić | IT-00-39 & 40/1 | Sentencing Judgement | Feb. 27, 2003 |
| 3 | Prosecutor v. Blagoje Simić, Miroslav Tadić and Simo Zarić | IT-95-9-T | Judgement | Oct. 17, 2003 |
| | | IT-95-9-A | Judgement | Nov. 28, 2006 |
| 4 | Prosecutor v. Dario Kordić and Mario Čerkez | IT-95-14/2-A | Judgement | Dec. 17, 2004 |
| 5 | Prosecutor v. Darko Mrđa | IT-02-59-S | Sentencing Judgement | March 31, 2004 |
| 6 | Prosecutor v. Dragan Obrenović | IT-02-60/2-S | Sentencing Judgement | Dec. 10, 2003 |
| 7 | Prosecutor v. Dragan Zelenović | IT-96-23/2-A | Judgement on Sentencing Appeal | Oct. 31, 2007 |
| 8 | Prosecutor v. Dragoljub Kunarac, Radomir Kovac and Zoran Vukovic | IT-96-23/1-T | Judgement | Feb. 22, 2001 |
| | | IT-96-23/1-A | Judgement | June 12, 2002 |
| 9 | Prosecutor v. Dragomir Milošević | IT-98-29/1-T | Judgement | Dec. 12, 2007 |
| | Prosecutor v. Dragomir Milošević | IT-98-29/1-A | Judgement | Nov. 12, 2009 |
| 10 | Prosecutor v. Duško Sikirica, Damir | IT-95-8-T | Judgement on Defence | Sept. 3, 2001 |

| | | | | |
|---|---|---|---|---|
| | Došen & Dragan Ko- lundžija | | Motions to Acquit | |
| 11 | Prosecutor v. Duško Tadic | IT-94-1-T | Opinion and Judge- ment | May 7, 1997 |
| | | IT-94-1-A | Judgement | July 15, 1999 |
| | | IT-94-1-T *bis*- R117 | Judgement | Nov. 11, 1999 |
| | | IT-94-1-Abis | Judgement on Senten- cing Appeals | Jan. 26, 2000 |
| | | IT-94-1-Abis | Separate Opinion of Judge Sha- habuddeen | Jan. 26, 2001 |
| 12 | Prosecutor v. Enver Hadžihasanović and Amir Kubura | IT-01-47-A | Judgement | Apr. 22, 2008 |
| 13 | Prosecutor v. Naser Orić | IT-03-68-A | Judgement | July 3, 2008 |
| 14 | Prosecutor v. Fatmir Limaj, Haradin Bala and Isak Musliu | IT-03-66-T | Judgement | Nov. 30, 2005 |
| 15 | Prosecutor v. Goran Jelisić | IT-95-10-T | Judgement | Dec. 14, 1999 |
| | | IT-95-10-A | Judgement | July 5, 2001 |
| 16 | Prosecutor v. Jad- ranko Prlić, Bruno Stojić, Slobodan Praljak, Milivoj Pet- ković, Valentin Ćorić & Berislav Pušić | IT-04-74-T | Judgement, vol. I | May 29, 2013 |
| | | | Judgement, vol. II | |
| | | | Judgement, vol. III | |
| | | | Judgement, vol. IV | |

| | | | | |
|---|---|---|---|---|
| | | | Judgement, vol. V | |
| | | | Judgement, vol. VI | |
| | Prosecutor v. Jadranko Prlić, Bruno Stojić, Slobodan Praljak, Milivoj Petković, Valentin Ćorić & Berislav Pušić | IT-04-74-A | Judgement, vol. I | Nov. 29, 2017 |
| | | | Judgement, vol. II | |
| | | | Judgement, vol. III | |
| 17 | Prosecutor v. Jovica Stanišić and Franko Simatović | IT-03-69-T | Judgement, vol. I | May 30, 2013 |
| | | | Judgement, vol. II | |
| 18 | Prosecutor v. Mićo Stanišić, Stojan Župljanin | IT-08-91-T | Judgement, vol. I | Mar. 27, 2013 |
| | | | Judgement, vol. II | |
| | | | Judgement, vol. III | |
| 19 | Prosecutor v. Milan Babić | IT-03-72-S | Sentencing Judgement | June 29, 2004 |
| 20 | Prosecutor v. Milan Lukić, Sredoje Lukić | IT-98-32/1-T | Judgement | July 20, 2009 |
| 21 | Prosecutor v. Milan Martić | IT-95-11-T | Judgement | June 12, 2007 |
| | | IT-95-11-A | Judgement | Oct. 8, 2008 |
| 22 | Prosecutor v. Milan Simić | IT-95-9/2-S | Sentencing Judgement | Oct. 17, 2002 |
| 23 | Prosecutor v. Mile Mrkšić, Miroslav Radić and Veselin Šljivančanin | IT-95-13/1-T | Judgement | Sept. 27, 2007 |
| 24 | Prosecutor v. Milomir Stakić | IT-97-24-T | Judgement | July 31, 2003 |
| | | IT-97-24-A | Judgement | Mar. 22, 2006 |

| 25 | Prosecutor v. Milorad Krnojelac | IT-97-25-T | Judgement | Mar. 15, 2002 |
|----|---------------------------------|------------|-----------|---------------|
|    |                                 | IT-97-25-A | Judgement | Sept. 17, 2003 |
| 26 | Prosecutor v. Miroslav Deronjić | IT-02-61-A | Judgement on Sentencing Appeal | July 20, 2005 |
| 27 | Prosecutor v. Miroslav Kvočka, Mlađo Radić, Dragoljub Prcač, Zoran Zigićand Milojica Kos | IT-98-30/1-T | Judgement | Nov. 2, 2001 |
|    |                                 | IT-98-30/1-A | Judgement | Fev. 28, 2005 |
| 28 | Prosecutor v. Miodrag Jokić | IT-01-42/1-S | Sentencing Judgement | March 18, 2004 |
| 29 | Prosecutor v. Mitar Vasiljević | IT-98-32-T | Judgement | Nov. 29, 2002 |
|    |                                 | IT-98-32-A | Judgement | Feb. 25, 2004 |
| 30 | Prosecutor v. Mladen Naletilić, a.k.a. "Tuta", and Vinko Martinović, a.k.a. "Štela" | IT-98-34-T | Judgement | Mar. 31, 2003 |
|    |                                 | IT-98-34-A | Judgement | May 3, 2006 |
| 31 | Prosecutor v. Momčilo Krajišnik | IT-00-39-T | Judgement | Sept. 27, 2006 |
|    |                                 | IT-00-39-A | Judgement | March 17, 2009 |
| 32 | Prosecutor v. Momčilo Perišić | IT-04-81-T | Judgement | Sept. 6, 2011 |
| 33 | Prosecutor v. Momir Nikolić | IT-02-60/1-A | Judgement | Mar. 8, 2006 |
| 34 | Prosecutor v. Nikola Šainović, Nebojša Pavković, Vladimir Lazarević | IT-05-87-T | Judgement, vol. I | Feb. 26, 2009 |
|    |                                 |            | Judgement, vol. II | |
|    |                                 |            | Judgement, vol. III | |
|    |                                 |            | Judgement, vol. IV | |

| | Prosecutor v. Nikola Šainović, Nebojša Pavković, Vladimir Lazarević | IT-05-87-A | Judgement | Jan. 23, 2014 |
|---|---|---|---|---|
| 35 | Prosecutor v. Predrag Banović | IT-02-65/1-S | Sentencing Judgement | Oct. 28, 2003 |
| 36 | Prosecutor v. Radislav Krstić | IT-98-33-T | Judgement | Aug. 2, 2001 |
| | | IT-98-33-A | Judgement | Apr. 19, 2004 |
| 37 | Prosecutor v. Radoslav Brđanin | IT-99-36-T | Judgement | Sept. 1, 2004 |
| | | IT-99-36-A | Judgement | Apr. 3, 2007 |
| 38 | Prosecutor v. Radovan Karadžić | IT-95-5/18-AR73.4 | Decision on Karadžić's Appeal of Trial Chamber's Decision on Alleged Holbrooke Agreement | Oct. 12, 2009 |
| | | IT-95-5/18-AR98bis | Judgement | July 13, 2013 |
| | | IT-95-5/18-T | Judgement, vol. I | Mar. 24, 2016 |
| | | | Judgement, vol. II | |
| | | | Judgement, vol. III | |
| | | | Judgement, vol. IV | |
| 39 | Prosecutor v. Ramush Haradinaj, Idriz Balaj, and Lahi Brahimaj | IT-04-84-T | Judgement | Apr. 3, 2008 |
| 40 | Prosecutor v. Ranko Češić | IT-95-10/1-S | Sentencing Judgement | March 11, 2004 |

| 41 | Prosecutor v. Ratko Mladić | IT-09-92-T | Judgement, vol. I | Nov. 22, 2017 |
|---|---|---|---|---|
| | | | Judgement, vol. II | |
| | | | Judgement, vol. III | |
| | | | Judgement, vol. IV | |
| 42 | Prosecutor v. Sefer Halilović | IT-01-48-A | Judgement | Oct. 16, 2007 |
| 43 | Prosecutor v. Slobodan Milošević | IT-02-54-T | Decision on Motion for Judgement of Acquittal | June 16, 2004 |
| 44 | Prosecutor v. Stanislav Galić | IT-98-29-T | Judgement and O-pinion | Dec. 5, 2003 |
| | | IT-98-29-A | Judgement | Nov. 30, 2006 |
| 45 | Prosecutor v. Stevan Todorović | IT-95-9/1-S | Sentencing Judgement | July 31, 2001 |
| 46 | Prosecutor v. Tihomir Blaškić | IT-95-14-T | Judgement | Mar. 3, 2000 |
| | | IT-95-14-A | Judgement | July 29, 2004 |
| 47 | Prosecutor v. Vojislav Šešelj | IT-03-67-T | Judgement, vol. I | Mar. 31, 2016 |
| | | | Judgement, vol. III Partially Dissenting Opinion of Judge Flavia Lattanzi | |
| 48 | Prosecutor v. Vidoje Blagojević | IT-02-60-T | Judgement | Jan. 17, 2005 |
| | | IT-02-60-A | Judgement | May 9, 2007 |
| 49 | Prosecutor v. Vlastimir Đorđević | IT-05-87/1-A | Judgement | Jan. 27, 2014 |

| 50 | Prosecutor v. Vujadin Popović et al. | IT-05-88-T | Judgement | June 10, 2010 |
|---|---|---|---|---|
| | | IT-05-88-A | Judgement | Jan. 30, 2015 |
| 51 | Prosecutor v. Zdravko Tolimir | IT-05-88/2-T | Judgement | Dec. 12, 2012 |
| | | IT-05-88/2-A | Judgement | Apr. 8, 2015 |
| | | IT-05-88/2-A A172-1/2054bis | Separate and Partly Dissenting Opinion of Judge Antonetti | July 14, 2015 |
| 52 | Prosecutor v. Zlatko Aleksovski | IT-95-14/1-A | Judgement | Mar. 24, 2000 |
| 53 | Prosecutor v. Zoran Kupreškić, Mirjan Kupreškić, Vlatko Kupreškić, Vladimir Šantić ("Vlado"), Stipo Alilovic ("BRKO"), Drago Josipović, Marinko Katava, Dragan Papić | IT-95-16-T | Judgement | Jan. 14, 2000 |

# International Criminal Tribunal for Rwanda – ICTR

| # | Case Name (Alphabetical Order) | Case Number | Type of Decision | Date |
|---|---|---|---|---|
| 1 | Prosecutor v. André Ntagerura, Emmanuel Bagambiki, Samuel Imanishimwe | ICTR-99-46-T | Judgement and Sentence | Feb. 25, 2004 |
| 2 | Prosecutor v. Athanase Seromba | ICTR-2001-66-I | Judgement | Dec. 13, 2006 |
| | | ICTR-2001-66-A | Judgement | Mar. 12, 2008 |
| 3 | Prosecutor v. Augustin Ndindiliyimana, Augustin | ICTR-00-56-T | Judgement and Sentence | May 17, 2011 |

|    | Bizimungu, François-Xavier Nzuwonemeye | | | |
|----|---------------------------------------|------------------------|-----------------------|------------------|
|    | Augustin Bizimungu v. Prosecutor | ICTR-00-56B-A | Judgement | June 30, 2014 |
| 4  | Prosecutor v. Augustin Ngirabatware | ICTR-99-54-T | Judgement and Sentence | Dec. 20, 2012 |
|    | Augustin Ngirabatware v. Prosecutor | MICT-12-29 | Judgement | Dec. 18, 2014 |
| 5  | Prosecutor v. Callixte Kalimanzira | ICTR-05-88-T | Judgement | June 22, 2009 |
|    | Callixte Kalimanzira v. Prosecutor | ICTR-05-88-A | Judgement | Oct. 20, 2010 |
| 6  | Prosecutor v. Callixte Nzabonimana | ICTR-98-44D-T | Judgement and Sentence | May 31, 2012 |
|    | Callixte Nzabonimana v. Prosecutor | ICTR-98-44D-A | Judgement | Sept. 29, 2014 |
| 7  | Prosecutor v. Dominique Ntawukulilyayo | ICTR-05-82-T | Judgement and Sentence | Aug. 3, 2010 |
|    | Dominique Ntawukulilyayo v. Prosecutor | ICTR-05-82-A | Judgement | Dec. 14, 2011 |
| 8  | Prosecutor v. Édouard Karemera et al. | ICTR-98-44-T | Judgement and Sentence | Feb. 2, 2012 |
|    | Édouard Karemera et al v. Prosecutor | ICTR-98-44-A | Judgement | Sept. 29, 2014 |
| 9  | Eliézer Niyitegeka v. Prosecutor | ICTR-96-14-A | Judgement | July 9, 2014 |
| 10 | Prosecutor v. Elizaphan and Gérard Ntakirutimana | ICTR-96-10 & ICTR-96-17-T | Judgement and Sentence | Feb. 21, 2003 |
|    | | ICTR-96-10 & ICTR-96-17-T | Judgement | Dec. 13, 2004 |
| 11 | Prosecutor v. Emmanuel Ndindabahizi | ICTR-2001-71-I | Judgement and Sentence | July 15, 2004 |
|    | Emmanuel Ndindabahizi v. Prosecutor | ICTR-01-71-A | Judgement | Jan. 16, 2007 |

| | Jean-Baptiste Gatete v. Prosecutor | ICTR-00-61-A | Judgement | Oct. 9, 2012 |
|---|---|---|---|---|
| 24 | Prosecutor v. Ildephonse Hategekimana | ICTR-00-55B-T | Judgement and Sentence | Dec. 6, 2010 |
| 25 | Prosecutor v. Ildéphonse Nizeyimana | ICTR-2000-55C-T | Judgement and Sentence | June 19, 2012 |
| 26 | Prosecutor v. Jean Kambanda | ICTR-97-23 | Judgement and Sentence | Sept. 4, 1998 |
| 27 | Prosecutor v. Jean de Dieu Kamuhanda | ICTR-95-54A-T | Judgement | Jan. 22, 2004 |
| | Jean de Dieu Kamuhanda v. Prosecutor | ICTR-95-54A-A | Judgement | Sept. 19, 2005 |
| 28 | Prosecutor v. Jean Mpambara | ICTR-01-65-T | Judgement | Sept. 11, 2006 |
| 29 | Prosecutor v. Jean-Paul Akayesu | ICTR-96-4-T | Judgement | Sept. 2, 1998 |
| | | ICTR-96-4-A | Judgement | June 1, 2001 |
| 30 | Prosecutor v. Joseph Nzabirinda | ICTR-2001-77-T | Judgement and Sentence | Feb. 23, 2007 |
| 31 | Justin Mugenzi et al v. Prosecutor | ICTR-99-50-A | Judgement | Feb. 4, 2013 |
| 32 | Prosecutor v. Juvénal Kajelijeli | ICTR-98-44A-T | Judgement and Sentence | Dec. 1, 2003 |
| 33 | Prosecutor v. Juvénal Rugambarara | ICTR-00-59-T | Judgement and Sentence | Nov. 16, 2007 |
| 34 | Prosecutor v. Clément Kayishema et al. | ICTR 95-1-T | Judgement | May 21, 1999 |
| | | ICTR 95-1-A | Judgement | June 1, 2001 |
| 35 | Prosecutor v. Laurent Semanza | ICTR-97-20-T | Judgement and Sentence | May 15, 2003 |
| 36 | Prosecutor v. Léonidas Nshogoza | ICTR-07-91-T | Judgement | July 7, 2009 |

| 48 | Tharcisse Muvunyi v. Prosecutor | ICTR-2000-55A-A | Judgement | Aug. 29, 2008 |
|---|---|---|---|---|
| | Prosecutor v. Tharcisse Muvunyi | ICTR-00-55A-T | Judgement | Feb. 11, 2010 |
| 49 | Prosecutor v. Tharcisse Renzaho | ICTR-97-31-T | Judgement and Sentence | July 14, 2009 |
| | Tharcisse Renzaho v. Prosecutor | ICTR-97-31-A | Judgement | Apr. 1, 2011 |
| 50 | Prosecutor v. Théoneste Bagosora, Gratien Kabiligi, Aloys Ntabakuze, Anatole Nsengiyumva | ICTR-98-41-T | Judgement and Sentence | Dec. 18, 2008 |
| 51 | Prosecutor v. Vincent Rutaganira | ICTR-95-1C-T | Judgement and Sentence | Mar. 14, 2005 |
| 52 | Prosecutor v. Yussuf Munyakazi | ICTR-97-36A-T | Judgement and Sentence | July 5, 2010 |
| | | ICTR-97-36A-A | Judgement | Sept. 28, 2011 |

# The Special Court for Sierra Leone – SCSL

| # | Case Name (Alphabetical Order) | Case Number | Type of Decision | Date |
|---|---|---|---|---|
| 1 | Prosecutor v. Brima, Kamara, Kanu (*AFRC case*) | SCSL-04-16-T | Judgement | June 20, 2007 |
| | | SCSL-04-16-A | Judgement | Feb. 22, 2008 |
| 2 | Prosecutor v. Fofana, Kondewa (*CDF case*) | SCSL-04-14-T | Judgement | Aug. 2, 2007 |
| | | | Partially Dissenting Opinion of Honorable Justice Renate Winter | |
| | | SCSL-04-14-A | Judgement | May 28, 2008 |

| 3 | Prosecutor v. Norman | SCSL-04-14-PT | Motion to Recuse judge Winter From Deliberating in the Preliminary Motion on the Recruitment of Child Soldiers | Mar. 24, 2004 |
|---|---|---|---|---|
| | | | Judge Winter's Response to Motion to Recuse Her From Deliberating on the Preliminary Motion on the Recruitment of Child Soldiers | May 14, 2004 |
| | | SCSL-04-14 | Motion to Recuse Judge Winter from Deliberating in the Preliminary Motion on the Recruitment of Child Soldiers | May 28, 2004 |
| | | SCSL-2004-14-AR72(E) | Decision on Preliminary Motion Based on Lack of Jurisdiction (Child Recruitment) | May 31, 2004 |
| 4 | Prosecutor v. Sesay, Kallon and Gbao (*RUF case*) | SCSL-2004-15-PT | Decision on Prosecution Request for Leave to Amend the Indictment | May 6, 2004 |
| | | SCSL-04-15-T | Prosecution Application for Leave to Amend Indictment | Feb. 20, 2006 |
| | | | Oral Rule 98 Decision, Transcript | Oct. 25, 2006 |
| | | | Judgement | Mar. 2, 2009 |
| | | | Sentencing Judgement | Apr. 8, 2009 |

| 5 | Prosecutor v. Taylor | SCSL-03-01-T | Judgement | May 18, 2012 |

# International Criminal Court – ICC

| # | Case Name (Alphabetical Order) | Case Number | Type of Decision | Date |
|---|---|---|---|---|
| 1 | Prosecutor v. Ahmad Muhammad Harun ("Ahmad Harun") and Ali Muhammad Ali Abd-Al-Rahman ("Ali Kushayb") | ICC-02/05-01/07 | Decision on the Prosecution Application Under Article 58(7) of the Rome Statute | Apr. 27, 2007 |
| 2 | Prosecutor v. Bosco Ntaganda | ICC-01/04-02/06 | Judgement | July 8, 2019 |
|   |   |   | Sentencing Judgement | Nov. 7, 2019 |
|   |   |   | Decision Pursuant to Article 61(7)(a) and (b) of the Rome Statute | June 9, 2014 |
| 3 | Prosecutor v. Callixte Mbarushimana | ICC-01/04-01/10 | Decision on the Confirmation of Charges | Dec. 16, 2011 |
| 4 | Prosecutor v. Francis Kirimi Muthaura, Uhuru Muigai Kenyatta and Mohammed Hussein Ali | ICC-01/09-02/11 | Decision on the Confirmation of Charges Pursuant to Article 61(7)(a) and (b) of the Rome Statute | Jan. 23, 2012 |

| 5 | Prosecutor v. Germain Katanga | ICC-01/04-01/07 | Decision on the Confirmation of Charges | Sept. 30, 2008 |
|---|---|---|---|---|
| | | | Judgement Pursuant to article 74 of the Statute | March 7, 2014 |
| 6 | Prosecutor v. Jean-Pierre Bemba Gombo | ICC-01/05-01/08 | Decision Pursuant to Article 61(7)(a) and (b) of the Rome Statute on the Charges of the Prosecutor Against Jean-Pierre Bemba Gombo | June 15, 2009 |
| | | | Judgement Pursuant to Article 74 of the Statute | Mar. 21, 2016 |
| 7 | Prosecutor v. Omar Hassan Ahmad Al Bashir | ICC-02/05-01/09 | Second Decision on the Prosecution's Application For a Warrant of Arrest | July 12, 2010 |
| 8 | Prosecutor v. Thomas Lubanga Dyilo | ICC-01/04-01/06 | Decision on the Confirmation of Charges | Jan. 29, 2007 |
| | | ICC-01/04-01/06-1229-AnxA | Written Submissions of the United Nations Special Representative of the Secretary-General on Children and Armed Conflict Submitted in Application of Rule 103 of the Rules of Proce- | Mar. 18, 2008 |

|   |   |   | dure and Evidence |   |
|---|---|---|---|---|
|   |   | ICC-01/04-01/06 | Redacted Version of Decision on "Indirect Victims" | Apr. 8, 2009 |
|   |   |   | Judgement Pursuant to Art. 74 of the Statute | Mar. 14, 2012 |
|   |   |   | Decision on Sentence Pursuant to Article 76 of the Statute | July 10, 2012 |
|   |   |   | Separate and Dissenting Opinion of Judge Odio Benito, Trial judgement |   |
|   |   |   | Judgement on the Appeal of Mr. Thomas Lubanga Dyilo Against His Conviction | Dec. 1, 2014 |
| 9 | Prosecutor v. William Samoei Ruto, Henry Kiprono Kosgey and Joshua Arap Sang | ICC-01/09-01/11 | Decision on the Confirmation of Charges Pursuant to Article 61(7)(a) and (b) of the Rome Statute | Jan. 23, 2012 |

# Inter-American Court of Human Rights – Inter-Am. Ct. H.R.

| # | Case Name (Alphabetical Order) | Case Number | Type of Decision | Date |
|---|---|---|---|---|

| 1 | Chitay Nech et al. v Guatemala | Inter-Am. Ct. H.R. (ser. C) No. 212 | Preliminary Objections, Merits, Reparations, and Costs, Judgement | May 25, 2010 |
|---|---|---|---|---|
| 2 | Gudiel Álvarez et al ("Diario Militar") v. Guatemala | Inter-Am. Ct. H.R. (ser. C) No. 253 | Judgement, Merits, Reparations and Costs | Nov. 20, 2012 |
| 3 | Río Negro Massacres v. Guatemala | Inter-Am. Ct. H.R. (ser. C) No. 250 | Preliminary Objection, Merits, Reparations and Costs, Judgement | Sept.4, 2012 |

# European Court of Human Rights – Eur. Ct. H.R.

| # | Case Name | Case Number | Type of Decision | Date |
|---|---|---|---|---|
| 1 | Vasiliauskas v. Lithuania | Eur. Ct. H.R. App. No. 35343/05 | | Oct. 20, 2015 |

> "Blessed are those who are persecuted for the sake of righteousness, for theirs is the kingdom of heaven."
>
> (The Gospel of Matthew, Chapter 5, verse 10)

# Introduction

## A. Problem statement, significance of the research, main research question and sub-research questions, and objectives of this book

> Some mothers, to avoid that ISIL/DAESH fighters took their sons, firmly embraced their children and "had thrown themselves off the mountains in desperation."[2]

In areas under its control in Iraq, the fighters of the self-proclaimed Islamic State of Iraq and the Levant (ISIL) – also known as IS (Islamic State) ISIS (Islamic State of Iraq and Syria), and DAESH (Ad-Dawlah al-Islāmiyah fı 'l-'Irāq wa-sh-Shām) – engaged in multiple persecutory acts and omissions against Christians, from 2014 to 2017. These acts and omissions violated several international humanitarian and criminal laws, resulted in devastating physical and mental consequences for ISIL/DAESH victims, particularly women and children, and left an enduring legacy of religious vulnerability of catastrophic proportions in Iraq.

ISIL/DAESH acts and omissions against Christians in Iraq can be grouped as follows: 1) Physical and mental harm; 2) Use of economic measures against the civilian population; 3) Attacks against property of sacred religious relevance; 4) Infringements upon the right to physical liberty and security; and 5) Infringements upon the right to privacy, and deprivation, destruction, and plunder of private property. Evidence collected by different local and international actors demonstrated that these violations were premeditated, systematic, and strategic, constituting a serious threat to international peace and security.

ISIL/DAESH violations of international criminal law represent a severe challenge to the international legal system. Therefore, this book took the form of a case study of the international criminal responsibility for international crimes committed by the ISIL/DAESH in Iraq against Christians.

---

[2]    UNAMI (July 6, 2014 – Sept. 10, 2014). p. 14.

This book aims to answer the following main research question: "whether the existing evidence of crimes against Christians in Iraq by members of the ISIL/DAESH (2014-2017) may amount to the crime of genocide, or if not, to crimes against humanity." Three sub-research questions were elucidated throughout this work: 1) "If ISIL/DAESH actions could amount to genocide, to what extent? Can genocidal *mens rea* be proved?" 2) "Whether genocide can be perpetrated by members of terrorist groups." 3) "Whether the labeling of an armed group as a "terrorist group" modifies the crimes of such group under the International Criminal Law regime."

This study's main objectives were twofold: 1) to determine the legal nature and typification of ISIL/DAESH fighters' acts and omissions against Christians in Iraq, and 2) to determine the criminal responsibility for these acts and omissions. With these objectives, the author implicitly assumes that ISIL/DAESH did not act in a legal vacuum. On the other hand, the "modality" of responsibility which attaches to such acts (for example, whether the perpetrators are to be classified as principals or mere participants/accomplices, the issue of command responsibility, etc.) is not within the sphere of this book.

This book aims to advance the understanding of the atrocities that ISIL/DAESH perpetrated against Christians in Iraq. Through a detailed analysis of hundreds of cases from international criminal tribunals, the book intends to make a significant and original contribution to the field of genocide and crimes against humanity studies. Ultimately, the purpose of this research work is to serve in the near future as an important tool for the investigation, prosecution, and punishment of ISIL/DAESH terrorist fighters in Iraq's local courts or internationally.

## B. The structure of the book.

This book has four chapters, along with introductory and concluding remarks. Here in these introductory remarks, the reader will find a vast, detailed, and methodical review of the literature on the crimes of genocide and crimes against humanity. Research for this book concentrated on academic works, international criminal case-law, official documents from states, reports from inter-governmental and intra-governmental organizations, reports from NGOs, and documents from ISIL/DAESH's official propaganda machine (*Dabiq* and *Rumiyah* issues). These works were selected with the objective of legally assessing whether ISIL/DAESH violations of international criminal law against Christians in Iraq would fall under the definition of genocide, as prescribed by the Rome Statute in its Article 6, or would fall under the crime of persecution, as a crime against humanity as prescribed by the Rome Statute in Article 7.1.h. The definitions provided in those articles are generally accepted in academic writings as reflective of customary international law.

The author researched the works of several scholars who published sound works exploring the substantive law of genocide and crimes against humanity and the origin of laws against these crimes. The author also meticulously explored the historical evolution of International Criminal Law and traced in detail the evolutionary status of the recognition of individual criminal responsibility in International Criminal Law, and the various forms of criminal responsibility. Besides, the author explored a large body of literature on the notions of the general principles, theories, and practice of International Criminal Law, the very concept of an international crime, accepted methods of investigation, rules of pre-trial and trial procedure, rules of evidence, and issues regarding retroactivity and *nullum crimen sine lege*.

Later, the author introduced the pertinent case law on genocide and crimes against humanity of various international criminal tribunals, namely the International Military Tribunal (IMT, Nuremberg), the International Criminal Tribunal for the former Yugoslavia (ICTY), the International Criminal Tribunal for Rwanda (ICTR), the Special Court for Sierra Leone (SCSL), and the International Criminal Court (ICC). Finally, the author analyzed specific literature on the hypothetical genocide of Christians in Iraq perpetrated by ISIL/DAESH fighters.

After reviewing the literature, the author provided the methodology employed in this book to determine the legal nature of the atrocities perpetrated by ISIL/DAESH against Christians in Iraq from 2014 to 2017. This section explores the qualitative approach methods (doctrinal and comparative), historical-comparative research, *black law* and qualitative analysis of legal texts, in-depth analysis of genocide and crimes against humanity case-law, and triangulation research methods. Finally, the author presents other documentary research and in-depth readings employed throughout this project.

In Chapter 1, the author provides a documental description of the ISIL/DAESH regime in Iraq, starting with the origins of the group and a comprehensive timeline of their acts, omissions, money, and power in the region. The author explores the plethora of deliberate, widespread, systematic, and gross human rights and humanitarian abuses and international crimes against persons belonging to various religious and ethnic communities in areas under their control in Iraq. This chapter focuses on ISIL/DAESH targeting Christians in Iraq: Physical destruction of human lives, ISIL/DAESH's self-appointed sharia courts, public executions, forced conversions, destruction of churches, and general violations of humanitarian law such as recruitment and use of child rape, sexual violence, displacement, forced disappearances, and mass graves.

The research data in this Chapter were drawn from several United Nations (U.N.) documents, for instance, UNAMI reports (United Nations Assistance Mission for Iraq), General Assembly resolutions, Human Rights Council resolutions, and solemn meetings, reports from the U.N. General Assembly, U.N. Secretary-General, Ad Hoc Committees, the High Commissioner on Human Rights and from the General Assembly Special Representatives on Iraq. Reports from other U.N. Representatives were also scrutinized, for instance, Rep. of the Committee on the Rights of the Child, Special Representative of the Secretary-General for Children and Armed Conflict, Rep. of the Office of the United Nations High Commissioner for Human Rights, Rep. of the Office of the United Nations High Commissioner for Human Rights, Rep. of the Committee on the Elimination of Racial Discrimination, and the Rep. of the Committee on the Elimination of Discrimination against Women. Reports from international non-governmental organizations (NGOs), from Governments and their bodies, such as from the US Congress, the US White House, the US Department of State, and from the Council of Europe – European Parliament, were also assessed to provide bases for additional evidence.

In Chapter 2, the author appraises the vast factual matrix of human rights and humanitarian law violations contained in the case law from the Nuremberg, the ICTR, the ICTY, the SCSL, and ICC tribunals. The factual matrix was methodically read, scrutinized, compared, and divided into ten categories, as follows: 1) destruction and appropriation of private property; 2) use of derogatory language and religious discrimination; 3) mass executions; 4) physical violence; 5) malnutrition and water scarcity; 6) violations related to Water, Sanitation, and Hygiene (WASH); 7) sexual violence and rape; 8) forced labor and enslavement; 9) child recruitment and use; and 10) other general violations connected with the conditions of accommodation in detention and concentration camps.

Chapter 3 analyzes the legal definitions and contours of the crimes of genocide and crimes against humanity in the case-law from the Nuremberg, ICTR, ICTY, SCSL, and ICC tribunals. In relation to the crime of genocide, the author assessed these courts' approach to the legal definition (typification), applicable law, protected legal values, protected groups, *actus reus*, genocidal plan or policy, *mens rea*, evidence of *mens rea*, and the meaning of essential elements and terms, such as "destroy," or "in whole or in part." In relation to crimes against humanity, the author explored its definition and *chapeau* elements, the definition of attack, and the definition of terms, such as "civilian population," and "widespread or systematic." The prohibited acts and the policy element were also scrutinized. Specific crimes against humanity were analyzed, such as extermination and torture. Nevertheless, this Chapter's main focus was placed on the legal analysis of the underlying crime of persecution.

Chapter 4 constitutes the essence of this book. The author meticulously assessed whether the perpetrators' *actus reus* and *mens rea* behind ISIL/DAESH conducted against Christians in Iraq fall under the definition of genocide, as prescribed by the Rome Statute in Article 6, or fall under the crime of persecution as a crime against humanity, as defined in the Rome Statute in Article 7.1.a-k – the *test of equal gravity*. To perform this assessment, ISIL/DAESH violations of international human rights, humanitarian and criminal law were grouped in seven different categories in this chapter, as follows: 1) Physical and mental harm; 2) Use of economic measures against the civilian population; 3) Attacks against property of sacred religious relevance; 4) Infringement of the right to physical liberty and security; 5) Infringement of the right to privacy, and deprivation, destruction, and plunder of private property; and 6) The imposition and maintenance of other "restrictive and discriminatory measures involving denial of fundamental rights" and 7) Other violations of Humanitarian Law. In the Conclusion, the author provides a substantial and reasoned conclusion regarding the legal typification of ISIL/DAESH acts against Christians in Iraq.

While in Chapter 3, the book extensively discusses various aspects of the International Criminal Law on Genocide, Crimes Against Humanity, and persecution, this was done in an open exploratory manner (*theoretical legal analysis*), covering the generic aspects of a myriad of cases from international criminal courts. In Chapter 4, however, the book aims to show the reader explicitly which specific aspects of the International Criminal Law were exclusively and directly applicable to ISIL/DAESH's actions in Iraq. More than sixty cases from the ICC, ICTY, ICTR, and SCSL were reread, from scratch, in a work that took more than 12 hours a day for 28 days. Therefore, the legal analysis in Chapter 4 is not a repetition of the legal analysis performed in Chapter 3.

## C. Literature Review

In areas under its control in Iraq, ISIL/DAESH fighters engaged in multiple persecutory acts and omissions against Christians, which can be grouped as follows: 1) Physical and mental harm; 2) Use of economic measures against the civilian population; 3) Attacks against property of sacred religious relevance; 4) Infringements of the right to physical liberty and security; 5) Infringements of the right to privacy, and deprivation, destruction, and plunder of private property; and 6) Other violations of International Humanitarian Law. The literature review of the present book concentrates on academic works, international criminal case-law, official documents from states, reports from inter-governmental and intra-governmental organizations, reports from NGOs, and documents from ISIL/DAESH official propaganda machine that could help in the legal assessment of whether the *actus reus* and the perpetrators *mens rea* behind these conducts fall under the definition of genocide, as prescribed by the Rome Statute in its Article 6,[3] or fall under the crime of persecution, as a crime against humanity – the *test of equal gravity*[4] –, as prescribed by the Rome Statute in Article 7.1.h.[5]

## C.I. Works on the general theory of the crime of genocide, crimes against humanity, and persecution.

Many scholars have already published sound works exploring the substantive law of genocide and the origins of the legal prohibition of this crime, starting with the inaugural work of Raphael Lemkin – *Genocide as a Crime Under International Law* (1947)[6][7][8] – who himself coined and developed the term *genocide* in the early 1940s. Some pieces constitute the bedrock of the criminal justice curriculum and scholarship on genocide: Dinah L. Shelton, *Encyclopedia of Genocide and Crimes Against Humanity*, volumes I (2005),[9] II (2005),[10] and III (2005).[11] Professor William A. Schabas handbook *Genocide in*

---

[3]    United Nations. Rome Statute (July 17, 1998) 2187 UNTS 38544. Article 6.
[4]    *Idem.* Article 7.1.a–k
[5]    *Idem.* Article 7.1.h
[6]    Raphael Lemkin, Genocide as a Crime Under International Law *in* Genocide and Human Rights 3–9 (Mark Lattimer ed., Ashgate Publishing Limited, 2007).
[7]    Douglas Irvin-Erickson, Raphaël Lemkin and the Concept of Genocide (University of Pennsylvania Press, 2017).
[8]    Payam Akhavan, Reducing Genocide to Law: Definition, Meaning, and the Ultimate Crime (Cambridge University Press, 2012), Chapter *Raphaël Lemkin: A Biographical Sketch*, pp. 91–101.
[9]    Dinah L. Shelton, Encyclopedia of Genocide and Crimes Against Humanity (Thomson Gale, v. I, 2005).
[10]   Dinah L. Shelton, Encyclopedia of Genocide and Crimes Against Humanity (Thomson Gale, v. II, 2005).
[11]   Dinah L. Shelton, Encyclopedia of Genocide and Crimes Against Humanity (Thomson Gale, v. III, 2005).

*International Law: The Crime of Crimes* (2009),[12] and other substantial works on the topic – see, for example, (2007)[13], (2008),[14] and (2010)[15] – constitute a bedrock on the study of genocide. It is also worth noting Adam Jones' *Genocide: A Comprehensive Introduction* (2006),[16] Ralph Henham & Paul Behrens' *The Criminal Law of Genocide: International, Comparative and Contextual Aspects* (2007),[17] and Donald Bloxham & A. Dirk Moses' *The Oxford Handbook of Genocide Studies* (2010).[18] [19]

In their handbooks of International Criminal Law, M. Cherif Bassiouni (2003),[20] Robert Cryer (2007),[21] Gideon Boas et al. (2011),[22] Antonio Cassese (2013),[23] and Gerhard Werle (2014)[24] have meticulously detailed the historical evolution of International Criminal Law. In a comprehensive analysis of the history of international criminal investigations and prosecutions, Steven R. Ratner & Jason S. Abrams (2001),[25] Herbert R. Reginbogin & Chris-

---

[12] William A. Schabas, Genocide in International Law: The Crime of Crimes (Cambridge University Press, 2009).

[13] William A. Schabas, Origins of the Genocide Convention: From Nuremberg to Paris, 40 Case W. Res. J. Int'l L. 35 (2007).

[14] William A. Schabas, Genocide Law in a Time of Transition: Recent Developments in the Law of Genocide, 61 Rutgers L. Rev. 161 (2008).

[15] William A. Schabas, Retroactive Application of the Genocide Convention, 4 U. St. Thomas J.L. & Pub. Pol'y 36 (2010).

[16] Adam Jones, Genocide: A Comprehensive Introduction (Routledge, 2006).

[17] Ralph Henham & Paul Behrens eds., The Criminal Law of Genocide: International, Comparative and Contextual Aspects (Ashgate Publishing Limited, 2007).

[18] Donald Bloxham & A. Dirk Moses eds., The Oxford Handbook of Genocide Studies (Oxford University Press, 2010).

[19] See also: Johan D. van der Vyver, Prosecution and Punishment of the Crime of Genocide, 23 Fordham Int'l L.J. 286 (1999).

[20] M. Cherif. Bassiouni, Introduction to International Criminal Law (Transnational Publishers Inc., 2003).

[21] Robert Cryer, Håkan Friman, Darryl Robinson & Elizabeth Wilmshurst, An introduction to International Criminal Law and Procedure (Cambridge University Press, 3rd ed. 2014). pp. 91–102; 115–126.

[22] Gideon Boas et al, International Criminal Law Practitioner Library, Volume III: International Criminal Procedure (Cambridge university Press, 2011). pp. 23–54.

[23] Antonio Cassese, International Criminal Law (Oxford University Press, 2013). pp. 317–335.

[24] Gerhard Werle & Florian Jessberger, Principles of International Criminal Law (Oxford University Press, 2014).

[25] Steven R. Ratner & Jason S. Abrams, Accountability for Human Rights Atrocities in International Law: Beyond the Nuremberg Legacy (Oxford University Press, 2001). pp. 187–206.

toph J. M. Safferling (2006),[26] Hisakazu Fujita (2009),[27] Kevin Jon Heller (2011),[28] Yuki Tanaka, Tim McCormack & Gerry Simpson eds. (2011),[29] and Kai Ambos (2013),[30] thoroughly examined the establishment, the law, the functioning, the challenges and the outcomes of the Nuremberg and Tokyo Military Tribunals, from 1945 to 1948 and their importance for the current state of the International Criminal Law scholarship.[31] The aspects of retributive and restorative justice in the Nuremberg and Tokyo Military Tribunals, particularly to the references to them as 'victors' justice,' were mainly addressed by Alexander Boraine (2004).[32] Very importantly, Nanci Adler (2004),[33] Gideon Boas, James L. Bischoff and Natalie L. Reid (2007),[34] Ciara Damgaard (2008),[35] Geert-Jan Alexander Knoops (2008),[36] and Kai Ambos (2013)[37] traced, in a detailed and comprehensive manner, the evolutionary status of the recognition of individual criminal responsibility in International Criminal Law and the forms of criminal responsibility.

---

[26]   Herbert R. Reginbogin & Christoph J. M. Safferling eds., The Nuremberg Trials International Criminal Law Since 1945 60th Anniversary International Conference (K.G. Saur, 2006).

[27]   Hisakazu Fujita, The Tokyo Trial Revisited *in* The Legal Regime of the International Criminal Court: Essays in Honour of Professor Igor Blishchenko 23–49 (Martinus Nijhoff Publishers, 2009). pp. 23–49.

[28]   Kevin Jon Heller, The Nuremberg Military Tribunals and the Origins of International Criminal Law (Oxford University Press, 2011).

[29]   Yuki Tanaka, Tim McCormack & Gerry Simpson eds., Beyond Victor's Justice? The Tokyo War Crimes Trial Revisited (Martinus Nijhoff Publishers, 2011).

[30]   Kai Ambos, Treatise on International Criminal Law, Volume I: Foundations and General Part (Oxford University Press, 2013). pp. 1–10.

[31]   Concerning the constitution of the International Military Tribunal, the Nuremberg Tribunal, its jurisdiction and principles, please refer to: 1 Trial of the Major War Criminals before the International Military Tribunal (1947). p. 66; United States of America vs. Friedrich Flick *et al.* Case 5 (1947). p. XIII.

[32]   Alexander Boraine, Retributive Justice and Restorative Justice: Contradictory or Complimentary? *in* Genocide and Accountability: Three Public Lectures by Simone Veil, Geoffrey Nice, Alex Boraine 39–52 (Nanci Adler ed., Vossiuspers UvA, 2004).

[33]   Nanci Adler ed., Genocide and Accountability: Three Public Lectures by Simone Veil, Geoffrey Nice, Alex Boraine (Amsterdam University Press – Vossiuspers UvA, 2004).

[34]   Gideon Boas, James L. Bischoff & Natalie L. Reid, International Criminal Law Practitioner Library, Vol. I, Forms of Responsibility in International Criminal Law (Cambridge University Press, 2007).

[35]   Ciara Damgaard, Individual Criminal Responsibility for Core International Crimes: Selected Pertinent Issues (Springer, 2008).

[36]   Geert-Jan Alexander Knoops, Defenses in Contemporary International Criminal Law (Martinus Nijhoff, 2d ed. 2008).

[37]   Kai Ambos. *Supra* note 30.

Leaning on the efforts and work of Raphael Lemkin, the United Nations General Assembly adopted, on December 9, 1948, the Convention on the Prevention and Punishment of the Crime of Genocide by approving Resolution 260 as the first instrument of international law that codified the crime of genocide.[38] Comprehensive works were published on the background and preparation, drafting, ratification, multiform interpretation, dimensions, international analysis, and recent developments of the 1948 Convention. They explored the prosecution and punishment of the crime of genocide before the U.N. *ad hoc* tribunals as well as before the permanent International Criminal Court, which was established later – see, for example, Henry King *et al.* (2007),[39] Matthew Lippman (1985)[40] (1998),[41] Martin M. Sychold (1998)[42], Jennifer Balint (1998),[43] Johan D. van der Vyver (1999),[44] Steven R. Ratner & Jason S. Abrams (2001),[45] Edward Day *et al.* (2003),[46] Cherif Bassiouni M. (2003),[47] Dominic McGoldrick and Eric Donnell (2004),[48] Peter Quayle (2005),[49] John B. Quigley (2006),[50] Cryer, Robert (2007),[51] Alberto Costi

---

[38]  G. A. Res. 260 A (III), Convention on the Prevention and Punishment of the Crime of Genocide (Dec. 9, 1948).

[39]  Henry T. Jr. King; Benjamin B. Ferencz; Whitney R. Harris, Origins of the Genocide Convention, 40 Case W. Res. J. Int'l L. 13 (2007).

[40]  Matthew Lippman, The Drafting of the 1948 Convention on the Prevention and Punishment of the Crime of Genocide, 3 B.U. Int'l L. J. 1 (1985).

[41]  Matthew Lippman, The Convention on the Prevention and Punishment of the Crime of Genocide: Fifty Years Later, 15 Ariz. J. Int'l & Comp. L. 415 (1998).

[42]  Martin M. Sychold, Ratification of the Genocide Convention: The Legal Effects in Light of Reservations and Objections, 8 Swiss. Rev. Int'l & Eur. L. 533 (1998).

[43]  Jennifer Balint, Genocide and Law: International and National Dimensions, 14 World Bull. 1 (1998).

[44]  Johan D. van der Vyver. *Supra* note 19.

[45]  Steven R. Ratner & Jason S. Abrams. *Supra* note 25. pp. 26–45.

[46]  L. Edward Day; Margaret Vandiver; W. Richard Janikowski, Teaching the Ultimate Crime: Genocide and International Law in the Criminal Justice Curriculum, 14 J. Crim. Just. Educ. 119 (2003).

[47]  M. Cherif. Bassiouni. *Supra* note 20.

[48]  Christine Byron, The Crime of Genocide *in* The Permanent International Criminal Court: Legal and Policy Issues 143–177 (Dominic McGoldrick & Eric Donnelly eds., Hart Publishing, 2004).

[49]  Peter Quayle, Unimaginable Evil: The Legislative of the Genocide Convention, 5 Int'l Crim. L. Rev. 363 (2005).

[50]  John B. Quigley, The Genocide Convention: An International Law Analysis (Ashgate, 2006).

[51]  Robert Cryer, Håkan Friman, Darryl Robinson & Elizabeth Wilmshurst. *Supra* note 21.

(2009)[52] and Devrim Aydin (2014).[53] Hirad Abtahi & Philippa Webb – *The Genocide Convention: The Travaux Préparatoires*, Volume I (2008)[54] pieces together more than 300 background documents of the drafting process of the Genocide Convention produced between 1946 and 1948 – notes, corrections, letters from national delegations, official communications, recordings of the sessions and working papers.

The author also explored a large body of literature on the notions of the general principles, theories, and practice of International Criminal Law, the very concept of an international crime, accepted methods of investigation, rules of pre-trial and trial procedure, rules of evidence, issues regarding retroactivity and *nullum crimen sine lege* – see, for example, Cherif Bassiouni, M. (2003),[55] William A. Schabas (2006),[56] Leila Nadya Sadat & Michael P. Scharf (2008),[57] Gerhard Werle and Jessberger Florian (2014),[58] Sarah Nouwen (2016)[59] and Kevin Jon Heller (2017)[60]. Respective to the contextual and mental elements of the crime of genocide, some authors mainly explored this issue within the meaning employed by the International Court of Justice, the International Criminal Court as well as within the scope utilized by the Ad Hoc Tribunals: Claus Kress (2007),[61] Gideon Boas, James L. Bischoff and Natalie L. Reid (2009),[62] Kai Ambos

---

[52]   Alberto Costi, The 60th Anniversary of the Genocide Convention, 39 Victoria U. Wellington L. Rev. 831 (2009).

[53]   Devrim Aydin, The Interpretation of Genocidal Intent under the Genocide Convention and the Jurisprudence of International Courts, 78 J. Crim. L. 423 (2014).

[54]   Hirad Abtahi & Philippa Webb, The Genocide Convention: The Travaux Préparatoires, Volume I (Martinus Nijhoff Publishers, 2008).

[55]   M. Cherif. Bassiouni. *Supra* note 20.

[56]   William A. Schabas, The UN International Criminal Tribunals: The Former Yugoslavia, Rwanda and Sierra Leone (Cambridge University Press, 2006).

[57]   Leila Nadya Sadat & Michael P. Scharf eds., The Theory and Practice of International Criminal Law Essays in Honor of M. Cherif Bassiouni (Martinus Nijhoff Publishers, 2008).

[58]   Gerhard Werle & Florian Jessberger. *Supra* note 24.

[59]   Sarah Nouwen, International Criminal Law: Theory all over the place *in* The Oxford Handbook of the Theory of International Law 738–762 (Anne Orford & Florian Hoffmann eds. Oxford University Press, 2016).

[60]   Kevin Jon Heller, What Is an International Crime: (A Revisionist History), 58 Harv. Int'l L.J. 353 (2017).

[61]   Claus Kress, The International Court of Justice and the Elements of the Crime of Genocide, 18 Eur. J. Int'l L. 619 (2007).

[62]   Gideon Boas, James L. Bischoff & Natalie L. Reid, International Criminal Law Practitioner Library, Vol. II, Elements of Crime under International Criminal Law (Cambridge University Press, 2009). pp. 1–13.

(2014),[63] Robert Cryer (2014),[64] Mohamed Elewa Badar and Sara Porro (2015),[65] and Nasour Koursami (2018).[66] To explore the ICJ jurisprudence on genocide, the following cases and advisory opinions were scrutinized in this book (in chronological order): *Reservations to Convention on the Prevention and Punishment of the Crime of Genocide* (1951);[67] *Application of the Convention on the Prevention and Punishment of the Crime of Genocide* (July 11, 1996);[68] the *Democratic Republic of the Congo v. Belgium* (2000);[69] *Bosnia and Herzegovina v. Yugoslavia* (2003);[70] *Bosnia and Herzegovina v. Serbia and Montenegro* (2007);[71] *Croatia v. Serbia* (2008);[72] and *Croatia v. Serbia* (2015).[73]

Later, in the 1990s, the Security Council established The International Criminal Tribunal for the former Yugoslavia (ICTY)[74] and The United Nations International Criminal Tribunal for Rwanda (ICTR).[75] These tribunals have had the duty to investigate, prosecute and punish individuals responsible for committing genocide and other serious violations of International Criminal Law in the Rwandan (Hutus against the Tutsis, 1994) and Yugo-

---

[63]  Kai Ambos, Treatise on International Criminal Law, Volume II: The Crimes and Sentencing (Oxford University Press, 2014).

[64]  Robert Cryer, Håkan Friman, Darryl Robinson & Elizabeth Wilmshurst. *Supra* note 21. pp. 165–186.

[65]  Mohamed Elewa Badar and Sara Porro, Rethinking the Mental Elements in the Jurisprudence of the ICC *in* The Law and Practice of the International Criminal Court 649–668 (Carsten Stahn ed., Oxford University Press, 2015).

[66]  Nasour Koursami, The 'Contextual Elements' of the Crime of Genocide (Asser Press, 2018).

[67]  Reservations to Convention on the Prevention and Punishment of the Crime of Genocide, Advisory Opinion, 1951 I.C.J. 15 (May 28).

[68]  Application of the Convention on the Prevention and Punishment of the Crime of Genocide, Preliminary Objections, judgment, 1996 1. C. J. 595 (July 11, 1996).

[69]  Arrest Warrant of 11 April 2000 (Democratic Republic of the Congo v. Belgium), judgement, 2000, I.C.J. 3 (Feb. 14).

[70]  Application for Revision of the Judgment of 11 July 1996 in the Case concerning Application of the Convention on the Prevention and Punishment of the Crime of Genocide (Bosnia and Herzegovina v. Yugoslavia), preliminary objections (Yugoslavia v. Bosnia and Herzegovina), 2003, I.C.J. 7 (Feb. 3).

[71]  Application of the Convention on the Prevention and Punishment of the Crime of Genocide (Bosnia and Herzegovina v. Serbia and Montenegro), Judgment, 2007, I.C.J. 43 (Feb. 26).

[72]  Application of the Convention on the Prevention and Punishment of the Crime of Genocide (Croatia v. Serbia), judgement, 2008, I.C.J. 412 (Nov. 18).

[73]  Application of the Convention on the Prevention and Punishment of the Crime of Genocide (Croatia v. Serbia), 2015 I.C.J. 3 (Feb. 3).

[74]  S.C. Res. 827 (May 25, 1993).

[75]  S.C. Res. 955 (Nov. 8, 1994).

slavian territories (the conflict in the Balkans in the 1990s), such as crimes against humanity and the crime of persecution.

The ICTY has produced extensive jurisprudence on these crimes that will be analyzed in this book – in alphabetical order: *Ante Gotovina, Ivan Čermak, and Mladen Markač* (April 15, 2011);[76] *Biljana Plavšić* (Feb. 27, 2003);[77] *Blagoje Simić, Miroslav Tadić and Simo Zarić* (Oct. 17, 2003),[78] (Nov. 28, 2006);[79] *Dario Kordić and Mario Čerkez* (Feb 26, 2001), (Dec. 17, 2004);[80] *Darko Mrđa* (March 31, 2004);[81] *Dragan Obrenović* (Dec. 10, 2003);[82] *Dragan Zelenović* (Oct. 31, 2007);[83] *Dragoljub Kunarac, Radomir Kovac and Zoran Vukovic* (Feb. 22, 2001),[84] (June 12, 2002);[85] *Dragomir Milošević* (Dec. 12, 2007),[86] (Nov. 12, 2009);[87] *Duško Sikirica, Damir Došen & Dragan Kolundžija* (Sept. 3, 2001);[88] *Duško Tadic* (May 7, 1997),[89] (July 15, 1999),[90] (Nov.

[76] Prosecutor v. Ante Gotovina, Ivan Čermak, and Mladen Markač, Case No. IT-06-90-T, judgement, vols. I–II, (April 15, 2011).
[77] Prosecutor v. Biljana Plavšić, Case No. IT-00-39 & 40/1, sentencing judgement, (Feb. 27, 2003).
[78] Prosecutor v. Blagoje Simić, Miroslav Tadić and Simo Zarić, Case No. IT-95-9-T, (Oct. 17, 2003).
[79] Prosecutor v. Blagoje Simić, Miroslav Tadić and Simo Zarić, Case No. IT-95-9-A, (Nov. 28, 2006).
[80] Prosecutor v. Dario Kordić and Mario Čerkez, Case No. IT-95-14/2-T, judgement, (Feb 26, 2001); Prosecutor v. Dario Kordić and Mario Čerkez, Case No. IT-95-14/2-A, judgement, (Dec. 17, 2004).
[81] Prosecutor v. Darko Mrđa, Case No. IT-02-59-S, sentencing judgement, (March 31, 2004).
[82] Prosecutor v. Dragan Obrenović, Case No. IT-02-60/2-S, sentencing judgement, (Dec. 10, 2003).
[83] Prosecutor v. Dragan Zelenović, Case No. IT-96-23/2-A, judgement on sentencing appeal, (Oct. 31, 2007).
[84] Prosecutor v. Dragoljub Kunarac, Radomir Kovac and Zoran Vukovic, Case No. IT-96-23/1-T, judgement, (Feb. 22, 2001).
[85] Prosecutor v. Dragoljub Kunarac, Radomir Kovac and Zoran Vukovic, Case No. IT-96-23/1-A, judgement, (June 12, 2002).
[86] Prosecutor v. Dragomir Milošević, Case No. IT-98-29/1-T, judgement, (Dec. 12, 2007).
[87] Prosecutor v. Dragomir Milošević, Case No. IT-98-29/1-A, judgement, (Nov. 12, 2009).
[88] Prosecutor v. Duško Sikirica, Damir Došen & Dragan Kolundžija, Case No. IT-95-8-T, judgement on defence motions to acquit, (Sept. 3, 2001).
[89] Prosecutor v. Duško Tadic, Case No. IT-94-1-T, opinion and judgement, (May 7, 1997).
[90] Prosecutor v. Duško Tadic, Case No. IT-94-1-A, judgement, (July 15, 1999).

11, 1999),[91] (Jan. 26, 2000);[92] [93] *Enver Hadžihasanović and Amir Kubura* (Apr. 22, 2008);[94] *Naser Orić* (July 3, 2008);[95] *Fatmir Limaj, Haradin Bala and Isak Musliu* (Nov. 30, 2005);[96] *Goran Jelisić* (Dec. 14, 1999),[97] (July 5, 2001);[98] *Jadranko Prlić et al* (May 29, 2013),[99] (Nov. 29, 2017);[100] *Jovica Stanišić and Franko* Simatović (May 30, 2013);[101] *Mićo Stanišić, Stojan Župljanin* (Mar. 27, 2013);[102] *Milan Babić* (June 29, 2004);[103] *Milan Lukić, Sredoje Lukić* (July 20, 2009);[104] *Milan Martić* (June 12, 2007),[105] (Oct. 8, 2008);[106] *Milan Simić* (Oct. 17, 2002);[107] *Mile Mrkšić, Miroslav Radić and Veselin Šljivančanin* (Sept. 27, 2007);[108] *Milomir Stakić* (July 31, 2003),[109] (Mar. 22, 2006);[110] *Milorad Krnojelac* (Mar. 15, 2002),[111] , (Sept. 17, 2003);[112] *Miro-*

[91]  Prosecutor v. Duško Tadic, Case No. IT-94-1-T *bis*-R117, judgement, (Nov. 11, 1999).
[92]  Prosecutor v. Duško Tadic, Case No. IT-94-1-Abis, judgement in sentencing appeals, (Jan. 26, 2000).
[93]  Prosecutor v. Duško Tadic, Case No.: IT-94-1-Abis, judgement in sentencing appeals, separate opinion of Judge Shahabuddeen (Jan. 26, 2000).
[94]  Prosecutor v. Enver Hadžihasanović and Amir Kubura, Case No. IT-01-47-A, judgement, (Apr. 22, 2008).
[95]  Prosecutor v. Naser Orić, Case No. IT-03-68-A, judgement, (July 3, 2008).
[96]  Prosecutor v. Fatmir Limaj, Haradin Bala and Isak Musliu, Case No. IT-03-66-T, judgement, (Nov. 30, 2005).
[97]  Prosecutor v. Goran Jelisić., Case No. IT-95-10-T, judgement, (Dec. 14, 1999).
[98]  Prosecutor v. Goran Jelisić, Case No. IT-95-10-A, judgement, (July 5, 2001).
[99]  Prosecutor v. Jadranko Prlić, Bruno Stojić, Slobodan Praljak, Milivoj Petković, Valentin Ćorić & Berislav Pušić, Case No. IT-04-74-T, vols. I–VI, (May 29, 2013).
[100]  Prosecutor v. Jadranko Prlić, Bruno Stojić, Slobodan Praljak, Milivoj Petković, Valentin Ćorić & Berislav Pušić, Case No. IT-04-74-A, vols. I–III, (Nov. 29, 2017).
[101]  Prosecutor v. Jovica Stanišić and Franko Simatović, Case No. IT-03-69-T, judgement, vols. I–II, (May 30, 2013).
[102]  Prosecutor v. Mićo Stanišić, Stojan Župljanin, Case No. IT-08-91-T, judgement, vols. I–III, (Mar. 27, 2013).
[103]  Prosecutor v. Milan Babić, Case No. IT-03-72-S, sentencing judgement, (June 29, 2004).
[104]  Prosecutor v. Milan Lukić, Sredoje Lukić, Case No. IT-98-32/1-T, judgement, (July 20, 2009).
[105]  Prosecutor v. Milan Martić, Case No. IT-95-11-T, judgement, (June 12, 2007).
[106]  Prosecutor v. Milan Martić, Case No. IT-95-11-A, judgement, (Oct. 8, 2008).
[107]  Prosecutor v. Milan Simić, Case No. IT-95-9/2-S, sentencing judgement, (Oct. 17, 2002).
[108]  Prosecutor v. Mile Mrkšić, Miroslav Radić and Veselin Šljivančanin, Case No. IT-95-13/1, judgement, (Sept. 27, 2007).
[109]  Prosecutor v. Milomir Stakić, Case No. IT-97-24-T, judgement, (July 31, 2003).
[110]  Prosecutor v. Milomir Stakić, Case No. IT-97-24-A, judgement, (Mar. 22, 2006).
[111]  Prosecutor v. Milorad Krnojelac, Case No. IT-97-25-T, judgement, (Mar. 15, 2002).
[112]  Prosecutor v. Milorad Krnojelac, Case No. IT-97-25-A, judgement, (Sept. 17, 2003).

*slav Deronjić* (July 20, 2005);[113] *Miroslav Kvočka, Mlađo Radić, Dragoljub Prcač, Zoran Zigićand Milojica Kos* (Nov. 2, 2001),[114] (Fev. 28, 2005);[115] *Miodrag Jokić* (March 18, 2004);[116] *Mitar Vasiljević* (Nov. 29, 2002),[117] (Feb. 25, 2004);[118] *Mladen Naletilić* (Mar. 31, 2003),[119](May 3, 2006);[120] *Momčilo Krajišnik* (Sept. 27, 2006),[121] (March 17, 2009);[122] *Momčilo Perišić* (Sept. 6, 2011);[123] *Momir Nikolić* (Mar. 8, 2006);[124] *Nikola Šainović, Nebojša Pavković, Vladimir Lazarević* (Feb. 26, 2009),[125] (Jan. 23, 2014);[126] *Predrag Banović* (Oct. 28, 2003);[127] *Radislav Krstić* (Aug. 2, 2001),[128] (Apr. 19, 2004);[129] *Radoslav Brđanin* (Sept. 1, 2004),[130] (Apr. 3, 2007);[131] *Radovan Karadžić* (Oct. 12, 2009),[132] (Jul. 13, 2013),[133] (March

---

[113]   Prosecutor v. Miroslav Deronjić, Case No. IT-02-61-A, judgement on sentencing appeal, (July 20, 2005).

[114]   Prosecutor v. Miroslav Kvočka, Mlađo Radić, Dragoljub Prcač, Zoran Zigićand Milojica Kos, Case No. IT-98-30/1-T, judgment, (Nov. 2, 2001).

[115]   Prosecutor v. Miroslav Kvočka, Mlađo Radić, Dragoljub Prcač, Zoran Zigićand Milojica Kos, Case No. IT-98-30/1-A, judgment, (Fev. 28, 2005).

[116]   Prosecutor v. Miodrag Jokić, Case No. IT-01-42/1-S, sentencing judgement, (March 18, 2004).

[117]   Prosecutor v. Mitar Vasiljević, Case No. IT-98-32-T, judgement, (Nov. 29, 2002).

[118]   Prosecutor v. Mitar Vasiljević, Case No. IT-98-32-A, judgement, (Feb. 25, 2004).

[119]   Prosecutor v. Mladen Naletilić, a.k.a. "Tuta", and Vinko Martinović, a.k.a. "Štela", Case No. IT-98-34-T, judgement, (Mar. 31, 2003).

[120]   Prosecutor v. Mladen Naletilić, a.k.a. "Tuta", and Vinko Martinović, a.k.a. "Štela", Case No. IT-98-34-T, judgement, (May 3, 2006).

[121]   Prosecutor v. Momčilo Krajišnik, Case No. IT-00-39-T, judgement, (Sept. 27, 2006).

[122]   Prosecutor v. Momčilo Krajišnik, Case No. IT-00-39-A, judgement, (March 17, 2009).

[123]   Prosecutor v. Momčilo Perišić, Case No. IT-04-81-T, judgement, (Sept. 6, 2011).

[124]   Prosecutor v. Momir Nikolić, Case No. IT-02-60/1-A, judgement, (Mar. 8, 2006).

[125]   Prosecutor v. Nikola Šainović, Nebojša Pavković, Vladimir Lazarević, Case No. IT-05-87-T, judgement, vols. I–IV, (Feb. 26, 2009).

[126]   Prosecutor v. Nikola Šainović, Nebojša Pavković, Vladimir Lazarević, Case No. IT-05-87-A, judgement, (Jan. 23, 2014).

[127]   Prosecutor v. Predrag Banović, Case No. IT-02-65/1-S, sentencing judgement, (Oct. 28, 2003).

[128]   Prosecutor v. Radislav Krstić, Case No. IT-98-33-T, judgement, (Aug. 2, 2001).

[129]   Prosecutor v. Radislav Krstić, Case No. IT-98-33-A, judgement, (Apr. 19, 2004).

[130]   Prosecutor v. Radoslav Brđanin, Case No. IT-99-36-T, judgement, (Sept. 1, 2004).

[131]   Prosecutor v. Radoslav Brđanin, Case No. IT-99-36-A, judgement, (Apr. 3, 2007).

[132]   Prosecutor v. Radovan Karadžić, Case No. IT-95-5/18-AR73.4, decision on Karadžić's appeal of trial chamber's decision on alleged Holbrooke agreement (Oct. 12, 2009).

[133]   Prosecutor v. Radovan Karadžić, Case No. IT-95-5/18-AR98*bis*, judgement, (Jul. 13, 2013).

24, 2016);[134] *Ramush Haradinaj, Idriz Balaj, and Lahi Brahimaj* (Apr. 3, 2008);[135] *Ranko Češić* (March 11, 2004);[136] *Ratko Mladić* (Nov. 22, 2017);[137] *Sefer Halilović* (Oct. 16, 2007);[138] *Slobodan Milošević* (June 16, 2004);[139] *Stanislav Galić* (Dec. 5, 2003),[140] (Nov. 30, 2006);[141] *Stevan Todorović* (July 31, 2001);[142] *Tihomir Blaškić* (Mar. 3, 2000),[143] (July 29, 2004);[144] *Vojislav Šešelj* (Mar. 31, 2016);[145] [146] *Vidoje Blagojević, Dragan Jokić* (Jan. 17, 2005),[147] (May 9, 2007);[148] *Vlastimir Đorđević* (Jan. 27, 2014);[149] *Vujadin Popović et al.,* (June 10, 2010),[150] (Jan. 30, 2015);[151] *Zdravko Tolimir* (April 8, 2015),[152] (Dec. 12, 2012),[153] (Jul. 14, 2015);[154] *Prosecu-*

---

[134] Prosecutor v. Radovan Karadžić, Case No. IT-95-5/18-T, judgement, vols. I–IV, (March 24, 2016).

[135] Prosecutor v. Ramush Haradinaj, Idriz Balaj, and Lahi Brahimaj, Case No. IT-04-84-T, (Apr. 3, 2008).

[136] Prosecutor v. Ranko Češić, Case No. IT-95-10/1-S, sentencing judgement, (March 11, 2004).

[137] Prosecutor v. Ratko Mladić, Case No. IT-09-92-T, judgement, vols. I–V (Nov. 22, 2017).

[138] Prosecutor v. Sefer Halilović, Case No. IT-01-48-A, judgement, (Oct. 16, 2007).

[139] Prosecutor v. Slobodan Milošević, Case No. IT-02-54-T, decision on motion for judgement of acquittal, (June 16, 2004).

[140] Prosecutor v. Stanislav Galić, Case No. IT-98-29-T, judgement and opinion, (Dec. 5, 2003).

[141] Prosecutor v. Stanislav Galić, Case No. IT-98-29-A, judgement, (Nov. 30, 2006).

[142] Prosecutor v. Stevan Todorović, Case No. IT-95-9/1-S, sentencing judgement, (July 31, 2001).

[143] Prosecutor v. Tihomir Blaškić, Case No. IT-95-14-T, judgment, (Mar. 3, 2000).

[144] Prosecutor v. Tihomir Blaškić, Case No. IT-95-14-A, judgment, (July 29, 2004).

[145] Prosecutor v. Vojislav Šešelj, Case No. IT-03-67-T, judgement, vol. I–III, (Mar. 31, 2016).

[146] Prosecutor v. Vojislav Šešelj, Case No. IT-03-67-T, judgement, vol. 3, partially dissenting opinion of Judge Flavia Lattanzi – amended version, (Mar. 31, 2016).

[147] Prosecutor v. Vidoje Blagojević, Dragan Jokić, Case No. IT-02-60-T, judgement, (Jan. 17, 2005).

[148] Prosecutor v. Vidoje Blagojević, Dragan Jokić, Case No. IT-02-60-A, judgement, (May 9, 2007).

[149] Prosecutor v. Vlastimir Đorđević, Case No. IT-05-87/1-A, judgement, (Jan. 27, 2014).

[150] Prosecutor v. Vujadin Popović et al., Case No. IT-05-88-T, judgement, (June 10, 2010).

[151] Prosecutor v. Vujadin Popović et al., Case No. IT-05-88-A, judgement, (Jan. 30, 2015).

[152] Prosecutor v. Zdravko Tolimir, Case No. IT-05-88/2-A, judgement, (Apr. 8, 2015).

[153] Prosecutor v. Zdravko Tolimir, Case No. IT-05-88/2-T, judgement, (Dec. 12, 2012).

[154] Prosecutor v. Zdravko Tolimir, Case No. IT-05-88/2-A A172-1/2054*bis*, separate and partly dissenting opinion of Judge Antonetti, (Jul. 14, 2015).

*tor v. Zlatko Aleksovski* (Mar. 24, 2000);[155] and *Zoran Kupreškić et al* (Jan. 14, 2000).[156]

Such jurisprudence will be explored comparing it to the ICTR case-law – in alphabetical order: *Aloys Simba* (Dec. 13, 2005),[157] (Nov. 27, 2007);[158] *André Ntagerura, Emmanuel Bagambiki, Samuel Imanishimwe* (Feb. 25, 2004);[159] *Athanase Seromba* (Dec. 13, 2006),[160] (March 12, 2008);[161] *Augustin Bizimungu* (June 30, 2014);[162] *Augustin Ndindiliyimana* (May 17, 2011);[163] *Augustin Ngirabatware* (Dec. 20, 2012),[164] (Dec. 18, 2014);[165] *Callixte Kalimanzira* (June 22, 2009),[166] (Oct. 20, 2010);[167] *Callixte Nzabonimana* (May 31, 2012),[168] (Sept. 29, 2014);[169] *Dominique Ntawukulilyayo* (Aug. 3, 2010),[170] (Dec. 14, 2011);[171] *Édou-*

---

[155] Prosecutor v. Zlatko Aleksovski, Case No. IT-95-14/1-A, judgment, (Mar. 24, 2000).

[156] Prosecutor v. Zoran Kupreškić, Mirjan Kupreškić, Vlatko Kupreškić, Vladimir Šantić ("Vlado"), Stipo Alilovic ("BRKO"), Drago Josipović, Marinko Katava, Dragan Papić, Case No. IT-95-16-T, judgment, (Jan. 14, 2000).

[157] Prosecutor v. Aloys Simba, Case No. ICTR-01-76-T, judgement and sentence, (Dec. 13, 2005).

[158] Aloys Simba v. Prosecutor, Case No. ICTR-01-76-A, judgement, (Nov. 27, 2007).

[159] Prosecutor v. André Ntagerura, Emmanuel Bagambiki, Samuel Imanishimwe, Case No. ICTR-99-46-T, judgment and sentence, (Feb. 25, 2004).

[160] Prosecutor v. Athanase Seromba, Case No. ICTR-2001-66-I, judgement, (Dec. 13, 2006).

[161] Prosecutor v. Athanase Seromba, Case No. ICTR-2001-66-A, judgement, (March 12, 2008).

[162] Augustin Bizimungu v. Prosecutor, Case No. ICTR-00-56B-A, judgement, (June 30, 2014).

[163] Prosecutor v. Augustin Ndindiliyimana, Augustin Bizimungu, François-Xavier Nzuwonemeye, Case No: ICTR-00-56-T, judgement and sentence, (May 17, 2011).

[164] Prosecutor v. Augustin Ngirabatware, Case No. ICTR-99-54-T, judgement and sentence, (Dec. 20, 2012).

[165] Augustin Ngirabatware v. Prosecutor, Case No. MICT-12-29, judgement, Dec. 18, 2014.

[166] Prosecutor v. Callixte Kalimanzira, Case No. ICTR-05-88-T, judgement, (June 22, 2009).

[167] Callixte Kalimanzira v. Prosecutor, Case No. ICTR-05-88-A, judgement, (Oct. 20, 2010).

[168] Prosecutor v. Callixte Nzabonimana, Case No. ICTR-98-44D-T, judgement and sentence, (May 31, 2012).

[169] Callixte Nzabonimana v. Prosecutor, Case No. ICTR-98-44D-A, judgement, (Sept. 29, 2014).

[170] Prosecutor v. Dominique Ntawukulilyayo, Case No. ICTR-05-82-T, judgement and sentence, (Aug. 3, 2010).

[171] Dominique Ntawukulilyayo v. Prosecutor, Case No. ICTR-05-82-A, judgement, (Dec. 14, 2011).

*ard Karemera et al.* (Feb. 2, 2012),[172] (Sept. 29, 2014);[173] *Eliézer Niyitegeka* (July 9, 2014);[174] *Elizaphan and Gérard Ntakirutimana* (Feb. 21, 2003),[175] (Dec. 13, 2004);[176] *Emmanuel Ndindabahizi* (July 15, 2004),[177] (Jan. 16, 2007);[178] *Emmanuel Rukundo* (Feb. 27, 2009),[179] (Oct. 20, 2010);[180] *Ephrem Setako* (Feb. 25, 2010);[181] *Ferdinand Nahimana et al.* (Dec. 3, 2003),[182] (Nov. 28, 2007);[183] *François Karera* (Dec. 7, 2007),[184] (Feb. 2, 2009);[185] *GAA1* (Dec. 4, 2007);[186] *Gaspard Kanyarukiga* (Nov. 1, 2010);[187] *Georges Anderson Nderubumwe Rutaganda* (Dec. 6, 1999),[188] (May 26, 2003);[189] *Georges Ruggiu* (June 1, 2000);[190] *Grégoire*

---

[172] Prosecutor v. Édouard Karemera et al, Case No. ICTR-98-44-T, judgement and sentence, (Feb. 2, 2012).

[173] Édouard Karemera et al v. Prosecutor, Case No. ICTR-98-44-A, judgement, (Sept. 29, 2014).

[174] Eliézer Niyitegeka v. Prosecutor, Case No. ICTR-96-14-A, judgement, (July 9, 2014).

[175] Prosecutor v. Elizaphan and Gérard Ntakirutimana, Case No. ICTR- ICTR-96-10 & ICTR-96-17-T, judgement and sentence, (Feb. 21, 2003).

[176] Prosecutor v. Elizaphan and Gérard Ntakirutimana, Case No. ICTR-96-10-A & ICTR-96-17-A, judgement, (Dec. 13, 2004).

[177] Prosecutor v. Emmanuel Ndindabahizi, Case No. ICTR-2001-71-I, judgement and sentence, (July 15, 2004).

[178] Emmanuel Ndindabahizi v. Prosecutor, Case No. ICTR-01-71-A, judgement, (Jan. 16, 2007).

[179] Prosecutor v. Emmanuel Rukundo, Case No. ICTR-2001-70-T, judgement, (Feb. 27, 2009).

[180] Emmanuel Rukundo v. Prosecutor, Case No. ICTR-2001-70-A, judgement, (Oct. 20, 2010).

[181] Prosecutor v. Ephrem Setako, Case No. ICTR-04-81-T, judgement and sentence, (Feb. 25, 2010).

[182] Prosecutor v. Ferdinand Nahimana et al, Case No. ICTR-99-52-T, judgement, (Dec. 3, 2003).

[183] Ferdinand Nahimana et al v. Prosecutor, Case No. ICTR-99-52-A, judgement, (Nov. 28, 2007).

[184] Prosecutor v. François Karera, Case No. ICTR-01-74-T, Judgement and sentence, (Dec. 7, 2007).

[185] François Karera v. Prosecutor, Case No. ICTR-01-74-A, judgement, (Feb. 2, 2009).

[186] Prosecutor v. GAA1, Case No. ICTR-07-90-R77-I, judgement and sentence, (Dec. 4, 2007).

[187] Prosecutor v. Gaspard Kanyarukiga, Case No. ICTR-2002-78-T, judgement and sentence, (Nov. 1, 2010).

[188] Prosecutor v. Georges Anderson Nderubumwe Rutaganda, Case No. ICTR-96-3-T, judgement, (Dec. 6, 1999).

[189] Prosecutor v. Georges Anderson Nderubumwe Rutaganda, Case No. ICTR-96-3-A, judgement, (May 26, 2003).

[190] Prosecutor v. Georges Ruggiu, Case No. ICTR-97-32-I, judgement and sentence, (June 1, 2000).

*Ndahimana* (Dec. 30, 2011),[191] (Dec. 16, 2013);[192] *Hormisdas Nsengimana* (Nov. 17, 2009);[193] *Ignace Bagilishema* (June 7, 2001);[194] *Jean-Baptiste Gatete* (March 31, 2011),[195] (Oct. 9, 2012);[196] *Ildephonse Hategekimana* (Dec. 6, 2010);[197] *Ildéphonse Nizeyimana* (June 19, 2012);[198] *Jean Kambanda* (Sept. 4, 1998);[199] *Jean de Dieu Kamuhanda* (Jan. 22, 2004),[200] (Sept. 19, 2005);[201] *Jean Mpambara* (Sept. 11, 2006);[202] *Jean-Paul Akayesu* (Sept. 2, 1998),[203] (June 1, 2001);[204] *Joseph Nzabirinda* (Feb. 23, 2007);[205] *Justin Mugenzi et al* (Feb. 4, 2013);[206] *Juvénal Kajelijeli* (Dec. 1, 2003);[207] *Juvénal Rugambarara* (Nov. 16, 2007);[208] *Kayishema and Ruzindana* (May 21, 1999),[209] (June 1, 2001);[210] *Laurent Semanza* (May 15,

---

[191] Prosecutor v. Grégoire Ndahimana, Case No. ICTR-01-68-T, judgement and sentence, (Dec. 30, 2011).

[192] Grégoire Ndahimana v. Prosecutor, Case No. ICTR-01-68-A, judgement, (Dec. 16, 2013).

[193] Prosecutor v. Hormisdas Nsengimana, Case No. ICTR-01-69-T, (Nov. 17, 2009).

[194] Prosecutor v. Ignace Bagilishema, Case No. ICTR-95-1A, judgement, (June 7, 2001).

[195] Prosecutor v. Jean-Baptiste Gatete, Case No. ICTR-2000-61-T, judgement and sentence, (March 31, 2011).

[196] Jean-Baptiste Gatete v. Prosecutor, Case No. ICTR-00-61-A, judgement, (Oct. 9, 2012).

[197] Prosecutor v. Ildephonse Hategekimana, Case No. ICTR-00-55B-T, judgement and sentence, (Dec. 6, 2010).

[198] Prosecutor v. Ildéphonse Nizeyimana, Case No. ICTR-2000-55C-T, judgement and sentence, (June 19, 2012).

[199] Prosecutor v. Jean Kambanda, Case No. ICTR-97-23, judgement and sentence, (Sept. 4, 1998).

[200] Prosecutor v. Jean de Dieu Kamuhanda, Case No. ICTR-95-54A-T, judgement, (Jan. 22, 2004).

[201] Jean de Dieu Kamuhanda v. Prosecutor, Case No. ICTR-95-54A-A, judgement, (Sept. 19, 2005).

[202] Prosecutor v. Jean Mpambara, Case No. ICTR-01-65-T, judgement, (Sept. 11, 2006).

[203] Prosecutor v. Jean-Paul Akayesu, Case No. ICTR-96-4-T, judgement, (Sept. 2, 1998).

[204] Prosecutor v. Jean-Paul Akayesu, Case No. ICTR-96-4-A, judgement, (June 1, 2001).

[205] Prosecutor v. Joseph Nzabirinda, Case No. ICTR-2001-77-T, judgement and sentence, (Feb. 23, 2007).

[206] Justin Mugenzi et al v. Prosecutor, Case No. ICTR-99-50-A, judgement, (Feb. 4, 2013).

[207] Prosecutor v. Juvénal Kajelijeli, Case No. ICTR-98-44A-T, judgment and sentence, (Dec. 1, 2003).

[208] Prosecutor v. Juvénal Rugambarara, Case No. ICTR-00-59-T, sentencing judgement, (Nov. 16, 2007).

[209] Prosecutor v. Clément Kayishema and Ruzindana, Case No. ICTR 95-1-T, judgement, (May 21, 1999).

[210] Prosecutor v. Clément Kayishema and Ruzindana, Case No. ICTR-95-1-A, judgement, (June 1, 2001).

2003);[211] *Léonidas Nshogoza* (July 7, 2009);[212] *Michel Bagaragaza* (Nov. 17, 2009);[213] *Mikaeli Muhimana* (April 28, 2005),[214] (May 21, 2007);[215] *Musema* (Jan. 27, 2000);[216] *Omar Serushago* (Feb. 5, 1999);[217] *Paul Bisengimana* (Apr. 13, 2006);[218] *Pauline Nyiramasuhuko et al.* (June 24, 2011), [219] (Dec. 14, 2015);[220] *Protais Zigiranyirazo* (Dec. 18, 2008),[221] (Nov. 16, 2009);[222] *Rutaganda* (Dec. 6, 1999);[223] *Siméon Nchamihigo* (Nov. 12, 2008),[224] (March 18, 2010);[225] *Simon Bikindi* (Dec. 2, 2008),[226] (March 18, 2010);[227] *Sylvestre Gacumbitsi* (June 17, 2004),[228] (July 7, 2006);[229] *Tharcisse Muvunyi* (August 29, 2008),[230] (Feb. 11,

---

[211]  Prosecutor v. Laurent Semanza, Case No. ICTR-97-20-T, judgement and sentence, (May 15, 2003).

[212]  Prosecutor v. Léonidas Nshogoza, Case No. ICTR-07-91-T, judgement (July 7, 2009).

[213]  Prosecutor v. Michel Bagaragaza, Case No. ICTR-05-86-S, sentencing judgement, (Nov. 17, 2009).

[214]  Prosecutor v. Mikaeli Muhimana, Case No. ICTR-95-1B-T, judgement and sentence, (April 28, 2005).

[215]  Mikaeli Muhimana v. Prosecutor, Case No. ICTR-95-1B-A, judgement, (May 21, 2007).

[216]  Prosecutor v. Musema, Case No. ICTR-96-13-A, judgement and sentence, (Jan. 27, 2000).

[217]  Prosecutor v. Omar Serushago, Case No. ICTR-98-39-S, sentence, (Feb. 5, 1999).

[218]  Prosecutor v. Paul Bisengimana, Case No. ICTR-00-60-T, judgment and sentence, (Apr. 13, 2006).

[219]  Prosecutor v. Pauline Nyiramasuhuko *et al.*, Case No. ICTR-98-42-T, judgement and sentence, (June 24, 2011).

[220]  Prosecutor v. Pauline Nyiramasuhuko *et al.*, Case No. ICTR-98-42-A, judgement, (Dec. 14, 2015).

[221]  Prosecutor v. Protais Zigiranyirazo, Case No. ICTR-01-73-T, judgement, (Dec. 18, 2008).

[222]  Protais Zigiranyirazo v. Prosecutor, Case No. ICTR-01-73-A, judgement, (Nov. 16, 2009).

[223]  Prosecutor v. Rutaganda, Case No. ICTR-96-3-T, judgement and sentence, (Dec. 6, 1999).

[224]  Prosecutor v. Siméon Nchamihigo, Case No. ICTR-01-63-T, judgement and sentence, (Nov. 12, 2008).

[225]  Siméon Nchamihigo v. Prosecutor, Case No. ICTR-2001-63-A, judgement, (March 18, 2010).

[226]  Prosecutor v. Simon Bikindi, Case No. ICTR-01-72-T, judgement, (Dec. 2, 2008).

[227]  Simon Bikindi v. Prosecutor, Case No. ICTR-01-72-A, judgement, (March 18, 2010).

[228]  Prosecutor v. Sylvestre Gacumbitsi, Case No. ICTR-2001-64-T, judgement, (June 17, 2004).

[229]  Sylvestre Gacumbitsi v. Prosecutor, Case No. ICTR-2001-64-A, judgement, (July 7, 2006).

[230]  Tharcisse Muvunyi v. Prosecutor, Case No. ICTR-2000-55A-A, judgement, (Aug. 29, 2008).

2010);[231] *Tharcisse Renzaho* (July 14, 2009),[232] (Apr. 1, 2011);[233] *Théoneste Bagosora* (Dec. 18, 2008);[234] *Vincent Rutaganira* (March 14, 2005);[235] and *Yussuf Munyakazi* (July 5, 2010),[236] (Sept. 28, 2011).[237]

Many authors have explored the legitimacy, legality, and the legacy of the former ICTY and ICTR criminal tribunals and explored the accountability for human rights atrocities in International Law. Collectively, their studies presented the judicial responses/mechanisms to the crime of genocide and how these Tribunals helped to pave the way to the International Criminal Court. See, for example, Yusuf Aksar, in *Implementing International Humanitarian Law: From The Ad Hoc Tribunals to a Permanent International Criminal Court* (2004),[238] Guénaël Mettraux, *International Crimes and the Ad Hoc Tribunals*, (2006),[239] William A. Schabas, in *The UN International Criminal Tribunals: The Former Yugoslavia, Rwanda and Sierra Leone* (2006),[240] Anne-Marie de Brouwer and Alette Smeulers in *The Elgar Companion to the International Criminal Tribunal for Rwanda* (2016),[241] and others such as M. Cherif Bassiouni (1995),[242] Rachel Kerr (2004),[243]

---

[231]  Prosecutor v. Tharcisse Muvunyi, Case No. ICTR-00-55A-T, judgement, (Feb. 11, 2010).

[232]  Prosecutor v. Tharcisse Renzaho, Case No. ICTR-97-31-T, judgement and sentence, (July 14, 2009).

[233]  Tharcisse Renzaho v. Prosecutor, Case No. ICTR-97-31-A, judgement, (Apr. 1, 2011).

[234]  Prosecutor v. Théoneste Bagosora, Gratien Kabiligi, Aloys Ntabakuze, Anatole Nsengiyumva, Case No. ICTR-98-41-T, judgement and sentence, (Dec. 18, 2008).

[235]  Prosecutor v. Vincent Rutaganira, Case No. ICTR-95-1C-T, judgment and sentence, (March 14, 2005).

[236]  Prosecutor v. Yussuf Munyakazi, Case No. ICTR-97-36A-T, judgement and sentence, (July 5, 2010).

[237]  Prosecutor v. Yussuf Munyakazi, Case No. ICTR-97-36A-A, judgement, (Sept. 28, 2011).

[238]  Yusuf Aksar, Implementing International Humanitarian Law: From The Ad Hoc Tribunals to a Permanent International Criminal Court (Routledge, 2004). pp. 7–42.

[239]  Guénaël Mettraux, International Crimes and the Ad Hoc Tribunals, (Oxford University Press, 2006). pp. 193–265.

[240]  William A. Schabas *Supra* note 56.

[241]  Anne-Marie de Brouwer & Alette Smeulers eds., The Elgar Companion to the International Criminal Tribunal for Rwanda (Edward Elgar Publishing, 2016).

[242]  M. Cherif Bassiouni, Former Yugoslavia: Investigating Violations of International Humanitarian Law and Establishing an International Criminal Tribunal, 18 Fordham Int'l L.J. 1191 (1995).

[243]  Rachel Kerr, The International Criminal Tribunal for the Former Yugoslavia: An Exercise in Law, Politics, and Diplomacy (Oxford University Press, 2004).

Thierry Cruvellier (2006),[244] Fred Grünfeld & Anke Huijboom (2007),[245] Jackson Maogoto (2009),[246] Nicholas A. Jones (2010),[247] Helen Hintjens (2016),[248] Barbora Holá & Alette Smeulers (2016),[249] Payam Akhavan (2016),[250] Kai Ambos & Stefanie Bock (2016),[251] Justice Hassan Bubacar Jallow (2016).[252]

From June 15 to July 17, 1998, in Rome, following a report of the International Law Commission of July 8, 1994,[253] the United Nations Diplomatic Conference of Plenipotentiaries on the Establishment of an International Criminal Court drafted and approved the Rome Statute.[254] The Statute entered into force on 1 July 2002, when the International Criminal Court (ICC) was vested with temporal jurisdiction. The ICC was created as the first permanent criminal tribunal with jurisdiction over genocide and other serious violations of International Criminal Law. Almost ten years before the ICC was granted temporal jurisdiction, M. Cherif Bassiouni published a paper – *The Time Has Come for an International Criminal Court* (1991) – in which

---

[244]  Thierry Cruvellier, Court of Remorse: Inside the International Criminal Tribunal for Rwanda, Translated by Chari Voss (University of Wisconsin Press, 2006).

[245]  Fred Grünfeld & Anke Huijboom, The Failure to Prevent Genocide in Rwanda: The Role of Bystanders (Martinus Nijhoff Publishers, 2007).

[246]  Jackson Maogoto, The Experience of the Ad Hoc Tribunals for the Former Yugoslavia and Rwanda *in* The Legal Regime of the International Criminal Court: Essays in Honour of Professor Igor Blishchenko 63–74 (Martinus Nijhoff Publishers, 2009).

[247]  Nicholas A. Jones, The Courts of Genocide: Politics and the Rule of Law in Rwanda and Arusha (Routledge, 2010).

[248]  Helen Hintjens, The Creation of the ICTR *in* The Elgar Companion to the International Criminal Tribunal for Rwanda 15–43 (Anne-Marie de Brouwer & Alette Smeulers eds., Edward Elgar Publishing, 2016).

[249]  Barbora Holá & Alette Smeulers, Rwanda and the ICTR: facts and figures *in* The Elgar Companion to the International Criminal Tribunal for Rwanda 44–75 (Anne-Marie de Brouwer & Alette Smeulers eds., Edward Elgar Publishing, 2016).

[250]  Payam Akhavan, Genocide in the ICTR *in* The Elgar Companion to the International Criminal Tribunal for Rwanda 79–109 (Anne-Marie de Brouwer & Alette Smeulers eds., Edward Elgar Publishing, 2016).

[251]  Kai Ambos & Stefanie Bock, Individual Criminal Responsibility in the ICTR *in* The Elgar Companion to the International Criminal Tribunal for Rwanda 202–231 (Anne-Marie de Brouwer & Alette Smeulers eds., Edward Elgar Publishing, 2016).

[252]  Justice Hassan Bubacar Jallow, The ICTR's Elaboration of the Core International Crimes of Genocide, Crimes Against Humanity and War Crimes and Modes of Liability *in* The Elgar Companion to the International Criminal Tribunal for Rwanda 447–487 (Anne-Marie de Brouwer & Alette Smeulers eds., Edward Elgar Publishing, 2016).

[253]  U.N. Doc. A/CN.4/L.491/Rev.1 (July 8, 1994).

[254]  United Nations. Rome Statute (July 17, 1998) 2187 UNTS 38544.

he described the pressing need for a permanent court with jurisdiction over genocide.[255]

Some of the international struggles to establish the ICC were presented by Leila Sadat Wexler (1996)[256] and by Jackson Maogoto in their paper *Early Efforts to Establish an International Criminal Court*.[257] Robert Cryer et al. handbook – *An introduction to International Criminal Law and Procedure* (2014) –,[258] provided a systematic study of the creation of the ICC, its structure and composition, material jurisdiction, and enforcement mechanisms. Otto Triffterer and Kai Ambos put together a collective work – *The Rome Statute of the International Criminal Court: A Commentary* (2016),[259] that provided a detailed analysis of the drafting history of the Rome Statute, its legal importance, the interpretation of its elements, and the process in which the Court was established.

A detailed analysis of the International Criminal Court was also conducted by Yusuf Aksar (2004),[260] William A. Schabas 2007),[261] Benjamin N. Schiff (2008),[262] and Carsten Stahn (2015).[263] Professor M. Cherif Bassiouni, in his colossal *The Legislative History of the International Criminal Court* (2005),[264] [265] [266] provided a meticulous description and analysis of the chronology of relevant historical dates and events of the international criminal prosecution history.

---

[255]  M. Cherif Bassiouni, The Time Has Come for an International Criminal Court, 1 Ind. Int'l & Comp. L. Rev. 1 (1991).

[256]  Leila Sadat Wexler, The Proposed Permanent International Criminal Court: An Appraisal, 29 Cornell Int'l L.J. 665 (1996).

[257]  Jackson Maogoto, Early Efforts to Establish an International Criminal Court *in* The Legal Regime of the International Criminal Court: Essays in Honour of Professor Igor Blishchenko 3–22 (Martinus Nijhoff Publishers, 2009).

[258]  Robert Cryer, Håkan Friman, Darryl Robinson & Elizabeth Wilmshurst. *Supra* note 21. pp. 119–164.

[259]  Otto Triffterer & Kai Ambos eds., The Rome Statute of the International Criminal Court: A Commentary (Hart Publishing, 3d ed. 2016).

[260]  Yusuf Aksar. *Supra* note 238. pp. 43–68.

[261]  William A. Schabas, An Introduction to the International Criminal Court (Cambridge University Press, 2007).

[262]  Benjamin N. Schiff, Building the International Criminal Court (Cambridge University Press, 2008).

[263]  Carsten Stahn ed., The Law and Practice of the International Criminal Court (Oxford University Press, 2015).

[264]  M. Cherif Bassiouni, The Legislative History of the International Criminal Court, Vol. 1 (Transnational Publishers Inc., 2005).

[265]  M. Cherif Bassiouni, The Legislative History of the International Criminal Court, Vol. 2 (Transnational Publishers Inc., 2005).

[266]  M. Cherif Bassiouni, The Legislative History of the International Criminal Court, Vol. 3 (Transnational Publishers Inc., 2005).

Bassiouni also provided a thorough examination of the integrated text – article-by-article – of the Rome Statute, the Court's Elements of Crimes, its nature, functions, mechanisms, Rules of Procedure, and Evidence. Years later, in 2009, M. Cherif Bassiouni again co-edited *The Legal Regime of the International Criminal Court: Essays in Honour of Professor Igor Blishchenko,*[267] with new insights on the then-recent developments of the Court.

In 2002, an agreement between the United Nations and Sierra Leone's Government established the Special Court for Sierra Leone (SCSL). The Court's mandate was "to prosecute those persons who [bore] the greatest responsibility for serious violations of international humanitarian law and Sierra Leonean law committed in the territory of Sierra Leone since 30 November 1996."[268] The Court was vested with the power to analyze and prosecute a broad spectrum of horrific, "widespread or systematic attacks against the civilian population of Sierra Leone,"[269] committed by the members of the Armed Forces Revolutionary Council (AFRC) and the Revolutionary United Front (RUF). Such groups "launched an insurgency from Liberia's Lofa County into Sierra Leone's Kailahun District," that continued until president Ahmad Tejan Kabbah of Sierra Leone declared the end of hostilities on January 18, 2002.[270] The jurisprudence of the SCSL will be thoroughly scrutinized in this book, notably the *Norman Case* (March 24, 2004),[271] (May 14, 2004),[272] (May 28, 2004),[273] (May 31, 2004);[274] the *RUF case* (May 6, 2004),[275]

---

[267] José Doria, Hans-Peter Gasser & M. Cherif Bassiouni eds., The Legal Regime of the International Criminal Court: Essays in Honour of Professor Igor Blishchenko (Martinus Nijhoff Publishers, 2009).

[268] Prosecutor v. Sesay, Kallon and Gbao, Case No. SCSL-04-15-T, judgment, (March 2, 2009). (*RUF case*). ¶ 1.

[269] *Ibidem.* ¶ 1567.

[270] Prosecutor v. Taylor, Case No. SCSL-03-01-T, judgment, (May 18, 2012). ¶ 19.

[271] Prosecutor v. Norman, Case No. SCSL-04-14-PT, motion to recuse judge Winter from deliberating in the preliminary motion on the recruitment of child soldiers, (March 24, 2004).

[272] Prosecutor v. Norman, Case No. SCSL-04-14-PT, judge Winter's response to motion to recuse her from deliberating on the preliminary motion on the recruitment of child soldiers, (May 14, 2004).

[273] Prosecutor v. Norman, Case No. SCSL-04-14, motion to recuse judge Winter from deliberating in the preliminary motion on the recruitment of child soldiers, (May 28, 2004).

[274] Prosecutor v. Norman, Case No. SCSL-2004-14-AR72(E), decision on preliminary motion based on lack of jurisdiction (child recruitment), (May 31, 2004).

[275] Prosecutor v. Sesay, Kallon, Gbao, Case No. SCSL-2004-15-PT, decision on prosecution request for leave to amend the indictment (May 6, 2004). (RUF case).

(Feb. 20, 2006),[276] (Oct. 25, 2006),[277] (March 2, 2009),[278] (Apr. 8, 2009);[279] the *AFRC case* (June 20, 2007);[280] the *CDF case* (Aug. 2, 2007),[281] (Aug. 2, 2007),[282] (May 28, 2008);[283] the *Brima, Kamara, Kanu Case* (Feb. 22, 2008);[284] and the *Taylor Case* (May 18, 2012).[285]

More recently, several papers were written after the Prosecutor of the Court opened its investigation of the first case of genocide against Al Bashir – see, for example, *The ICC's First Encounter with the Crime of Genocide: The Case against Al Bashir*, from the University of Cologne Professor Claus Kress (2015).[286] The issue concerning the Prosecutor's investigation against Al Bashir is highly controversial. In 2005, an International Commission of Inquiry on Darfur, Sudan, was established by the Secretary-General according to Security Council Resolution 1564 (2004).[287] The Commission was assigned to respond to the question: "Do the crimes perpetrated in Darfur constitute acts of genocide?" After collecting "substantial and reliable material" and performing an in-depth analysis, the Commission concluded that Al Bashir's Government had not pursued a policy of genocide against an ethnic group.[288] The dichotomy between the findings of the U.N. Commission and the findings of the ICC Pre-Trial in issuing the Warrant of Arrest against Al

---

[276] Prosecutor v. Sesay, Kallon and Gbao, Case No. SCSL-04-15-T, prosecution application for leave to amend indictment, (Feb. 20, 2006). (RUF case).

[277] Prosecutor v. Sesay, Kallon and Gbao, Case No. SCSL-04-15-T, oral Rule 98 decision, transcript, (Oct. 25, 2006). (RUF case).

[278] Prosecutor v. Sesay, Kallon and Gbao. SCSL-04-15-T. *Supra* note 268.

[279] Prosecutor v. Sesay, Kallon and Gbao, Case No. SCSL-04-15-T, sentencing judgment, (Apr. 8, 2009). (RUF case).

[280] Prosecutor v. Brima, Kamara, Kanu, Case No. SCSL-04-16-T, judgment, (June 20, 2007 as revised on 19 July 2007). (AFRC case).

[281] Prosecutor v. Fofana, Kondewa, Case No. SCSL-04-14-T, judgment (Aug. 2, 2007). (CDF case).

[282] Prosecutor v. Fofana, Kondewa, Case No. SCSL-04-14-T, judgment, partially dissenting opinion of honorable justice Renate Winter (Aug. 2, 2007). (CDF case).

[283] Prosecutor v. Fofana, Kondewa, Case No. SCSL-04-14-A, judgment (May 28, 2008). (CDF case).

[284] Prosecutor v. Brima, Kamara, Kanu, Case No. SCSL-04-16-A, judgment, (Feb. 22, 2008).

[285] Prosecutor v. Taylor. SCSL-03-01-T. *Supra* note 270.

[286] Claus Kress, The ICC's First Encounter with the Crime of Genocide: The Case against Al Bashir *in* The Law and Practice of the International Criminal Court 669–704 (Carsten Stahn ed., Oxford University Press, 2015).

[287] U.N. Doc. S/2005/60 (Feb. 1, 2005).

[288] *Idem.* ¶¶ 507–518.

Bashir[289] is of pivotal importance for the academic investigation of this thesis as to whether the acts of killings and forcible displacements of persons committed by ISIS against Christians in Iraq configure genocide. In Darfur, the Commission considered that "killing and forcibly displacing members of some tribes did not (automatically) evince a specific intent to annihilate, in whole or in part, a group distinguished on racial, ethnic, national or religious grounds." Instead, the Commission considered that the planned and organized attacks on villages "pursued the intent to drive the victims from their homes, primarily for purposes of counter-insurgency warfare."[290]

Whether there was genocide or not in Darfur is an open question in legal scholarship. Its answer is of fundamental importance. For example, Professor Schabas questioned in his paper on the *State Plan or Policy Element in the Crime of Genocide* (2007):[291] *Has Genocide Been Committed in Darfur?* In this regard, Philip Alston (2005)[292] and Claus Kress (2005),[293] Nina Bang-Jensen, and Stefanie Frease (2006)[294] raised essential questions on the model of the Darfur Commission, the model of documenting atrocities and *reporting* for future responses to the crisis. Samuel Totten and Eric Markusen (2006),[295] as well as Gérard Prunier (2011),[296] made significant considerations as to how to reconcile theory and practice when confronting atrocities hard to prove intent, like genocide.

William A. Schabas (2006)[297] and Gregor Noll (2016)[298] very well theorized the issue of jurisdiction in International Criminal Law and lectured on the ma-

---

[289] Prosecutor v. Omar Hassan Ahmad Al Bashir, ICC-02/05-01/09, second decision on the prosecution's application for a warrant of arrest, (July 12, 2010).

[290] U.N. Doc. S/2005/60 (Feb. 1, 2005). Session I and II.

[291] William A. Schabas, Has Genocide Been Committed in Darfur? The State Plan or Policy Element in the Crime of Genocide *in* The Criminal Law of Genocide: International, Comparative and Contextual Aspects 39–47 (Ralph Henham & Paul Behrens eds., Ashgate Publishing Limited, 2007).

[292] Philip Alston, The Darfur Commission as a Model for Future Responses to Crisis Situations, 3 J. Int'l Crim. Just. 600 (2005).

[293] Claus Kress, The Darfur Report and Genocidal Intent, 3 J. Int'l Crim. Just. 562 (2005).

[294] Nina Bang-Jensen & Stefanie Frease, Creating the ADT: turning a Good Idea into Reality *in* Genocide in Darfur: Investigating the Atrocities in the Sudan 45–57 (Samuel Totten & Eric Markusen eds., Routledge, 2006).

[295] Samuel Totten & Eric Markusen eds., Genocide in Darfur: Investigating the Atrocities in the Sudan (Routledge, 2006).

[296] Gérard Prunier, Darfur: Genocidal Theory and Practical Atrocities *in* Confronting genocide 45–56 (René Provost & Payam Akhavan eds., Springer, 2011).

[297] William A. Schabas *Supra* note 56.

[298] Gregor Noll, Theorizing Jurisdiction *in* The Oxford Handbook of the Theory of International Law 600–617 (Anne Oford & Florian Hoffmann eds., Oxford University Press, 2016).

terial, temporal, and personal admissibility issues under the ICC Statute as well as under the former Yugoslavia, Rwanda, and Sierra Leone tribunal statutes. Professor Gregor Noll paid particular attention to the early developments of the ICC case-law with the *Thomas Lubanga Dyilo* case (January 29, 2007),[299] (March 18, 2008),[300] (April 8, 2009),[301] (March 14, 2012),[302] and (July 10, 2012).[303] [304] Ianin Cameron (2004),[305] and Victor Tsilonis (2019),[306] gave particular attention to the policy issues of jurisdiction and reflected upon the consequences of this approach over the permanent International Criminal Court. Pertaining to the intricate and controversial issue of universal jurisdiction for international crimes, M. Cherif Bassiouni (2001)[307] and (2003)[308], David A. Tallman (2003),[309] Diane F. Orentlicher (2008),[310] Władysław Czapliński (2009),[311]

---

[299] Prosecutor v. Thomas Lubanga Dyilo, Case No. ICC-01/04-01/06, decision on the confirmation of charges, (Jan. 29, 2007).

[300] Prosecutor v. Thomas Lubanga Dyilo, Case No. ICC-01/04-01/06-1229-AnxA, written submissions of the United Nations Special Representative of the Secretary-General on Children and Armed Conflict submitted in application of Rule 103 of the Rules of Procedure and Evidence, (March 18, 2008).

[301] Prosecutor v. Thomas Lubanga Dyilo, Case No. ICC-01/04-01/06, redacted version of decision on "indirect victims," (Apr. 8, 2009).

[302] Prosecutor v. Thomas Lubanga Dyilo, Case No. ICC-01/04-01/06, judgment pursuant to Art. 74 of the Statute, (March 14, 2012).

[303] Prosecutor v. Thomas Lubanga Dyilo, Case No. ICC-01/04-01/06, decision on sentence pursuant to Article 76 of the Statute, (July 10, 2012).

[304] Prosecutor v. Thomas Lubanga Dyilo, Case No. ICC-01/04-01/06, separate and dissenting opinion of judge Odio Benito, trial judgment, (July 10, 2012).

[305] Cameron, Ianin. Jurisdiction and admissibility issues under the ICC Statute *in* The Permanent International Criminal Court: Legal and Policy Issues 65–94 (Dominic McGoldrick & Eric Donnelly eds., Hart Publishing, 2004).

[306] Victor Tsilonis, The Jurisdiction of the International Criminal Court (Springer, 2019). pp. 75–102.

[307] M. Cherif Bassiouni, Universal Jurisdiction for International Crimes: Historical Perspectives and Contemporary Practice, 42 Va. J. Int'l L. 81 (2001).

[308] M. Cherif. Bassiouni. *Supra* note 20.

[309] David A Tallman, Universal Jurisdiction: Lessons From Belgium's Experience *in* Accountability for Atrocities: National and International Responses 375–409 (Jane E. Stromseth ed., Transnational Publishers Inc: Ardsley, 2003).

[310] Diane F. Orentlicher, Universal Jurisdiction: A Pragmatic Strategy in Pursuit of a Moralist's Vision *in* The Theory and Practice of International Criminal Law Essays in Honor of M. Cherif Bassiouni 127–154 (Leila Nadya Sadat & Michael P. Scharf eds., Martinus Nijhoff Publishers, 2008).

[311] Władysław Czapliński, Jus Cogens, Obligations Erga Omnes and International Criminal Responsibility *in* The Legal Regime of the International Criminal Court: Essays in Honour of Professor Igor Blishchenko 403–420 (Martinus Nijhoff Publishers, 2009).

Gerhard Werle (2014)[312] and Aisling O'Sullivan (2017)[313] shed light on the historical perspectives, jurisdictional responses and the contemporary practice on the *erga omnes* duty to prosecute crimes in violation of *jus cogens* norms. In 2019, Victor Tsilonis wrote extensively about current challenges concerning the Jurisdiction of the International Criminal Court.[314]

Regarding the jurisdiction of the International Criminal Court over crimes against humanity, Professors M. Larry May (2005),[315] Cherif Bassiouni (2011),[316] Norman Geras (2011),[317] Christopher K. Hall, Joseph Powderly & Niamh Hayes (2016),[318] Victor Tsilonis (2019),[319] and Robert Dubler SC & Matthew Kalyk (2018)[320] wrote comprehensive works on the historical evolution, philosophical foundations, and developments on the typicity of such crime and in its relation with Customary International Law.[321] The works of Gideon Boas, James L. Bischoff & Natalie L. Reid (2009),[322] Cherif Bassiouni (2011),[323] and Kai Ambos (2014)[324] were also scrutinized in the legal analysis of the crime of persecution on religious grounds, as a crime against humanity, according to Article 7.1.h of the Rome Statute.[325] A significant portion of the ICC case-law concerning genocide and crimes against humanity was also scrutinized in the present book, for instance (in alphabetical order), *Ahmad Muhammad Harun and Ali Muhammad Ali Abd-Al-*

---

[312]  Gerhard Werle & Florian Jessberger. *Supra* note 24.

[313]  Aisling O'Sullivan, Universal Jurisdiction in International Criminal Law: The Debate and the Battle for Hegemony (Routledge, 2017).

[314]  Victor Tsilonis. *Supra* note 306. pp. 103–127.

[315]  Larry May, Crimes Against Humanity: A Normative Account (Cambridge University Press, 2005).

[316]  M. Cherif Bassiouni, Crimes Against Humanity: Historical Evolution and Contemporary Application (Cambridge University Press, 2011).

[317]  Norman Geras, Crimes Against Humanity: Birth of a Concept (Manchester University Press, 2011). pp. 1–31.

[318]  Christopher K. Hall, Joseph Powderly & Niamh Hayes, Article 7. Crimes Against Humanity *in* The Rome Statute of the International Criminal Court: A Commentary 144–294 (Otto Triffterer & Kai Ambos eds., Hart Publishing, 3d ed. 2016).

[319]  Victor Tsilonis. *Supra* note 306. pp. 103–126

[320]  Robert Dubler SC & Matthew Kalyk, Crimes Against Humanity in the 21st Century: Law, Practice and Threats to International Peace and Security (Brill/Nijhoff, 2018). pp. 1–34.

[321]  *Idem.* pp. 745–958.

[322]  Gideon Boas, James L. Bischoff & Natalie L. Reid. *Supra* note 62. pp. 88–99.

[323]  M. Cherif Bassiouni. *Supra* note 316. pp. 396–405.

[324]  Kai Ambos. *Supra* note 63. pp. 104–108.

[325]  United Nations. Rome Statute (July 17, 1998) 2187 UNTS 38544. Article 7.1.h

*Rahman* (Apr. 27, 2007);[326] *Bosco Ntaganda* (June 9, 2014),[327] (July 8, 2019),[328] (Nov. 7, 2019);[329] *Callixte Mbarushimana* (Dec. 16, 2011);[330] *Francis Kirimi Muthaura, Uhuru Muigai Kenyatta and Mohammed Hussein Ali* (Jan. 23, 2012);[331] *Germain Katanga* (Sept. 30, 2008),[332] (March 7, 2014);[333] *Jean-Pierre Bemba Gombo* (June 15, 2009),[334] (March 21, 2016);[335] *Omar Hassan Ahmad Al Bashir* (July 12, 2010);[336] *Thomas Lubanga Dyilo* (Jan. 29, 2007)[337] (March 18, 2008),[338] (Apr. 8, 2009),[339] (March 14, 2012),[340] (July 10, 2012),[341] (July 10, 2012),[342] (Dec. 1, 2014);[343] and *William Samoei Ruto, Henry Kiprono Kosgey and Joshua Arap Sang* (Jan. 23, 2012).[344]

---

[326] Prosecutor v. Ahmad Muhammad Harun ("Ahmad Harun") and Ali Muhammad Ali Abd-Al-Rahman ("Ali Kushayb"), Case No. ICC-02/05-01/07, decision on the prosecution application under Article 58(7) of the Rome Statute, (Apr. 27, 2007).

[327] Prosecutor v. Bosco Ntaganda, Case No. ICC-01/04-02/06, decision pursuant to Article 61(7)(a) and (b) of the Rome Statute, (June 9, 2014).

[328] Prosecutor v. Bosco Ntaganda, Case No. ICC-01/04-02/06, judgment, (July 8, 2019).

[329] Prosecutor v. Bosco Ntaganda, Case No. ICC-01/04-02/06, sentencing judgment, (Nov. 7, 2019).

[330] Prosecutor v. Callixte Mbarushimana, Case No. ICC-01/04-01/10, decision on the confirmation of charges, (Dec. 16, 2011).

[331] Prosecutor v. Francis Kirimi Muthaura, Uhuru Muigai Kenyatta and Mohammed Hussein Ali, Case No. ICC-01/09-02/11, decision on the confirmation of charges pursuant to Article 61(7)(a) and (b) of the Rome Statute, (Jan. 23, 2012).

[332] Prosecutor v. Germain Katanga, Case No. ICC-01/04-01/07, decision on the confirmation of charges, (Sept. 30, 2008).

[333] Prosecutor v. Germain Katanga, Case No. ICC-01/04-01/07, judgment pursuant to article 74 of the Statute, (March 7, 2014).

[334] Prosecutor v. Jean-Pierre Bemba Gombo, Case No. ICC-01/05-01/08, Decision Pursuant to Article 61(7)(a) and (b) of the Rome Statute on the charges of the Prosecutor against Jean-Pierre Bemba Gombo, (June 15, 2009).

[335] Prosecutor v. Jean-Pierre Bemba Gombo, Case No. ICC-01/05-01/08, judgment pursuant to article 74 of the Statute, (March 21, 2016).

[336] Prosecutor v. Omar Hassan Ahmad Al Bashir, Case No. ICC-02/05-01/09, second decision on the prosecution's application for a warrant of arrest, (July 12, 2010).

[337] Prosecutor v. Thomas Lubanga Dyilo. ICC-01/04-01/06. *Supra* note 299.

[338] Prosecutor v. Thomas Lubanga Dyilo. ICC-01/04-01/06-1229-AnxA. *Supra* note 300.

[339] Prosecutor v. Thomas Lubanga Dyilo. ICC-01/04-01/06. *Supra* note 301.

[340] Prosecutor v. Thomas Lubanga Dyilo. ICC-01/04-01/06. *Supra* note 302.

[341] Prosecutor v. Thomas Lubanga Dyilo. ICC-01/04-01/06. *Supra* note 303.

[342] Prosecutor v. Thomas Lubanga Dyilo. ICC-01/04-01/06. *Supra* note 304.

[343] Prosecutor v. Thomas Lubanga Dyilo, Case No. ICC-01/04-01/06 A 5, judgment on the appeal of Mr. Thomas Lubanga Dyilo against his conviction, (Dec. 1, 2014).

[344] Prosecutor v. William Samoei Ruto, Henry Kiprono Kosgey and Joshua Arap Sang, Case No. ICC-01/09-01/11, decision on the confirmation of charges pursuant to Article 61(7)(a) and (b) of the Rome Statute, (Jan. 23, 2012).

A critical and practical aspect of the jurisdiction and the power of the Prosecutor of the ICC is related to two essential issues: First) the issue of selectivity in International Criminal Law and Second) the issue related to the decision as to what cases should be investigated. For example, Robert Cryer delineated profound aspects of this issue in *Prosecuting International Crimes: Selectivity and the International Criminal Law Regime* (2005).[345] Conversely, Fabricio Guariglia and Emeric Rogier wrote the Selection of Situations and Cases by the OTP of the ICC (2015).[346] William A. Schabas addressed the process of selecting the crimes which most seriously violated international public order in his handbook *The UN International Criminal Tribunals* (2006),[347] as well as in his specific works on the topic: *Victor's Justice* (2010),[348] and *Selecting Situations and Cases in The Law and Practice of the International Criminal Court* (2015).[349]

Another major issue related to jurisdiction resides in the relationship between national and the international system efforts in holding perpetrators of atrocities accountable. In this regard, see, for example, the critical contribution of Jane E. Stromseth in *Challenges in the Pursuit of Accountability* (2003).[350] This discussion is essential to analyze four crucial aspects: Firstly) to analyze the states' cooperation with the international courts and tribunals – see, for example, Robert Cryer *et al.* (2007)[351] –; secondly) to analyze the prosecution of crimes under International Criminal Law by domestic courts; thirdly) to analyze the challenges related to the Principle of Complementarity; and fourthly) to analyze reparations for victims of genocide – see, for example, William A. Schabas (2003),[352] Jane E. Stromseth

---

[345]   Robert Cryer, Prosecuting International Crimes: Selectivity and International Criminal Law Regime (Cambridge University Press, 2005).

[346]   Fabricio Guariglia and Emeric Rogier, The Selection of Situations and Cases by the OTP of the ICC *in* The Law and Practice of the International Criminal Court 350–364 (Carsten Stahn ed., Oxford University Press, 2015).

[347]   William A. Schabas *Supra* note 56.

[348]   William A. Schabas, Victor's Justice: Selecting Situations at the International Criminal Court, 43 J. Marshall L. Rev. 535 (2010).

[349]   William A. Schabas, Selecting Situations and Cases *in* The Law and Practice of the International Criminal Court 365–381 (Carsten Stahn ed., Oxford University Press, 2015).

[350]   Jane E. Stromseth, Challenges in the Pursuit of Accountability *in* Accountability for Atrocities: National and International Responses 1–36 (Jane E. Stromseth ed., Transnational Publishers Inc: Ardsley, 2003).

[351]   Robert Cryer, Håkan Friman, Darryl Robinson & Elizabeth Wilmshurst. *Supra* note 21.

[352]   William A. Schabas. *Supra* note 12.

(2003),[353] Aram A. Schvey (2003),[354] Larry Charles Dembowski (2003),[355] Carla Ferstman, Mariana Goetz, and Alan Stephens (2009)[356] and Gerhard Werle (2014).[357]

The interconnection between the international criminal accountability and the domestic obligation to prosecute human rights violations of prior regimes was meticulously explored in the magisterial work of Diane F. Orentlicher (1991)[358] and Juan E. Méndez (2007),[359] along with David A. Tallman (2003),[360] Amoury Combs Nancy (2018),[361] Jason Strain and Elizabeth Keyes (2003).[362] Importantly, Cherif Bassiouni M. (2003),[363] E. van. Sliedregt (2003),[364] Guénaël Mettraux (2006),[365] and Sarah Nouwen (2016)[366] wrote about the genocide's perpetrator, as well as about superior responsibility, the international criminal responsibility of non-state actors, and the issue of state criminality v. individual criminality, in the context of the crime of genocide.

---

[353]  Jane E. Stromseth, Challenges in the Pursuit of Accountability *in* Accountability for Atrocities: National and International Responses 1–36 (Jane E. Stromseth ed., Transnational Publishers Inc: Ardsley, 2003).

[354]  Aram A. Schvey, Striving for Accountability in the Former Yugoslavia *in* Accountability for Atrocities: National and International Responses 39–85 (Jane E. Stromseth ed., Transnational Publishers Inc: Ardsley, 2003).

[355]  Larry Charles Dembowski, The International Criminal Court: Complementarity *in* Accountability for Atrocities: National and International Responses 135–169 (Jane E. Stromseth ed., Transnational Publishers Inc: Ardsley, 2003).

[356]  Carla Ferstman, Mariana Goetz & Alan Stephens eds., Reparations for Victims of Genocide, War Crimes and Crimes against Humanity Systems in Place and Systems in the Making (Martinus Nijhoff Publishers, 2009).

[357]  Gerhard Werle & Florian Jessberger. *Supra* note 24.

[358]  Diane F. Orentlicher, Settling Accounts: The Duty to Prosecute Human Rights Violations of a Prior Regime, 100 Yale L.J. 2537 (1991).

[359]  Juan E. Méndez, Accountability for Past Abuses *in* Genocide and Human Rights 429–456 (Mark Lattimer ed., Ashgate Publishing Limited, 2007).

[360]  David A Tallman *Supra* note 309. pp. 375–409.

[361]  Nancy Amoury Combs, Deconstructing the Epistemic Challenges to Mass Atrocity Prosecutions, 75 Wash. & Lee L. Rev. 223 (2018).

[362]  Jason Strain & Elizabeth Keyes, Accountability in the Aftermath of Rwanda's Genocide *in* Accountability for Atrocities: National and International Responses 87–133 (Jane E. Stromseth ed., Transnational Publishers Inc: Ardsley, 2003).

[363]  M. Cherif. Bassiouni. *Supra* note 20.

[364]  E. Van. Sliedregt, The Criminal Responsibility of Individuals for Violations of International Humanitarian Law (Asser Press, 2003).

[365]  Guénaël Mettraux *Supra* note 239.

[366]  Sarah Nouwen *Supra* note 59. pp. 738–762.

Regarding the responsibility to protect and the duty to prevent genocide as well as the Security Council's role in humanitarian intervention, this issue was substantively addressed in the International Criminal Law scholarship, with particular highlight to the leading work of William A. Schabas, "Genocide and the International Court of Justice: Finally, a duty to prevent the crime of crimes" (2007).[367] Other scholars shed essential light on the issue – see, for example, Jack Donnelly (2007),[368] Jonathan I. Charney (2007),[369] Helene de Pooter (2009),[370] Jeremy Sarkin and Carly Fowler (2010),[371] Serena Forlati (2011),[372] Mark Gibney (2011),[373] Inger Skjelsbaek (2012),[374] Andreas Zimmermann (2012),[375] Milena Sterio (2015),[376] Caroline E. Nabity (2016),[377] Sarah Lesser (2017),[378] and Marquise Houle (2017-2018).[379] Particular attention is dedicated to selected ICJ case-law: *Reservations to Convention on the Prevention and Punishment of the Crime of*

---

[367] William A. Schabas. *Supra* note 12.

[368] Jack Donnelly, Genocide and humanitarian intervention *in in* Genocide and Human Rights 385–401 (Mark Lattimer ed., Ashgate Publishing Limited, 2007).

[369] Jonathan I. Charney, Anticipatory Humanitarian Intervention in Kosovo *in* Genocide and Human Rights 403–426 (Mark Lattimer ed., Ashgate Publishing Limited, 2007).

[370] Helene de Pooter, Obligation to Prevent Genocide: A Large Shell Yet to Be Filled, The, 17 Afr. Y.B. Int'l L. 287 (2009).

[371] Jeremy Sarkin; Carly Fowler, The Responsibility to Protect and the Duty to Prevent Genocide: Lessons to Be Learned from the Role of the International Community and the Media during the Rwandan Genocide and the Conflict in Former Yugoslavia, 33 Suffolk Transnat'l L. Rev. 35 (2010).

[372] Serena Forlati, Legal Obligation to Prevent Genocide: Bosnia v. Serbia and beyond, The, 31 Polish Y.B. Int'l L. 189 (2011).

[373] Mark Gibney, Universal Duties: The Responsibility to Protect, the Duty to Prevent (Genocide) and Extraterritorial Human Rights Obligations, 3 Global Resp. Protect 123 (2011).

[374] Inger Skjelsbaek, Responsibility to Protect or Prevent: Victims and Perpetrators of Sexual Violence Crimes in Armed Conflicts, 4 Global Resp. Protect 154 (2012).

[375] Andreas Zimmermann, Security Council and the Obligation to Prevent Genocide and War Crimes, The, 32 Polish Y.B. Int'l L. 307 (2012).

[376] Milena Sterio, The Applicability of the Humanitarian Intervention Exception to the Middle Eastern Refugee Crisis: Why the International Community Should Intervene against ISIS, 38 Suffolk Transnat'l L. Rev. 325 (2015).

[377] Caroline E. Nabity, It's Genocide, Now What: The Obligations of the United States under the Convention to Prevent and Punish Genocide Being Committed at the Hands of ISIS, 8 Creighton Int'l & Comp. L.J. 70 (2016).

[378] Sarah Lesser, Early Non-Military Intervention to Prevent Atrocity Crimes, 10 Am. J. Mediation 84 (2017).

[379] Marquise Houle, The Responsibility to Protect, Military Intervention and Genocide, 8 Int'l L. Y.B. 139 (2017-2018).

*Genocide*, 1951 (May 28),[380] *Application of the Convention on the Prevention and Punishment of the Crime of Genocide*, 1996 (July 11, 1996),[381] the *Democratic Republic of the Congo v. Belgium*, 2000 (February 14),[382] *Yugoslavia v. Bosnia and Herzegovina*, 2003, (Feb. 3),[383] *Bosnia and Herzegovina v. Serbia and Montenegro*, 2007 (February 26),[384] *Croatia v. Serbia*, 2008 (Nov. 18),[385] and *Croatia v. Serbia*, 2015 (February 3).[386] Notably, in 2019, Professor Robert Frau wrote in *The International Criminal Court and the Security Council*[387] about the political issues and challenges in the relation between the United Nations Security Council and the International Criminal Court.

Significantly, back in 1997, Kurt Jonassohn had already considered the study of genocide from a comparative perspective with human rights.[388] He also proposed a methodology for studying genocide through a comparative research approach. This same approach was lately adopted by Mark Lattimer, in 2007,[389] and by Antonio Cassese, in 2008,[390] who interpreted the atrocities of war through a human dimension. In two superlative works, Martin Shaw analyzed genocide through its moral and philosophical perspectives – *War and genocide: Organized Killing in Modern Societies* (2003),[391] and through its sociological aspect. Considering the sociological aspect of it, William A. Schabas analyzed the similarities and distinctions of both concepts in *Ethnic Cleansing and Genocide* (2003-

---

[380] Reservations to Convention on the Prevention and Punishment of the Crime of Genocide, Advisory Opinion, 1951 I.C.J. 15 (May 28).

[381] Application of the Convention on the Prevention and Punishment of the Crime of Genocide, Preliminary Objections, judgment, 1996 1. C. J. 595 (July 11, 1996).

[382] Democratic Republic of the Congo v. Belgium. I.C.J. 3. *Supra* note 69.

[383] Bosnia and Herzegovina v. Yugoslavia. I.C.J. 7. *Supra* note 70.

[384] Bosnia and Herzegovina v. Serbia and Montenegro. I.C.J. 43. *Supra* note 71.

[385] Croatia v. Serbia. I.C.J. 412. *Supra* note 72.

[386] Croatia v. Serbia. I.C.J. 3. *Supra* note 73.

[387] Robert Frau, The International Criminal Court and the Security Council: The International Criminal Court as a Political Tool? *In* The International Criminal Court in Turbulent Times 112–130 (Gerhard Werle & Andreas Zimmermann eds., Asser Press, 2019).

[388] Kurt Jonassohn & Karin Solveig Björnson, Genocide and Gross Human Rights Violation in Comparative Perspective (Transaction Publishers, 1997).

[389] Mark Lattimer ed., Genocide and Human Rights (Ashgate Publishing Limited, 2007).

[390] Antonio Cassese, The Human Dimension of International Law: Selected Papers (Oxford University Press, 2008).

[391] Martin Shaw, War and genocide: Organized Killing in Modern Societies (Polity Press, 2003).

2004).[392] Later on, Martin Shaw, leaning on the sociological aspects of the issue, adopted, in *What is genocide?* (2007),[393] a critical theoretical approach to point out the contradictions in the genocide legal theory. In the same year, Jacqes Semelin explored, in *Purify and Destroy*, the political uses of genocide by governments to establish and uphold political power.

## C.2. The literature on the hypothetical genocide of Christians in Iraq, perpetrated by ISIL/DAESH fighters

The Islamic State in Iraq and the Levant (ISIL/DAESH) occupied large parts of Iraq from 2014 to 2017. During this time, ISIL/DAESH members committed grave violations of International Criminal Law and international humanitarian law. In March 2015, an OHCHR[394] mission field investigation in Iraq reported "reliable information about acts of violence perpetrated against civilians because of their affiliation or perceived affiliation to a religious group."[395] Later on, several other reports from states, official governmental organizations, and inter-governmental organizations – recounted atrocities committed by ISIL/DAESH in Iraq from 2014 to 2017. For instance, reports from the U.N. Secretary-General (June 5, 2015),[396] (Aug. 28, 2018),[397] from the Representative of the Office of the United Nations High Commissioner for Human Rights,[398] the Representative of the Committee on the Elimination of Discrimination against Women,[399] from the Representative of the UN Secretary-General (July 9, 2018),[400] (Aug. 8, 2018),[401] the Representative of the Special Rapporteur on Extrajudicial, Summary or Arbitrary Executions,[402] from the Security Council,[403] from the European Parliament (Feb. 4, 2016),[404] (2017),[405] the UK Parliament,[406] as well as from the US Department of State.[407]

---

[392]  William A. Schabas, Ethnic Cleansing and Genocide: Similarities and Distinctions, 3 Eur. Y.B. Minority Issues 109 (2003–2004).
[393]  Martin Shaw, What is Genocide? (Polity Press, 2007).
[394]  The Office of the United Nations High Commissioner for Human Rights – OHCHR.
[395]  U.N. Doc. A/HRC/28/18 (March 27, 2015). *Preamble.*
[396]  U.N. Doc. A/69/926–S/2015/409 (June 5, 2015). ¶ 71.
[397]  U.N. Doc. A/73/347 (Aug. 28, 2018). ¶ 9.
[398]  U.N. Doc. A/HRC/28/18 (March 27, 2015). ¶ 78.
[399]  U.N. Doc. CEDAW/C/IRQ/7 (Aug. 15, 2018). ¶ 9.
[400]  U.N. Doc. S/2018/677 (July 9, 2018). ¶ 3.
[401]  U.N. Doc. S/PV.8324 (Aug. 8, 2018). ¶ 3.
[402]  U.N. Doc. A/HRC/38/44/Add.1 (June 20, 2018). ¶¶ 23, 25, 28, 73.
[403]  S.C. Res. 2379 (Sept. 21, 2017). ¶ 1.
[404]  Eur. Parl., Systematic Mass Murder of Religious Minorities by the so-called 'ISIS/Daesh' (2016/2529(RSP)), Resolution (Feb. 4, 2016). p. 35/79. h.

Besides, several *reports* from international non-governmental organizations explicitly indicated that ISIL/DAESH committed egregious atrocities against Christians in Iraq from 2014 to 2017. See, for example, the reports from 1) Genocide Watch, *ISIS is Committing Genocide* (2015);[408] 2) Knights of Columbus, *Genocide Against Christians in the Middle East: A Report Submitted to Secretary of State John Kerry by the Knights of Columbus and in Defense of Christians* (2016);[409] 3) The Hudson Institute, *The ISIS Genocide of Middle Eastern Christian Minorities and Its Jizya Propaganda Ploy* (2016)[410] and 4) Human Rights Watch, *Accountability for ISIS Crimes in Iraq* (2017).[411] Such reports indicate that ISIL/DAESH fighters perpetrated mass and individual killings, executions by, *inter alia*, hanging, stoning, drowning, throwing persons off buildings, beheadings, crucifixions, shootings, burnings, and other forms of murders.

These reports also indicate the perpetration of the following acts specifically against Christians in Iraq, from 2014 to 2017: the taking of hostages, use of persons as human shields, torture, beatings, mutilation, amputation, rape, enslavement, extensive violence, and inhuman and degrading treatment, causing serious bodily or mental harm, sexual slavery and abuse of women and girls, abductions, enforced disappearances, intentional displacement of the Christian population, the kidnapping of children, separation of children from their mothers, systematic destruction of Christian places of worship, forced conversions, the destruction of their Christian cultural heritage and historic sites and monuments. There is a debate about whether the existing evidence of persecution of Chris-

---

[405]   Eur. Parl., Prosecuting and Punishing the Crimes Against Humanity or Even Possible Genocide Committed by Daesh, Resolution 2190 (2017). ¶¶ 3, 3.1, 4.

[406]   UK Parliament, Genocide in Syria and Iraq, Early Day Motion, Sponsored by Robert Flello (Jan. 26, 2016).

[407]   U.S. Dep't of State, Department Press, Remarks by Secretary of State John Kerry (Mar. 17, 2016).

[408]   ISIS is Committing Genocide, GENOCIDE WATCH (Oct. 14, 2015). Conclusions, ¶ 2.

[409]   Knights of Columbus affirmed in its report that there is "overwhelming direct and circumstantial evidence" that ISIS and its affiliates committed genocide against Christians in Iraq (Genocide Against Christians in the Middle East: A Report Submitted to Secretary of State John Kerry by the Knights of Columbus and in Defense of Christians, KNIGHTS OF COLUMBUS, Observatory on intolerance and discrimination against Christians, Mar. 9, 2016). pp. 27, 38, 39, 54–131, 135–199.)

[410]   The ISIS Genocide of Middle Eastern Christian Minorities and Its *Jizya* Propaganda Ploy, THE HUDSON INSTITUTE, Center for Religious Freedom, Nina Shea (August 2016). *passim.*

[411]   Flawed Justice Report: Accountability for ISIS Crimes in Iraq, HUMAN RIGHTS WATCH (December 2017). pp. 16, 21 and 27.

tians in Iraq by terrorist members of the ISIL/DAESH regime (2014-2017) amounts to genocide. Much of the controversy indicates that the documentation of ISIL/DAESH crimes against Christians is substantial yet incomplete.[412]

Some crucial reasons for the incompleteness of data are: 1) Due to security concerns, access to different parts of Iraq was restricted until ISIL/DAESH's defeat in December 2017. Despite ISIL/DAESH's defeat in Iraq in December 2017, the terrorist group reportedly continues to attempt isolated attacks against civilians and security forces, particularly in the Baghdad region.[413] On October 18, 2018, the U.S. Department of State, through its Bureau of Consular Affairs, issued a red flag travel advisory for Iraq, the highest level of concern for visitors/foreigners.[414] In addition, from August 2018, eyewitnesses reported active foreign terrorist fighters in search of children for the purposes of trafficking and sexual slavery. This seriously impeded the verification and documentation of cases of genocide against Christians; 2) Owing to the fear of police involvement with armed groups, several families of victims were reluctant to report violations of rights to the Iraqi national police authorities; and 3) Most of the humanitarian advocacy agencies placed in the Autonomous Administration in Northern Iraq lack official access permits from the Iraqi government to the areas affected by conflict in Bagdad and in Mosul. This compromises the reporting and documentation of possible cases of genocide.[415]

Nevertheless, despite the incompleteness of data, various bodies have suggested that these acts are consistent with the crime of genocide: In the United States, The Senate,[416] The House of Representatives,[417] separately,

---

[412] Huma Haider, The Persecution of Christians in the Middle East. University of Birmingham. London: Assets Publishing Service – UK Government. February 16, 2017. pp. 11–12.

[413] Rep. of the S.C., Monthly Forecast: Situation in Iraq, February 2018 (Jan. 31, 2018).

[414] U.S. Dep't of State, Bureau of Consular Affairs. Iraq Travel Advisory. October 18, 2018.

[415] U.N. Doc. S/2018/770 (August 16, 2018). ¶ 10).

[416] S. 2377, 114th Cong. (Dec. 9, 2015). ¶ 7.

[417] 163 Cong. Rec. H5368 (daily ed. June 29, 2017) (statement of Rep. Ted Poe). p. H5369; 163 Cong. Rec. E1315 (daily ed. Oct. 3, 2017) (statement of Rep. Christopher H. Smith). Preamble; 164 Cong. Rec. S6876 (daily ed. Oct. 11, 2018) (statement of Rep. Mitch McConnell). ¶ 1; 164 Cong. Rec. H9600 (daily ed. Nov. 27, 2018) (statement of Rep. Christopher H. Smith). P. H9603; 164 Cong. Rec. E1606 – H.R. 390 (daily ed. Dec. 6, 2018) (statement of Rep. Anna G. Eshoo). Drafting. preamble; 165 Cong. Rec. X 1.1/A: X/A (daily ed. Jan. 10, 2017) (statement of Rep. Christopher H. Smith). Preamble; 165 Cong. Rec. H349 (daily ed. Jan. 9, 2019) (statement of Rep. Jeff Fortenberry). p. H352; 163 Cong. Rec. H4632 (daily ed. June 6, 2017) (statement of

as well as assembled,[418] The Department of State Secretary,[419] and its Office of the Spokesperson,[420] its Office of the Legal Adviser,[421] the Special Presidential Envoy for the Global Coalition to Defeat ISIS,[422] as well as the U.S. Permanent Representative to the United Nations.[423]

Likewise, on numerous occasions, the European Parliament formally recognized that some of these atrocities might sustain a formal accusation of genocide, particularly the killings, slaughtering, beatings, extortion, torture, and other inhuman and degrading treatment, extermination, and systematic cleansing, forced displacement, abduction/kidnappings, deprivation of liberty, enslavement, human trafficking, hostage-taking, use of persons as human shields, or for suicide bombing, forced

---

Rep. Edward Royce). p. H4633; 165 Cong. Rec. H2350 (daily ed. Mar. 5, 2019) (statement of Rep. Jeff Fortenberry). p. H2350.

[418] H.R.Con.Res. 75, 114th Cong. (Sept. 9, 2015). ¶ 1; H.R. 4017, 114th Cong. (Nov. 16, 2015). Preamble; H.R.Con.Res. 75, 114th Cong. (Mar. 15, 2016). Dispositive part, p.2; H.R.Con.Res. 41, 114th Cong. (July 18, 2016). ¶ 7; H.R. 407, 115th Cong. (Dec. 12, 2017). Preamble; H. Res. 1117, 115th Cong. (Oct. 5, 2018). Preamble; H.R. 390, 115th Cong. (Nov. 29, 2018). Drafting. Preamble; Sec. 2. Findings. ¶ 3; H. Res. 259, 116th Cong. (Mar. 27, 2019). p. 2; 165 Cong. Rec. H349 (daily ed. Jan. 9, 2019) (statement of Rep. Jeff Fortenberry). p. H351; H. Res. 259, 116th Cong. (Mar. 27, 2019). p. 2.

[419] U.S. Dep't of State, Department Press, Remarks by Secretary of State John Kerry (Mar. 17, 2016).

[420] U.S. Dep't of State, Office of the Spokesperson, Department Press, Briefing by Heather Nauert (Aug. 3, 2017); U.S. Dep't of State, Office of the Spokesperson, Department Press, Briefing by Heather Nauert (Aug. 15, 2017); U.S. Dep't of State, Office of the Spokesperson, Department Press, Briefing by Heather Nauert (Oct. 26, 2017); U.S. Dep't of State, Office of the Spokesperson, Department Press, Readout of USAID Administrator Green and Ambassador-at-Large for International Religious Freedom Samuel Brownback's Trip to Northern Iraq (July 5, 2018).

[421] U.S. Dep't of State, Office of the Legal Adviser, Digest of the United States Practice in International Law (2016). p. 780; U.S. Dep't of State, Office of the Legal Adviser, Digest of the United States Practice in International Law (2017). p. 283.

[422] U.S. Dep't of State, Department Press, Remarks by Special Presidential Envoy for the Global Coalition to Defeat ISIS Brett McGurk (June 22, 2017); U.S. Dep't of State, Department Press, Remarks by Special Presidential Envoy for the Global Coalition to Defeat ISIS Brett McGurk (July 8, 2017); U.S. Dep't of State, Department Press, Remarks by Special Presidential Envoy for the Global Coalition to Defeat ISIS Brett McGurk (July 13, 2017); U.S. Dep't of State, Department Press, Special Briefing by Special Presidential Envoy for the Global Coalition to Defeat ISIS Brett McGurk (Dec. 21, 2017); U.S. Dep't of State, Department Press, Remarks by Special Presidential Envoy for the Global Coalition to Defeat ISIS Brett McGurk (June 26, 2018).

[423] U.S. Permanent Representative to the United Nations, Ambassador Nikki Haley, Explanation of Vote Following the Adoption of UN Security Council Resolution 2379 on Accountability for ISIS Atrocities (Sept. 21, 2017).

marriage, rape, sexual slavery of Christian women and children and other forms of sexual violence, separation of Christian children from their mothers, forcibly transferring them to another group, forceful conversions to Islam, systematic destruction of Christian places of worship and religious artifacts, the kidnapping of priests, vandalization of tombs and cemeteries, declarations and statements of doctrine and policy encompassing the destruction of Christians.[424] Most of these declarations and statements were clearly broadcasted by ISIL/DAESH itself in their propaganda magazines *Dabiq*[425] and *Rumiyah*.[426] The number of Christians in Iraq

---

[424]   Eur. Parl., Committee on Legal Affairs and Human Rights, Threats Against Humanity Posed by the Terrorist Group Known as "IS": Violence Against Christians and Other Religious or Ethnic Communities, Compendium of Amendments (Final version), Doc. No. 13618 (Sept. 30, 2014); Eur. Parl., Systematic Mass Murder of Religious Minorities by the so-called 'ISIS/Daesh' (2016/2529(RSP)), Resolution (Feb. 4, 2016); Eur. Parl., Situation in Northern Iraq/Mosul (TA(2016)0422), Resolution (Oct. 27, 2016). d; Eur. Parl., Prosecuting and Punishing the Crimes Against Humanity or Even Possible Genocide Committed by Daesh, Resolution 2190 (2017). ¶ 1; Eur. Parl., EU priorities for the UN Human Rights Council Sessions in 2017 (2017/2598(RSP)), Resolution (Mar. 16, 2017). ¶ 21; Eur. Parl., Committee on Legal Affairs and Human Rights, Humanitarian Consequences of the Actions of the Terrorist Group Known as "Islamic State", Draft Resolution, Compendium of Amendments (Revised version), Doc. No. 13741 (Apr. 21, 2017); Eur. Parl., Committee on Legal Affairs and Human Rights, Prosecuting and Punishing the Crimes Against Humanity or Even Possible Genocide Committed by Daesh, Report, Doc. No. 14402 (Sept. 22, 2017); Eur. Parl., Annual Report on Human Rights and Democracy in the World 2016 and the European Union's Policy on the Matter (2017/2122(INI)), Resolution (Dec. 13, 2017).

[425]   This book analyzes the following Dabiq Magazine issues: Dabiq, Issue 1, Ramadan 1435 (July 2014); Dabiq, Issue 2, Ramadan 1435 (July 2014); Dabiq, Issue 3, Shawwal 1435 (July/August 2014); Dabiq, Issue 4, Dhul-Hijah 1435 (September 2014); Dabiq, Issue 5, Muharram 1436 (October 2014); Dabiq, Issue 6, Rabi'Al-Awwal 1436 (December, 2014); Dabiq, Issue 7, Rabi 'Al Akhir 1436 (February, 2015); Dabiq, Issue 8, Jumada Al-Akhirah 1436 (March, 2015); Dabiq, Issue 9, Sha'ban 1436 (May, 2015); Dabiq, Issue 10, Ramadan 1436 (July, 2015); Dabiq, Issue 11, Dhul-Qa'dah 1436 (September, 2015); Dabiq, Issue 12, Safar 1437 (November, 2015); Dabiq, Issue 13, Rabi' Al-Akhir 1437 (January, 2016); Dabiq, Issue 14, Rajab 1437 (April, 2016); and Rumiyah, Issue 1, Dhul Hijah 1437 (September 2016).

[426]   This book analyzes the following Rumiyah Magazine issues: Rumiyah, Issue 2, Muharram 1438 (October 2016); Rumiyah, Issue 3, Safar 1438 (November 2016); Rumiyah, Issue 4, Rabi' al-Awwal 1438 (December 2016); Rumiyah, Issue 5, Rabi' al-Akhir 1438 (January 2017); Rumiyah, Issue 6, Jumada al-Ula 1438 (February 2017); Rumiyah, Issue 7, Jumada al-Akhirah 1438 (March 2017); Rumiyah, Issue 8, Rajab 1438 (April 2017); Rumiyah, Issue 9, Sha'ban 1438 (May 2017); and Rumiyah, Issue 10, Ramadan 1438 (June 2017).

is thought to have declined during the ISIL/DAESH regime, particularly in Mosul and in the Ninewa Plains.[427]

The international criminal law scholarship lacks works that analyze the specific issue of whether the ISIL/DAESH persecution of Christians in Iraq, from 2014 to early 2017, constituted genocide, within the meaning and scope of the 1948 Genocide Convention, or persecution, within the meaning of the 1998 Rome Statute. Four works are worthy of attention in this regard. They are rare texts that explore some of the research questions of this *thesis*: 1) Mindy Belz's book: *They Say We Are Infidels: On the Run From ISIS With Persecuted Christians in the Middle East* (2016);[428] 2) The book edited by Ronald Rychlak and Jane Adolphe: *The Persecution and Genocide of Christians in Middle East: Prevention, Prohibition & Prosecution* (2017);[429] 3) Sarah Myers Raben's paper: *The ISIS Eradication of Christians and Yazidis: Human Trafficking, Genocide, and the Missing International Efforts to Stop It* (2018)[430] and Eric Osborne, Matthew Dowd, and Ryan McBrearty's paper: *Intending the Worst: The Case of ISIS's Specific Intent to Destroy the Christians of Iraq* (2019).[431]

Three other pieces addressed the issue, but incidentally alone. They considered much more the general aspects and the machinery of ISIL/DAESH and its threat to global security, rather than what risks ISIL/DAESH directly posed for Christians in Iraq: the paper from Frederic Gilles Sourgens, *The End of Law: The ISIL/DAESH Case Study for a Comprehensive Theory of Lawlessness* (2015)[432] and the books from 1) Patrick Cockburn, *The Rise of Islamic State: ISIS and the New Sunni Revolution* (2015);[433] 2) Robert Spencer, *The Complete Infidel's Guide to ISIS* (2015);[434] 3) Lawrence Wright, *The Terror Years: From Al-Qaeda to the Islamic State* (2016);[435] 4) Daniel Silander and John Janzekovic's book: *In-*

---

[427]  U.N. Doc. A/HRC/34/53/Add.1 (Jan. 9, 2017). ¶ 32.

[428]  Mindy Belz, They Say We Are Infidels: On the Run From ISIS With Persecuted Christians in the Middle East (Tyndale House Publishers Inc., 2016).

[429]  Ronald Rychlak & Jane Adolphe eds., The Persecution and Genocide of Christians in Middle East: Prevention, Prohibition & Prosecution (Angelico Press, 2017).

[430]  Sarah Myers Raben, The ISIS Eradication of Christians and Yazidis: Human Trafficking, Genocide, and the Missing International Efforts to Stop It, 15 Braz. J. Int'l L. 239 (2018).

[431]  Eric Osborne; Matthew Dowd; Ryan McBrearty, Intending the Worst: The Case of ISIS's Specific Intent to Destroy the Christians of Iraq, 46 Pepp. L. Rev. 545 (2019).

[432]  Frederic Gilles Sourgens, The End of Law: The ISIL/DAESH Case Study for a Comprehensive Theory of Lawlessness, 39 Fordham Int'l L.J. 355 (2015).

[433]  Patrick Cockburn, The Rise of Islamic State: ISIS and the New Sunni Revolution (Verso, 2015).

[434]  Robert Spencer, The Complete Infidel's Guide to ISIS (Regnery Publishing, 2015).

[435]  Lawrence Wright, The Terror Years: From Al-Qaeda to the Islamic State (Alfred A. Knopf, 2016).

*ternational Organizations and the Rise of ISIL/DAESH: Global Responses to Human Security Threats* (2017)[436] and 5) Robert Manne, *The Mind of the Islamic State* (2017).[437] Also, two manuscripts in the book edited by Jacob Eriksson & Ahmed Khaleel, *Iraq After ISIS: The Challenges of Post-War Recovery*, are relevant in this context: 1) the text from Simon Mabon & Ana Maria Kumarasamy, *Da'ish, Stasis and Bare Life in Iraq*,[438] contributes to understanding the political aspects in the process of the emergence of ISIL/DAESH and 2) the text from Razaw Salihy, *Terror and Torment: The Civilian Journey to Escape Iraq's War Against the "Islamic State,"*[439] brings a civilian perspective on surviving Iraq's war against the Islamic State.

Although the papers and books cited above stand out in a scarcity of works, the epistemological approach of these works mentioned above regarded the crimes against Christians in Iraq much more through a political/policy and sociological lens than from a legal standpoint. Some scholars did indeed address the legal aspects related to ISIL/DAESH acts – see, for example, George S. Jr. Yacoubian *et al.* (2005),[440] Coman Kenny (2017),[441] and Gabor Kajtar (2017)[442] –, but they did not consider – or did not address – the possibility of a genocide perpetrated by ISIL/DAESH against Christians in Iraq. The pertinent hundreds of Security Council's reports, resolutions, and other Councils' documents on the topic are scarcely mentioned by those works on ISIS in Iraq. Consequentially, the facts described in those documents are not tried against the elements of the crime of genocide. Therefore, there is an open flank in the field yet to be unpassionately clarified and academically investigated.

---

[436]  Daniel Silander, Don Wallace & John Janzekovic eds. International Organizations and the rise of ISIL/DAESH: Global Responses to Human Security Threats (Routledge, 2017).

[437]  Robert Manne, The Mind of the Islamic State (Prometheus Books, 2017).

[438]  Simon Mabon & Ana Maria Kumarasamy, Da'ish, Stasis and Bare Life in Iraq *in* Iraq After ISIS: The Challenges of Post-War Recovery 9–28 (Jacob Eriksson & Ahmed Khaleel eds., Palgrave Macmillan, 2019).

[439]  Razaw Salihy, Terror and Torment: The Civilian Journey to Escape Iraq's War Against the "Islamic State" *in* Iraq After ISIS: The Challenges of Post-War Recovery 79–98 (Jacob Eriksson & Ahmed Khaleel eds., Palgrave Macmillan, 2019).

[440]  George S. Jr. Yacoubian; Anna N. Astvatsaturova; Tracy M. Proietti, Iraq and the ICC: Should Iraq Nationals by Prosecuted for the Crime of Genocide before the International Criminal Court, 1 War Crimes Genocide & Crimes against Human. 47 (2005).

[441]  Coman Kenny, Prosecuting Crimes of International Concern: Islamic State at the ICC, 33 Utrecht J. Int'l & Eur. L. 120 (2017).

[442]  Gabor Kajtar, The Use of Force against ISIL/DAESH in Iraq and Syria – A Legal Battlefield, 34 Wis. Int'l L.J. 535 (2017).

## D. Methodology

This book aims to determine the legal nature of the atrocities perpetrated by ISIL/DAESH against Christians in Iraq from 2014 to 2017 and to respond more appropriately to the critical issue of criminal accountability for international crimes. In doing so, this research ultimately intends to further the International Criminal Law scholarship on genocide and persecution as a crime against humanity.

This research employs both a doctrinal and comparative approach, with thoroughly scrutinized texts and detailed analyses as the primary research keys.[443] However, this research intends to develop a body of theory that moves beyond simple descriptive research. After a thorough and meticulous reading of all the sources found, the work proceeds with a critical interpretation of them, striving to find the meanings, the connections, and the legal significance behind the ordinary text.[444]

This work encompasses a *historical-comparative* research method that analyzes both the international legislative history of genocide and crimes against humanity as well as the evolution of such crimes in the jurisprudence of international courts.[445] In doing so, this research *piece* proceeds with a detailed, meticulous, methodical, and technical verification – *doctrinal research* – whether these two bodies of law allow for an interpretation of the elements of the crime of genocide to give substratum for an allegation of genocide against Christians in Iraq. This dragnet approach encompasses a close and robust *black law* and qualitative analysis of legal texts – laws, treaties, Security Council resolutions, and International Criminal Law jurisprudence – that support the research hypothesis.

The research methods used throughout this study also involve in-depth genocide case-law studies and their analyses. Employing both quantitative and qualitative analyses, it proceeds with a three-fold comparison: firstly, a comparison among the UN Tribunals – The ICJ, SCSL, the ICTR, ICTY, and their Residual Mechanism – and the ICC; secondly, a comparison between the international and the domestic (Iraqi) judicial mechanisms to hold perpetrators of genocide accountable and thirdly, a comparison between the Security Council Resolutions on Iraq and the compliance of states with them.

---

[443]  Please refer to: W. Lawrence Neuman, Social Research Methods: Qualitative and Quantitative Approaches (Pearson Education Limited, 7th. ed. 2014). p. 38.

[444]  *Idem.* p. 17.

[445]  *Idem.* p. 52.

The Security Council's Resolutions constitute a benchmark for protecting persons from direct and indirect consequences of armed conflicts. They establish a framework upon which states, armed/extremist groups, individuals, and private entities can be targets for specific sanctions. Conscious of its responsibility towards international peace and security, both in its duty to protect groups from genocide as well as in its obligation to prevent genocide, the United Nations Security Council is of paramount importance in keeping the relevant parties in line with the principles of international humanitarian law.

To better understand the juridical pattern of the Security Council in protecting groups from genocide, this research methodically scrutinized ordinary Security Council Resolutions, Security Council Resolutions under the authority of Chapter VII of the Charter of United Nations, reports from the Counter-Terrorism Committee (CCT), and the Counter-Terrorism Committee Executive Directorate (CTED), Presidential Statements, and conclusions of the Security Council Thematic Working Groups, such as the one on Iraq and the other on Children and Armed Conflict. Ultimately, the most critical Security Council organ that this research painstakingly followed was the Investigative Team in Iraq, whose primary duties, under Resolution 2379 (2017), included: *collecting, preserving, and storing evidence in Iraq of acts that may amount to war crimes, crimes against humanity and genocide committed by the terrorist group ISIL/DAESH (Da'esh) in Iraq.*

Several other UN documents were analyzed utilizing the triangulation research method,[446] [447] both in tandem and separately: UNAMI reports, General Assembly resolutions, Human Rights Council resolutions, and solemn meetings; reports from the UN General Assembly, the UN Secretary-General, Ad Hoc Committees, the High Commissioner on Human Rights and from the General Assembly Special Representatives on Iraq, and these Representatives: Rep. of the Committee on the Rights of the Child, Special Representative of the Secretary-General for Children and Armed Conflict, Rep. of the Office of the United Nations High Commissioner for Human Rights, Rep. of the Office of the United Nations High Commissioner for Human Rights, Rep. of the Committee on the Elimination of Racial Discrimination, and the Rep. of the Committee on the Elimination of Discrimination

---

[446] "Triangulation departs from the idea that looking at something from multiple points of view improves accuracy." (W. Lawrence Neuman. *Supra* note 443. p. 166).

[447] The term *triangulation* "has been employed somewhat more broadly by Denzin (1970: 310) to refer to an approach that uses 'multiple observers, theoretical perspectives, sources of data, and methodologies', but the emphasis has tended to be on methods of investigation and sources of data. (Alan Bryman, Social Research Methods (Oxford University Press, 4th. ed. 2012. p. 312).

against Women. Reports from international non-governmental organizations (NGOs), as well as documents from Governments and their bodies, such as from the US Congress, the US White House, the US Department of State, and from the Council of Europe – European Parliament, provided additional evidentiary bases.

Other documentary research and in-depth readings were necessary throughout this book. Electronic literature for analysis was available through Hein-Online. Similarly, daily news items related to the research topic were also followed-up. Speeches, statements, and memoranda made by various actors in this research were taken into consideration. Finally, the author aimed to liaise with experts in International Criminal Law and victims of ISIL/DAESH atrocities – through reports from international NGOs –, thus employing a mixed methodology approach, inclusive of interviews, courses, and seminars to better understand the interconnectivity and complexity of the terrorism phenomena with the practice of genocidal or persecutory acts.

As the search for existing evidence of ISIL/DAESH violations unfolded, the author encountered significant limitations to determine the exact magnitude of ISIL/DAESH acts. Due to several practical constraints, local and international actors found it very difficult to interview victims and collect material and documental evidence in the areas under the former regime of ISIL/DAESH, or under the influence of the terrorist groups. Among these reasons, the following may be indicated as examples: 1) the victims' fear of reprisal or retaliation by the perpetrators; 2) chronic instability in the region; 3) administrative restrictions in accessing the affected regions; 4) limited psychosocial support and counseling services for the victims; 5) a climate of widespread impunity for perpetrators; and 6) weak law enforcement.

Given the controversial character of the crime of genocide, this book did not dedicate time to analyzing the ISIL/DAESH atrocities against Christians in Iraq through an interdisciplinary approach (sociological, political, and international relations). The work exclusively focused on the foundational crime elements of *typicity* and legality of the criminal conduct perpetrated by ISIL/DAESH fighters.

## E. Important caveats

Before the reader proceeds, there are some important caveats and clarifications:

1) Given the controversial character of the crime of genocide, this book did not dedicate time to analyzing the ISIL/DAESH atrocities against Christians in Iraq through an interdisciplinary approach, namely from a sociological, political, and international relations standpoint. This book exclusively focused on the foundational crime elements of *typicity* and *legality* of the criminal conduct perpetrated by ISIL/DAESH fighters;

2) The author recognizes that several reports from international and inter-governmental organizations accounted that ISIL/DAESH perpetrated war crimes in Iraq. Although these are serious crimes, they were excluded from the scope of examination in this work due to the critical time constraints the author was submitted to, while analyzing the possible perpetration of genocide and crimes against humanity by ISIL/DAESH in Iraq;

3) Because hundreds of cases are cited throughout the book, the author did not proceed with a full citation of them every time they are referenced in the footnotes. In order to find the full citation of the case, please refer to the first call number indicated with the Latin term *Supra* note #. When a citation makes an *exact* reference to an *immediate* previous citation, the author used the Latin terms *ibidem* and *idem;*

4) When multiple case law is cited in the very same reference call, the cases are all cited in chronological order and grouped according to the international courts that decided the cases;

5) Because hundreds of United Nations (U.N.) documents were cited throughout Chapters 1 to 4, the author, in an attempt to ease the readers' work, did not provide a full citation of the source in the footnotes, with the exception of U.N. Treaty Law, and Security Council Resolutions. In this sense, the author provides a citation exclusively with the U.N. Document call reference (U.N. Doc.). The reader may find at the end of each chapter a chart with the complete citation of U.N. sources, including the documents from the United Nations Assistance Mission for Iraq (UNAMI).

6) The term "child" refers to a human being under the age of 18 years-old;

7) The United Nations Body of Principles for the Protection of All Persons under Any Form of Detention or Imprisonment[448] indicates

---

[448] United Nations. Commission on Human Rights. Body of principles for the protection of all persons under any form of detention or imprisonment. 7 March 1978. Resolution E/CN.4/RES/19(XXXIV).

that "arrest" refers to the *act* of apprehending a person and that "detention" refers to the *condition* of a detained person. Despite this indication, this research used these terms interchangeably;

8) The use of the term "human rights" – and interchangeably "fundamental rights" – is only and exclusively a reflection of the fact that the international laws regarding crimes against humanity and persecution necessarily require a substantial violation of "fundamental rights" – see, for example, Article 7.2.g of the Rome Statute. Therefore, this book does not explore the different meanings, the scope, and the theoretical aspects regarding the terms "human rights" and "fundamental rights."

9) Finally, in this book, there are plenty of references to the terms "terrorism," "terrorist groups," "terrorist attacks," "terrorist practices," and "for terrorist purposes." However, the author will not discuss the meaning, the scope, or other implications of these terms for the international legal and jurisprudential scholarship. Several U.N. mechanisms specifically name the Islamic State in Iraq and the Levant/IS/DAESH as "terrorist group," and its fighters as "terrorist fighters."[449] Therefore, this Thesis only follows this approach.

---

[449]  See, for example: S.C. Res. 2170 (Aug. 15, 2014). ¶ 1, 4; S.C. Res. 2199 (Feb. 12, 2015). ¶ 15; S.C. Res. 2249 (Nov. 20, 2015). ¶ 3.

*Chart of United Nations documents cited in the Introduction – Chronological order*

## 1994

U.N. Doc. A/CN.4/L.491/Rev.1 (July 8, 1994).
Rep. of the Working Group on a Draft Statute for An International Criminal Court, International Law Commission.

## 2005

U.N. Doc. S/2005/60 (Feb. 1, 2005).
Rep. of the International Commission of Inquiry on Darfur to the Secretary-General Pursuant to Security Council Resolution 1564 (2004).

## 2015

U.N. Doc. A/HRC/28/18 (March 27, 2015).
Rep. of the Office of the United Nations High Commissioner for Human Rights, submitted to the Human Rights Council, Human Rights Situation in Iraq in the Light of Abuses Committed by The so Called Islamic State in Iraq and The Levant and Associated Groups.

U.N. Doc. A/69/926–S/2015/409 (June 5, 2015).
U.N. Secretary-General, Children and Armed Conflict.

## 2017

U.N. Doc. A/HRC/34/53/Add.1 (Jan. 9, 2017).
Rep. of the Special Rapporteur on Minority Issues, submitted to the Human Rights Council concerning her mission to Iraq.

## 2018

U.N. Doc. A/HRC/38/44/Add.1 (June 20, 2018).
Rep. of the Special Rapporteur on Extrajudicial, Summary or Arbitrary Executions, submitted to the Human Rights Council concerning her mission to Iraq.

U.N. Doc. S/2018/677 (July 9, 2018).
Rep. of the U.N. Secretary-General submitted to the S.C, pursuant to the implementation of Res. 2367 (2017).

U.N. Doc. S/PV.8324 (Aug. 8, 2018).
Rep. of the U.N. Secretary-General submitted to the S.C, The Situation Concerning Iraq, pursuant to Res. 2367 (2017).

U.N. Doc. CEDAW/C/IRQ/7 (Aug. 15, 2018).
Rep. of the Committee on the Elimination of Discrimination against Women, Seventh Periodic Report Submitted by Iraq Under Article 18 of the Convention.

U.N. Doc. S/2018/770 (August 16, 2018).
Rep. of the U.N. Secretary-General submitted to the S.C, pursuant to the Threat Posed by ISIL/DAESH (Da'esh) to International Peace and Security.

U.N. Doc. A/73/347 (Aug. 28, 2018).
U.N. Secretary-General, Effects of terrorism on the enjoyment of human rights.

*Chart of documents from the United Nations Assistance Mission for Iraq (UNAMI) — Chronological order*

## 2014

July 6, 2014 – Sept. 10, 2014.
Rep. of the Office of the United Nations High Commissioner for Human Rights, United Nations Assistance Mission for Iraq (UNAMI), Report on the Protection of Civilians in the Armed Conflict in Iraq.

# 1. ISIL/DAESH atrocities in Iraq

## 1.1. Timeline of ISIL/DAESH operations

### 1.1.1. The origins in Syria and Iraq

The origin of the Islamic State of Iraq and the Levant (ISIL/DAESH) dates back to 1999 with the establishment of the group *Jama'at al-Tawhid wal-Ji-had*, under the leadership of a Jordanian national named Abu Musab al-Zarqawi.[450][451] In 2003, the group was fully engaged in the Iraqi insurgency against Iraq's American-led invasion and occupation.[452][453] In 2006, Sunni insurgents joined the group. They formed the *Mujahideen Shura Council*, which established the Islamic State of Iraq, in October 2006, as one of the divisions of Al-Qaida in Iraq.[454] The newly established organization "emulated their adversaries and learned how to effectively conduct organized information activities."[455]

In 2011, following the waves of the civil war in Syria, the leader of the Islamic State of Iraq at that time, Abu Bakr al-Baghdadi, decided to expand the presence, the visibility, and the operations of the group in vast Sunni provinces of Syria, particularly in Raqqa, Idlib, Deir ez-Zor, and Allepo.[456] Following the occupation of these areas, al-Baghdadi announced the merging of the *Jabhat an-Nuṣrah li-Ahli ash-Sham* (al-Nusra Front) together with the Islamic State of Iraq, forming a new single group under the name the Islamic State of Iraq and Al-Sham.[457]

However, a cojoined statement from al-Qaida's leader, Ayman al-Zawahiri, and the al-Nusra Front leader, Abu Mohammad Al-Julani, denied the merger, "stating that neither they nor anyone else in al-Nusra's leader-

---

[450] NATO, "DAESH Information Campaign and its influence: Results of the Study" (Jan. 2016). p. 13.
[451] The legal foundations of the Islamic State, THE BROOKINGS INSTITUTION, The Brookings Project on U.S. Relations with the Islamic World (July 2016).
[452] NATO. *Supra* note 450. p. 13.
[453] Fawaz A. Gerges, ISIS: A History (Princeton University Press, 2016). p. 50.
[454] U.N. Doc. S/2011/366 (June 15, 2011). ¶ 14; U.N. Doc. S/2015/852 (Nov. 9, 2015). ¶ 15; U.N. Doc. A/HRC/38/44/Add.1 (June 20, 2018). ¶ 18.
[455] NATO. *Supra* note 450. p. 13.
[456] *Ibidem.*
[457] *Ibidem.*

ship, had been consulted."[458] The issuance of this statement by al-Qaeda and the al-Nusra Front "cut all connections with al-Baghdadi's organization."[459] In 2013, several armed groups and foreign fighters joined the group forming an "all-encompassing entity" named the Islamic State of Iraq and al-Sham (Levant) – ISIL/DAESH, or Daesh.[460][461] The group then occupied large parts of Syria and northern Iraq, particularly the Governorates of Anbar, Ninawa, Salah al-Din, Kirkuk, and Diyala.[462][463]

## 1.1.2. The terrorist group names.

Daesh' is the acronym of ad-Dawlah al-Islāmiyah fī 'l-'Irāq wa-sh-Shām. Depending on the Arabic conjugation, "the acronym 'Daesh' sounds like an Arabic word that can have several shades of meaning from 'to trample down and crush' to 'a bigot who imposes his view on others,'"[464] State members of the North Atlantic Treaty Organization (NATO) argued that the term *'Daesh,'* instead of *'ISIL/DAESH,'* should be the correct term to refer to the Islamic State, "because it is much more undermining to the organization than the use of their chosen name, 'Islamic State/IS/ISIS/ISIL/DAESH,' together with an epithet."[465] NATO considers that with the use of the term 'ISIL/DAESH,' member states are somehow acknowledging and recognizing that the group indeed comprises a state (the Islamic State of Iraq and the Levant) and recognizing its legitimacy.[466]

NATO also argued that "by using the name 'the Islamic State,' chosen by the terrorists themselves, news agencies participate in Daesh's propaganda campaign."[467] Instead, "the use of the name Daesh in the public media," argued NATO, would "send a clear message to the terrorists about the overwhelming majority of people worldwide that do not support their

---

[458]  *Ibidem.*

[459]  *Ibidem.*

[460]  U.N. Doc. S/2011/366 (June 15, 2011). ¶ 14; U.N. Doc. A/HRC/38/44/Add.1 (June 20, 2018). ¶ 18.

[461]  According to the NATO data, twenty-five organizations pledged their allegiance to ISIL/DAESH and ten more offered global support to it. (NATO. *Supra* note 450. p. 19).

[462]  U.N. Doc. A/HRC/30/NGO/116 (Sept. 8, 2015). p. 2; U.N. Doc. A/HRC/38/44/Add.1 (June 20, 2018). ¶ 18; U.N. Doc. A/73/352/Add.6 (Oct. 2018). ¶ 1; U.N. Doc. S/2019/984 (Dec. 23, 2019). ¶ 5.

[463]  NATO. *Supra* note 450. p. 14.

[464]  *Idem.* p. 10.

[465]  *Ibidem.*

[466]  *Ibidem.*

[467]  *Ibidem.*

campaign of violence to achieve their goals."[468] Notwithstanding NATO's approach, this book will employ the terms 'ISIL/DAESH' and 'Daesh' interchangeably to refer to the self-proclaimed Islamic State of Iraq and the Levant for the sole reason that the former is the term extensively used in documents from the major organisms of the United Nations (U.N.) umbrella. The use of the term ISIL/DAESH in this book does not imply that the author supports ISIL/DAESH ideology or ISIL/DAESH atrocious acts in Iraq and Syria.

## 1.1.3. ISIL/DAESH power in Iraq

At the peak of its power, ISIL/DAESH seized, controlled, and exercised multiple layers of power on approximately 40 percent of the Iraqi territory.[469] ISIL/DAESH then divided Ninewa Governorate into three governing entities, Jazeera, Tigris, and Ninewa.[470] The group established a leader (*wali*) for each of these regions.[471] On June 29, 2014, the group 1) proclaimed itself a Caliphate, self-claiming the monopoly of law and order;[472] 2) asserted the role of unifying Sunni insurgent groups under goals similar to those of Al-Qaida; and 3) declared its "exclusive theological and political authority over the world's Muslims."[473]

Politically, ISIL/DAESH organized the Caliphate into several councils and departments: the Leadership Council, the Intelligence Council; the Military Council; the Fighter Assistance Council; the Legal Council; the Security Council, the Financial Council, and the Media Council.[474] Operationally, ISIL/DAESH organized its fighters in small cells and lone wolves to carry out its "targeted hit-and-run operations."[475] Tactically, ISIL/DAESH "established safe havens in the Hamrin mountain range of north-eastern Iraq."[476] Taking advantage of flaws between the Iraqi forces and *Kurdish* forces,[477] ISIL/DAESH commanded up to 30,000 fighters in the Levant.[478] Of

---

[468] *Idem.* pp. 10–11.

[469] U.N. Doc. A/HRC/38/44/Add.1 (June 20, 2018). ¶ 18.

[470] U.N. Doc. A/HRC/30/66 (July 27, 2015). ¶ 12.

[471] *Ibidem.*

[472] William Harris, Quicksilver War: Syria, Iraq and the Spiral of Conflict (Oxford University Press, 2018). pp. 59–60.

[473] U.N. Doc. A/HRC/38/44/Add.1 (June 20, 2018). ¶ 18.

[474] NATO. *Supra* note 450. p. 21.

[475] U.N. Doc. S/2020/717 (July 23, 2020). ¶ 10.

[476] *Ibidem.*

[477] The forces of the Autonomous Administration in Northern Iraq.

[478] U.N. Doc. S/2015/739 (July 19, 2016). ¶ 11.

this total, 25,000 persons comprised "foreign terrorist fighters" (FTFs), coming from more than 100 (one hundred) countries.[479] FTFs constituted the most crucial asset of the ISIL/DAESH terrorist network. They used to make regular daily movements between Iraq and the Syrian Arab Republic, particularly in the Anbar and Ninawa Provinces.[480]

Between June 2014 and December 2017, local and foreign ISIL/DAESH fighters waged war on Iraq and left the country in a situation of extreme political, economic, social, and military volatility.[481] [482] Internationally, ISIL/DAESH became a "global and unprecedented threat to international peace and security" "through its terrorist acts and its violent extremist ideology."[483] [484] During this period, several U.N. entities reported that ISIL/DAESH fighters and commanders committed systematic and wide-spread violations of international human rights, humanitarian law, and criminal law against populations living in areas under ISIL/DAESH's control, particularly against women and children.[485] [486] [487]

Operating with broad impunity, ISIL/DAESH restricted several fundamental freedoms and instilled fear in the population living under its regime.[488] [489]In a systematic fashion, they committed murder, mass killings, ill-treatment, torture, arbitrary deprivation of liberty, forced conversions into Islam, kidnapping, hostage-taking, suicide bombings, use of civilians as human shields during the hostilities, and recruitment and use of children. They also perpetrated enslavement, human trafficking, forced trans-

[479]  U.N. Doc. S/2015/975 (Dec. 29, 2015). ¶ 78; U.N. Doc. A/HRC/38/44/Add.1 (June 20, 2018). ¶ 18; U.N. Doc. S/2019/984 (Dec. 23, 2019). ¶ 5.
[480]  U.N. Doc. A/HRC/38/44/Add.1 (June 20, 2018). ¶ 18; U.N. Doc. S/2019/984 (Dec. 23, 2019). ¶ 5; U.N. Doc. S/2020/717 (July 23, 2020). ¶ 10.
[481]  UNAMI (Nov. 6, 2018). p. 3.
[482]  U.N. Doc. S/2014/774 (Oct. 31, 2014). ¶ 19.
[483]  S.C. Res. 2490 (Sept. 20, 2019). Preamble, p. 1.
[484]  See also: S.C. Res. 2249 (Nov. 20, 2015). Preamble, p. 1; S.C. Res. 2379 (Sept. 21, 2017). Preamble, p.1.
[485]  U.N. Doc. S/2015/82 (Feb. 2, 2015). ¶ 48; U.N. Doc. S/2016/92 (Jan. 29, 2016). ¶ 9; U.N. Doc. A/HRC/38/44/Add.1 (June 20, 2018). ¶¶ 18, 22; U.N. Doc. A/73/352/Add.6 (Oct. 12, 2018). ¶ 1; U.N. Doc. S/2018/1031 (Nov. 16, 2018). ¶ 8.
[486]  UNAMI (Sept. 11, 2014 – Dec. 10, 2014). p. 6; UNAMI (Dec. 11, 2014 – April 30, 2015). p. 10; UNAMI (Nov. 6, 2018). p. 3.
[487]  S.C. Res. 2299 (July 25, 2016). Preamble, p. 4; S.C. Res. 2367 (July 14, 2017). Preamble, p. 4; S.C. Res. 2490 (Sept. 20, 2019). Preamble, p.1.
[488]  U.N. Doc. S/2015/530 (July 13, 2015). ¶ 51; U.N. Doc. CERD/C/IRQ/22-25 (Nov. 22, 2017). ¶ 15; U.N. Doc. A/HRC/38/44/Add.1 (June 20, 2018). ¶ 23; U.N. Doc. CEDAW/C/IRQ/7 (Aug. 15, 2018). ¶ 10; U.N. Doc. S/2018/1031 (Nov. 16, 2018). ¶ 8.
[489]  UNAMI (May 1, 2015 – Oct. 31, 2015). p. 19.

fers of civilians, sale of women and children as spoils of war, forced marriage, rape, sexual slavery, and other forms of sexual violence. ISIL/DAESH fighters installed landmines, used weaponized chemical agents, and shelled civilian areas. They committed attacks on critical infrastructure, systematic destruction of places of worship, destruction of cultural heritage, trafficking of cultural property, and other violent acts seeking to destroy/eradicate/exterminate entire religious and ethnic groups.[490] [491] [492] [493] [494] [495]

ISIL/DAESH reportedly conducted a deliberate series of mass executions against Iraqi Security Forces in areas under its control.[496] For instance, in one of the most notorious mass massacres in Iraq, ISIL/DAESH summarily executed 1,700 air force cadets on June 12, 2014, at Camp Speicher in Salah al-Din governorate.[497] [498] In another instance, they killed 175 Iraqi air force cadets at an airbase in Tikrit.[499] ISIL/DAESH also mass executed a large number of unarmed Iraqi soldiers.[500] On August 8, 2015, ISIL/DAESH reportedly "executed at least 300 civil servants employed by the Independent High Electoral Commission (IHEC) in Mosul, Ninewa."[501]

The escalation of crossfire attacks and asymmetric armed clashes between ISIL/DAESH, the NATO Coalition, and the Iraqi Security Forces

---

[490]	U.N. Doc. S/2014/774 (Oct. 31, 2014). ¶ 76; U.N. Doc. A/HRC/28/18 (March 27, 2015). ¶¶ 35, 76; U.N. Doc. A/HRC/30/66 (July 27, 2015). ¶ 32; U.N. Doc. S/2016/92 (Jan. 29, 2016). ¶ 9; U.N. Doc. S/2017/75 (Jan. 26, 2017). ¶ 36; U.N. Doc. CCPR/C/IRQ/CO/5/Add.1 (Aug. 18, 2017). ¶ 19; U.N. Doc. S/2017/881 (Oct. 19, 2017). ¶ 63; U.N. Doc. A/HRC/38/44/Add.1 (June 20, 2018). ¶ 23; U.N. Doc. CEDAW/C/IRQ/7 (Aug. 15, 2018). ¶¶ 9, 10, 12.

[491]	UNAMI (July 6, 2014 – Sept. 10, 2014). p. 14; UNAMI (Dec. 11, 2014 – April 30, 2015). p. 4; UNAMI (Nov. 6, 2018). p. 4.

[492]	S.C. Res. 2490 (Sept. 20, 2019). Preamble, p.1.

[493]	163 Cong. Rec. H4632 (daily ed. June 6, 2017) (statement of Rep. Edward Royce). p. H4633.

[494]	Eur. Parl., Systematic Mass Murder of Religious Minorities by the so-called 'ISIS/Daesh' (2016/2529(RSP)), Resolution (Feb. 4, 2016). B; Eur. Parl., Prosecuting and Punishing the Crimes Against Humanity or Even Possible Genocide Committed by Daesh, Resolution 2190 (2017). ¶ 3.2.

[495]	Punished for Daesh's Crimes: Displaced Iraqis Abused by Militias and Government Forces, AMNESTY INTERNATIONAL (Oct. 18, 2016). p. 15.

[496]	UNAMI (July 6, 2014 – Sept. 10, 2014). pp. 6, 8, 14, 16; UNAMI (Nov. 6, 2018). p. 4.

[497]	U.N. Doc. A/HRC/28/18 (March 27, 2015). ¶ 32; U.N. Doc. A/HRC/38/44/Add.1 (June 20, 2018). ¶ 77; U.N. Doc. CEDAW/C/IRQ/7 (Aug. 15, 2018). ¶ 11.

[498]	AMNESTY INTERNATIONAL. *Supra* note 495. p. 7.

[499]	U.N. Doc. CEDAW/C/IRQ/7 (Aug. 15, 2018). ¶ 11.

[500]	U.N. Doc. A/69/53/Add.1 (Sept. 1, 2014). Preamble, p.7.

[501]	UNAMI (May 1, 2015 – Oct. 31, 2015). p. 9.

caused the indirect killing and maiming of thousands of children in urban centers.[502] [503] In several of these attacks, ISIL/DAESH denied humanitarian relief access to affected children.[504] From June 2014 until the end of 2017, The United Nations Assistance Mission for Iraq (UNAMI) recorded at least 30,000 civilians killed and 55,150 injured in Iraq, either due to direct or indirect result of ISIL/DAESH actions.[505] [506] International observers concluded that some of these incidents might have constituted war crimes and crimes against humanity.[507] [508] The devastating impact of ISIL/DAESH attacks on civilians and civilian infrastructure was unfathomable.[509]

Following ISIL/DAESH's self-proclamation of the Caliphate, ISIL/DAESH imposed the *takfiri* doctrine with their own interpretation of the Islam faith and Muslim ideologies. By then, ISIL/DAESH started its systematic and deliberate intent to persecute and to destroy Christians in Iraq. Issuing a series of ultimatums, ISIL/DAESH declared Christians as "slaves of the cross"[510] and threatened them with executions.[511] [512] At the time, Christians in Iraq lived in an atmosphere of fear and intimidation.

In March 2015, an OHCHR mission field investigation in Iraq reported "reliable information about acts of violence perpetrated against civilians because of their affiliation or perceived affiliation to a religious group."[513]

---

[502]   U.N. Doc. A/68/878–S/2014/339 (May 15, 2014). ¶ 73; U.N. Doc. A/69/212 (July 31, 2014). ¶ 4; U.N. Doc. S/2015/82 (Feb. 2, 2015). ¶¶ 22, 51; U.N. Doc. A/69/926–S/2015/409 (June 5, 2015). ¶¶ 71, 74; U.N. Doc. S/2016/77 (Jan. 26, 2016). ¶ 57; U.N. Doc. A/70/836–S/2016/360 (Apr. 20, 2016). ¶¶ 8.a, 61; U.N. Doc. S/2016/396 (Apr. 27, 2016). ¶¶ 42, 46; U.N. Doc. A/71/205 (July 25, 2016). ¶ 4; U.N. Doc. A/72/361–S/2017/821 (Aug. 24, 2017). ¶ 78; U.N. Doc. S/2018/677 (July 9, 2018). ¶ 45; U.N. Doc. S/2019/984 (Dec. 23, 2019). ¶ 53.

[503]   UNAMI (July 6, 2014 – Sept. 10, 2014). p. 9.

[504]   U.N. Doc. A/72/361–S/2017/821 (Aug. 24, 2017). ¶ 83.

[505]   UNAMI (Nov. 6, 2018). p. 3.

[506]   See also: U.N. Doc. A/HRC/38/44/Add.1 (June 20, 2018). ¶ 1.

[507]   UNAMI (Dec. 11, 2014 – April 30, 2015). pp. 4, 10.

[508]   See also: U.N. Doc. A/HRC/38/44/Add.1 (June 20, 2018). ¶¶ 22, 48; U.N. Doc. A/73/352/Add.6 (Oct. 12, 2018). ¶ 1; U.N. Doc. A/73/352/Add.6 (Oct. 2018). ¶ 1; U.N. Doc. S/2018/1031 (Nov. 16, 2018). ¶ 8.

[509]   U.N. Doc. A/69/926–S/2015/409 (June 5, 2015). ¶ 76; U.N. Doc. A/HRC/30/66 (July 27, 2015). ¶ 15; U.N. Doc. A/70/836–S/2016/360 (Apr. 20, 2016). ¶ 58, 61; S.C. Res. 2379 (Sept. 21, 2017). ¶ 1; U.N. Doc. S/2018/677 (July 9, 2018). ¶¶ 20, 38, 39; U.N. Doc. A/HRC/38/44/Add.1 (June 20, 2018). ¶ 1.

[510]   Eur. Parl., Prosecuting and Punishing the Crimes Against Humanity or Even Possible Genocide Committed by Daesh, Resolution 2190 (2017). ¶ 4.

[511]   UNAMI (July 6, 2014 – Sept. 10, 2014). p. 11.

[512]   U.N. Doc. A/HRC/34/53/Add.1 (Jan. 9, 2017). ¶ 32.

[513]   U.N. Doc. A/HRC/28/18 (March 27, 2015).

These reports indicated that ISIL/DAESH'S acts were particularly directed against the Christian and the Yazidi groups in the Iraqi territory.[514] Later on, several United Nations bodies considered the possibility that the acts perpetrated by ISIL/DAESH against Christians in Iraq, from 2014 to 2017, could fall within the definition of genocide, as determined by the 1948 U.N. Convention on the Prevention and Punishment of Genocide.[515] Likewise, at the end of 2014, Iraq's Cabinet issued Decision No. 92 (2014), "designating the suffering inflicted on Iraqi Yazidis, Turkmens, Christians, and the Shabak and other minority groups by ISIL/DAESH terrorist gangs as genocide."[516]

Intending to provide logistical and financial support to its actions, recruit and indoctrinate new fighters, and to destabilize States outside Iraq, by "provoking a confrontation between 'believers' and 'apostates,'" ISIL/DAESH maintained a highly effective propaganda machinery throughout the internet and the social media.[517] With the use of sophisticated technologies and encryption tools, ISIL/DAESH fighters used to publish videos and photographs showing the group's atrocities against civilians every week.[518] [519]

As an attempted tactic to demonstrate the group's power, ISIL/DAESH extensively portrayed videos of their training sessions, of "blood-soaked battles scenes," and images of innocent persons being tortured, stoned to death, drowned, shot, or being thrown from tall buildings.[520] Alarmingly,

---

[514]  See, for example: U.N. Doc. A/HRC/28/18 (March 27, 2015); U.N. Doc. S/2016/92 (Jan. 29, 2016); U.N. Doc. A/HRC/34/53/Add.1 (Jan. 9, 2017); U.N. Doc. S/2018/773 (Aug. 17, 2017); U.N. Doc. CCPR/C/IRQ/CO/5/Add.1 (Aug. 18, 2017); S.C. Res. 2379 (Sept. 21, 2017); U.N. Doc. CERD/C/IRQ/22-25 (Nov. 22, 2017); U.N. Doc. A/HRC/38/44/Add.1 (June 20, 2018); U.N. Doc. CEDAW/C/IRQ/7 (Aug. 15, 2018); U.N. Doc. A/HRC/39/NGO/X (Aug. 23, 2018); U.N. Doc. A/73/347 (Aug. 28, 2018); U.N. Doc. A/73/352/Add.6 (Oct. 2018).

[515]  Contrary to this argument that ISIL/DAESH specifically intended the sole destruction of the group of Christians in Iraq, other arguments comprehend that ISIL/DAESH "intended war with everyone it encountered and terrorized even its own sympathizers." (William Harris. *Supra* note 472. p. 60).

[516]  U.N. Doc. CEDAW/C/IRQ/7 (Aug. 15, 2018). ¶ 104.

[517]  U.N. Doc. S/2016/92 (Jan. 29, 2016). ¶¶ 39, 41.

[518]  U.N. Doc. A/HRC/30/66 (July 27, 2015). ¶ 37; U.N. Doc. S/2016/92 (Jan. 29, 2016). ¶ 41.

[519]  UNAMI (Dec. 11, 2014 – April 30, 2015). pp. 13, 20–21; UNAMI (May 1, 2015 – Oct. 31, 2015). p. 11.

[520]  Cubs in the Lions' Den: Indoctrination and Recruitment of Children Within Islamic State Territory, THE INTERNATIONAL CENTRE FOR THE STUDY OF RADICALISATION (ICSR) (July 23, 2018).

ISIL/DAESH fighters continually used children for propaganda on social media. Pictures of children being trained, wearing ISIL/DAESH uniforms and images and videos of boys perpetrating violent acts were commonplace in ISIL/DAESH online pamphlets.[521] [522]

## 1.1.4. The Global Coalition to Defeat ISIL/DAESH.

In September 2014, at the request of the Iraqi Government, a group comprising a myriad of actors formed a coalition to counter ISIL/DAESH (the "Coalition"; the "Counter-ISIL/DAESH Coalition"; the "International Coalition"; the "Global Coalition to Defeat ISIL/DAESH").[523] [524] Domestically, the Coalition received open support from the Iraqi Government, the Iraqi security forces,[525] from diverse actors of the Autonomous Administration in Northern Iraq,[526] the People's Defence Forces of the *Kurdish Workers Party*,[527] the Sinjar Resistance Units,[528] the Protection Force of Ezidkhan,[529] and the Popular Mobilization Force.[530] Internationally, the Coalition was

---

[521]  UNAMI (July 6, 2014 – Sept. 10, 2014). p. 18; UNAMI (Dec. 11, 2014 – April 30, 2015). pp. 11, 13, 20; UNAMI (May 1, 2015 – Oct. 31, 2015). pp. 16–17.

[522]  U.N. Doc. A/HRC/30/66 (July 27, 2015). ¶ 37; U.N. Doc. S/2015/852 (Nov. 9, 2015). ¶¶ 33–34.

[523]  Claire Mills, *ISIS/Daesh: the military response in Iraq and Syria*, HOUSE OF COMMONS PUBLISHING HOUSE, Mar. 8, 2017. p. 4.

[524]  U.N. Doc. S/2019/984 (Dec. 23, 2019). ¶ 18.

[525]  "The Iraqi security forces, include[ed] entities such as the Iraqi police, under the Ministry of the Interior, and the Iraqi armed forces, under the [coordination of the] Ministry of Defence." (*Idem.* ¶ 16).

[526]  "Kurdish actors in Iraq contributed significantly to the fight against ISIL/DAESH, notably the Kurdistan Regional Government, including the Kurdish Peshmerga (the armed forces of the Kurdistan Regional Government), the Peshmerga Zeravani (the military police) and the Peshmerga Asayish (the internal security forces)." (*Idem.* ¶ 19).

[527]  *Idem.* ¶ 20.

[528]  "The Sinjar Resistance Units were established in 2007 to protect Yazidi communities. [It] played a key role in the fight against ISIL/DAESH in and around Sinjar since 2014." (*Idem.* ¶ 21).

[529]  "The Protection Force of Ezidkhan, a Yazidi armed group, was established in 2014 to support efforts against ISIL/DAESH." (*Ibidem*).

[530]  "Following the capture of Mosul by ISIL/DAESH in June 2014, the Popular Mobilization Forces, operating as an umbrella organization composed primarily of Shi'a but also Sunni tribal mobilization groups and minority groups (for example, brigade 36, comprising Yazidis and Turkmen), supported the [Iraqi] Government in combating ISIL/DAESH. On 26 November 2016, pursuant to the Popular Mobilization Commission Law, the Popular Mobilization Forces were recognized as an in-

initially supported by 68 states,[531] led by the United States.[532] [533] On August 29, 2015, Turkey formally joined the coalition,[534] "allowing US aircraft to launch airstrikes against ISIS from Incirlik air force base."[535] [536] In May 2017, at the Iraqi government's request, NATO became a member of the "Global Coalition to Defeat ISIS" (NATO Mission in Iraq – NMI),[537] expanding the scope of its operations held from 2004 to the end of 2011.[538]

Large-scale conjoined military tactics of the Coalition and domestic forces in Iraq defeated ISIL/DAESH's operations in the Iraqi territory in December 2017.[539] [540] On December 9, 2017, Iraq's Prime Minister declared the "final victory" over ISIL/DAESH.[541] [542] The group was then confined to "small pockets" in the territories of Iraq and the Syrian Arab Republic.[543] With the intensification of the Coalition attacks against ISIL/DAESH, several of the terrorist group's "fighters, planners and senior doctrinal, security and military commanders" were killed in targeted strikes or "left the immediate conflict zone."[544] [545] From December 2017 onwards, ISIL/DAESH

---

dependent military formation within the Iraqi armed forces under the direct command of the Prime Minister." (*Idem.* ¶ 17).

[531] Claire Mills. *Supra* note 523. p. 4.

[532] *Ibidem.*

[533] By July 2020, the U.S. currently still had about 5,000 troops stationed in Iraq. (Rep. of the S.C., Monthly Forecast: Situation in Iraq, August 2020 (July 31, 2020). p. 7).

[534] Claire Mills. *Supra* note 523. p. 33.

[535] *Ibidem.*

[536] "After December 2015, Turkey maintained a 1,000 strong military base at Bashiqa, to the north-east of Mosul, and has been training local tribal forces, largely comprised of Sunni Arabs, Turkmen and Kurdish Peshmerga. Once trained, those forces [operated] under the control of the Iraqi government." (*Idem.* pp. 39–40).

[537] NATO. *Supra* note 450. pp. 1–2, 157.

[538] "From 2004 to end 2011, NATO helped Iraq provide for its own security by training Iraqi personnel and supporting the development of the country's security institutions. NATO trained and mentored middle- and senior-level personnel from the Iraqi security forces in Iraq and outside of Iraq, at NATO schools and training centres." (*Idem.* p. 232).

[539] U.N. Doc. CCPR/C/IRQ/CO/5/Add.1 (Aug. 18, 2017). ¶ 1; U.N. Doc. A/HRC/38/44/Add.1 (June 20, 2018). ¶ 18; U.N. Doc. S/2018/770 (August 16, 2018). ¶ 4.

[540] United Nations. Security Council. Security Council Report: Monthly Forecast. February 2018. Situation in Iraq. p.14.

[541] U.N. Doc. A/HRC/38/44/Add.1 (June 20, 2018). ¶ 5; U.N. Doc. CEDAW/C/IRQ/7 (Aug. 15, 2018). ¶ 16; U.N. Doc. S/2019/984 (Dec. 23, 2019). ¶ 5.

[542] William Harris. *Supra* note 472. p. 93.

[543] U.N. Doc. S/2018/705 (July 27, 2018). ¶¶ 1, 3–4.

[544] *Idem.* ¶ 2.

[545] U.N. Doc. S/2018/770 (August 16, 2018). ¶¶ 5, 8.

started a transitional period "from a proto-State structure into a [global] terrorist network."[546] [547]

Despite the setbacks caused by the Coalition at the time, ISIL/DAESH collective discipline was still intact and the terrorist group maintained its determination to control Iraq's territory and population.[548] In a report dated July 27, 2018, U.N. Security Council member states estimated that, by then, between 20,000 and 30,000 individuals were still "fully engaged militarily" with ISIL/DAESH] in Iraq and the Syrian Arab Republic, "roughly equally distributed between the two countries."[549] Back on March 18, 2019, ISIL/DAESH had already circulated a *communiqué* "reasserting its presence and calling upon supporters to intensify the fight and take revenge for [the recent attacks against mosques in different countries]."[550] These fighters "remain[ed] (...) fully engaged militarily and others concealed in sympathetic communities and urban areas."[551]

U.N. Security Council Reports showed that, despite the damage to the so-called Caliphate's bureaucratic structures, many other ISIL/DAESH structures of the Caliphate remained intact. For instance, the collective discipline of ISIL/DAESH, the general security and finance bureaus,[552] the group's immigration and logistics coordination office,[553] the financial structures,[554] the ability to channel funds across borders,[555] and the ability to invest and infiltrate businesses in the region.[556] These reports indicated that "ISIL/DAESH continue[d] to transition from a proto-State structure into a terrorist network."[557] By June 2018, ISIL/DAESH was still able "to extract and sell some oil and mount attacks [...] across the border into Iraq."[558]

Recent reports from 2019 and 2020 indicated that, through sleeper cells, the Islamic State's remnants in Iraq and the Levant continued to pose

---

[546] U.N. Doc. S/2018/705 (July 27, 2018). ¶ 12.
[547] See also: U.N. Doc. S/2018/80 (Jan. 31, 2018). ¶ 6; U.N. Doc. S/2018/705 (July 27, 2018). p.3, ¶ 12.
[548] U.N. Doc. S/2018/770 (August 16, 2018). ¶ 6; U.N. Doc. S/2020/717 (July 23, 2020). p. 3.
[549] U.N. Doc. S/2018/705 (July 27, 2018). ¶¶ 2–3.
[550] U.N. Doc. S/2019/365 (May 2, 2019). ¶ 22.
[551] U.N. Doc. S/2018/770 (2018). ¶ 5.
[552] U.N. Doc. S/2018/705 (July 27, 2018). ¶ 4.
[553] *Ibidem.*
[554] *Idem.* ¶ 16.
[555] *Idem.* ¶ 17.
[556] *Idem.* ¶ 4.
[557] *Idem.* ¶ 12.
[558] U.N. Doc. S/2018/705 (July 27, 2018). p. 3.

resilient, serious, and evolving threats in Iraq.[559] ISIL/DAESH continued launching "frequent asymmetrical attacks" against the Iraqi people,[560] including against children,[561] by carrying out deadly attacks, particularly in Anbar, Baghdad, Diyala, Kirkuk, Ninawa, and Salah al-Din Governorates.[562]

A report from the French Ministry for Europe and Foreign Affairs, from November 2019, indicated that, by then, ISIL/DAESH: 1) continued its presence in Syria and Iraq through "active clandestine cells;[563] 2) persisted, through its affiliates, as a terrorist group "in Africa, the Arabian Peninsula, South Asia, and South-East Asia;"[564] and 3) continued the "spread of sophisticated propaganda calling for violence."[565] This *persistence* means that "ISIL/DAESH [was] adapting, consolidating and creating conditions for an eventual resurgence in its Iraqi and Syrian heartlands."[566]

Alarmingly, a report from the U.N. Secretary-General informed that "the temporary stabilization of [ISIL/DAESH] 's military position in the east of the Syrian Arab Republic in early 2018 may have encouraged significant numbers of foreign terrorist fighters to remain in the conflict zone."[567] [568] In October 2018, trying to tackle ISIL/DAESH's resurgence, NATO established a training and capacity-building mission in Iraq to help "strengthen[ing] Iraqi security forces and Iraqi military education institutions so that Iraqi forces [could] prevent the return of ISIS/Da'esh."[569] In 2019, the Coalition to counter the Islamic State in Iraq and the Levant comprised 81 nations.[570] [571]

---

[559]   U.N. Doc. S/2018/80 (Jan. 31, 2018). ¶ 4; U.N. Doc. S/2018/705 (July 27, 2018). ¶¶ 1, 11; U.N. Doc. S/2018/705 (July 27, 2018). ¶ 13; U.N. Doc. S/2018/770 (August 16, 2018). ¶ 5; U.N. Doc. S/2019/101 (Feb. 1, 2019). ¶ 14; U.N. Doc. S/2020/140 (Feb. 21, 2020). ¶ 23; U.N. Doc. S/2020/363 (May 6, 2020). ¶ 24; U.N. Doc. S/2020/717 (July 23, 2020). p. 3.

[560]   U.N. Doc. S/2019/903 (Nov. 22, 2019). ¶ 29; U.N. Doc. S/2019/984 (Dec. 23, 2019). ¶ 22.

[561]   U.N. Doc. A/73/907–S/2019/509 (June 20, 2019). ¶ 70.

[562]   U.N. Doc. S/2019/903 (Nov. 22, 2019). ¶ 29.

[563]   France Ministry for Europe and Foreign Affairs, "Has Daesh been defeated?", France Diplomacy (Nov. 2019).

[564]   *Ibidem.*

[565]   *Ibidem.*

[566]   U.N. Doc. S/2019/570 (July 15, 2019). ¶ 3.

[567]   U.N. Doc. S/2018/770 (August 16, 2018). ¶ 7.

[568]   See also: U.N. Doc. S/2019/103 (Feb. 1, 2019). ¶ 6.

[569]   NATO. *Supra* note 450. p. 1.

[570]   U.N. Doc. S/2019/984 (Dec. 23, 2019). ¶ 18.

[571]   By July 2020, the Coalition against ISIL/DAESH had about 2,500 troops in Iraq. (Rep. of the S.C., Monthly Forecast: Situation in Iraq, August 2020 (July 31, 2020). p. 7).

Iraqi judicial authorities have been unable to prosecute most of ISIL/DAESH's atrocious acts due to its courts' lack of material jurisdiction.[572] Genocide and crimes against humanity are not typified under Iraqi law.[573] Consequently, domestic judicial authorities are prevented from prosecuting such crimes.[574] [575] Internationally, Iraq is not a signatory to the Rome Statute of the International Criminal Court, whose material jurisdiction comprises genocide.[576] Consequently, Iraq did not grant jurisdiction to the Court. Also, Iraq has not acceded to the Protocol Additional to the Geneva Conventions of 12 August 1949 relative to the protection of victims of non-international armed conflicts (Additional Protocol II).[577]

## 1.1.5. International efforts to hold ISIL/DAESH terrorist fighters accountable

Following international efforts to hold ISIL/DAESH accountable for its acts, the Security Council, through Resolution 2379, from September 2017, established an Investigative Team "to support Iraqi efforts to [prosecute ISIL/DAESH fighters]," by "assisting with the collection, preservation, and storage of evidence."[578] [579] The Investigative Team was created with three substantive investigative priorities:

"(a) Attacks committed by ISIL/DAESH against the Yazidi community in the Sinjar district in August 2014;
(b) Crimes committed by ISIL/DAESH in Mosul between 2014 and 2016, including the execution of religious minorities, crimes involving sexual and gender-based violence and crimes against children;
(c) The mass killing of unarmed Iraqi air force cadets from Tikrit Air Academy in June 2014."[580]

Although the Investigative Team was generally vested with the competence to investigate the *execution of religious minorities,* no express mention of crimes committed by ISIL/DAESH against Christians in Iraq was made.

---

[572]  HUMAN RIGHTS WATCH. *Supra* note 411. p. 27.
[573]  *Idem.* p. 21.
[574]  U.N. Doc. A/HRC/38/44/Add.1 (June 20, 2018). ¶ 19.
[575]  HUMAN RIGHTS WATCH. *Supra* note 411. p. 27.
[576]  U.S. Dep't of State, Bureau of Democracy, H.R. and Lab., International Religious Freedom Report (2016). *passim.*
[577]  U.N. Doc. A/HRC/38/44/Add.1 (June 20, 2018). ¶¶ 10, 13.
[578]  *Idem.* ¶ 19.
[579]  See also: U.N. Doc. A/73/352/Add.6 (Oct. 12, 2018). ¶ 2.
[580]  U.N. Doc. S/2019/407 (May 17, 2019). ¶ 13.a, b, c

The Investigative Team was composed of experienced "international experts and Iraqi investigative judges and other criminal experts, including experienced members of the prosecution services, who will /work on an equal footing, under the authority of the Special Adviser."[581]

Upon creation, the Investigative Team's mandate comprised twelve major commands:

## Concerning the evidence:

1) to collect and preserve forensic material and excavation of mass graves;[582]
2) to collect, preserve, store, and analyze documentary and digital evidentiary material "pertaining to acts that may amount to war crimes, crimes against humanity and genocide committed by ISIL/DAESH (Da'esh) in Iraq,"[583] [584] and to "ensure an uninterrupted chain of custody of the evidence in its possession";[585]
3) to collect and preserve testimonial evidence and protect witnesses following international standards;[586]
4) to collect and preserve existing documentary evidence from "Iraqi national authorities, other national Governments, victims and witness groups, civil society bodies and international and regional organizations, in accordance with international standards."[587]

## Concerning the ISIL/DAESH victims:

5) to protect and support survivors of ISIL/DAESH atrocities.[588]

## Concerning the engagement with Iraqi authorities:

6) to promote accountability domestically as well as globally;[589]
7) to engage and cooperate with the Government of Iraq;[590]

---

[581]  U.N. Doc. S/2018/118 (Feb. 14, 2018). ¶ 14.
[582]  U.N. Doc. S/2019/407 (May 17, 2019). ¶¶ 34–42; U.N. Doc. S/2019/878 (Nov. 13, 2019). p. 9; U.N. Doc. S/2020/386 (May 11, 2020). p. 8.
[583]  U.N. Doc. S/2018/118 (Feb. 14, 2018). ¶ 5.
[584]  See also: U.N. Doc. S/2019/407 (May 17, 2019). ¶¶ 26–29.
[585]  U.N. Doc. S/2018/118 (Feb. 14, 2018). ¶ 8.
[586]  U.N. Doc. S/2018/1031 (Nov. 16, 2018). ¶ 30.d; U.N. Doc. S/2019/407 (May 17, 2019). ¶ 43; U.N. Doc. S/2019/878 (Nov. 13, 2019). p. 10; U.N. Doc. S/2020/386 (May 11, 2020). p. 9.
[587]  U.N. Doc. S/2018/1031 (Nov. 16, 2018). ¶ 30.a, d.
[588]  Idem. p. 10.
[589]  U.N. Doc. S/2018/118 (Feb. 14, 2018). ¶ 2; U.N. Doc. S/2018/1031 (Nov. 16, 2018). p. 12; U.N. Doc. S/2020/386 (May 11, 2020). pp. 15, 18; U.N. Doc. S/2019/407 (May 17, 2019). p. 17; U.N. Doc. S/2019/878 (Nov. 13, 2019). pp. 12, 15, 18.

8)  to strengthen the capacity of Iraqi authorities;[591]
9)  to partner with all elements of Iraqi society.[592]

## Concerning the engagement with international and intergovernmental authorities:

10) to support the United Nations Assistance Mission in Iraq;[593]
11) to engage with Security Council Member States in the fight against ISIL/DAESH;[594]
12) to ensure coherence with United Nations system entities.[595] [596]

The Government of Iraq expressly accepted the assistance through a "Term of Reference," dated February 8, 2018, upon the condition that the Investigative Team would operate with full respect for the Guiding Principles[597] and "for the sovereignty of Iraq and its jurisdiction over crimes committed in its territory."[598] The main tenet of the Term of Reference sought to promote

---

[590]  U.N. Doc. S/2018/1031 (Nov. 16, 2018). p. 9; U.N. Doc. S/2020/386 (May 11, 2020). p. 12; U.N. Doc. S/2019/407 (May 17, 2019). p. 12; U.N. Doc. S/2019/878 (Nov. 13, 2019). p. 12.

[591]  U.N. Doc. S/2019/878 (Nov. 13, 2019). p. 14; U.N. Doc. S/2020/386 (May 11, 2020). p. 13.

[592]  U.N. Doc. S/2019/407 (May 17, 2019). p. 13; U.N. Doc. S/2019/878 (Nov. 13, 2019). p. 14; U.N. Doc. S/2020/386 (May 11, 2020). p. 14.

[593]  U.N. Doc. S/2018/1031 (Nov. 16, 2018). p. 11; U.N. Doc. S/2019/407 (May 17, 2019). p. 16.

[594]  U.N. Doc. S/2018/1031 (Nov. 16, 2018). p. 15; U.N. Doc. S/2019/407 (May 17, 2019). p. 14; U.N. Doc. S/2019/878 (Nov. 13, 2019). p. 16; U.N. Doc. S/2020/386 (May 11, 2020). p. 16.

[595]  Namely: the Office of the Special Representative of the Secretary-General for Sexual Violence in Conflict, the Office on Genocide Prevention and the Responsibility to Protect, the Office of the Special Representative of the Secretary-General for Children and Armed Conflict, the United Nations Office on Drugs and Crime, the Counter-Terrorism Committee, the Counter-Terrorism Committee Executive Directorate, the Office of Counter-Terrorism, the United Nations Mine Action Service, the Office of the United Nations High Commissioner for Human Rights and the Human Rights Office of the United Nations Assistance Mission for Iraq. (U.N. Doc. S/2018/1031 (Nov. 16, 2018). p. 13).

[596]  U.N. Doc. S/2019/407 (May 17, 2019). p. 14; U.N. Doc. S/2019/878 (Nov. 13, 2019). p. 17; U.N. Doc. S/2020/386 (May 11, 2020). p. 16.

[597]  The Guiding Principles of the Investigative Team are: *"Principle 1: Operating with impartiality and independence; Principle 2: Fostering collective support in Iraq; Principle 3: Adhering to international standards and best practices; Principle 4: Focusing on those who bear the greatest responsibility."* (U.N. Doc. S/2018/1031 (Nov. 16, 2018). ¶¶ 19–27).

[598]  U.N. Doc. S/2018/118 (Feb. 14, 2018). ¶ 4.

"accountability for acts that may amount to war crimes, crimes against humanity and genocide committed by ISIL/DAESH (Da'esh) and work[ing] with survivors, in a manner consistent with relevant national laws, to ensure that their interests in achieving accountability for ISIL/DAESH (Da'esh) are fully recognized."[599]

Since then, "Iraq has therefore committed itself to prosecute international crimes, and the international community has committed itself to support such efforts."[600] Nevertheless, the investigation, documentation, and assessment of all violations of human rights and humanitarian law that occurred in ISIL/DAESH-controlled areas in Iraq, from 2014 to 2017, remained a challenge for the United Nations and particularly for most international NGOs.[601] The challenge involves a lack of documentation, lack of security, access constraints to conflict-affected areas, logistical limitations, and the victims' fear of retaliation, fear of retribution, fear of repercussions, and stigma, particularly in cases of widespread sexual violence perpetrated by ISIL/DAESH against women and children.[602] Therefore, most of the violations demonstrated in international reports from this period in Iraq are considered to be significantly underreported or "illustrative of broader trends"[603] due to the impossibility of obtaining data in the territories once controlled by ISIL/DAESH.[604]

## 1.2. Acts of persecution and discrimination against ethnic and religious minorities

Between June 2014 and December 2017, ISIL/DAESH fighters committed a plethora of deliberate, widespread, and systematic gross human rights and humanitarian abuses and international crimes against persons belonging to various religious and ethnic communities in areas under their control

---

[599] U.N. Doc. A/HRC/38/44/Add.1 (June 20, 2018). ¶ 19.

[600] *Ibidem.*

[601] U.N. Doc. A/HRC/28/18 (March 27, 2015). ¶ 61; U.N. Doc. S/2015/852 (Nov. 9, 2015). ¶ 53.

[602] U.N. Doc. A/HRC/28/18 (March 27, 2015). ¶ 49; U.N. Doc. S/2015/852 (Nov. 9, 2015). ¶¶ 42, 55; U.N. Doc. A/70/836–S/2016/360 (Apr. 20, 2016). ¶ 62; U.N. Doc. A/72/361–S/2017/821 (Aug. 24, 2017). ¶ 79; U.N. Doc. S/2017/881 (Oct. 19, 2017). ¶ 49; U.N. Doc. A/73/907–S/2019/509 (June 20, 2019). ¶ 75; U.N. Doc. S/2019/984 (Dec. 23, 2019). ¶¶ 62, 74.

[603] U.N. Doc. S/2015/852 (Nov. 9, 2015). ¶ 41.

[604] U.N. Doc. A/HRC/32/35/Add.1 (April 5, 2016). ¶ 4; U.N. Doc. A/70/836–S/2016/360 (Apr. 20, 2016). ¶ 58; U.N. Doc. S/2019/984 (Dec. 23, 2019). ¶ 62.

in Iraq, including the perpetration of atrocious acts against women, children, persons with disabilities and the elderly.[605] [606] [607] ISIL/DAESH systematically targeted, persecuted, killed, injured, abducted, tortured, raped, sexually abused, enslaved, and forced to flee thousands of Christians, Yezidis (Yazidis), Shi'a Muslims, Sunni Muslims, Shi'a Shabaks, Shia Turkmen, Baha'is, Kaka'es, Assyrians, Zoroastrians, Faili Kurds, and Sabea-Mandeans.[608] [609] [610] [611] [612]

---

[605]   U.N. Doc. A/69/53/Add.1 (Sept. 1, 2014). ¶ 1; U.N. Doc. A/HRC/RES/S-22/1 (Sept. 3, 2014). Preamble, p.1; U.N. Doc. S/2014/774 (Oct. 31, 2014). ¶ 46; U.N. Doc. S/2015/82 (Feb. 2, 2015). ¶ 46; U.N. Doc. S/2015/530 (July 13, 2015). ¶ 44; U.N. Doc. A/HRC/30/NGO/116 (Sept. 8, 2015). p. 2; U.N. Doc. S/2016/77 (Jan. 26, 2016). ¶ 48; U.N. Doc. S/2016/92 (Jan. 29, 2016). ¶ 9; U.N. Doc. A/HRC/32/35/Add.1 (April 5, 2016). ¶ 55; U.N. Doc. S/2016/897 (Oct. 25, 2016). ¶ 44; U.N. Doc. A/HRC/34/50 (Jan. 17, 2017). ¶ 54; U.N. Doc. CEDAW/C/IRQ/7 (Aug. 15, 2018). ¶ 10; U.N. Doc. CERD/C/IRQ/22-25 (Nov. 22, 2017). ¶¶ 15–16.

[606]   S.C. Res. 2233 (July 29, 2015). Preamble, p. 3; S.C. Res. 2249 (Nov. 20, 2015). Preamble, p. 1; S.C. Res. 2299 (July 25, 2016). Preamble, pp. 1, 4; S.C. Res. 2367 (July 14, 2017). Preamble, p. 1; S.C. Res. 2388 (Nov. 21, 2017). Preamble, pp. 2–3.

[607]   UNAMI (July 6, 2014 – Sept. 10, 2014). p. 11; UNAMI (Dec. 11, 2014 – April 30, 2015). p. 20; UNAMI (May 1, 2015 – Oct. 31, 2015). pp. 19–20; U.N. Doc. A/HRC/30/66 (July 27, 2015). ¶ 18; UNAMI (Jan. 2020). p. iv.

[608]   U.N. Doc. A/69/53/Add.1 (Sept. 1, 2014). Preamble, p.7; U.N. Doc. A/HRC/RES/S-22/1 (Sept. 3, 2014). Preamble, p.1; UNAMI (Sept. 11, 2014 – Dec. 10, 2014). p. 15; U.N. Doc. S/2014/774 (Oct. 31, 2014). ¶¶ 49–50; U.N. Doc. A/HRC/28/18 (March 27, 2015). ¶¶ 16, 23; U.N. Doc. A/HRC/30/66 (July 27, 2015). ¶ 48; U.N. Doc. A/HRC/30/NGO/116 (Sept. 8, 2015). p. 2; U.N. Doc. S/2016/77 (Jan. 26, 2016). ¶ 50; U.N. Doc. S/2016/92 (Jan. 29, 2016). ¶ 9; U.N. Doc. A/HRC/32/35/Add.1 (April 5, 2016). ¶¶ 50, 55–56, 58; U.N. Doc. A/70/836–S/2016/360 (Apr. 20, 2016). ¶ 62; U.N. Doc. A/HRC/34/53/Add.1 (Jan. 9, 2017). ¶¶ 29–30, 36–39, 40–47, 61; U.N. Doc. CERD/C/IRQ/22-25 (Nov. 22, 2017). ¶ 16; U.N. Doc. CEDAW/C/IRQ/7 (Aug. 15, 2018). ¶ 11; U.N. Doc. S/2019/984 (Dec. 23, 2019). ¶ 60.

[609]   UNAMI (July 6, 2014 – Sept. 10, 2014). p. 8; UNAMI (Sept. 11, 2014 – Dec. 10, 2014). pp. 15–17; UNAMI (Dec. 11, 2014 – April 30, 2015). p. 20; UNAMI (May 1, 2015 – Oct. 31, 2015). pp. 15–16; UNAMI (Nov. 6, 2018). p. 4.

[610]   S.C. Res. 2388 (Nov. 21, 2017). ¶ 10.

[611]   UK Parliament, Genocide in Syria and Iraq, Early Day Motion, Sponsored by Robert Flello (Jan. 26, 2016).

[612]   AMNESTY INTERNATIONAL. *Infra* note 785. p. 15; AMNESTY INTERNATIONAL. *Supra* note 495. p. 15; Flawed Justice Report: Accountability for ISIS Crimes in Iraq, HUMAN RIGHTS WATCH (December 2017). p. 16; AMNESTY INTERNATIONAL. *Infra* note 961. p. 15.

In areas under its control, ISIL/DAESH extensively submitted Christians and Yazidis to forced conversions to the Muslim faith.[613] [614] [615] Most of the men who allegedly converted were ordered by ISIL/DAESH to "be transported to new locations where their conversion would be monitored."[616] Alarmingly, married women who converted "were told by ISIL/DAESH that their previous marriages were not recognized in Islamic law and that they, as well as unmarried women who converted, would be given to ISIL/DAESH fighters as wives."[617] ISIL/DAESH then issued orders that these women and girls should be forcibly married to its commanders and fighters.[618] [619] Women and girls who refused to convert or refused to be married to ISIL/DAESH fighters were subjected to physical violence. Many of these women were later reportedly killed.[620]

ISIL/DAESH continually and deliberately destroyed and looted cultural heritage, historic cities, cultural sites, archaeological sites, historical monuments, and symbols in Iraq. The group has also damaged Christian religious objects and removed crosses from the domes of churches by replacing them with ISIL/DAESH black flags. ISIL/DAESH destroyed places of worship/religious buildings and other sites dedicated to religion, such as churches, convents, monasteries, and Christian cemeteries, by blowing them up, burning, detonating them with grenades or other types of explosives, or by demolishing using bulldozers. The group also destroyed Sunni and Shi'a mosques, ancient Shrines belonging to the Kaka'e, Shabak Shi'a, Sufi, and Sunni communities, demolished public and private libraries, and burned thousands of books.[621] [622] [623] [624] In addition, ISIL/DAESH deliberately

---

[613] AMNESTY INTERNATIONAL. *Supra* note 495. *passim.*

[614] U.N. Doc. A/69/53/Add.1 (Sept. 1, 2014). Preamble, p.7; U.N. Doc. A/HRC/RES/S-22/1 (Sept. 3, 2014). Preamble, p.1; U.N. Doc. A/HRC/32/35/Add.1 (April 5, 2016). ¶ 55; U.N. Doc. CEDAW/C/IRQ/7 (Aug. 15, 2018). ¶ 9.

[615] UNAMI (Nov. 6, 2018). p. 4.

[616] UNAMI (July 6, 2014 – Sept. 10, 2014). p. 15.

[617] *Ibidem.*

[618] U.N. Doc. A/HRC/32/35/Add.1 (April 5, 2016). ¶ 50; U.N. Doc. CCPR/C/IRQ/CO/5/Add.1 (Aug. 18, 2017). ¶ 19; U.N. Doc. S/2017/939 (Nov. 10, 2017). ¶ 4; U.N. Doc. A/72/865–S/2018/465 (May 16, 2018). ¶ 79; U.N. Doc. S/2019/984 (Dec. 23, 2019). ¶¶ 33, 60.

[619] S.C. Res. 2199 (Feb. 12, 2015). Preamble, p.2; S.C. Res. 2299 (July 25, 2016). Preamble, p. 5; S.C. Res. 2368 (July 20, 2017). Preamble, p. 6; S.C. Res. 2388 (Nov. 21, 2017). Preamble, pp. 2–3; S.C. Res. 2379 (Sept. 21, 2017). Preamble, p.1.

[620] UNAMI (Dec. 11, 2014 – April 30, 2015). p. 22.

[621] U.N. Doc. A/69/53/Add.1 (Sept. 1, 2014). Preamble, p.7; U.N. Doc. S/2014/774 (Oct. 31, 2014). ¶ 46; U.N. Doc. S/2015/82 (Feb. 2, 2015). ¶¶ 46, 50; U.N. Doc. A/HRC/28/18 (March 27, 2015). ¶ 76; U.N. Doc. A/HRC/30/66 (July 27, 2015). ¶ 25; U.N. Doc.

perpetrated acts of wanton destruction of private property and denied religious and ethnic groups access to essential humanitarian services.[625] [626]

In vast areas of Iraq under its control, ISIL/DAESH expelled or attempted to destroy the Yazidi group. ISIL/DAESH fighters: 1) tortured, severely ill-treated, enslaved, submitted to rape, forced marriages, sexual enslavement, and other forms of sexual violence thousands of women and girls from the Yazidi community; 2) recruited, indoctrinated, and used children in hostilities; 3) abducted women and children and submitted them to human trafficking; and 4) forced Yazidis, including young girls, to convert to Islam. Those who refused to convert were summarily killed or treated as sex slaves, if women. Yazidis attempting to flee were being killed or captured by ISIL/DAESH.[627] [628] [629] [630] According to reports from states, supranational organizations, international and domestic NGOs, and intergovernmental organizations, the atrocities perpetrated by ISIL/DAESH

---

S/2015/852 (Nov. 9, 2015). ¶ 21; U.N. Doc. S/2016/77 (Jan. 26, 2016). ¶ 50; U.N. Doc. S/2016/92 (Jan. 29, 2016). ¶ 12; U.N. Doc. A/HRC/32/35/Add.1 (April 5, 2016). ¶ 55; U.N. Doc. S/2016/77 (Jan. 26, 2016). ¶ 50; U.N. Doc. S/2016/592 (July 5, 2016). ¶ 17; U.N. Doc. A/HRC/34/53/Add.1 (Jan. 9, 2017). ¶ 7; U.N. Doc. CERD/C/IRQ/22-25 (Nov. 22, 2017). ¶ 15; U.N. Doc. CEDAW/C/IRQ/7 (Aug. 15, 2018). ¶ 10.

[622]  S.C. Res. 2233 (July 29, 2015). Preamble, p. 4; S.C. Res. 2249 (Nov. 20, 2015). Preamble, p. 1, ¶ 3; S.C. Res. 2299 (July 25, 2016). Preamble, pp. 4–5; S.C. Res. 2367 (July 14, 2017). Preamble, p. 4; S.C. Res. 2368 (July 20, 2017). Preamble, p. 6.

[623]  UNAMI (Dec. 11, 2014 – April 30, 2015). pp. 17–19; UNAMI in Iraq (May 1, 2015 – Oct. 31, 2015). pp. 16–17; UNAMI (July 6, 2014 – Sept. 10, 2014). pp. 9–10, 16; UNAMI (Sept. 11, 2014 – Dec. 10, 2014). p. 12.

[624]  AMNESTY INTERNATIONAL. *Supra* note 495. *passim*.

[625]  UNAMI (July 6, 2014 – Sept. 10, 2014). p. 11; UNAMI (Dec. 11, 2014 – April 30, 2015). p. 13.

[626]  U.N. Doc. S/2014/774 (Oct. 31, 2014). ¶ 50; U.N. Doc. A/HRC/32/35/Add.1 (April 5, 2016). ¶ 58.

[627]  U.N. Doc. A/HRC/28/18 (March 27, 2015). ¶¶ 17, 20, 35–37, 40, 45; U.N. Doc. A/69/926–S/2015/409 (June 5, 2015). ¶ 77; U.N. Doc. S/2015/530 (July 13, 2015). ¶¶ 44, 50; U.N. Doc. A/HRC/30/66 (July 27, 2015). ¶¶ 32, 37, 48–49; U.N. Doc. A/HRC/30/NGO/116 (Sept. 8, 2015). pp. 2–3; U.N. Doc. S/2015/852 (Nov. 9, 2015). ¶¶ 33, 42, 52–53; U.N. Doc. S/2016/77 (Jan. 26, 2016). ¶ 48; U.N. Doc. S/2016/92 (Jan. 29, 2016). ¶ 22; U.N. Doc. S/2016/361 (Apr. 20, 2016). ¶¶ 20, 40; U.N. Doc. S/2016/396 (Apr. 27, 2016). ¶ 43; U.N. Doc. A/71/303 (Aug. 5, 2016). ¶ 33; U.N. Doc. S/2016/1090 (Dec. 21, 2016). p. 7; U.N. Doc. A/HRC/34/53/Add.1 (Jan. 9, 2017). Preamble, p.1, ¶ 57; U.N. Doc. S/2017/75 (Jan. 26, 2017). ¶ 41; U.N. Doc. A/72/164 (July 18, 2017). ¶ 25; U.N. Doc. S/2017/881 (Oct. 19, 2017). ¶ 48; U.N. Doc. CED/C/IRQ/22-25 (Nov. 22, 2017). ¶ 16; U.N. Doc. A/72/865–S/2018/465 (May 16, 2018). ¶ 79; U.N. Doc. S/2018/677 (July 9, 2018). ¶ 40; U.N. Doc. A/HRC/41/46 (Abr. 23, 2019). ¶ 21; U.N. Doc. S/2019/984 (Dec. 23, 2019). ¶¶ 28, 60.

could amount to war crimes, crimes against humanity, and possibly the crime of genocide.[631] [632]

## 1.2.1. ISIL/DAESH targeting Christians in Iraq: Physical destruction of human lives, forced conversions, destruction of churches, rape, sexual violence, displacement, and mass graves

Throughout the hundreds of years of Iraqi history, different groups and entities have historically targeted Christian communities in the country because of their religious faith and their "perceived ties with the West."[633] The religious group of those who profess the Christian faith in Iraq consists of a myriad of communities with a broad spectrum of professing values:

> "Armenian Catholics and Orthodox Christians, members of the Assyrian Church of the East, Assyrian Orthodox Christians, Chaldean Catholics, Evangelicals, other Protestants, Syriac Catholics, and Orthodox Christians, and other distinct religious groups that fall within the category of 'Christian.'"[634] [635] [636]

---

[628]  UNAMI (July 6, 2014 – Sept. 10, 2014). pp. 14–15; UNAMI (Sept. 11, 2014 – Dec. 10, 2014). p. 13; UNAMI (Dec. 11, 2014 – April 30, 2015). p. 20; UNAMI (May 1, 2015 – Oct. 31, 2015). p. 18; UNAMI (Aug. 2016). pp. 9–16.

[629]  Office of the United Nations High Commissioner for Human Rights, Internal Communication Clearance Form, UA, IRQ 4/2014 (July 24, 2014). p. 2; Office of the United Nations High Commissioner for Human Rights, Internal Communication Clearance Form, UA, IRQ 5/2014 (Aug. 18, 2014). p. 2; Office of the United Nations High Commissioner for Human Rights, Internal Communication Clearance Form, UA, IRQ 1/2015 (May 4, 2015). pp. 1–2.

[630]  AMNESTY INTERNATIONAL. *Infra* note 961. p. 11; ICSR. *Supra* note 520. p. 13.

[631]  UNAMI (Jan. 2020). p. iv.

[632]  See also: U.N. Doc. S/2016/897 (Oct. 25, 2016). ¶ 44.

[633]  U.N. Doc. A/HRC/34/53/Add.1 (Jan. 9, 2017). ¶ 31.

[634]  *Ibidem.*

[635]  "Approximately 67 percent of Christians are Chaldean Catholics (an eastern rite of the Roman Catholic Church), and nearly 20 percent are members of the Assyrian Church of the East. The remainder are Syriac Orthodox, Syriac Catholic, Armenian Catholic, Armenian Apostolic, and Anglican and other Protestants. [...] There are approximately 2,000 registered members of evangelical Christian churches in the IKR, while an unknown number, mostly converts from Islam, practice the religion secretly." (U.S. Dep't of State, Bureau of Democracy, H.R. and Lab., International Religious Freedom Report (2019). p. 3).

[636]  "Shia Muslims, predominantly Arabs but also including Turkoman, Faili (Shia) Kurds, and others, constitute 55 to 60 percent of the population. [...] Sunni Mus-

The United States State Department estimated that, in 2002, the number of the Christian population in Iraq ranged from 800,000 to 1.4 million. After the 2003 invasion of US troops, these figures dramatically declined. In the years that followed until 2014, the group of Christians in Iraq was reduced to between 250,000 to 350,000, majorly living in the Ninewa Plain and the Autonomous Administration in Northern Iraq.[637][638]

The Republic of Iraq's Constitution establishes Islam as the State's official religion[639] and as a "foundational source" of legislation.[640] The Constitution also establishes that "no law may be enacted contradicting the established provisions of Islam."[641] Domestic laws forbid the conversion of Muslims to other religions.[642] In case of a parent converting to Islam, the child must receive an "administrative designation."[643] Islamic education and the study of the Quran is compulsory in primary and secondary schools.[644] Although freedom of religious belief and practice is safeguarded in the Iraqi Constitution, the document mainly protects the "Islamic identity" and the "Islamic religion" of the Iraqi people, which is professed by 97 percent of the total population, which comprises 38.9 million (midyear 2019 estimate).[645][646]

The Republic of Iraq "is a single, federal, independent and fully sovereign State with a republican, representative (parliamentary) and democratic system of government." The State is "an active founding member of the League of Arab States, the Organization of Islamic Cooperation, and the Movement of Non-Aligned Countries."[647] Iraq has been a member-state of

---

lims are approximately 40 percent of the population, of which Arabs constitute 24 percent, Kurds 15 percent, and Turkomans the remaining 1 percent." (*Ibidem*).

[637] U.S. Dep't of State, Bureau of Democracy, H.R. and Lab., International Religious Freedom Report (2019). p. 3.

[638] U.N. Doc. A/HRC/32/35/Add.1 (April 5, 2016). ¶ 57; U.N. Doc. A/HRC/34/53/Add.1 (Jan. 9, 2017). ¶¶ 31–32.

[639] U.N. Doc. CERD/C/IRQ/22-25 (Nov. 22, 2017). ¶ 7.

[640] U.S. Dep't of State, Bureau of Democracy, H.R. and Lab., International Religious Freedom Report (2019). p. 4–5.

[641] *Idem*. p. 1.

[642] *Idem*. p. 5.

[643] *Ibidem*.

[644] *Idem*. p. 8.

[645] U.S. Dep't of State, Bureau of Democracy, H.R. and Lab., International Religious Freedom Report (2019). pp. 3, 5.

[646] Rep. of the Committee on the Elimination of Racial Discrimination, Combined Twenty-Second to Twenty-Fifth Periodic Reports Submitted by Iraq Under Article 9 of the Convention, U.N. Doc. CERD/C/IRQ/22-25 (Nov. 22, 2017). ¶ 7.

[647] U.N. Doc. CERD/C/IRQ/22-25 (Nov. 22, 2017). ¶ 8.

the United Nations since 1945.[648] Iraq is party to key international conventions on International Human Rights, International Humanitarian Law, and International Criminal Law, particularly those related to the right to life and physical integrity,[649] the right of non-discrimination, and the rights of minorities.[650] Iraq "has endured decades of authoritarianism, followed by a difficult transition that was marked by international presence, unrest, and continuous violence, resulting in thousands of civilian casualties."[651]

In June 2014, the Islamic State in Iraq and the Levant (ISIL/DAESH) occupied North Iraq and self-proclaimed the 'Caliphate' as "the only legitimate [Muslim] authority on the planet."[652] [653] ISIL/DAESH then started a campaign to persecute and destroy religious and ethnic groups in Iraq, particularly the Christians and the Yazidis, through the perpetration of systematic and widespread violations and abuses of International Criminal Law, International Human Rights Law, and International Humanitarian Law in the territories under the control of the group.[654] Evidence suggests that these acts may amount to war crimes, crimes against humanity, and genocide.[655]

Following the ISIL/DAESH self-proclamation of the Caliphate, the group imposed the *takfiri* doctrine with their own interpretation of the Islamic faith and Muslim ideologies. At the beginning of July 2014, ISIL/DAESH "significantly increased its restrictions on the Christian [...]

---

[648]   U.N. Doc. CRC/C/OPAC/IRQ/1 (May 9, 2012). ¶ 3.

[649]   Iraq is party to the International Covenant on Civil and Political Rights, the Convention against Torture and Other Cruel, Inhuman or Degrading Treatment or Punishment, the Convention on the Rights of the Child and the Optional Protocol thereto on the involvement of children in armed conflict, the International Convention for the Protection of All Persons from Enforced Disappearance, the Convention on the Elimination of All Forms of Discrimination against Women, the 1949 Geneva Conventions and the Protocol additional to the Geneva Conventions of 12 August 1949 (Additional Protocol I), the Convention on the Prevention and Punishment of the Crime of Genocide, and the International Convention for the Protection of All Persons from Enforced Disappearance.

[650]   Iraq is party to the International Covenant on Civil and Political Rights, the International Covenant on Economic, Social and Cultural Rights and the International Convention on the Elimination of All Forms of Racial Discrimination.

[651]   U.N. Doc. A/HRC/28/18 (March 27, 2015). ¶ 1.

[652]   William Harris. *Supra* note 472. pp. 59–60.

[653]   See also: U.N. Doc. A/HRC/30/NGO/116 (Sept. 8, 2015). p. 2.

[654]   UNAMI (Sept. 11, 2014 – Dec. 10, 2014). p. 6; UNAMI (Dec. 11, 2014 – April 30, 2015). p. 10; U.N. Doc. S/2018/1031 (Nov. 16, 2018). ¶ 8.

[655]   U.N. Doc. S/2018/1031 (Nov. 16, 2018). ¶ 8.

communities within [Mosul]."[656] An ultimatum followed these restrictions for Christians to leave Mosul and surrounding northern areas by July 14, 2014, or face execution.[657]

Although perceived as the "People of the Book" – 'Ahl Al-Kitab' in Arabic –, the ISIL/DAESH ultimatum to Christians declared them as "slaves of the cross."[658] [659] [660] [661] [662] In the ultimatum, ISIL/DAESH threatened Christians: "We will conquer your Rome, break your crosses, and enslave your women, by the permission of Allah, the Exalted."[663] ISIL/DAESH fighters proclaimed the "great glory of Allah" in allowing them to sell Christians' sons and daughters as slaves at the slave market (malak yamiin),[664] a slave market that "will commence in Rome by Allah's power and might."[665] ISIL/DAESH solemnly ordered war against the apostates,[666] a war against the Christians

---

[656]   UNAMI (July 6, 2014 – Sept. 10, 2014). pp. 11–12.

[657]   Ibidem.

[658]   The expression People of the Book "is used in the Quran to refer to Jews, Christians and Sabeeans and emphasises the community of faith between those who possess monotheistic scriptures." (Valeria Cetorelli & Ashraph, Sareta, A Demographic Documentation of ISIS's Attack on the Yazidi Village of Kocho (The London School of Economics and Political Science – LSE, 2019). p. 8).

[659]   William Harris. Supra note 472. p. 60.

[660]   U.N. Doc. A/HRC/28/18 (March 27, 2015). ¶ 21.

[661]   Valeria Cetorelli & Ashraph, Sareta. Supra note 658. p. 8.

[662]   Eur. Parl., Prosecuting and Punishing the Crimes Against Humanity or Even Possible Genocide Committed by Daesh, Resolution 2190 (2017). ¶ 4.

[663]   The complete ultimatum from ISIL/DAESH to Christians in Iraq reads: "We will conquer your Rome, break your crosses, and enslave your women, by the permission of Allah, the Exalted. This is His promise to us; He is glorified and He does not fail in His promise. If we do not reach that time, then our children and grandchildren will reach it, and they will sell your sons as slaves at the slave market. Finally, this certainty is the one that should pulse in the heart of every mujćhid from the Islamic State and every supporter outside until he fights the Roman crusaders near Dćbiq." (KNIGHTS OF COLUMBUS. Supra note 409. pp. 8–9).

[664]   Ibidem.

[665]   Another part of the ultimatum from ISIL/DAESH to Christians in Iraq reads: "And nothing changes for the Islamic State, as it will continue to pronounce takfir [abandonment of Islam] upon the Jews, the Christians, the pagans, and the apostates from the Rćfidah, the Nusayriyyah, the Sahwah, and the tawćghīt [disbelievers]. It will continue to wage war against the apostates until they repent from apostasy. It will continue to wage war against the pagans until they accept Islam. It will continue to wage war against the Jewish state until the Jews hide behind their gharqad trees. And it will continue to wage war against the Christians until the truce decreed sometime before the Malhamah. Thereafter, the slave markets will commence in Rome by Allah's power and might." (Idem. p. 9).

[666]   Apostates, which can be understood as those not accepting Islam. Ibidem.

"until the truce decreed sometime before the *Malhamah*."[667] ISIL/DAESH
had then started its systematic and deliberate intent to persecute and destroy Christians in Iraq.

Some reports suggested that, in pursuing their campaign to destroy
Christians in Iraq, ISIL/DAESH fighters chose extremely efficient methods
of direct physical destruction of lives, as well as *slow death* methods. Some
of these *efficient methods* included: 1) mass and individual killings; and 2)
executions by, *inter alia*, hanging, stoning, drowning, throwing persons off
buildings, beheadings, crucifixions, shootings, burnings, and other forms
of murder. *Slow death* methods included: 1) taking of hostages; 2) use of
persons as human shields; 3) torture, beatings, mutilations, and amputations; 4) rape, sexual slavery, and abuse of women and girls; 5) inhuman
and degrading treatment, causing serious bodily or mental harm; 5) abductions, human trafficking, enforced disappearances, and intentional displacement of the Christian population; 6) separation of children from their
mothers; 7) systematic destruction of Christian places of worship; 8) forced
conversions; 9) deprivation of liberty; and 10) use of persons as human
shields or for suicide bombing.[668 669 670 671 672] The bodies of an unknown
number of Christian faith civilians continue to be discovered in mass
graves in areas previously under the ISIL/DAESH domain.[673]

Issuing orders, declarations, and statements of doctrine, ISIL/DAESH
compelled members of Christian communities, including young children,
to either 1) convert to Islam; 2) pay a fine – in accordance with Sharia Law

---

[667]  *Ibidem.*

[668]  U.N. Doc. A/HRC/28/18 (March 27, 2015). ¶ 78; U.N. Doc. A/69/926–S/2015/409
       (June 5, 2015). ¶ 71; S.C. Res. 2379 (Sept. 21, 2017). ¶ 1; U.N. Doc. CEDAW/C/IRQ/7
       (Aug. 15, 2018). ¶ 9; U.N. Doc. S/2018/677 (July 9, 2018). p.3; U.N. Doc. S/PV.8324
       (Aug. 8, 2018). p.3; U.N. Doc. A/73/347 (Aug. 28, 2018). ¶ 9; U.N. Doc.
       A/HRC/38/44/Add.1 (June 20, 2018). ¶¶ 23, 25, 28, 73.

[669]  Michelle Nichols, Iraq Tells United Nations That Islamic State Committed Geno-
       cide, REUTERS, Feb. 17, 2015; Anugrah Kumar, ISIS Burns Christians Alive in
       Locked Caskets, Escaped Prisoner Reveals, CHRISTIAN POST, Jan. 6, 2016.

[670]  Eur. Parl., Systematic Mass Murder of Religious Minorities by the so-called
       'ISIS/Daesh' (2016/2529(RSP)), Resolution (Feb. 4, 2016). p. 35/79. H; Eur. Parl.,
       Prosecuting and Punishing the Crimes Against Humanity or Even Possible Geno-
       cide Committed by Daesh, Resolution 2190 (2017). ¶¶ 3, 3.1, 4.

[671]  U.S. Dep't of State, Department Press, Remarks by Secretary of State John Kerry
       (Mar. 17, 2016).

[672]  UK Parliament, Genocide in Syria and Iraq, Early Day Motion, Sponsored by Robert
       Flello (Jan. 26, 2016).

[673]  U.N. Doc. A/HRC/34/53/Add.1 (Jan. 9, 2017). ¶ 63; U.N. Doc. A/HRC/38/44/Add.1
       (June 20, 2018). ¶ 77; U.N. Doc. S/2018/677 (July 9, 2018). ¶¶ 42, 43.

– called *jizyah* (toleration/protection tax); 3) face expulsion; or 4) face summary killings – death by the sword.[674] [675] [676] [677] [678] Children were reported being beheaded by ISIL/DAESH members for refusing to convert to Islam.[679] These orders were announced publicly in leaflets and through all the mosques' loudspeakers during Friday's prayers.[680] [681]

ISIL/DAESH systematically destroyed Christian places of worship or converted Christian churches/places of worship into mosques and bases. ISIL/DAESH intentionally looted or destroyed religious monuments, Christian cemeteries, religious artifacts, cultural heritage sites, and historic sites. The group also removed crosses and vandalized tombs. Several reports accounted for ISIL/DAESH's kidnapping and executions of the clergy, priests, and pastors.[682] [683] [684] [685] [686] [687] Several reports suggest that ISIL/

---

[674]  U.N. Doc. A/HRC/S-22/NGO/8 (Aug. 29, 2014). p.3; U.N. Doc. A/HRC/RES/S-22/1 (Sept. 3, 2014). p.1; U.N. Doc. A/HRC/28/18 (March 27, 2015). ¶ 21; U.N. Doc. A/HRC/34/53/Add.1 (Jan. 9, 2017). ¶ 32.

[675]  UNAMI (July 6, 2014 – Sept. 10, 2014). p.11; UNAMI (Dec. 11, 2014 – Apr. 30, 2015). p.21.

[676]  Hamdi Alkhshali & Joshua Berlinger, *Facing Fines, Conversion or Death, Christian Families Flee Mosul*, CNN, July 20, 2014; Eleftheriou-Smith, Loulla-Mae. The Independent: British 'Vicar of Baghdad' claims Isis beheaded four children for refusing to convert to Islam. December 8, 2014; Jane Corbin, *Could Christianity Be Driven From Middle East?* BBC, April 15, 2015; Moni Basu, *Being Christian in Iraq after ISIS: In Biblical Lands of Iraq, Christianity in Peril After ISIS*, CNN, Nov. 21, 2016; Myers, Russell. The Mirror: ISIS behead four children in Iraq after they refuse to convert to Islam. December 8, 2017.

[677]  AMNESTY INTERNATIONAL. *Supra* note 495. p. 15; HUMAN RIGHTS WATCH. (December 2017). p. 16.

[678]  KNIGHTS OF COLUMBUS. *Supra* note 409. p. 4, 6).

[679]  Loulla-Mae Eleftheriou-Smith, *British 'Vicar of Baghdad' Claims Isis Beheaded Four Children For Refusing to Convert to Islam*, THE INDEPENDENT, Dec. 8, 2014; Russell Myers, *ISIS Behead Four Children in Iraq After They Refuse to Convert to Islam*, THE MIRROR, Dec. 8, 2017.

[680]  UNAMI, Protection of Civilians in the Armed Conflict in Iraq (July 6, 2014 – Sept. 10, 2014). p.11.

[681]  THE HUDSON INSTITUTE. *Supra* note 410. p. 6.

[682]  U.N. Doc. A/69/53/Add.1 (Sept. 1, 2014). Preamble, p.7; U.N. Doc. A/HRC/28/18 (March 27, 2015). ¶¶ 22, 78.

[683]  UNAMI (July 6, 2014 – Sept. 10, 2014). p.12; UNAMI (Sept. 11, 2014 – Dec. 10, 2014). p. 12; UNAMI (Dec. 11, 2014 – Apr. 30, 2015). p.19; UNAMI (May 1, 2015 – Oct. 31, 2015). p.16.

DAESH declarations encompassed a policy of destroying, eradicating, and exterminating the entire Christian community in Iraq.[688] [689] [690]

After ISIL/DAESH's takeover of Mosul, Christian families and children fled Qaraqosh and other villages in the Nineveh Plains in massive numbers. Disabled, aged, and those unable to travel were left behind.[691] [692] [693] ISIL/DAESH occupied and destroyed the houses of those who refused to convert to Islam and seized all their belongings, including identity docu-

---

[684] Eur. Parl., Systematic Mass Murder of Religious Minorities by the so-called 'ISIS/Daesh' (2016/2529(RSP)), Resolution (Feb. 4, 2016). ¶ 8; Eur. Parl., Prosecuting and Punishing the Crimes Against Humanity or Even Possible Genocide Committed by Daesh, Resolution 2190 (2017). ¶¶ 3–4; Eur. Parl., Prosecuting and Punishing the Crimes Against Humanity or Even Possible Genocide Committed by Daesh, Report, Doc. No. 14402 (Sept. 22, 2017). ¶¶ 4, 22; Eur. Parl., Annual Report on Human Rights and Democracy in the World 2016 and the European Union's Policy on the Matter (2017/2122(INI)), Resolution (Dec. 13, 2017). ¶ 36.

[685] 163 Cong. Rec. H5368 (daily ed. June 29, 2017) (statement of Rep. Ted Poe). p. H5369.

[686] AMNESTY INTERNATIONAL. *Supra* note 495. p. 15.

[687] *Iraq's Oldest Christian Monastery Destroyed by Islamic State,* BBC.COM, Jan. 20, 2016.

[688] Eur. Parl., Threats Against Humanity Posed by the Terrorist Group Known as "IS": Violence Against Christians and Other Religious or Ethnic Communities (Final version), Doc. No. 13618 (Sept. 30, 2014). ¶ 7; Eur. Parl., Prosecuting and Punishing the Crimes Against Humanity or Even Possible Genocide Committed by Daesh, Resolution 2190 (2017). ¶¶ 3.2, 4; Eur. Parl., Annual Report on Human Rights and Democracy in the World 2016 and the European Union's Policy on the Matter (2017/2122(INI)), Resolution (Dec. 13, 2017). ¶ 36.

[689] H.R.Con.Res. 75, 114th Cong. (Mar. 15, 2016). p. 2; H.R. 407, 115th Cong. (Dec. 12, 2017). Preamble; H.R. 390, 115th Cong. (Nov. 29, 2018). Drafting. Sec. 2. Findings. ¶ 3; 165 Cong. Rec. H349 (daily ed. Jan. 9, 2019) (statement of Rep. Jeff Fortenberry). p. H351.

[690] 163 Cong. Rec. H4632 (daily ed. June 6, 2017) (statement of Rep. Edward Royce). p. H4633; 163 Cong. Rec. H5368 (daily ed. June 29, 2017) (statement of Rep. Ted Poe). p. H5369; 165 Cong. Rec. H2350 (daily ed. Mar. 5, 2019) (statement of Rep. Jeff Fortenberry). p. H2350; H. Res. 259, 116th Cong. (Mar. 27, 2019). p. 2.

[691] U.N. Doc. A/HRC/S-22/NGO/8 (Aug. 29, 2014). p.3; U.N. Doc. A/HRC/28/18 (March 27, 2015). ¶ 21; U.N. Doc. A/HRC/34/53/Add.1 (Jan. 9, 2017). ¶¶ 32, 62; U.N. Doc. A/HRC/44/NGO/115 (June 30, 2020). p. 2.

[692] UNAMI (July 6, 2014 – Sept. 10, 2014). pp. 11–12.

[693] Hamdi Alkhshali & Joshua Berlinger, *Facing Fines, Conversion or Death, Christian Families Flee Mosul,* CNN, July 20, 2014; Jane Corbin, *Could Christianity Be Driven From Middle East?* BBC, April 15, 2015; Eliza Griswold, *Is this the end of Christianity in the Middle East?* THE NEW YORK TIMES, July 22, 2015; Moni Basu, *Being Christian in Iraq after ISIS: In Biblical Lands of Iraq, Christianity in Peril After ISIS,* CNN, Nov. 21, 2016; Hollie McKay, *Life After ISIS: Christians Say They Can't Go Home Without International Protection,* FOX NEWS, Dec. 14, 2017.

ments and indispensable survival items.[694][695][696] In Mosul, the walls of houses, businesses, and farms belonging to Christians were marked with an Arabic letter "N" (ن) – the first letter of the Arabic word 'nasara,' nasrane ("Nazarene"), the Quran word referring to Christians)[697][698] – as well as marked with the sign of "property of the Islamic State" (al-Dawla al-Islamiyya).[699][700][701][702]

As the *mass exodus* of Christians advanced over other municipalities, ISIL/DAESH reportedly cut the water and electricity supply to these areas, such as the Nineveh Plain and Qaraqosh.[703][704][705][706] ISIL/DAESH left the Christian group in Iraq in an atmosphere of fear and intimidation. As Christian women and girls were fleeing, they were physically and sexually abused and raped by ISIL/DAESH fighters at checkpoints.[707] In ISIL/DAESH-controlled areas, these women and girls were systematically sold as sexual slaves.[708] Prohibited by ISIL/DAESH fighters from going back to their

---

[694] U.N. Doc. A/HRC/28/18 (March 27, 2015). ¶¶ 21–22; U.N. Doc. A/HRC/44/NGO/115 (June 30, 2020). p. 2.

[695] UNAMI (July 6, 2014 – Sept. 10, 2014). pp. 11–12; UNAMI (Dec. 11, 2014 – April 30, 2015). p. 21; UNAMI (May 1, 2015 – Oct. 31, 2015). p. 15.

[696] Eur. Parl., Systematic Mass Murder of Religious Minorities by the so-called 'ISIS/Daesh' (2016/2529(RSP)), Resolution (Feb. 4, 2016). p. 35/79. h.

[697] U.N. Doc. A/HRC/34/53/Add.1 (Jan. 9, 2017). ¶ 32.

[698] UNAMI (July 6, 2014 – Sept. 10, 2014). p. 11.

[699] *Ibidem.*

[700] Office of the United Nations High Commissioner for Human Rights, Internal Communication Clearance Form, UA, IRQ 4/2014 (July 24, 2014). p. 2; U.N. Doc. A/HRC/S-22/NGO/8 (Aug. 29, 2014). p.3; U.N. Doc. A/HRC/34/53/Add.1 (Jan. 9, 2017). ¶ 62.

[701] U.S. Dep't of State, Bureau of Democracy, H.R. and Lab., International Religious Freedom Report (2017). p.160.

[702] Eliza Griswold, *Is this the end of Christianity in the Middle East?* THE NEW YORK TIMES, July 22, 2015.

[703] UNAMI (July 6, 2014 – Sept. 10, 2014). p. 12.

[704] Eur. Parl. Plenary sitting. Joint Motion for a Resolution Pursuant to Rule 123(2) and (4), of the Rules of Procedure. Systematic Mass Murder of Religious Minorities by The So-called ISIS/Daesh 2014–2019. (Feb. 3, 2016). ¶ 11.

[705] THE HUDSON INSTITUTE. *Supra* note 410. p. 6.

[706] Eliza Griswold, *Is this the end of Christianity in the Middle East?* THE NEW YORK TIMES, July 22, 2015.

[707] UNAMI (July 6, 2014 – Sept. 10, 2014). p. 12.

[708] U.N. Doc. A/69/926–S/2015/409 (June 5, 2015). ¶ 71; U.N. Doc. S/2016/92 (Jan. 29, 2016). ¶ 9; U.N. Doc. A/70/836–S/2016/360 (Apr. 20, 2016). ¶ 62; U.N. Doc. S/2018/677 (July 9, 2018). ¶ 75; U.N. Doc. A/73/263 (July 27, 2018). ¶ 11; U.N. Doc. S/2018/770 (August 16, 2018). ¶ 10.

houses, Christians' inability to reconstitute themselves indicated to the international community the terrorist group's intent to destroy the religious group in Iraq. A Non-Governmental Organization with Special Consultative Status in the Human Rights Council estimated that, following ISIL/DAESH control of the Iraqi territory, "the Christian population of Iraq has shrunk to only 150,000 members, about 0.39 percent of the country's population."[709] [710]

Several United Nations bodies considered that the acts perpetrated by ISIL/DAESH against Christians in Iraq, from 2014 to 2017, could fall within the definition of genocide, as determined by the 1948 U.N. Convention on the Prevention and Punishment of Genocide: the United Nations Assistance Mission for Iraq (UNAMI),[711] the United Nations Human Rights Committee,[712] the United Nations Human Rights Council,[713] and United Nations Committee on the Elimination of Racial Discrimination.[714] Likewise, on numerous occasions, the Parliamentary Assembly of the Council of Europe[715] and the European Parliament formally recognized that evidence might sustain an accusation of genocide against ISIL/DAESH members for their acts against Christians in Iraq.[716] France[717] and the United Kingdom[718] [719] [720]

---

[709] U.N. Doc. A/HRC/44/NGO/115 (June 30, 2020). p. 2.

[710] See also: The United Nations High Commissioner for Human Rights estimated this figure in approximately 200,000 Christians. (U.N. Doc. A/HRC/28/18 (March 27, 2015). ¶ 21); U.N. Doc. A/HRC/34/53/Add.1 (Jan. 9, 2017). ¶ 32.

[711] UNAMI (Dec. 11, 2014 – Apr. 30, 2015). p. i.

[712] U.N. Doc. CCPR/C/IRQ/CO/5/Add.1 (Aug. 18, 2017). ¶¶ 1, 3.

[713] U.N. Doc. A/HRC/RES/S-22/1 (Sept. 3, 2014). p.1; U.N. Doc. A/HRC/38/44/Add.1 (June 20, 2018).

[714] U.N. Doc. CERD/C/IRQ/22-25 (Nov. 22, 2017). ¶ 16.

[715] Eur. Parl., Prosecuting and Punishing the Crimes Against Humanity or Even Possible Genocide Committed by Daesh, Resolution 2190 (2017). ¶¶ 1, 2, 3, 3.1, 4.

[716] Eur. Parl., Threats Against Humanity Posed by the Terrorist Group Known as "IS": Violence Against Christians and Other Religious or Ethnic Communities (Final version), Doc. No. 13618 (Sept. 30, 2014); Eur. Parl., Prosecuting and Punishing the Crimes Against Humanity or Even Possible Genocide Committed by Daesh, Resolution 2190 (2017). ¶ 1; Eur. Parl., EU priorities for the UN Human Rights Council Sessions in 2017 (2017/2598(RSP)), Resolution (Mar. 16, 2017). ¶ 21; Eur. Parl., Prosecuting and Punishing the Crimes Against Humanity or Even Possible Genocide Committed by Daesh, Compendium of Amendments, Doc. No. 14402 (Oct. 11, 2017); Eur. Parl., Annual Report on Human Rights and Democracy in the World 2016 and the European Union's Policy on the Matter (2017/2122(INI)), Resolution (Dec. 13, 2017).

[717] Permanent Mission of France to the United Nations, "The Fight Against Impunity for Atrocities: Bringing Daesh to Justice," Remarks by François Delattre, (Mar. 9, 2017).

also recognized the existence of at least circumstantial evidence to sustain that ISIL/DAESH might have committed genocide against Christians. Several international organizations followed this approach.[721]

Also, several instances of political power in the United States considered ISIL/DAESH's atrocities against Christians in Iraq. In the US Congress, the Senate,[722] and the House of Representatives,[723] separately, as well as assembled with concurring resolutions,[724] recognized that the crimes committed by ISIL/DAESH against Christians in Iraq, from 2014 to 2017, could constitute genocide. In the U.S. Department of State, different spheres have also considered that the acts perpetrated by ISIL/DAESH against Christians had the required legal elements for the consideration of genocide: the Department of State Secretary,[725] [726] the Office of the Spokesper-

---

[718]   UK Parliament, Genocide in Syria and Iraq, Early Day Motion, Sponsored by Robert Flello (Jan. 26, 2016).

[719]   Arabella Lang & Ben Smith, *Declaring Daesh Massacres' Genocide,* HOUSE OF COMMONS PUBLISHING HOUSE, Apr. 15, 2016.

[720]   Patrick Wintour, *MPs Unanimously Declare Yazidis and Christians Victims of Isis Genocide: British Parliament Defies Government to Condemn Barbarity of Islamic State in Syria and Iraq,* THE GUARDIAN, April 20, 2016.

[721]   For example: KNIGHTS OF COLUMBUS. *Supra* note 409. p. 10, 11, 27; THE HUDSON INSTITUTE. *Supra* note 410. pp. 1–2; AMNESTY INTERNATIONAL. *Supra* note 495. p.15; HUMAN RIGHTS WATCH. (December 2017). p. 16.

[722]   S. 2377, 114th Cong. (Dec. 9, 2015). ¶ 7.

[723]   H.R. 4017, 114th Cong. (Nov. 16, 2015). Preamble; H. Res. 1117, 115th Cong. (Oct. 5, 2018). Preamble; H.R. 390, 115th Cong. (Nov. 29, 2018). Drafting. Preamble; H. Res. 259, 116th Cong. (Mar. 27, 2019). p. 2.

[724]   H.R.Con.Res. 75, 114th Cong. (Sept. 9, 2015). ¶ 1; H.R.Con.Res. 75, 114th Cong. (Mar. 15, 2016). Dispositive part; H.R.Con.Res. 41, 114th Cong. (July 18, 2016). ¶ 7; 165 Cong. Rec. X 1.1/A: X/A (daily ed. Jan. 10, 2017) (statement of Rep. Christopher H. Smith). Preamble; 163 Cong. Rec. E1315 (daily ed. Oct. 3, 2017) (statement of Rep. Christopher H. Smith). Preamble; 164 Cong. Rec. S6876 (daily ed. Oct. 11, 2018) (statement of Rep. Mitch McConnell). ¶ 1; 164 Cong. Rec. H9600 (daily ed. Nov. 27, 2018) (statement of Rep. Christopher H. Smith). P. H9603; 164 Cong. Rec. E1606 – H.R. 390 (daily ed. Dec. 6, 2018) (statement of Rep. Anna G. Eshoo). Drafting. Preamble; 165 Cong. Rec. H349 (daily ed. Jan. 9, 2019) (statement of Rep. Jeff Fortenberry). p. H352.

[725]   Amanda Holpuch, Harriet Sherwood & Owen Bowcott, *John Kerry: Isis Is Committing Genocide in Syria and Iraq, says US House,* THE GUARDIAN, Mar. 17, 2016; John Hudson, *Obama Administration Declares Islamic State Genocide Against Christians,* FOREIGN POLICY, Mar. 17, 2016; Andrea Mitchell, Cassandra Vinograd, F. Brinley Bruton & Abigail Williams, *Daesh Is Responsible For Genocide: Kerry: ISIS Is Committing Genocide Against Yazidis, Christians and* Shiite Muslims, NBC NEWS, Mar. 17, 2016.

[726]   U.S. Dep't of State, Department Press, Remarks by Secretary of State John Kerry (Mar. 17, 2016).

son,[727] the Department Press,[728] and the Office of the Legal Adviser[729] In 2017, the U.S. Commission on International Religious Freedom[730] and the U.S. Permanent Representative to the United Nations[731] indicated that ISIL/DAESH might have executed Christians near extinction in Iraq solely because they were Christians. However, none of these instances presented pieces of evidence to support their allegation of genocide, although their reports actually mentioned the existence of such evidence.

## 1.3. ISIL/DAESH self-appointed sharia courts: Sharia Law, sentences, the use of public executions, and mass graves

In areas under its control, ISIL/DAESH engaged in numerous unlawful detentions. The group "ran detention facilities managed by various entities: the Islamic police, the military police, the morality police, raid squads, and security forces."[732] Moreover, ISIL/DAESH established self-appointed sharia courts that extrajudicially sentenced civilians to cruel, inhuman, de-

---

[727] U.S. Dep't of State, Office of the Spokesperson, Department Press, Briefing by Heather Nauert (Aug. 3, 2017); U.S. Dep't of State, Office of the Spokesperson, Department Press, Briefing by Heather Nauert (Aug. 15, 2017); U.S. Dep't of State, Office of the Spokesperson, Department Press, Briefing by Heather Nauert (Oct. 26, 2017); U.S. Dep't of State, Office of the Spokesperson, Department Press, Readout of USAID Administrator Green and Ambassador-at-Large for International Religious Freedom Samuel Brownback's Trip to Northern Iraq (July 5, 2018).

[728] U.S. Dep't of State, Department Press, Remarks by Special Presidential Envoy for the Global Coalition to Defeat ISIS Brett McGurk (June 22, 2017); U.S. Dep't of State, Department Press, Remarks by Special Presidential Envoy for the Global Coalition to Defeat ISIS Brett McGurk (July 8, 2017); U.S. Dep't of State, Department Press, Remarks by Special Presidential Envoy for the Global Coalition to Defeat ISIS Brett McGurk (July 13, 2017); U.S. Dep't of State, Department Press, Special Briefing by Special Presidential Envoy for the Global Coalition to Defeat ISIS Brett McGurk (Dec. 21, 2017); U.S. Dep't of State, Department Press, Remarks by Special Presidential Envoy for the Global Coalition to Defeat ISIS Brett McGurk (June 26, 2018).

[729] U.S. Dep't of State, Office of the Legal Adviser, Digest of the United States Practice in International Law (2016). p. 780; U.S. Dep't of State, Office of the Legal Adviser, Digest of the United States Practice in International Law (2017). p. 283.

[730] U.S. Dep't of State, Bureau of Democracy, H.R. and Lab., International Religious Freedom Report (2017).

[731] U.S. Permanent Representative to the United Nations, Ambassador Nikki Haley, Explanation of Vote Following the Adoption of UN Security Council Resolution 2379 on Accountability for ISIS Atrocities (Sept. 21, 2017).

[732] U.N. Doc. A/HRC/38/44/Add.1 (June 20, 2018). ¶ 24.

grading treatment, and death. Women, young children, and persons with disabilities were among the long list of victims.[733] [734] [735] [736] [737] Such "courts" lacked any power to exercise judicial authority, in total violation of international law.[738] Through such "courts," ISIL/DAESH ultimately instituted a state in which violence became a "necessary and 'normal' way of life,"[739] instilling on civilians in Iraq "feelings of fear, insecurity, and disorientation."[740]

The passing of "sentences" and the summary executions did not respect any fundamental principle of due process or fair trial guarantees.[741] [742] ISIL/DAESH victims were punished under the "guilty until proven innocent" rule without a previous lawful judgement.[743] The executions were 1) often preceded by the enforced disappearances of victims, and 2) most of the time were held in public, in front of a civilian crowd.[744]

ISIL/DAESH courts punished civilians for a myriad of reasons:

1) For failing to comply with ISIL/DAESH's strict code of conduct: civilians were rigidly and brutally punished on charges of adultery; charges for the practice of homosexual acts (sodomy); charges for watching football matches; charges for smoking cigarettes; charges for practicing magic; and

[733] "In Mosul alone, Ninewa governorate, ISIL/DAESH has established at least 14 so-called 'courts'." (UNAMI (Sept. 11, 2014 – Dec. 10, 2014). p. 10).

[734] U.N. Doc. S/2014/774 (Oct. 31, 2014). ¶ 49; U.N. Doc. S/2015/82 (Feb. 2, 2015). ¶ 48; U.N. Doc. A/HRC/28/18 (March 27, 2015). ¶¶ 35, 48–49, 76; U.N. Doc. A/HRC/30/66 (July 27, 2015). ¶¶ 11, 20; U.N. Doc. A/HRC/38/44/Add.1 (June 20, 2018). ¶ 24; U.N. Doc. A/73/347 (Aug. 28, 2018). ¶ 9; U.N. Doc. S/2019/984 (Dec. 23, 2019). ¶ 6.

[735] UNAMI (July 6, 2014 – Sept. 10, 2014). pp. 6, 15; UNAMI (Sept. 11, 2014 – Dec. 10, 2014). p. 10; UNAMI (Dec. 11, 2014 – April 30, 2015). pp. 11, 13–14, 22; UNAMI (May 1, 2015 – Oct. 31, 2015). pp. 9, 11–12, 17, 32; UNAMI (Aug. 2016). p. 11; UNAMI (Nov. 6, 2018). p. 4.

[736] S.C. Res. 2379 (Sept. 21, 2017). Preamble, p.1.

[736] Office of the United Nations High Commissioner for Human Rights, Internal Communication Clearance Form, UA, IRQ 5/2014 (Aug. 18, 2014). p. 1.

[737] AMNESTY INTERNATIONAL. *Supra* note 495. *passim.*

[738] UNAMI (May 1, 2015 – Oct. 31, 2015). p. 11.

[739] ICSR. *Supra* note 520.

[740] U.N. Doc. A/HRC/28/18 (March 27, 2015). ¶ 36

[741] UNAMI (May 1, 2015 – Oct. 31, 2015). p. 11.

[742] U.N. Doc. A/HRC/28/18 (March 27, 2015). ¶ 48; U.N. Doc. A/HRC/38/44/Add.1 (June 20, 2018). ¶ 24.

[743] U.N. Doc. A/HRC/28/18 (March 27, 2015). ¶ 76

[744] U.N. Doc. A/HRC/38/44/Add.1 (June 20, 2018). ¶ 25.

charges for using telephones, cellphones, and the internet.[745] [746] [747] Music and CD stores were utterly banned in Mosul.[748] In one instance, ISIL/DAESH "stopped a wedding procession in the Ghabat area of northern Mosul because of the decorated cars and loud music."[749] After much disagreement, "ISIL/DAESH fighters started shooting at the wedding party, killing the bride and the groom and injuring others."[750]

2) ISIL/DAESH imposed a strict dress code on men and women. Women and girls above thirteen years of age who had refused to wear the veil (*niqab*) were sentenced to brutal beatings or stoning in public.[751] [752] Female students starting from the age of 10 were forced to cover their faces and hands in school premises.[753] In the holy month of Ramadan, women were prohibited from leaving their homes from dawn to sunset.[754] ISIL/DAESH also imposed harsh sentences on female doctors who did not abide by the group's dress code.[755] Reportedly, ISIL/DAESH inquired that hospitals make known "the marital status of the female doctors and stated that married women should wear black, while unmarried females other colours [sic], so as to be easily distinguishable."[756] On one occasion, "a female doctor reported that she was stopped from attending to an urgent case because she was not covered properly."[757] [758] Male residents of Mosul were

---

[745] UNAMI (July 6, 2014 – Sept. 10, 2014). pp. 6, 15–16; UNAMI (Sept. 11, 2014 – Dec. 10, 2014). p. 14; UNAMI (Dec. 11, 2014 – April 30, 2015). pp. 13–14, 21, 24; UNAMI (May 1, 2015 – Oct. 31, 2015). pp. 17, 32.

[746] U.N. Doc. A/HRC/28/18 (March 27, 2015). ¶ 49; U.N. Doc. S/2016/77 (Jan. 26, 2016). ¶ 49; U.N. Doc. S/2016/592 (July 5, 2016). ¶ 37; U.N. Doc. S/2017/75 (Jan. 26, 2017). ¶ 39; U.N. Doc. A/HRC/38/44/Add.1 (June 20, 2018). ¶ 27; U.N. Doc. A/73/347 (Aug. 28, 2018). ¶ 9.

[747] AMNESTY INTERNATIONAL. *Supra* note 495. p. 15; Jacob Eriksson & Ahmed Khaleel eds., Iraq After ISIS: The Challenges of Post-War Recovery. (Palgrave Macmillan, 2019). p. 84.

[748] UNAMI (Sept. 11, 2014 – Dec. 10, 2014). p. 14.

[749] UNAMI (Dec. 11, 2014 – April 30, 2015). p. 16.

[750] *Ibidem.*

[751] UNAMI (July 6, 2014 – Sept. 10, 2014). p. 11; UNAMI (Dec. 11, 2014 – April 30, 2015). p. 24.

[752] U.N. Doc. S/2015/530 (July 13, 2015). ¶ 51; U.N. Doc. S/2019/984 (Dec. 23, 2019). ¶ 6.

[753] UNAMI (Sept. 11, 2014 – Dec. 10, 2014). p. 14.

[754] U.N. Doc. S/2015/530 (July 13, 2015). ¶ 51; U.N. Doc. A/HRC/30/66 (July 27, 2015). ¶ 12.

[755] UNAMI (July 6, 2014 – Sept. 10, 2014). p. 10.

[756] *Ibidem.*

[757] *Ibidem.*

[758] See also: U.N. Doc. A/HRC/30/66 (July 27, 2015). ¶ 19.

instructed by ISIL/DAESH fighters to adopt an Afghan-style of dressing (*shalwar kamiz*), to grow beards, and shave mustaches.[759]

3) For refusal to swear allegiance to ISIL/DAESH: ISIL/DAESH imposed charges on people for refusing to pledge allegiance to the group;[760] [761] for failing to support ISIL/DAESH fighters, as, for example, "for allegedly refusing to allow ISIL/DAESH to install and launch rockets from the rooftops of their houses;"[762] [763] persons were sentenced for allegedly assisting civilian residents in leaving areas under ISIL/DAESH's control;[764] civilians were punished for allegedly cooperating/collaborating with the Iraqi security forces (ISF) and its affiliated forces, and for supporting or aiding the Government of Iraq;[765] [766] ISIL/DAESH murdered victims for attempting to flee from Iraq or for assisting others in fleeing.[767]

4) For opposing ISIL/DAESH's extreme ideology and *Takfiri* doctrines: ISIL/DAESH fighters sentenced to death those accused of blasphemy, apostasy, those considered infidels, and those who allegedly strayed from the group's own interpretation of Islam and own interpretation of religious rulings.[768] [769] [770] [771] ISIL/DAESH killed even *Imams* who allegedly did not conform to the group's ideologies, failed to praise the group's atrocities, refused to join the insurgents, or denounced ISIL/DAESH fighters in their sermons and prayers.[772] ISIL/DAESH also imposed brutal punishments on civilians who failed to memorize the Quran and recite it publicly.[773] [774]

---

[759]  U.N. Doc. S/2015/530 (July 13, 2015). ¶ 51.

[760]  U.N. Doc. A/HRC/28/18 (March 27, 2015). ¶ 29.

[761]  UNAMI (July 6, 2014 – Sept. 10, 2014). p. 7.

[762]  Office of the United Nations High Commissioner for Human Rights, Spokesperson for the UN High Commissioner for Human Rights: Ravina Shamdasani (Nov. 29, 2016). (2).

[763]  See also: UNAMI (May 1, 2015 – Oct. 31, 2015). p. 10.

[764]  U.N. Doc. S/2015/530 (July 13, 2015). ¶ 50; UNAMI (May 1, 2015 – Oct. 31, 2015). p. 9.

[765]  U.N. Doc. S/2015/82 (Feb. 2, 2015). ¶ 49; U.N. Doc. S/2016/396 (Apr. 27, 2016). ¶ 44; U.N. Doc. S/2016/592 (July 5, 2016). ¶ 37; U.N. Doc. S/2017/75 (Jan. 26, 2017). ¶ 39; U.N. Doc. S/2017/881 (Oct. 19, 2017). ¶ 51.

[766]  UNAMI (Dec. 11, 2014 – April 30, 2015). p. 12; UNAMI (May 1, 2015 – Oct. 31, 2015). pp. 9–12.

[767]  UNAMI (May 1, 2015 – Oct. 31, 2015). p. 9.

[768]  U.N. Doc. S/2014/774 (Oct. 31, 2014). ¶ 49; U.N. Doc. A/HRC/30/66 (July 27, 2015). ¶¶ 19, 48; U.N. Doc. S/2016/77 (Jan. 26, 2016). ¶ 49; U.N. Doc. S/2016/92 (Jan. 29, 2016). ¶ 9; U.N. Doc. S/2016/897 (Oct. 25, 2016). ¶ 45; U.N. Doc. A/HRC/38/44/Add.1 (June 20, 2018). ¶ 26.

[769]  UNAMI (June 5 – July 5, 2014). p. 13; UNAMI (May 1, 2015 – Oct. 31, 2015). pp. 8, 11.

[770]  Office of the United Nations High Commissioner for Human Rights, Internal Communication Clearance Form, UA, IRQ 4/2014 (July 24, 2014). p. 2.

[771]  AMNESTY INTERNATIONAL. *Supra* note 495.

5) ISIL/DAESH tortured or killed persons accused of banditry, such as theft/stealing.[775] [776]

6) ISIL/DAESH killed members of its own group "for refusing to fight or acting against its interests."[777]

ISIL/DAESH imposed punishments/sentences included:

1) Deliberate torture and physical ill-treatment: mutilations and amputations, particularly of hands, fingers, and arms, including the amputation of children; floggings; lashings; and beating of the victims with cables and with plastic pipes.[778] [779] [780]

2) Deliberate, systematic, unlawful execution/killing of civilians in areas under ISIL/DAESH control: killings through gunshots in the head; executions by firing squad; killings through public beheadings, including the beheading of children, elderly people, and members of the same family together; killings by throwing the victims from the top of tall buildings; killings by stoning, hanging; death by immolation; death by burning civilians alive, including the burning of children; death by the burying of persons alive, including children; killing by a sword bit above the person's neck; killing by inflicting deep knife wounds on the victims' bodies; death by drowning, by placing civilians in an iron cage that was submerged into the water; killing of civilian adults and children by rocket-propelled grenades; killings through crucifixion, including the crucifixions of children; the killing of entire families at once; the execution of prisoners.[781] [782] [783] [784] [785] In different instances, ISIL/DAESH forced sons to behead their own fathers.[786]

---

[772]  UNAMI (June 5 – July 5, 2014). p. 10; UNAMI (July 6, 2014 – Sept. 10, 2014). pp. 7, 9; UNAMI (May 1, 2015 – Oct. 31, 2015). pp. 10–11.

[773]  ICSR. *Supra* note 520. pp. 17, 21.

[774]  UNAMI (May 1, 2015 – Oct. 31, 2015). p. 18.

[775]  U.N. Doc. A/HRC/28/18 (March 27, 2015). ¶ 49

[776]  UNAMI (Dec. 11, 2014 – April 30, 2015). pp. 13–14; UNAMI (May 1, 2015 – Oct. 31, 2015). p. 12.

[777]  UNAMI (May 1, 2015 – Oct. 31, 2015). pp. 12, 32.

[778]  UNAMI (Dec. 11, 2014 – April 30, 2015). pp. 13–14, 24; UNAMI (May 1, 2015 – Oct. 31, 2015). p. 12; UNAMI (Aug. 2016). pp. 11, 16.

[779]  U.N. Doc. A/HRC/28/18 (March 27, 2015). ¶¶ 48–49, 76; U.N. Doc. A/HRC/30/66 (July 27, 2015). ¶ 11; U.N. Doc. S/2016/92 (Jan. 29, 2016). ¶ 9; U.N. Doc. S/2016/396 (Apr. 27, 2016). ¶ 44; U.N. Doc. A/73/347 (Aug. 28, 2018). ¶ 9; U.N. Doc. S/2019/984 (Dec. 23, 2019). ¶¶ 6, 48, 56.

[780]  AMNESTY INTERNATIONAL. *Supra* note 495. pp. 15, 44.

[781]  U.N. Doc. A/69/53/Add.1 (Sept. 1, 2014). Preamble, p.7; U.N. Doc. A/HRC/RES/S-22/1 (Sept. 3, 2014). Preamble, p.1; U.N. Doc. S/2014/774 (Oct. 31, 2014). ¶¶ 46, 76; U.N. Doc. S/2015/82 (Feb. 2, 2015). ¶ 46; U.N. Doc. CRC/C/IRQ/CO/2-4 (March 3,

Several victims were blindfolded before being tortured or executed, and their hands were tied behind their backs.[787] Commonly, ISIL/DAESH made use of bulldozer tractors to its victims by forcing them to lie down on the street, and a tractor was driven over them, smashing them to death.[788] Frequently, ISIL/DAESH fighters used to throw their victims' corpses into the Tigris River or simply leave the bodies on the side of the road.[789] [790]

Most of the ISIL/DAESH executions, beatings, and mutilations were performed during public events, in public places, and in front of a crowd,

---

2015). ¶ 23.a; U.N. Doc. A/HRC/28/18 (March 27, 2015). ¶¶ 31, 35, 49, 76; U.N. Doc. S/2015/530 (July 13, 2015). ¶¶ 44, 50; U.N. Doc. A/HRC/30/66 (July 27, 2015). ¶¶ 11, 32; U.N. Doc. S/2016/77 (Jan. 26, 2016). ¶ 49; U.N. Doc. S/2016/92 (Jan. 29, 2016). ¶ 9; U.N. Doc. A/HRC/32/35/Add.1 (April 5, 2016). ¶ 55; U.N. Doc. S/2016/396 (Apr. 27, 2016). ¶¶ 44, 78; U.N. Doc. S/2016/592 (July 5, 2016). ¶ 37; U.N. Doc. S/AC.51/2016/2 (Aug. 18, 2016). ¶ 8.a; U.N. Doc. S/2016/897 (Oct. 25, 2016). ¶ 45; U.N. Doc. S/2017/75 (Jan. 26, 2017). ¶ 39; U.N. Doc. CCPR/C/IRQ/CO/5/Add.1 (Aug. 18, 2017). ¶ 19; U.N. Doc. A/72/361–S/2017/821 (Aug. 24, 2017). ¶ 78; U.N. Doc. S/2017/881 (Oct. 19, 2017). ¶¶ 51, 63; U.N. Doc. CERD/C/IRQ/22-25 (Nov. 22, 2017). ¶¶ 15–16; U.N. Doc. S/2018/359 (Apr. 17, 2018). ¶ 18; U.N. Doc. A/HRC/38/44/Add.1 (June 20, 2018). ¶¶ 25–28; U.N. Doc. CEDAW/C/IRQ/7 (Aug. 15, 2018). ¶ 11; U.N. Doc. A/73/347 (Aug. 28, 2018). ¶ 9; U.N. Doc. S/2019/984 (Dec. 23, 2019). ¶¶ 6, 56); U.N. Doc. S/2019/984 (Dec. 23, 2019). ¶ 6; U.N. Doc. A/74/845–S/2020/525 (June 9, 2020). ¶ 71).

[782] UNAMI (June 5 – July 5, 2014). pp. 10–11; UNAMI (July 6, 2014 – Sept. 10, 2014). pp. 5–7, 14–15; UNAMI (Sept. 11, 2014 – Dec. 10, 2014). pp. 7–10; UNAMI (Dec. 11, 2014 – April 30, 2015). pp. 12–13, 21; UNAMI (May 1, 2015 – Oct. 31, 2015). pp. 8–12, 17, 32.

[783] S.C. Res. 2233 (July 29, 2015). Preamble, p. 3; S.C. Res. 2299 (July 25, 2016). Preamble, p. 4; S.C. Res. 2367 (July 14, 2017). Preamble, p. 4.

[784] Office of the United Nations High Commissioner for Human Rights, Internal Communication Clearance Form, UA, IRQ 5/2014 (Aug. 18, 2014). p. 1; Office of the United Nations High Commissioner for Human Rights, Spokesperson for the UN High Commissioner for Human Rights: Ravina Shamdasani (Nov. 29, 2016). (2).

[785] Iraq: Barwana Massacre – Botched Investigation, Families Waiting for Justice, AMNESTY INTERNATIONAL (June 10, 2015). L.

[786] U.N. Doc. A/HRC/38/44/Add.1 (June 20, 2018). ¶ 28.

[787] UNAMI (Dec. 11, 2014 – April 30, 2015). p. 21; UNAMI (May 1, 2015 – Oct. 31, 2015). pp. 11, 17.

[788] UNAMI (May 1, 2015 – Oct. 31, 2015). p. 9; UNAMI (Aug. 2016). p. 13.

[789] UNAMI (July 6, 2014 – Sept. 10, 2014). p. 14; UNAMI (Sept. 11, 2014 – Dec. 10, 2014). p. 11; UNAMI (Dec. 11, 2014 – April 30, 2015). p. 12.

[790] U.N. Doc. CERD/C/IRQ/22-25 (Nov. 22, 2017). ¶ 16; U.N. Doc. CEDAW/C/IRQ/7 (Aug. 15, 2018). ¶ 11.

which often included a large number of children.[791] [792] [793] For example, in February 2016, following a "judgement" for theft by ISIL/DAESH, the group publicly amputated with a sword the right hands of three boys in Mosul.[794] In another incident, in April 2016, in Tall Afar, Ninawa Governorate, ISIL/DAESH "killed a 15-year-old boy accused of being a disbeliever by tearing him apart between two cars driving in opposite directions."[795] [796] In many instances, the public was encouraged to participate in the killings, for example, by stoning the victims.[797] Following executions, ISIL/DAESH often displayed deceased bodies publicly, particularly by hanging them on the scaffolding of buildings, on electricity poles, or at the entrances of towns under the Group's control.[798] [799] Such public spectacles in front of dozens of people were usually intended to warn those considering diso-beying the group's authority and rules.[800] [801]

ISIL/DAESH also targeted for public executions persons related to the public life of Iraq and Iraqi's security forces, including 1) candidates to for-mer and current members of parliament, including female representatives; 2) former candidates and candidates for public offices; 3) current and for-mer public servants and officials of the Government of Iraq; 4) former and current local mayors (*Mukhtar*); 5) employees of local Iraqi City Councils and members of governorate councils; 6) employees and former employees of The Independent High Electoral Commission (IHEC); 7) female commu-nity and political leaders; 8) members and former members/officers of Iraqi security forces (ISF), and current and former members of the police,

---

[791]  U.N. Doc. S/2015/82 (Feb. 2, 2015). ¶ 47; U.N. Doc. A/HRC/30/66 (July 27, 2015). ¶ 19; U.N. Doc. S/2016/77 (Jan. 26, 2016). ¶ 49; U.N. Doc. S/2016/92 (Jan. 29, 2016). ¶ 9; U.N. Doc. A/73/347 (Aug. 28, 2018). ¶ 9..

[792]  UNAMI (Sept. 11, 2014 – Dec. 10, 2014). pp. 6, 11; UNAMI (Dec. 11, 2014 – April 30, 2015). pp. 11–12; UNAMI (May 1, 2015 – Oct. 31, 2015). pp. 8–9, 12, 17; UNAMI (Aug. 2016). p. 11.

[793]  Office of the United Nations High Commissioner for Human Rights, Internal Com-munication Clearance Form, UA, IRQ 5/2014 (Aug. 18, 2014). p. 1.

[794]  U.N. Doc. S/2019/984 (Dec. 23, 2019). ¶ 56.

[795]  *Ibidem.*

[796]  See also: UNAMI (Dec. 11, 2014 – April 30, 2015). p. 12.

[797]  U.N. Doc. A/HRC/38/44/Add.1 (June 20, 2018). ¶ 27.

[798]  UNAMI (Sept. 11, 2014 – Dec. 10, 2014). p. 8; UNAMI (May 1, 2015 – Oct. 31, 2015). p. 9.

[799]  U.N. Doc. A/73/347 (Aug. 28, 2018). ¶ 9.

[800]  UNAMI (Sept. 11, 2014 – Dec. 10, 2014). p. 10; UNAMI (Dec. 11, 2014 – April 30, 2015). p. 21; UNAMI (May 1, 2015 – Oct. 31, 2015). pp. 9, 11–12.

[801]  U.N. Doc. A/73/347 (Aug. 28, 2018). ¶ 9.

Iraqi Army officers, and other Iraqi security personnel; and 9) the Deputy Attorney General of Mosul Court of Appeal.[802] [803] [804]

ISIL/DAESH fighters also sentenced Iraq's public figures to be tortured and publicly executed. The group deliberately tortured and murdered: 1) journalists, media workers, and associated personnel, including female journalists; 2) lawyers, for carrying out their professional duties, including female lawyers; 3) human rights activists and community leaders, including an alarming number of women leaders; 4) doctors and health workers, particularly "for refusing to work in field hospitals or treat wounded ISIL/DAESH fighters;"[805] [806] [807] 5) a vast number of *imams*; 6) any kind of professionals "perceived to be associated with the [Iraqi] Government."[808]

As one of the most atrocious legacies of ISIL/DAESH's terror in Iraq, international investigations have already found more than two hundred mass graves in areas formerly controlled by ISIL/DAESH. The overwhelming majority of the deceased bodies and remains of victims found contain civilian men, women, and children. However, it also contains the corpses and remains of Iraqi Security Forces, police officers, and associated forces killed and buried by ISIL/DAESH.[809] [810] Shockingly, UNAMI estimated that

---

[802]   U.N. Doc. S/2014/774 (Oct. 31, 2014). ¶¶ 48, 51; U.N. Doc. S/2015/82 (Feb. 2, 2015). ¶ 47; U.N. Doc. A/HRC/28/18 (March 27, 2015). ¶¶ 29, 31; U.N. Doc. A/HRC/30/66 (July 27, 2015). ¶¶ 6, 19, 32; U.N. Doc. S/2016/77 (Jan. 26, 2016). ¶ 49; U.N. Doc. S/2018/359 (Apr. 17, 2018). ¶ 44; U.N. Doc. S/2018/975 (Oct. 31, 2018). ¶ 46.

[803]   UNAMI (June 5 – July 5, 2014). p. 10; UNAMI (July 6, 2014 – Sept. 10, 2014). pp. 6, 11; UNAMI (Sept. 11, 2014 – Dec. 10, 2014). pp. 6–7, 10; UNAMI (Dec. 11, 2014 – April 30, 2015). p. 12; UNAMI (May 1, 2015 – Oct. 31, 2015). pp. 8–12, 15.

[804]   Office of the United Nations High Commissioner for Human Rights, Internal Communication Clearance Form, UA, IRQ 5/2014 (Aug. 18, 2014). p. 1.

[805]   U.N. Doc. S/2014/774 (Oct. 31, 2014). ¶ 48; U.N. Doc. A/HRC/28/14 (Dec. 12, 2014). ¶ 19; U.N. Doc. A/HRC/28/18 (March 27, 2015). ¶ 49; U.N. Doc. A/HRC/30/66 (July 27, 2015). ¶ 19; U.N. Doc. S/2015/852 (Nov. 9, 2015). ¶ 48; U.N. Doc. A/HRC/38/44/Add.1 (June 20, 2018). ¶ 27; U.N. Doc. CEDAW/C/IRQ/7 (Aug. 15, 2018). ¶ 14.

[806]   S.C. Res. 2299 (July 25, 2016). Preamble, p. 1; S.C. Res. 2367 (July 14, 2017). Preamble, p. 1.

[807]   UNAMI (June 5 – July 5, 2014). p. 12; UNAMI (July 6, 2014 – Sept. 10, 2014). pp. 5–6, 8, 10; UNAMI (Sept. 11, 2014 – Dec. 10, 2014). pp. 7, 9–10; UNAMI (Dec. 11, 2014 – April 30, 2015). pp. 10–11, 13, 24; UNAMI (May 1, 201 – Oct. 31, 2015). pp. 8, 10–11, 32.

[808]   U.N. Doc. A/HRC/30/66 (July 27, 2015). ¶ 19.

[809]   U.N. Doc. A/HRC/RES/28/32 (April 8, 2015). ¶ 3; U.N. Doc. S/2015/82 (Feb. 2, 2015). ¶ 48; U.N. Doc. A/HRC/28/18 (March 27, 2015). ¶ 70; U.N. Doc. S/2016/396 (Apr. 27, 2016). ¶ 47; U.N. Doc. S/2017/75 (Jan. 26, 2017). ¶ 42; U.N. Doc. S/2017/881 (Oct. 19, 2017). ¶ 53; U.N. Doc. S/2018/42 (Jan. 17, 2018). ¶ 51; U.N. Doc. S/2018/975 (Oct. 31,

these mass graves contain from 6,000 to more than 12,000 ISIL/DAESH victims, most of whom have not yet been identified.[811] [812] To date, numerous mass graves have already been discovered by the ISF, the Iraqi Federal Police, the *Peshmerga* forces, international authorities, and by the Investigative Team (S.C. Res. 2379).[813] In Jalawla, Mosul, and Ramadi's sub-districts, authorities have found mass graves containing two hundred bodies.[814] In the Ninawa governorate, authorities found a mass grave containing at least four hundred corpses, which demonstrates that these ISIL/DAESH crime scenes were "sites of harrowing human loss, profound suffering, and shocking cruelty."[815] [816]

A 2016 Report from the Special Rapporteur on Extrajudicial, Summary or Arbitrary Executions showed that "many [of these] mass grave sites lack the necessary protection, leaving them exposed to damage by the elements and are subject to uncontrolled excavations."[817] In a report from the U.N. Secretary-General submitted to the Security Council, Iraqi Government officials informed UNAMI that "they had neither the resources nor the expertise to adequately protect or excavate these sites, with the possible loss or damage of forensic evidence and means of identification of the remains."[818] Forensics staff in Iraq lacked storage systems, DNA testing facilities, and basic tools, such as gloves and bleach.[819] The Special Rapporteur on Extrajudicial, Summary or Arbitrary Executions reported that, at the current pace, professionals of the Iraqi Medico-Legal Institute would take over 800 years to complete their task of identifying bodies found in ISIL/DAESH mass graves.[820]

---

2018). ¶ 47; U.N. Doc. S/2018/1031 (Nov. 16, 2018). ¶ 9; U.N. Doc. S/2019/984 (Dec. 23, 2019). ¶ 50.

[810]   UNAMI (July 6, 2014 – Sept. 10, 2014). p. 7; UNAMI (Sept. 11, 2014 – Dec. 10, 2014). p. 9; UNAMI (May 1, 2015 – Oct. 31, 2015). p. 30; UNAMI (Nov. 6, 2018). pp. 1–2.

[811]   U.N. Doc. S/2018/975 (Oct. 31, 2018). ¶ 47.

[812]   UNAMI (Nov. 6, 2018). pp. 1–2.

[813]   U.N. Doc. S/2016/77 (Jan. 26, 2016). ¶ 50.

[814]   UNAMI (Sept. 11, 2014 – Dec. 10, 2014). p. 9; U.N. Doc. S/2015/82 (Feb. 2, 2015). ¶ 49.

[815]   U.N. Doc. S/2018/1031 (Nov. 16, 2018). ¶ 9.

[816]   See also: U.N. Doc. S/2017/75 (Jan. 26, 2017). ¶ 42

[817]   U.N. Doc. A/HRC/38/44/Add.1 (June 20, 2018). ¶ 78.

[818]   U.N. Doc. S/2016/77 (Jan. 26, 2016). ¶ 50.

[819]   U.N. Doc. A/HRC/38/44/Add.1 (June 20, 2018). ¶ 78.

[820]   *Idem.* ¶ 79.

## 1.4. ISIL/DAESH money

At the time of ISIL/DAESH atrocities in Iraq, the group was frequently portrayed as the wealthiest terrorist organization in the world. In 2014, the terrorist group's annual revenue reached a fortune of 1.9 billion dollars.[821][822] Reports show that despite the damage to ISIL/DAESH bureaucratic structures, after its defeat in Iraq, in December 2017, the group's finance bureaus were intact.[823] It is estimated that the remaining ISIL/DAESH fighters possessed between $50 million and $300 million of financial reserves in 2019.[824] Reports show that it is very likely that ISIL/DAESH will redevelop financial self-sufficiency in the future to fund larger-scale attacks.[825]

ISIL/DAESH has possessed a wide degree of diversification in its sources of financing since 2014. It has been reported that a potential dwindling in the group's revenue streams is always fixed by quickly replacing the loss with other sources of income.[826] There are seven major categories of income that have usually been utilized by ISIL/DAESH as its primary source of revenue:

1) Oil and agricultural products: the ISIL/DAESH seizure of oil fields and infrastructure, pipelines, storage tanks, and refineries and the direct or indirect selling/smuggling/trade of oil and gas; the selling of agricultural lands and smuggled agricultural products.[827][828][829]

2) Extortion, confiscation, and robbery: the organized and systematic extortion of businesses, individuals, and of individuals seeking to flee from ISIL/DAESH's conflict zones; looting, confiscation, and selling of goods and

---

[821] U.N. Doc. S/2016/92 (Jan. 29, 2016). ¶ 16.

[822] Caliphate in Decline: An Estimate of Islamic State's Financial Fortunes, THE INTERNATIONAL CENTRE FOR THE STUDY OF RADICALISATION (ICSR) (Feb. 17, 2018). p. 3.

[823] U.N. Doc. S/2018/705 (July 27, 2018). ¶ 4.

[824] U.N. Doc. S/2019/103 (Feb. 1, 2019). ¶ 12; U.N. Doc. S/2019/612 (July 31, 2019). ¶ 11.

[825] See, for example: U.N. Doc. S/2019/103 (Feb. 1, 2019). ¶¶ 5, 9, 13; U.N. Doc. S/2020/53 (Jan. 20, 2020). ¶ 1.

[826] U.N. Doc. S/2015/739 (Sept. 25, 2015). ¶ 3; U.N. Doc. S/2016/92 (Jan. 29, 2016). ¶ 17.

[827] U.N. Doc. S/2014/774 (Oct. 31, 2014). ¶ 22; U.N. Doc. A/HRC/30/66 (July 27, 2015). ¶ 4; U.N. Doc. S/2015/739 (Sept. 25, 2015). ¶ 5; U.N. Doc. S/2016/92 (Jan. 29, 2016). ¶¶ 16–17, 20; U.N. Doc. S/2017/573(Aug. 7, 2017). ¶ 21; U.N. Doc. S/2018/705 (July 27, 2018). ¶ 15; U.N. Doc. CEDAW/C/IRQ/7 (Aug. 15, 2018). ¶ 10; U.N. Doc. S/2019/103 (Feb. 1, 2019). ¶ 14).

[828] S.C. Res. 2199 (Feb. 12, 2015). Preamble, p.1; S.C. Res. 2299 (July 25, 2016). Preamble, p. 5; S.C. Res. 2367 (July 14, 2017). Preamble, p. 5.

[829] ICSR. *Supra* note 822. p. 8.

property, such as money, home furniture, vehicles, phones, electronics, and other possessions; confiscation and sale of precious metals, such as gold, silver, copper, and diamonds.[830] [831] [832] [833]

3) Taxes and fees: taxing the population living in territories under ISIL/DAESH control, including the collection of religious taxes, mobility/delivery taxes, taxes on basic food and raw materials for the population, taxes for electricity and water, taxes on businesses, financial transactions and cash withdrawals from banks, taxes on utilities, salaries, pensions and benefits, and customs duties and passage fees at checkpoints.[834] [835] [836] [837] [838] [839]

---

[830] U.N. Doc. S/2014/774 (Oct. 31, 2014). ¶ 22; U.N. Doc. S/2015/739 (Sept. 25, 2015). ¶ 4; U.N. Doc. S/2016/92 (Jan. 29, 2016). ¶¶ 16, 18, 22; U.N. Doc. S/2015/739 (July 19, 2016). ¶¶ 14, 15; U.N. Doc. S/2017/881 (Oct. 19, 2017). ¶ 63; U.N. Doc. CEDAW/C/IRQ/7 (Aug. 15, 2018). ¶ 10; U.N. Doc. S/2019/103 (Feb. 1, 2019). ¶ 15; U.N. Doc. S/2019/570 (July 15, 2019). ¶ 72.

[831] S.C. Res. 2199 (Feb. 12, 2015). Preamble, p.2; S.C. Res. 2253 (Dec. 17, 2015). Preamble, p. 3.

[832] UNAMI (July 6, 2014 – Sept. 10, 2014). p. 16; UNAMI (Sept. 11, 2014 – Dec. 10, 2014). pp. 13–14; UNAMI (Aug. 2016). p. 13.

[833] ICSR. *Supra* note 822. pp. 7–8.

[834] Estimated 8 million people lived in territories under ISIL/DAESH control between 2014 and 2017. (U.N. Doc. S/2016/92 (Jan. 29, 2016). ¶ 18).

[835] ISIL/DAESH attempted to legitimize a taxing system "by calling the "tax" a "religious tax" or "zakat". The tax amounted "to at least 2.5 per cent of the capital earned from businesses, goods and agricultural products, including wheat, barley, cotton and livestock; from services of contractors and traders in Iraq's western and northern provinces and from trucks entering the territories under ISIL/DAESH control." (U.N. Doc. S/2016/92 (Jan. 29, 2016). ¶ 18).

[836] "According to UNAMI, the ISIL/DAESH tax on trucks generated around $900 million per year. In some cases, the group extorted up to 10 per cent, on the grounds that "it is a nation in time of war." (U.N. Doc. S/2016/92 (Jan. 29, 2016). ¶ 18).

[837] ISIL/DAESH also demanded "*jizyah*" tax on minorities in territory under its control. See Also: U.N. Doc. S/2015/739 (Sept. 25, 2015). ¶ 4).

[838] "Based on figures for total revenue from zakat (Islamic alms-giving) and sums extrapolated from taxation income in Islamic State's largest city of Mosul following its capture in the summer of 2014, the group received $300–400m from taxation in 2014. Despite losing territory throughout the year, its tax income increased to $400–800m in 2015, as the group consolidated and exploited its control over major population centers in Iraq." (ICSR. *Supra* note 822. p. 7).

[839] See also: U.N. Doc. A/HRC/30/66 (July 27, 2015). ¶ 11; U.N. Doc. S/2015/739 (Sept. 25, 2015). ¶ 4; U.N. Doc. S/2015/739 (July 19, 2016). ¶ 14. U.N. Doc. S/2016/92 (Jan. 29, 2016). ¶ 20; U.N. Doc. S/2017/573(Aug. 7, 2017). ¶ 21; U.N. Doc. S/2018/705 (July 27, 2018). ¶ 15); U.N. Doc. S/2019/984 (Dec. 23, 2019). ¶ 6.

4) Trafficking: drug trafficking; human trafficking, sale/trading of women and children for purposes of organ removal, enslavement (*'malak yamiin'*), for sexual slavery, for sexual exploitation and abuse; trafficking of arms; looting, smuggling, and illicit trafficking/selling of cultural heritage/property and antiquities from archaeological sites, museums, libraries, public archives, and religious sites from ISIL/DAESH-controlled territory in Iraq; illicit trade of wildlife and illicit trade of charcoal.[840][841][842][843][844]

5) Money operations: money laundering; donations and revenue from foreign terrorist fighters, ISIL/DAESH's family members and from other various individuals seeking the advance of the "Caliphate"; cash couriers, unregistered money service businesses (*hawaladars*), wire transfers, and credit card withdrawals; imposition of rents on the looted property; the systematic use of the internet, mobile payment platforms, and financial technologies, such as cryptocurrencies, to raise funds and collect donations, particularly through social media.[845][846][847]

6) Legitimate businesses: investing in "clean" individuals, legitimate businesses, and commercial fronts, both locally and beyond the Syrian Arab Republic and Iraq, "such as construction companies, money exchanges, agricultural entities, fisheries, and real estate, including hotels."[848]

---

[840]  U.N. Doc. S/2014/774 (Oct. 31, 2014). ¶ 22; U.N. Doc. A/HRC/28/18 (March 27, 2015). ¶¶ 35, 40; U.N. Doc. S/2016/92 (Jan. 29, 2016). ¶¶ 12, 16, 22; U.N. Doc. S/2015/739 (July 19, 2016). ¶ 16; U.N. Doc. A/71/303 (Aug. 5, 2016). ¶ 24; U.N. Doc. S/2016/949 (Nov. 10, 2016). ¶ 10; U.N. Doc. A/72/164 (July 18, 2017). ¶ 25; U.N. Doc. S/2017/939 (Nov. 10, 2017). ¶ 4; U.N. Doc. CEDAW/C/IRQ/7 (Aug. 15, 2018). ¶ 10; U.N. Doc. S/2018/770 (August 16, 2018). ¶ 11; U.N. Doc. S/2019/570 (July 15, 2019). ¶ 10; U.N. Doc. S/2019/984 (Dec. 23, 2019). ¶ 33.

[841]  S.C. Res. 2199 (Feb. 12, 2015). ¶ 16; S.C. Res. 2233 (July 29, 2015). Preamble, pp. 3–4; S.C. Res. 2249 (Nov. 20, 2015). Preamble, p. 1; S.C. Res. 2253 (Dec. 17, 2015). Preamble, p. 3; S.C. Res. 2299 (July 25, 2016). Preamble, pp. 4–5; S.C. Res. 2367 (July 14, 2017). Preamble, pp. 4–5; S.C. Res. 2379 (Sept. 21, 2017). Preamble, p.1.

[842]  UNAMI (Aug. 2016). p. 16; UNAMI (Nov. 6, 2018). pp. 3–4.

[843]  Supplement to the International Protocol on the Documentation and Investigation of Sexual Violence in Conflict, Iraq: Guidance for Practitioners in Iraq, INSTITUTE FOR INTERNATIONAL CRIMINAL INVESTIGATIONS (IICI) (March 2018). p. 5.

[844]  ICSR. *Supra* note 822. p. 7.

[845]  U.N. Doc. S/2016/92 (Jan. 29, 2016). ¶¶ 16, 20, 22, 24; U.N. Doc. S/2018/705 (July 27, 2018). ¶ 17; U.N. Doc. S/2019/103 (Feb. 1, 2019). ¶¶ 13, 16; U.N. Doc. S/2019/570 (July 15, 2019). ¶¶ 11, 73–74; U.N. Doc. S/2019/612 (July 31, 2019). ¶ 11; U.N. Doc. S/2019/984 (Dec. 23, 2019). ¶ 6; U.N. Doc. S/2020/53 (Jan. 20, 2020). ¶ 14).

[846]  S.C. Res. 2199 (Feb. 12, 2015). Preamble, p.2.

[847]  ICSR. *Supra* note 822. p. 7.

[848]  U.N. Doc. S/2017/573(Aug. 7, 2017). ¶ 22; U.N. Doc. S/2018/14/Rev.1 (Feb. 27, 2018). ¶¶ 12–13; U.N. Doc. S/2018/705 (July 27, 2018). ¶ 16; U.N. Doc. S/2019/103 (Feb. 1,

7) Kidnapping: the kidnapping of persons for ransom.[849] [850] [851]

## 1.5. Violations of International Humanitarian Law: ISIL/DAESH warfare machine

Throughout the ISIL/DAESH regime in Iraq, international organizations, governments, and several U.N. bodies reported that the terrorist group committed several International Humanitarian Law violations. ISIL/DAESH reportedly breached the principles of distinction, proportionality, and precaution numerous times. Thousands of innocent civilians perished due to direct and deliberate actions or due to secondary effects of the violence.

ISIL/DAESH reportedly closed gates of dams – or totally destroyed them –, deliberately cut off – attempted to cut off – clean water supplies and water connections. The group also took control of water barrages on the Euphrates River to redirect water flows and deliberately caused extensive flooding, which caused "the displacement of local residents and the destruction of agrarian land, livestock, and irrigation networks."[852] [853] As secondary effects, thousands of civilians lacked access to clean water, and several children died from dehydration.[854] [855] Also, ISIL/DAESH cut electricity supply /connections and destroyed electricity stations in the areas under the group's control, which meant, in most cases, that electrical water pumps would no longer work.[856] As a consequence, access to public water was limited to one day per week in some locations.[857]

---

2019). ¶ 13; U.N. Doc. S/2019/570 (July 15, 2019). ¶ 10; U.N. Doc. S/2020/53 (Jan. 20, 2020). ¶ 13.

[849] U.N. Doc. S/2014/774 (Oct. 31, 2014). ¶ 22; U.N. Doc. S/2018/705 (July 27, 2018). ¶ 15; U.N. Doc. S/2019/103 (Feb. 1, 2019). ¶ 14; U.N. Doc. S/2019/570 (July 15, 2019). ¶ 72.

[850] S.C. Res. 2199 (Feb. 12, 2015). Preamble, p.2, ¶ 18; S.C. Res. 2253 (Dec. 17, 2015). Preamble, p. 3.

[851] ICSR. *Supra* note 822. p. 7.

[852] UNAMI (July 6, 2014 – Sept. 10, 2014). pp. 8, 12; UNAMI (Dec. 11, 2014 – April 30, 2015). p. 17.

[853] U.N. Doc. S/2014/485 (July 11, 2014). ¶ 13; U.N. Doc. S/2015/530 (July 13, 2015). ¶ 18; U.N. Doc. A/HRC/30/66 (July 27, 2015). ¶ 8; U.N. Doc. A/72/865–S/2018/465 (May 16, 2018). ¶ 83.

[854] UNAMI (July 6, 2014 – Sept. 10, 2014). pp. 13, 16.

[855] U.N. Doc. CRC/C/IRQ/CO/2-4 (March 3, 2015). ¶ 23.b.

[856] UNAMI (July 6, 2014 – Sept. 10, 2014). pp. 8, 12, 16; UNAMI (Dec. 11, 2014 – April 30, 2015). p. 17.

[857] U.N. Doc. S/2016/396 (Apr. 27, 2016). ¶ 57.

ISIL/DAESH deliberately destroyed bridges, including railway bridges, mined routes out of the cities, and took over major intersections and important roads leading out of Iraq.[858] [859] In districts like Muqdadiyah, in Diyala, ISIL/DAESH had destroyed 90 percent of vital facilities after the Caliphate's self-proclamation.[860] Also, ISIL/DAESH blew up the headquarters of several local Police Departments. It also blew up several government buildings, including local Council buildings and buildings belonging to the Ministry of Justice, Finance, and Municipalities.[861]

Concerning access to food, ISIL/DAESH systematically demanded a share of the harvest from farmers.[862] Deliberately, the terrorist group burned crops and trapped civilians when they tried to collect humanitarian food packages dropped from airplanes.[863] [864] The group left the civilian population, including women and children, without food for periods of up to three days.[865] On one occasion, "one woman was breastfeeding her three-month-old baby and, as ISIL/DAESH had not brought food and water for three days, [she] resorted to drinking water from the toilets of the building where [she was] being held."[866] As secondary effects, during the ISIL/DAESH regime in Iraq, there have been severe shortages of food in the areas controlled by the group in Iraq.[867] From January to April 2016, the prices of essential food commodities skyrocketed by over 800 percent.[868] Several children, some as young as three years old, died from hunger.[869]

ISIL/DAESH attacks deliberately targeted hospitals, clinics, and health services, leaving them partially or entirely nonfunctional because of the damages. The group also used hospitals to secure military positions and looted medical supplies.[870] [871] ISIL/DAESH deliberately attacked medical

---

858   UNAMI (Dec. 11, 2014 – April 30, 2015). p. 17.
859   U.N. Doc. S/2015/82 (Feb. 2, 2015). ¶ 22; U.N. Doc. A/HRC/32/35/Add.1 (April 5, 2016). ¶ 40.
860   UNAMI (Dec. 11, 2014 – April 30, 2015). p. 17.
861   *Ibidem.*
862   U.N. Doc. A/HRC/30/66 (July 27, 2015). ¶ 12.
863   U.N. Doc. S/2019/612 (July 31, 2019). ¶ 7.
864   UNAMI (Aug. 2016). p. 10.
865   *Idem.* p. 11.
866   *Ibidem.*
867   UNAMI (July 6, 2014 – Sept. 10, 2014). p. 16; U.N. Doc. A/HRC/30/66 (July 27, 2015). ¶ 11.
868   U.N. Doc. S/2016/396 (Apr. 27, 2016). ¶ 57.
869   UNAMI (July 6, 2014 – Sept. 10, 2014). p. 13; U.N. Doc. CRC/C/IRQ/CO/2-4 (March 3, 2015). ¶ 23.b.
870   U.N. Doc. S/2015/852 (Nov. 9, 2015). ¶¶ 21, 48; U.N. Doc. A/HRC/32/35/Add.1 (April 5, 2016). ¶ 31; U.N. Doc. A/73/907–S/2019/509 (June 20, 2019). ¶ 76.

personnel, their homes, and their family members.[872] ISIL/DAESH systematically denied civilians critical medical assistance, frequently causing their death or severe health complications due to a lack of assistance.[873] In addition, ISIL/DAESH constantly abducted civilians, including women, to force them to give blood to injured ISIL/DAESH members.[874]

Starting in early 2015, ISIL/DAESH extensively and consistently imposed severe restrictions on civilians' freedom of movement living in the areas under the group's control. In many instances, ISIL/DAESH leaders issued orders to close checkpoints to prevent residents from leaving controlled areas. Civilians attempting to flee ISIL/DAESH-controlled areas, including children as young as seven years old, were severely punished with corporal punishments and death if caught.[875] [876] [877] [878] To punish those who attempted to flee, ISIL/DAESH planted improvised explosive devices (IEDs) and mines along roads used as escape routes for civilians and left booby-traps and IEDs in civilian houses so that the victims would be severely injured or killed upon return from their attempted escape.[879] [880]

---

[871]  U.N. Doc. A/69/926–S/2015/409 (June 5, 2015). ¶ 76; U.N. Doc. S/2015/852 (Nov. 9, 2015). ¶ 48; U.N. Doc. A/72/361–S/2017/821 (Aug. 24, 2017). ¶ 81; U.N. Doc. A/72/865–S/2018/465 (May 16, 2018). ¶ 83; U.N. Doc. A/73/907–S/2019/509 (June 20, 2019). ¶ 76; U.N. Doc. S/2019/984 (Dec. 23, 2019). ¶ 71.

[872]  U.N. Doc. S/2015/852 (Nov. 9, 2015). ¶ 48; U.N. Doc. A/73/907–S/2019/509 (June 20, 2019). ¶ 76.

[873]  UNAMI (July 6, 2014 – Sept. 10, 2014). p. 16; U.N. Doc. S/2016/396 (Apr. 27, 2016). ¶ 57; U.N. Doc. A/72/361–S/2017/821 (Aug. 24, 2017). ¶ 83.

[874]  UNAMI (Aug. 2016). p. 12.

[875]  U.N. Doc. S/2015/530 (July 13, 2015). ¶ 50; U.N. Doc. A/HRC/30/66 (July 27, 2015). ¶¶ 6, 12; U.N. Doc. A/HRC/32/35/Add.1 (April 5, 2016). ¶ 40; U.N. Doc. S/2016/396 (Apr. 27, 2016). ¶ 45; U.N. Doc. S/2016/592 (July 5, 2016). ¶ 37; U.N. Doc. S/2017/881 (Oct. 19, 2017). U.N. Doc. A/72/865–S/2018/465 (May 16, 2018). ¶ 83; ¶ 63; U.N. Doc. S/2019/984 (Dec. 23, 2019). ¶ 51.

[876]  UNAMI (Sept. 11, 2014 – Dec. 10, 2014). p. 14; UNAMI (Dec. 11, 2014 – April 30, 2015). p. 23; UNAMI (May 1, 2015 – Oct. 31, 2015). p. 9; UNAMI (Aug. 2016). p. 10.

[877]  Office of the United Nations High Commissioner for Human Rights, Spokesperson for the UN High Commissioner for Human Rights: Ravina Shamdasani (Nov. 29, 2016). (2).

[878]  Jacob Eriksson & Ahmed Khaleel eds., Iraq After ISIS: The Challenges of Post-War Recovery. (Palgrave Macmillan, 2019). p. 84.

[879]  U.N. Doc. A/HRC/30/66 (July 27, 2015). ¶ 24; U.N. Doc. A/HRC/32/35/Add.1 (April 5, 2016). ¶ 69; U.N. Doc. S/2017/881 (Oct. 19, 2017). ¶ 52; U.N. Doc. S/2019/984 (Dec. 23, 2019). ¶ 54.

[880]  UNAMI (Dec. 11, 2014 – April 30, 2015). p. 16;

Many civilians, including women, the elderly, and children, died while trying to leave Iraqi provinces on foot due to: heat waves, freezing temperatures during the winter, dehydration, starvation, or when caught in the coalition's crossfire against ISIL/DAESH.[881] [882] With the execution of such barbaric acts, ISIL/DAESH intended to create a state of fear among civilians to prevent them from leaving controlled areas in Iraq.[883] On rare occasions, ISIL/DAESH fighters permitted that specific individuals traveled outside the controlled areas upon the imposition of a bail system, "guaranteeing that they will return within a set time limit, otherwise face forfeiture of their properties."[884] [885]

Deliberate actions of ISIL/DAESH fighters and active hostilities between ISIL/DAESH and the Coalition, particularly between 2015 and 2017, "significantly restricted humanitarian access to conflict-affected areas," particularly in Anbar, Kirkuk, Salah al-Din, and Ninawa Governorates.[886] Constraints on the delivery of humanitarian assistance imposed by ISIL/DAESH imposed devastating effects on children.[887] Trapped civilians caught in the crossfire remained in critical need of humanitarian aid.[888] [889] [890] For instance, in July 2015,

> "more than 8.2 million people across Iraq, or nearly 25 percent of the country's population, [were] estimated to require humanitarian assistance, including over 3 million internally displaced persons living in over 3,000 locations. Nearly half of all displaced persons [were] children. [...] Since 8 April, over 290,000 people ha[d] been internally displaced from Ramadi district. An

---

[881]   U.N. Doc. CRC/C/IRQ/CO/2-4 (March 3, 2015). ¶ 23.b; U.N. Doc. S/2016/77 (Jan. 26, 2016). ¶ 66; U.N. Doc. A/HRC/32/35/Add.1 (April 5, 2016). ¶ 40; U.N. Doc. S/2016/592 (July 5, 2016). ¶ 37; U.N. Doc. S/2019/984 (Dec. 23, 2019). ¶¶ 51–52.

[882]   UNAMI (July 6, 2014 – Sept. 10, 2014). pp. 12–14.

[883]   U.N. Doc. A/HRC/32/35/Add.1 (April 5, 2016). ¶ 69.

[884]   UNAMI (Sept. 11, 2014 – Dec. 10, 2014). p. 14.

[885]   In early January, 2015, "UNAMI/OHCHR received reports that residents of Mosul wishing to travel outside the city [had] to identify a family member to stand as guarantor for their return." (UNAMI (Dec. 11, 2014 – April 30, 2015). p. 23).

[886]   U.N. Doc. S/2019/984 (Dec. 23, 2019). ¶ 75.

[887]   U.N. Doc. A/69/926–S/2015/409 (June 5, 2015). ¶ 74.

[888]   "The Iraqi Air Force delivered food and relief through a humanitarian airdrop operation over the [Iraqi] mountains on 4 and 5 August [of 2014]. However, civilians trapped on the mountain informed UNAMI that the supplies had not reached the intended targets and those that were insufficient to meet the needs of those trapped there." (UNAMI (July 6, 2014 – Sept. 10, 2014). pp. 5, 12–13).

[889]   UNAMI (June 5 – July 5, 2014). p. 9; UNAMI (Dec. 11, 2014 – April 30, 2015). p. 17.

[890]   U.N. Doc. S/2015/82 (Feb. 2, 2015). ¶ 22; U.N. Doc. S/2015/530 (July 13, 2015). ¶¶ 50, 57; U.N. Doc. S/2015/852 (Nov. 9, 2015). ¶ 56.

estimated 4.4 million people [were] in need of food assistance, 7.8 million people require[d] essential health-care services and 4.1 million [were] in critical need of access to safe water and sanitation."[891]

A year later, Iraq's humanitarian operation became "one of the largest and most complex in the world."[892] The number of persons in need of humanitarian assistance escalated to an estimated 10 million Iraqis, "including over 3.3 million internally displaced persons, [...] and the 3 million people believed to be living under ISIL/DAESH control."[893] [894] In Mosul alone, over one million people were directly affected by the Coalition's military operations.[895] In December 2019, two years after ISIL/DAESH was declared defeated by the Coalition, over two million people still lacked humanitarian assistance, including an alarming number of at least 1 million children and internally displaced persons.[896] The Iraqi Government's assistance to those civilians who escaped ISIL/DAESH-controlled areas was minimal throughout the ISIL/DAESH regime in Iraq.[897]

ISIL/DAESH perpetrated extreme violence and brutality, specifically targeting civilians and public areas or simply carrying out indiscriminate attacks to terrorize the population.[898] [899] ISIL/DAESH made no "distinction between men and women, children and old people."[900] Therefore, the group violated the core principles of international humanitarian laws, such as distinction, precaution, and proportionality.[901]

---

[891]   U.N. Doc. S/2015/530 (July 13, 2015). ¶ 57.
[892]   U.N. Doc. S/2016/592 (July 5, 2016). ¶ 48.
[893]   *Ibidem.*
[894]   See also: UNAMI (July 6, 2014 – Sept. 10, 2014). p. 13; U.N. Doc. S/2016/77 (Jan. 26, 2016). ¶ 66.
[895]   U.N. Doc. S/2016/592 (July 5, 2016). ¶ 48.
[896]   U.N. Doc. S/2019/984 (Dec. 23, 2019). ¶ 8.
[897]   U.N. Doc. A/HRC/32/35/Add.1 (April 5, 2016). ¶ 52.
[898]   U.N. Doc. S/2015/852 (Nov. 9, 2015). ¶ 21; U.N. Doc. S/2018/359 (Apr. 17, 2018). ¶ 18; U.N. Doc. CCPR/C/IRQ/CO/5/Add.1 (Aug. 18, 2017). ¶ 19; U.N. Doc. S/2019/984 (Dec. 23, 2019). ¶ 4.
[899]   S.C. Res. 2249 (Nov. 20, 2015). Preamble, p. 1.
[900]   U.N. Doc. CEDAW/C/IRQ/7 (Aug. 15, 2018). ¶ 15.
[901]   U.N. Doc. S/2015/852 (Nov. 9, 2015). ¶ 25

Systematically, ISIL/DAESH fighters' warfare methods included:

1) The use of airstrikes, shelling, and other weaponized air operations on an almost daily basis;[902]
2) The systematic detonation of improvised explosive devices (IEDs), placed particularly in places of extensive agglomeration of civilians and on traffic routes;[903] [904]
3) The installation of rocket launchers on the rooftops of civilian houses;[905] [906]
4) Attacks with mortar shells;[907]
5) The launching of complex attacks with explosive-laden vehicles, including the use of cars and boats rigged with explosives;[908] [909]
6) The use of high-yield imported explosive devices, land mines, and booby-traps planted in the houses of internally displaced persons to prevent their return;[910] [911]
7) The use of weaponized commercial drones;[912] [913]

---

[902] UNAMI (July 6, 2014 – Sept. 10, 2014). pp. 9, 11–12, 16; UNAMI (Dec. 11, 2014 – April 30, 2015). p. 16; U.N. Doc. S/2019/984 (Dec. 23, 2019). ¶ 50.

[903] UNAMI (June 5 – July 5, 2014). p. 9; UNAMI (Dec. 11, 2014 – April 30, 2015). p. 16.

[904] U.N. Doc. S/2015/82 (Feb. 2, 2015). ¶ 24; U.N. Doc. S/PV.7556 (Nov. 11, 2015). p. 3; U.N. Doc. S/2017/573(Aug. 7, 2017). ¶ 18; U.N. Doc. A/72/361–S/2017/821 (Aug. 24, 2017). ¶ 78; U.N. Doc. S/2017/881 (Oct. 19, 2017). ¶¶ 26, 52; U.N. Doc. S/2018/677 (July 9, 2018). ¶ 39; U.N. Doc. S/2019/365 (May 2, 2019). ¶ 22; U.N. Doc. A/73/907–S/2019/509 (June 20, 2019). ¶ 74; U.N. Doc. S/2019/984 (Dec. 23, 2019). ¶¶ 7, 54.

[905] UNAMI (May 1, 2015 – Oct. 31, 2015). p. 16; Office of the United Nations High Commissioner for Human Rights, Spokesperson for the UN High Commissioner for Human Rights: Ravina Shamdasani (Nov. 29, 2016). (2).

[906] U.N. Doc. S/2016/396 (Apr. 27, 2016). ¶ 46; U.N. Doc. S/2017/75 (Jan. 26, 2017). ¶ 39; U.N. Doc. S/2019/984 (Dec. 23, 2019). ¶ 70.

[907] UNAMI (July 6, 2014 – Sept. 10, 2014). p. 9; U.N. Doc. S/2016/396 (Apr. 27, 2016). ¶ 46; U.N. Doc. S/2019/984 (Dec. 23, 2019). ¶ 50.

[908] UNAMI (July 6, 2014 – Sept. 10, 2014). p. 9; UNAMI (Sept. 11, 2014 – Dec. 10, 2014). p. 8; UNAMI (Dec. 11, 2014 – April 30, 2015). p. 16.

[909] U.N. Doc. S/2016/592 (July 5, 2016). ¶ 18; U.N. Doc. S/2017/881 (Oct. 19, 2017). ¶ 50; U.N. Doc. S/2019/984 (Dec. 23, 2019). ¶ 50.

[910] UNAMI (Dec. 11, 2014 – April 30, 2015). pp. 16–17.

[911] U.N. Doc. S/2016/592 (July 5, 2016). ¶ 18; U.N. Doc. S/2019/984 (Dec. 23, 2019). ¶ 50.

[912] U.N. Doc. S/2019/103 (Feb. 1, 2019). ¶ 23; U.N. Doc. S/2019/984 (Dec. 23, 2019). ¶ 50.

[913] "In addition to using commercially available drones, ISIL/DAESH has developed the capacity to modify them and to build its own models, using recycled parts from commercially available drones." (U.N. Doc. S/2017/573(Aug. 7, 2017). ¶ 18). See also: U.N. Doc. S/2018/770 (August 16, 2018). ¶ 12.

8) The use of weaponized chemical agents on the battlefield, such as sulfur mustard, chlorine, and other toxic industrial chemicals (TICs);[914][915]

9) The use of snipers to shoot civilians;[916]

10) The use of firing squads to execute civilians;[917]

11) Suicide bomb attacks, using children as young as 9 years old for vesting explosive devices;[918][919][920][921]

12) The constant use of bulldozers to destroy houses, and religious sites, to force entry to towns, and to kill people by laying them on streets and passing the bulldozer over them;[922]

13) The continued and systematic seizing of military hardware and equipment from the Iraqi security forces;[923]

14) ISIL/DAESH used civilian infrastructure and civilians as human shields, including an alarming number of women and children;[924][925]

---

[914] UNAMI (Sept. 11, 2014 – Dec. 10, 2014). p. 11; UNAMI (Dec. 11, 2014 – April 30, 2015). p. 19; UNAMI (May 1, 2015 – Oct. 31, 2015). p. 17.

[914] U.N. Doc. A/HRC/28/18 (March 27, 2015). ¶ 47; U.N. Doc. S/PV.7556 (Nov. 11, 2015). p. 3; U.N. Doc. S/2016/92 (Jan. 29, 2016). ¶ 42; U.N. Doc. S/2016/396 (Apr. 27, 2016). ¶ 46; U.N. Doc. S/2016/592 (July 5, 2016). ¶ 38; U.N. Doc. S/2015/739 (July 19, 2016). ¶ 10; U.N. Doc. S/2016/897 (Oct. 25, 2016). ¶ 45; U.N. Doc. A/72/53/Add.1 (Sept. 29, 2017). ¶ 25; U.N. Doc. A/73/53/Add.1 (Sept. 28, 2018). ¶ 34; U.N. Doc. S/2019/984 (Dec. 23, 2019). ¶ 50.

[915] The White House, Report of the President of the USA Donald J. Trump, National Strategy for Countering Weapons of Mass Destruction (Dec. 2018). p. 1.

[916] UNAMI (Dec. 11, 2014 – April 30, 2015). p. 16; U.N. Doc. CEDAW/C/IRQ/7 (Aug. 15, 2018). ¶ 15; U.N. Doc. S/2019/984 (Dec. 23, 2019). ¶ 50.

[917] UNAMI (May 1, 2015 – Oct. 31, 2015). p. 8.

[918] U.N. Doc. S/PV.7556 (Nov. 11, 2015). p. 3; U.N. Doc. S/2016/77 (Jan. 26, 2016). ¶ 20; U.N. Doc. S/2016/92 (Jan. 29, 2016). ¶ 42; U.N. Doc. S/2016/592 (July 5, 2016). ¶¶ 17–18; U.N. Doc. S/2018/677 (July 9, 2018). ¶ 38..

[919] S.C. Res. 2299 (July 25, 2016). Preamble, p. 4; S.C. Res. 2367 (July 14, 2017). Preamble, p. 4; S.C. Res. 2379 (Sept. 21, 2017). Preamble, p.1.

[920] UNAMI (July 6, 2014 – Sept. 10, 2014). p. 8; UNAMI (Sept. 11, 2014 – Dec. 10, 2014). p. 12; UNAMI (Dec. 11, 2014 – April 30, 2015). pp. 11, 16; UNAMI (May 1, 2015 – Oct. 31, 2015). pp. 14–15.

[921] U.S. Dep't of State, Bureau of Counterterrorism, Country Reports on Terrorism (2019). p. 118).

[922] UNAMI (July 6, 2014 – Sept. 10, 2014). p. 9; UNAMI (May 1, 2015 – Oct. 31, 2015). p. 16; UNAMI (Aug. 2016). p. 13.

[923] U.N. Doc. S/2015/82 (Feb. 2, 2015). ¶ 24.

[924] UNAMI (June 5 – July 5, 2014). p. 9; UNAMI (July 6, 2014 – Sept. 10, 2014). pp. 5, 9; UNAMI (Sept. 11, 2014 – Dec. 10, 2014). pp. 13–14; UNAMI (Dec. 11, 2014 – April 30, 2015). p. 16; UNAMI (May 1, 2015 – Oct. 31, 2015). p. 14.

15) The systematic destruction of civilian homes and civilian infrastructure by looting, pillaging, burning, and demolishing them as a
punishment for families allegedly supporting the coalition against
ISIL/DAESH fighters;[926] [927] [928] [929]

16) The implementation of systematic policies of violence, fear, persecution, and elimination of fundamental rights;[930] [931] and

17) The targeting of schools for destruction, particularly with the use
of explosive devices.[932]

Recent reports showed that ISIL/DAESH still maintains the weaponry capacity of the so-called Caliphate times.[933] Reports also showed alarming
levels of civilian casualties, particularly children, trapped in the crossfire
between ISIL/DAESH and the coalition forces battling the group.[934] [935]

---

[925]  U.N. Doc. S/2017/75 (Jan. 26, 2017). ¶¶ 35, 51; U.N. Doc. CEDAW/C/IRQ/7 (Aug. 15,
2018). ¶¶ 9, 15; U.N. Doc. S/2019/984 (Dec. 23, 2019). ¶¶ 33, 51.

[926]  U.N. Doc. S/2014/774 (Oct. 31, 2014). ¶ 46; U.N. Doc. S/2015/82 (Feb. 2, 2015). ¶¶
46, 49; U.N. Doc. A/HRC/28/18 (March 27, 2015). ¶¶ 33, 76; U.N. Doc. S/2015/530
(July 13, 2015). ¶ 44; U.N. Doc. A/HRC/30/66 (July 27, 2015). ¶ 24; U.N. Doc.
A/HRC/32/35/Add.1 (April 5, 2016). ¶ 55; U.N. Doc. S/2016/592 (July 5, 2016). ¶ 17.

[927]  S.C. Res. 2253 (Dec. 17, 2015). Preamble, pp. 1, 3.

[928]  UNAMI (June 5 – July 5, 2014). p. 13; UNAMI (July 6, 2014 – Sept. 10, 2014). p. 8;
UNAMI (Sept. 11, 2014 – Dec. 10, 2014). p. 9; UNAMI (May 1, 2015 – Oct. 31, 2015).
pp. 15–16.

[929]  AMNESTY INTERNATIONAL. *Supra* note 495. *passim.*

[930]  UNAMI (June 5 – July 5, 2014). p. 9; UNAMI (July 6, 2014 – Sept. 10, 2014). p. 5; UN-
AMI (Sept. 11, 2014 – Dec. 10, 2014). p. 6; UNAMI (May 1, 2015 – Oct. 31, 2015). p.
32.

[931]  U.N. Doc. A/69/53/Add.1 (Sept. 1, 2014). Preamble, p.7; U.N. Doc. A/HRC/RES/S-
22/1 (Sept. 3, 2014). Preamble, p.1; U.N. Doc. S/2015/530 (July 13, 2015). ¶ 44; U.N.
Doc. S/2016/592 (July 5, 2016). ¶ 17.

[932]  U.N. Doc. S/2015/852 (Nov. 9, 2015). ¶ 21; U.N. Doc. A/72/865–S/2018/465 (May 16,
2018). ¶ 80.

[933]  U.N. Doc. S/2019/103 (Feb. 1, 2019). ¶ 24.

[934]  UNAMI (July 6, 2014 – Sept. 10, 2014). p. 9.

[935]  U.N. Doc. S/2015/852 (Nov. 9, 2015). ¶¶ 20, 23, 25; U.N. Doc. S/2016/92 (Jan. 29,
2016). ¶ 10; U.N. Doc. S/2016/592 (July 5, 2016). ¶ 18; U.N. Doc. A/72/361–
S/2017/821 (Aug. 24, 2017). ¶ 6; U.N. Doc. S/2019/984 (Dec. 23, 2019). ¶¶ 8, 47; U.N.
Doc. A/74/845–S/2020/525 (June 9, 2020). ¶ 71.

## 1.5.1. Attacks against schools and education personnel.

ISIL/DAESH deliberately targeted schools for destruction.[936] Besides, ISIL/DAESH used schools for military purposes, for instance, as detention centers, military training centers, depots, interrogation sites, recruiting points for minors to join ISIL/DAESH, and as bases to launch attacks.[937] [938] International reports revealed that ISIL/DAESH was involved in numerous incidents of deliberate attacks or threats of attacks on professors, teachers, and students, such as seizing belongings, threatening, abducting, torturing, executing, injuring, and killing educational personnel and pupils.[939] [940]

ISIL/DAESH has also reportedly used schools in areas under its control to 1) implement its own educational curriculum following its *takfiri* doctrines; 2) to spread its militarized radical ideological views; and 3) to "transform the pedagogical system into a system of mass indoctrination."[941] [942] [943] ISIL/DAESH prohibited most universities from teaching humanities disciplines, which the group considered "blasphemous."[944] Educators and professors that refused to submit to ISIL/DAESH educational rules, doctrines, and values were summarily tortured to death in public.[945]

---

[936]  U.N. Doc. S/2015/852 (Nov. 9, 2015). ¶ 21; U.N. Doc. A/72/865–S/2018/465 (May 16, 2018). ¶ 80.

[937]  UNAMI (Sept. 11, 2014 – Dec. 10, 2014). p. 13; UNAMI (May 1, 2015 – Oct. 31, 2015). p. 18.

[938]  U.N. Doc. A/69/926–S/2015/409 (June 5, 2015). ¶¶ 75, 77; U.N. Doc. S/2015/530 (July 13, 2015). ¶ 49; U.N. Doc. A/HRC/30/66 (July 27, 2015). ¶ 37; U.N. Doc. S/2015/852 (Nov. 9, 2015). ¶ 45; U.N. Doc. A/70/836–S/2016/360 (Apr. 20, 2016). ¶ 63; U.N. Doc. A/72/361–S/2017/821 (Aug. 24, 2017). ¶ 80; U.N. Doc. A/72/865–S/2018/465 (May 16, 2018). ¶ 81; U.N. Doc. A/73/907–S/2019/509 (June 20, 2019). ¶ 76; U.N. Doc. S/2019/984 (Dec. 23, 2019). ¶¶ 8, 67–68.

[939]  UNAMI (Sept. 11, 2014 – Dec. 10, 2014). p. 14; UNAMI (Dec. 11, 2014 – April 30, 2015). p. 14; UNAMI (July 6, 2014 – Sept. 10, 2014). pp. 5–6.

[940]  U.N. Doc. S/2015/852 (Nov. 9, 2015). ¶ 46; U.N. Doc. S/2016/77 (Jan. 26, 2016). ¶ 49; U.N. Doc. A/72/361–S/2017/821 (Aug. 24, 2017). ¶ 80; U.N. Doc. CEDAW/C/IRQ/7 (Aug. 15, 2018). ¶ 14.

[941]  UNAMI (July 6, 2014 – Sept. 10, 2014). p. 5; UNAMI (Sept. 11, 2014 – Dec. 10, 2014). pp. 6, 14; UNAMI (Dec. 11, 2014 – April 30, 2015). p. 24.

[942]  U.N. Doc. A/HRC/30/66 (July 27, 2015). ¶ 11; U.N. Doc. S/2015/852 (Nov. 9, 2015). ¶ 45; U.N. Doc. S/2016/77 (Jan. 26, 2016). ¶ 49; U.N. Doc. S/2019/984 (Dec. 23, 2019). ¶¶ 6, 65–66, 68.

[943]  ICSR. *Supra* note 520.

[944]  William Harris. *Supra* note 472. p. 68.

[945]  UNAMI (Dec. 11, 2014 – April 30, 2015). p. 24; U.N. Doc. A/70/836–S/2016/360 (Apr. 20, 2016). ¶ 63; U.N. Doc. S/2019/984 (Dec. 23, 2019). ¶ 66.

## 1.5.2. Displacement

As ISIL/DAESH gained full control over entire regions in Iraq, the group triggered a mass exodus of millions of people, creating "a scenario of mass and unpredictable internal displacement."[946] [947] [948] For instance, only the taking over of Mosul by ISIL/DAESH made more than 500,000 people flee their homes.[949] Between 2014 and 2017, over six million Iraqi civilians became internally displaced due to ISIL/DAESH's direct and indirect actions.[950] ISIL/DAESH directly and expressly ordered that Christians and the Yazidis leave the villages they had lived in for centuries.[951] The humanitarian crisis created by the fight between ISIL/DAESH, the Coalition, and the Iraqi Security Forces indirectly affected millions in the region. The Special Rapporteur on the human rights of internally displaced persons on his mission to Iraq estimated that 8 million Iraqis required "some form of humanitarian assistance" in Iraq's three years of violent internal conflict.[952] Hundreds of thousands of displaced women, children, people with disabilities, and the elderly were "left behind," facing "extreme hardship" as a result of the displacement.[953] [954]

Since the Iraqi Government and the Coalition declared ISIL/DAESH's defeat in December 2017, more than 4 million internally displaced persons "have returned to over 1,400 areas of origin across 35 districts and seven governorates of Iraq."[955] [956] A report from the U.N. Secretary-General from May 2019 submitted to the Security Council pointed out that as of March 2019, "approximately 1.75 million people remain[ed] internally displaced in Iraq in approximately 3,200 locations across 104 districts."[957] The report

---

[946]  UNAMI (Aug. 2016). p. 6.
[947]  See also: U.N. Doc. A/HRC/29/NGO/95 (June 10, 2015). p. 2; U.N. Doc. A/HRC/30/66 (July 27, 2015). ¶ 39; U.N. Doc. A/HRC/32/35/Add.1 (April 5, 2016). ¶¶ 4, 6, 77.
[948]  See also: S.C. Res. 2367 (July 14, 2017). Preamble, p. 1.
[949]  U.N. Doc. A/HRC/32/35/Add.1 (April 5, 2016). ¶ 6; U.N. Doc. A/HRC/44/41/Add.1 (May 13, 2020). ¶ 7.
[950]  U.N. Doc. A/HRC/44/41/Add.1 (May 13, 2020). ¶ 6.
[951]  UNAMI (July 6, 2014 – Sept. 10, 2014). p. 9; U.N. Doc. A/HRC/28/18 (March 27, 2015). ¶¶ 35, 76; U.N. Doc. CERD/C/IRQ/22-25 (Nov. 22, 2017). ¶ 15; U.N. Doc. CEDAW/C/IRQ/7 (Aug. 15, 2018). ¶ 10.
[952]  U.N. Doc. A/HRC/32/35/Add.1 (April 5, 2016). ¶ 4.
[953]  U.N. Doc. A/HRC/38/44/Add.1 (June 20, 2018). ¶ 73.
[954]  See also: UNAMI (July 6, 2014 – Sept. 10, 2014). p. 12; U.N. Doc. A/HRC/44/41/Add.1 (May 13, 2020). ¶ 11.
[955]  U.N. Doc. S/2019/101 (Feb. 1, 2019). ¶¶ 50, 59.
[956]  See also: U.N. Doc. A/HRC/44/41/Add.1 (May 13, 2020). ¶¶ 7, 19.
[957]  U.N. Doc. S/2019/365 (May 2, 2019). ¶ 59.

also demonstrated that more than half of this amount of people faced displacement for longer than three years.[958] Another report from the Special Rapporteur on the human rights of internally displaced persons on her mission to Iraq, from May 2020, showed that, by then, over four million people still remained in need of humanitarian assistance in the region.[959] Ms. Cecilia Jimenez-Damary indicated that "two-thirds of the [Iraqi] displaced population, internally displaced persons in and out of camp settings lack[ed] or [had] limited access to food, shelter, potable water, sanitation, health care, education, and livelihood opportunities."[960]

Children with alleged links to ISIL/DAESH faced even more significant hurdles and serious human rights violations in IDP camps in Iraq.[961] Many of these infants lacked official documentation or birth certificates or were generally blocked from accessing general civil documents.[962] [963] [964] As a consequence, they could not access fundamental rights, such as being enrolled in schools. Many of them faced the risk of statelessness.[965] The IDP camp administration severely restricts these children's freedom of movement "due to their alleged affiliation with ISIL/DAESH or because their parents were [or still are] ISIL/DAESH fighters or commanders."[966] [967] [968] These children live in crowded camps under miserable conditions, "where

---

[958]  *Ibidem.*

[959]  U.N. Doc. A/HRC/44/41/Add.1 (May 13, 2020). ¶ 19.

[960]  *Idem.* ¶¶ 19, 43–44.

[961]  The Condemned: Woman and Children Isolated, Trapped and Exploited in Iraq, AMNESTY INTERNATIONAL (Apr. 17, 2018). p. 20.

[962]  "Without these documents, many women are unable to work, move freely or inherit property or pensions, and their children are often unable to attend school and are at risk of becoming stateless." (*Idem.* pp. 22–23).

[963]  "Internally displaced persons face numerous barriers when they seek to obtain or renew civil documentation. Many have lost their documents or had them destroyed or confiscated in the course of displacement. Those having lived in areas controlled by ISIL/DAESH might hold documents that are not recognized by the Government of Iraq. Iraqi law requires that civil documents be obtained in one's place of origin, to which internally displaced persons are often unable to travel." (U.N. Doc. A/HRC/44/41/Add.1 (May 13, 2020). ¶ 25).

[964]  See also: U. N. Office of Counter-Terrorism (UNOCT), *Children affected by the foreign-fighter phenomenon: Ensuring a child rights-based approach,* (Oct. 7, 2019). p. 5.

[965]  *Ibidem.*

[966]  AMNESTY INTERNATIONAL. *Supra* note 961. p. 34.

[967]  "Some children are held in de facto detention in IDP camps; some are prevented from leaving by camp authorities; and others are unable to cross through checkpoints outside of the camps, either because they do not have their identity cards or fear they will be arrested." (*Idem.* p. 24).

[968]  See also: U.N. Doc. S/2019/984 (Dec. 23, 2019). ¶ 80.

they suffer from limited access to basic humanitarian services, such as food, water, shelter, medical care, and other essential services, along with a lack of respect for due process, the right to a fair trial and other fundamental rights."[969] [970] [971] [972]

In virtue of these children's perceived links with ISIL/DAESH, they are verbally harassed, sexually abused, subjected to rape and sexual exploitation, or otherwise intimidated and abused by the Iraqi military and by police forces or even by the administration of the IDP camp itself.[973] [974] Under anti-terrorism laws, several of these internally displaced children were subjected to arbitrary arrest by the authorities of the Autonomous Administration in Northern and Iraqi authorities. In detention centers, almost always held in unknown locations, these authorities perpetrated ill-treatment and torture against displaced boys and girls for their alleged involvement with armed groups.[975] [976]

Children were frequently detained along with adults and submitted to long detention periods.[977] Under the 2005 Iraqi anti-terrorism, the Iraqi judicial system prescribed the death penalty to these minors, "regardless of age at the time of the alleged commission of the crime or time of conviction,"[978] conduct that frontally violates international juvenile justice standards.[979] Several internally displaced children in Iraq face the additional risk of suffering radicalization and indoctrination from terrorist

---

[969] U.N. Doc. S/2019/984 (Dec. 23, 2019). ¶ 42.

[970] "In Iraq, for example, up to 13,000 children younger than 12 years old reportedly lack birth certificates or other documentation to establish their nationalities. Some may be of Iraqi parentage, while others may have one or two foreign parents." (U. N. Office of Counter-Terrorism (UNOCT), *Children affected by the foreign-fighter phenomenon: Ensuring a child rights-based approach*, (Oct. 7, 2019). p. 5).

[971] See also: U.N. Doc. S/2019/103 (Feb. 1, 2019). ¶ 21.

[972] See also: Eur. Parl., Committee on Social Affairs, Health and Sustainable Development, International obligations concerning the repatriation of children from war and conflict zones, Report, Doc. No. 15055 (Jan. 29, 2020). ¶¶ 1, 9.

[973] AMNESTY INTERNATIONAL. *Supra* note 961. pp. 26–29.

[974] U.N. Doc. S/2019/984 (Dec. 23, 2019). ¶ 42.

[975] AMNESTY INTERNATIONAL. *Supra* note 961. *passim*.

[976] U.N. Doc. S/2015/852 (Nov. 9, 2015). ¶ 39; U.N. Doc. A/70/836–S/2016/360 (Apr. 20, 2016). ¶ 60; U.N. Doc. A/72/361–S/2017/821 (Aug. 24, 2017). ¶ 77; U.N. Doc. A/73/907–S/2019/509 (June 20, 2019). ¶ 72; U.N. Doc. S/2019/984 (Dec. 23, 2019). ¶¶ 43–44.

[977] U.N. Doc. A/69/926–S/2015/409 (June 5, 2015). ¶ 73; U.N. Doc. S/2015/852 (Nov. 9, 2015). ¶ 39.

[978] U.N. Doc. S/2015/852 (Nov. 9, 2015). ¶ 40.

[979] U.N. Doc. A/73/907–S/2019/509 (June 20, 2019). ¶ 82.

groups, including from the remaining pockets of ISIL/DAESH.[980] For instance, the situation in *Al Hol*, an IDP camp in Iraq where 90% of the camp residents are women and children, is considered a "timebomb."[981]

In all *strata* of Iraqi society, these displaced children face "social marginalization and are at a high risk of exploitation and abuse."[982] Internationally, a report from the U.N. Secretary-General submitted to the Security Council demonstrated that several countries of origin have refused to repatriate these children.[983] Several of these children end up being victims of trafficking and sexual slavery at the hands of terrorist groups and militias.[984] In a report from May 2020, the Special Rapporteur on the human rights of internally displaced persons on her mission to Iraq stated that the situation of internally displaced children in Iraq "– a generation traumatized by violence, deprived of education and opportunities – is among the most tragic legacies of the conflict against ISIL/DAESH."[985]

## 1.5.3. Crimes of sexual order

In areas under ISIL/DAESH control, the group carried out deliberate and systematic acts of rape and other harrowing acts of sexual abuse/violence against women, girls, and boys.[986] [987] [988] [989] Children as young as 6 years of

---

[980]   U.N. Doc. S/2019/103 (Feb. 1, 2019). ¶ 20.

[981]   Eur. Parl., Committee on Social Affairs, Health and Sustainable Development, International obligations concerning the repatriation of children from war and conflict zones, Report, Doc. No. 15055 (Jan. 29, 2020). ¶ 14.

[982]   U.N. Doc. A/HRC/44/41/Add.1 (May 13, 2020). ¶ 43.

[983]   U.N. Doc. A/73/907–S/2019/509 (June 20, 2019). ¶ 83; U.N. Doc. S/2019/984 (Dec. 23, 2019). ¶ 43.

[984]   U.N. Doc. S/2018/770 (August 16, 2018). ¶ 10.

[985]   U.N. Doc. A/HRC/44/41/Add.1 (May 13, 2020). ¶ 42.

[986]   "The term conflict-related sexual violence refers to rape, sexual slavery, forced prostitution, forced pregnancy, forced abortion, enforced sterilization, forced marriage and any other form of sexual violence of comparable gravity perpetrated against women, men, girls or boys that is directly or indirectly linked (temporally, geographically or causally) to a conflict." (U.N. Doc. S/2016/361/Rev.1 (June 22, 2016). ¶ 2).

[987]   UNAMI (Dec. 11, 2014 – April 30, 2015). p. 22; UNAMI (Nov. 6, 2018). p. 4.

[988]   U.N. Doc. S/2014/774 (Oct. 31, 2014). ¶¶ 46, 76; U.N. Doc. S/2015/82 (Feb. 2, 2015). ¶ 46; U.N. Doc. A/HRC/28/18 (March 27, 2015). ¶¶ 35, 39, 76; U.N. Doc. S/2015/530 (July 13, 2015). ¶ 44; U.N. Doc. S/2015/852 (Nov. 9, 2015). ¶¶ 3, 42; U.N. Doc. A/HRC/32/35/Add.1 (April 5, 2016). ¶¶ 50, 55; U.N. Doc. S/2016/361 (Apr. 20, 2016). ¶ 40; U.N. Doc. S/2016/396 (Apr. 27, 2016). ¶ 78; U.N. Doc. S/AC.51/2016/2 (Aug. 18, 2016). ¶¶ 3, 8.a; U.N. Doc. CCPR/C/IRQ/CO/5/Add.1 (Aug. 18, 2017). ¶ 19; U.N. Doc. CEDAW/C/IRQ/7 (Aug. 15, 2018). ¶ 9; U.N. Doc. A/74/845–S/2020/525 (June 9, 2020). ¶ 72.

age were taken and raped by ISIL/DAESH fighters and commanders, most of the time daily.[990] [991] ISIL/DAESH leaders also used to gift women and girls to its fighters as sex slaves, as a reward for winning battles, or simply for winning Quran memorization competitions.[992] [993] [994] Frequently, ISIL/DAESH fighters drugged women and girls to facilitate rape and render the victims into a more "docile" state.[995] [996] Severely traumatized women and children often attempted suicide after the incidents of rape and sexual abuse by members of ISIL/DAESH.[997]

Using communication platforms and encrypted messaging technology, ISIL/DAESH sold and traded abducted women and girls from approximately 20 different countries.[998] ISIL/DAESH forced victims to smile while fighters took photographs to be used by the group in online bidding processes.[999] Some girls were as young as seven-year-old.[1000] Tragically, ISIL/DAESH reportedly used medical professionals "to procure drugs and administer harmful treatments not justified by medical concerns, including hormone treatments, to accelerate the physical maturation of young girls in order to expedite their sale."[1001]

---

[989] S.C. Res. 2299 (July 25, 2016). Preamble, p p. 1, 4; S.C. Res. 2233 (July 29, 2015). Preamble, p. 3; S.C. Res. 2367 (July 14, 2017). Preamble, pp. 1, 4; S.C. Res. 2368 (July 20, 2017). Preamble, p. 6; S.C. Res. 2379 (Sept. 21, 2017). Preamble, p.1; S.C. Res. 2388 (Nov. 21, 2017). Preamble, pp. 2–3, ¶ 18.

[989] AMNESTY INTERNATIONAL. *Supra* note 495. p. 15.

[990] UNAMI (Sept. 11, 2014 – Dec. 10, 2014). p. 13; UNAMI (Dec. 11, 2014 – April 30, 2015). p. 22.

[991] U.N. Doc. A/HRC/28/18 (March 27, 2015). ¶ 40; U.N. Doc. S/2015/852 (Nov. 9, 2015). ¶ 42; U.N. Doc. A/72/865–S/2018/465 (May 16, 2018). ¶ 79; U.N. Doc. A/73/347 (Aug. 28, 2018). ¶ 31; U.N. Doc. S/2019/984 (Dec. 23, 2019). ¶ 60.

[992] UNAMI (July 6, 2014 – Sept. 10, 2014). p. 15; UNAMI (Sept. 11, 2014 – Dec. 10, 2014); UNAMI (May 1, 2015 – Oct. 31, 2015). p. 18.

[993] U.N. Doc. A/HRC/28/18 (March 27, 2015). ¶ 37; U.N. Doc. S/2016/1090 (Dec. 21, 2016). p. 7.

[994] ICSR. *Supra* note 520.

[995] U.N. Doc. S/2016/1090 (Dec. 21, 2016). pp. 8–9.

[996] See also: U.N. Doc. S/2016/361 (Apr. 20, 2016). ¶ 19; U.N. Doc. S/2016/361/Rev.1 (June 22, 2016). ¶ 19.

[997] UNAMI (June 5 – July 5, 2014). p. 11; U.N. Doc. A/HRC/28/18 (March 27, 2015). ¶ 43; U.N. Doc. CEDAW/C/IRQ/7 (Aug. 15, 2018). ¶ 13.

[998] U.N. Doc. S/2016/1090 (Dec. 21, 2016). pp. 7, 9.

[999] U.N. Doc. A/HRC/28/18 (March 27, 2015). ¶ 37; U.N. Doc. S/2016/1090 (Dec. 21, 2016). p. 7.

[1000] UNAMI (Aug. 2016). p. 16.

[1001] U.N. Doc. S/2016/1090 (Dec. 21, 2016). p. 8.

ISIL/DAESH destined women and girls to destinations such as Turkey, Syria, Palestine, Saudi Arabia, Qatar, Egypt, and Tunisia.[1002] Routinely, ISIL/DAESH used to sell the very same woman or girl several times to enhance their profitability.[1003] Reports show that some women and girls were resold as many as 15 times.[1004] Additionally, to "maintain the girls' financial value when sold on the market," ISIL/DAESH also forced the victims to take contraceptive pills or injections or use drugs to induce abortion.[1005] Furthermore, ISIL/DAESH fighters and buyers were encouraged "not to ejaculate [inside] the women during the intercourse" to avoid pregnancies.[1006]

After ISIL/DAESH abducted women and girls with the intent of selling them, the group kept their victims under captivity in appalling conditions for periods of up to nineteen months.[1007] While "waiting" to be sold, women and girls were brutally raped, subjected to sexual slavery, or severely beaten with sticks, clubs, plastic pipes, and other instruments until the point of passing out.[1008] In several public statements, ISIL/DAESH openly advocated for officially institutionalizing, regulating, and codifying sexual slavery.[1009] ISIL/DAESH fighters kept some of the victims in isolation for up to five days, with no food or water, even when victims were nourishing mothers.[1010] In some cases, ISIL/DAESH held them in underground prisons with dirty water up to their knees.[1011]

Women and girls who rarely managed to escape reported an existence filled with fear, deep emotional wounds, stigma, and repudiation as they returned to their communities.[1012] A survivor, who was subjected to slavery for 19 months by ISIL/DAESH, told international human rights investigators how ISIL/DAESH men "hit her when she tried to prevent them from taking her 13-year old daughter away from her."[1013] [1014] She

---

[1002]  UNAMI (Aug. 2016). p. 16.

[1003]  *Ibidem.*

[1004]  IICI. *Supra* note 843. p. 5.

[1005]  U.N. Doc. S/2016/1090 (Dec. 21, 2016). p. 9.

[1006]  *Ibidem.*

[1007]  UNAMI (Aug. 2016). p. 17.

[1008]  *Idem.* p. 16.

[1009]  U.N. Doc. S/2016/361 (Apr. 20, 2016). ¶ 21; UNAMI (Aug. 2016). p. 14; U.N. Doc. S/2016/949 (Nov. 10, 2016). ¶ 10.

[1010]  UNAMI (Aug. 2016). p. 16.

[1011]  *Ibidem.*

[1012]  U.N. Doc. S/2019/984 (Dec. 23, 2019). ¶ 60.

[1013]  UNAMI (Aug. 2016). p. 15.

[1014]  *Ibidem.*

"screamed, begging them to leave the child. While she held her daughter's hand tightly to prevent them from taking her away, an ISIL/DAESH member hit her on her hand, fracturing it, and dragged the child out. Since her escape, she stated that she has suffered from repeated nightmares of the event."[1015]

ISIL/DAESH instituted a pattern of sexual violence as a multifaceted tool for multifold purposes:

1) As a systematic, widespread, and deliberate instrument of terrorizing, humiliating, and subjugating entire civilian communities, particularly religious and ethnic minorities;[1016]

2) As part of its strategy for controlling territory and "to advance key strategic priorities;"[1017] [1018]

3) As a tool "to suppress communities opposing its radical ideology;"[1019]

4) As a "tool of genocide against indigenous, religious, ethnic or political minorities;"[1020] [1021]

5) As a punishment instrument for women and girls who refused to convert;[1022]

6) As a tactic of war against children belonging to minority groups;[1023] and

7) To broadcast ISIL/DAESH's view that female bodies are "vessels for producing a new generation that can be raised in their own image, according to their radical ideology, and control over women's sexuality and reproduction."[1024]

---

[1015] *Ibidem.*

[1016] U.N. Doc. S/2016/92 (Jan. 29, 2016). ¶ 9; U.N. Doc. S/2019/984 (Dec. 23, 2019). ¶ 33

[1017] UNAMI (Dec. 11, 2014 – April 30, 2015). p. 22.

[1018] See also: U.N. Doc. S/2016/92 (Jan. 29, 2016). ¶ 9; U.N. Doc. S/2019/984 (Dec. 23, 2019). ¶ 33.

[1019] UNAMI (Dec. 11, 2014 – April 30, 2015). p. 22; U.N. Doc. S/2019/984 (Dec. 23, 2019). ¶ 33.

[1020] U.N. Doc. S/2016/361 (Apr. 20, 2016). ¶ 14.

[1021] "Extremists groups such as ISIL/DAESH have raped women pursuant to a plan of self-perpetuation aimed at transmitting their ideology to a new generation who can be raised in their own image. In this way, women's bodies [were] used as "biological weapons" to alter the demography of a region and to unravel existing kinship ties." (*Ibidem*).

[1022] UNAMI (Dec. 11, 2014 – April 30, 2015). pp. 20, 22.

[1023] U.N. Doc. CRC/C/IRQ/CO/2-4 (March 3, 2015). ¶ 44; U.N. Doc. S/2015/852 (Nov. 9, 2015). ¶ 42; U.N. Doc. S/2016/92 (Jan. 29, 2016). ¶ 9; U.N. Doc. S/AC.51/2016/2 (Aug. 18, 2016). ¶ 3; U.N. Doc. S/2016/1090 (Dec. 21, 2016). p. 5.

[1024] U.N. Doc. S/2016/92 (Jan. 29, 2016). ¶ 9.

## 1.5.4. Recruitment and use of children in armed conflict.

Several instances and bodies of the United Nations have already recognized that ISIL/DAESH carried out systematic and deliberate recruitment and use of children in all areas under its control, including across borders. For example, the Secretary-General,[1025] the Security Council,[1026] [1027] the Office of the United Nations High Commissioner for Human Rights,[1028] [1029] the Human Rights Committee,[1030] the Committee on the Elimination of Racial Discrimination,[1031] and the Committee on the Elimination of Discrimination against Women.[1032] Reports showed that girls and boys as young as five were recruited and used by the group.[1033] [1034] The recruitment and use of children constituted "a central component of the political, military and ideological aims of ISIL/DAESH in Iraq."[1035] [1036] [1037]

There is abundant evidence that children from minority groups, including the Christian group, were recruited both to take part in hostili-

---

[1025] U.N. Doc. S/2014/774 (Oct. 31, 2014). ¶¶ 46, 54, 76; U.N. Doc. A/69/926–S/2015/409 (June 5, 2015). ¶¶ 7, 71–72; U.N. Doc. S/2015/852 (Nov. 9, 2015). ¶¶ 3, 29, 31–33; U.N. Doc. S/2016/77 (Jan. 26, 2016). ¶ 57; U.N. Doc. S/2015/530 (July 13, 2015). ¶¶ 44, 49; U.N. Doc. A/70/836–S/2016/360 (Apr. 20, 2016). ¶¶ 59, 67; U.N. Doc. S/2016/592 (July 5, 2016). ¶ 45; U.N. Doc. A/72/361–S/2017/821 (Aug. 24, 2017). ¶ 76; U.N. Doc. S/2017/881 (Oct. 19, 2017). ¶ 49; U.N. Doc. A/72/865–S/2018/465 (May 16, 2018). ¶¶ 16, 75, 82.

[1026] S.C. Res. 2169 (July 30, 2014). Preamble, p. 3; S.C. Res. 2233 (July 29, 2015). Preamble, p. 3; S.C. Res. 2299 (July 25, 2016). Preamble, p. 4; S.C. Res. 2379 (Sept. 21, 2017). p.1, ¶ 1.

[1027] U.N. Doc. S/AC.51/2016/2 (Aug. 18, 2016). ¶¶ 3, 7.d, 8.a.

[1028] UNAMI (July 6, 2014 – Sept. 10, 2014). pp. iii, 17; UNAMI (Dec. 11, 2014 – April 30, 2015). p. 22; UNAMI (May 1, 2015 – Oct. 31, 2015). p. 18.

[1029] U.N. Doc. A/HRC/30/66 (July 27, 2015). ¶¶ 3637.

[1030] U.N. Doc. CCPR/C/IRQ/CO/5/Add.1 (Aug. 18, 2017). ¶ 19.

[1031] U.N. Doc. CERD/C/IRQ/22-25 (Nov. 22, 2017). ¶ 15.

[1032] U.N. Doc. CEDAW/C/IRQ/7 (Aug. 15, 2018). ¶ 9.

[1033] UNAMI (Dec. 11, 2014 – April 30, 2015). p. 22.

[1034] U.N. Doc. A/HRC/28/18 (March 27, 2015). ¶ 44; U.N. Doc. A/HRC/30/66 (July 27, 2015). ¶ 37; U.N. Doc. S/2015/852 (Nov. 9, 2015). ¶ 32; U.N. Doc. S/2016/92 (Jan. 29, 2016). ¶ 10; U.N. Doc. S/2017/75 (Jan. 26, 2017). ¶ 40; U.N. Doc. S/2019/984 (Dec. 23, 2019). ¶ 27.

[1035] U.N. Doc. S/2019/984 (Dec. 23, 2019). ¶ 27.

[1036] "While recruitment below the age of 18 has been prohibited in Iraq since 2010, child recruitment is not criminalized." (*Idem.* ¶ 85).

[1037] For a more comprehensive understanding of the problem of ISIL/DAESH recruitment and use of children, please refer to: The children of Islamic State, QUILLIAM INTERNATIONAL, Noman Benotman, Nikita Malik (March 2016).

ties directly and actively engage in attacks or to be used for support functions:[1038]

**1) Active roles.** ISIL/DAESH used children as combatants, actively participating in hostilities to: carry out suicide attacks; perform executions on civilians, soldiers, prisoners, and even on other ISIL/DAESH fighters; carry out shootings; conduct beheadings; launch small and medium-sized rockets; stay in the front line shielding ISIL/DAESH fighters during the fighting. ISIL/DAESH also used children for police functions, such as patrolling, manning checkpoints, and arresting and detaining individuals.[1039][1040]

**2) Support roles.** ISIL/DAESH used children for: cooking; cleaning; carrying and transporting weapons; loading and unloading guns; manufacturing explosive devices; for videotaping attacks for propaganda purposes; and for donating blood for treating injured ISIL/DAESH fighters.[1041] Children were also used for logistics: girl children were used as wives for fighters; children were used as informants, and acted as spies, scouts, and lookouts.[1042] Under the group's surveillance, ISIL/DAESH also forced children to work as farmers and shepherds.[1043]

ISIL/DAESH indoctrinated and trained large numbers of children through its courses in schools and youth military training camps, customized textbooks, and mobile apps.[1044][1045][1046] Boys were reportedly being

---

[1038] U.N. Doc. S/2015/852 (Nov. 9, 2015). ¶ 29; U.N. Doc. A/HRC/28/18 (March 27, 2015). ¶ 78; U.N. Doc. A/70/836–S/2016/360 (Apr. 20, 2016). ¶ 59; U.N. Doc. CEDAW/C/IRQ/7 (Aug. 15, 2018). ¶ 9; U.N. Doc. A/73/347 (Aug. 28, 2018). ¶ 35.

[1039] UNAMI (July 6, 2014 – Sept. 10, 2014). pp. 17–18; UNAMI, UNAMI (Sept. 11, 2014 – Dec. 10, 2014). p. 6; UNAMI (May 1, 2015 – Oct. 31, 2015). p. 18.

[1040] U.N. Doc. A/HRC/28/18 (March 27, 2015). ¶¶ 45–46, 76; U.N. Doc. A/69/926–S/2015/409 (June 5, 2015). ¶ 72; U.N. Doc. S/2015/852 (Nov. 9, 2015). ¶¶ 21, 29, 32 ,34, 52; U.N. Doc. S/2016/77 (Jan. 26, 2016). ¶ 57; U.N. Doc. S/2016/92 (Jan. 29, 2016). ¶ 10; U.N. Doc. A/72/361–S/2017/821 (Aug. 24, 2017). ¶ 9; U.N. Doc. A/72/865–S/2018/465 (May 16, 2018). ¶¶ 75, 82; U.N. Doc. CEDAW/C/IRQ/7 (Aug. 15, 2018). ¶ 9; U.N. Doc. S/2019/984 (Dec. 23, 2019). ¶¶ 6–7, 29, 31–34, 54.

[1041] UNAMI (July 6, 2014 – Sept. 10, 2014). pp. 17–18.
U.N. Doc. A/HRC/28/18 (March 27, 2015). ¶ 45; U.N. Doc. S/2015/852 (Nov. 9, 2015). ¶¶ 29, 32; U.N. Doc. A/72/865–S/2018/465 (May 16, 2018). ¶¶ 75, 79; U.N. Doc. S/2019/984 (Dec. 23, 2019). ¶¶ 32–33.

[1042] U.N. Doc. S/2015/852 (Nov. 9, 2015). ¶ 29; U.N. Doc. A/72/865–S/2018/465 (May 16, 2018). ¶ 75; U.N. Doc. S/2019/984 (Dec. 23, 2019). ¶ 32.

[1043] UNAMI (Dec. 11, 2014 – April 30, 2015). p. 20.

[1044] UNAMI (July 6, 2014 – Sept. 10, 2014). p. 17; UNAMI (May 1, 2015 – Oct. 31, 2015). p. 14; UNAMI (Aug. 2016). p. 12.

[1045] U.N. Doc. CRC/C/IRQ/CO/2-4 (March 3, 2015). ¶ 23.c; U.N. Doc. A/HRC/28/18 (March 27, 2015). ¶ 46; U.N. Doc. S/2016/92 (Jan. 29, 2016). ¶ 10.

[1046] ICSR. *Supra* note 520. *passim.*

forced to watch videos of beheadings and other atrocities. If they refused, ISIL/DAESH fighters would severely beat them.[1047] Through manipulation, inducement, desensitization, constant exposure to violent images, and "normalization" of atrocities, the group sought to "'re-programme' [sic] children to disregard normal behaviour, [sic] judgements, ethics, and values," and to "numb them to the value of human life."[1048] [1049]

In youth training camps, ISIL/DAESH forced children as young as five-years-old to convert to Islam and to memorize the Quran.[1050] Children received training on combat tactics, the use of weapons, and the perpetration of acts of extreme violence.[1051] To numb and embolden the children, ISIL/DAESH extensively resorted to forcing or inducing the minors to take drugs during the training sessions.[1052] To ensure obedience, instill fear, and exert control over the recruited minors, ISIL/DAESH committed horrifying violence against children "using executions, amputations, physical mutilations, and other brutalities."[1053] Children who rebelled or attempted to flee "were severely punished, including by being detained or executed."[1054] Children who survived such atrocities were lately reported showing critical "signs of trauma, including extreme fatigue, sleep disturbances, dizziness, and difficulty concentrating."[1055]

The ISIL/DAESH campaign to recruit children included methods of forcefully taking minors from their family homes, schools, from IDPs and refugee camps, and orphanages, and in front of mosques during Friday prayers.[1056] [1057] [1058] A 2014 report from the Office of the United Nations High Commissioner for Human Rights showed that some mothers, to avoid that ISIL/DAESH fighters took their sons and daughters, firmly embraced their children and "had thrown themselves off the mountains in despera-

---

[1047] U.N. Doc. A/HRC/28/18 (March 27, 2015). ¶ 45.
[1048] ICSR. *Supra* note 520. p. 13.
[1049] See also: U.N. Doc. S/2019/984 (Dec. 23, 2019). ¶ 28
[1050] U.N. Doc. S/2015/852 (Nov. 9, 2015). ¶ 33; UNAMI (Aug. 2016). p. 12.
[1051] UNAMI (May 1, 2015 – Oct. 31, 2015). p. 14; U.N. Doc. S/2015/852 (Nov. 9, 2015). ¶ 33; UNAMI (Aug. 2016). p. 12; U.N. Doc. S/2019/984 (Dec. 23, 2019). ¶ 29.
[1052] U.N. Doc. S/2019/984 (Dec. 23, 2019). ¶ 29.
[1053] *Idem.* ¶ 56.
[1054] *Idem.* ¶ 31.
[1055] UNAMI (Aug. 2016). pp. 15–16.
[1056] UNAMI (July 6, 2014 – Sept. 10, 2014). p. 17; UNAMI (May 1, 2015 – Oct. 31, 2015). pp. 18–19.
[1057] U.N. Doc. A/69/926–S/2015/409 (June 5, 2015). ¶ 72; U.N. Doc. A/HRC/30/66 (July 27, 2015). ¶ 37; U.N. Doc. S/2015/852 (Nov. 9, 2015). ¶¶ 32–33; U.N. Doc. S/2019/984 (Dec. 23, 2019). ¶ 28.
[1058] ICSR. *Supra* note 520. p. 3.

tion."[1059] Vulnerable children, such as street children or children from families facing extreme economic hardship, were mainly targeted by ISIL/DAESH.[1060] ISIL/DAESH frequently displayed videos promising children "power and economic support."[1061] In some cases, ISIL/DAESH reportedly recruited even the sons and relatives of its own fighters.[1062]

The exact number of child recruitment and use incidents by ISIL/DAESH remains considerably underdocumented still at the time of this book's writing.[1063] Lack of access to conflict-affected areas and the fear of retaliation by the victims' families account for the two main reasons for this lack of documentation.[1064] For instance, despite ISIL/DAESH's defeat in Iraq in December 2017, the terrorist group reportedly continues to attempt isolated attacks against civilians and security forces, particularly in the Baghdad region.[1065] On October 18, 2018, the U.S. Department of State, through its Bureau of Consular Affairs, issued a red flag travel advisory for Iraq, the highest level of concern for visitors/foreigners.[1066] Also, many international humanitarian advocacy and reporting agencies placed in the Autonomous Administration in Northern Iraq lack official access permits from the Iraqi Government to the areas affected by the conflict in Bagdad and Mosul, which compromises the reporting of violations in these areas. Mostly, individual permission to visit certain areas and specific camps in Iraq is given on a case-by-case basis exclusively made on the field. Due to the fear of police involvement with armed groups, several families of victims were reluctant to report violations of rights to the Iraqi national police authorities.

However, the forced recruitment and use of children in Iraq is not a recent issue in the country's history and does not constitute a problem created exclusively by ISIL/DAESH. For decades, other parties to the continuous conflict in Iraq have been recruiting as combatants for direct participation in the hostilities as well as to play support roles, such as the Iraqi military and other security forces, the pro-government forces, the Peo-

---

[1059] UNAMI (July 6, 2014 – Sept. 10, 2014). p. 14.

[1060] U.N. Doc. S/2019/984 (Dec. 23, 2019). ¶¶ 28, 30.

[1061] *Idem.* ¶ 29.

[1062] UNAMI (July 6, 2014 – Sept. 10, 2014). p. 17; U.N. Doc. S/2015/852 (Nov. 9, 2015). ¶ 32.

[1063] U.N. Doc. S/2015/852 (Nov. 9, 2015). ¶¶ 32, 49

[1064] U.N. Doc. A/69/926–S/2015/409 (June 5, 2015). ¶ 77; U.N. Doc. S/2015/852 (Nov. 9, 2015). ¶¶ 53, 55.

[1065] United Nations. Security Council. Security Council Report: Monthly Forecast. (Feb. 2018). Situation in Iraq. p.14.

[1066] US Department of State. Bureau of Consular Affairs. Iraq Travel Advisory. (Oct. 18, 2018).

ple's Defence Forces of the *Kurdish Workers Party*, the Popular Mobilization Forces, the Protection Force of Ezidkhan, the Peshmerga Zeravani, Sunni tribal mobilization groups, the *Shasho*, various Turkmen-based self-defense groups, the Sinjar Resistance Units, the Protection Force of Ezidkhan, the Awakening Council (also known as the "Sons of Iraq"), non-State armed groups, armed militias, insurgent groups in the Iraqi territory, and terrorist groups such as the Al-Qaida in Iraq.[1067]

## 1.5.5. Forced disappearances

In areas under its control, ISIL/DAESH carried out deliberate abductions/ kidnappings of civilians, including thousands of women and children as young as six-years-old, both isolated and mass abductions.[1068] [1069] [1070] Although the motives of why ISIL/DAESH used to perpetrate abductions are often unknown,[1071] information suggests that the victims were targeted in virtue of varied reasons, such as:

---

[1067] U.N. Doc. A/61/529–S/2006/826 (Oct. 26, 2006). ¶ 44; U.N. Doc. A/62/609– S/2007/757 (Dec. 21, 2007). ¶ 53; U.N. Doc. A/63/785–S/2009/158 (Mar. 26, 2009). ¶¶ 59–60; U.N. Doc. A/64/742–S/2010/181 (Apr. 13, 2010). ¶ 81; U.N. Doc. A/65/820–S/2011/250 (Apr. 23, 2011). ¶ 97; U.N. Doc. S/AC.51/2011/6 (Oct. 3, 2011). ¶ 6; U.N. Doc. A/66/782–S/2012/261 (Apr. 6, 2012). ¶ 42; U.N. Doc. CRC/C/OPAC/IRQ/1 (May 9, 2012). ¶ 30; U.N. Doc. A/67/845–S/2013/245 (May 15, 2013). ¶ 69; U.N. Doc. S/2015/530 (July 13, 2015). ¶ 49; U.N. Doc. S/2015/852 (Nov. 9, 2015). ¶¶ 35, 37; U.N. Doc. A/70/836–S/2016/360 (Apr. 20, 2016). ¶ 59; U.N. Doc. A/72/361–S/2017/821 (Aug. 24, 2017). ¶¶ 76, 84; U.N. Doc. S/2017/881 (Oct. 19, 2017). ¶ 49; U.N. Doc. S/2019/984 (Dec. 23, 2019). ¶¶ 35–36, 38–40.

[1068] UNAMI (July 6, 2014 – Sept. 10, 2014). p. 14; UNAMI (May 1, 2015 – Oct. 31, 2015). pp. 8–9, 13–14; UNAMI (June 5 – July 5, 2014). p. 12; UNAMI (Aug. 2016). p. 11; UNAMI (Nov. 6, 2018). p. 4.

[1069] U.N. Doc. S/2014/774 (Oct. 31, 2014). ¶¶ 46, 48, 76; U.N. Doc. S/2015/82 (Feb. 2, 2015). ¶¶ 46–47, 52; U.N. Doc. A/69/926–S/2015/409 (June 5, 2015). ¶ 7; U.N. Doc. S/2015/530 (July 13, 2015). ¶ 44; U.N. Doc. A/70/162 (July 20, 2015). ¶ 5; U.N. Doc. A/HRC/30/66 (July 27, 2015). ¶¶ 6, 32; U.N. Doc. S/2015/852 (Nov. 9, 2015). ¶¶ 32, 49; U.N. Doc. S/2016/77 (Jan. 26, 2016). ¶ 49; U.N. Doc. A/HRC/32/35/Add.1 (April 5, 2016). ¶ 55; U.N. Doc. A/70/836–S/2016/360 (Apr. 20, 2016). ¶ 65; U.N. Doc. S/2016/396 (Apr. 27, 2016). ¶ 78; U.N. Doc. S/2016/592 (July 5, 2016). ¶ 37; U.N. Doc. S/2016/897 (Oct. 25, 2016). ¶ 45; U.N. Doc. S/2017/75 (Jan. 26, 2017). ¶ 38; U.N. Doc. CCPR/C/IRQ/CO/5/Add.1 (Aug. 18, 2017). ¶ 19; U.N. Doc. A/72/361–S/2017/821 (Aug. 24, 2017). ¶ 82; U.N. Doc. CEDAW/C/IRQ/7 (Aug. 15, 2018). ¶ 9; U.N. Doc. A/73/347 (Aug. 28, 2018). ¶ 35; U.N. Doc. S/2019/984 (Dec. 23, 2019). ¶ 72; U.N. Doc. A/74/845–S/2020/525 (June 9, 2020). ¶ 74.

[1070] S.C. Res. 2388 (Nov. 21, 2017). Preamble, pp. 2–3.

[1071] UNAMI (Dec. 11, 2014 – April 30, 2015). p. 14; U.N. Doc. A/HRC/30/66 (July 27, 2015). ¶ 20.

1) For the victims belonging to minority religious and ethnic groups;[1072]
2) For human trafficking, slave trade, sexual exploitation, and for the payment of ransoms;[1073]
3) For the victims' refusal to volunteer in fighting alongside ISIL/DAESH;[1074]
4) For the victims' alleged cooperation with the international press;[1075]
5) For the victims' alleged cooperation with the Iraqi Security Forces and with the Iraqi Government;[1076] [1077]
6) For victims merely being leaders from the Sunni Arab tribes;[1078]
7) For shopkeepers allegedly raising food prices;[1079]
8) For recruitment and use of children in forced military training;[1080]
9) For the punishment of children or their families for trying to flee ISIL/DAESH-held areas;[1081] or
10) For perpetrating killings and persecution of those who opposed ISIL/DAESH ideology, control, and rules.[1082]

ISIL/DAESH reportedly abducted countless people from government and security force backgrounds and other persons of influence in the Iraqi society, such as former Government security officers, former parliamentary candidates, employees and former employees of the Independent High Electoral Commission (IHEC), Governors of Iraq provinces, current and former Iraqi Army officers and their families, *Imams*, staff from consular missions, and university professors and their families.[1083] [1084]

---

[1072] U.N. Doc. A/69/926–S/2015/409 (June 5, 2015). ¶ 77; U.N. Doc. A/60/335 (Sept. 7, 2005). ¶ 13.
[1073] U.N. Doc. S/2016/361 (Apr. 20, 2016). ¶ 20.
[1074] UNAMI (May 1, 2015 – Oct. 31, 2015). p. 13.
[1075] *Idem.* p. 14.
[1076] UNAMI (Sept. 11, 2014 – Dec. 10, 2014). pp. 6, 9.
[1077] U.N. Doc. S/2017/75 (Jan. 26, 2017). ¶ 38.
[1078] UNAMI (Sept. 11, 2014 – Dec. 10, 2014). p. 6.
[1079] U.N. Doc. S/2017/75 (Jan. 26, 2017). ¶ 38.
[1080] U.N. Doc. S/2019/984 (Dec. 23, 2019). ¶ 73.
[1081] *Ibidem.*
[1082] UNAMI (Dec. 11, 2014 – April 30, 2015). pp. 10, 14; U.N. Doc. S/2016/396 (Apr. 27, 2016). ¶ 44.
[1083] UNAMI (July 6, 2014 – Sept. 10, 2014). p. 10; UNAMI (Sept. 11, 2014 – Dec. 10, 2014). p. 9; UNAMI (Dec. 11, 2014 – April 30, 2015). pp. 12–14; UNAMI (May 1, 2015 – Oct. 31, 2015). pp. 8, 13–14.
[1084] U.N. Doc. S/2017/75 (Jan. 26, 2017). ¶ 38.

Several victims of ISIL/DAESH were being taken by the group from their homes, workplaces, or checkpoints.[1085] [1086] The exact fate and where-abouts of the vast majority of these forcibly disappeared victims remain still unknown at the time of the writing of this book.[1087] [1088]

Numerous sources confirmed that, after abduction/capture, ISIL/DAESH usually separated men from women, particularly Christian and Yazidi groups. Then, married women were separated from single ones; children were separated from their parents, and, finally, girl children were separated from the boys for further selling and recruitment and use.[1089] [1090] In one instance that ISIL/DAESH fighters were separating the young girls from the women, around 500 young girls were taken away.[1091] Tragically, in this particular event, a thirteen-year-old girl was taken to a hall in Mo-sul that was full of young girls.[1092] After seven days, she "was sold to an Iraqi ISIL/DAESH member, at the premises of a former court in Mosul, for 1,000 US dollars."[1093]

*Chart of United Nations documents cited in Chapter 1 – Chronological or-der*

## 2005

U.N. Doc. A/60/335 (Sept. 7, 2005).
Rep. of the Special Representative of the Secretary-General for Children and Armed Conflict, addressed to the G.A. on its Sixtieth session.

---

[1085] U.N. Doc. A/HRC/28/18 (March 27, 2015). ¶ 30.

[1086] Office of the United Nations High Commissioner for Human Rights, Spokesperson for the UN High Commissioner for Human Rights: Ravina Shamdasani (Nov. 29, 2016). (2).

[1087] UNAMI (June 5 – July 5, 2014). p. 12; UNAMI (July 6, 2014 – Sept. 10, 2014). pp. 7–8, 13; UNAMI (Sept. 11, 2014 – Dec. 10, 2014). p. 9; UNAMI (Dec. 11, 2014 – April 30, 2015). pp. 10, 13, 20; UNAMI (May 1, 2015 – Oct. 31, 2015). pp. 8, 13–14; UNAMI (Aug. 2016). pp. 13, 15.

[1088] U.N. Doc. S/2015/82 (Feb. 2, 2015). ¶ 52; U.N. Doc. A/HRC/38/44/Add.1 (June 20, 2018). ¶ 73; U.N. Doc. S/2019/984 (Dec. 23, 2019). ¶ 28.

[1089] UNAMI (Sept. 11, 2014 – Dec. 10, 2014). pp. 13–14; UNAMI (Dec. 11, 2014 – April 30, 2015). p. 22; UNAMI (Aug. 2016). p. 15.

[1090] U.N. Doc. CRC/C/IRQ/CO/2-4 (March 3, 2015). ¶ 52; U.N. Doc. A/69/926–S/2015/409 (June 5, 2015). ¶ 77.

[1091] UNAMI (Aug. 2016). p. 15.

[1092] *Ibidem.*

[1093] *Ibidem.*

## 2006

U.N. Doc. A/61/529–S/2006/826 (Oct. 26, 2006).
Rep. of the Special Representative of the Secretary-General for Children and Armed Conflict, addressed to the G.A. on its Sixty-first session.

## 2007

U.N. Doc. A/62/609–S/2007/757 (Dec. 21, 2007).
Rep. of the Special Representative of the Secretary-General for Children and Armed Conflict, addressed to the G.A. on its Sixty-second session.

## 2009

U.N. Doc. A/63/785–S/2009/158 (Mar. 26, 2009).
Rep. of the Special Representative of the Secretary-General for Children and Armed Conflict, addressed to the G.A. on its Sixty-third session.

## 2010

U.N. Doc. A/64/742–S/2010/181 (Apr. 13, 2010).
Rep. of the Special Representative of the Secretary-General for Children and Armed Conflict, addressed to the G.A. on its Sixty-fourth session.

## 2011

U.N. Doc. A/65/820–S/2011/250 (Apr. 23, 2011).
U.N. Secretary-General, *Children and Armed Conflict.*

U.N. Doc. S/2011/366 (June 15, 2011).
Rep. of the U.N. Secretary-General submitted to the S.C, pursuant to *Children and Armed Conflict in Iraq.*

U.N. Doc. S/AC.51/2011/6 (Oct. 3, 2011).
Rep. of the S.C. Working Group on Children and Armed Conflict, *Conclusions on Children and Armed Conflict in Iraq.*

## 2012

U.N. Doc. A/66/782–S/2012/261 (Apr. 6, 2012).
U.N. Secretary-General, *Children and Armed Conflict.*

U.N. Doc. CRC/C/OPAC/IRQ/1 (May 9, 2012).
Rep. of the Committee on the Rights of the Child, Consideration of reports submitted by States parties under article 8, paragraph 1, of the Optional Protocol to the Convention on the Rights of the Child on the involvement of children in armed conflict Initial reports of States parties due in 2010 Iraq.

## 2013

U.N. Doc. A/67/845–S/2013/245 (May 15, 2013).
U.N. Secretary-General, *Children and Armed Conflict*

## 2014

U.N. Doc. A/68/878–S/2014/339 (May 15, 2014).
U.N. Secretary-General, *Children and Armed Conflict.*

U.N. Doc. S/2014/485 (July 11, 2014).
Rep. of the U.N. Secretary-General submitted to the S.C, pursuant to *Paragraph 6 of Rresolution 2110 (2013).*

U.N. Doc. A/69/212 (July 31, 2014).
Rep. of the Special Representative of the Secretary-General for Children and Armed Conflict, addressed to the G.A. on its Sixty-eighth session.

U.N. Doc. A/HRC/S-22/NGO/8 (Aug. 29, 2014).
U.N. Human Rights Council, Written Statement Submitted by the European Centre for Law and Justice, A Non-Governmental Organization in Special Consultative Status.

U.N. Doc. A/69/53/Add.1 (Sept. 1, 2014).
Rep. of the Human Rights Council.

U.N. Doc. A/HRC/RES/S-22/1 (Sept. 3, 2014).
Human Rights Council Res. S-22/1

U.N. Doc. S/2014/774 (Oct. 31, 2014).
Rep. of the U.N. Secretary-General submitted to the S.C, pursuant to *paragraph 6 or Res. 2169.*

U.N. Doc. A/HRC/28/14 (Dec. 12, 2014).
Human Rights Council. Report of the Working Group on the Universal Periodic Review: Iraq.

## 2015

U.N. Doc. S/2015/82 (Feb. 2, 2015).
Rep. of the U.N. Secretary-General submitted to the S.C, pursuant *to Paragraph 6 or Res. 2169* (2014).

U.N. Doc. CRC/C/IRQ/CO/2-4 (March 3, 2015).
Committee on the Rights of the Child, Concluding observations on the combined second to fourth periodic reports of Iraq. U.N. Doc. CRC/C/IRQ/CO/2-4 (March 3, 2015).

U.N. Doc. A/HRC/28/18 (March 27, 2015).
Rep. of the Office of the United Nations High Commissioner for Human Rights, submitted to the Human Rights Council, *Human Rights Situation in Iraq in the Light of Abuses Committed by The so Called Islamic State in Iraq and The Levant and Associated Groups.*

U.N. Doc. A/HRC/RES/28/32 (April 8, 2015).
Human Rights Council Res. 28/32.

U.N. Doc. A/69/926–S/2015/409 (June 5, 2015).
U.N. Secretary-General, *Children and Armed Conflict.*

U.N. Doc. A/HRC/29/NGO/95 (June 10, 2015).
U.N. Human Rights Council, Written Statement Submitted by the Al-khoei Foundation, A Non-Governmental Organization in Special Consultative Status.

U.N. Doc. S/2015/530 (July 13, 2015).
Rep. of the U.N. Secretary-General submitted to the S.C, pursuant to *Paragraph 6 or Res. 2169 (2014).*

U.N. Doc. A/HRC/30/66 (July 27, 2015).
Rep. of the Office of the United Nations High Commissioner for Human Rights, submitted to the Human Rights Council, Technical Assistance Provided to Assist in The Promotion and Protection of Human Rights in Iraq.

U.N. Doc. A/HRC/30/NGO/116 (Sept. 8, 2015).
U.N. Human Rights Council, Written statement submitted by the International Youth and Student Movement for the United Nations, A Non-Governmental Organization in Special Consultative Status.

U.N. Doc. S/2015/739 (Sept. 25, 2015).
U.N. Chair of the S.C., United Nations. Security Council. Letter dated 25 September 2015 from the Chair of the Security Council Committee pursuant to resolutions 1267 (1999) and 1989 (2011) concerning Al-Qaida and associated individuals and entities addressed to the President of the Security Council.

U.N. Doc. S/2015/852 (Nov. 9, 2015).
Rep. of the U.N. Secretary-General submitted to the S.C, pursuant to *Children and Armed Conflict in Iraq*.

U.N. Doc. S/PV.7556 (Nov. 11, 2015).
Rep. of the U.N. Secretary-General submitted to the S.C, pursuant to *Res. 2233 (2015)*.

U.N. Doc. S/2015/975 (Dec. 29, 2015).
U.N. Chair of the S.C., Letter dated 15 December 2015 from the Chair of the Security Council Committee established pursuant to resolution 1373 (2001) concerning counter-terrorism addressed to the President of the Security Council.

## 2016

U.N. Doc. S/2016/77 (Jan. 26, 2016).
Rep. of the U.N. Secretary-General submitted to the S.C, pursuant to *Paragraph 7 or Res. 2233 (2015)*.

U.N. Doc. S/2016/92 (Jan. 29, 2016).
Rep. of the U.N. Secretary-General submitted to the S.C, pursuant to the *Threat Posed by ISIL/DAESH (Da'esh) to International Peace and Security*.

U.N. Doc. A/HRC/32/35/Add.1 (April 5, 2016).
U.N. Human Rights Council, Report of the Special Rapporteur on the Human Rights of Internally Displaced Persons, Chaloka Beyani, Visit to Iraq.

U.N. Doc. S/2016/361 (Apr. 20, 2016).
Rep. of the U.N. Secretary-General submitted to the S.C, on *Conflict-Related Sexual Violence.*

U.N. Doc. A/70/836–S/2016/360 (Apr. 20, 2016).
U.N. Secretary-General, *Children and Armed Conflict.*

U.N. Doc. S/2016/396 (Apr. 27, 2016).
Rep. of the U.N. Secretary-General submitted to the S.C, pursuant to *Paragraph 7 or Res. 2233 (2015).*

U.N. Doc. S/2016/361/Rev.1 (June 22, 2016).
Rep. of the U.N. Secretary-General submitted to the S.C, on *Conflict-Related Sexual Violence.*

U.N. Doc. S/2016/592 (July 5, 2016).
Rep. of the U.N. Secretary-General submitted to the S.C, pursuant to the *Paragraph 7 of Res. 2233 (2015).*

U.N. Doc. S/2015/739 (July 19, 2016).
U.N. Chair of the S.C., Letter dated 25 September 2015 from the Chair of the Security Council Committee pursuant to resolutions 1267 (1999) and 1989 (2011) concerning Al-Qaida and associated individuals and entities addressed to the President of the Security Council.

U.N. Doc. A/71/205 (July 25, 2016).
Rep. of the Special Representative of the Secretary-General for Children and Armed Conflict, addressed to the G.A. on its Seventy-first session.

U.N. Doc. A/71/303 (Aug. 5, 2016).
Rep. of the Special Rapporteur on Trafficking in persons, especially women and children, Maria Grazia Giammarinaro, submitted to the Human Rights Council concerning her mission to Iraq.

U.N. Doc. S/AC.51/2016/2 (Aug. 18, 2016).
Rep. of the S.C. Working Group on Children and Armed Conflict, *Conclusions on Children and Armed Conflict in Iraq.*

U.N. Doc. S/2016/897 (Oct. 25, 2016).
Rep. of the U.N. Secretary-General submitted to the S.C, pursuant to the *Implementation of Res. 2299 (2016).*

U.N. Doc. S/2016/949 (Nov. 10, 2016).
Rep. of the U.N. Secretary-General submitted to the S.C, pursuant to the
*Implementation of Measures to Counter Trafficking in Persons.*

U.N. Doc. S/2016/1090 (Dec. 21, 2016).
U.N. Chair of the S.C., Letter dated 20 December 2016 from the Secretary-
General addressed to the President of the Security Council.

## 2017

U.N. Doc. A/HRC/34/53/Add.1 (Jan. 9, 2017).
Rep. of the Special Rapporteur on Minority Issues, submitted to the Human
Rights Council concerning her mission to Iraq.

U.N. Doc. A/HRC/34/50 (Jan. 17, 2017).
U.N. Human Rights Council, Report of the Special Rapporteur on freedom
of religion and belief.

U.N. Doc. S/2017/75 (Jan. 26, 2017).
Rep. of the U.N. Secretary-General submitted to the S.C, pursuant to *the
Implementation of Res. 2299 (2016).*

U.N. Doc. A/72/164 (July 18, 2017).
Joint Rep. of the Special Rapporteur on the sale and sexual exploitation of
children, including child prostitution, child pornography and other child
sexual abuse material and the Special Rapporteur on trafficking in persons,
especially women and children.

U.N. Doc. S/2017/573 (Aug. 7, 2017).
U.N. Chair of the S.C., Letter dated 7 August 2017 from the Chair of the Security Council Committee pursuant to resolutions 1267 (1999), 1989 (2011)
and 2253 (2015) concerning Islamic State in Iraq and the Levant (Da'esh),
Al-Qaida and associated individuals, groups, undertakings and entities addressed to the President of the Security Council, U.N. Doc. S/2017/573
(Aug. 7, 2017).

U.N. Doc. CCPR/C/IRQ/CO/5/Add.1 (Aug. 18, 2017).
Rep. of the Human Rights Committee, Concluding Observations on the
Fifth Periodic Report of Iraq.

U.N. Doc. A/72/361–S/2017/821 (Aug. 24, 2017).
U.N. Secretary-General, *Children and Armed Conflict.*

U.N. Doc. A/72/53/Add.1 (Sept. 29, 2017).
Rep. of the Human Rights Council, U.N. Doc. A/72/53/Add.1 (Sept. 29, 2017).

U.N. Doc. S/2017/881 (Oct. 19, 2017).
Rep. of the U.N. Secretary-General submitted to the S.C, pursuant to *Res. 2367 (2017)*, U.N. Doc. S/2017/881 (Oct. 19, 2017).

U.N. Doc. S/2017/939 (Nov. 10, 2017).
Rep. of the U.N. Secretary-General submitted to the S.C, pursuant *Trafficking in Persons in Armed Conflict,* according to the S. C. Res. 2331 (2016).

U.N. Doc. CERD/C/IRQ/22-25 (Nov. 22, 2017).
Rep. of the Committee on the Elimination of Racial Discrimination, Concluding Observations on the Combined Twenty-Second to Twenty-Fifth Periodic Reports of Iraq.

U.N. Doc. S/2017/966 (2017).
U.N. Secretary-General, Letter dated Nov. 15, 2017 from the Secretary-General addressed to the President of the Security Council.

## 2018

U.N. Doc. S/2018/42 (Jan. 17, 2018).
Rep. of the U.N. Secretary-General submitted to the S.C, pursuant to *Res. 2367 (2017).*

U.N. Doc. S/2018/80 (Jan. 31, 2018).
Rep. of the U.N. Secretary-General submitted to the S.C, pursuant to the *Threat Posed by ISIL/DAESH (Da'esh) to International Peace and Security.*

U.N. Doc. S/2018/14/Rev.1 (Feb. 27, 2018).
U.N. Chair of the S.C., Letter dated 17 January 2018 from the Chair of the Security Council Committee pursuant to resolutions 1267 (1999), 1989 (2011), and 2253 (2015) concerning Islamic State in Iraq and the Levant (Da'esh), Al-Qaida and associated individuals, groups, undertakings and entities addressed to the President of the Security Council.

U.N. Doc. S/2018/118 (Feb. 14, 2018).
U.N. Chair of the S.C., Letter dated 9 February 2018 from the Secretary-General addressed to the President of the Security Council, U.N. Doc. S/2018/118 (Feb. 14, 2018).

U.N. Doc. S/2018/359 (Apr. 17, 2018).
Rep. of the U.N. Secretary-General submitted to the S.C, pursuant to *Res. 2367 (2017)*.

U.N. Doc. A/72/865–S/2018/465 (May 16, 2018).
U.N. Secretary-General, *Children and Armed Conflict.*

U.N. Doc. A/HRC/38/44/Add.1 (June 20, 2018).
Rep. of the Special Rapporteur on Extrajudicial, Summary or Arbitrary Executions, submitted to the Human Rights Council concerning her mission to Iraq.

U.N. Doc. S/2018/677 (July 9, 2018).
Rep. of the U.N. Secretary-General submitted to the S.C, pursuant to *the Implementation of Res. 2367* (2017).

U.N. Doc. S/2018/705 (July 27, 2018).
U.N. Chair of the S.C., United Nations. Security Council. Letter dated July 16, 2018 from the Chair of the Security Council addressed to the President of the Security Council pursuant to resolutions 1267 (1999), 1989 (2011) and 2253 (2015) concerning Islamic State in Iraq and the Levant.

U.N. Doc. A/73/263 (July 27, 2018).
U.N. Secretary-General, *Trafficking in women and girls.*

U.N. Doc. S/PV.8324 (Aug. 8, 2018).
Rep. of the U.N. Secretary-General submitted to the S.C, *The Situation Concerning Iraq,* pursuant to Res. 2367 (2017).

U.N. Doc. CEDAW/C/IRQ/7 (Aug. 15, 2018).
Rep. of the Committee on the Elimination of Discrimination against Women, Seventh Periodic Report Submitted by Iraq Under Article 18 of the Convention.

U.N. Doc. S/2018/770 (August 16, 2018).
Rep. of the U.N. Secretary-General submitted to the S.C, pursuant to the *Threat Posed by ISIL/DAESH (Da'esh) to International Peace and Security.*

U.N. Doc. S/2018/773 (Aug. 17, 2017).
U.N. Secretary-General, Letter dated Aug. 15, 2018 from the Secretary-General addressed to the President of the Security Council.

U.N. Doc. A/HRC/39/NGO/X (Aug. 23, 2018)
U.N. Human Rights Council, Written Statement Submitted by the European Centre for Law and Justice, A Non-Governmental Organization in Special Consultative Status, Request that the U.N. Recognize ISIS Atrocities Against Christians and Other Religious and Ethnic Minorities as Genocide and Take Immediate Appropriate Action.

U.N. Doc. A/73/347 (Aug. 28, 2018)
U.N. Secretary-General, *Effects of terrorism on the enjoyment of human rights.*

U.N. Doc. A/73/53/Add.1 (Sept. 28, 2018).
Rep. of the Human Rights Council.

U.N. Doc. A/73/352/Add.6 (Oct. 12, 2018).
U.N. Secretary-General, *United Nations Investigative Team to Promote Accountability for Crimes Committed by Da'esh/Islamic State in Iraq and the Levant.*

U.N. Doc. S/2018/975 (Oct. 31, 2018).
Rep. of the U.N. Secretary-General submitted to the S.C, pursuant to the *Implementation of Res. 2421 (2018).*

U.N. Doc. S/2018/1031 (Nov. 16, 2018).
Rep. of the Special Adviser and Head of the U. N. Investigative Team to Promote Accountability for Crimes Committed by Da'esh/Islamic State in Iraq and the Levant submitted to the S.C, First report of the Special Adviser and Head of the United Nations Investigative Team to Promote Accountability for Crimes Committed by Da'esh/Islamic State in Iraq and the Levant.

U.N. Doc. S/2018/770 (2018).
Rep. of the U.N. Secretary-General submitted to the S.C, pursuant to the *Threat Posed by ISIL/DAESH (Da'esh) to International Peace and Security.*

## 2019

U.N. Doc. S/2019/101 (Feb. 1, 2019).
Rep. of the U.N. Secretary-General submitted to the S.C, on the *Implementation of resolution 2421 (2018),* U.N. Doc. S/2019/101 (Feb. 1, 2019).

U.N. Doc. S/2019/103 (Feb. 1, 2019).
Rep. of the U.N. Secretary-General submitted to the S.C, pursuant to the *Threat Posed by ISIL/DAESH (Da'esh) to International Peace and Security.*

U.N. Doc. A/HRC/41/46 (Abr. 23, 2019).
Rep. of the Special Rapporteur on Trafficking in persons, especially women and children, Maria Grazia Giammarinaro, submitted to the Human Rights Council.

U.N. Doc. S/2019/365 (May 2, 2019).
Rep. of the U.N. Secretary-General submitted to the S.C, pursuant to the *Implementation of Res. 2421 (2018)*.

U.N. Doc. S/2019/407 (May 17, 2019).
Rep. of the Special Adviser and Head of the U. N. Investigative Team to Promote Accountability for Crimes Committed by Da'esh/Islamic State in Iraq and the Levant submitted to the S.C, Second report of the Special Adviser and Head of the United Nations Investigative Team to Promote Accountability for Crimes Committed by Da'esh/Islamic State in Iraq and the Levant.

U.N. Doc. A/73/907–S/2019/509 (June 20, 2019).
U.N. Secretary-General, *Children and Armed Conflict.*

U.N. Doc. S/2019/570 (July 15, 2019).
U.N. Chair of the S.C., Letter dated 15 July 2019 from the Chair of the Security Council Committee pursuant to resolutions 1267 (1999), 1989 (2011) and 2253 (2015) concerning Islamic State in Iraq and the Levant (Da'esh), Al-Qaida and associated individuals, groups, undertakings and entities addressed to the President of the Security Council.

U.N. Doc. S/2019/612 (July 31, 2019).
Rep. of the U.N. Secretary-General submitted to the S.C, on the *Threat posed by ISIL (Da'esh) to international peace and security and the range of United Nations efforts in support of Member States in countering the threat,* U.N. Doc. S/2019/612 (July 31, 2019).

U.N. Doc. S/2019/878 (Nov. 13, 2019).
Rep. of the Special Adviser and Head of the U. N. Investigative Team to Promote Accountability for Crimes Committed by Da'esh/Islamic State in Iraq and the Levant submitted to the S.C, Third report of the Special Adviser and Head of the United Nations Investigative Team to Promote Accountability for Crimes Committed by Da'esh/Islamic State in Iraq and the Levant.

U.N. Doc. S/2019/903 (Nov. 22, 2019).
Rep. of the U.N. Secretary-General submitted to the S.C, on the *Implementation of resolution 2470 (2019)*.

U.N. Doc. S/2019/984 (Dec. 23, 2019).
Rep. of the U.N. Secretary-General submitted to the S.C, pursuant to *Children and Armed Conflict in Iraq*.

## 2020

U.N. Doc. S/2020/53 (Jan. 20, 2020).
U.N. Chair of the S.C., Letter dated 20 January 2020 from the Chair of the Security Council Committee pursuant to resolutions 1267 (1999), 1989 (2011) and 2253 (2015) concerning Islamic State in Iraq and the Levant (Da'esh), Al-Qaida and associated individuals, groups, undertakings and entities addressed to the President of the Security Council.

U.N. Doc. S/2020/140 (Feb. 21, 2020).
Rep. of the U.N. Secretary-General submitted to the S.C, on the *Implementation of resolution 2470 (2019)*.

U.N. Doc. S/2020/363 (May 6, 2020).
Rep. of the U.N. Secretary-General submitted to the S.C, on the *Implementation of resolution 2470 (2019)*.

U.N. Doc. S/2020/386 (May 11, 2020).
Rep. of the Special Adviser and Head of the U. N. Investigative Team to Promote Accountability for Crimes Committed by Da'esh/Islamic State in Iraq and the Levant submitted to the S.C, Fourth report of the Special Adviser and Head of the United Nations Investigative Team to Promote Accountability for Crimes Committed by Da'esh/Islamic State in Iraq and the Levant.

U.N. Doc. A/HRC/44/41/Add.1 (May 13, 2020).
U.N. Human Rights Council, Report of the Special Rapporteur on the Human Rights of Internally Displaced Persons, Cecilia Jimenez-Damary, Visit to Iraq.

U.N. Doc. A/74/845–S/2020/525 (June 9, 2020).
Rep. of the U.N. Secretary-General submitted to the S.C, on *Children and Armed Conflict,* U.N. Doc. A/74/845–S/2020/525.

U.N. Doc. A/HRC/44/NGO/115 (June 30, 2020).
U.N. Human Rights Council, Written Statement Submitted by the Society
for Threatened Peoples, A Non-Governmental Organization in Special Consultative Status.

U.N. Doc. S/2020/717 (July 23, 2020).
U.N. Chair of the S.C., Letter dated 16 July 2020 from the Chair of the Security Council Committee pursuant to resolutions 1267 (1999), 1989 (2011)
and 2253 (2015) concerning Islamic State in Iraq and the Levant (Da'esh),
Al-Qaida and associated individuals, groups, undertakings and entities addressed to the President of the Security Council.

*Chart of documents from the United Nations Assistance Mission for Iraq
(UNAMI) – Chronological order*

## 2014

July 6, 2014 – Sept. 10, 2014.
UNAMI, Protection of Civilians in the Armed Conflict in Iraq.

Sept. 11, 2014 – Dec. 10, 2014.
UNAMI, Protection of Civilians in the Armed Conflict in Iraq.

Dec. 11, 2014 – April 30, 2015.
UNAMI, Protection of Civilians in the Armed Conflict in Iraq.

## 2015

May 1, 2015 – Oct. 31, 2015.
UNAMI, Protection of Civilians in the Armed Conflict in Iraq.

## 2016

Aug. 2016.
UNAMI, Report: A Call for Accountability and Protection: Yezidi Survivors
of Atrocities Committed by ISIL/DAESH.

Aug. 2016.
UNAMI, Report: A Call for Accountability and Protection: Yezidi Survivors
of Atrocities Committed by ISIL/DAESH.

## 2018

Nov. 6, 2018.
UNAMI, Unearthing Atrocities: Mass Graves in territory formerly controlled by ISIL/DAESH.

## 2020

Jan. 2020.
UNAMI, Human Rights in the Administration of Justice in Iraq: Trials under the anti-terrorism laws and implications for justice, accountability and social cohesion in the aftermath of ISIL/DAESH.

# 2. The factual matrix of human rights and humanitarian law violations: an appraisal of the facts from the Nuremberg, the ICTR, the ICTY, the SCSL, and ICC tribunals

## A. Germany

Following Adolf Hitler becoming the supreme leader or Führer of the Nationalsozialistische Deutsche Arbeiterpartei (National Socialist German Workers Party), the doctrines, practices, and policies of the Nazi Party were put in place in Germany and the occupied territories during the Second World War.[1094] Hitler's colossal doctrine conceived that "persons of so-called 'German blood' [as specified by the Nazi conspirators] were a 'master race' and were accordingly entitled to subjugate, dominate, or exterminate other' races.'"[1095]

The Nazi party, with the support of the Schutzstaffel (the SS), then started the "Common Plan" of destroying and persecuting all opponents "whose political belief or spiritual aspirations were deemed to be in conflict with the aims of the Nazis."[1096] [1097] The SS painstakingly planned, prepared, and executed crimes against peace, crimes against humanity, and war crimes both within Germany and within occupied territories, violating international treaties, agreements, assurances, rules, and war customs.[1098]

Crimes of unspeakable evil were perpetrated, for instance: murder, mass killings, extermination, mutilations, amputations, beatings, torture, the taking and killing of hostages, kidnapping of children, forced medical experiments, slave labor, ill-treatment of prisoners of war, and persons on the high seas, the plunder and confiscation of public and private property, the indiscriminate destruction of cities, towns, and villages, forced displacement of civilians, deportation, devastation not justified by military necessity, and other inhumane acts committed against civilian popula-

---

[1094] 1 Trial of the Major War Criminals before the International Military Tribunal (1947). p. 30.

[1095] *Idem.* p. 31.

[1096] *Idem.* p. 66.

[1097] See also: *Idem.* p. 31.

[1098] 1 Trial of the Major War Criminals before the International Military Tribunal (1947). p. 29; United States of America vs. Friedrich Flick *et al.* Case 5 (1947). p. XIII.

tions.[1099] Hundreds of thousands of Jews, in particular, were systematically persecuted by the Nazis since 1933.[1100] They were killed, tortured, locked in concentration camps, and deprived of their property/belongings."[1101]

At Nazi concentration camps, civilian inmate victims had all sorts of ailments, such as gangrenous wounds, tuberculosis, typhus, and other infectious diseases.[1102] The premises where inmates were placed had "appalling conditions."[1103] Very frequently, SS officers gave inmates little or nothing to eat.[1104] At all times, the camps were surrounded by an electrically charged fence and by barbed wire.[1105] Prisoners were tattooed with numbers for prison control.[1106] Those who tried to escape were summarily shot to death.[1107] Many prisoners were executed by gas or shooting or by injections. Mostly those who survived, showed "scars of a miserable existence under Nazi prison rule."[1108]

## B. Sierra Leone

In Sierra Leone, eleven years of internal civil conflict that commenced on March 23, 1991, left the country with a complex net of armed groups.[1109] In particular, armed fighters formed two major rebel groups, the Armed Forces Revolutionary Council (AFRC) and the Revolutionary United Front (RUF). Such groups launched an insurgency movement from Liberia's Lofa County into Sierra Leone's Kailahun District that "continued until president Ahmad Tejan Kabbah of Sierra Leone announced the cessation of hostilities on January 18, 2002." Thousands of civilians remained under the control of AFRC/RUF, including women and children.[1110] [1111] Documentary and witness evidence established that such groups and other retreating

---

[1099] 1 Trial of the Major War Criminals before the International Military Tribunal (1947). p. 29.

[1100] Idem. p. 66.

[1101] Ibidem.

[1102] 30 Trial of the Major War Criminals before the International Military Tribunal (1948). pp. 462–463.

[1103] Ibidem.

[1104] Ibidem.

[1105] **United States of America v. Oswald Pohl, et al. Case 4** (Pohl case) (1947). p. 385.

[1106] Idem. p. 416.

[1107] Idem. p. 394.

[1108] 30 Trial of the Major War Criminals before the International Military Tribunal (1948). pp. 462–463.

[1109] Prosecutor v. Taylor. SCSL-03-01-T. Supra note 270. ¶ 19.

[1110] Idem. ¶ 936.

[1111] Idem. ¶ 18.

forces committed a broad-spectrum of horrific, systematic, and wide-spread attacks against Sierra Leone's civilian population.[1112] [1113]

## C. Rwanda

In Rwanda, following the death of Rwandan president Juvénal Habya-rimana in a plane crash, persons belonging to the Tutsi ethnicity were singled out and targeted in their communities by persons belonging to the Hutu ethnicity.[1114] [1115] Hutus accused the Tutsi of being involved in the shooting down with missiles of the president's Habyarimana aircraft on the evening of April 6, 1994. Hutu political forces associated with presi-dent Habyarimana then formed two militia groups after the crash: the Interahamwe and the Impuzamugambi. Both received training, support, weapons, ammunition, and intelligence from the official Rwandan army and from Rwandan police for a settling of accounts with the Tutsi.[1116] The plane crash event then triggered, in the territory of Rwanda, between April 6 and July 17, 1994, the widespread persecution, torture, rape, and killing of hundreds of thousands of civilians, solely because of their mem-bership to the Tutsi ethnicity, including women, children, and the el-derly.[1117]

Fearing threats of death and different kinds of attacks on the physical and mental integrity of the Hutu, thousands of Tutsis fled their homes.

---

[1112] Prosecutor v. Sesay, Kallon and Gbao. SCSL-04-15-T. *Supra* note 268. ¶ 1567.

[1113] See also: Prosecutor v. Brima, Kamara, Kanu. SCSL-04-16-T. *Supra* note 280. ¶ 233; Prosecutor v. Sesay, Kallon and Gbao. SCSL-04-15-T. *Supra* note 268. ¶¶ 1522, 1606; Prosecutor v. Sesay, Kallon and Gbao. SCSL-04-15-T. *Supra* note 279. ¶ 153.

[1114] Prosecutor v. Gaspard Kanyarukiga. ICTR-2002-78-T. *Supra* note 187. ¶ 660.

[1115] "In the early 1930s, Belgian authorities introduced a permanent distinction by di-viding the population into three groups which they called ethnic groups, with the Hutu representing about 84% of the population, while the Tutsi (about 15%) and Twa (about 1%) accounted for the rest. In line with this division, it became man-datory for every Rwandan to carry an identity card mentioning his or her ethnic-ity. [...] The reference to ethnic background on identity cards was maintained, even after Rwanda's independence and was, at last, abolished only after the tragic events the country experienced in 1994." (Prosecutor v. Jean-Paul Akayesu. ICTR-96-4-T. *Supra* note 203. ¶ 83).

[1116] Prosecutor v. Tharcisse Renzaho. ICTR-97-31-T. *Supra* note 232.

[1117] Prosecutor v. Jean-Paul Akayesu. ICTR-96-4-T. *Supra* note 203. ¶ 1; Prosecutor v. Gaspard Kanyarukiga. ICTR-2002-78-T. *Supra* note 187. ¶¶ 659-660.

They sought refuge in the country's communal bureaus, parishes, and churches.[1118] While seeking refuge,

> "displaced female civilians were regularly taken by armed local militia and/or communal police and subjected to sexual violence, and/or beaten on or near the bureau communal premises. Displaced civilians were also murdered frequently on or near the bureau communal premises."[1119]

Dozens of women suffered atrocious acts of sexual nature, generally "accompanied by explicit threats of death or bodily harm."[1120] As a result of these acts perpetrated by police personnel and local militia fighters, female civilians "lived in constant fear, and their physical and psychological health deteriorated as a result of the sexual violence and beatings and killings."[1121]

Also, the Interahamwe erected roadblocks and checkpoints throughout Rwanda. Two main reasons were behind this procedure: 1) preventing Tutsi refugees from fleeing and 2) killing influential Tutsi people, such as primary teachers and university professors. Under the orders and supervision of the Hutu Jean-Paul Akayesu, the mayor of Rwandan Taba commune, the Interahamwe conducted house-to-house searches, interrogated and beat with rifles and sticks a significant number of Tutsi individuals.[1122]

## D. Former Yugoslavia

During the dismantling of former Yugoslavia in the late 1990s, Serbian authorities – government personnel, the military, and the police – submitted thousands of Bosnian Muslim civilians to intolerable conditions of life exclusively for their religious background/identity, violating numerous human rights recognized in international instruments.[1123] Serbian authorities adopted "cleaning-up," restrictive, intimidatory, verbally abusive, and wide and systematic discriminatory measures against the victims, notably restrictions on freedom of movement, denial of employment, violations to

---

[1118]  Prosecutor v. Jean-Paul Akayesu. ICTR-96-4-T. *Supra* note 203. ¶ 12a; Prosecutor v. Yussuf Munyakazi. ICTR-97-36A-T. *Supra* note 236. ¶ 321; Prosecutor v. Jean-Baptiste Gatete. ICTR-2000-61-T. *Supra* note 195. ¶ 633.
[1119]  Prosecutor v. Jean-Paul Akayesu. ICTR-96-4-T. *Supra* note 203. ¶ 12a.
[1120]  *Ibid.*
[1121]  *Ibid.*
[1122]  *Idem.* ¶¶ 12, 16.
[1123]  Prosecutor v. Vujadin Popović *et al.* IT-05-88-A. *Supra* note 151. ¶ 753; Prosecutor v. Radovan Karadžić. IT-95-5/18-T, vol. 1. *Supra* note 134. ¶¶ 991, 1165.

the right to privacy, and discriminatory measures on equal access to public services.[1124] They were submitted to horrific acts of physical violence and subjected to severe psychological abuse by Bosnian Serb, in a context of an atmosphere of "intimidation, suffering, misery, the threat of execution, and pain."[1125] Most of these acts of violence took place in the context in which Serbian soldiers and police personnel arbitrarily arrested thousands of Muslim civilians in detention camps for indiscriminate periods of time.[1126]

Detained Bosnian Muslims, including women, young children, and elderly persons, were subjected to multiple severe beatings on a daily basis for long periods, day and night.[1127] Serbian police authorities and soldiers perpetrated such atrocious violent acts on discriminatory grounds. The majority of victims were Bosnian Muslims and some Bosnian Croat detainees.[1128] Majorly, the detainees were kept in cellars, guarded by the police

---

[1124] Prosecutor v. Milomir Stakić. IT-97-24-T. *Supra* note 109. ¶ 261; Prosecutor v. Radislav Krstić. IT-98-33-A. *Supra* note 129. ¶ 37; Prosecutor v. Vidoje Blagojević, Dragan Jokić. IT-02-60-T. *Supra* note 147. ¶¶ 308, 311, 328; Prosecutor v. Momčilo Krajišnik. IT-00-39-T. *Supra* note 121. ¶¶ 784, 787, 804-805; Prosecutor v. Milan Lukić, Sredoje Lukić. IT-98-32/1-T. *Supra* note 104. ¶ 664; Prosecutor v. Radovan Karadžić. IT-95-5/18-T, vol. 1. *Supra* note 134. ¶¶ 991, 1064, 1337, 2496, 2512-2513, 2568; Prosecutor v. Ratko Mladić. IT-09-92-T, vol. 2. *Supra* note 137. ¶ 1485.

[1125] Prosecutor v. Milorad Krnojelac. IT-97-25-T. *Supra* note 111. ¶ 143.

[1126] The terms "unlawful," "arbitrary," and "illegal" detention/imprisonment employed here is regarded as the "deprivation of liberty of the individual without due process of law". It consists of the following elements: "(1) an individual is deprived of his or her liberty; (2) the deprivation of liberty is carried out arbitrarily, that is, there is no legal basis for it; and (3) the perpetrator acted with the intent to deprive the individual arbitrarily of his or her liberty." (Prosecutor v. Mićo Stanišić, Stojan Župljanin. IT-08-91-T, vol. 1. *Supra* note 102. ¶ 238). See also: Prosecutor v. Momčilo Krajišnik. IT-00-39-T. *Supra* note 121. ¶ 752).

[1127] Prosecutor v. Milorad Krnojelac. IT-97-25-T. *Supra* note 111. ¶¶ 143, 272, 280; Prosecutor v. Blagoje Simić, Miroslav Tadić and Simo Zarić. IT-95-9-T. *Supra* note 78. ¶¶ 696, 703, 711, 770; Prosecutor v. Slobodan Milošević. IT-02-54-T. *Supra* note 139. ¶ 173; Prosecutor v. Milan Martić. IT-95-11-T. *Supra* note 105. ¶ 288; Prosecutor v. Milan Lukić, Sredoje Lukić. IT-98-32/1-T. *Supra* note 104. ¶ 978; Prosecutor v. Mićo Stanišić, Stojan Župljanin. IT-08-91-T, vol. 1. *Supra* note 102. ¶¶ 289, 603, 683; Prosecutor v. Vujadin Popović *et al.* IT-05-88-A. *Supra* note 151. ¶ 753; Prosecutor v. Radovan Karadžić. IT-95-5/18-T, vol. 1. *Supra* note 134. ¶¶ 1013, 1015, 1156, 1165, 1167, 1190, 1201, 1306, 1333, 1346, 1353, 2497; Prosecutor v. Ratko Mladić. IT-09-92-T, vol. 2. *Supra* note 137. ¶ 1762.

[1128] Prosecutor v. Blagoje Simić *et al.* IT-95-9-T. *Supra* note 78. ¶¶ 771–772; Prosecutor v. Slobodan Milošević. IT-02-54-T. *Supra* note 139. ¶ 189; Prosecutor v. Mićo Stanišić, Stojan Župljanin. IT-08-91-T, vol. 1. *Supra* note 102. ¶¶ 676, 683.

the whole time for the duration of their detention.[1129] Serbian soldiers kept many of the detainees in solitary confinement cells, isolation rooms, and dark rooms or kept them in incommunicado detention in many instances.[1130] On rare occasions, some of the detainees were allowed outside the cell for 30 minutes a day.[1131] Those who tried to escape the prison facilities were killed immediately.[1132]

## E. Darfur, Sudan.

In the early 2000s in Darfur, Sudan, the Sudanese government forces, the National Security and Intelligence Service, the Military Intelligence, the Janjaweed, and the rebels committed indiscriminate attacks against civilians.[1133] These forces deliberately and extensively submitted civilians in Darfur to egregious forms of physical and mental torture and cruel and degrading treatment. Sudanese forces perpetrated barbaric acts such as killing by crucifixion, burning people to death, including children, extremely violent beatings, whippings, and skinning people. They stripped women of their clothes and raped them. These forces also committed extreme mental torture, verbal abuse, and humiliation, being "dragged along the ground by horses and camels from a noose placed around their necks." Also, they performed forced extraction of eyes, keeping persons under the scorching sun for days on, suspending persons from the ceiling, and beating them repeatedly, among other cruel forms of torture.[1134][1135] These forces also forced many mothers to watch their children being burned alive.[1136]

---

[1129] Prosecutor v. Radoslav Brđanin. IT-99-36-T. *Supra* note 130. ¶¶ 923, 931, 949; Prosecutor v. Mićo Stanišić, Stojan Župljanin. IT-08-91-T, vol. 1. *Supra* note 102. ¶¶ 584, 678; Prosecutor v. Radovan Karadžić. IT-95-5/18-T, vol. 1. *Supra* note 134. ¶¶ 1392, 1477, 1479.

[1130] Prosecutor v. Milorad Krnojelac. IT-97-25-T. *Supra* note 111. ¶ 272; Prosecutor v. Radovan Karadžić. IT-95-5/18-T, vol. 1. *Supra* note 134. ¶¶ 1399, 1427; Prosecutor v. Blagoje Simić *et al.* IT-95-9-T. *Supra* note 78. ¶ 696; Prosecutor v. Radovan Karadžić. IT-95-5/18-T, vol. 1. *Supra* note 134. ¶ 1479.

[1131] Prosecutor v. Radoslav Brđanin. IT-99-36-T. *Supra* note 130. ¶ 951.

[1132] Prosecutor v. Slobodan Milošević. IT-02-54-T. *Supra* note 139. ¶ 212.

[1133] U.N. Doc. S/2005/60 (Feb. 1, 2005). ¶¶ 238, 241–250, 254–256, 269–279, 285–288, 301–317, 364–367.

[1134] *Idem.* ¶¶ 274, 362, 365–373, 379.

[1135] Reports showed that some civilians lost up to 17 family members due to Sudan Government attacks in the mountains. (*Idem.* ¶ 274).

[1136] *Idem.* ¶ 365.

With the use of heavy weaponry, such as AK-47s, RPGs, Garanovs, Kal-ashnikovs, G-3s, G-4 assault rifles, Katyusha Hawns 106, Hawns 120 DShK, 12.7-mm machine guns mounted on vehicles, and rocket-propelled gre-nades, Government forces, and rebels killed thousands of civilians, includ-ing women, children, and the elderly. They perpetrated abductions, en-forced disappearances and summary executions, burned civilian houses, destroyed schools and hospitals, perpetrated wanton destruction of vil-lages or devastation not justified by military necessity, destroyed wells, and looted private properties and livestock.[1137] Helicopters and Antonov aircraft were used during many of the attacks.[1138]

Government soldiers, acting together with Janjaweed planned, orga-nized, and perpetrated several attacks against civilians involving sexual violence and rape.[1139] In Wadi Tina, Northern Darfur, at about 6 in the morning on 7 January 2003, a woman

"was at her home in the village of Tarne. Around 3,000 Janjaweed riding horses and camels attacked the village. Around 8 in the morning on the sec-ond day at the wadi, [she] was raped for the first time. A very large group of Janjaweed arrived at the wadi. They selected a woman each and raped them. Over a period of a week, [she] was raped 14 times by different Janjaweed. [She] told them to stop. They said 'you are women of *Torabora* and we will not stop this'. [Women] were called slaves and frequently beaten with leather straps, punched and slapped. [She] feared for [her] life if [she] [did] not have sex with them. [The women] were humiliated in front of other women and were forced to have sex in front of them. Other Janjaweed were watching."[1140]

In another chilling incident outside the Zam Zam camp, three separate groups of women were sexually attacked at a government road checkpoint in Northern Darfur:

"Approximately 2 km after the checkpoint, around 20 soldiers dressed in camouflage uniforms drove up to the group of women and ordered them to stop while firing some gunshots. The women were told to get down off their donkeys and lie on the ground. The witness was holding her sister-in-law's one-year-old child, who started to cry. One of the soldiers grabbed the child and threw it away on the side of the road. [...] Some soldiers held one of the other women down and started raping her. At the same time, the witness

---

[1137]  *Idem.* p. 3, ¶¶ 242, 252–253, 255, 269, 274. 349, 387–388.
[1138]  *Idem.* ¶¶ 186, 253, 277, 280, 282, 301, 387.
[1139]  *Idem.* ¶¶ 248, 275, 335, 346, 348, 353.
[1140]  *Idem.* ¶ 345.

was held down on the ground by soldiers who also pulled her clothing over her head. Four soldiers then had vaginal intercourse with her, one after the other. The soldiers were about finished raping the five women when the second group of women who went to El Fashir to sell wood arrived at the same location [and also raped the women]."[1141]

Women and young girls, as young as eight years old, were reportedly gang-raped in public, beaten, and whipped while suffering sexual violence, repeatedly raped while held in confinement for several days, and made sexual slaves.[1142] All over Darfur, Government soldiers and the Janjaweed raped women in front of their family members.[1143] Many women and girls became pregnant as a result of rape.[1144] The International Commission of Inquiry on Darfur, created by the U.N. Security Council, concluded that the Janjaweed and Government soldiers perpetrated such patterns of rape and sexual violence with a deliberate strategy to terrorize the civilian population.[1145]

Sudanese government forces and the Janjaweed shelled mountains with mortars, forcing the civilian population to leave their homes and villages.[1146] The United Nations estimated that, in virtue of the attacks, around 1.65 million became internally displaced in Darfur, and more than 200,000 persons became refugees in neighboring Chad.[1147] Thousands suffered from thirst and hunger.[1148] Displaced persons were kept in overcrowded premises with limited food and water. Reportedly, several hundred children died due to disease outbreaks.[1149] Over several days and months, civilians were attacked early in the morning before sunrise and during prayer time.[1150]

Sudanese government detainees were kept in incommunicado detention, locked 24 hours a day in cells with little or no light and ventilation at all for periods reaching months.[1151] Proper medical treatment for sick detainees was inexistent or insufficient.[1152] Reportedly, personnel from the

---

[1141] *Idem.* ¶ 350.
[1142] *Idem.* ¶¶ 333–334, 340–341, 348–349, 351, 353.
[1143] *Idem.* ¶ 346.
[1144] *Idem.* ¶ 334.
[1145] *Idem.* ¶ 353.
[1146] *Idem.* ¶ 325.
[1147] *Idem.* p. 3, ¶¶ 186, 226.
[1148] *Idem.* ¶ 274.
[1149] *Idem.* ¶ 367.
[1150] *Idem.* ¶ 241.
[1151] *Idem.* ¶¶ 370–371.
[1152] *Idem.* ¶ 370.

National Security and Intelligence Service and the Military Intelligence used to extensively torture the detained.[1153]

Most of the victims in Sudan belonged to African tribes, particularly the Fur, Masalit, and Zaghawa tribes.[1154] Nevertheless, the International Commission of Inquiry on Darfur concluded later that "the intent of the attackers was not to destroy an ethnic group as such or part of the group."[1155] Instead, the Commission concluded that the intention of all the attacking forces in Darfur "was to murder all those men they considered as rebels, as well as forcibly expel the whole population so as to vacate the villages and prevent rebels from hiding among or getting support from the local population."[1156]

## 2.1. Destruction and appropriation of private property

### 2.1.1. The Nazi context

Destruction or appropriation of private property constitutes an immemorial practice in armed conflicts, whether internal or international. During the Nazi regime, the SS committed pillage and appropriation of properties on a large scale, particularly goods belonging to the Jewish population. Among the long list of items appropriated from the Jews by the SS were currency in notes or gold, foreign currency, gold bars, gold brooches, gold rings, rings with brilliants, gold earrings, cuff links with brilliants, gold bracelets with brilliants, thousands of watches of most expensive Swiss makes, gold watches, jewels, trinkets, brilliants, thousands of kilos of pearls, hundreds of diamonds, precious stones, corals, old gold and silver coins of high collector's value, valuable stamp collections, pure gold mechanical pencils, binoculars, textiles of all sorts, clothing of all types, linen, feathers for bedding, rags, wallets, razor blades, hair-cutting machines, scissors of all kinds, silver and gold cigarette cases, clinical thermometers, valuable furniture and household items, and other highly valuable items of different types.[1157] [1158]

---

[1153] *Idem.* ¶ 379.

[1154] *Idem.* ¶ 245.

[1155] *Idem.* ¶ 514

[1156] *Ibidem.*

[1157] **United States of America v. Oswald Pohl,** *et al.* **Case 4** (Pohl case) (1947). pp. 706–712, 727–728.

[1158] Pieces containing gold were either to be sold abroad or for melting down. (**United States of America v. Oswald Pohl,** *et al.* **Case 4** (Pohl case) (1947). pp. 711–712).

Other items of low value, such as soap, lotions, and plates, were also confiscated.[1159] SS also appropriated porcelain, platinum, and gold extracted from the teeth of concentration camp inmates.[1160] Items of little value "were either destroyed or given to the population as premiums for good harvests."[1161]

## 2.1.2. The context of the Former Yugoslavia

In the late 1990s, radical governmental discriminatory policies against Bosnian Muslims took place in the Former Yugoslavia, mainly seeking their expulsion from the Yugoslavian territory. Municipalities, mostly inhabited by Muslim civilians, were taken by the military and the police. During and after the take-over of towns and villages, Serb forces systematically and extensively expelled Bosnian Muslims from their homes.[1162]

Serb forces forced Muslims and Serb Croats to surrender their personal belongings to the municipality, to local authorities, or to Bosnian Serb governmental authorities.[1163] Serb forces ordered Muslim detainees to hand over all money and surrender identification documents.[1164] Jewelry and valuables were confiscated.[1165] Even the dead bodies of killed Bosnian Muslims, after mass executions, were searched for valuables by Serb soldiers before burial.[1166]

Acts of destruction, confiscation, appropriation, and plunder of private houses were carried out in multiple municipalities on a permanent basis with the deliberate discriminatory intent against Bosnian Muslims and Bosnian Croats. These acts were based on the victims' identity *as belonging*

---

[1159]  *Idem.* p. 727.

[1160]  *Idem.* pp. 476–478.

[1161]  *Idem.* pp. 727–728.

[1162]  Prosecutor v. Momčilo Krajišnik. IT-00-39-T. *Supra* note 121. ¶ 824; Prosecutor v. Radovan Karadžić. IT-95-5/18-T, vol. 1. *Supra* note 134. ¶¶ 2539–2540.

[1163]  Prosecutor v. Radislav Krstić. IT-98-33-A. *Supra* note 129. ¶ 37; Prosecutor v. Momčilo Krajišnik. IT-00-39-T. *Supra* note 121. ¶¶ 765, 821, 823; Prosecutor v. Milan Martić. IT-95-11-T. *Supra* note 105. ¶ 288; Prosecutor v. Radovan Karadžić. IT-95-5/18-T, vol. 1. *Supra* note 134. ¶¶ 1342, 2539, 2542, 2544.

[1164]  Prosecutor v. Mićo Stanišić, Stojan Župljanin. IT-08-91-T, vol. 1. *Supra* note 102. ¶ 585; Prosecutor v. Radovan Karadžić. IT-95-5/18-T, vol. 1. *Supra* note 134. ¶¶ 1201, 1306, 2542.

[1165]  Prosecutor v. Blagoje Simić *et al.* IT-95-9-T. *Supra* note 78. ¶ 846; Prosecutor v. Momčilo Krajišnik. IT-00-39-T. *Supra* note 121. ¶ 823; Prosecutor v. Radovan Karadžić. IT-95-5/18-T, vol. 1. *Supra* note 134. ¶¶ 1201, 1306, 2542.

[1166]  Prosecutor v. Radovan Karadžić. IT-95-5/18-T, vol. 1. *Supra* note 134. ¶ 2542.

*to a legally protected group.*[1167] Serb forces looted businesses and other establishments, such as restaurants, shops, offices, cafés, and gas stations belonging to Muslims.[1168] Goods taken out of factories were appropriated.[1169] While Serb Forces were specifically ordered to destroy all Bosnian Muslim private and commercial property and finally give them to the Serbs, private property/houses owned by Serbs were not touched.[1170]

## 2.2. Use of derogatory language, religious discrimination, and destruction of Mosques in the former Yugoslavia

Frequently, the Serbian military and police personnel verbally abused the Muslims, calling them "Balijas"/"Balija's mothers" and forced them to sing "Chetnik" songs, used derogatory language against women, and stated that they should leave the territory or suffer.[1171] Serbian authorities cursed, threatened, warned, humiliated, and insulted Bosnian Muslims with ethnic slurs and ethnic affirmations such as: "Muslims were simply going to disappear," "Muslims cannot live with others," "Muslims are fictitious people," or "Muslims and Croats must be separated forever."[1172] Serb Forces also forced the detainees to make the sign of the cross, carve crosses with a knife on their bodies, or forced them to sign papers saying that they had "voluntarily joined the Serbian Orthodox religion."[1173] Some

---

[1167] Prosecutor v. Blagoje Simić *et al.* IT-95-9-T. *Supra* note 78. ¶ 873; Prosecutor v. Momčilo Krajišnik. IT-00-39-T. *Supra* note 121. ¶¶ 820–821, 823, 825, 829–830, 833; Prosecutor v. Radovan Karadžić. IT-95-5/18-T, vol. 1. *Supra* note 134. ¶ 2542–2545, 2546, 2555, 2558.

[1168] Prosecutor v. Blagoje Simić *et al.* IT-95-9-T. *Supra* note 78. ¶ 846; Prosecutor v. Momčilo Krajišnik. IT-00-39-T. *Supra* note 121. ¶¶ 773, 823, 829; Prosecutor v. Radovan Karadžić. IT-95-5/18-T, vol. 1. *Supra* note 134. ¶ 2543.

[1169] Prosecutor v. Blagoje Simić *et al.* IT-95-9-T. *Supra* note 78. ¶ 846.

[1170] Prosecutor v. Momčilo Krajišnik. IT-00-39-T. *Supra* note 121. ¶¶ 823, 827; Prosecutor v. Radovan Karadžić. IT-95-5/18-T, vol. 1. *Supra* note 134. ¶¶ 2543, 2555; Prosecutor v. Ratko Mladić. IT-09-92-T, vol. 2. *Supra* note 137. ¶ 1762.

[1171] Prosecutor v. Blagoje Simić *et al.* IT-95-9-T. *Supra* note 78. ¶ 726; Prosecutor v. Radovan Karadžić. IT-95-5/18-T, vol. 1. *Supra* note 134. ¶¶ 1325, 1332, 1361, 2494, 2514.

[1172] Prosecutor v. Zdravko Tolimir. IT-05-88/2-A. *Supra* note 152. ¶ 576; Prosecutor v. Radovan Karadžić. IT-95-5/18-T, vol. 1. *Supra* note 134. ¶¶ 1033, 1035, 1477, 1306, 1826, 2516, 2494, 2496, 2514, 2756.

[1173] Prosecutor v. Radovan Karadžić. IT-95-5/18-T, vol. 1. *Supra* note 134. ¶¶ 1013, 1325, 2494, 2277.

victims were also forced to commit acts contrary to the Muslim faith, such as eating pork and drinking beer.[1174]

Through loudspeakers and radio broadcasts, Bosnian Serb leaders and soldiers made announcements with the objective of "creating fear and inciting inter-ethnic hatred amongst the population."[1175] They ordered that Muslim men should surrender their documents, women, and children or else be killed.[1176] In Foča, for example,

> "Bosnian Serb leaders made radio announcements that it was no longer possible for Bosnian Serbs to live with their Bosnian Muslim neighbors, that they could not be woken every morning by the hodza from the mosque, and that 'the time had come for the Serbs to settle accounts with the balijas once and for all, and that the Serbs would no longer allow their ribs to be broken.'"[1177]

In a context of a wider discriminatory attack against Muslims in the Former Yugoslavia, Serbian military and police intentionally targeted for wanton destruction of personal religious symbols of significance to the Bosnian Muslim or Bosnian Croat people.[1178] The perpetrators' intent was "to wipe out traces of the Muslim culture and religion."[1179] Mosques – even those under UNESCO protection –, were intentionally damaged, demolished with heavy machinery, burned, used to store weapons and for training, shelled, destroyed by Serb Forces with tanks or explosives, or converted for another use such as being flattened and used as a parking lot.[1180] Serb forces used the minarets of the mosques to play Serbian music.[1181] The minarets were also targeted and blown up with explosives to be finally razed to the ground.[1182] Even the tombs of mosques' adjacent cemeteries were also removed.[1183]

---

[1174] *Idem.* ¶ 2494.

[1175] *Idem.* ¶ 2598.

[1176] *Idem.* ¶¶ 759, 983.

[1177] *Idem.* ¶ 2515.

[1178] Prosecutor v. Milomir Stakić. IT-97-24-T. *Supra* note 109. ¶ 811; Prosecutor v. Momčilo Krajišnik. IT-00-39-T. *Supra* note 121. ¶¶ 780, 838; Prosecutor v. Mićo Stanišić, Stojan Župljanin. IT-08-91-T, vol. 1. *Supra* note 102. ¶ 524.

[1179] Prosecutor v. Momčilo Krajišnik. IT-00-39-T. *Supra* note 121. ¶ 838.

[1180] Prosecutor v. Mićo Stanišić, Stojan Župljanin. IT-08-91-T, vol. 1. *Supra* note 102. ¶¶ 525–526; Prosecutor v. Radovan Karadžić. IT-95-5/18-T, vol. 1. *Supra* note 134. ¶ ¶ 925, 927, 1039, 1068, 1354, 1356–1357, 1359, 1453, 1455, 1606, 1887, 1889, 2552.

[1181] *Idem.* ¶ 1355.

[1182] Prosecutor v. Mićo Stanišić, Stojan Župljanin. IT-08-91-T, vol. 1. *Supra* note 102. ¶ 526.

## 2.3. Mass executions

### 2.3.1. Mass executions in Rwanda

Throughout 1994, an official policy of mass extermination of Tutsis was put into action in Rwanda by the Hutus. It involved different levels of government power and local officials, with the participation of Rwandan soldiers, gendarmes, militia, and demobilized soldiers.[1184] Under the instructions of military Tharcisse Renzaho, which were broadcast on Radio Rwanda, roadblocks and checkpoints were built by Hutus with the intent to "intercept, identify and kill Tutsis."[1185] Tutsi civilians had been targeted solely based on their ethnicity.[1186] Following the crash of Rwanda's President's plane on 6 April 1994, Hutus alleged that Tutsis were involved in the event.[1187] Since then, Hutus regarded the Tutsi as the "enemies" of Rwanda.[1188] Hutus widely and systematically abducted and killed thousands of Tutsis in these interceptions.[1189]

During the same period, the Hutu Jean-Paul Akayesu, the mayor of Taba, one of Rwanda's communes, instructed the Interahamwe, militias, the communal police, and local people to perpetrate mass killings of intellectual and influential Tutsi people at the roadblocks and in the bureaus communal.[1190] Tutsi intellectuals, particularly teachers of all instruction levels, were considered by Hutus as "the source of all of the misery in Rwanda."[1191] [1192] Under the orders of Akayesu, teachers were bound, tied, kicked in the chest, beaten with guns, clubs, hoes, and sticks, and suffered other atrocious kinds of torture.[1193] Akayesu also ordered the killing of teachers with machetes and blows to the neck with agricultural tools.[1194] Hutus also killed Tutsi teachers with bullets and grenades.[1195]

---

[1183] Prosecutor v. Radovan Karadžić. IT-95-5/18-T, vol. 1. *Supra* note 134. ¶ 1453.
[1184] Prosecutor v. Tharcisse Renzaho. ICTR-97-31-T. *Supra* note 232. ¶ 116.
[1185] *Ibidem.*
[1186] *Idem.* ¶ 5.
[1187] Prosecutor v. Jean-Paul Akayesu. ICTR-96-4-T. *Supra* note 203. ¶ 123.
[1188] Prosecutor v. Tharcisse Renzaho. ICTR-97-31-T. *Supra* note 232. ¶ 180.
[1189] Prosecutor v. Pauline Nyiramasuhuko *et al.* ICTR-98-42-A. *Supra* note 220. ¶ 2125.
[1190] Prosecutor v. Jean-Paul Akayesu. ICTR-96-4-T. *Supra* note 203. ¶¶ 20–21, 288–289, 313.
[1191] *Idem.* ¶ 288–289.
[1192] See also: *Idem.* ¶¶ 20, 427.
[1193] *Idem.* ¶¶ 21, 288.
[1194] *Idem.* ¶¶ 20, 313.
[1195] *Idem.* ¶ 288.

Many teachers were left to die a slow death, being buried alive in ditches and mass graves.[1196]

In Rwanda, Hutus persecuted Tutsis based on their ethnicity in a widespread and systematic manner, seeking to destroy them as they fled from mass executions.[1197] In 1994, thousands of Tutsi civilians, mostly women, children, and elderly people, suffering persecution from different entities, sought refuge in the premises of churches, parishes, mosques, and communal offices. As Tutsis took refuge in these places, the Rwandan Interahamwe attacked them with all sorts of guns, grenades, bladed weapons, and machetes.[1198]

At church premises, the Interahamwe deliberately slaughtered, tortured, and threatened Tutsi victims over multiple days.[1199] Women and girls were repeatedly raped.[1200] In many instances, the Interahamwe demolished the churches with the use of bulldozers to crush those inside to death.[1201] Some Interahamwe attacks killed 2,000 or 6,000 refugees at once.[1202] Such multiple large-scale attacks were deliberately planned, instigated, and ordered by Hutu's official commanders and Interahamwe leaders.[1203] These commanders and leaders knew that their acts formed part of a broader attack against the Tutsi.[1204] The International Criminal Tribunal for Rwanda later concluded that these atrocities were committed by Hutus "as part of a widespread or systematic attack against the Tutsi civilian population on ethnic grounds" and, therefore, constituted a crime against humanity.[1205]

---

[1196]  *Idem.* ¶¶ 288, 427.

[1197]  Prosecutor v. Gaspard Kanyarukiga. ICTR-2002-78-T. *Supra* note 187. ¶ 663.

[1198]  Prosecutor v. Jean-Paul Akayesu. ICTR-96-4-T. *Supra* note 203. ¶ 424; Prosecutor v. Yussuf Munyakazi. ICTR-97-36A-T. *Supra* note 236. ¶¶ 323, 341.

[1199]  Prosecutor v. Brima, Kamara, Kanu. SCSL-04-16-T. *Supra* note 280. ¶ 932; Prosecutor v. Yussuf Munyakazi. ICTR-97-36A-T. *Supra* note 236. ¶ 322; Prosecutor v. Gaspard Kanyarukiga. ICTR-2002-78-T. *Supra* note 187. ¶ 661.

[1200]  Prosecutor v. Jean-Paul Akayesu. ICTR-96-4-T. *Supra* note 203. ¶ 438.

[1201]  Prosecutor v. Gaspard Kanyarukiga. ICTR-2002-78-T. *Supra* note 187. ¶¶ 645, 649, 661, 663.

[1202]  *Idem.* ¶ 666.

[1203]  Prosecutor v. Yussuf Munyakazi. ICTR-97-36A-T. *Supra* note 236. ¶ 322; Prosecutor v. Gaspard Kanyarukiga. ICTR-2002-78-T. *Supra* note 187. ¶ 663; Prosecutor v. Jean-Baptiste Gatete. ICTR-2000-61-T. *Supra* note 195. ¶ 641.

[1204]  Prosecutor v. Gaspard Kanyarukiga. ICTR-2002-78-T. *Supra* note 187. ¶ 664.

[1205]  *Ibidem.* See also: ¶ 645.

## 2.3.2. Mass executions in the Former Yugoslavia

In the late 1990s in the former Yugoslavia, Serbian authorities subjected to mass executions Muslim detainees, including women, children as young as three years old, and elderly as old as 85 years old.[1206] Victims were shot multiple times with guns and automatic rifles, individually or in groups, while in seclusion in detention camps or while trying to escape.[1207] They were frequently shot through the mouth, blindfolded shot, shot with their hands tied behind their necks, shot lined up in rows, shot from behind, or even tied together in pairs.[1208] When the shooting stopped, Serbian soldiers proceeded to certify that all the victims were dead and to pile up the dead bodies with loaders, tractors, excavators, bulldozers, caterpillars, scrappers, and mechanical diggers.[1209] Soldiers then proceeded to transport/load the bodies onto trucks, buses, and containers and to dispose of them in mass graves.[1210] Majorly, the victims that were later found in the graves by independent international authorities were dressed in civilian clothing.[1211]

As a mass execution policy of Serbian authorities, Bosnian Muslims or Bosnian Croats were deliberately used as human shields on the front lines

---

[1206] Prosecutor v. Vidoje Blagojević, Dragan Jokić. IT-02-60-T. *Supra* note 147. ¶ 346, 354, 362; Prosecutor v. Radovan Karadžić. IT-95-5/18-T, vol. 1. *Supra* note 134. ¶¶ 1064, 1142–1143, 1146; Prosecutor v. Ratko Mladić. IT-09-92-T, vol. 2. *Supra* note 137. ¶ 1762.

[1207] Prosecutor v. Slobodan Milošević. IT-02-54-T. *Supra* note 139. ¶¶ 198, 211, 218; Prosecutor v. Vidoje Blagojević, Dragan Jokić. IT-02-60-T. *Supra* note 147. ¶¶ 295, 312–313, 328, 341, 346, 355; Prosecutor v. Radovan Karadžić. IT-95-5/18-T, vol. 1. *Supra* note 134. ¶¶ 1064, 1146.

[1208] Prosecutor v. Slobodan Milošević. IT-02-54-T. *Supra* note 139. ¶¶ 161, 211–212, 218; Prosecutor v. Vidoje Blagojević, Dragan Jokić. IT-02-60-T. *Supra* note 147. ¶¶ 295, 313, 341; Prosecutor v. Radovan Karadžić. IT-95-5/18-T, vol. 1. *Supra* note 134. ¶¶ 1064, 1142, 1146, 1869.

[1209] Prosecutor v. Vidoje Blagojević, Dragan Jokić. IT-02-60-T. *Supra* note 147. ¶¶ 310, 328, 342, 352–353, 360; Prosecutor v. Radovan Karadžić. IT-95-5/18-T, vol. 1. *Supra* note 134. ¶ 1143.

[1210] Prosecutor v. Milomir Stakić. IT-97-24-T. *Supra* note 109. ¶ 261; Prosecutor v. Slobodan Milošević. IT-02-54-T. *Supra* note 139. ¶¶ 161, 212, 217; Prosecutor v. Vidoje Blagojević, Dragan Jokić. IT-02-60-T. *Supra* note 147. ¶¶ 295, 310–314, 328, 341–342, 346, 352, 353–355; Prosecutor v. Momčilo Krajišnik. IT-00-39-T. *Supra* note 121. ¶ 1074; Prosecutor v. Radovan Karadžić. IT-95-5/18-T, vol. 1. *Supra* note 134. ¶¶ 1143, 1337, 1766, 1869.

[1211] Prosecutor v. Vidoje Blagojević, Dragan Jokić. IT-02-60-T. *Supra* note 147. ¶¶ 295, 346, 354, 362; Prosecutor v. Radovan Karadžić. IT-95-5/18-T, vol. 1. *Supra* note 134. ¶¶ 1064, 1146.

to protect Serb Forces or killed due to explosive blasts and grenades.[1212] As a consequence, the Muslim detainees lived in constant fear of being executed at any time by Bosnian soldiers and military personnel.[1213] Besides, Muslims were coercively forced to leave their homes based on discriminatory ethnic/religious grounds. As part of a widespread and systematic attack, Serbian soldiers and police separated men, women, and children with the objective of dissolution of the group through the commission of (i) attacks against their homes; (ii) shelling of villages; (iii) destruction of mosques and other property; (iv) forcible arrest and removal from their homes; (v) detention in multiple detention facilities; (vi) mistreatment and killings.[1214]

## 2.4. Physical violence

### 2.4.1. Physical violence in Nazi concentration camps and the occupied territories

SS Nazi troops committed atrocious cruelties against civilians in the occupied territories during German expansion. They also committed cruel acts against prisoners in protective custody in concentration camps, rendering the victims helpless.[1215] Among the brutalities imposed, SS officers: 1) perpetrated extreme beatings using guns, whips, clubs, and everything that was on the hand of SS men, causing deep unconsciousness or even death of victims; 2) tied persons in chains and then applied tourniquets; 3) crushed the fingers of persons with thumbscrews; 4) burned the skin of victims with cigarettes; 5) tortured with drip-apparatus, "under which the prisoners had to stand so long that they came away with serious purulent wounds on the scalp;" 6) lashed the back of concentration camp inmates

---

[1212] Prosecutor v. Vidoje Blagojević, Dragan Jokić. IT-02-60-T. *Supra* note 147. ¶¶ 312, 355; Prosecutor v. Momčilo Krajišnik. IT-00-39-T. *Supra* note 121. ¶¶ 763, 819; Prosecutor v. Radovan Karadžić. IT-95-5/18-T, vol. 1. *Supra* note 134. ¶¶ 2444, 2452, 2534, 2536–2537.

[1213] Prosecutor v. Radovan Karadžić. IT-95-5/18-T, vol. 1. *Supra* note 134. ¶ 1766.

[1214] Prosecutor v. Vidoje Blagojević, Dragan Jokić. IT-02-60-T. *Supra* note 147. ¶¶ 660, 675; Prosecutor v. Momčilo Krajišnik. IT-00-39-T. *Supra* note 121. ¶¶ 807–808; Prosecutor v. Mićo Stanišić, Stojan Župljanin. IT-08-91-T, vol. 1. *Supra* note 102. ¶ 686; Prosecutor v. Radovan Karadžić. IT-95-5/18-T, vol. 1. *Supra* note 134. ¶¶ 1004, 1006, 1039–1040, 1186, 1256, 1273, 1331, 1333, 1465.

[1215] 30 Trial of the Major War Criminals before the International Military Tribunal (1948). p. 465; 36 Trial of the Major War Criminals before the International Military Tribunal (1949). p. 91.

with barbed wire sticks; 7) castrated men; 8) perpetrated floggings; 9) placed persons in bloodstained coffins; 10) deliberately threw grenades against inmates; 11) perpetrated punitive detachments on civilians and concentration camp inmates for minor reasons such as be found smoking cigarettes; 12) urinated into the mouth of inmates.[1216] [1217] [1218] Although wounded victims cried in a loud voice for help, they could not be taken into care. Those who dared to help them were shot down by the SS men.[1219]

In 1944, the SS completed the construction of gas chambers to put into action the "final solution" – Hitler's plan to kill hundreds of thousands of Jews.[1220] In the Nuremberg Trials, the Nazi-German Colonel Amen provided a disturbing description of this process in Auschwitz, comparing it to Treblinka. In his own words:

> "Another improvement we made over Treblinka was that we built our gas chamber to accommodate 2,000 people at one time whereas at Treblinka their 10 gas chambers only accommodated 200 people each. The way we selected our victims was as follows: We had two SS doctors on duty at Auschwitz to examine the incoming transports of prisoners. The prisoners would be marched by one of the doctors who would make spot decisions as they walked by. Those who were fit for work were sent into the camp. Others were sent immediately to the extermination plants. Still another improve-

---

[1216] **United States of America v. Oswald Pohl, et al. Case 4** (Pohl case) (1947). pp. 471–472; 4 Trial of the Major War Criminals before the International Military Tribunal (1947). pp. 140–141; 30 Trial of the Major War Criminals before the International Military Tribunal (1948). pp. 389, 465; 36 Trial of the Major War Criminals before the International Military Tribunal (1949). p. 91.

[1217] "The inmates were harnessed before heavy rollers, and then they had to pull these rollers back and forth across a square of the newly established camp, and the new camp road which was being constructed. In this way they were to make the soil more solid on the square and on the road." (**United States of America v. Oswald Pohl, et al. Case 4** (Pohl case) (1947). p. 471).

[1218] "Apart from the work, the Jews received various forms of corporal punishment. I recall one case where one was hit over the head with a pick by a kapo. One of the usual punishments was to make the inmates carry bricks wherever they went, for each slight infraction. Sometimes an inmate would carry as many as 5 or 6 bricks. These he would have to take wherever he went, to eat, to sleep, everywhere. Also, just to amuse themselves, the Germans would ride their bicycles and have inmates trot behind them wherever they went, as dogs." (**United States of America v. Carl Krauch, et al.** Case 6, Volume 8 (I.G. Farben case) (1947). p. 624).

[1219] 36 Trial of the Major War Criminals before the International Military Tribunal (1949). p. 91.

[1220] 5 Trial of the Major War Criminals before the International Military Tribunal (1947). pp. 172–173.

ment we made over Treblinka was that at Treblinka the victims almost always knew that they were to be exterminated and at Auschwitz we endeavored to fool the victims into thinking that they were to go through a delousing process."[1221]

Two practices were common after the dead bodies were removed from the gas chambers, removing human skin from the backs and chests and removing teeth. After the removal, the human skin

> "was chemically treated and placed in the sun to dry. After that it was cut into various sizes for use as saddles, riding breeches, gloves, house slippers, and ladies" handbags. Tattooed skin was especially valued by SS men. Russians, Poles, and other inmates were used in this way, but it was forbidden to cut out the skin of a German. This skin had to be from healthy prisoners and free from defects."[1222]

Sometimes, when the number of human skins was inferior to what SS demanded, perfectly healthy young inmates would be killed exclusively to remove their skin.[1223] SS officers would inject deadly substances or shoot victims in the face so that the skin could be uninjured.[1224] After this process, all teeth containing gold and porcelain were extracted to be further sold.[1225] In this way, persons having good skin or good teeth in the concentration camps were always at imminent risk of being killed.[1226] In many cases, SS officers also requested that prisoners' skulls and skeletons were removed for further enterprises.[1227] In these cases, the skull or the body were boiled.[1228] After that, "the soft parts were removed, and the bones were bleached, dried and reassembled."[1229]

Because children of tender years were unable to work in the camps, they were invariably "exterminated."[1230] Because the gas chambers were usually full of adults, children were not gassed most of the time but just

---

[1221] 11 Trial of the Major War Criminals before the International Military Tribunal (1947). p. 417.

[1222] 5 Trial of the Major War Criminals before the International Military Tribunal (1947). pp. 171–172.

[1223] *Ibidem.*

[1224] *Idem.* pp. 172–173.

[1225] *Ibidem.*

[1226] *Ibidem.*

[1227] *Ibidem.*

[1228] *Ibidem.*

[1229] *Ibidem.*

[1230] 11 Trial of the Major War Criminals before the International Military Tribunal (1947). p. 417.

burned alive on big piles of sheets of wood and gasoline or burned in open fields with grills.[1231] As children cried helplessly in a loud voice,

> "the [Auschwitz] camp administration ordered that an orchestra be made by a hundred inmates and should play. They played very loud all the time. They played the Blue Danube or Rosamunde; so that even the people in the city of Auschwitz could not hear the screams. Without the orchestra, they would have heard the screams of horror; they would have been horrible screams. The people two kilometers from there could even hear those screams, namely, that came from the transports of children."[1232] [1233]

If a child happened to be burned to death by more "merciful" SS people, they would first beat the child's head "against a stone before putting it on the pile of fire and wood, so that the child lost consciousness [before being killed]."[1234] It is estimated that the Nazis killed several thousand children in this manner in the concentration camps.[1235]

## 2.4.2. Physical violence in the context of Rwanda and Sierra Leone

Throughout 1994, as part of a broad intent to destroy Rwanda's Tutsi population, Hutus submitted hundreds of thousands of Tutsis to barbaric acts of torture and physical violence in the Rwandan territory.[1236] As a hallmark of Hutu militia policy, Tutsis were beaten with clubs, machetes, small axes, and metal sticks to the point that their bones were broken or they could no longer walk.[1237] Tutsi women and girls were forcefully undressed in pub-

---

[1231] **United States of America v. Oswald Pohl, et al. Case 4** (Pohl case) (1947). pp. 662–663.

[1232] *Idem.* p. 663.

[1233] In a chilling hearing at Nuremberg, the Nazi Germain Colonel Amen stated that "very frequently women would hide their children under the clothes, but of course when we found them we would send the children in to be exterminated. We were required to carry out these exterminations in secrecy but of course the foul and nauseating stench from the continuous burning of bodies permeated the entire area and all of the people living in the surrounding communities knew that exterminations were going on at Auschwitz." (11 Trial of the Major War Criminals before the International Military Tribunal (1947). p. 417).

[1234] **United States of America v. Oswald Pohl, et al. Case 4** (Pohl case) (1947). p. 663.

[1235] *Ibidem.*

[1236] Prosecutor v. Gaspard Kanyarukiga. ICTR-2002-78-T. *Supra* note 187. ¶ 660; Édouard Karemera et al v. Prosecutor. ICTR-98-44-A. *Supra* note 173. ¶ 606.

[1237] Prosecutor v. Jean-Paul Akayesu. ICTR-96-4-T. *Supra* note 203. ¶¶ 17, 19, 396; Prosecutor v. Tharcisse Renzaho. ICTR-97-31-T. *Supra* note 232. ¶ 671.

lic, beaten, tortured, raped, and humiliated.[1238] Pregnant women were beaten on their bellies to the point of causing premature deliveries or miscarriages.[1239]

In Sierra Leone, after 1999, RUF and AFRC fighters, Kamajors, and rebels beat to death, shot to death, and hacked to death large numbers of civilians indiscriminately, including babies, children, and women, with the sole objective of humiliating and dominating Sierra Leone communities during the armed conflict.[1240] Frequently, captured civilians "were stripped naked and forced to laugh, and line-up before the rebels molested and defiled them."[1241] In one instance, "the Kamajors slit open the stomach of one victim and displayed his entrails in a bucket before the remaining civilians."[1242] On another occasion, rebels using a machete "cleaved" a child in two, ironically as a "sacrifice for peace."[1243] At the bridges near Kamboma, Kamajors ordered the killing of anyone who passed by.[1244]

In addition, AFRC/RUF, rebels, Kamajors, and other retreating forces perpetrated other horrific crimes of physical violence against a large number of civilians.[1245] They committed acts such as floggings, cutting off body parts, shootings in the stomach, beatings (while tied up, often to death), knocking out of teeth of victims' mouths, throwing of boiling water on victims, collective punishment, the carving of the letters "RUF" or "AFRC" on the victims' bodies, and beheadings.[1246] Civilians were also extensively used as human shields.[1247] As a demonstration of power, rebels systematically "disemboweled civilians, and their intestines were stretched across a road to form a barrier. Human heads were placed on sticks on either side of the road to mark such barriers."[1248]

---

[1238]  *Idem.* ¶¶ 437, 449.

[1239]  *Idem.* ¶ 437.

[1240]  Prosecutor v. Brima, Kamara, Kanu. SCSL-04-16-T. *Supra* note 280. ¶ 34; Prosecutor v. Sesay, Kallon and Gbao. SCSL-04-15-T. *Supra* note 279. ¶¶ 107, 118.

[1241]  Prosecutor v. Sesay, Kallon and Gbao. SCSL-04-15-T. *Supra* note 279. ¶ 118.

[1242]  Prosecutor v. Fofana, Kondewa. SCSL-04-14-T. *Supra* note 281. ¶ 386.

[1243]  Prosecutor v. Sesay, Kallon and Gbao. SCSL-04-15-T. *Supra* note 268. ¶ 1598.

[1244]  Prosecutor v. Fofana, Kondewa. SCSL-04-14-T. *Supra* note 281. ¶ 406.

[1245]  Prosecutor v. Sesay, Kallon and Gbao. SCSL-04-15-T. *Supra* note 279. ¶ 153.

[1246]  Prosecutor v. Brima, Kamara, Kanu. SCSL-04-16-T. *Supra* note 280. ¶ 34; Prosecutor v. Fofana, Kondewa. SCSL-04-14-T. *Supra* note 281. ¶¶ 405, 421, 653; Prosecutor v. Sesay, Kallon and Gbao. SCSL-04-15-T. *Supra* note 279. ¶¶ 146–147, 153; Prosecutor v. Taylor. SCSL-03-01-T. *Supra* note 270. ¶¶ 863, 1219, 1311, 1631.

[1247]  Prosecutor v. Sesay, Kallon and Gbao. SCSL-04-15-T. *Supra* note 268. ¶ 1598; Prosecutor v. Taylor. SCSL-03-01-T. *Supra* note 270. ¶ 936.

[1248]  Prosecutor v. Brima, Kamara, Kanu. SCSL-04-16-T. *Supra* note 280. ¶ 34.

As a widespread and systematic practice, AFRC troops and "Juntas" burned several innocent civilians alive, including an alarming number of children.[1249] Reports showed that children as young as a five-year-old girl were burned alive.[1250] Young children were usually locked in houses that were set ablaze or placed under mattresses set on fire.[1251] Pregnant women were also mainly targeted without any apparent reason, either by RUF or AFRC fighters or by Sierra Leone soldiers. Victims were violently beaten, stabbed, and raped, usually until death.[1252] For instance, AFRC troops and armed soldiers split open the belly of pregnant women and removed the fetuses.[1253] In a brutal demonstration of the insignificance of life and human dignity, "pregnant women were killed by having their stomachs slit open, and the foetus [sic] removed merely to settle a bet amongst the troops as to the gender of the foetus [sic]."[1254]

The suffering of civilians in their family unit was horrifying. Fighters or soldiers forced civilian families into brutal acts of cruelty and mental trauma: married couples were ordered to strip and to have sexual intercourse in public or otherwise face death; sons were forced by rebels and soldiers to rape mothers; daughters were forced to touch their fathers' penises publicly; brothers were forced to rape sisters; parents were subjected to physical and sexual violence in the presence of their children; victims "were made to choose between their own lives or those of their family members" and to observe one family member killed in their presence.[1255] After death, civilians received orders from soldiers or rebels to bury the corpses of their loved ones.[1256]

---

[1249]  Prosecutor v. Brima, Kamara, Kanu. SCSL-04-16-T. *Supra* note 280. ¶¶ 34, 888; Prosecutor v. Sesay, Kallon and Gbao. SCSL-04-15-T. *Supra* note 279. ¶ 107.

[1250]  Prosecutor v. Taylor. SCSL-03-01-T. *Supra* note 270. ¶ 1318.

[1251]  Prosecutor v. Brima, Kamara, Kanu. SCSL-04-16-T. *Supra* note 280. ¶¶ 888, 1561; Prosecutor v. Sesay, Kallon and Gbao. SCSL-04-15-T. *Supra* note 279. ¶ 147.

[1252]  Prosecutor v. Brima, Kamara, Kanu. SCSL-04-16-T. *Supra* note 280. ¶¶ 412, 888, 1561; Prosecutor v. Sesay, Kallon and Gbao. SCSL-04-15-T. *Supra* note 279. ¶ 125.

[1253]  Prosecutor v. Brima, Kamara, Kanu. SCSL-04-16-T. *Supra* note 280. ¶¶ 1555, 1561.

[1254]  *Idem.* ¶ 34.

[1255]  Prosecutor v. Brima, Kamara, Kanu. SCSL-04-16-T. *Supra* note 280. ¶ 34. See also: Prosecutor v. Sesay, Kallon and Gbao. SCSL-04-15-T. *Supra* note 268. ¶ 1560; Prosecutor v. Sesay, Kallon and Gbao. SCSL-04-15-T. *Supra* note 279. ¶¶ 109, 118, 120, 126, 148.

[1256]  Prosecutor v. Sesay, Kallon and Gbao. SCSL-04-15-T. *Supra* note 279. ¶ 118

## 2.4.2.1. Mutilations in Sierra Leone

Amputations and mutilations constituted a hallmark of the AFRC/RUF, rebels, Kamajors, and other retreating forces in Sierra Leone.[1257] An unknown number of innocent civilians – estimated to be in the thousands – were subjected to this type of crime from 1999 until the end of the civil conflict.[1258] Civilians were subjected to horrific amputations, including amputation of arms and hands (unilateral and bilateral), fingers, feet, breasts, lips, and ears.[1259] An extensive number of witnesses testified "that rebels asked civilians whether they wanted short sleeves or long sleeves and their arms were amputated either at the elbow or at the wrist accordingly."[1260] In bilateral amputations, the victims had both their right and left arms/hands amputated.

Shockingly, AFRC/RUF and other retreating forces would perform tongue amputations and eyeball amputations against civilians, including children, women, and young nursing mothers "to prevent [them] from telling others who had committed these acts against [them]."[1261] Chillingly, Kamajors used to sing songs while mutilating and amputating women and children.[1262] Amputated body parts were usually piled on the streets, tied together and displaced in public places, placed in big plastic bags, or simply buried in the dirt.[1263]

Such atrocity extensively affected children in at least three ways:

**First)** AFRC/RUF, rebels, Kamajors, and other retreating forces amputated hundreds of children. In one instance, a 13-year-old young girl had both hands amputated.[1264] In another instance, the rebels "captured a boy named Samuel, whom they suspected of being a Kamajor, and severed both his hands and cut out his tongue."[1265] Then, the rebels placed a bag over his

---

[1257] Prosecutor v. Brima, Kamara, Kanu. SCSL-04-16-T. *Supra* note 280. ¶ 34; Prosecutor v. Sesay, Kallon and Gbao. SCSL-04-15-T. *Supra* note 268. ¶ 1521.

[1258] Prosecutor v. Taylor. SCSL-03-01-T. *Supra* note 270. ¶ 1351.

[1259] Prosecutor v. Brima, Kamara, Kanu. SCSL-04-16-T. *Supra* note 280. ¶¶ 34, 412; Prosecutor v. Sesay, Kallon and Gbao. SCSL-04-15-T. *Supra* note 268. ¶¶ 1521, 1554, 1556; Prosecutor v. Sesay, Kallon and Gbao. SCSL-04-15-T. *Supra* note 279. ¶ 146; Prosecutor v. Taylor. SCSL-03-01-T. *Supra* note 270. ¶ 1269.

[1260] Prosecutor v. Sesay, Kallon and Gbao. SCSL-04-15-T. *Supra* note 268. ¶ 1521.

[1261] Prosecutor v. Taylor. SCSL-03-01-T. *Supra* note 270. ¶¶ 1269–1270, 1319.

[1262] Prosecutor v. Fofana, Kondewa. SCSL-04-14-T. *Supra* note 281. ¶ 421

[1263] Prosecutor v. Sesay, Kallon and Gbao. SCSL-04-15-T. *Supra* note 268. ¶ 1554; Prosecutor v. Sesay, Kallon and Gbao. SCSL-04-15-T. *Supra* note 279. ¶ 118; Prosecutor v. Taylor. SCSL-03-01-T. *Supra* note 270. ¶ 1319.

[1264] Prosecutor v. Taylor. SCSL-03-01-T. *Supra* note 270. ¶ 1319.

[1265] Prosecutor v. Sesay, Kallon and Gbao. SCSL-04-15-T. *Supra* note 268. ¶ 1559.

head with a written message for the ECOMOG, that the rebels "were around and would be back" to commit more atrocities.[1266] [1267] In Koidu, rebels inflicted severe physical violence on a 15-year-old boy. The boy had both hands "amputated at the wrist and both his legs were amputated at the ankle. He was then thrown alive into a latrine."[1268] Terrifyingly, "the boy was still crying as the rebels walked away."[1269]

**Second)** AFRC/RUF, rebels, Kamajors, and other retreating forces obliged children to watch their family and loved ones' amputations. On one occasion, after some children saw their mother gang-raped by rebels, they were ordered to watch their father being tied up to a tree and having his left hand amputated.[1270] The amputee later stated that: "My children were sitting in front of me. Where they were put, they were stirring, and they were looking, seeing me because they didn't hide them. They were in the open, and they were seeing what was happening."[1271]

**Third)** AFRC/RUF, rebels, Kamajors, and other retreating forces forced children to perform amputations on civilians.[1272] In one instance, rebels forced a victim to "place his left hand on the wooden log, and the Commando ordered a junior rebel to cut it off."[1273] As children usually did not have the same body strength as adult rebels, their blows sometimes did not entirely amputate the victims' limbs when they attempted to perform amputations.[1274] On different occasions, the Commando had to complete the amputations of victims performed by children.[1275]

Surviving victims of amputations suffered mental and physical consequences to an incalculable degree. Their suffering was immense once their lives "instantly and forever changed into one of dependence."[1276] In Sierra Leone, most of the victims "were turned into beggars, unable to earn any other living and even today cannot perform even the simplest of tasks without the help of others."[1277]

---

[1266] The Economic Community of West African States Monitoring Group (ECOMOG).
[1267] Prosecutor v. Sesay, Kallon and Gbao. SCSL-04-15-T. *Supra* note 268. ¶ 1559.
[1268] Prosecutor v. Sesay, Kallon and Gbao. SCSL-04-15-T. *Supra* note 279. ¶ 150.
[1269] *Ibidem.*
[1270] *Idem.* ¶ 148.
[1271] *Ibidem.*
[1272] Prosecutor v. Sesay, Kallon and Gbao. SCSL-04-15-T. *Supra* note 268. ¶ 1554.
[1273] *Idem.* ¶ 1549.
[1274] *Ibidem.*
[1275] *Ibidem.*
[1276] Prosecutor v. Sesay, Kallon and Gbao. SCSL-04-15-T. *Supra* note 279. ¶ 155.
[1277] Prosecutor v. Brima, Kamara, Kanu. SCSL-04-16-T. *Supra* note 280. ¶ 34.

## 2.4.3. Physical violence in the Former Yugoslavia detention camps

As a general practice, Muslim detainees were beaten/hit by the Serbian military with truncheons, metal bars, baseball bats, police batons, rifle butts, pistol butts, metal chains, thick pipes, grips of guns, sticks, thick electric cables, stakes, metal rods, rubber hoses, pieces of wood, wooden planks, wooden poles, wooden clubs, belts, chair legs, and pliers.[1278] The detainees were stripped to the waist and beaten on all parts of their bodies: on their heads, on their heads and stomachs, on their kidneys, on their hands, and on the soles of their feet.[1279] Prisoners were beaten on arrival, during the first hours of detention, while undergoing interrogations, or during their imprisonment in detention facilities. During beatings, soldiers jumped on detainees, and in many instances, the victims had their hands tied behind their backs.[1280]

After these intense periods of beatings, the floor and the walls of the premises where detainees were beaten were always covered with hair, teeth, skin, blood, and sweat.[1281] There are plenty of documented cases in which the victims were submitted to forced/non-anesthetic extraction of teeth or had their teeth knocked out with fists.[1282] Many of the victims were

---

[1278] Prosecutor v. Milorad Krnojelac. IT-97-25-T. *Supra* note 111. ¶ 280; Prosecutor v. Blagoje Simić *et al.* IT-95-9-T. *Supra* note 78. ¶¶ 696, 703, 711, 719, 733, 770; Prosecutor v. Slobodan Milošević. IT-02-54-T. *Supra* note 139. ¶ 196; Prosecutor v. Milan Martić. IT-95-11-T. *Supra* note 105. ¶ 288; Prosecutor v. Milan Lukić, Sredoje Lukić. IT-98-32/1-T. *Supra* note 104. ¶¶ 801, 821, 978; Prosecutor v. Mićo Stanišić, Stojan Župljanin. IT-08-91-T, vol. 1. *Supra* note 102. ¶¶ 289, 585, 677–678; Prosecutor v. Radovan Karadžić. IT-95-5/18-T, vol. 1. *Supra* note 134. ¶¶ 989, 1010, 1165, 1167, 1177, 1179, 1190, 1201, 1306, 1342, 1352, 1399, 1986.

[1279] Prosecutor v. Vidoje Blagojević, Dragan Jokić. IT-02-60-T. *Supra* note 147. ¶ 310; Prosecutor v. Milan Martić. IT-95-11-T. *Supra* note 105. ¶ 288; Prosecutor v. Radovan Karadžić. IT-95-5/18-T, vol. 1. *Supra* note 134. ¶ 1010.

[1280] Prosecutor v. Vidoje Blagojević, Dragan Jokić. IT-02-60-T. *Supra* note 147. ¶¶ 340, 349; Prosecutor v. Milan Martić. IT-95-11-T. *Supra* note 105. ¶ 288; Prosecutor v. Mićo Stanišić, Stojan Župljanin. IT-08-91-T, vol. 1. *Supra* note 102. ¶ 289, 585, 676; Prosecutor v. Radovan Karadžić. IT-95-5/18-T, vol. 1. *Supra* note 134. ¶¶ 1010, 1013, 1165, 1167, 2277.

[1281] Prosecutor v. Milorad Krnojelac. IT-97-25-T. *Supra* note 111. ¶ 273; Prosecutor v. Blagoje Simić *et al.* IT-95-9-T. *Supra* note 78. ¶ 722; Prosecutor v. Mićo Stanišić, Stojan Župljanin. IT-08-91-T, vol. 1. *Supra* note 102. ¶ 604; Prosecutor v. Radovan Karadžić. IT-95-5/18-T, vol. 1. *Supra* note 134. ¶¶ 991, 1000, 1010, 1300, 1337, 1344, 1399, 1766, 1811, 2502.

[1282] Prosecutor v. Blagoje Simić *et al.* IT-95-9-T. *Supra* note 78. ¶¶ 696, 703, 711, 721, 772; Prosecutor v. Radovan Karadžić. IT-95-5/18-T, vol. 1. *Supra* note 134. ¶¶ 1013, 1986.

ordered by Serbian soldiers to lick their own blood on the floor and walls.[1283] Howls/moans/screams of pain and crying for help were audible to the other detainees to the point that they could not sleep at night.[1284]

Civilians detained by the Serbian military were kicked with army boots, hit with fists, punched, stabbed, or cut on multiple places of the body with knives, penetrated with pointed stakes, truncheons, and all other kinds of objects into their anuses.[1285] Frequently, Serbian soldiers subjected the victims to attacks by dogs, forced detainees to graze grass like animals, urinated on the detainees, burned them with cigarettes, forced them to swallow bullets and extinguished cigarettes, forced them to eat their own excrement or to drink their own urine.[1286] Serb military and police forced the civilian detainees to stand for periods of up to twelve hours, to kneel on sharp stones until they fainted, and to lean on walls in stressful positions with their weight on the fingers spread out.[1287]

As a result of these brutal beatings and acts of violence, several detainees suffered injuries so severe to the point of losing consciousness, losing one or both eyes completely, having severe breathing difficulties, urinating blood, of having difficulty sleeping due to intense bone ache.[1288] Soldiers beat the victims to the point their bodies were all "black and blue," swollen and "kind of bluish," of being unable to sit, to stand on their feet, or to walk for days – or could not move anymore –, and other various

---

[1283] Prosecutor v. Blagoje Simić et al. IT-95-9-T. *Supra* note 78. ¶ 720.

[1284] Prosecutor v. Milorad Krnojelac. IT-97-25-T. *Supra* note 111. ¶¶ 143, 272; Prosecutor v. Vidoje Blagojević, Dragan Jokić. IT-02-60-T. *Supra* note 147. ¶¶ 338, 348; Prosecutor v. Radovan Karadžić. IT-95-5/18-T, vol. 1. *Supra* note 134. ¶¶ 990, 1026, 1344, 1348, 1427, 2502.

[1285] Prosecutor v. Blagoje Simić et al. IT-95-9-T. *Supra* note 78. ¶¶ 703, 719, 728; Prosecutor v. Milan Lukić, Sredoje Lukić. IT-98-32/1-T. *Supra* note 104. ¶¶ 821, 978; Prosecutor v. Mićo Stanišić, Stojan Župljanin. IT-08-91-T, vol. 1. *Supra* note 102. ¶¶ 289, 603; Prosecutor v. Radovan Karadžić. IT-95-5/18-T, vol. 1. *Supra* note 134. ¶¶ 999, 1165, 1167, 1177, 1179, 1190, 1201, 1301, 1306, 1332-1333, 1344, 2340, 2502–2503.

[1286] Prosecutor v. Blagoje Simić et al. IT-95-9-T. *Supra* note 78. ¶¶ 719–720, 733; Prosecutor v. Momčilo Krajišnik. IT-00-39-T. *Supra* note 121. ¶ 802; Prosecutor v. Milan Martić. IT-95-11-T. *Supra* note 105. ¶ 288; Prosecutor v. Radovan Karadžić. IT-95-5/18-T, vol. 1. *Supra* note 134. ¶¶ 999, 1013, 1015, 1477, 2276, 2494.

[1287] Prosecutor v. Radoslav Brđanin. IT-99-36-T. *Supra* note 130. ¶ 950; Prosecutor v. Mićo Stanišić, Stojan Župljanin. IT-08-91-T, vol. 1. *Supra* note 102. ¶ 676; Prosecutor v. Radovan Karadžić. IT-95-5/18-T, vol. 1. *Supra* note 134. ¶ 1192.

[1288] Prosecutor v. Milorad Krnojelac. IT-97-25-T. *Supra* note 111. ¶¶ 147, 149, 151, 272; Prosecutor v. Blagoje Simić et al. IT-95-9-T. *Supra* note 78. ¶ 696; Prosecutor v. Momčilo Krajišnik. IT-00-39-T. *Supra* note 121. ¶ 802; Prosecutor v. Radovan Karadžić. IT-95-5/18-T, vol. 1. *Supra* note 134. ¶¶ 1011, 1191, 1325, 1332, 1479, 2345, 2497.

health problems as a result of the unjust detention.[1289] Many detainees died following the beatings.[1290] In cases of death, the incident was usually followed by issuing false death reports by Serbian authorities.[1291]

As a routine practice, Serbian soldiers ordered Muslim detainees to beat each other, even their own family members.[1292] Muslims were made to carry the dead bodies of their relatives, ordered to witness the beatings of other inmates, commanded to walk over dead bodies barefooted, or to "bite or suck each others' penises while soldiers stood by and laughed."[1293] The victims were also forced to lick each others' buttocks and forced to eat their fellow detainees' severed body parts.[1294]

## 2.5. Malnutrition & water scarcity

### 2.5.1. Nazi concentration camps context and the occupied territories

In concentration camps such as Struthof, Belsen, Auschwitz, and Mauthausen, German commanders intentionally submitted civilian inmates to a starvation diet, leaving them without water or food for periods of up to 14 days.[1295] If food was ever provided, it was served in terrible conditions and

---

[1289]  Prosecutor v. Blagoje Simić et al. IT-95-9-T. Supra note 78. ¶¶ 711, 770; Prosecutor v. Vidoje Blagojević, Dragan Jokić. IT-02-60-T. Supra note 147. ¶ 310; Prosecutor v. Milan Lukić, Sredoje Lukić. IT-98-32/1-T. Supra note 104. ¶ 796; Prosecutor v. Mićo Stanišić, Stojan Župljanin. IT-08-91-T, vol. 1. Supra note 102. ¶ 676; Prosecutor v. Radovan Karadžić. IT-95-5/18-T, vol. 1. Supra note 134. ¶¶ 1012, 1399, 2497.

[1290]  Prosecutor v. Slobodan Milošević. IT-02-54-T. Supra note 139. ¶ 196; Prosecutor v. Radovan Karadžić. IT-95-5/18-T, vol. 1. Supra note 134. ¶¶ 718, 1021, 1205, 2345, 2347.

[1291]  Prosecutor v. Radovan Karadžić. IT-95-5/18-T, vol. 1. Supra note 134. ¶ 1426.

[1292]  Prosecutor v. Slobodan Milošević. IT-02-54-T. Supra note 139. ¶ 196; Prosecutor v. Momčilo Krajišnik. IT-00-39-T. Supra note 121. ¶ 802; Prosecutor v. Milan Lukić, Sredoje Lukić. IT-98-32/1-T. Supra note 104. ¶ 801; Prosecutor v. Mićo Stanišić, Stojan Župljanin. IT-08-91-T, vol. 1. Supra note 102. ¶ 585; Prosecutor v. Radovan Karadžić. IT-95-5/18-T, vol. 1. Supra note 134. ¶¶ 1015, 1298, 1301, 1325, 1345, 1986, 2423.

[1293]  Prosecutor v. Vidoje Blagojević, Dragan Jokić. IT-02-60-T. Supra note 147. ¶ 340. Se also: Prosecutor v. Mićo Stanišić, Stojan Župljanin. IT-08-91-T, vol. 1. Supra note 102. ¶ 289; Prosecutor v. Radovan Karadžić. IT-95-5/18-T, vol. 1. Supra note 134. ¶¶ 1345, 1869, 2503.

[1294]  Prosecutor v. Radovan Karadžić. IT-95-5/18-T, vol. 1. Supra note 134. ¶¶ 1298, 2503.

[1295]  5 Trial of the Major War Criminals before the International Military Tribunal (1947). p. 172.

in minimal rations per person, or even only liquid food.[1296] In most cases, commanders would give inmates only 1/12 of a loaf of bread.[1297] At one instance, the Red Cross sent 150 kilograms of chocolate to be distributed to children starving to death at the concentration camp. However, only ten kilograms were distributed. The commandant kept 140 kilograms of chocolate for himself and to "be used as barter to his personal advantage."[1298]

Lack of proper food in appropriate amounts would frequently leave the inmates with terrible immune system resistance and susceptible to infections to a horrible extent.[1299] An estimated 75 percent of the victims were bloated from hunger.[1300] Many of them would collapse several times a day and had to be carried by fellow victims.[1301] From 1941 to 1945, hundreds died every day in the camps due to starvation, malnutrition, and acute thirst.[1302] Jewish, Italian, Russian and French inmates accounted for most of the victims.[1303] In several cases, they "weighed 50 to 60 pounds at the time of death", and their "internal organs had often shrunk to one-third of their normal size."[1304]

Hunger in some Nazi concentration camps was so severe that many Jewish inmates had to resort to cannibalism practices to feed themselves.[1305] Abundant evidence shows that these inmates have eaten the flesh from fellow Jewish dead bodies. They used to cut out soft body parts such as the liver and the heart of the dead and ate them.[1306]

---

[1296] **United States of America v. Oswald Pohl, et al. Case 4** (Pohl case) (1947). pp. 396–397, 408–409; **United States of America v. Carl Krauch, et al.** Case 6, Volume 8 (I.G. Farben case) (1947). pp. 623–624; 30 Trial of the Major War Criminals before the International Military Tribunal (1948). p. 471.

[1297] 30 Trial of the Major War Criminals before the International Military Tribunal (1948). p. 471.

[1298] *Ibidem.*

[1299] **United States of America v. Oswald Pohl, et al. Case 4** (Pohl case) (1947). p. 396.

[1300] 30 Trial of the Major War Criminals before the International Military Tribunal (1948). p. 471.

[1301] **United States of America v. Carl Krauch, et al.** Case 6, Volume 8 (I.G. Farben case) (1947). p. 624.

[1302] 5 Trial of the Major War Criminals before the International Military Tribunal (1947). pp. 172, 174–175; 30 Trial of the Major War Criminals before the International Military Tribunal (1948). p. 471.

[1303] 5 Trial of the Major War Criminals before the International Military Tribunal (1947). p. 174–175.

[1304] *Ibidem.*

[1305] *Ibidem.*

[1306] 30 Trial of the Major War Criminals before the International Military Tribunal (1948). p. 471.

## 2.5.2. Nutritional conditions in the Former Yugoslavia detention camps

Nutritional conditions were harsh in the detention camps in Former Yugoslavia. At least four reasons accounted for this fact: 1) There was insufficient food in terms of quantity as well as in terms of quality; 2) Detainees were rarely fed during long intervals of time, even those who had to labor exhaustively; 3) Detainees were given a very short time to eat their food, or else they would be beaten; and 4) The premises used to make the hygienization of food and kitchen utensils were completely inadequate.[1307]

As a result of a deliberate policy to cause malnutrition, Serb soldiers made civilian Croats and Muslims suffer extreme weight loss of up to 60 kilograms per person during their detention at the camps.[1308] Hunger/starvation was so severe to some detainees that many of them had to resort to eating grass, insects, carbonized food, soldiers' leftovers, or food that was given to the dogs.[1309] When detainees were eventually given food, many of them had to eat it from the same cups used to relieve themselves or from the same bowls that the soldiers used to feed the dogs.[1310] The food was usually spoiled, which frequently caused them stomach problems and stomach aches.[1311] Very often, the guards would purposely spill on the detainees' meals.[1312]

---

[1307] Prosecutor v. Blagoje Simić et al. IT-95-9-T. *Supra* note 78. ¶ 738; Prosecutor v. Radoslav Brđanin. IT-99-36-T. *Supra* note 130. ¶¶ 912, 918, 928, 932, 938, 952; Prosecutor v. Milan Martić. IT-95-11-T. *Supra* note 105. ¶ 288; Prosecutor v. Mićo Stanišić, Stojan Župljanin. IT-08-91-T, vol. 1. *Supra* note 102. ¶¶ 584, 676, 683, 774, 907; Prosecutor v. Radovan Karadžić. IT-95-5/18-T, vol. 1. *Supra* note 134. ¶¶ 989, 1015, 1071, 1167, 1201, 1305, 1307, 1466, 1832, 1991, 1998, 2399.

[1308] Prosecutor v. Milorad Krnojelac. IT-97-25-T. *Supra* note 111. ¶¶ 139, 147–151; Prosecutor v. Blagoje Simić et al. IT-95-9-T. *Supra* note 78. ¶ 739; Prosecutor v. Slobodan Milošević. IT-02-54-T. *Supra* note 139. ¶ 193; Prosecutor v. Radoslav Brđanin. IT-99-36-T. *Supra* note 130. ¶¶ 912, 918, 932; Prosecutor v. Mićo Stanišić, Stojan Župljanin. IT-08-91-T, vol. 1. *Supra* note 102. ¶¶ 584, 678; Prosecutor v. Radovan Karadžić. IT-95-5/18-T, vol. 1. *Supra* note 134. ¶¶ 1478, 1483–1984, 2509.

[1309] Prosecutor v. Milorad Krnojelac. IT-97-25-T. *Supra* note 111. ¶ 148; Prosecutor v. Slobodan Milošević. IT-02-54-T. *Supra* note 139. ¶ 193; Prosecutor v. Radoslav Brđanin. IT-99-36-T. *Supra* note 130. ¶¶ 912, 923, 928, 932, 952; Prosecutor v. Mićo Stanišić, Stojan Župljanin. IT-08-91-T, vol. 1. *Supra* note 102. ¶ 584; Prosecutor v. Radovan Karadžić. IT-95-5/18-T, vol. 1. *Supra* note 134. ¶¶ 1325, 2339, 2399, 2508.

[1310] Prosecutor v. Mićo Stanišić, Stojan Župljanin. IT-08-91-T, vol. 1. *Supra* note 102. ¶ 774; Prosecutor v. Radovan Karadžić. IT-95-5/18-T, vol. 1. *Supra* note 134. ¶ 2399.

[1311] Prosecutor v. Radoslav Brđanin. IT-99-36-T. *Supra* note 130. ¶¶ 923, 932, 952; Prosecutor v. Radovan Karadžić. IT-95-5/18-T, vol. 1. *Supra* note 134. ¶ 1166.

[1312] Prosecutor v. Mićo Stanišić, Stojan Župljanin. IT-08-91-T, vol. 1. *Supra* note 102. ¶ 907.

Potable water for drinking and for ordinary/domestic chores was extremely insufficient in the camps in terms of quantity and quality.[1313] Due to the low quality of the water provided for detainees, intestinal and stomach problems were reported continuously.[1314] It was also reported that the Serb military and police forced detainees to drink and to use for personal hygiene water that was not fit for human consumption, destined, in fact, for industrial use,[1315] or to drink water stored in filthy glass bottles.[1316]

If women and children tried to collect rainwater or tried to escape the camp to get a drink of water, Serb soldiers would beat them with rifles, batons, and various other objects.[1317] Running water pump stations were usually placed in containers outside the premises of the camp and were at the discretion/control of the guards.[1318] Consequentially, at many times, Muslim detainees had to fight between themselves for a drink, to beg for water singing Serbian songs to obtain it, or to resort to drinking their own urine not to die from thirst.[1319] Water for the shower was particularly scarce. In some instances, icy cold water was given to the detainees in extreme conditions during the winter.[1320]

# 2.6. Water, Sanitation, and Hygiene (WASH-Cluster)

## 2.6.1. WASH in the context of the Nazi concentration camps and the occupied territories

The sanitary installations of the Nazi concentration camps were appalling. Toilets, latrines, and washrooms were absolutely inadequate, extremely filthy, muddy, and vermin-prevailing.[1321] As a deliberate policy of the ad-

---

[1313]   Prosecutor v. Radoslav Brđanin. IT-99-36-T. *Supra* note 130. ¶¶ 913, 918, 923; Prosecutor v. Radovan Karadžić. IT-95-5/18-T, vol. 1. *Supra* note 134. ¶¶ 989, 1021, 1201, 1388, 1984.

[1314]   Prosecutor v. Radovan Karadžić. IT-95-5/18-T, vol. 1. *Supra* note 134. ¶ 1388.

[1315]   Prosecutor v. Radoslav Brđanin. IT-99-36-T. *Supra* note 130. ¶ 933.

[1316]   *Idem.* ¶ 952.

[1317]   Prosecutor v. Radovan Karadžić. IT-95-5/18-T, vol. 1. *Supra* note 134. ¶¶ 1388, 2277.

[1318]   *Idem.* ¶ 1009.

[1319]   Prosecutor v. Radoslav Brđanin. IT-99-36-T. *Supra* note 130. ¶ 931; Prosecutor v. Vidoje Blagojević, Dragan Jokić. IT-02-60-T. *Supra* note 147. ¶ 338; Prosecutor v. Radovan Karadžić. IT-95-5/18-T, vol. 1. *Supra* note 134. ¶ 1418.

[1320]   Prosecutor v. Radoslav Brđanin. IT-99-36-T. *Supra* note 130. ¶ 919; Prosecutor v. Radovan Karadžić. IT-95-5/18-T, vol. 1. *Supra* note 134. ¶ 1984.

[1321]   **United States of America v. Oswald Pohl, *et al.* Case 4** (Pohl case) (1947). pp. 271, 394; 5 Trial of the Major War Criminals before the International Military Tribunal (1947). p. 174.

ministration of the camps, there was no cleaning material for toilets, and sanitary installations were never taken care of.[1322] If baths of inmates were ever allowed by German commanders, they would be authorized only once a month.[1323] Consequently, hundreds of cases of scabies, body lice, and cases of extensive impetigo were reported every day in the camps.[1324] Infections of all sorts were always prevailing in the camps.[1325] Diarrhea, dysentery, and epidemics of typhus and tuberculosis continually exposed the camps to severe dangers to its members, provoking hundreds of deaths daily.[1326]

## 2.6.2. WASH in the context of the Former Yugoslavia detention camps

Sanitation in the Former Yugoslavia detention camps was deplorable: 1) lice and scabies infestation were widespread; 2) flies made the situation unbearable; 3) skin diseases were prevalent; 4) there were widespread acute cases of diarrhea and dysentery; 5) toilet facilities were inadequate or non-existent; 6) the camps had limited or no shower or bath facilities. Some detainees had to resort to washing themselves in rivers, even during the winter; 7) there were no hygienic products or toiletries supplied, such as soap or toothpaste; 8) there was no water for bathing or for personal hygiene, and as a consequence, detainees could not bathe or brush their teeth; 9) there were no lavatory facilities for washing clothes.[1327]

---

[1322] **United States of America v. Oswald Pohl, et al. Case 4** (Pohl case) (1947). p. 396; 5 Trial of the Major War Criminals before the International Military Tribunal (1947). p. 174.

[1323] 5 Trial of the Major War Criminals before the International Military Tribunal (1947). p. 174.

[1324] **United States of America v. Oswald Pohl, et al. Case 4** (Pohl case) (1947). p. 360.

[1325] *Idem.* p. 396.

[1326] **United States of America v. Oswald Pohl, et al. Case 4** (Pohl case) (1947). pp. 360, 394; 5 Trial of the Major War Criminals before the International Military Tribunal (1947). p. 174–175; 30 Trial of the Major War Criminals before the International Military Tribunal (1948). p. 471.

[1327] Prosecutor v. Milorad Krnojelac. IT-97-25-T. *Supra* note 111. ¶ 136; Prosecutor v. Slobodan Milošević. IT-02-54-T. *Supra* note 139. ¶ 200; Prosecutor v. Radoslav Brđanin. IT-99-36-T. *Supra* note 130. ¶¶ 911, 919, 923, 927–928, 934, 937, 939, 943–944, 953, 957, 960, 962; Prosecutor v. Mićo Stanišić, Stojan Župljanin. IT-08-91-T, vol. 1. *Supra* note 102. ¶¶ 584, 678, 683, 774; Prosecutor v. Radovan Karadžić. IT-95-5/18-T, vol. 1. *Supra* note 134. ¶¶ 915, 989, 1189, 1201, 1225, 1388, 1479, 1755, 1797, 1823, 1996, 2016, 2145, 2509.

In most detention camps, there were no toilets in the cells of the prison.[1328] Detainees were often forced to defecate and urinate in the rooms where they were kept, sometimes in buckets, pots, or beakers (that were not emptied for days), in barrels or nylon/plastic bags, in army flasks, in canisters, in improvised shelters made out of blankets, or they used to simply relieve themselves in their own pants.[1329] As a consequence, the stench in the cells was unbearable.[1330]

In the camps served with outside toilets, the prisoners were systematically restricted from/denied the use of toilet facilities.[1331] Toilets were usually blocked and filthy and were served with cold water only.[1332] In some cases, Serbs sent detainees to isolation cells as punishment for having made a heater to heat water.[1333] Detainees were generally allowed five minutes in the morning and five minutes in the evening to use the toilets and had to wait hours before being allowed to use them.[1334] The soldiers severely beat many of the detainees with their rifles on their way to the toilets.[1335]

---

[1328]  Prosecutor v. Radoslav Brđanin. IT-99-36-T. *Supra* note 130. ¶¶ 923, 957; Prosecutor v. Radovan Karadžić. IT-95-5/18-T, vol. 1. *Supra* note 134. ¶¶ 1389, 1984, 1996.

[1329]  Prosecutor v. Radoslav Brđanin. IT-99-36-T. *Supra* note 130. ¶¶ 911, 923, 925, 937, 953, 960; Prosecutor v. Vidoje Blagojević, Dragan Jokić. IT-02-60-T. *Supra* note 147. ¶ 338; Prosecutor v. Mićo Stanišić, Stojan Župljanin. IT-08-91-T, vol. 1. *Supra* note 102. ¶¶ 584, 678, 774; Prosecutor v. Radovan Karadžić. IT-95-5/18-T, vol. 1. *Supra* note 134. ¶¶ 1189, 1755, 2145, 2400, 2508.

[1330]  Prosecutor v. Vidoje Blagojević, Dragan Jokić. IT-02-60-T. *Supra* note 147. ¶ 310; Prosecutor v. Mićo Stanišić, Stojan Župljanin. IT-08-91-T, vol. 1. *Supra* note 102. ¶¶ 678, 774; Prosecutor v. Radovan Karadžić. IT-95-5/18-T, vol. 1. *Supra* note 134. ¶ 2508.

[1331]  Prosecutor v. Vidoje Blagojević, Dragan Jokić. IT-02-60-T. *Supra* note 147. ¶ 348; Prosecutor v. Milan Martić. IT-95-11-T. *Supra* note 105. ¶ 288; Prosecutor v. Radovan Karadžić. IT-95-5/18-T, vol. 1. *Supra* note 134. ¶ 1755.

[1332]  Prosecutor v. Milorad Krnojelac. IT-97-25-T. *Supra* note 111. ¶ 136; Prosecutor v. Radoslav Brđanin. IT-99-36-T. *Supra* note 130. ¶ 934; Prosecutor v. Milan Martić. IT-95-11-T. *Supra* note 105. ¶ 288; Prosecutor v. Radovan Karadžić. IT-95-5/18-T, vol. 1. *Supra* note 134. ¶ 1984.

[1333]  Prosecutor v. Milorad Krnojelac. IT-97-25-T. *Supra* note 111. ¶ 151.

[1334]  Prosecutor v. Mićo Stanišić, Stojan Župljanin. IT-08-91-T, vol. 1. *Supra* note 102. ¶ 584; Prosecutor v. Radovan Karadžić. IT-95-5/18-T, vol. 1. *Supra* note 134. ¶¶ 1177, 1755, 1984.

[1335]  Prosecutor v. Radoslav Brđanin. IT-99-36-T. *Supra* note 130. ¶¶ 923, 960; Prosecutor v. Vidoje Blagojević, Dragan Jokić. IT-02-60-T. *Supra* note 147. ¶ 348; Prosecutor v. Mićo Stanišić, Stojan Župljanin. IT-08-91-T, vol. 1. *Supra* note 102. ¶ 774; Prosecutor v. Radovan Karadžić. IT-95-5/18-T, vol. 1. *Supra* note 134. ¶¶ 1009, 1755, 2277.

## 2.7. Other violations connected with the conditions of accommodation

### 2.7.1. Accommodation in the Nazi concentration camps and the occupied territories

The living conditions in the Nazi concentration camps were horrible.[1336] Due to overcrowding, the rooms in the concentration camps could not be cleaned.[1337] The ground was utterly bogged beyond control.[1338] There were no covers, sleeping bags, mattresses, or any kind of bedding.[1339] Inmates had to resort to sleeping directly on the floor.[1340] Without a heating system and proper clothing and shoes, thousands of prisoners had to stand in the cold during winter.[1341] Several became ill with pneumonia and died.[1342]

Thousands of inmates had to live underground in overcrowded tunnels built by themselves, especially for this purpose. Only a small part of the inmates had the "possibility to see the sunlight in the camp and to live in barracks."[1343] Others had to live by the hundreds in train cars. Several of them died from suffocation.[1344]

### 2.7.2. Accommodation in detention camps in the Former Yugoslavia

Serb military and police held Muslim detainees in unbearably over-crowded cells with insufficient room to sit, lie down, or move around.[1345]

---

[1336] **United States of America v. Oswald Pohl, et al. Case 4** (Pohl case) (1947). p. 396.
[1337] 5 Trial of the Major War Criminals before the International Military Tribunal (1947). p. 174.
[1338] **United States of America v. Oswald Pohl, et al. Case 4** (Pohl case) (1947). p. 393.
[1339] 30 Trial of the Major War Criminals before the International Military Tribunal (1948). p. 471.
[1340] *Ibidem.*
[1341] **United States of America v. Oswald Pohl, et al. Case 4** (Pohl case) (1947). p. 396; 5 Trial of the Major War Criminals before the International Military Tribunal (1947). p. 172; **United States of America v. Carl Krauch, et al.** Case 6, Volume 8 (I.G. Farben case) (1947). pp. 623–624.
[1342] *Ibidem.*
[1343] **United States of America v. Oswald Pohl, et al. Case 4** (Pohl case) (1947). p. 396.
[1344] 5 Trial of the Major War Criminals before the International Military Tribunal (1947). p. 172.
[1345] Prosecutor v. Milorad Krnojelac. IT-97-25-T. *Supra* note 111. ¶¶ 135–136; Prosecutor v. Blagoje Simić et al. IT-95-9-T. *Supra* note 78. ¶ 737; Prosecutor v. Slobodan Milošević. IT-02-54-T. *Supra* note 139. ¶ 191; Prosecutor v. Radoslav Brđanin. IT-

In one instance, more than 500 detainees had to share rooms smaller than 20 by 20 meters in size.[1346] There were documented cases in which detainees were simply kept in stables meant for livestock.[1347] During the winter, most of them were not provided with blankets.[1348]

Moreover, due to a lack of sleeping space, the Serb military and police frequently packed detainees one on top of the other.[1349] They were forced either 1) to take turns to lie down and sleep or 2) to sleep sitting up or standing up.[1350] Many had to resort to sleeping on cardboard on the concrete floor, on wooden palettes, or simply directly on the concrete floor, or generally outside of the cell.[1351] In extreme situations, Muslim detainees were also forced to lie amidst excrement.[1352]

In the summer, the temperature in the facilities was so intensely hot due to heat waves that people fainted due to the heat.[1353] During the winter, wet conditions due to leaking roofs caused the temperature to decrease.[1354] There was insufficient or no heating at all to the point that the

---

99-36-T. *Supra* note 130. ¶¶ 917, 931, 936; Prosecutor v. Mićo Stanišić, Stojan Župljanin. IT-08-91-T, vol. 1. *Supra* note 102. ¶¶ 584, 676; Prosecutor v. Radovan Karadžić. IT-95-5/18-T, vol. 1. *Supra* note 134. ¶¶ 1179, 1305, 1479, 1832, 1996, 2145–2146, 2277.

[1346] Prosecutor v. Mićo Stanišić, Stojan Župljanin. IT-08-91-T, vol. 1. *Supra* note 102. ¶ 678.

[1347] Prosecutor v. Radovan Karadžić. IT-95-5/18-T, vol. 1. *Supra* note 134. ¶¶ 1003, 1392.

[1348] Prosecutor v. Radoslav Brđanin. IT-99-36-T. *Supra* note 130. ¶¶ 917, 925, 941; Prosecutor v. Radovan Karadžić. IT-95-5/18-T, vol. 1. *Supra* note 134. ¶¶ 1393, 1479.

[1349] Prosecutor v. Milorad Krnojelac. IT-97-25-T. *Supra* note 111. ¶ 136; Prosecutor v. Slobodan Milošević. IT-02-54-T. *Supra* note 139. ¶ 191; Prosecutor v. Mićo Stanišić, Stojan Župljanin. IT-08-91-T, vol. 1. *Supra* note 102. ¶¶ 584, 774; Prosecutor v. Radovan Karadžić. IT-95-5/18-T, vol. 1. *Supra* note 134. ¶¶ 989, 1166, 1179, 1189, 1201, 1225, 2016, 2507-2008.

[1350] Prosecutor v. Radoslav Brđanin. IT-99-36-T. *Supra* note 130. ¶¶ 947, 950; Prosecutor v. Radovan Karadžić. IT-95-5/18-T, vol. 1. *Supra* note 134. ¶ 1996.

[1351] Prosecutor v. Blagoje Simić *et al.* IT-95-9-T. *Supra* note 78. ¶ 737; Prosecutor v. Radoslav Brđanin. IT-99-36-T. *Supra* note 130. ¶¶ 923, 941, 948, 950, 955, 959; Prosecutor v. Mićo Stanišić, Stojan Župljanin. IT-08-91-T, vol. 1. *Supra* note 102. ¶¶ 584, 678; Prosecutor v. Radovan Karadžić. IT-95-5/18-T, vol. 1. *Supra* note 134. ¶¶ 1166, 1393, 1479, 2339.

[1352] Prosecutor v. Slobodan Milošević. IT-02-54-T. *Supra* note 139. ¶ 191.

[1353] Prosecutor v. Radoslav Brđanin. IT-99-36-T. *Supra* note 130. ¶¶ 931, 959; Prosecutor v. Vidoje Blagojević, Dragan Jokić. IT-02-60-T. *Supra* note 147. ¶ 320; Prosecutor v. Mićo Stanišić, Stojan Župljanin. IT-08-91-T, vol. 1. *Supra* note 102. ¶ 584; Prosecutor v. Radovan Karadžić. IT-95-5/18-T, vol. 1. *Supra* note 134. ¶¶ 1418, 1823, 2008, 2507.

[1354] Prosecutor v. Radovan Karadžić. IT-95-5/18-T, vol. 1. *Supra* note 134. ¶ 2508.

detainees were exposed to freezing temperatures and contracted pneumonia and other respiratory diseases.[1355] Serb military punished those detainees who tried to make winter clothes out of blankets to solitary confinement cells, where temperatures were considerably lower than in the cells.[1356]

There was no light in many of the rooms occupied by the victims.[1357] Guards frequently refused to open the windows of the rooms crowded with detainees, including a significant number of women and children, making it difficult for the detainees to breathe due to the lack of ventilation.[1358]

## 2.7.3. Medical assistance in the detention camps

*2.7.3.1. Medical assistance to concentration camps' inmates in Germany and the occupied territories*

Medical assistance in Nazi concentration camps, including access to doctors and medication, was almost nonexistent.[1359] Overcrowded infirmaries had more than one prisoner sharing the same bed.[1360] Epidemics of all sorts were widespread, such as spotted fever, tuberculosis, and typhus.[1361] General debilities and heart diseases were also striking.[1362] Sick persons were not transported out of the barracks. Consequently, diseases were spread to a large number of people, and death rates were extremely high.[1363]

---

[1355] Prosecutor v. Milorad Krnojelac. IT-97-25-T. *Supra* note 111. ¶ 151; Prosecutor v. Radovan Karadžić. IT-95-5/18-T, vol. 1. *Supra* note 134. ¶¶ 2145, 2507–2508.

[1356] *Idem.* ¶ 138.

[1357] Prosecutor v. Radoslav Brđanin. IT-99-36-T. *Supra* note 130. ¶ 955; Prosecutor v. Mićo Stanišić, Stojan Župljanin. IT-08-91-T, vol. 1. *Supra* note 102. ¶ 584; Prosecutor v. Radovan Karadžić. IT-95-5/18-T, vol. 1. *Supra* note 134. ¶¶ 2507–2508.

[1358] Prosecutor v. Slobodan Milošević. IT-02-54-T. *Supra* note 139. ¶ 191; Prosecutor v. Radoslav Brđanin. IT-99-36-T. *Supra* note 130. ¶¶ 931, 951, 955, 959; Prosecutor v. Mićo Stanišić, Stojan Župljanin. IT-08-91-T, vol. 1. *Supra* note 102. ¶¶ 584, 678; Prosecutor v. Radovan Karadžić. IT-95-5/18-T, vol. 1. *Supra* note 134. ¶¶ 1305, 1418, 1420, 2507.

[1359] 5 Trial of the Major War Criminals before the International Military Tribunal (1947). p. 174; 30 Trial of the Major War Criminals before the International Military Tribunal (1948). p. 471.

[1360] **United States of America v. Oswald Pohl, *et al*. Case 4** (Pohl case) (1947). p. 359.

[1361] *Idem.* pp. 360, 416. See also: 5 Trial of the Major War Criminals before the International Military Tribunal (1947). p. 174.

[1362] **United States of America v. Oswald Pohl, *et al*. Case 4** (Pohl case) (1947). p. 394.

[1363] *Idem.* pp. 394, 416.

It was a common practice that SS medical doctors gave lethal injections of Phenol, Evipan, or Benzine to inmates invalid for work.[1364] Patients with sickness in the body were systematically killed.[1365] Frequently, "prisoners were killed only because they had dysentery or vomited and gave the nurses too much trouble."[1366] If an inmate fell sick or injured, they would often hide such condition, fearful that they would be sent to the gas chambers.[1367] Many would commit suicide out of fear of being gassed.[1368] Patients with mental disorders were summarily "liquidated by being led to the gas chamber and injected there or shot."[1369]

Under "the guise of medical science," SS medical doctors committed a group of crimes that shocked the human conscience and proved their complete disregard for human life.[1370] SS performed numerous types of medical experiments on thousands of healthy civilian inmates in concentration camps.[1371] Such medical experiments were always forced on thousands of victims, meaning that the persons submitted to such procedures were never volunteers.[1372]

SS medical doctors performed all sorts of medical experiments, for instance, malaria experiments,[1373] experiments to determine the effects of

---

[1364] 5 Trial of the Major War Criminals before the International Military Tribunal (1947). p. 172.

[1365] **United States of America v. Carl Krauch, et al.** Case 6, Volume 8 (I.G. Farben case) (1947). p. 624.

[1366] 5 Trial of the Major War Criminals before the International Military Tribunal (1947). pp. 172–173.

[1367] **United States of America v. Carl Krauch, et al.** Case 6, Volume 8 (I.G. Farben case) (1947). p. 624.

[1368] **United States of America v. Oswald Pohl, et al. Case 4** (Pohl case) (1947). p. 394.

[1369] 5 Trial of the Major War Criminals before the International Military Tribunal (1947). pp. 172–173.

[1370] **United States of America v. Oswald Pohl, et al. Case 4** (Pohl case) (1947). pp. 224–225.

[1371] *Ibidem.* See also: 30 Trial of the Major War Criminals before the International Military Tribunal (1948). p. 471.

[1372] 5 Trial of the Major War Criminals before the International Military Tribunal (1947). pp. 168–169.

[1373] "The victims were either bitten by mosquitoes or given injections of malaria sporozoites taken from mosquitoes. Different kinds of treatment were applied, including quinine, pyrifer, neosalvarsan, antipyrin, pyramidon, and a drug called 2516 Behring." Autopsies on the bodies of people showed that part of them died from these malaria experiments and other part died from the malaria itself. Hundreds "died later from diseases which were fatal because of the physical condition resulting from the malaria attacks. In addition, there were deaths resulting from poisoning due to overdoses of neosalvarsan and pyramidon." (*Idem.* p. 169).

changing air pressure on human beings,[1374][1375] experiments on the effect of cold water on human beings,[1376][1377] Phlegmon experiments,[1378] saltwater experiments,[1379] sterilization experiments,[1380] gynecological experiments performed on young girls,[1381] and applications of intravenous injections of

[1374] "As many as 25 persons were put at one time into a specially constructed van in which pressure could be increased or decreased as required. The purpose was to find out the effects on human beings of high altitude and of rapid descents by parachute." (*Ibidem*).

[1375] "Most of the prisoners used died from these experiments, from internal hemorrhage of the lungs or brain. The survivors coughed blood when taken out. [...] The survivors were sent to invalid blocks and liquidated shortly afterwards. Only a few escaped." (*Idem.* p. 170).

[1376] "This was done to find a way for reviving airmen who had fallen into the ocean. The subject was placed in ice cold water and kept there until he was unconscious. Blood was taken from his neck and tested each time his body temperature dropped one degree. This drop was determined by a rectal thermometer. Urine was also periodically tested. Some men stood it as long as 24 to 36 hours. The lowest body temperature reached was 19 degrees centigrade, but most men died at 25 or 26 degrees. When the men were removed from the ice water attempts were made to revive them by artificial sunshine, with hot water, by electro-therapy, or by animal warmth. For this last experiment prostitutes were used and the body of the unconscious man was placed between the bodies of two women. Himmler was present at one such experiment." (*Ibidem*).

[1377] "Of those who survived [this experiment], many became mentally deranged. Those who did not die were sent to invalid blocks and were killed just as were the victims of the air pressure experiments." (*Ibidem*).

[1378] In this experiment, patients were given "intramuscular and intravenous injections of pus from diseased persons." Then, any medical treatment was "forbidden for 3 days, by which time serious inflammation and in many cases general blood poisoning [occured]. Then each group was "divided into groups of 10. Half were given chemical treatment with liquid and special pills every 10 minutes for 24 hours. The remainder [were] treated with sulfanamide and surgery. In some cases, all the limbs [were] amputated." "[...] For these experiments Polish, Czech, and Dutch priests were ordinarily used. Pain was intense in such experiments. Most of the [...] persons who were used finally died. Most of the others became permanent invalids and were later killed." (*Idem.* p. 171).

[1379] "In the fall of 1944, there were 60 to 80 persons who were subjected to saltwater experiments. They were locked in a room and for 5 days were given nothing for food but salt water. During this time their urine, blood, and excrement were tested. None of these prisoners died, possibly because they received smuggled food from other prisoners. Hungarians and Gypsies were used for these experiments." (*Ibidem*).

[1380] 30 Trial of the Major War Criminals before the International Military Tribunal (1948). p. 471.

[1381] *Ibidem*.

benzine to test human resistance to this substance.[1382] Operations on the throat, stomach, gall bladder, and liver of healthy prisoners were executed simply to improve SS medical students' and doctors' surgical techniques.[1383] Even junior students with minimal surgical experience would perform complex, dangerous, and complicated medical procedures.[1384] Consequently, "many prisoners died on the operating table and many others from later complications."[1385]

## 2.7.3.2. Medical assistance in detention camps of the Former Yugoslavia

At detention camps of the Former Yugoslavia, medical care for Muslim detainees was majorly inadequate or non-existent, and there was a shortage of medicines and supplies – or no medicine provided at all.[1386] In most cases, the Serbian military and police did not provide detainees with any medical treatment for their pre-existing health conditions, such as diabetes, high blood pressure, asthma, heart disease, epilepsy, kidney disease, tuberculosis, and mental illness, or for the injuries caused by the beatings, such as spinal column fractures, severed limbs, broken ribs, multiple bone fractures, and fractured skulls.[1387]

---

[1382] *Ibidem.*

[1383] "For this purpose, a needle was jabbed into the liver of a person and a small piece of the liver was extracted. No anesthetic was used. The experiment is very painful and often had serious results, as the stomach or large blood vessels were often punctured, resulting in hemorrhage. Many persons died of these tests for which Polish, Russian, Czech, and German prisoners were employed." (5 Trial of the Major War Criminals before the International Military Tribunal (1947). p. 170). See also: pp. 168–169.

[1384] *Ibidem.*

[1385] *Ibidem.*

[1386] Prosecutor v. Milorad Krnojelac. IT-97-25-T. *Supra* note 111. ¶ 141; Prosecutor v. Radoslav Brđanin. IT-99-36-T. *Supra* note 130. ¶¶ 913, 934, 945; Prosecutor v. Radovan Karadžić. IT-95-5/18-T, vol. 1. *Supra* note 134. ¶¶ 1166–1167, 1179, 1188, 1201, 1225, 1823, 1832, 2507.

[1387] Prosecutor v. Milorad Krnojelac. IT-97-25-T. *Supra* note 111. ¶¶ 150, 272; Prosecutor v. Blagoje Simić *et al.* IT-95-9-T. *Supra* note 78. ¶ 711; Prosecutor v. Radoslav Brđanin. IT-99-36-T. *Supra* note 130. ¶¶ 913, 920, 928, 954; Prosecutor v. Momčilo Krajišnik. IT-00-39-T. *Supra* note 121. ¶ 1057; Prosecutor v. Milan Lukić, Sredoje Lukić. IT-98-32/1-T. *Supra* note 104. ¶ 796; Prosecutor v. Mićo Stanišić, Stojan Župljanin. IT-08-91-T, vol. 1. *Supra* note 102. ¶¶ 584, 676, 678; Prosecutor v. Radovan Karadžić. IT-95-5/18-T, vol. 1. *Supra* note 134. ¶¶ 1015, 1190, 1390, 1986, 2008, 2497.

Mentally disabled detainees did not receive any proper medical care either.[1388] Most of the victims suffered from deteriorated psychological health due to terrible mental trauma and fear.[1389] In many detention centers, Bosnian Muslims were frequently subjected to practices that caused deep mental suffering by Serbian authorities, such as sleep deprivation and having their heads pushed into buckets with human excrement.[1390] While these acts took place, the victims were usually ordered to laugh.[1391] As a result of all these ill-treatments, they commonly displayed lasting psychological effects, such as post-traumatic stress syndrome, shocks due to fear, flashbacks from traumatic events, mental blocks, anxiety attacks, heart attacks, frequent nightmares, and chronic insomnia.[1392] All of that required constant psychiatric supervision and continuous use of medication, which they did not have access to.[1393]

## 2.8. Sexual violence and rape

### 2.8.1. Sexual violence and rape in the context of the Former Yugoslavian detention camps

There is plenty of evidence that the Serbian military, police, and authorities subjected Bosnian Muslim women, men, girls, and boys to acts of sexual violence. The victims were raped or gang-raped by Serb soldiers/police who guarded the detention camps on multiple occasions.[1394] Some women

---

[1388]  Prosecutor v. Milorad Krnojelac. IT-97-25-T. *Supra* note 111. ¶ 148.

[1389]  Prosecutor v. Radovan Karadžić. IT-95-5/18-T, vol. 1. *Supra* note 134. ¶ 1831.

[1390]  Prosecutor v. Blagoje Simić *et al.* IT-95-9-T. *Supra* note 78. ¶ 720; Prosecutor v. Radoslav Brđanin. IT-99-36-T. *Supra* note 130. ¶ 950; Prosecutor v. Milan Martić. IT-95-11-T. *Supra* note 105. ¶ 288; Prosecutor v. Milan Lukić, Sredoje Lukić. IT-98-32/1-T. *Supra* note 104. ¶ 821; Prosecutor v. Radovan Karadžić. IT-95-5/18-T, vol. 1. *Supra* note 134. ¶ 990.

[1391]  Prosecutor v. Blagoje Simić *et al.* IT-95-9-T. *Supra* note 78. ¶ 733.

[1392]  Prosecutor v. Milorad Krnojelac. IT-97-25-T. *Supra* note 111. ¶¶ 143–144, 147, 149–150; Prosecutor v. Milan Lukić, Sredoje Lukić. IT-98-32/1-T. *Supra* note 104. ¶ 796.

[1393]  Prosecutor v. Milorad Krnojelac. IT-97-25-T. *Supra* note 111. ¶ 151.

[1394]  Prosecutor v. Blagoje Simić *et al.* IT-95-9-T. *Supra* note 78. ¶¶ 728, 772; Prosecutor v. Slobodan Milošević. IT-02-54-T. *Supra* note 139. ¶¶ 193, 200; Prosecutor v. Momčilo Krajišnik. IT-00-39-T. *Supra* note 121. ¶ 800; Prosecutor v. Milan Martić. IT-95-11-T. *Supra* note 105. ¶ 288; Prosecutor v. Milan Lukić, Sredoje Lukić. IT-98-32/1-T. *Supra* note 104. ¶ 701; Prosecutor v. Mićo Stanišić, Stojan Župljanin. IT-08-91-T, vol. 1. *Supra* note 102. ¶¶ 678, 682–683; Prosecutor v. Radovan Karadžić. IT-95-5/18-T, vol. 1. *Supra* note 134. ¶¶ 916, 920, 990–991, 1015, 1021, 1201, 1225, 1269,

and children were taken away every day for the course of their detention. Some were chosen randomly, while others were systematically/intentionally called by their names and taken.[1395] Some were taken for a few hours and returned, while others were raped and sexually abused several times a day on a continuous basis for periods of up to two and a half months.[1396] For example, at Foča High School detention center, a woman was raped by Serbian soldiers approximately 150 times in the course of 40 days of detention.[1397]

There were several manners in which members of Serb Forces forced Muslim detainees to perform sexual acts: 1) Male prisoners were forced to engage in "degrading sexual acts" with each other and to perform oral sex on each other in the presence of other detainees; 2) Muslim women, girls as young as seven and young boys were taken out at night and were forced to strip and perform sexual acts with elderly men or to dance and perform sexual acts in front of Bosnian Serb soldiers; 3) Frequently, naked women were taken to "rape rooms" for approximately 20 minutes or were taken away in the following days to be sexually abused and severely beaten; 4) Hundreds of Muslim men and women were frequently ordered "to undress completely and to dance together around the Serb soldiers while touching each others' breasts and penises."[1398]

The victims had no choice but to obey the soldiers. Those who tried to resist were severely beaten and submitted to additional horrific acts of sexual violence. Victims were commonly taken to separate rooms, tied to desks, tied with chains that were for leading cattle, and raped with all sorts of objects such as police truncheons and knives, and had their lips, necks, and breasts bitten, causing them terrible pain, fear, and mental trauma.[1399]

---

1346, 2500, 2504, 2506; Prosecutor v. Ratko Mladić. IT-09-92-T, vol. 2. *Supra* note 137. ¶ 1485.

[1395] Prosecutor v. Mićo Stanišić, Stojan Župljanin. IT-08-91-T, vol. 1. *Supra* note 102. ¶ 682; Prosecutor v. Ratko Mladić. IT-09-92-T, vol. 2. *Supra* note 137. ¶ 1485.

[1396] Prosecutor v. Slobodan Milošević. IT-02-54-T. *Supra* note 139. ¶ 193; Prosecutor v. Mićo Stanišić, Stojan Župljanin. IT-08-91-T, vol. 1. *Supra* note 102. ¶ 682; Prosecutor v. Radovan Karadžić. IT-95-5/18-T, vol. 1. *Supra* note 134. ¶¶ 916, 990–991, 2500.

[1397] Prosecutor v. Radovan Karadžić. IT-95-5/18-T, vol. 1. *Supra* note 134. ¶ 917.

[1398] Prosecutor v. Blagoje Simić *et al.* IT-95-9-T. *Supra* note 78. ¶ 728; Prosecutor v. Momčilo Krajišnik. IT-00-39-T. *Supra* note 121. ¶ 800; Prosecutor v. Mićo Stanišić, Stojan Župljanin. IT-08-91-T, vol. 1. *Supra* note 102. ¶¶ 603, 682; Prosecutor v. Radovan Karadžić. IT-95-5/18-T, vol. 1. *Supra* note 134. ¶¶ 916, 920, 922–923, 990, 1016–1017, 1269, 1831, 2500–2503; Prosecutor v. Ratko Mladić. IT-09-92-T, vol. 2. *Supra* note 137. ¶¶ 1485, 1493.

[1399] Prosecutor v. Slobodan Milošević. IT-02-54-T. *Supra* note 139. ¶¶ 162, 200; Prosecutor v. Momčilo Krajišnik. IT-00-39-T. *Supra* note 121. ¶ 800; Prosecutor v. Milan

Many times, pliers were used to mistreat the victims, and many of them were beaten after the rape and needed medical assistance due to excessive bleeding.[1400]

## 2.8.2. Sexual violence and rape in Sierra Leone

As a standard policy to terrorize the civilian population, AFRC and RUF fighters committed thousands of rapes against civilian women and girls throughout Sierra Leone.[1401] Throughout the city of Freetown and the Western Area, hundreds of women and young girls – as young as nine years old – were brutally gang-raped by rebels, sometimes until death.[1402] Evidence showed that at least seven armed rebels gang-raped some girls at the same time.[1403] Several victims were raped in the presence of their family members.[1404] For instance, on one occasion

> "[the witness'] wife was gang-raped by eight rebels as he and his children were forced to watch. He was ordered to count each rebel as they consecutively raped his wife, as they laughed and mocked him. After this ordeal, one of the rapists, Tamba Joe, took a knife and stabbed [the witness'] wife in front of her entire family."[1405]

In addition to the penetration of the penis into the victims' vaginas and anuses, AFRC/RUF fighters used to insert all sorts of objects into victims' genitalia and anal areas, such as sticks, pieces of wood, and even pistols.[1406] Most of the victims were traumatically injured and mutilated due to the

---

Lukić, Sredoje Lukić. IT-98-32/1-T. *Supra* note 104. ¶ 701; Prosecutor v. Radovan Karadžić. IT-95-5/18-T, vol. 1. *Supra* note 134. ¶¶ 916, 920, 991, 1225, 2501, 2504; Prosecutor v. Ratko Mladić. IT-09-92-T, vol. 2. *Supra* note 137. ¶ 1493.

[1400] Prosecutor v. Slobodan Milošević. IT-02-54-T. *Supra* note 139. ¶ 193; Prosecutor v. Mićo Stanišić, Stojan Župljanin. IT-08-91-T, vol. 1. *Supra* note 102. ¶ 682; Prosecutor v. Radovan Karadžić. IT-95-5/18-T, vol. 1. *Supra* note 134. ¶ 991; Prosecutor v. Ratko Mladić. IT-09-92-T, vol. 2. *Supra* note 137. ¶ 1485.

[1401] Prosecutor v. Brima, Kamara, Kanu. SCSL-04-16-T. *Supra* note 280. ¶ 412; Prosecutor v. Taylor. SCSL-03-01-T. *Supra* note 270. ¶ 876; Prosecutor v. Taylor. SCSL-03-01-T. *Supra* note 270. ¶ 1016.

[1402] Prosecutor v. Brima, Kamara, Kanu. SCSL-04-16-T. *Supra* note 280. ¶¶ 34, 992; Prosecutor v. Sesay, Kallon and Gbao. SCSL-04-15-T. *Supra* note 268. ¶ 1574; Prosecutor v. Sesay, Kallon and Gbao. SCSL-04-15-T. *Supra* note 279. ¶ 126.

[1403] Prosecutor v. Taylor. SCSL-03-01-T. *Supra* note 270. ¶ 1270.

[1404] Prosecutor v. Brima, Kamara, Kanu. SCSL-04-16-T. *Supra* note 280. ¶ 991.

[1405] Prosecutor v. Sesay, Kallon and Gbao. SCSL-04-15-T. *Supra* note 279. ¶ 125.

[1406] *Idem.* ¶¶ 125–126, 130.

insertion of such foreign objects.[1407] Several times, fighters would deliberately slit the genitalia of several males and females exclusively to inflict pain and humiliation.[1408]

AFRC/RUF rebels also submitted to forced marriages thousands of women and girls as young as 10-years-old.[1409] The most beautiful girls were brought to the senior commanders.[1410] In addition to "serve" the rebels with forced sexual relations, women victims were expected to perform domestic chores.[1411] In addition to committing several acts of sexual violence, plenty of evidence showed that AFRC/RUF fighters abducted thousands of women and girls of school-going age to use them as sexual slaves, exercising powers of ownership over them.[1412]

The victims of such barbaric acts displayed clear signs of mental trauma, such as post-traumatic stress disorder and depression, and physical consequences, such as contamination with sexually transmitted infections, unwanted pregnancies due to sexual violence, and miscarriages as a result of the rapes.[1413] Due to the well-founded fear of stigmatization, shame, rejection, retribution, and reprisal, several cases of sexual violence against women and children perpetrated by AFRC/RUF fighters were considered significantly underreported in Sierra Leone.[1414]

## 2.9. Forced labor & enslavement

### 2.9.1. Forced labor & enslavement in the Nazi concentration camps and the occupied territories

During the Nazi regime in Germany and occupied territories, the SS's policy toward Germany's slave laborers was clear: to make inmates under the

---

[1407] Prosecutor v. Brima, Kamara, Kanu. SCSL-04-16-T. *Supra* note 280. ¶ 34; Prosecutor v. Taylor. SCSL-03-01-T. *Supra* note 270. ¶ 882.

[1408] Prosecutor v. Sesay, Kallon and Gbao. SCSL-04-15-T. *Supra* note 279. ¶ 126.

[1409] *Idem.* ¶ 128.

[1410] Prosecutor v. Brima, Kamara, Kanu. SCSL-04-16-T. *Supra* note 280. ¶ 1045.

[1411] *Idem.* ¶ 412. See also: Prosecutor v. Sesay, Kallon and Gbao. SCSL-04-15-T. *Supra* note 268. ¶¶ 1561–1562, 1565.

[1412] Prosecutor v. Brima, Kamara, Kanu. SCSL-04-16-T. *Supra* note 280. ¶ 412; Prosecutor v. Sesay, Kallon and Gbao. SCSL-04-15-T. *Supra* note 268. ¶ 1574; Prosecutor v. Sesay, Kallon and Gbao. SCSL-04-15-T. *Supra* note 279. ¶ 128; Prosecutor v. Taylor. SCSL-03-01-T. *Supra* note 270. ¶¶ 936, 1094.

[1413] Prosecutor v. Brima, Kamara, Kanu. SCSL-04-16-T. *Supra* note 280. ¶ 991; Prosecutor v. Taylor. SCSL-03-01-T. *Supra* note 270. ¶ 882.

[1414] Prosecutor v. Taylor. SCSL-03-01-T. *Supra* note 270. ¶ 882.

custody of the SS to literally "work to death."[1415] [1416] SS guards would force inmates into hard jobs for days straight without any kind of rest, such as carrying rails around and pieces of machinery, working in the construction of tunnels, digging cellars, working in cement factories, and hardening road surfaces.[1417] While performing a 12-hour shift of forced labor, Nazi personnel brutally tortured, beat, or whipped inmates to the point of victims losing consciousness.[1418] Some inmates would receive harsh punitive detachments without any plausible reason.[1419] Others were shot during their work by the SS guards.[1420] Consequentially, the death rate of inmates was correspondingly high.[1421]

## 2.9.2. Forced labor & enslavement in the Former Yugoslavia detention camps

Serbian military, police, and authorities forced Muslim detainees at the detention camps to perform several types of forced labor, such as clearing

---

[1415] In Nazi Heinrich Himmler's abominable own words on "the attitude of the SS toward Germany's slave laborers," in the Poznan speech of 4 October 1943: "What happens to a Russian, to a Czech, does not interest me in the slightest. [...] Whether nations live in prosperity or starve to death interests me only insofar as we need them as slaves for our Kultur; otherwise, it is of no interest to me. Whether 10,000 Russian females fall down from exhaustion while digging an anti-tank ditch interests me only insofar as the anti-tank ditch for Germany is finished. We shall never be rough and heartless when it is not necessary, but it is clear, we Germans, who are the only people in the world who have a decent attitude towards animals, will also assume a decent attitude towards these man animals. But it is a crime against our own blood to worry about them and give them ideals, thus causing our sons and grandsons to have a more difficult time with them." (**United States of America v. Oswald Pohl,** *et al.* **Case 4** (Pohl case) (1947). pp. 230–231).

[1416] "[Inmates] had no color in their faces whatsoever. They were practically living corpses, covered with skin and bone, and completely broken in spirit. Everyone who was there knew that the inmates were kept there as long as they turn out work and that when they were physically unable to continue, they were disposed of." (**United States of America v. Carl Krauch,** *et al.* **Case 6**, Volume 8 (I.G. Farben case) (1947). p. 624).

[1417] **United States of America v. Oswald Pohl,** *et al.* **Case 4** (Pohl case) (1947). pp. 248–249, 396, 472; **United States of America v. Carl Krauch,** *et al.* **Case 6**, Volume 8 (I.G. Farben case) (1947). pp. 623–624. See also: p. 472.

[1418] **United States of America v. Oswald Pohl,** *et al.* **Case 4** (Pohl case) (1947). pp. 396, 408–409, 472.

[1419] *Idem.* p. 472.

[1420] *Idem.* pp. 408–409.

[1421] *Idem.* p. 472.

forests, felling trees, working in fields and factories, assisting in the construction of infrastructure projects, transporting bodies, and burying them in mass graves, digging of trenches, carrying of munitions at frontlines, and working on the frontline.[1422] Detainees were guarded by members of the police as well as of armed forces in olive-drab uniforms. They were kept working without any food or water, in freezing conditions, suffering exhaustion, being beaten with rifle butts if they refused to work, and being exposed to injuries and killings in crossfire operations.[1423] Muslims and Croats were chosen by the Serbian military, police, and authorities to perform acts of forced labor with an explicit discriminatory nature by virtue of their religion/nationality.[1424]

## 2.9.3. Forced labor & enslavement in Sierra Leone

AFRC/RUF fighters forced thousands of civilians to work in diamond mining pits in various locations of Sierra Leone.[1425] Civilians had to perform extensive shifts of work without rest for periods of up to two years.[1426] Duties varied from directly mining pits to other tasks such as carrying loads, farming, going on food-finding missions, and general domestic chores.[1427]

Many civilian miners had to work naked, "in chains and tied with rope around their waists."[1428] Fighters' guns would always be pointed at the miners all over the diamond pits, so the victims could not escape.[1429] AFRC/RUF fighters would give miners only one plantain a day to eat.[1430] There was no medical assistance or medication for miners at all.[1431]

If civilians refused to mine or failed to find diamonds, AFRC/RUF fighters would often strip naked civilians, flog, stab, beat, rub with mud, shoot,

---

[1422] Prosecutor v. Radoslav Brđanin. IT-99-36-T. *Supra* note 130. ¶ 921; Prosecutor v. Momčilo Krajišnik. IT-00-39-T. *Supra* note 121. ¶¶ 759, 815; Prosecutor v. Mićo Stanišić, Stojan Župljanin. IT-08-91-T, vol. 1. *Supra* note 102. ¶ 908; Prosecutor v. Radovan Karadžić. IT-95-5/18-T, vol. 1. *Supra* note 134. ¶¶ 1021, 1179, 1195, 1201, 1255, 1298, 1300, 1394, 1479, 2424.

[1423] Prosecutor v. Mićo Stanišić, Stojan Župljanin. IT-08-91-T, vol. 1. *Supra* note 102. ¶ 908–909; Prosecutor v. Radovan Karadžić. IT-95-5/18-T, vol. 1. *Supra* note 134. ¶¶ 1196, 2424.

[1424] Prosecutor v. Momčilo Krajišnik. IT-00-39-T. *Supra* note 121. ¶ 816.

[1425] Prosecutor v. Taylor. SCSL-03-01-T. *Supra* note 270. ¶ 1744.

[1426] *Idem.* ¶ 1743.

[1427] *Idem.* ¶ 1970.

[1428] *Idem.* ¶ 1742.

[1429] *Idem.* ¶¶ 1698, 1742.

[1430] *Idem.* ¶ 1742.

[1431] *Ibidem.*

and eventually kill them as an example to the other workers.[1432] Whenever civilians found diamonds, the gemstones would be immediately taken by the fighters and given to the superior commanders.[1433]

## 2.10. Child recruitment in Sierra Leone

Throughout Sierra Leone, children were an indispensable "tool" at the hands of RUF and AFRC forces from February 1998 onwards.[1434] Thousands of children as young as six, eight, nine, ten, and eleven years old were abducted, separated from their families, forcibly trained, and forced to actively participate in hostilities and to be used in support/logistical tasks in various locations throughout the country.[1435] The RUF and AFRC rebels regarded children as "fearless," "full of agility," and "more obedient than adults:"[1436] [1437]

> "Young boys were of particular value [...] due to their loyalty to the movement and their ability to effectively conduct espionage activities, as their small size and agility made them particularly suitable for hazardous assignments. The younger children were particularly aggressive when armed and were known to kill human beings as if they were nothing more than 'chickens'."[1438]

After being recruited, RUF subjected children to military training, which was, most of the time, the same training given to adults.[1439] Lessons included "military discipline, physical endurance, armour [sic] and artillery classes, and how to mount ambushes."[1440] [1441] RUF and AFRC fighters as-

---

[1432]  *Idem.* ¶¶ 1631, 1742–1743.

[1433]  *Idem.* ¶ 1742.

[1434]  Prosecutor v. Fofana, Kondewa. SCSL-04-14-T. *Supra* note 281. ¶ 688; Prosecutor v. Sesay, Kallon and Gbao. SCSL-04-15-T. *Supra* note 268. ¶¶ 1616, 1708.

[1435]  Prosecutor v. Sesay, Kallon and Gbao. SCSL-04-15-T. *Supra* note 268. ¶¶ 1617, 1649, 1661, 1674, 1677, 1691, 1699, 1701-1702, 1747; Prosecutor v. Sesay, Kallon and Gbao. SCSL-04-15-T. *Supra* note 279. ¶ 180.

[1436]  Prosecutor v. Taylor. SCSL-03-01-T. *Supra* note 270. ¶ 1356.

[1437]  See also: Prosecutor v. Sesay, Kallon and Gbao. SCSL-04-15-T. *Supra* note 268. ¶ 1703.

[1438]  *Idem.* ¶ 1616.

[1439]  *Idem.* ¶¶ 1619, 1633, 1647, 1684, 1707.

[1440]  *Ibidem.*

[1441]  See also: Prosecutor v. Brima, Kamara, Kanu. SCSL-04-16-T. *Supra* note 280. ¶ 34; Prosecutor v. Sesay, Kallon and Gbao. SCSL-04-15-T. *Supra* note 268. ¶ 1638.

signed children both to "active combat" functions and "logistical support" functions.[1442]

Active combat functions included: 1) to commit crimes such as killing, looting, burning civilian houses, burning civilians alive, raping civilians flogging civilians; 2) to actively participate in hostilities; 3) to attack officers of peacekeeping missions, particularly UNAMSIL peacekeepers; 4) to decapitate or behead civilians; 5) to mutilate and amputate civilians, including other children; 6) to take part in patrols; 7) to serve as bodyguards for higher-ranking Commanders; 8) to spy on enemy positions and to collect intelligence; 9) to gather information from civilians and opposition camps; 10) to guard military objectives; and 11) to carry guns and armament, such as light and heavy weapons, rocket launchers, and grenades.[1443]

Tasks of logistical importance included: 1) to dig diamonds for their adult commanders; 2) to guard diamond mining pits; 3) to participate in food-finding missions; and 4) cooking and undertaking "laundry duties, fetch[ing] water and carry[ing] goods, including looted property and food for the forces."[1444]

RUF often drugged children during the training and after this period when child soldiers were in active combat.[1445] The most common substances that RUF habitually gave to children included "alcohol or drugs such as marijuana, amphetamines, and cocaine."[1446] The administration of drugs usually followed the same pattern:

> "The children's legs would sometimes be "cut with blades [so] cocaine [could be] rubbed in the wounds," which made them feel "like a big person" and see other people "like chickens and rats" that they could kill. Drugs were often ingested by smoke inhalation or by sniffing."[1447] [1448]

---

[1442] Prosecutor v. Sesay, Kallon and Gbao. SCSL-04-15-T. *Supra* note 268. ¶ 1620.

[1443] *Idem.* ¶¶ 146, 1618, 1620, 1638, 1654, 1672, 1682, 1687, 1711, 1714–1715, 1719, 1725, 1729, 1731–1733. See also: Prosecutor v. Sesay, Kallon and Gbao. SCSL-04-15-T. *Supra* note 279. ¶ 180; Prosecutor v. Taylor. SCSL-03-01-T. *Supra* note 270. ¶¶ 1311, 1356, 1403, 1483–1490, 1496, 1523, 1604, 1618, 1665, 1674, 1681, 1684, 1711–1712, 1719.

[1444] Prosecutor v. Sesay, Kallon and Gbao. SCSL-04-15-T. *Supra* note 268. ¶¶ 1618, 1620, 1660, 1664, 1675; Prosecutor v. Taylor. SCSL-03-01-T. *Supra* note 270. ¶¶ 1459, 1491–1496, 1523.

[1445] Prosecutor v. Brima, Kamara, Kanu. SCSL-04-16-T. *Supra* note 280. ¶ 34.

[1446] Prosecutor v. Sesay, Kallon and Gbao. SCSL-04-15-T. *Supra* note 268. ¶ 1623.

[1447] *Ibidem.*

[1448] See also: Prosecutor v. Taylor. SCSL-03-01-T. *Supra* note 270. ¶ 1356.

Those children who were "unable to endure the training regime,"[1449] or who attempted escaping, or that refused to carry out orders were summarily killed by RUF fighters.[1450] If they survived, these child soldiers "were robbed of a childhood and most of them lost the chance of an education."[1451] [1452]

---

[1449] Prosecutor v. Sesay, Kallon and Gbao. SCSL-04-15-T. *Supra* note 268. ¶ 1641.

[1450] *Idem.* ¶ 1619.

[1451] Prosecutor v. Brima, Kamara, Kanu. SCSL-04-16-T. *Supra* note 280. ¶ 34.

[1452] On March 14, 2012, the ICC Trial Chamber considered Thomas Lubanga Dyilo guilty of the crime of conscripting and enlisting children under the age of fifteen years into the Patriotic Forces for the Liberation of Congo (FPLC) and using them to participate actively in hostilities within the meaning of Articles 8(2)(e)(vii) and 25(3)(a) of the Rome Statute. Please refer to: Prosecutor v. Thomas Lubanga Dyilo. ICC-01/04-01/06. *Supra* note 340. ¶ 1358.

# 3. An assessment of the caselaw from Nuremberg, the ICTR, the ICTY, the SCSL, and ICC tribunals on genocide and crimes against humanity

## 3.1. Genocide

### 3.1.1. Overview, definition, protected legal values, elements, and the applicable law

In 1944, the Polish-Jewish jurist Raphael Lemkin coined and developed the term *genocide* as a new legal concept to portray the conduct perpetrated by the Nazis against certain groups of people, particularly the Jews – the Holocaust –, and, to a lesser degree, against the Gypsies.[1453][1454][1455][1456][1457] The neologism *genocide* was formed by the juxtaposition of the Greek word *genos* (meaning tribe, race, or nation), followed by the Latin suffix *cide* (meaning killing).[1458] With his inaugural piece *Axis Rule in Occupied Europe*, Lemkin laid the foundations "for a definition of what would become the gravest of international crimes."[1459] The Nuremberg Military Tribunal trials, which took place from 1945 to 1949 to hold accountable Nazi war criminals, did not profit from Lemkin's work, in obedience to the foundations of *nullum crimen sine lege*.[1460] Consequently, the Nuremberg judgements "dealt with genocide as a crime against humanity."[1461]

---

[1453] Raphael Lemkin. *Supra* note 6. pp. 3–9.

[1454] Douglas Irvin-Erickson. *Supra* note 7. *passim.*

[1455] Payam Akhavan. *Supra* note 8. pp. 91–101.

[1456] Gideon Boas, James L. Bischoff & Natalie L. Reid. *Supra* note 62. p.145.

[1457] Robert Cryer, Håkan Friman, Darryl Robinson & Elizabeth Wilmshurst. *Supra* note 21. p. 166.

[1458] Gideon Boas, James L. Bischoff & Natalie L. Reid. *Supra* note 62. p.145.

[1459] *Ibidem.*

[1460] In this regard, The ICTR Trial Chamber noted that "the crimes prosecuted by the Nuremberg Tribunal, namely the holocaust of the Jews or the *Final Solution*, were very much constitutive of genocide, but they could not be defined as such because the crime of genocide was not defined until later." (Prosecutor v. Jean Kambanda. ICTR-97-23. *Supra* note 199. ¶ 14).

[1461] Kevin Jon Heller. *Supra* note 28. p. 388.

It was only after World War II that "genocide developed from a cate-
gory of crimes against humanity to an autonomous crime."[1462] [1463] The General Assembly of the then-recently created United Nations subsequently
recognized that genocide constituted an "odious scourge" that inflicted
"great losses on humanity" "at all periods of history."[1464] On December 9,
1948, through its Resolution 260 A (III), the General Assembly approved the
Convention on the Prevention and Punishment of the Crime of Genocide
(*hereinafter* The Genocide Convention, The U.N. Genocide Convention),
which came into force on January 12, 1951. From then on, "genocide is,
first and foremost, a legal concept."[1465] In Article I, the Contracting Parties
on the novel Genocide Convention confirmed that genocide might be committed in times of peace or in times of war.[1466] The crime of genocide was
later typified in other instruments of international treaty law, namely in
the Statutes of the ICTY,[1467] ICTR,[1468] and ICC (The Rome Statute).[1469] Both
the Genocide Convention[1470] and the Rome Statute[1471] define the crime of
genocide with the same *verbatim*: an act "committed with intent to destroy,
in whole or in part, a national, ethnical, racial or religious group, as such."
Genocide is incontestably considered a *jus cogens* norm and also part of the
customary International Criminal Law.[1472] [1473] [1474]

---

[1462] Kai Ambos. *Supra* note 63. p. 1.

[1463] "The legal concept of genocide was forged in the crucible of post-Second World
War efforts to prosecute Nazi atrocities. Its development took place in conjunction with that of other international crimes, especially crimes against humanity,
with which it bears a close but complex and difficult relationship. The development and history of genocide as a legal concept cannot be properly understood
without considering the parallel existence of crimes against humanity." (William
A. Schabas, The Law and Genocide 123–141 *in* The Oxford Handbook of Genocide
Studies (Donald Bloxham & A. Dirk Moses eds. *Supra* note 18. p. 124–125).

[1464] G. A. Res. 260 A (III), Convention on the Prevention and Punishment of the Crime
of Genocide (Dec. 9, 1948). *Preamble.*

[1465] William A. Schabas, The Law and Genocide 123–141 *in* The Oxford Handbook of
Genocide Studies (Donald Bloxham & A. Dirk Moses eds. *Supra* note 18. p. 123).

[1466] G. A. Res. 260 A (III), Convention on the Prevention and Punishment of the Crime
of Genocide (Dec. 9, 1948). Article I.

[1467] Statute of the International Tribunal for the Prosecution of Persons Responsible
for Serious Violations of International Humanitarian Law Committed in the Territory of the Former Yugoslavia since 1991, U.N. Doc. S/RES/827 (May 25, 1993).

[1468] Statute of the International Criminal Tribunal for Rwanda, U.N. Doc. S/RES/955
(Nov. 8, 1994).

[1469] United Nations. Rome Statute (July 17, 1998) 2187 UNTS 38544.

[1470] G. A. Res. 260 A (III), Convention on the Prevention and Punishment of the Crime
of Genocide (Dec. 9, 1948). Article II.

[1471] United Nations. Rome Statute (July 17, 1998) 2187 UNTS 38544. Article 6.

The instruments of international treaty law on genocide aim to protect at least three values:

Firstly, they aim to protect the very right of the physical existence of entire human groups,[1475] their moral integrity, and very dignity as "distinct entities."[1476] In doing so, they aim to safeguard the manifold social, economic, cultural, historical, political, moral, and anthropological "future contributions" that human groups bring to humanity;[1477] [1478]

Secondly, recognizing that genocide is a "crime against all of humankind,"[1479] which affects "not only the group targeted for destruction,"[1480] they aim to protect humanity as a whole;

Thirdly, recognizing that genocide "constitutes a threat to international peace and security,"[1481] they aim to establish "effective measures to bring to justice the persons who are responsible for [such crime]"[1482] – individual criminal responsibility. In doing so, it aims to contribute to the process of international cooperation, "national reconciliation, restoration, and maintenance of peace."[1483]

In the present 1948 Convention, genocide means an act "committed with intent to destroy, in whole or in part, a national, ethnical, racial or religious group, as such."[1484] For the Convention, genocide is characterized by two legal elements: the *mens rea* (moral elements/subjective elements) and the *actus reus* (material elements/objective elements).[1485] [1486] [1487] [1488]

---

[1472] Prosecutor v. Musema. ICTR-96-13-A. *Supra* note 216. ¶ 151.

[1473] To date (March 11, 2023), the Convention on the Prevention and Punishment of the Crime of Genocide has been ratified by 153 contracting states.

[1474] Kai Ambos. *Supra* note 63. p. 2

[1475] G. A. Res. 96(I), The Crime of Genocide, Fifty-fifth plenary meeting, U.N. Doc. A/RES/96 (Dec. 11, 1946). *preamble.*

[1476] Prosecutor v. Milomir Stakić. IT-97-24-A. *Supra* note 110. ¶ 21.

[1477] *Ibidem.*

[1478] G. A. Res. 96(I), The Crime of Genocide, Fifty-fifth plenary meeting, U.N. Doc. A/RES/96 (Dec. 11, 1946). *preamble.*

[1479] Prosecutor v. Radislav Krstić. IT-98-33-A. *Supra* note 129. ¶ 36.

[1480] *Ibidem.*

[1481] S.C. Res. 955 (Nov. 8, 1994). *preamble.*

[1482] *Ibidem.*

[1483] *Ibidem.*

[1484] G. A. Res. 260 A (III), Convention on the Prevention and Punishment of the Crime of Genocide (Dec. 9, 1948). Article II.

[1485] Prosecutor v. Kayishema and Ruzindana. ICTR 95-1-T. *Supra* note 209. ¶ 90; Prosecutor v. Goran Jelisić. IT-95-10-T. *Supra* note 97. ¶ 62.

[1486] U.N. Doc. A/CN.4/SER.A/1996/Add.l (Part 2) (1996). p. 44, ¶ 4.

[1487] U.N. Doc. A/51/10 (May 6, 1996 – July 26, 1996). p. 45. ¶ 8.

The *mens rea* refers to the specific *intent* to destroy, in whole or in part, specific groups of people – a national, ethnical, racial, or religious group – because of their "unique distinguishing characteristics (particular group identity)."[1489] [1490] [1491] The *actus reus* refers to the *numerus clausus* list of acts that may be considered genocide if perpetrated with genocidal *intent*. Both the Genocide Convention and the Rome Statute define the genocide *actus reus* with the same *verbatim*: "Killing members of the group";[1492] [1493] "Causing serious bodily or mental harm to members of the group;"[1494] "Deliberately inflicting on the group conditions of life calculated to bring about its physical destruction in whole or in part";[1495] [1496] "Imposing measures intended to prevent births within the group";[1497] "Forcibly transferring children of the group to another group."[1498] In Article III, the Genocide Convention punishes the inchoate forms of the crime, namely: conspiracy to commit genocide; direct and public incitement to commit genocide; attempt to commit genocide; and complicity in genocide.[1499]

---

[1488] Kai Ambos suggests that "as opposed to what is suggested by some of the case law the structure of the genocide crime may be characterized by three constitutive elements: 1) the actus reus (objective elements) of the offence, which consists of one or several of the acts enumerated under Article 6(2) ICC Statute; 2) the corresponding mens rea (subjective element), as described in Article 30 ICC; and 3) an extended (ulterior) mental element, namely the intent to destroy (special subjective element), in whole or in part, a national, ethnical, racial or religious group as such." (Kai Ambos. *Supra* note 63. p. 5).

[1489] Prosecutor v. Ratko Mladić., IT-09-92-T, vol. 3. *Supra* note 137. ¶ 3436.

[1490] See also: Prosecutor v. Milomir Stakić. IT-97-24-T. *Supra* note 109. ¶ 521; Prosecutor v. Radoslav Brđanin. IT-99-36-T. *Supra* note 130. ¶ 698.

[1491] See also: U.N. Doc. A/51/10 (May 6, 1996 – July 26, 1996). p. 44. ¶ 5.

[1492] United Nations. Rome Statute (July 17, 1998) 2187 UNTS 38544. Art. 6. (a).

[1493] The Rome Statute follows the verbatim of the Genocide Convention, Article II. (G. A. Res. 260 A (III), Convention on the Prevention and Punishment of the Crime of Genocide (Dec. 9, 1948).

[1494] United Nations. Rome Statute (July 17, 1998) 2187 UNTS 38544. Art. 6. (b).

[1495] *Idem.* Art. 6. (c).

[1496] In *Akayesu*, the ICTR Trial Chamber held that "the expression deliberately inflicting on the group conditions of life calculated to bring about its physical destruction in whole or in part, should be construed as the methods of destruction by which the perpetrator does not immediately kill the members of the group, but which, ultimately, seek their physical destruction. (...) inter alia, subjecting a group of people to a subsistence diet, systematic expulsion from homes and the reduction of essential medical services below minimum requirement." (Prosecutor v. Jean-Paul Akayesu. ICTR-96-4-T. *Supra* note 203. ¶¶ 505–506).

[1497] United Nations. Rome Statute (July 17, 1998) 2187 UNTS 38544. Art. 6. (d).

[1498] *Idem.* Art. 6. (e).

[1499] G. A. Res. 260 A (III), Convention on the Prevention and Punishment of the Crime of Genocide (Dec. 9, 1948). III(b), (c), (d), (e).

The physical/biological destruction of the group, in whole or in part, must be the objective of the underlying conduct of the crime of genocide.[1500] [1501] [1502] Nevertheless, "it is not necessary to prove the *de facto* destruction of the group."[1503] [1504] Cultural destruction was not contemplated in the Genocide Convention nor the statutes that followed it. Concerning this issue, the ICTY Appeals Chamber in *Krstić* stated:

"Customary international law limits the definition of genocide to those acts seeking the physical or biological destruction of all or part of the group. [A]n enterprise attacking only the cultural or sociological characteristics of a human group in order to annihilate these elements which give to that group its own identity distinct from the rest of the community would not fall under the definition of genocide."[1505] [1506]

---

[1500]  Prosecutor v. Emmanuel Ndindabahizi. ICTR-2001-71-I. *Supra* note 177. ¶ 454; Prosecutor v. Radoslav Brđanin. IT-99-36-T. *Supra* note 130. ¶ 963; Prosecutor v. Vidoje Blagojević, Dragan Jokić. IT-02-60-T. *Supra* note 147. ¶ 656; Prosecutor v. Mikaeli Muhimana. ICTR-95-1B-T. *Supra* note 214. ¶ 497; Prosecutor v. Jean Mpambara. ICTR-01-65-T. *Supra* note 202. ¶ 8.

[1501]  U.N. Doc. A/CN.4/SER.A/1996/Add.l (Part 2) (1996). p. 45, ¶ 12.

[1502]  U.N. Doc. A/51/10 (May 6, 1996 – July 26, 1996). pp. 45–46. ¶ 12.

[1503]  "Nevertheless, the *de facto* destruction of the group may constitute evidence of the specific intent and may also serve to distinguish the crime of genocide from the inchoate offences (...) such as the attempt to commit genocide." (Prosecutor v. Radoslav Brđanin. IT-99-36-T. *Supra* note 130. ¶ 697).

[1504]  In Stakić, the ICTY stated that, in cases of forced deportation, "it does not suffice to deport a group or a part of a group." The Trial Chamber considered that "a clear distinction must be drawn between physical destruction and mere dissolution of a group. The expulsion of a group or part of a group does not in itself suffice for genocide." (Prosecutor v. Milomir Stakić. IT-97-24-T. *Supra* note 109. ¶ 519).

[1505]  Prosecutor v. Radislav Krstić. IT-98-33-A. *Supra* note 129. ¶ 25.

[1506]  This was also the conclusion of the ICTY when *Krstić* was still in the first instance at the Trial Chamber: "An enterprise attacking only the cultural or sociological characteristics of a human group in order to annihilate these elements which give to that group its own identity distinct from the rest of the community would not fall under the definition of genocide." Interestingly, however, the Trial Chamber pointed out that "where there is physical or biological destruction there are often simultaneous attacks on the cultural and religious property and symbols of the targeted group as well, attacks which may legitimately be considered as evidence of an intent to physically destroy the group." The Court then concluded: "In this case, the Trial Chamber will thus take into account as evidence of intent to destroy the group the deliberate destruction of mosques and houses belonging to members of the group." (Prosecutor v. Radislav Krstić., IT-98-33-T. *Supra* note 128. ¶ 580).

The correct determination of the targeted group, which is the object of international protection, must always be made on a case-by-case basis, considering both objective and subjective elements.[1507] [1508] This means that the victims of the attacked group are targeted because of "particular, distinct, and (...) common characteristics."[1509] Groups are targeted due to their identity (*positive* approach), rather than a lack thereof (*negative* approach).[1510] The victims of genocide are generally perceived as belonging to a group because the perpetrator of the crime identifies them as belonging to such a group. Nevertheless, in some instances, "the victim may perceive himself or herself to belong to the aforesaid group"[1511] – *self-identification*.[1512]

On September 2, 1998, the ICTR held a conviction of genocide against the Rwandan mayor of the Taba Commune, Jean-Paul Akayesu.[1513] The Trial Chamber unanimously convicted Akayesu on the counts of "genocide" and "direct and public incitement to commit genocide"[1514] for having planned, instigated, ordered, committed, or otherwise aided genocidal attacks of the Hutu ethnic group against the Tutsi in Rwanda.[1515] Importantly, in such a ruling, rape was considered a form of genocide.[1516] Also, the Trial Chamber held that no special status is required for the perpetrator of genocidal acts.[1517] The ICTR Appeals Chamber later upheld the sentence on June 1, 2001, which unanimously dismissed each of the grounds of appeal raised

---

[1507] Prosecutor v. Radoslav Brđanin. IT-99-36-T. *Supra* note 130. ¶¶ 683–684; Prosecutor v. Vidoje Blagojević, Dragan Jokić. IT-02-60-T. *Supra* note 147. ¶ 667; Prosecutor v. Vidoje Blagojević, Dragan Jokić. IT-02-60-T. *Supra* note 147. ¶ 667; Prosecutor v. Zdravko Tolimir. IT-05-88/2-T. *Supra* note 153. ¶ 735; Prosecutor v. Radovan Karadžić. IT-95-5/18-T, vol. I. *Supra* note 134. ¶ 541.

[1508] Prosecutor v. Laurent Semanza. ICTR-97-20-T. *Supra* note 211. ¶ 317; Prosecutor v. Jean de Dieu Kamuhanda. ICTR-95-54A-T. *Supra* note 200. ¶ 630; Prosecutor v. Sylvestre Gacumbitsi. ICTR-2001-64-T. *Supra* note 228. ¶ 254; Prosecutor v. Athanase Seromba. ICTR-2001-66-T. *Supra* note 160. ¶ 318.

[1509] Prosecutor v. Zdravko Tolimir. IT-05-88/2-T. *Supra* note 153. ¶ 735.

[1510] Prosecutor v. Milomir Stakić. IT-97-24-T. *Supra* note 109. ¶ 512; Prosecutor v. Radoslav Brđanin. IT-99-36-T. *Supra* note 130. ¶ 685; Prosecutor v. Vujadin Popović *et al.* IT-05-88-T. *Supra* note 150. ¶ 809; Prosecutor v. Radovan Karadžić. IT-95-5/18-T, vol. I. *Supra* note 134. ¶ 541.

[1511] Prosecutor v. Radoslav Brđanin. IT-99-36-T. *Supra* note 130. ¶ 683.

[1512] Prosecutor v. Clément Kayishema and Ruzindana. ICTR 95-1-T. *Supra* note 209. ¶ 98.

[1513] Prosecutor v. Jean-Paul Akayesu. ICTR-96-4-T. *Supra* note 203.

[1514] *Idem.* Section 8. Verdict.

[1515] *Idem.* ¶¶ 672–675.

[1516] *Idem.* ¶¶ 731–734.

[1517] *Idem. Passim.*

by Jean-Paul Akayesu.[1518] The Chamber confirmed all the counts on which Akayesu was convicted and upheld the sentence of life imprisonment handed down by the Trial Chamber.[1519] Later, both the ICJ[1520] and the ICTY[1521] acknowledged the perpetration of genocide in Srebrenica.

Notably, Professor Schabas lectures that "in addition to genocide itself, which is defined in Article II of the Convention on the Prevention and Punishment of the Crime of Genocide, Article III describes four forms of participation in the crime: conspiracy, direct and public incitement, attempt, and complicity."[1522] Schabas explains that, concerning the attempted form of genocide, there are striking differences between "result-based" and "conduct-based" patterns of action.[1523] He clarifies that in conducts such as killing, inflicting harm, and transferring children, the perpetrator of such acts responds for the *attempted* form of the crime when they fail to achieve the desired result of the action, the destruction of a protected group.[1524] [1525] On the other hand, when the perpetrators' actions concern an act such as preventing births, the perpetrators are fully responsible for their conduct, regardless of the outcome of their actions.[1526] [1527] [1528]

## 3.1.2. The Protected Groups

Not all human groups fall under the protection of genocide.[1529] The most distinctive trait of the crime of genocide resides in its victims. The ultimate

---

[1518] *Idem.* Section V. Disposition.

[1519] *Ibidem.*

[1520] Bosnia and Herzegovina v. Serbia and Montenegro. I.C.J. 43. *Supra* note 71. ¶¶ 278–297.

[1521] Prosecutor v. Radislav Krstić. IT-98-33-T. *Supra* note 128; Prosecutor v. Radislav Krstić. IT-98-33-A. *Supra* note 129; Prosecutor v. Momir Nikolić IT-02-60/1-A. *Supra* note 124. Prosecutor v. Vujadin Popović *et al.* IT-05-88-T. *Supra* note 150; Prosecutor v. Vujadin Popović *et al.* IT-05-88-A. *Supra* note 151; Prosecutor v. Zdravko Tolimir. IT-05-88/2-A. *Supra* note 152; Prosecutor v. Radovan Karadžić. IT-95-5/18-T, vols. 1, 2,3, 4. *Supra* note 134.

[1522] William A. Schabas. *Supra* note 12. p. 307.

[1523] *Idem.* pp. 334–339.

[1524] Prosecutor v. Jean-Paul Akayesu. ICTR-96-4-T. *Supra* note 203. ¶ 509.

[1525] U.N. Doc. A/CN.4/SER.A/1996/Add.l (Part 2) (1996). p. 46, ¶ 17.

[1526] William A. Schabas. *Supra* note 12. pp. 334–339.

[1527] See also: **United States of America v.** Ulrich Greifelt, *et al.* Case 5 (RuSHA case) (1947). p. 110; Prosecutor v. Jean-Paul Akayesu. ICTR-96-4-T. *Supra* note 203. ¶¶ 507–508.

[1528] See also: U.N. Doc. A/CN.4/SER.A/1996/Add.l (Part 2) (1996). p. 46, ¶ 16.

[1529] Robert Cryer, Håkan Friman, Darryl Robinson & Elizabeth Wilmshurst. *Supra* note 21. p. 169.

victim of genocide is always a group protected by law.[1530] The U.N. Genocide Convention prescribes, in an exhaustive list, that the victim must belong to a specific national, ethnical, racial, or religious group *as such*.[1531] Such *verbatim* was transliterated in the statutes of the ICTR,[1532] ICTY,[1533] and of the ICC.[1534] [1535] In *Prosecutor v. Blagojević & Jokić*, the ICTY considered that a group comprises its individuals and the "history, traditions, the relationship between its members, the relationship with other groups, [and] the relationship with the land."[1536]

The genocide perpetrator targets the victims because of their membership in the aforesaid protected groups.[1537] [1538] This means that the genocide law aims to protect "mainly a collective legal interest, that is, the right of certain groups to exist, and to contribute to a pluralistic world."[1539] Therefore, the destruction of the members belonging to these groups constitutes "the means used to achieve the ultimate criminal objective with respect to the group."[1540] This ultimately means that the prohibited genocidal act – or acts – is (are) committed against an individual because of their membership in a particular group rather than by virtue of their particular identity, characteristics, and singularities.[1541] [1542] These individuals "are important not per se but only as members of the group to which they belong."[1543]

---

[1530]  Prosecutor v. Duško Sikirica *et al.* IT-95-8-T. *Supra* note 88. ¶ 89; Prosecutor v. Jean Mpambara. ICTR-01-65-T. *Supra* note 202. ¶ 8.

[1531]  G. A. Res. 260 A (III), Convention on the Prevention and Punishment of the Crime of Genocide (Dec. 9, 1948). Article II.

[1532]  Statute of the International Criminal Tribunal for Rwanda, U.N. Doc. S/RES/955 (Nov. 8, 1994). Article 2.2.

[1533]  Statute of the International Tribunal for the Prosecution of Persons Responsible for Serious Violations of International Humanitarian Law Committed in the Territory of the Former Yugoslavia since 1991, U.N. Doc. S/RES/827 (May 25, 1993). Article 4.2.

[1534]  United Nations. Rome Statute (July 17, 1998) 2187 UNTS 38544. Article 6, *caput.*

[1535]  See also: U.N. Doc. A/CN.4/SER.A/1996/Add.l (Part 2) (1996). p. 45, ¶ 9.

[1536]  Prosecutor v. Vidoje Blagojević, Dragan Jokić. IT-02-60-T. *Supra* note 147. ¶ 666.

[1537]  Prosecutor v. Jean Mpambara. ICTR-01-65-T. *Supra* note 202. ¶ 8; Prosecutor v. François Karera. ICTR-01-74-T. *Supra* note 184. ¶ 534; Prosecutor v. Emmanuel Rukundo. ICTR-2001-70-T. *Supra* note 179. ¶ 556; Prosecutor v. Gaspard Kanyarukiga. ICTR-2002-78-T. *Supra* note 187. ¶ 635.

[1538]  U.N. Doc. A/CN.4/SER.A/1996/Add.l (Part 2) (1996). p. 45, ¶ 9.

[1539]  Kai Ambos. *Supra* note 63. p. 3.

[1540]  U.N. Doc. A/CN.4/SER.A/1996/Add.l (Part 2) (1996). p. 45, ¶ 6.

[1541]  *Ibidem.*

[1542]  Prosecutor v. Jean-Paul Akayesu. ICTR-96-4-T. *Supra* note 203. ¶ 521; Prosecutor v. Musema. ICTR-96-13-A. *Supra* note 216. ¶ 165; Prosecutor v. Emmanuel Ndindabahizi. ICTR-2001-71-I. *Supra* note 177. ¶ 454.

[1543]  U.N. Doc. A/CN.4/SER.A/1996/Add.l (Part 2) (1996). p. 45, ¶ 9.

Neither the Genocide Convention nor other international statutes clearly define the meaning and scope of the protected groups (national, ethnical, racial, or religious groups *as such*).[1544] [1545] The preparatory work on the U.N. Convention itself made considerations that such concepts may, sometimes, overlap in practical considerations.[1546] In different instances, the ICTR recognized this very fact that the concepts of *national, ethnical, racial,* and *religious* groups do not share a "generally or internationally accepted definition."[1547] [1548]

In *Prosecutor v. Ignace Bagilishema*, the ICTR considered that such concepts must always be assessed "in the light of a particular political, social, historical, and cultural context."[1549] [1550] This means that, "although membership of the targeted group must be an objective feature of the society in question, there is also a subjective dimension."[1551] For instance, the Court regarded that

> "a group may not have precisely defined boundaries and there may be occasions when it is difficult to give a definitive answer as to whether or not a victim was a member of a protected group. Moreover, the perpetrators of genocide may characterize the targeted group in ways that do not fully correspond to conceptions of the group shared generally, or by other segments of society."[1552]

The ICTR, in *Akayesu*, defined a "national" group taking into consideration the *Nottebohm* decision rendered by the International Court of Justice. Based on the such ruling, the Trial Chamber held that a national group is defined "as a collection of people who are perceived to share a legal bond based on common citizenship, coupled with reciprocity of rights and duties."[1553] The International Commission of Inquiry on Darfur regarded "na-

---

[1544] Prosecutor v. Radislav Krstić., IT-98-33-T. *Supra* note 128. ¶ 555; Prosecutor v. Radoslav Brđanin. IT-99-36-T. *Supra* note 130. ¶ 682; Prosecutor v. Zdravko Tolimir. IT-05-88/2-T. *Supra* note 153. ¶ 735.

[1545] Prosecutor v. Jean de Dieu Kamuhanda. ICTR-95-54A-T. *Supra* note 200. ¶ 630.

[1546] *Ibidem.*

[1547] Prosecutor v. Ignace Bagilishema. ICTR-95-1A-T. *Supra* note 194. ¶ 65.

[1548] See also: Prosecutor v. Georges Anderson Nderubumwe Rutaganda. ICTR-96-3-T. *Supra* note 188. ¶ 56.

[1549] Prosecutor v. Ignace Bagilishema. ICTR-95-1A-T. *Supra* note 194. ¶ 65.

[1550] See also: Prosecutor v. Georges Anderson Nderubumwe Rutaganda. ICTR-96-3-T. *Supra* note 188. ¶ 56.

[1551] Prosecutor v. Ignace Bagilishema. ICTR-95-1A-T. *Supra* note 194. ¶ 65.

[1552] *Ibidem.*

[1553] Prosecutor v. Jean-Paul Akayesu. ICTR-96-4-T. *Supra* note 203. ¶ 512.

tional" groups as "those sets of individuals which have a distinctive identity in terms of nationality or national origin."[1554] In 1986, the Special Rapporteur on the Draft Code of Offences against the Peace and Security of Mankind recognized a conceptual controversy with the terms "national" and "ethnical" groups. Doudou Thiam acknowledged that "a national group often comprises several different ethnic groups."[1555] Doudou Thiam recognized that states that are perfectly homogeneous from an ethnic point of view are rare.[1556] For instance:

> "In Africa, in particular, territories were divided without taking account of ethnic groups, and that has often created problems for young States shaken by centrifugal movements which are often aimed at ethnic regrouping. With rare exceptions (Somalia, for example), almost all African States have an ethnically mixed population. On other continents, migrations, trade, the vicissitudes of war and conquests have created such mixtures that the concept of the ethnic group is only relative or may no longer have any meaning at all."[1557]

An "ethnic" group was considered by the ICTR and by the International Commission of Inquiry on Darfur as a group whose members share a common language, shared traditions, or common cultural heritage.[1558] [1559] [1560] On the other hand, both the ICTR and the Commission considered that a "racial" group "comprise those sets of individuals sharing some hereditary physical traits or characteristics,"[1561] that are "often identified with a geographical region, irrespective of linguistic, cultural, national, or religious factors."[1562] Tracing the differences between the terms "ethnic" and "racial," the Special Rapporteur on the Draft Code of Offences against the Peace and Security of Mankind considered that:

---

[1554] U.N. Doc. S/2005/60 (Feb. 1, 2005). ¶ 494.

[1555] *Idem.* ¶ 57.

[1556] *Ibidem.*

[1557] *Ibidem.*

[1558] Prosecutor v. Jean-Paul Akayesu. ICTR-96-4-T. *Supra* note 203. ¶ 513.

[1559] U.N. Doc. S/2005/60 (Feb. 1, 2005). ¶ 494.

[1560] "The word *ethnical* used in the [Genocide] Convention has been replaced by the word *ethnic* in article 17 to reflect modern English usage without in any way affecting the substance of the provision. Furthermore, the Commission was of the view that the article covered the prohibited acts when committed with the necessary intent against members of a tribal group." (U.N. Doc. A/CN.4/SER.A/1996/Add.l (Part 2) (1996). p. 45, ¶ 9).

[1561] U.N. Doc. S/2005/60 (Feb. 1, 2005). ¶ 494.

[1562] Prosecutor v. Jean-Paul Akayesu. ICTR-96-4-T. *Supra* note 203. ¶ 514.

"It seems that the ethnic bond is more cultural. It is based on cultural values and is characterized by a way of life, a way of thinking and the same way of looking at life and things. On a deeper level, the ethnic group is based on a cosmogony. The racial element, on the other hand, refers more typically to common physical traits."[1563]

A "religious" group was regarded by the ICTR, in *Akayesu*, as a group in which its "members share the same religion, denomination or mode of worship."[1564] The International Commission of Inquiry on Darfur, by its turn, considered the membership element of religion, encompassing "sets of individuals having the same religion, as opposed to other groups adhering to a different religion."[1565]

These definitions are not absolute. Both the ICTR and the ICTY considered that such determination takes into consideration both objective and subjective criteria. According to the Courts, this criterion is always assessed on a case-by-case basis.[1566] The objective criteria consider aspects such as biological aspects, as well as the social or historical context.[1567] In contrast, the subjective criteria consider the perceptions of the perpetrators and the victims themselves (self-perception).[1568] According to the ICTR, the subjective aspect means that the perpetrator of genocide perceives the victim as belonging to a group slated for destruction.[1569] In some instances, "the victim may perceive himself/herself as a member of said group."[1570] [1571] [1572] [1573] This being the case, it is crucially important that the group under consideration must be "stable" and "coherent,"[1574] [1575] consti-

---

[1563] U.N. Doc. A/CN.4/398 (March 11, 1986). ¶ 58.

[1564] Prosecutor v. Jean-Paul Akayesu. ICTR-96-4-T. *Supra* note 203. ¶ 515.

[1565] U.N. Doc. S/2005/60 (Feb. 1, 2005). ¶ 494.

[1566] Prosecutor v. Laurent Semanza. ICTR-97-20-T. *Supra* note 211. ¶ 317; Prosecutor v. Radoslav Brđanin. IT-99-36-T. *Supra* note 130. ¶ 684; Prosecutor v. Vidoje Blagojević, Dragan Jokić. IT-02-60-T. *Supra* note 147. ¶ 667.

[1567] Prosecutor v. Laurent Semanza. ICTR-97-20-T. *Supra* note 211. ¶ 317.

[1568] *Ibidem.*

[1569] Prosecutor v. Musema. ICTR-96-13-A. *Supra* note 216. ¶ 161.

[1570] *Ibidem.*

[1571] See also: Prosecutor v. Ignace Bagilishema. ICTR-95-1A-T. *Supra* note 194. ¶ 65; Prosecutor v. Vidoje Blagojević, Dragan Jokić. IT-02-60-T. *Supra* note 147. ¶ 667.

[1572] U.N. Doc. S/2005/60 (Feb. 1, 2005). ¶¶ 498–500, 518.

[1573] For the International Commission of Inquiry on Darfur, "the self-perception of people as members of tribes and the social networks connected to the tribal structures constituted the central feature of the demographics of Darfur." (*Idem.* ¶ 53).

[1574] Hirad Abtahi & Philippa Webb. *Supra* note 54. p. 1312.

[1575] See also: Gideon Boas, James L. Bischoff & Natalie L. Reid. *Supra* note 62. p. 147.

tuted in a continuous, irremediable, and permanent fashion.[1576] This excludes "mobile" groups, whose commitment to the group is based on a
voluntary      fashion,     such     as     political,     social,     and     economic
groups.[1577] [1578] [1579] [1580]

When considering genocide offenses, Customary International Criminal Law has a well-established rule that groups must always be defined by
their *positive* characteristics — i.e., national, ethical, racial, or religious –
rather than by their *negative* characteristics – i.e., not possessing a specific
"distinct identity."[1581] [1582] In *Stakić*, the ICTY Appeals Chamber considered
that "the drafting history of the Genocide Convention (...) was meant to
incorporate an understanding [that is] incompatible with the negative definition of target groups."[1583] [1584] This, however, does not mean that more

[1576]  Prosecutor v. Jean-Paul Akayesu. ICTR-96-4-T. *Supra* note 203. ¶ 511.
[1577]  Prosecutor v. Goran Jelisić. IT-95-10-T. *Supra* note 97. ¶ 69; Prosecutor v. Musema.
        ICTR-96-13-A. *Supra* note 216. ¶ 162.
[1578]  U.N. Doc. A/CN.4/SER.A/1996/Add.l (Part 2) (1996). p. 45, ¶ 9.
[1579]  In *Vasiliauskas v. Lithuania*, the European Court of Human Rights Considered that
        "there are some arguments to the effect that political groups were protected by
        customary international law on genocide in 1953." However, the Court considered
        that "there are equally strong contemporaneous countervailing views. At this
        juncture, the Court reiterates that notwithstanding those views favouring the in-
        clusion of political groups in the definition of genocide, the scope of the codified
        definition of genocide remained narrower in the Genocide Convention and was
        retained in all subsequent international-law instruments." Therefore, the Court
        concluded: "In sum, the Court finds that there is no sufficiently strong basis for
        finding that customary international law as it stood in 1953 included "political
        groups" among those falling within the definition of genocide." (Vasiliauskas v.
        Lithuania, App. No. 35343/05 (Eur. Ct. H.R. Oct. 20, 2015). ¶ 175. See also: ¶¶ 178,
        181).
[1580]  During the drafting of the Rome Statute, "there was a suggestion to expand the
        definition of the crime of genocide contained in the [Genocide] Convention to en-
        compass social and political groups. This suggestion was supported by some dele-
        gations who felt that any gap in the definition should be filled. However, other
        delegations expressed opposition to amending the definition [of genocide] con-
        tained in the [Genocide] Convention, which was binding on all States as a matter
        of customary law and which had been incorporated in the implementing legisla-
        tion of the numerous States parties do the Convention." (M. Cherif Bassiouni. *Su-
        pra* note 265. p. 42).
[1581]  Prosecutor v. Radoslav Brđanin. IT-99-36-T. *Supra* note 130. ¶ 685; Prosecutor v.
        Vujadin Popović *et al.* IT-05-88-T. *Supra* note 150. ¶ 809.
[1582]  "A negatively defined group — for example all *non-Serbs* in a particular region—
        thus does not meet the definition." (Prosecutor v. Vujadin Popović *et al.* IT-05-88-
        T. *Supra* note 150. ¶ 809).
[1583]  Prosecutor v. Milomir Stakić. IT-97-24-A. *Supra* note 110. ¶ 22.

than one characteristic could be targeted at the same time. More than one group may be targeted for genocide at the same time.[1585] [1586]

## 3.1.3. Actus reus: Objective elements

The Genocide Convention and the Rome Statute establish a *numerus clausus* list of the underlying prohibited acts of genocide – *actus reus*: "killing members of the group,"[1587] "causing serious bodily or mental harm to members of the group,"[1588] "deliberately inflicting on the group conditions of life calculated to bring about its physical destruction in whole or in part,"[1589] "imposing measures intended to prevent births within the group,"[1590] and "forcibly transferring children of the group to another group."[1591] [1592] [1593] The existence of a genocidal plan or policy is not a legal constituent element of the crime of genocide. However, it might be an essential element in facilitating proof of the crime and the perpetrator's intent.[1594]

### 3.1.3.1. Destroy

The underlying act of killing members of a group as an act of genocide refers to the group's *destruction*. Such destruction entails two requirements: 1) the perpetrator of the genocidal act must *intentionally* kill one or more group members and 2) proof of a result.[1595] [1596] The term *destroy* in the Genocide

---

[1584] For the ICTY, "given that negatively defined groups lack specific characteristics, defining groups by reference to a negative would run counter to the intent of the Genocide Convention's drafters." (*Ibidem*).

[1585] Prosecutor v. Radoslav Brđanin. IT-99-36-T. *Supra* note 130. ¶¶ 686, 735.

[1586] In such cases, "the elements of the crime of genocide must be considered in relation to each group separately." (*Idem.* ¶ 686).

[1587] United Nations. Rome Statute (July 17, 1998) 2187 UNTS 38544. Art. 6. (a).

[1588] *Idem.* Art. 6. (b).

[1589] *Idem.* Art. 6. (c).

[1590] *Idem.* Art. 6. (d).

[1591] *Idem.* Art. 6. (e).

[1592] G. A. Res. 260 A (III), Convention on the Prevention and Punishment of the Crime of Genocide (Dec. 9, 1948). Article II.

[1593] See also: United Nations. Rome Statute (July 17, 1998) 2187 UNTS 38544. Article 6.

[1594] Prosecutor v. Goran Jelisić., IT-95-10-A. *Supra* note 98. ¶ 48; Prosecutor v. Vujadin Popović *et al.* IT-05-88-T. *Supra* note 150. ¶ 830.

[1595] Prosecutor v. Clément Kayishema and Ruzindana. ICTR 95-1-T. *Supra* note 209. ¶ 100; Prosecutor v. Laurent Semanza. ICTR-97-20-T. *Supra* note 211. ¶ 319; Prosecutor v. Jean de Dieu Kamuhanda. ICTR-95-54A-T. *Supra* note 200. ¶ 632; Prosecutor v. Gaspard Kanyarukiga. ICTR-2002-78-T. *Supra* note 187. ¶ 637; Prosecutor v. Il-

Convention, as well as in Customary International Law, means, exclusively, the physical or biological destruction of a human group[1597] [1598] – through death or other destructive means.[1599] The term excludes the possibility of *cultural* genocide or *sociological* genocide.[1600] [1601] [1602] [1603] Nevertheless, while attacks on cultural and religious symbols of the targeted group while such attacks "may not constitute underlying acts of genocide, they may be considered evidence of intent to physically destroy the group."[1604] [1605] For the ICTR Trial Chamber, in *Prosecutor v. Jean Mpambara*, "the commission of even a single instance of one of the prohibited acts is sufficient [to prove genocide], provided that the accused genuinely intends by that act to destroy at least a substantial part of the group."[1606]

### 3.1.3.2. Causing serious bodily or mental harm to members of the group

Although directly killing persons through the immediate cessation of human life – the complete failure of the neuronal and cardiorespiratory functions – may represent the most precise method of committing genocide,

---

dephonse Hategekimana. ICTR-00-55B-T. *Supra* note 197. ¶ 687; Prosecutor v. Édouard Karemera *et al.* ICTR-98-44-T. *Supra* note 172. ¶ 1608.

[1596] Prosecutor v. Radoslav Brđanin. IT-99-36-T. *Supra* note 130. ¶ 689; Prosecutor v. Zdravko Tolimir. IT-05-88/2-T. *Supra* note 153. ¶ 736; Prosecutor v. Radovan Karadžić. IT-95-5/18-T, vol. I. *Supra* note 134. ¶ 542.

[1597] Prosecutor v. Vidoje Blagojević, Dragan Jokić. IT-02-60-T. *Supra* note 147. ¶ 657.

[1598] See also: Prosecutor v. Laurent Semanza. ICTR-97-20-T. *Supra* note 211. ¶ 315; Prosecutor v. Mikaeli Muhimana. ICTR-95-1B-T. *Supra* note 214. ¶ 497.

[1599] Prosecutor v. Vidoje Blagojević, Dragan Jokić. IT-02-60-T. *Supra* note 147. ¶ 666; Prosecutor v. Momčilo Krajišnik. IT-00-39-T. *Supra* note 121. ¶ 854.

[1600] Prosecutor v. Vujadin Popović *et al.* IT-05-88-T. *Supra* note 150. ¶ 822. See also: Prosecutor v. Vidoje Blagojević, Dragan Jokić. IT-02-60-T. *Supra* note 147. ¶ 658; Prosecutor v. Radovan Karadžić. IT-95-5/18-T, vol. 1. *Supra* note 134. ¶ 553.

[1601] "The (International Court of Justice) notes that the travaux préparatoires of the Convention show that the drafters originally envisaged two types of genocide, physical or biological genocide, and cultural genocide, but that this latter concept was eventually dropped in this context." (Croatia v. Serbia. I.C.J. 3. *Supra* note 73. ¶ 136).

[1602] See also: Prosecutor v. Jean-Paul Akayesu. ICTR-96-4-T. *Supra* note 203. ¶ 500; Prosecutor v. Juvénal Kajelijeli. ICTR-98-44A-T. *Supra* note 207. ¶ 813; Prosecutor v. Mikaeli Muhimana. ICTR-95-1B-T. *Supra* note 214. ¶ 497.

[1603] See also: Robert Cryer, Håkan Friman, Darryl Robinson & Elizabeth Wilmshurst. *Supra* note 21. p. 179.

[1604] Prosecutor v. Radovan Karadžić. IT-95-5/18-T, vol. 1. *Supra* note 134. ¶ 553.

[1605] See also: Prosecutor v. Vujadin Popović *et al.* IT-05-88-T. *Supra* note 150. ¶ 822.

[1606] Prosecutor v. Jean Mpambara. ICTR-01-65-T. *Supra* note 202. ¶ 8.

serious bodily or mental harm may also constitute genocide when committed with genocidal intent against protected groups.[1607] [1608] Serious harm has been constructed as a genocidal act in which the perpetrator inflicts on the victim either physical injury (*bodily* harm) or "some type of impairment of mental faculties" (*mental* harm) with the intent to destroy a national, ethnical, racial or religious group as such, in whole or in part.[1609]

The determination of what constitutes *harm* and *serious* depends on each case's particular circumstances, using a *common-sense* approach.[1610] [1611] To establish the *mens rea* for the underlying offense, the threshold of such determination requires that the acts that cause bodily or mental harm must be inflicted intentionally and be of a serious nature sufficient to threaten the destruction of the targeted group *in whole or in part*.[1612] [1613] Importantly, this determination does not require proof of a result.[1614]

In *Prosecutor v. Sylvestre Gacumbitsi* and in *Prosecutor v. Vidoje Blagojević, Dragan Jokić*, the ICTR, and the ICTY, respectively, specified that the harm need not be permanent or irremediable.[1615] However, a serious bodily or mental harm to suffice an accusation on counts of genocide must result "in a grave and long-term disadvantage to a person's ability to lead a normal and constructive life," such as those that cause "disfigurement or causes

---

[1607] Prosecutor v. Jean-Paul Akayesu. ICTR-96-4-T. *Supra* note 203. ¶¶ 502, 504; Prosecutor v. Jean-Baptiste Gatete. ICTR-2000-61-T. *Supra* note 195. ¶ 584; Prosecutor v. Augustin Ndindiliyimana *et al.* ICTR-00-56-T. *Supra* note 163. ¶ 2075.

[1608] U.N. Doc. A/CN.4/SER.A/1996/Add.l (Part 2) (1996). p. 46, ¶ 15.

[1609] Prosecutor v. Jean de Dieu Kamuhanda. ICTR-95-54A-T. *Supra* note 200. ¶ 633.

[1610] Prosecutor v. Vujadin Popović *et al.* IT-05-88-T. *Supra* note 150. ¶ 811; Prosecutor v. Zdravko Tolimir. IT-05-88/2-T. *Supra* note 153. ¶ 738; Prosecutor v. Radovan Karadžić. IT-95-5/18-T, vol. I. *Supra* note 134. ¶ 545.

[1611] Prosecutor v. Clément Kayishema and Ruzindana. ICTR 95-1-T. *Supra* note 209. ¶¶ 108, 110, 113; Prosecutor v. Jean de Dieu Kamuhanda. ICTR-95-54A-T. *Supra* note 200. ¶ 634.

[1612] Prosecutor v. Radoslav Brđanin. IT-99-36-T. *Supra* note 130. ¶ 690; Prosecutor v. Vujadin Popović *et al.* IT-05-88-T. *Supra* note 150. ¶ 811; Prosecutor v. Zdravko Tolimir. IT-05-88/2-T. *Supra* note 153. ¶ 738; Prosecutor v. Radovan Karadžić. IT-95-5/18-T, vol. I. *Supra* note 134. ¶ 544.

[1613] Prosecutor v. Laurent Semanza. ICTR-97-20-T. *Supra* note 211. ¶ 323; Prosecutor v. Jean de Dieu Kamuhanda. ICTR-95-54A-T. *Supra* note 200. ¶ 633; Prosecutor v. Gaspard Kanyarukiga. ICTR-2002-78-T. *Supra* note 187. ¶ 637; Prosecutor v. Jean-Baptiste Gatete. ICTR-2000-61-T. *Supra* note 195. ¶ 584; Prosecutor v. Grégoire Ndahimana. ICTR-01-68-T. *Supra* note 191. ¶ 805; Prosecutor v. Édouard Karemera *et al.* ICTR-98-44-T. *Supra* note 172. ¶ 1609.

[1614] Prosecutor v. Vujadin Popović *et al.* IT-05-88-T. *Supra* note 150. ¶ 811.

[1615] Prosecutor v. Sylvestre Gacumbitsi. ICTR-2001-64-T. *Supra* note 228. ¶ 291; Prosecutor v. Vidoje Blagojević, Dragan Jokić. IT-02-60-T. *Supra* note 147. ¶ 645.

any serious injury to the external, internal organs or senses."[1616] In this vein, the bodily or the mental harm perpetrated on members of a group must be serious enough "as to threaten its destruction in whole or in part."[1617] In *Prosecutor v. Augustin Ndindiliyimana, Augustin Bizimungu,* and *François-Xavier Nzuwonemeye,* the ICTR established that torture and other serious physical violence, as well as sexual violence and rape, may constitute serious bodily or mental harm for the effects of accountability for genocide crimes.[1618] [1619] [1620]

In the international criminal case-law, serious bodily harm is referred to as 1) acts "so violent or of such intensity that they immediately cause the malfunctioning of one or many essential mechanisms of the human body;" 2) acts that have an "impact on one or more elements of the human structure, which disables the organs of the body and prevents them from functioning as normal;" or 3) acts that handicap the victims making them "unable to be a socially useful unit or a socially existent unit of the group."[1621] The harm caused by these acts "need not bring about death."[1622]

---

[1616] Prosecutor v. Vidoje Blagojević, Dragan Jokić. IT-02-60-T. *Supra* note 147. ¶ 645.

[1617] U.N. Doc. A/51/10 (May 6, 1996 – July 26, 1996). p. 46. ¶ 14.

[1618] Prosecutor v. Augustin Ndindiliyimana *et al.* ICTR-00-56-T. *Supra* note 163. ¶ 2075.

[1619] In *Croatia v. Serbia,* the parties disagreed "on whether causing serious bodily or mental harm to members of the group must contribute to the destruction of the group, in whole or in part, in order to constitute the actus reus of genocide for purposes of Article II (b) of the Convention." Croatia argued that "there is no need to show that the harm itself contributed to the destruction of the group." On the other hand, Serbia contended that the harm "must be so serious that it threatens the group with destruction." Then, the ICJ considered that, in the context of Genocide Convention, article II, *caput,* and considering the Convention's object and purpose, "the ordinary meaning of 'serious' is that the bodily or mental harm referred to in subparagraph (b) of that Article must be such as to contribute to the physical or biological destruction of the group, in whole or in part." (Croatia v. Serbia. I.C.J. 3. *Supra* note 73. ¶ 157.

[1620] For the ICTY Trial Chamber, in *Krajišnik,* the scope and meaning of the condition of "causing serious bodily" is "somewhat open to interpretation, but a fair and consistent construction of this clause alongside the four other types of actus reus is that, in order to pass as the actus reus of genocide under (ii), the act must inflict such "harm" as to contribute, or tend to contribute, to the destruction of the group or part thereof. Harm amounting to "a grave and long-term disadvantage to a person's ability to lead a normal and constructive life" has been said to be sufficient for this purpose." (Prosecutor v. Momčilo Krajišnik. IT-00-39-T. *Supra* note 121. ¶ 862).

[1621] Prosecutor v. Clément Kayishema and Ruzindana. ICTR 95-1-T. *Supra* note 209. ¶ 107.

[1622] *Ibid.*

The scope of actions which may constitute serious bodily or mental harm depends on the circumstances of each case (case-by-case basis).[1623] [1624] [1625] [1626] [1627] However, the perpetration of certain conducts strongly suggests the infliction of such serious bodily or mental harm as a genocidal act. For instance: 1) torture, inhumane or degrading treatment; 2) rape and other forms of sexual violence; 3) interrogations combined with beatings; 4) inflicting intense fear or terror, intimidation or threat, such as threats of death; 5) harm that causes serious damage, deformity, malfunctioning, extensive injury or impairment of the body senses or the body external or internal organs; 6) the fear of being captured; 7) confiscation of identification documents; 8) systematic expulsion from homes; 9) separation/forcibly transference of the women, children, and elderly people; 10) imposition of inhumane living conditions; 11) forced labor, excessive work, or physical exertion; 12) failure to provide adequate accommodation/shelter/housing; 13) failure to provide food and water; 14) lack

---

[1623] Prosecutor v. Radovan Karadžić. IT-95-5/18-T, vol. 1. *Supra* note 134. ¶¶ 545, 2586.

[1624] Prosecutor v. Clément Kayishema and Ruzindana. ICTR 95-1-T. *Supra* note 209. ¶ 110; Prosecutor v. Sylvestre Gacumbitsi. ICTR-2001-64-T. *Supra* note 228. ¶ 291; Prosecutor v. Mikaeli Muhimana. ICTR-95-1B-T. *Supra* note 214. ¶ 502; Prosecutor v. Théoneste Bagosora *et al.* ICTR-98-41-T. *Supra* note 234. ¶ 2117; Prosecutor v. Callixte Kalimanzira. ICTR-05-88-T. *Supra* note 166. ¶ 159; Prosecutor v. Tharcisse Renzaho. ICTR-97-31-T. *Supra* note 232. ¶ 762; Prosecutor v. Gaspard Kanyarukiga. ICTR-2002-78-T. *Supra* note 187. ¶ 637.

[1625] The jurisprudence of International Criminal Law considers that serious mental harm refers to "more than minor or temporary impairment of mental faculties." (Prosecutor v. Augustin Ndindiliyimana *et al.* ICTR-00-56-T. *Supra* note 163. ¶ 2075).

[1626] Importantly, in the Eichmann case, the District Court of Jerusalem considered that serious bodily or mental harm of members of the group can be caused " by the enslavement, starvation, deportation and persecution [...] and by their detention in ghettos, transit camps and concentration camps in conditions which were designed to cause their degradation, deprivation of their rights as human beings, and to suppress them and cause them inhumane suffering and torture." (Eichmann case *apud* Prosecutor v. Jean-Paul Akayesu. ICTR-96-4-T. *Supra* note 203. ¶ 503).

[1627] For the ICTY Trial Chamber, in *Tolimir*, "the determination of the seriousness of the bodily or mental harm inflicted on members of a group must be made on a case-by-case basis, with appropriate consideration given to the particular circumstances of each case." For the Chamber, "the harm must be of such a serious nature as to contribute or tend to contribute to the destruction of all or part of the group; although it need not be permanent or irreversible, it must go 'beyond temporary unhappiness, embarrassment or humiliation' and inflict 'grave and long-term disadvantage to a person's ability to lead a normal and constructive life.'" (Prosecutor v. Zdravko Tolimir. IT-05-88/2-T. *Supra* note 153. ¶ 738.

of clothing; 15) failure to provide medical care; 16) failure to provide hygienic sanitation facilities; 17) persecution; 18) deportation; 19) mutilation; and 20) other "serious acts of physical violence falling short of killing that seriously injure the health, cause disfigurement, or cause any serious injury to the external or internal organs or senses (to members of the targeted national, ethnical, racial or religious group)."[1628] [1629]

The *seriousness* of such (bodily and mental) *harm* is not assessed based on their capability of being permanent or irremediable.[1630] It suffices that the *harm* is serious enough to go "beyond temporary unhappiness, embarrassment or humiliation."[1631] [1632] Accordingly, the bodily harm inflicted on

---

[1628] Prosecutor v. Radoslav Brđanin. IT-99-36-T. *Supra* note 130. ¶ 690; Prosecutor v. Vidoje Blagojević, Dragan Jokić. IT-02-60-T. *Supra* note 147. ¶¶ 645, 647, 652; Prosecutor v. Vujadin Popović *et al.* IT-05-88-T. *Supra* note 150. ¶¶ 812, 815, 992; Prosecutor v. Zdravko Tolimir. IT-05-88/2-T. *Supra* note 153. ¶ 737; Prosecutor v. Radovan Karadžić. IT-95-5/18-T, vol. 1. *Supra* note 134. ¶ 545; Prosecutor v. Ratko Mladić., IT-09-92-T, vol. 3. *Supra* note 137. ¶ 3453.

[1629] Prosecutor v. Jean-Paul Akayesu. ICTR-96-4-T. *Supra* note 203. ¶ 504; Prosecutor v. Clément Kayishema and Ruzindana. ICTR 95-1-T. *Supra* note 209. ¶¶ 108–111; Prosecutor v. Musema. ICTR-96-13-A. *Supra* note 216. ¶ 156; Prosecutor v. Jean de Dieu Kamuhanda. ICTR-95-54A-T. *Supra* note 200. ¶ 634; Prosecutor v. Sylvestre Gacumbitsi. ICTR-2001-64-T. *Supra* note 228. ¶¶ 29, 291; Prosecutor v. Mikaeli Muhimana. ICTR-95-1B-T. *Supra* note 214. ¶ 502; Prosecutor v. Théoneste Bagosora *et al.* ICTR-98-41-T. *Supra* note 234. ¶ 2117; Prosecutor v. Callixte Kalimanzira. ICTR-05-88-T. *Supra* note 166. ¶ 159; Prosecutor v. Tharcisse Renzaho. ICTR-97-31-T. *Supra* note 232. ¶ 762; Prosecutor v. Dominique Ntawukulilyayo. ICTR-05-82-T. *Supra* note 170. ¶ 452; Prosecutor v. Gaspard Kanyarukiga. ICTR-2002-78-T. *Supra* note 187. ¶ 637; Prosecutor v. Jean-Baptiste Gatete. ICTR-2000-61-T. *Supra* note 195. ¶ 584; Prosecutor v. Augustin Ndindiliyimana *et al.* ICTR-00-56-T. *Supra* note 163. ¶ 2075; Prosecutor v. Grégoire Ndahimana. ICTR-01-68-T. *Supra* note 191. ¶ 805; Prosecutor v. Édouard Karemera *et al.* ICTR-98-44-T. *Supra* note 172. ¶ 1609.

[1630] Prosecutor v. Jean-Paul Akayesu. ICTR-96-4-T. *Supra* note 203. ¶ 502; Prosecutor v. Clément Kayishema and Ruzindana. ICTR 95-1-T. *Supra* note 209. ¶¶ 108, 110; Prosecutor v. Musema. ICTR-96-13-A. *Supra* note 216. ¶ 156; Prosecutor v. Jean de Dieu Kamuhanda. ICTR-95-54A-T. *Supra* note 200. ¶ 634; Prosecutor v. Sylvestre Gacumbitsi. ICTR-2001-64-T. *Supra* note 228. ¶ 291; Prosecutor v. Radoslav Brđanin. IT-99-36-T. *Supra* note 130. ¶ 690; Prosecutor v. Mikaeli Muhimana. ICTR-95-1B-T. *Supra* note 214. ¶ 502; Prosecutor v. Théoneste Bagosora *et al.* ICTR-98-41-T. *Supra* note 234. ¶ 2117; Prosecutor v. Callixte Kalimanzira. ICTR-05-88-T. *Supra* note 166. ¶ 159; Prosecutor v. Tharcisse Renzaho. ICTR-97-31-T. *Supra* note 232. ¶ 762; Prosecutor v. Dominique Ntawukulilyayo. ICTR-05-82-T. *Supra* note 170. ¶ 452; Prosecutor v. Augustin Ndindiliyimana *et al.* ICTR-00-56-T. *Supra* note 163. ¶ 2075.

[1631] Prosecutor v. Vujadin Popović *et al.* IT-05-88-T. *Supra* note 150. ¶ 811.

[1632] See also: Prosecutor v. Clément Kayishema and Ruzindana. ICTR 95-1-T. *Supra* note 209. ¶ 107; Prosecutor v. Jean de Dieu Kamuhanda. ICTR-95-54A-T. *Supra* note 200.

the victim need not be irreversible,[1633] [1634] but must impose a long-lasting impact on the victims' ability to lead a normal and constructive life."[1635] Consequentially, even when the genocidal methods chosen by the perpetrator are inefficient or do not bring a *de facto* destruction of the group, such fact does not preclude a finding of genocidal intent.[1636]

### 3.1.3.3. Deliberately inflicting on the group conditions of life calculated to bring about its physical destruction in whole or in part

Genocide can also be perpetrated by *inflicting on the group conditions of life calculated to bring about its physical destruction in whole or in part*.[1637] This refers to circumstances/conditions of life that do not immediately kill the members of a protected group but which purposefully will lead them to a slow death/physical destruction, in whole or in part.[1638] [1639] Examples of such conditions are abundant in international criminal case law: lack of proper housing/accommodation for a reasonable period, systematic expulsion of persons from their homes, resettlement, lack of clothing, lack of hygiene, reducing required medical services and essential medical supplies below a minimum, excessive work or physical exertion, rape, the contamination of water pumps, the starving of a group of people or subjecting a group of people to a subsistence diet.[1640] [1641] [1642]

---

¶ 634; Prosecutor v. Jean-Baptiste Gatete. ICTR-2000-61-T. *Supra* note 195. ¶ 584; Prosecutor v. Grégoire Ndahimana. ICTR-01-68-T. *Supra* note 191. ¶ 805; Prosecutor v. Édouard Karemera *et al.* ICTR-98-44-T. *Supra* note 172. ¶ 1609.

[1633] Prosecutor v. Radoslav Brđanin. IT-99-36-T. *Supra* note 130. ¶ 690; Prosecutor v. Vujadin Popović *et al.* IT-05-88-T. *Supra* note 150. ¶ 811; Prosecutor v. Zdravko Tolimir. IT-05-88/2-T. *Supra* note 153. ¶ 738; Prosecutor v. Radovan Karadžić. IT-95-5/18-T, vol. I. *Supra* note 134. ¶ 543.

[1634] Prosecutor v. Jean-Paul Akayesu. ICTR-96-4-T. *Supra* note 203. ¶ 502; Prosecutor v. Laurent Semanza. ICTR-97-20-T. *Supra* note 211. ¶¶ 320, 322; Prosecutor v. Édouard Karemera *et al.* ICTR-98-44-T. *Supra* note 172. ¶ 1609.

[1635] Prosecutor v. Zdravko Tolimir. IT-05-88/2-A. *Supra* note 152. ¶ 207.

[1636] Prosecutor v. Milomir Stakić. IT-97-24-T. *Supra* note 109. ¶ 522; Prosecutor v. Radislav Krstić. IT-98-33-A. *Supra* note 129. ¶ 32.

[1637] Prosecutor v. Kayishema and Ruzindana. ICTR 95-1-T. *Supra* note 209. ¶ 115.

[1638] Prosecutor v. Jean-Paul Akayesu. ICTR-96-4-T. *Supra* note 203. ¶ 505; Prosecutor v. Kayishema and Ruzindana. ICTR 95-1-T. *Supra* note 209. ¶¶ 115, 116; Prosecutor v. Musema. ICTR-96-13-A. *Supra* note 216. ¶ 157; Prosecutor v. Milomir Stakić. IT-97-24-T. *Supra* note 109. ¶ 518; Prosecutor v. Zdravko Tolimir. IT-05-88/2-T. *Supra* note 153. ¶ 741; Prosecutor v. Radovan Karadžić. IT-95-5/18-T, vol. I. *Supra* note 134. ¶ 546.

[1639] Prosecutor v. Vujadin Popović *et al.* IT-05-88-T. *Supra* note 150. ¶ 814.

Customary international law does not require proof that a result – the destruction of the group – was accomplished.[1643] This consideration means that international criminal tribunals do not require proof that the methods of destruction "actually led to death or serious bodily or mental harm of members of the protected group."[1644] In practice, when direct evidence of "whether the conditions of life imposed on the group were deliberately calculated to bring about its physical destruction" is lacking, a trial chamber "can be guided by the objective probability of these conditions leading to the physical destruction of the group in part."[1645] [1646]

### 3.1.3.4. Imposing measures intended to prevent births within the group

International Criminal Law jurisprudence does not require that the perpetrator chooses the most efficient method to accomplish their objective of destroying the targeted part.[1647] According to ICTR's *Prosecutor v. Clément Kayishema et al* rationale, the perpetrator needs not to choose a "persistent pattern of conduct" in their genocidal acts.[1648] So, for instance, *imposing measures intended to prevent births within the group* constitutes a *slow method* of destroying a group as opposed to a *more efficient* method of destruction. In *Prosecutor v. Radovan Karadžić* and *Prosecutor v. Zdravko Tolimir*, the ICTY defined that *slow death* methods are those that do not immediately kill the members of the groups but which, ultimately, seek to cause serious bodily or mental harm and final physical destruction.[1649] [1650] [1651]

---

[1640] Prosecutor v. Jean-Paul Akayesu. ICTR-96-4-T. *Supra* note 203. ¶ 506; Prosecutor v. Kayishema and Ruzindana. ICTR 95-1-T. *Supra* note 209. ¶¶ 115–116; Prosecutor v. Musema. ICTR-96-13-A. *Supra* note 216. ¶ 157.

[1641] Prosecutor v. Omar Hassan Ahmad Al Bashir. ICC-02/05-01/09. *Supra* note 289. ¶ 38.

[1642] Prosecutor v. Milomir Stakić. IT-97-24-T. *Supra* note 109. ¶ 517; Prosecutor v. Radoslav Brđanin. IT-99-36-T. *Supra* note 130. ¶ 691; Prosecutor v. Vujadin Popović *et al.* IT-05-88-T. *Supra* note 150. ¶ 815; Prosecutor v. Zdravko Tolimir. IT-05-88/2-T. *Supra* note 153. ¶ 740; Prosecutor v. Radovan Karadžić. IT-95-5/18-T, vol. I. *Supra* note 134. ¶ 547.

[1643] Prosecutor v. Milomir Stakić. IT-97-24-T. *Supra* note 109. ¶ 517; Prosecutor v. Radoslav Brđanin. IT-99-36-T. *Supra* note 130. ¶ 691; Prosecutor v. Vujadin Popović *et al.* IT-05-88-T. *Supra* note 150. ¶ 814; Prosecutor v. Zdravko Tolimir. IT-05-88/2-T. *Supra* note 153. ¶ 741; Prosecutor v. Radovan Karadžić. IT-95-5/18-T, vol. I. *Supra* note 134. ¶ 546.

[1644] Prosecutor v. Radovan Karadžić. IT-95-5/18-T, vol. I. *Supra* note 134. ¶ 546.

[1645] *Idem.* ¶ 548.

[1646] See also: Prosecutor v. Zdravko Tolimir. IT-05-88/2-T. *Supra* note 153. ¶ 742.

[1647] Prosecutor v. Radislav Krstić. IT-98-33-A. *Supra* note 129. ¶ 32.

[1648] Prosecutor v. Clément Kayishema *et al.* ICTR-95-1-A. *Supra* note 210. ¶ 163.

In *Prosecutor v. Athanase Seromba*, the ITCR's Appeals Chamber recalled that, in the context of genocide, "direct and physical perpetration is not limited to direct physical killing" and that "other acts can constitute direct participation in the *actus reus* of the crime."[1652] Therefore, the act of *imposing measures intended to prevent births within the group* may be constructed as including not only physical acts but also mental ones.[1653] [1654] Examples of such punishable methods under the Genocide Convention abound once it establishes a *numerus apertus* list.[1655] In *Prosecutor v. Zdravko Tolimir*, the ICTY conceived that the determination of the seriousness of the *harm* – or the determination of the efficiency of the destruction method – is always made on a case-by-case basis.[1656] They may include, for example, using persons as human shields, the forcible transfer of children, the recruitment and use of children of a protected group, providing the victims extremely insufficient food, poisoned food, severely insufficient water for drinking and personal hygiene, rape, sexual mutilation, the practice of enforced sterilization, forced birth control, forced separation of males and females, prohibition of marriages, and forceful procreation/impregnation.[1657] [1658] [1659]

---

[1649] Please refer to: Prosecutor v. Zdravko Tolimir. IT-05-88/2-A. *Supra* note 152. ¶ 203. See also: ¶ 225

[1650] For the ICTY jurisprudence, serious bodily or mental harm "must be of such a serious nature as to contribute or tend to contribute to the destruction of all or part of the group." Although it "need not be permanent or irreversible, it must go beyond temporary unhappiness, embarrassment or humiliation and inflict "grave and long-term disadvantage to a person's ability to lead a normal and constructive life." (*Idem*. ¶ 201).

[1651] See also: Prosecutor v. Radovan Karadžić. IT-95-5/18-T. *Supra* note 134. ¶ 2586.

[1652] Prosecutor v. Athanase Seromba. ICTR-2001-66-A. *Supra* note 161. ¶ 161.

[1653] Prosecutor v. Jean-Paul Akayesu. ICTR-96-4-T. *Supra* note 203. ¶ 508; Prosecutor v. Musema. ICTR-96-13-A. *Supra* note 216. ¶ 158.

[1654] Prosecutor v. Vujadin Popović *et al*. IT-05-88-T. *Supra* note 150. ¶ 818; Prosecutor v. Zdravko Tolimir. IT-05-88/2-T. *Supra* note 153. ¶ 743.

[1655] These conducts include, *inter alia*, "subjecting the group to a subsistence diet; failing to provide adequate medical care; systematically expelling members of the group from their homes; and generally creating circumstances that would lead to a slow death such as the lack of proper food, water, shelter, clothing, sanitation, or subjecting members of the group to excessive work or physical exertion." (Prosecutor v. Zdravko Tolimir. IT-05-88/2-A. *Supra* note 152. ¶ 225).

[1656] *Idem*. ¶ 201.

[1657] Prosecutor v. Radoslav Brđanin. IT-99-36-T. *Supra* note 130. ¶ 691; Prosecutor v. Vidoje Blagojević, Dragan Jokić. IT-02-60-T. *Supra* note 147. ¶ 665; Prosecutor v. Momčilo Krajišnik. IT-00-39-T. *Supra* note 121. ¶ 854; Prosecutor v. Zdravko Tolimir. IT-05-88/2-T. *Supra* note 153. ¶ 743; Prosecutor v. Zdravko Tolimir. IT-05-

In *Prosecutor v. Radovan Karadžić*, the ICTY considered that intentionally subjecting persons to rape and other acts of sexual violence, in virtue of being part of a protected group, as such, could cause profound mental or physical suffering or injury, one of the elements of the crime of genocide.[1660] In *Prosecutor v. Jean-Paul Akayesu*, the ICTR explicitly considered the possibility of sexual crimes to constitute genocide.[1661] In *Édouard Karemera et al. v. Prosecutor*, the ITCR's Appeals Chamber went even further in considering that when genocidal crimes of a sexual nature "are allegedly perpetrated by subordinates in multiple locations, an indication of location is not always possible."[1662] The Court, therefore, established that, in the circumstances like these, an indictment is not defective when it "fails to specify the exact location and dates of the rapes and sexual assaults."[1663] [1664]

## 3.1.3.5. Is a genocidal plan or policy required?

The jurisprudence of international *ad hoc* criminal courts has repeatedly recognized that the existence of a genocidal plan is not an element required for a conviction for genocide.[1665] [1666] In *Siméon Nchamihigo v. Prosecutor*,[1667] *Prosecutor v. Clément Kayishema et al.*,[1668] *Prosecutor v. Vujadin Popović et*

---

88/2-A. *Supra* note 152. ¶ 225; Prosecutor v. Radovan Karadžić. IT-95-5/18-T. *Supra* note 134. ¶ 447.

[1658] Prosecutor v. Clément Kayishema and Ruzindana. ICTR 95-1-T. *Supra* note 209. ¶ 117; Prosecutor v. Musema. ICTR-96-13-A. *Supra* note 216. ¶ 158.

[1659] Forceful procreation is constituted when female victims of genocide are impregnated "by a man of another group [the perpetrator of genocide], with the intent to have her give birth to a child who will consequently not belong to its mother's group." (Prosecutor v. Jean-Paul Akayesu. ICTR-96-4-T. *Supra* note 203. ¶¶ 507–508).

[1660] Prosecutor v. Radovan Karadžić. IT-95-5/18-T. *Supra* note 134. ¶¶ 2500, 2501, 2581.

[1661] Prosecutor v. Jean-Paul Akayesu. ICTR-96-4-T. *Supra* note 203. *passim*; Prosecutor v. Jean-Paul Akayesu. ICTR-96-4-A. *Supra* note 204. *passim*.

[1662] Édouard Karemera et al v. Prosecutor. ICTR-98-44-A. *Supra* note 173. ¶ 594.

[1663] *Ibidem*.

[1664] "The Appeals Chamber is not convinced that the Indictment is defective in failing to specify the exact location and dates of the rapes and sexual assaults for which Karemera and Ngirumpatse were convicted. (...) Where crimes are alleged to have been perpetrated by subordinates in multiple locations, indication of location is not always possible." (*Ibidem*.)

[1665] Aloys Simba v. Prosecutor. ICTR-01-76-A. *Supra* note 158. ¶ 260.

[1666] See also: Kai Ambos. *Supra* note 63. p. 17.

[1667] Siméon Nchamihigo v. Prosecutor. ICTR-2001-63-A. *Supra* note 225. ¶ 363.

[1668] Prosecutor v. Clément Kayishema *et al.* ICTR-95-1-A. *Supra* note 210. ¶¶ 94, 134, 138.

al.,[1669] *Prosecutor v. Goran Jelisić,*[1670] and *Prosecutor v. Goran Jelisić,*[1671] both the ICTR and the ICTY repeated such *motto* – that, in the context of proving specific intent, premeditation, and a "high-level genocidal plan" are not required in order to convict an accused of genocide.[1672] [1673]

However, international criminal courts recognized that it would be hard to conceive that a genocidal enterprise could be made effective without the guidelines of such a plan or organization.[1674] Consequently, the existence of such a plan or policy may become a crucial element in order to constitute further evidence to support/facilitate proof of genocide.[1675] For instance, in *Prosecutor v. Radislav Krstić,* the ICTY Appeals Chamber stated that the definition of genocide in the Elements of Crimes adopted by the ICC "indicates clearly that genocide requires that 'the conduct took place in the context of a manifest pattern of similar conduct.'"[1676] In *Prosecutor v. Goran Jelisić,* the ICTY Appeals Chamber considered that, in genocide cases, "the evidence may be consistent with the existence of a plan or policy, or may even show such existence, and the existence of a plan or policy may facilitate proof of the crime."[1677]

In *Prosecutor v. Fatmir Limaj et al.*[1678] and *Ferdinand Nahimana et al. v. Prosecutor,*[1679] the ICTY and the ICTR, respectively, defined "plan" as an intentional design of criminal conduct that will be perpetrated later in time. Such a *plan* may be constituted of a myriad of elements. In *Prosecutor v. Vujadin Popović et al.,* for example, the ICTY considered that "attacks on cul-

---

[1669] Prosecutor v. Vujadin Popović *et al.* IT-05-88-T. *Supra* note 150. ¶ 830.

[1670] Prosecutor v. Goran Jelisić. IT-95-10-T. *Supra* note 97. ¶ 85.

[1671] Prosecutor v. Goran Jelisić., IT-95-10-A. *Supra* note 98. ¶ 48.

[1672] Prosecutor v. Kayishema and Ruzindana. ICTR 95-1-T. *Supra* note 209. ¶ 91; Prosecutor v. Goran Jelisić. IT-95-10-T. *Supra* note 97. ¶ 85; Prosecutor v. Vidoje Blagojević, Dragan Jokić. IT-02-60-T. *Supra* note 147. ¶ 656; Siméon Nchamihigo v. Prosecutor. ICTR-2001-63-A. *Supra* note 225. ¶ 363; Prosecutor v. Vujadin Popović *et al.* IT-05-88-T. *Supra* note 150. ¶ 830; Prosecutor v. Vujadin Popović *et al.* IT-05-88-A. *Supra* note 151. ¶¶ 435, 440.

[1673] The element of premeditation as a necessary condition for the perpetration of genocide was rejected during the *travaux préparatoires* of the Genocide Convention. (Prosecutor v. Jean-Paul Akayesu. ICTR-96-4-T. *Supra* note 203. ¶ 501).

[1674] Prosecutor v. Kayishema and Ruzindana. ICTR 95-1-T. *Supra* note 209. ¶ 94.

[1675] Prosecutor v. Goran Jelisić., IT-95-10-A. *Supra* note 98. ¶ 48; Prosecutor v. Vujadin Popović *et al.* IT-05-88-A. *Supra* note 151. ¶ 435; Prosecutor v. Radovan Karadžić. IT-95-5/18-T, vol. 1. *Supra* note 134. ¶ 550.

[1676] Prosecutor v. Radislav Krstić. IT-98-33-A. *Supra* note 129. ¶ 224.

[1677] Prosecutor v. Goran Jelisić., IT-95-10-A. *Supra* note 98. ¶ 48.

[1678] Prosecutor v. Fatmir Limaj *et al.* IT-03-66-T. *Supra* note 96. ¶ 513.

[1679] Ferdinand Nahimana et al v. Prosecutor. ICTR-99-52-A. *Supra* note 183. ¶ 479.

tural and religious property and symbols of the targeted group often occur alongside physical and biological destruction and may legitimately be considered as evidence of an intent to physically destroy the group."[1680]

In *Prosecutor v. Radovan Karadžić*, the court considered that the plan/policy of the burning of several mosques in Foča constituted a clear evidence of genocidal intent.[1681] In *Prosecutor v. Goran Jelisić* and *Prosecutor v. Vidoje Blagojević, Dragan Jokić*, the ICTY also considered that the policy of grouping members of a protected group for their deliberate and systematic killing and subsequent piling of the bodies into mass graves could serve as an indication of genocide.[1682] Also, in *Prosecutor v. Milomir Stakić*,[1683] the ICTY made considerations as to whether an allegation of systematic expulsion from homes could constitute part of a *plan* or *policy* to create circumstances that would lead to a slow death of persons in a protected group. In *Prosecutor v. Radovan Karadžić*, the court considered whether the complete perpetrator's knowledge of the inability of victims from protected groups to reconstitute themselves would sustain an allegation of genocidal intent/genocidal plan.[1684]

The strategy of making speeches via loudspeakers – or by other public means – to create fear and incite hatred against ethnic and or religious groups was proved as evidence of a genocide plan in *Prosecutor v. Radovan Karadžić* (ICTY)[1685] and *Prosecutor v. Vujadin Popović et al.* (ICTY).[1686] The court's *rationale* in *Prosecutor v. Goran Jelisić* (ICTY) is that certain statements issued by alleged perpetrators of genocide have the potential to demonstrate 1) a "general context of public persecutions"[1687] and 2) full awareness of the discriminatory nature of biological/physical killing/destruction operations of persons belonging to a protected group.

### 3.1.4. Mens rea: Subjective elements

The most distinguishable, unique, specific, predominant characteristic of the crime of genocide is the *dollus specialis* – "specific intent" (*mens rea*)[1688] –,

---

[1680]  Prosecutor v. Vujadin Popović *et al.* IT-05-88-A. *Supra* note 151. ¶ 822.

[1681]  Prosecutor v. Radovan Karadžić. IT-95-5/18-T. *Supra* note 134. ¶¶ 925, 926.

[1682]  Prosecutor v. Goran Jelisić. IT-95-10-T. *Supra* note 97. ¶ 90; Prosecutor v. Vidoje Blagojević, Dragan Jokić. IT-02-60-T. *Supra* note 147. ¶ 674.

[1683]  Prosecutor v. Milomir Stakić. IT-97-24-T. *Supra* note 109. ¶ 517.

[1684]  Prosecutor v. Radovan Karadžić. IT-95-5/18-T. *Supra* note 134. ¶¶ 920, 2589.

[1685]  *Idem.* ¶¶ 983, 2598.

[1686]  Prosecutor v. Vujadin Popović *et al.* IT-05-88-A. *Supra* note 151. ¶ 1318.

[1687]  Prosecutor v. Goran Jelisić. IT-95-10-T. *Supra* note 97. ¶ 73.

present at the moment of the commission of the criminal act.[1689] [1690] Therefore, the *intent* is a constitutive element of the crime, which requires evidence beyond a reasonable doubt that the genocide perpetrator sought to execute the act for which he was charged (proof of the mental state).[1691] [1692]

The intent refers to the deliberate will to commit the underlying legal acts of physically destroying, in whole or in part, protected groups of people, *as such* – a national, ethnic, racial, or religious group (*actus reus*).[1693] It is this very aim intended by the perpetrator, rather than the "actual physical destruction," that suffices the legal requirements of the crime of genocide.[1694] Unlike crimes such as murder and persecution *per se*, the ultimate victim of genocide is always a distinct group protected by International Criminal Law rather than the individuals who are a part of such a group.[1695] [1695]

---

[1688] "The *mens rea* required for the crime of genocide—intent to destroy, in whole or in part, a national, ethnical, racial or religious group" (...) has been referred to variously as, for instance, special intent, specific intent, *dolus specialis*, particular intent and genocidal intent" and they may be used interchangeably. (Prosecutor v. Milomir Stakić. IT-97-24-T. *Supra* note 109. ¶ 520); (Prosecutor v. Radovan Karadžić. IT-95-5/18-T, vol. 1. *Supra* note 134. ¶ 549).

[1689] Prosecutor v. Jean Kambanda. ICTR-97-23. *Supra* note 199. ¶ 16; Prosecutor v. Zdravko Tolimir. IT-05-88/2-A. *Supra* note 152. ¶ 564.

[1690] "Insofar as Tolimir suggests that *ex post facto* evidence cannot support an inference of genocidal intent, the Appeals Chamber reiterates that, as a general principle, it is not an error of law to rely on material originating from outside the time period of the Indictment, so long as it has probative value." (Prosecutor v. Zdravko Tolimir. IT-05-88/2-A. *Supra* note 152. ¶ 569).

[1691] Prosecutor v. Jean-Paul Akayesu. ICTR-96-4-T. *Supra* note 203. ¶ 498.

[1692] Prosecutor v. Milomir Stakić. IT-97-24-T. *Supra* note 109. ¶ 520; Prosecutor v. Vujadin Popović *et al.* IT-05-88-T. *Supra* note 150. ¶ 823; Prosecutor v. Zdravko Tolimir. IT-05-88/2-T. *Supra* note 153. ¶ 744; Prosecutor v. Radovan Karadžić. IT-95-5/18-T, vol. I. *Supra* note 134. ¶ 549.

[1693] Prosecutor v. Jean-Paul Akayesu. ICTR-96-4-T. *Supra* note 203. ¶ 498; Prosecutor v. Kayishema and Ruzindana. ICTR 95-1-T. *Supra* note 209. ¶ 91; Prosecutor v. Musema. ICTR-96-13-A. *Supra* note 216. ¶ 164; Prosecutor v. Milomir Stakić. IT-97-24-T. *Supra* note 109. ¶¶ 520–522; Prosecutor v. Radislav Krstić. IT-98-33-A. *Supra* note 129. ¶ 8; Prosecutor v. Momčilo Krajišnik. IT-00-39-T. *Supra* note 121. ¶ 851; Prosecutor v. Ephrem Setako. ICTR-04-81-T. *Supra* note 181. ¶ 466; Prosecutor v. Vujadin Popović *et al.* IT-05-88-T. *Supra* note 150. ¶¶ 817, 820; Prosecutor v. Dominique Ntawukulilyayo. ICTR-05-82-T. *Supra* note 170. ¶ 452; Prosecutor v. Jean-Baptiste Gatete. ICTR-2000-61-T. *Supra* note 195. ¶ 582; Prosecutor v. Augustin Ndindiliyimana *et al.* ICTR-00-56-T. *Supra* note 163. ¶¶ 2072, 2074; Prosecutor v. Zdravko Tolimir. IT-05-88/2-A. *Supra* note 152. ¶ 246.

[1694] Prosecutor v. Milomir Stakić. IT-97-24-T. *Supra* note 109. ¶ 522; Prosecutor v. Slobodan Milošević. IT-02-54-T. *Supra* note 139. ¶ 126.

Intent, then, means, in practice, that the acts of the accused against a national, ethnical, racial, or religious group are not accidental or consequential of negligence.[1697] [1698] The accused must have committed the prohibited acts with a "particular state of mind,"[1699] in a "conscious, intentional or volitional" fashion,[1700] with proved evidence of knowledge that their actions can (and will) cause the destruction of a separate, distinct group protected by international law, in whole or in part, *as such*.[1701]

The expression "as such" in this context reveals the *dollus specialis* – surplus of intent – of the perpetrator as a critical element for the crime of genocide.[1702] [1703] [1704] [1705] [1706] This means that the persons targeted by the per-

---

[1695]  Prosecutor v. Kayishema and Ruzindana. ICTR 95-1-T. *Supra* note 209. ¶ 98; Prosecutor v. Musema. ICTR-96-13-A. *Supra* note 216. ¶ 165; Prosecutor v. François Karera. ICTR-01-74-T. *Supra* note 184. ¶ 534.

[1696]  This specific intent "is what differentiates genocide from the crime against humanity of persecution. Even though they both have discriminatory elements, some of which are common to both crimes, in the case of persecution, the perpetrator commits crimes against individuals, on political, racial or religious grounds. It is this factor that establishes a demarcation between genocide and most cases of ethnic cleansing." (Prosecutor v. Duško Sikirica *et al.* IT-95-8-T. *Supra* note 88. ¶ 89).

[1697]  Prosecutor v. Mikaeli Muhimana. ICTR-95-1B-T. *Supra* note 214. ¶ 495.

[1698]  U.N. Doc. A/CN.4/SER.A/1996/Add.l (Part 2) (1996). p. 44, ¶¶ 4, 5.

[1699]  *Idem.* p. 44. ¶ 5.

[1700]  *Ibidem.*

[1701]  Prosecutor v. Vidoje Blagojević, Dragan Jokić. IT-02-60-T. *Supra* note 147. ¶ 670.

[1702]  Prosecutor v. Radislav Krstić., IT-98-33-T. *Supra* note 128. ¶ 551; Prosecutor v. Milomir Stakić. IT-97-24-T. *Supra* note 109. ¶ 520; Prosecutor v. Radoslav Brđanin. IT-99-36-T. *Supra* note 130. ¶ 698; Prosecutor v. Vidoje Blagojević, Dragan Jokić. IT-02-60-T. *Supra* note 147. ¶ 670; Prosecutor v. Vujadin Popović *et al.* IT-05-88-T. *Supra* note 150. ¶ 821; Prosecutor v. Radovan Karadžić. IT-95-5/18-T, vol. I. *Supra* note 134. ¶ 551.

[1703]  Prosecutor v. Musema. ICTR-96-13-A. *Supra* note 216. ¶ 166.

[1704]  Bosnia and Herzegovina v. Serbia and Montenegro. I.C.J. 43. *Supra* note 71. ¶ 187.

[1705]  U.N. Doc. A/51/10 (May 6, 1996 – July 26, 1996). p. 45. ¶ 7.

[1706]  In *Niyitegeka*, the ICTR Appeals Chamber considered that the term *as such*, "constituted an important element of genocide, the crime of crimes." For the Court, "the expression *as such* was deliberately included by the authors of the Genocide Convention in order to reconcile the two diverging approaches in favour of and against including a motivational component as an additional element of the crime." The term *as such* "has the *effet utile* of drawing a clear distinction between mass murder and crimes in which the perpetrator targets a specific group because of its nationality, race, ethnicity or religion." In other words, the Appeals Chamber recognized that the term *as such* "clarifies the specific intent requirement. It does not prohibit a conviction for genocide in a case in which the perpetrator was also

petrator are not randomly/accidentally attacked but rather chosen exclusively because of their membership in a group.[1707] [1708] According to Professor Kai Ambos, the Article 30 of the Rome Statute[1709] prescribes the general rule in International Criminal Law for the *mens rea*.[1710] It requires that the acts of the accused (*actus reus*) are committed under a specific mental state that can be divided into *cognitive knowledge* [Article 30 (2)(b), (3)], and *volitional will* [Article 30 (2)(a).[1711]

In the term *as such* resides the crucial differentiation between genocide and the crime against humanity of persecution.[1712] Both crimes are committed on a discriminatory basis. Still, while the perpetrator of persecution targets *individuals* because of their affiliation with a racial or religious group, for example, the perpetrator of genocide necessarily intends to destroy the group itself and to destroy the very right of existence of that group as an autonomous entity.[1713] [1714]

Determining that the perpetrator specifically and purposefully intended the result of their action – specific *cognitive* genocidal intent –[1715] is often impossible. This is so due to two main reasons: 1) The intent is founded on the mental state of the perpetrator of genocide[1716] – the "psychological nexus between the physical result and the mental state of the perpetrator."[1717] Only the perpetrator himself has first-hand [*cognitive*] knowledge of his own mental state, and he is unlikely to testify to his own

---

driven by other motivations that are legally irrelevant in this context." (Eliézer Niyitegeka v. Prosecutor. ICTR-96-14-A. *Supra* note 174. ¶ 53).

[1707] Prosecutor v. Jean-Paul Akayesu. ICTR-96-4-T. *Supra* note 203. ¶ 498; Prosecutor v. Duško Sikirica *et al.* IT-95-8-T. *Supra* note 88. ¶ 89; Prosecutor v. Vidoje Blagojević, Dragan Jokić. IT-02-60-T. *Supra* note 147. ¶ 669.

[1708] United Nation, Report of the Commission to the General Assembly on the work of its forty-eighth session, Yearbook of the International Law Commission, Vol. II, U.N. Doc. A/CN.4/SER.A/1996/Add.l (Part 2) (1996). p. 45, ¶ 7.

[1709] United Nations. Rome Statute (July 17, 1998) 2187 UNTS 38544.

[1710] Kai Ambos. *Supra* note 30. p. 266.

[1711] *Idem.* pp. 18, 24, 269.

[1712] Prosecutor v. Duško Sikirica *et al.* IT-95-8-T. *Supra* note 87. ¶ 89.

[1713] Prosecutor v. Radislav Krstić., IT-98-33-T. *Supra* note 128. ¶ 553; Prosecutor v. Duško Sikirica *et al.* IT-95-8-T. *Supra* note 87. ¶ 89; Prosecutor v. Radoslav Brđanin. IT-99-36-T. *Supra* note 130. ¶ 699; Prosecutor v. Zdravko Tolimir. IT-05-88/2-T. *Supra* note 153. ¶ 746; Prosecutor v. Radovan Karadžić. IT-95-5/18-T, vol. I. *Supra* note 134. ¶ 551.

[1714] Prosecutor v. Clément Kayishema and Ruzindana. ICTR 95-1-T. *Supra* note 209. ¶ 89.

[1715] Prosecutor v. Musema. ICTR-96-13-A. *Supra* note 216. ¶ 164.

[1716] Prosecutor v. Jean-Paul Akayesu. ICTR-96-4-T. *Supra* note 203. ¶ 523.

[1717] Prosecutor v. Musema. ICTR-96-13-A. *Supra* note 216. ¶ 166.

genocidal intent;"[1718] [1719] 2) It must be proved that the *mens rea* was formed prior to the commission of the genocidal acts.[1720] Unveiling this perpetrator's *particular intent* to destroy a protected group *as such* is judicially challenging, as the ICTY well recognized in *Prosecutor v. Vujadin Popović* et al.,[1721] *Prosecutor v. Milomir Stakić*[1722] , and *Prosecutor v. Goran Jelisić*.[1723]

The U.N. International Law Commission considered that the extent of such *cognitive* knowledge "of the details of a plan or a policy to carry out the crime of genocide" may "vary depending on the position of the perpetrator in the governmental hierarchy or the military command structure."[1724] In practice, this means that the perpetrator need not have a full "knowledge of every detail of a comprehensive plan or policy of genocide."[1725] Indeed, the preparatory work of the Genocide Convention did not consider that premeditations were a legal ingredient of the crime of genocide.[1726] Professor Kai Ambos proposed a manner to infer the nature of such perpetrator's knowledge. Ambos explained that, in order to assess *intent*, the following quantitative and qualitative sub-issues need to be formulated:

> "(1) Is it necessary to intend the destruction of a significant number of members of the group (quantitative element)?
> (2) Would it be sufficient to intend to destroy a significant section of the group, for example, the leaders (qualitative element)?
> (3) Would it be sufficient to intend to destroy a reasonably significant number or section of a part of a group?"[1727]

In 2007, *in Bosnia and Herzegovina v. Serbia and Montenegro*, the International Court of Justice recognized that, in assessing the occurrence of genocide, it is not enough to verify the occurrence of certain acts prohibited by International Criminal Law.[1728] However, the occurrence of certain acts may provide a substantial substratum to infer the will of the genocide perpe-

---

[1718] Prosecutor v. Vujadin Popović *et al.* IT-05-88-T. *Supra* note 150. ¶ 823.
[1719] See also: Prosecutor v. Jean-Paul Akayesu. ICTR-96-4-T. *Supra* note 203. ¶ 523; Prosecutor v. Callixte Kalimanzira. ICTR-05-88-T. *Supra* note 166. ¶ 731.
[1720] Prosecutor v. Kayishema and Ruzindana. ICTR 95-1-T. *Supra* note 209. ¶ 91.
[1721] Prosecutor v. Vujadin Popović *et al.* IT-05-88-A. *Supra* note 151. ¶ 823.
[1722] Prosecutor v. Milomir Stakić. IT-97-24-T. *Supra* note 109. ¶ 522.
[1723] Prosecutor v. Goran Jelisić. IT-95-10-T. *Supra* note 97. ¶ 78.
[1724] U.N. Doc. A/CN.4/SER.A/1996/Add.l (Part 2) (1996). p. 45, ¶ 10.
[1725] *Ibidem.*
[1726] Prosecutor v. Goran Jelisić. IT-95-10-T. *Supra* note 97. ¶ 100.
[1727] See also: Kai Ambos. *Supra* note 30. p. 41.
[1728] Bosnia and Herzegovina v. Serbia and Montenegro. I.C.J. 43. *Supra* note 71. ¶ 187.

trator, when *direct* evidence of *cognitive* genocidal intent is lacking. Such intent may still be *inferred* (*inferential*/circumstantial/indirect evidence) from several facts and circumstances – all circumstantial evidence taken together.[1729] [1730] [1731] Therefore, the *factual matrix* can prove the genocidal intent *beyond any reasonable doubt.*[1732] [1733]

---

[1729] Prosecutor v. Clément Kayishema and Ruzindana. ICTR 95-1-T. *Supra* note 209. ¶ 93; Prosecutor v. Laurent Semanza. ICTR-97-20-T. *Supra* note 211. ¶ 313; Prosecutor v. Emmanuel Ndindabahizi. ICTR-2001-71-I. *Supra* note 177. ¶ 454; Prosecutor v. Aloys Simba. ICTR-01-76-T. *Supra* note 157. ¶ 413; Sylvestre Gacumbitsi v. Prosecutor. ICTR-2001-64-A. *Supra* note 229. ¶¶ 40-41; Prosecutor v. Jean Mpambara. ICTR-01-65-T. *Supra* note 202. ¶ 8; Ferdinand Nahimana et al v. Prosecutor. ICTR-99-52-A. *Supra* note 183. ¶ 524; Prosecutor v. François Karera. ICTR-01-74-T. *Supra* note 184. ¶ 534; Prosecutor v. Emmanuel Rukundo. ICTR-2001-70-T. *Supra* note 179. ¶ 557; Prosecutor v. Yussuf Munyakazi. ICTR-97-36A-T. *Supra* note 236. ¶ 494; Prosecutor v. Gaspard Kanyarukiga. ICTR-2002-78-T. *Supra* note 187. ¶ 636; Prosecutor v. Grégoire Ndahimana. ICTR-01-68-T. *Supra* note 191. ¶ 804; Prosecutor v. Callixte Nzabonimana. ICTR-98-44D-T. *Supra* note 168. ¶ 1704; Prosecutor v. Augustin Ngirabatware. ICTR-99-54-T. *Supra* note 164. ¶ 1327.

[1730] Prosecutor v. Goran Jelisić., IT-95-10-A. *Supra* note 98. ¶ 47; Prosecutor v. Duško Sikirica *et al.* IT-95-8-T. *Supra* note 87. ¶ 61; Prosecutor v. Radislav Krstić. IT-98-33-A. *Supra* note 129. ¶¶ 32, 34; Prosecutor v. Radoslav Brđanin. IT-99-36-T. *Supra* note 130. ¶ 704; Prosecutor v. Vujadin Popović *et al.* IT-05-88-T. *Supra* note 150. ¶¶ 820, 823; Prosecutor v. Radovan Karadžić. IT-95-5/18-AR98*bis*. *Supra* note 133. ¶ 80; Prosecutor v. Radovan Karadžić. IT-95-5/18-T, vol. I. *Supra* note 134. ¶ 550.

[1731] Prosecutor v. Jean-Pierre Bemba Gombo. ICC-01/05-01/08. *Supra* note 335. ¶ 239; Prosecutor v. Bosco Ntaganda. ICC-01/04-02/06. *Supra* note 328. ¶ 69.

[1732] Prosecutor v. Jean-Paul Akayesu. ICTR-96-4-T. *Supra* note 203. ¶ 523; Prosecutor v. Kayishema and Ruzindana. ICTR 95-1-T. *Supra* note 209. ¶ 93; Prosecutor v. Mikaeli Muhimana. ICTR-95-1B-T. *Supra* note 214. ¶ 496; Sylvestre Gacumbitsi v. Prosecutor. ICTR-2001-64-A. *Supra* note 229. ¶ 40; Aloys Simba v. Prosecutor. ICTR-01-76-A. *Supra* note 158. ¶ 264; Prosecutor v. François Karera. ICTR-01-74-T. *Supra* note 184. ¶ 534; Ferdinand Nahimana et al v. Prosecutor. ICTR-99-52-A. *Supra* note 183. ¶ 524; Prosecutor v. Siméon Nchamihigo. ICTR-01-63-T. *Supra* note 224. ¶ 331; Prosecutor v. Protais Zigiranyirazo. ICTR-01-73-T. *Supra* note 221. ¶ 398; Prosecutor v. Théoneste Bagosora *et al.* ICTR-98-41-T. *Supra* note 234. ¶ 2116; Prosecutor v. Emmanuel Rukundo. ICTR-2001-70-T. *Supra* note 179. ¶ 557; Prosecutor v. Callixte Kalimanzira. ICTR-05-88-T. *Supra* note 166. ¶ 731; Prosecutor v. Tharcisse Renzaho. ICTR-97-31-T. *Supra* note 232. ¶ 761; Prosecutor v. Ephrem Setako. ICTR-04-81-T. *Supra* note 181. ¶ 467; Prosecutor v. Yussuf Munyakazi. ICTR-97-36A-T. *Supra* note 236. ¶ 494; Prosecutor v. Dominique Ntawukulilyayo. ICTR-05-82-T. *Supra* note 170. ¶ 451; Prosecutor v. Ildephonse Hategekimana. ICTR-00-55B-T. *Supra* note 197. ¶ 669; Prosecutor v. Jean-Baptiste Gatete. ICTR-2000-61-T. *Supra* note 195. ¶ 583; Prosecutor v. Édouard Karemera *et al.* ICTR-98-44-T. *Supra* note 172. ¶ 1607; Prosecutor v. Callixte Nzabonimana. ICTR-98-44D-T. *Supra* note 168. ¶ 1704; Prosecutor v. Ildéphonse Nizeyimana. ICTR-2000-55C-T. *Supra* note 198. ¶ 1492.

In the light of the ICTY's and ICTR's jurisprudence, genocidal intent may be inferred from a certain number of concrete facts, circumstances, presumptions of facts or indicia,[1734][1735] including, but not limited to: 1) the general context of the perpetration of the underlying prohibited acts of genocide; 2) the specific characteristics of the members of the protected group targeted for destruction; 3) the systematic and repetitive culpable acts of targeting of persons in virtue of their belonging to a particular group; 4) the scale and frequency of atrocities committed; 5) the geographical location of the perpetrator's attacks; 6) the weapons employed in the attack(s); 7) the objective probability that the perpetrator's imposition of conditions of life on a protected group will lead to the effective physical destruction of such group, in whole or in part; 8) the extent of bodily injuries perpetrated against the victims of the protected group; 9) the length of time that the members of the protected group were exposed to genocidal acts; 10) the impact that the disappearance or the destruction of *part* of the protected group would have for the survival of the *entire* group; 11) objective proofs of the accused's mental state with respect to the deliberate perpetration of the underlying acts of genocide; 12) the perpetrator's statements, deeds, use of derogatory language, and public demonstrations in support of destructive acts against a protected group; 13) the methodical way of planning genocidal acts; 14) the participation/involvement of government or military personnel in the genocidal acts; 15) the existence of underlying discriminatory political doctrines against a protected group; 16) the confiscation or destruction of the targeted group's property; 17) the exclusion of members of other groups from the perpetrator's attacks against the targeted group; and 18) other perpetrator's culpable acts committed against the targeted group.[1736][1737]

---

[1733] Prosecutor v. Radislav Krstić. IT-98-33-A. *Supra* note 129. ¶¶ 32–33; Prosecutor v. Radoslav Brđanin. IT-99-36-T. *Supra* note 130. ¶¶ 704, 968; Prosecutor v. Zdravko Tolimir. IT-05-88/2-A. *Supra* note 152. ¶¶ 246–247, 561, 564; Prosecutor v. Vujadin Popović *et al.* IT-05-88-T. *Supra* note 150. ¶¶ 820, 823; Prosecutor v. Ratko Mladić., IT-09-92-T, vol. 3. *Supra* note 137. ¶ 3435.

[1734] Prosecutor v. Jean-Paul Akayesu. ICTR-96-4-T. *Supra* note 203. ¶ 523.

[1735] The International Commission of Inquiry on Darfur also considered that "whenever direct evidence of genocidal intent is lacking, as is mostly the case, intent can be inferred from many acts and manifestations or factual circumstances." (U.N. Doc. S/2005/60 (Feb. 1, 2005). ¶ 502).

[1736] Prosecutor v. Jean-Paul Akayesu. ICTR-96-4-T. *Supra* note 203. ¶ 523; Prosecutor v. Kayishema and Ruzindana. ICTR 95-1-T. *Supra* note 209. ¶ 93; Prosecutor v. Mikaeli Muhimana. ICTR-95-1B-T. *Supra* note 214. ¶ 496; Prosecutor v. Siméon Nchamihigo. ICTR-01-63-T. *Supra* note 224. ¶ 331; Prosecutor v. Emmanuel Rukundo. ICTR-2001-70-T. *Supra* note 179. ¶ 557; Prosecutor v. Callixte Kalimanzira. ICTR-05-88-T.

Examples abound regarding the admission of indirect evidence in genocide case law. The jurisprudence of the ICTR, for example, has extensively ruled in this regard: *Prosecutor v. Emmanuel Ndindabahizi*,[1738] *Prosecutor v. Jean Mpambara*,[1739] *Aloys Simba v. Prosecutor*.[1740] *Ferdinand Nahimana et al. v. Prosecutor*,[1741] *Prosecutor v. François Karera*,[1742] *Prosecutor v. Siméon Nchamihigo*, [1743] *Prosecutor v. Théoneste Bagosora et al.*,[1744] *Prosecutor v. Protais Zigiranyirazo*,[1745] *Prosecutor v. Emmanuel Rukundo*,[1746] *Prosecutor v. Callixte Kalimanzira*,[1747] *Prosecutor v. Tharcisse Renzaho*,[1748] *Prosecutor v. Hormisdas Nsengimana*,[1749] *Prosecutor v. Ephrem Setako*,[1750] *Siméon Nchamihigo v. Prosecutor*,[1751] *Prosecutor v. Yussuf Munyakazi*,[1752] *Prosecutor v. Gaspard Kanyarukiga*,[1753] *Prosecutor v. Jean-Baptiste Gatete*,[1754] *Prosecutor v. Augustin Ndindiliyimana et*

---

*Supra* note 166. ¶ 731; Prosecutor v. Tharcisse Renzaho. ICTR-97-31-T. *Supra* note 232. ¶ 761; Prosecutor v. Hormisdas Nsengimana, Case No. ICTR-01-69-T, (Nov. 17, 2009). ¶ 832; Prosecutor v. Ephrem Setako. ICTR-04-81-T. *Supra* note 181. ¶ 467; Prosecutor v. Dominique Ntawukulilyayo. ICTR-05-82-T. *Supra* note 170. ¶ 451; Callixte Kalimanzira v. Prosecutor. ICTR-05-88-A. *Supra* note 167. ¶ 89; Prosecutor v. Gaspard Kanyarukiga. ICTR-2002-78-T. *Supra* note 187. ¶ 636; Prosecutor v. Jean-Baptiste Gatete. ICTR-2000-61-T. *Supra* note 195. ¶ 583; Prosecutor v. Augustin Ndindiliyimana *et al.* ICTR-00-56-T. *Supra* note 163. ¶ 2073.

[1737] Prosecutor v. Goran Jelisić. IT-95-10-T. *Supra* note 97. ¶¶ 73, 75; Prosecutor v. Duško Sikirica *et al.* IT-95-8-T. *Supra* note 88. ¶ 77; Prosecutor v. Milomir Stakić. IT-97-24-T. *Supra* note 109. ¶ 526; Prosecutor v. Radoslav Brđanin. IT-99-36-T. *Supra* note 130. ¶¶ 704, 906, 970; Prosecutor v. Vidoje Blagojević *et al.* IT-02-60-A. *Supra* note 148. ¶ 123; Prosecutor v. Vujadin Popović *et al.* IT-05-88-T. *Supra* note 150. ¶ 823; Prosecutor v. Zdravko Tolimir. IT-05-88/2-A. *Supra* note 152. ¶¶ 246, 252–253; Prosecutor v. Radovan Karadžić. IT-95-5/18-T, vol. 1. *Supra* note 134. ¶ 550.

[1738] Prosecutor v. Emmanuel Ndindabahizi. ICTR-2001-71-I. *Supra* note 177. ¶ 454.

[1739] Prosecutor v. Jean Mpambara. ICTR-01-65-T. *Supra* note 202. ¶ 8.

[1740] Aloys Simba v. Prosecutor. ICTR-01-76-A. *Supra* note 158. ¶ 264.

[1741] Ferdinand Nahimana et al v. Prosecutor. ICTR-99-52-A. *Supra* note 183. ¶ 524.

[1742] Prosecutor v. François Karera. ICTR-01-74-T. *Supra* note 184. ¶ 615–616.

[1743] Prosecutor v. Siméon Nchamihigo. ICTR-01-63-T. *Supra* note 224. ¶ 331.

[1744] Prosecutor v. Théoneste Bagosora *et al.* ICTR-98-41-T. *Supra* note 234. ¶ 2116.

[1745] Prosecutor v. Protais Zigiranyirazo. ICTR-01-73-T. *Supra* note 221. ¶ 798.

[1746] Prosecutor v. Emmanuel Rukundo. ICTR-2001-70-T. *Supra* note 179. ¶ 557.

[1747] Prosecutor v. Callixte Kalimanzira. ICTR-05-88-T. *Supra* note 166. ¶ 731.

[1748] Prosecutor v. Tharcisse Renzaho. ICTR-97-31-T. *Supra* note 232. ¶ 761.

[1749] Prosecutor v. Hormisdas Nsengimana, Case No. ICTR-01-69-T, (Nov. 17, 2009). ¶ 832.

[1750] Prosecutor v. Ephrem Setako. ICTR-04-81-T. *Supra* note 181. ¶ 467.

[1751] Siméon Nchamihigo v. Prosecutor. ICTR-2001-63-A. *Supra* note 225. ¶ 136.

[1752] Prosecutor v. Yussuf Munyakazi. ICTR-97-36A-T. *Supra* note 236. ¶ 494.

[1753] Prosecutor v. Gaspard Kanyarukiga. ICTR-2002-78-T. *Supra* note 187. ¶¶ 636, 653.

[1754] Prosecutor v. Jean-Baptiste Gatete. ICTR-2000-61-T. *Supra* note 195. ¶ 583.

al.,[1755] and *Prosecutor v. Pauline Nyiramasuhuko.*[1756] Also, the ICTY has comprehensively ruled on the acceptance of inferential evidence to prove genocidal intent. See, for example: *Prosecutor v. Goran Jelisić,*[1757] *Prosecutor v. Milomir Stakić,*[1758] *Prosecutor v. Radislav Krstić,*[1759] *Prosecutor v. Radoslav Brđanin,*[1760] *Prosecutor v. Vidoje Blagojević, Dragan Jokić,*[1761] *Prosecutor v. Vujadin Popović et al.,*[1762] and *Prosecutor v. Ratko Mladić*

Importantly, the statutory and case-law frameworks allow the admittance of Press and NGO reports as 1) *prima facie* reliable evidence of mens rea, "provided that they offer sufficient guarantees of impartiality"; as 2) corroboratory evidence, determined on a case-by-case basis, and as 3) an instrumental tool to assess Prosecution's allegations.[1763] [1764] [1765] *The criminal intent to commit genocide need not be the sole motivation of the perpetrator's attack against a protected group.*[1766]

---

[1755]   Prosecutor v. Augustin Ndindiliyimana *et al.* ICTR-00-56-T. *Supra* note 163. ¶ 2073.

[1756]   Prosecutor v. Pauline Nyiramasuhuko *et al.* ICTR-98-42-A. *Supra* note 220. ¶ 1029.

[1757]   Prosecutor v. Goran Jelisić., IT-95-10-A. *Supra* note 98. ¶ 47.

[1758]   Prosecutor v. Milomir Stakić. IT-97-24-T. *Supra* note 109. ¶ 526.

[1759]   Prosecutor v. Radislav Krstić. IT-98-33-A. *Supra* note 129. ¶ 33.

[1760]   Prosecutor v. Radoslav Brđanin. IT-99-36-T. *Supra* note 130. ¶ ¶ 704, 968–970.

[1761]   Prosecutor v. Vidoje Blagojević *et al.* IT-02-60-A. *Supra* note 148. ¶ 123.

[1762]   Prosecutor v. Vujadin Popović *et al.* IT-05-88-T. *Supra* note 150. ¶ 823; Prosecutor v. Vujadin Popović *et al.* IT-05-88-A. *Supra* note 151. ¶¶ 544, 553.

[1763]   In *Prosecutor v. Jean-Paul Akayesu,* for example, the ICTR Trial Chamber considered as evidence photographs and videos of the British cameraman, Simon Cox. (Prosecutor v. Jean-Paul Akayesu. ICTR-96-4-T. *Supra* note 203. ¶¶ 116, 161–162).

[1764]   In *Prosecutor v. Callixte Mbarushimana,* for example, the ICC Pre-Trial Chamber, analyzing documents emanating from Human Rights Watch, considered that "the source of the documents, the purpose for which the information contained therein was gathered and the nature and relevance of the information contained therein," satisfied relevant *due process* elements and had, therefore, "probative value." (Prosecutor v. Callixte Mbarushimana. ICC-01/04-01/10. *Supra* note 330. ¶¶ 71, 78).

[1765]   See also: Prosecutor v. Jean-Pierre Bemba Gombo. ICC-01/05-01/08. *Supra* note 335. ¶¶ 269–271.

[1766]   Prosecutor v. Aloys Simba. ICTR-01-76-T. *Supra* note 157. ¶ 412; Prosecutor v. François Karera. ICTR-01-74-T. *Supra* note 184. ¶ 534; Prosecutor v. Théoneste Bagosora *et al.* ICTR-98-41-T. *Supra* note 234. ¶ 2115; Prosecutor v. Emmanuel Rukundo. ICTR-2001-70-T. *Supra* note 179. ¶ 557; Prosecutor v. Callixte Kalimanzira. ICTR-05-88-T. *Supra* note 166. ¶ 158; Prosecutor v. Tharcisse Renzaho. ICTR-97-31-T. *Supra* note 232. ¶ 760; Prosecutor v. Ephrem Setako. ICTR-04-81-T. *Supra* note 181. ¶ 466; Prosecutor v. Yussuf Munyakazi. ICTR-97-36A-T. *Supra* note 236. ¶ 493; Prosecutor v. Dominique Ntawukulilyayo. ICTR-05-82-T. *Supra* note 170. ¶ 450; Prosecutor v. Gaspard Kanyarukiga. ICTR-2002-78-T. *Supra* note 187. ¶ 636; Prosecutor v. Ildephonse Hategekimana. ICTR-00-55B-T. *Supra* note 197. ¶ 668; Prosecutor v.

The *de facto* destruction of the targeted group, in whole or in part, is not required to prove *mens rea*, although it might serve "to distinguish the crime of genocide from the inchoate offenses (...), such as the attempt to commit genocide."[1767] Besides, it is not also necessary to prove that the perpetrator of the genocidal acts "chose the most efficient method to accomplish his objective of destroying the targeted part."[1768] Customary international law considers that "even where the method selected will not implement the perpetrator's intent to the fullest, leaving that destruction incomplete, this ineffectiveness alone does not preclude a finding of genocidal intent."[1769] [1770]

The mere knowledge that certain genocidal acts are being committed against a protected group does not suffice the legal requirements for conviction and sentencing. The ICTY firmly consolidated such rationale in *Prosecutor v. Radislav Krstić* (ICTY),[1771] *Prosecutor v. Slobodan Milošević*,[1772] *Prosecutor v. Vidoje Blagojević*, Dragan Jokić,[1773] *Prosecutor v. Protais Zigiranyirazo*,[1774] *Prosecutor v. Vujadin Popović et al.*,[1775] and *Prosecutor v. Vujadin Popović et al.*,[1776] In *Prosecutor v. Milomir Stakić*, the court went even one step further in sustaining that proof of *de facto* destruction of the group in part would not be required in genocide cases.[1777] However, in *Prosecutor v. Radoslav Brđanin,* the ICTY concluded that the de facto destruction of the group "may constitute evidence of the specific intent and may also serve to distinguish the crime of genocide from the inchoate offenses (...) such as the attempt to commit genocide".[1778]

Regarding the genocidal *mens rea,* it is also important to highlight that the crime of genocide "do(es) not require that the aider and abettor share

---

Jean-Baptiste Gatete. ICTR-2000-61-T. *Supra* note 195. ¶ 582; Prosecutor v. Grégoire Ndahimana. ICTR-01-68-T. *Supra* note 191. ¶ 803; Prosecutor v. Édouard Karemera *et al.* ICTR-98-44-T. *Supra* note 172. ¶ 1606; Prosecutor v. Ildéphonse Nizeyimana. ICTR-2000-55C-T. *Supra* note 198. ¶ 1491.

[1767] Prosecutor v. Radoslav Brđanin. IT-99-36-T. *Supra* note 130. ¶ 697.

[1768] Prosecutor v. Radislav Krstić. IT-98-33-A. *Supra* note 129. ¶ 32.

[1769] *Ibidem.*

[1770] See also: Prosecutor v. Zdravko Tolimir. IT-05-88/2-T. *Supra* note 153. ¶ 748.

[1771] Prosecutor v. Radislav Krstić. IT-98-33-A. *Supra* note 129. ¶¶ 37, 134.

[1772] Prosecutor v. Slobodan Milošević. IT-02-54-T. *Supra* note 139. ¶ 126.

[1773] Prosecutor v. Vidoje Blagojević, Dragan Jokić. IT-02-60-T. *Supra* note 147. ¶ 656.

[1774] Prosecutor v. Protais Zigiranyirazo. ICTR-01-73-T. *Supra* note 221. ¶ 798.

[1775] Prosecutor v. Vujadin Popović *et al.* IT-05-88-T. *Supra* note 150. ¶ 820.

[1776] Prosecutor v. Vujadin Popović *et al.* IT-05-88-A. *Supra* note 151. ¶ 820.

[1777] Prosecutor v. Milomir Stakić. IT-97-24-T. *Supra* note 109. ¶¶ 517, 522.

[1778] Prosecutor v. Radoslav Brđanin. IT-99-36-T. *Supra* note 130. ¶ 697.

the *mens rea* of the principal perpetrator."[1779] Proving the principal perpetrator's specific intent is sufficient to prove genocidal intent,[1780] as well established by the ICTR in *Prosecutor v. Clément Kayishema et al.*,[1781] *Prosecutor v. Protais Zigiranyirazo*,[1782] *Prosecutor v. Tharcisse Renzaho*,[1783] and *Dominique Ntawukulilyayo v. Prosecutor*,[1784] and by the ICTY in *Prosecutor v. Vidoje Blagojević, Dragan Jokić*.[1785] The ICTR and the ICTY have a vast jurisprudence of persons convicted of committing genocide or aiding and abetting and ordering, or directly and publicly incitement to commit genocide. From the ICTR, see, for example: *Prosecutor v. Athanase Seromba*,[1786] *Prosecutor v. François Karera*,[1787] *Prosecutor v. Siméon Nchamihigo*,[1788] *Prosecutor v. Simon Bikindi*,[1789] *Prosecutor v. Protais Zigiranyirazo*,[1790] *Prosecutor v. Théoneste Bagosora, Anatole Nsengiyumva*,[1791] *Prosecutor v. Emmanuel Rukundo*,[1792] *Prosecutor v. Tharcisse Muvunyi*,[1793] *Prosecutor v. Dominique Ntawukulilyayo*,[1794] *Prosecutor v. Gaspard Kanyarukiga*,[1795] and *Prosecutor v. Jean-Baptiste*.[1796]

Notably, the existence of a personal motive does not preclude a finding of specific genocidal intent.[1797] [1798] [1799] In such instances, the International

---

[1779]  Dominique Ntawukulilyayo v. Prosecutor. ICTR-05-82-A. *Supra* note 171. ¶ 222.

[1780]  *Ibid.*

[1781]  Prosecutor v. Clément Kayishema *et al.* ICTR-95-1-A. *Supra* note 210. ¶ 170.

[1782]  Prosecutor v. Protais Zigiranyirazo. ICTR-01-73-T. *Supra* note 221. ¶ 798.

[1783]  Prosecutor v. Tharcisse Renzaho. ICTR-97-31-T. *Supra* note 232. ¶ 779.

[1784]  Dominique Ntawukulilyayo v. Prosecutor. ICTR-05-82-A. *Supra* note 171. ¶ 222.

[1785]  Prosecutor v. Vidoje Blagojević *et al.* IT-02-60-A. *Supra* note 148. ¶ 127.

[1786]  Prosecutor v. Athanase Seromba. ICTR-2001-66-I. *Supra* note 160. ¶ 372.

[1787]  Prosecutor v. François Karera. ICTR-01-74-T. *Supra* note 184. ¶ 569.

[1788]  Prosecutor v. Siméon Nchamihigo. ICTR-01-63-T. *Supra* note 224. ¶ 381.

[1789]  Prosecutor v. Simon Bikindi. ICTR-01-72-T. *Supra* note 226. Chapter V.

[1790]  Prosecutor v. Protais Zigiranyirazo. ICTR-01-73-T. *Supra* note 221. ¶ 447.

[1791]  Prosecutor v. Théoneste Bagosora *et al.* ICTR-98-41-T. *Supra* note 234. ¶ 2158.

[1792]  Prosecutor v. Emmanuel Rukundo. ICTR-2001-70-T. *Supra* note 179. ¶ 591.

[1793]  Prosecutor v. Tharcisse Muvunyi. ICTR-00-55A-T. *Supra* note 231. ¶ 134.

[1794]  Prosecutor v. Dominique Ntawukulilyayo. ICTR-05-82-T. *Supra* note 170. ¶ 460.

[1795]  Prosecutor v. Gaspard Kanyarukiga. ICTR-2002-78-T. *Supra* note 187. ¶ 667.

[1796]  Prosecutor v. Jean-Baptiste Gatete. ICTR-2000-61-T. *Supra* note 195. *passim.*

[1797] Prosecutor v. Goran Jelisić., IT-95-10-A. *Supra* note 98. ¶ 49; Prosecutor v. Milomir Stakić. IT-97-24-A. *Supra* note 110. ¶ 45; Prosecutor v. Vujadin Popović *et al.* IT-05-88-T. *Supra* note 150. ¶ 825; Prosecutor v. Radovan Karadžić. IT-95-5/18-T, vol. I. *Supra* note 134. ¶ 554.

[1798]  Prosecutor v. Aloys Simba. ICTR-01-76-T. *Supra* note 157. ¶ 412; Prosecutor v. François Karera. ICTR-01-74-T. *Supra* note 184. ¶ 534; Prosecutor v. Théoneste Bagosora *et al.* ICTR-98-41-T. *Supra* note 234. ¶ 2115; Prosecutor v. Emmanuel Rukundo. ICTR-2001-70-T. *Supra* note 179. ¶ 557; Prosecutor v. Callixte Kalimanzira. ICTR-05-88-T. *Supra* note 166. ¶ 158; Prosecutor v. Tharcisse Renzaho. ICTR-97-31-T. *Su-*

Commission of Inquiry on Darfur has already stated that "this special [genocidal] intent must not be confused with motive, namely, the particular reason that may induce a person to engage in criminal conduct."[1800] For the Commission, genocide perpetrators may possess underlying motives behind their genocidal acts, for example "the desire to appropriate the goods belonging to that ['targeted] group or set of persons," or "the urge to take revenge for prior attacks by members of that group or by the desire to please his superiors who despise that group."[1801] The Commission concluded that, "from the viewpoint of criminal law, what matters is not the motive, but rather whether or not there exists the requisite special intent to destroy a group."[1802]

This means that "in genocide cases, the reason(s) why the accused sought to destroy the victim group has no bearing on guilt."[1803] [1804] In *Prosecutor v. Tharcisse Renzaho*, the ICTR clearly stated that the existence of personal motive "does not preclude him from having the specific intent to commit genocide,"[1805] [1806] [1807] provided that the *intent* to destroy is proven

---

pra note 232. ¶ 760; Prosecutor v. Ephrem Setako. ICTR-04-81-T. *Supra* note 181. ¶ 466; Prosecutor v. Yussuf Munyakazi. ICTR-97-36A-T. *Supra* note 236. ¶ 493; Prosecutor v. Dominique Ntawukulilyayo. ICTR-05-82-T. *Supra* note 170. ¶ 450; Prosecutor v. Gaspard Kanyarukiga. ICTR-2002-78-T. *Supra* note 187. ¶ 636; Prosecutor v. Ildephonse Hategekimana. ICTR-00-55B-T. *Supra* note 197. ¶ 668; Prosecutor v. Jean-Baptiste Gatete. ICTR-2000-61-T. *Supra* note 195. ¶ 582; Prosecutor v. Grégoire Ndahimana. ICTR-01-68-T. *Supra* note 191. ¶ 803; Prosecutor v. Édouard Karemera *et al.* ICTR-98-44-T. *Supra* note 172. ¶ 1606; Prosecutor v. Ildéphonse Nizeyimana. ICTR-2000-55C-T. *Supra* note 198. ¶ 1491.

[1799] U.N. Doc. A/CN.4/SER.A/1989/Add.l (Part 2) (1989). ¶ 154.

[1800] U.N. Doc. S/2005/60 (Feb. 1, 2005). ¶ 493.

[1801] *Ibid.*

[1802] *Ibid.*

[1803] Prosecutor v. Milomir Stakić. IT-97-24-A. *Supra* note 110. ¶ 45.

[1804] See also: Prosecutor v. Goran Jelisić., IT-95-10-A. *Supra* note 98. ¶ 49; Prosecutor v. Vujadin Popović *et al.* IT-05-88-T. *Supra* note 150. ¶ 825.

[1805] Prosecutor v. Tharcisse Renzaho. ICTR-97-31-T. *Supra* note 232. ¶ 760.

[1806] Kai Ambos teaches that "while the motive inquires about the reasons behind a certain conduct ('why'), the intent merely goes to the psychological state of mind during the act. Thus, the fact that the perpetrators may act with motives other than destruction does not exclude the existence of genocidal intent." (Kai Ambos. *Supra* note 63. p. 40).

[1807] See also: Prosecutor v. Emmanuel Rukundo. ICTR-2001-70-T. *Supra* note 179. ¶ 557; Prosecutor v. Callixte Kalimanzira. ICTR-05-88-T. *Supra* note 166. ¶ 158; Prosecutor v. Hormisdas Nsengimana, Case No. ICTR-01-69-T, (Nov. 17, 2009). ¶ 831; Prosecutor v. Ephrem Setako. ICTR-04-81-T. *Supra* note 181. ¶ 466; Prosecutor v. Dominique Ntawukulilyayo. ICTR-05-82-T. *Supra* note 170. ¶ 450; Prosecutor v. Gaspard

beyond a reasonable doubt, as established in *Prosecutor v. Clément Kayishema et al.* (ICTR),[1808] *Eliézer Niyitegeka v. Prosecutor* (ICTR),[1809] *Prosecutor v. Emmanuel Rukundo* (ICTR),[1810] *Prosecutor v. Gaspard Kanyarukiga* (ICTR).[1811] [1812] It is also not necessary that the perpetrator is exclusively/solely motivated by a genocidal intent.[1813]

### 3.1.5. "In whole or in part."

In establishing specific genocidal intent, proof that the perpetrator intended the "complete annihilation of a group" is not necessary[1814] – the extermination of the group in its entirety throughout the world.[1815] It is well established in the International Criminal Law jurisprudence that a large number of victims does not constitute an element of the crime of genocide.[1816] [1817] See, for example, *Grégoire Ndahimana v. Prosecutor* (ICTR),[1818] *Prosecutor v. Ratko Mladić* (ICTY),[1819] and *Callixte Nzabonimana v.*

---

  Kanyarukiga. ICTR-2002-78-T. *Supra* note 187. ¶ 636; Prosecutor v. Jean-Baptiste Gatete. ICTR-2000-61-T. *Supra* note 195. ¶ 582; Prosecutor v. Augustin Ndindiliyimana *et al.* ICTR-00-56-T. *Supra* note 163. ¶ 2072.

[1808] Prosecutor v. Clément Kayishema *et al.* ICTR-95-1-A. *Supra* note 210. ¶ 161.

[1809] Eliézer Niyitegeka v. Prosecutor. ICTR-96-14-A. *Supra* note 174. ¶ 53.

[1810] Prosecutor v. Emmanuel Rukundo. ICTR-2001-70-T. *Supra* note 179. ¶ 557.

[1811] Prosecutor v. Gaspard Kanyarukiga. ICTR-2002-78-T. *Supra* note 187. ¶ 635.

[1812] See also: Prosecutor v. Goran Jelisić. IT-95-10-T. *Supra* note 97. ¶ 49; Prosecutor v. Vidoje Blagojević, Dragan Jokić. IT-02-60-T. *Supra* note 147. ¶ 669.

[1813] Prosecutor v. Emmanuel Rukundo. ICTR-2001-70-T. *Supra* note 179. ¶ 557; Prosecutor v. Callixte Kalimanzira. ICTR-05-88-T. *Supra* note 166. ¶ 158; Prosecutor v. Tharcisse Renzaho. ICTR-97-31-T. *Supra* note 232. ¶ 760; Prosecutor v. Hormisdas Nsengimana, Case No. ICTR-01-69-T, (Nov. 17, 2009). ¶ 831; Prosecutor v. Ephrem Setako. ICTR-04-81-T. *Supra* note 181. ¶ 466; Prosecutor v. Dominique Ntawukulilyayo. ICTR-05-82-T. *Supra* note 170. ¶ 450; Prosecutor v. Gaspard Kanyarukiga. ICTR-2002-78-T. *Supra* note 187. ¶ 636; Prosecutor v. Jean-Baptiste Gatete. ICTR-2000-61-T. *Supra* note 195. ¶ 582; Prosecutor v. Augustin Ndindiliyimana *et al.* ICTR-00-56-T. *Supra* note 163. ¶ 2072.

[1814] Prosecutor v. Athanase Seromba. ICTR-2001-66-T. *Supra* note 160. ¶ 319.

[1815] Prosecutor v. Jean-Paul Akayesu. ICTR-96-4-T. *Supra* note 203. ¶ 497.

[1816] Grégoire Ndahimana v. Prosecutor. ICTR-01-68-A. *Supra* note 192. ¶ 231.

[1817] However, it is authoritative to mention that "where only part of a protected group is targeted that part must constitute a substantial part of that group such that it is significant enough to have an impact on the group as a whole. In determining substantiality, considerations may include: the relative numerical size of the targeted part, the prominence of the part of the group within the larger whole, and the area of the perpetrators' activity and control". (Prosecutor v. Ratko Mladić., IT-09-92-T. *Supra* note 137. ¶ 172).

[1818] Grégoire Ndahimana v. Prosecutor. ICTR-01-68-A. *Supra* note 192. ¶ 231.

*Prosecutor* (ITCR).[1820] Therefore, there is no numeric threshold.[1821] [1822] It is sufficient to prove the perpetrator's intent to destroy a substantial part thereof (in part).[1823] Accordingly, the genocidal *mens rea* may be manifested in two forms: 1) the intent to destroy a group *en masse* (in whole), or 2) the intent to destroy a group *selectively* (in part).[1824] [1825] The first refers to the aim of destroying large numerical portions of the targeted group through the perpetration of certain prohibited acts prescribed in the statutes of International Criminal Law courts.[1826] [1827] The second refers to the desire to exterminate a limited/'selected number of persons whose disappearance would have a huge impact upon the survival of the group.[1828] [1829]

---

[1819] Prosecutor v. Ratko Mladić., IT-09-92-T. *Supra* note 137.

[1820] Callixte Nzabonimana v. Prosecutor. ICTR-98-44D-A. *Supra* note 169. ¶ 126.

[1821] Prosecutor v. Laurent Semanza. ICTR-97-20-T. *Supra* note 211. ¶ 316; Prosecutor v. Sylvestre Gacumbitsi. ICTR-2001-64-T. *Supra* note 228. ¶ 258; Prosecutor v. Aloys Simba. ICTR-01-76-T. *Supra* note 157. ¶ 412; Prosecutor v. Théoneste Bagosora *et al.* ICTR-98-41-T. *Supra* note 234. ¶ 2115; Prosecutor v. Callixte Kalimanzira. ICTR-05-88-T. *Supra* note 166. ¶ 158; Prosecutor v. Tharcisse Renzaho. ICTR-97-31-T. *Supra* note 232. ¶ 760; Prosecutor v. Ephrem Setako. ICTR-04-81-T. *Supra* note 181. ¶ 466; Prosecutor v. Yussuf Munyakazi. ICTR-97-36A-T. *Supra* note 236. ¶ 493; Prosecutor v. Dominique Ntawukulilyayo. ICTR-05-82-T. *Supra* note 170. ¶ 450; Prosecutor v. Ildephonse Hategekimana. ICTR-00-55B-T. *Supra* note 197. ¶ 668; Prosecutor v. Jean-Baptiste Gatete. ICTR-2000-61-T. *Supra* note 195. ¶ 582; Prosecutor v. Grégoire Ndahimana. ICTR-01-68-T. *Supra* note 191. ¶ 803; Prosecutor v. Édouard Karemera *et al.* ICTR-98-44-T. *Supra* note 172. ¶ 1606.

[1822] Prosecutor v. Milomir Stakić. IT-97-24-T. *Supra* note 109. ¶ 522; Prosecutor v. Vujadin Popović *et al.* IT-05-88-T. *Supra* note 150. ¶ 831; Prosecutor v. Zdravko Tolimir. IT-05-88/2-T. *Supra* note 153. ¶ 749; Prosecutor v. Zdravko Tolimir. IT-05-88/2-A A172-1/2054bis. *Supra* note 154. p. 98/2054 BIS; Prosecutor v. Radovan Karadžić. IT-95-5/18-T, vol. I. *Supra* note 134. ¶ 555.

[1823] Prosecutor v. Athanase Seromba. ICTR-2001-66-T. *Supra* note 160. ¶ 319.

[1824] According to the ICTY, "genocidal intent may therefore be manifest in two forms. It may consist of desiring the extermination of a very large number of the members of the group, in which case it would constitute an intention to destroy a group *en masse*. However, it may also consist of the desired destruction of a more limited number of persons selected for the impact that their disappearance would have upon the survival of the group as such." (Prosecutor v. Vujadin Popović *et al.* IT-05-88-A. *Supra* note 151. ¶ 82).

[1825] See also: Prosecutor v. Kayishema and Ruzindana. ICTR 95-1-T. *Supra* note 209. ¶ 97; Prosecutor v. Goran Jelisić. IT-95-10-T. *Supra* note 97. ¶ 82; Prosecutor v. Radislav Krstić. IT-98-33-A. *Supra* note 129. ¶ 8.

[1826] Prosecutor v. Goran Jelisić. IT-95-10-T. *Supra* note 97. ¶ 82.

[1827] Prosecutor v. Georges Anderson Nderubumwe Rutaganda. ICTR-96-3-A. *Supra* note 189. ¶ 524

[1828] Prosecutor v. Goran Jelisić. IT-95-10-T. *Supra* note 97. ¶ 82.

Importantly, although the determination of the occurrence of genocide does not require a numeric threshold of victims, it must be proved, beyond a reasonable doubt, "that the perpetrator acted with the intent to destroy the group as such, in whole or in part." The intent to destroy a protected group must be to destroy at least a relatively considerable portion of individuals whose destruction would jeopardize the existence of the whole group as such.[1830] [1831] According to the *rationale* of *Prosecutor v. Milomir Stakić*, "it is not necessary to establish, with the assistance of a demographer, the size of the victimized population in numerical terms."[1832] It suffices to prove, without reasonable doubt, that the perpetrator had the intent to destroy at least a substantial part of the group, whose elimination would be significant to the survival of the entire group, such as the elimination of the group's leadership or the elimination of its male members.[1833] [1834]

The determination of whether the destruction of a fractioned part of the targeted group is substantial enough (*substantiality requirement*) to

---

[1829] In *Jelisić*, the ICTY considered that "the character of the attack on the leadership must be viewed in the context of the fate or what happened to the rest of the group. If a group has its leadership exterminated, and at the same time or in the wake of that, has a relatively large number of the members of the group killed or subjected to other heinous acts, for example deported on a large scale or forced to flee, the cluster of violations ought to be considered in its entirety in order to interpret the provisions of the [Genocide] Convention in a spirit consistent with its purpose." (*Ibidem*).

[1830] Prosecutor v. Duško Sikirica *et al.* IT-95-8-T. *Supra* note 87. ¶ 65; Prosecutor v. Vidoje Blagojević, Dragan Jokić. IT-02-60-T. *Supra* note 147. ¶ 668; Prosecutor v. Zdravko Tolimir. IT-05-88/2-T. *Supra* note 153. ¶ 749.

[1831] Prosecutor v. Clément Kayishema and Ruzindana. ICTR 95-1-T. *Supra* note 209. ¶¶ 96–97; Prosecutor v. Goran Jelisić. IT-95-10-T. *Supra* note 97. ¶ 82; Prosecutor v. Laurent Semanza. ICTR-97-20-T. *Supra* note 211. ¶ 316; Prosecutor v. Emmanuel Ndindabahizi. ICTR-2001-71-I. *Supra* note 177. ¶ 454; Prosecutor v. Aloys Simba. ICTR-01-76-T. *Supra* note 157. ¶ 412; Prosecutor v. François Karera. ICTR-01-74-T. *Supra* note 184. ¶ 534; Prosecutor v. Gaspard Kanyarukiga. ICTR-2002-78-T. *Supra* note 187. ¶ 635; Prosecutor v. Ildephonse Hategekimana. ICTR-00-55B-T. *Supra* note 197. ¶ 668.

[1832] Prosecutor v. Milomir Stakić. IT-97-24-T. *Supra* note 109. ¶ 522.

[1833] Prosecutor v. François Karera. ICTR-01-74-T. *Supra* note 184. ¶ 534; Prosecutor v. Callixte Kalimanzira. ICTR-05-88-T. *Supra* note 166. ¶¶ 158, 730; Prosecutor v. Tharcisse Renzaho. ICTR-97-31-T. *Supra* note 232. ¶ 760; Prosecutor v. Ephrem Setako. ICTR-04-81-T. *Supra* note 181. ¶ 466; Prosecutor v. Dominique Ntawukulilyayo. ICTR-05-82-T. *Supra* note 170. ¶ 450; Prosecutor v. Jean-Baptiste Gatete. ICTR-2000-61-T. *Supra* note 195. ¶ 582; Prosecutor v. Augustin Ndindiliyimana *et al.* ICTR-00-56-T. *Supra* note 163. ¶ 2072.

[1834] Prosecutor v. Vujadin Popović *et al.* IT-05-88-T. *Supra* note 150. ¶¶ 865-866.

meet such legal requirement and represent a danger of destruction to the entire group – *relative weight* –involves the consideration of several factors that must always be analyzed on a case-by-case basis.[1835] These factors include but are not limited to: 1) the "numeric size of the targeted part of the group," "measured not only in absolute terms but also in relation to the overall size of the entire group;" 2) whether the targeted portion of the group is *emblematic* of the overall group, such as its leadership; 3) the prominence of the targeted portion; and 4) whether the targeted portion is essential to the survival of the whole group, such as the destruction of its male members.[1836] [1837] Also, customary international law supports the understanding that genocide might be perpetrated "even when the discriminatory intent only extends to "a limited geographic zone."[1838] [1839]

A crucial question regarding the targeting of a specific group and the numeric threshold of victims necessary to establish genocide is whether more than one group can be targeted at the same time by the same perpetrators. In making considerations about genocidal acts committed against both Bosnian Muslims as well as Bosnian Croats in the Former Yugoslavia, the ICTY concluded, in *Prosecutor v. Radoslav Brđanin*, on the possibility of perpetrators to target *at the same time* more than one protected group, provided that the elements of the crime of genocide are considered in relation to each group separately.[1840]

Besides, Customary International Law also allows the possibility of the characterization of the crime of genocide even when the perpetrators' intent to destroy a group is limited to a geographical area or a single community, which means the possibility that the elimination of a certain por-

---

[1835] Prosecutor v. Radislav Krstić. IT-98-33-A. *Supra* note 129. ¶ 12; Prosecutor v. Radoslav Brđanin. IT-99-36-T. *Supra* note 130. ¶ 702; Prosecutor v. Vujadin Popović *et al.* IT-05-88-T. *Supra* note 150. ¶ 832; Prosecutor v. Zdravko Tolimir. IT-05-88/2-T. *Supra* note 153. ¶ 749.

[1836] Prosecutor v. Duško Sikirica *et al.* IT-95-8-T. *Supra* note 87. ¶ 65. See also: Prosecutor v. Milomir Stakić. IT-97-24-T. *Supra* note 109. ¶ 525; Prosecutor v. Radislav Krstić. IT-98-33-A. *Supra* note 129. ¶ 12; Prosecutor v. Radoslav Brđanin. IT-99-36-T. *Supra* note 130. ¶¶ 701–702; Prosecutor v. Vujadin Popović *et al.* IT-05-88-T. *Supra* note 150. ¶¶ 832, 865–866; Prosecutor v. Zdravko Tolimir. IT-05-88/2-T. *Supra* note 153. ¶ 749; Prosecutor v. Zdravko Tolimir. IT-05-88/2-A A172-1/2054bis. *Supra* note 154. p. 98/2054 BIS.

[1837] Prosecutor v. Clément Kayishema and Ruzindana. ICTR 95-1-T. *Supra* note 209. ¶ 96.

[1838] Prosecutor v. Duško Sikirica *et al.* IT-95-8-T. *Supra* note 87. ¶ 68.

[1839] See also: Prosecutor v. Milomir Stakić. IT-97-24-T. *Supra* note 109. ¶ 523; Prosecutor v. Radoslav Brđanin. IT-99-36-T. *Supra* note 130. ¶ 703.

[1840] Prosecutor v. Radoslav Brđanin. IT-99-36-T. *Supra* note 130. ¶ 735.

tion of the group may accomplish the intent of "purifying an entire region" inhabited by such group.[1841] In *Prosecutor v. Radoslav Brđanin*, the ICTY confirmed the characterization of genocide even when the specific intent to destroy a group, in part, extends to an area "difficult to precisely determine."[1842]

Likewise, the ITCR's Appeals Chamber understood, in *Callixte Kalimanzira v. Prosecutor*, that the local concentration of crimes – specifically at Kalimanzira's prefecture – rather than at the national level was not a relevant factor to assess the gravity of such crimes.[1843] Most importantly, the Chamber conceived the idea of the *indivisible character* of the crime of genocide. For the Chamber, "the genocide that was committed in Rwanda between 6 April 1994 and 17 July 1994, which resulted in the killings of hundreds of thousands of Tutsis, is indivisible."[1844]

## 3.2. Crimes against humanity.

### 3.2.1. Legal Definition and chapeau elements

It is a core principle of Customary International Law that civilians must always be protected at all times, in peacetime and in circumstances of armed conflicts.[1845] Therefore, the targeting of civilians and civilian objects is absolutely forbidden under Customary International Law and may not be derogated under the allegation of military necessity.[1846] Likewise, attacks on the civilian population are not also supported by "*tu quoque*" allegations.[1847] Therefore, certain acts purposefully directed against any civil-

---

[1841]  Prosecutor v. Goran Jelisić. IT-95-10-T. *Supra* note 97. ¶ 83; Prosecutor v. Duško Sikirica *et al.* IT-95-8-T. *Supra* note 88. ¶ 68; Prosecutor v. Radoslav Brđanin. IT-99-36-T. *Supra* note 130. ¶ 703; Prosecutor v. Radislav Krstić. IT-98-33-A. *Supra* note 129. ¶¶ 15, 16, 28.

[1842]  Prosecutor v. Radoslav Brđanin. IT-99-36-T. *Supra* note 130. ¶ 967.

[1843]  Callixte Kalimanzira v. Prosecutor. ICTR-05-88-A. *Supra* note 167. ¶ 229.

[1844]  *Ibidem.*

[1845]  Prosecutor v. Vidoje Blagojević, Dragan Jokić. IT-02-60-T. *Supra* note 147. ¶ 544.

[1846]  Prosecutor v. Dragoljub Kunarac *et al.* IT-96-23/1-A. *Supra* note 85. ¶ ¶ 87, 91; Prosecutor v. Vidoje Blagojević, Dragan Jokić. IT-02-60-T. *Supra* note 147. ¶ 544; Prosecutor v. Stanislav Galić. IT-98-29-A. *Supra* note 141. ¶ 130; Prosecutor v. Brima, Kamara, Kanu. SCSL-04-16-T. *Supra* note 280. ¶ 216.

[1847]  "The existence of an attack from one side against the other side's civilian population would neither justify the attack by that other side against the civilian population of its opponent nor displace the conclusion that the other side's forces were in fact targeting a civilian population as such." (Prosecutor v. Dragoljub Kunarac *et al.* IT-96-23/1-A. *Supra* note 85. ¶ 87).

ian population – *actus reus* –, when committed in a context of widespread or systematic attacks, may constitute a crime against humanity within the scope and jurisdiction of international criminal courts.[1848] The Rome Statute defines a "crime against humanity" as an act "committed as part of a widespread or systematic attack directed against any civilian population, with knowledge of the attack."[1849] [1850] Crimes against humanity may be perpetrated in peace times and in times of armed conflict.[1851] [1852]

In different instances, the ICTR, the ICTY, and the SCSL had already had the opportunity to define the general distinguishable elements or conditions to determine whether a particular act – or a set of acts – may amount to a crime against humanity (*chapeau* elements): (i) there must be an attack; (ii) the attack must be either widespread or systematic; (iii) a civilian population must be the specific target of the attack; (iv) the perpetrator must know that there is a such widespread or systematic attack targeting a civilian population; (v) the perpetrator must understand that their acts are part of the attack.[1853] [1854] [1855] [1856] The ICTR, in addition to these elements, still considers the following: (vi) "the act must be inhumane in nature and character, causing great suffering, or serious injury to body or to mental or physical health;"[1857] and (vii) "the act must be committed on one or more discriminatory grounds, namely, national, political, ethnic, racial or religious grounds."[1858]

---

[1848]  Prosecutor v. Dragoljub Kunarac *et al.* IT-96-23/1-A. *Supra* note 85. ¶¶ 85, 99; Prosecutor v. Radoslav Brđanin. IT-99-36-A. *Supra* note 131. ¶ 257; Prosecutor v. Zdravko Tolimir. IT-05-88/2-A. *Supra* note 152. ¶ 142.

[1849]  United Nations. Rome Statute (July 17, 1998) 2187 UNTS 38544. Article 7.

[1850]  See also: Prosecutor v. Sesay, Kallon and Gbao. SCSL-04-15-T. *Supra* note 268. ¶ 75; Prosecutor v. Jean-Paul Akayesu. ICTR-96-4-T. *Supra* note 203. ¶ 585; Prosecutor v. Laurent Semanza. ICTR-97-20-T. *Supra* note 211. ¶ 333.

[1851]  M. Cherif Bassiouni. *Supra* note 316. p. 30.

[1852]  U.N. Doc. S/2005/60 (Feb. 1, 2005). ¶ 178.

[1853]  Prosecutor v. Dragoljub Kunarac *et al.* IT-96-23/1-A. *Supra* note 85. ¶¶ 85–86; Prosecutor v. Momčilo Krajišnik. IT-00-39-T. *Supra* note 121. ¶ 705; Prosecutor v. Milan Lukić, Sredoje Lukić. IT-98-32/1-T. *Supra* note 104. ¶ 876.

[1854]  Prosecutor v. Jean-Paul Akayesu. ICTR-96-4-T. *Supra* note 203. ¶ 578.

[1855]  Prosecutor v. Sesay, Kallon and Gbao. SCSL-04-15-T. *Supra* note 268. ¶ 76.

[1856]  **See also: The Nuremberg Tribunal: United States of America v. Oswald Pohl, *et al.* Case 4** (Pohl case) (1947). p. 207; United States of America vs. Friedrich Flick *et al.* Case 5 (1947). p. XIX.

[1857]  Prosecutor v. Jean-Paul Akayesu. ICTR-96-4-T. *Supra* note 203. ¶ 578.

[1858]  *Ibid.*

## 3.2.1.1. Attack

The concepts of "attack" against a civilian population and "armed conflict" in customary international law are not identical and must be distinguished from one another.[1859] [1860] The former is considered "an element of a crime against humanity" and the latter "a jurisdictional requirement pursuant to the [the law of crimes against humanity]."[1861] The distinction between an attack and an armed conflict "reflects the position in customary international law that crimes against humanity may be committed in peacetime and independent of an armed conflict."[1862] [1863] Different from the jurisdictional requirements from the ICTR, SCSL, and ICC, the Statute of the ICTY required that the underlying crimes were "committed in armed conflict, whether international or internal in character."[1864]

---

[1859] Prosecutor v. Goran Jelisić., IT-95-10-A. *Supra* note 98. ¶ 141; Prosecutor v. Dragoljub Kunarac *et al*. IT-96-23/1-A. *Supra* note 85. ¶ 86; Prosecutor v. Mitar Vasiljević. IT-98-32-T. *Supra* note 117. ¶ 30; Prosecutor v. Milomir Stakić. IT-97-24-T. *Supra* note 109. ¶ 623; Prosecutor v. Radoslav Brđanin. IT-99-36-T. *Supra* note 130. ¶ 131; Prosecutor v. Vidoje Blagojević, Dragan Jokić. IT-02-60-T. *Supra* note 147. ¶ 543; Prosecutor v. Momčilo Krajišnik. IT-00-39-T. *Supra* note 121. ¶ 706; Prosecutor v. Nikola Šainović *et al*. IT-05-87-T, vol. 1. *Supra* note 125. ¶ 144; Prosecutor v. Milan Lukić, Sredoje Lukić. IT-98-32/1-T. *Supra* note 104. ¶ 873; Prosecutor v. Ante Gotovina *et al*. IT-06-90-T, vol. I. *Supra* note 76. ¶ 1702; Prosecutor v. Momčilo Perišić. IT-04-81-T. *Supra* note 123. ¶ 82; Prosecutor v. Taylor. SCSL-03-01-T. *Supra* note 270. ¶ 506; Prosecutor v. Zdravko Tolimir. IT-05-88/2-T. *Supra* note 153. ¶ 693; Prosecutor v. Mićo Stanišić, Stojan Župljanin. IT-08-91-T, vol. 1. *Supra* note 102. ¶ 24; Prosecutor v. Jovica Stanišić and Franko Simatović. IT-03-69-T, vol. I. *Supra* note 101. ¶ 962; Prosecutor v. Radovan Karadžić. IT-95-5/18-T, vol. I. *Supra* note 134. ¶ 473; Prosecutor v. Ratko Mladić. IT-09-92-T, vol. III. *Supra* note 137. ¶ 3024.

[1860] Prosecutor v. Brima, Kamara, Kanu. SCSL-04-16-T. *Supra* note 280. ¶ 214; Prosecutor v. Sesay, Kallon and Gbao. SCSL-04-15-T. *Supra* note 268. ¶ 77; Prosecutor v. Taylor. SCSL-03-01-T. *Supra* note 270. ¶ 506.

[1861] Prosecutor v. Blagoje Simić *et al*. IT-95-9-T. *Supra* note 78. ¶ 39.

[1862] Prosecutor v. Fofana, Kondewa. SCSL-04-14-T. *Supra* note 281. ¶ 111.

[1863] See also: Prosecutor v. Sesay, Kallon and Gbao. SCSL-04-15-T. *Supra* note 268. ¶ 77

[1864] Prosecutor v. Vidoje Blagojević, Dragan Jokić. IT-02-60-T. *Supra* note 147. ¶ 542. See also: Prosecutor v. Duško Tadic. IT-94-1-T. *Supra* note 89. ¶¶ 627, 928; Prosecutor v. Duško Tadic. IT-94-1-A. *Supra* note 90. ¶¶ 249, 271; Prosecutor v. Zoran Kupreškić, *et al*. IT-95-16-T. *Supra* note 156. ¶ 545; Prosecutor v. Dragoljub Kunarac *et al*. IT-96-23/1-T. *Supra* note 84. ¶¶ 411, 413; Prosecutor v. Goran Jelisić., IT-95-10-A. *Supra* note 98. ¶ 139; Prosecutor v. Dragoljub Kunarac *et al*. IT-96-23/1-A. *Supra* note 85. ¶¶ 83-84, 105; Prosecutor v. Mitar Vasiljević. IT-98-32-T. *Supra* note 117. ¶ 38; Prosecutor v. Blagoje Simić *et al*. IT-95-9-T. *Supra* note 78. ¶¶ 36, 38; Prosecutor v. Radoslav Brđanin. IT-99-36-T. *Supra* note 130. ¶ 133; Prosecutor v. Momčilo Krajišnik. IT-00-39-T. *Supra* note 121. ¶ 704; Prosecutor v. Ante Gotovina

According to the SCSL Trial Chamber, an attack constitutes a "campaign, operation or course of conduct directed against a civilian population and encompasses any mistreatment of the civilian population."[1865] [1866] [1867] An attack can be comprised of a single act or multiple acts.[1868] International criminal case-law considers that an attack is not "limited to the use of armed force," or other acts of *military* nature, and can encompass any mistreatment of the civilian population, including persons taking no active part in hostilities.[1869] [1870] [1871] An "armed conflict" is

---

*et al.* IT-06-90-T, vol. I. *Supra* note 76. ¶¶ 1699-1700; Prosecutor v. Momčilo Perišić. IT-04-81-T. *Supra* note 123. ¶ 80; Prosecutor v. Zdravko Tolimir. IT-05-88/2-T. *Supra* note 153. ¶¶ 690-691; Prosecutor v. Jovica Stanišić and Franko Simatović. IT-03-69-T, vol. I. *Supra* note 101. ¶¶ 959-960; Prosecutor v. Radovan Karadžić. IT-95-5/18-T, vol. I. *Supra* note 134. ¶ 471; Prosecutor v. Ratko Mladić. IT-09-92-T, vol. III. *Supra* note 137. ¶¶ 3021–3022.

[1865] Prosecutor v. Brima, Kamara, Kanu. SCSL-04-16-T. *Supra* note 280. ¶¶ 213-214. See also: Prosecutor v. Fofana, Kondewa. SCSL-04-14-T. *Supra* note 281. ¶ 111; Prosecutor v. Sesay, Kallon and Gbao. SCSL-04-15-T. *Supra* note 268. ¶ 77; Prosecutor v. Taylor. SCSL-03-01-T. *Supra* note 270. ¶ 506.

[1866] See also: Prosecutor v. Jean-Paul Akayesu. ICTR-96-4-T. *Supra* note 203. ¶ 581; Prosecutor v. Hormisdas Nsengimana, Case No. ICTR-01-69-T, (Nov. 17, 2009). ¶ 843; Prosecutor v. Yussuf Munyakazi. ICTR-97-36A-T. *Supra* note 236. ¶ 503; Prosecutor v. Ildephonse Hategekimana. ICTR-00-55B-T. *Supra* note 197. ¶ 701; Prosecutor v. Augustin Ndindiliyimana *et al.* ICTR-00-56-T. *Supra* note 163. ¶ 2087.

[1867] See also: Prosecutor v. Dragoljub Kunarac *et al.* IT-96-23/1-T. *Supra* note 84. ¶ 415; Prosecutor v. Dragoljub Kunarac *et al.* IT-96-23/1-A. *Supra* note 85. ¶ 86; Prosecutor v. Mitar Vasiljević. IT-98-32-T. *Supra* note 117. ¶ 29; Prosecutor v. Milomir Stakić. IT-97-24-T. *Supra* note 109. ¶ 623; Prosecutor v. Blagoje Simić *et al.* IT-95-9-T. *Supra* note 78. ¶ 39; Prosecutor v. Radoslav Brđanin. IT-99-36-T. *Supra* note 130. ¶ 131; Prosecutor v. Vidoje Blagojević, Dragan Jokić. IT-02-60-T. *Supra* note 147. ¶ 543; Prosecutor v. Mile Mrkšić *et al.* IT-95-13/1. *Supra* note 108. ¶ 436; Prosecutor v. Nikola Šainović *et al.* IT-05-87-T, vol. 1. *Supra* note 125. ¶ 144; Prosecutor v. Milan Lukić, Sredoje Lukić. IT-98-32/1-T. *Supra* note 104. ¶ 873; Prosecutor v. Ante Gotovina *et al.* IT-06-90-T, vol. I. *Supra* note 76. ¶ 1702; Prosecutor v. Momčilo Perišić. IT-04-81-T. *Supra* note 123. ¶ 82; Prosecutor v. Jovica Stanišić and Franko Simatović. IT-03-69-T, vol. I. *Supra* note 101. ¶ 962; Prosecutor v. Ratko Mladić. IT-09-92-T, vol. III. *Supra* note 137. ¶ 3024.

[1868] Prosecutor v. Zoran Kupreškić, *et al.* IT-95-16-T. *Supra* note 156. ¶ 550; Prosecutor v. Dragoljub Kunarac *et al.* IT-96-23/1-A. *Supra* note 85. ¶ 96; Prosecutor v. Nikola Šainović *et al.* IT-05-87-T, vol. 1. *Supra* note 125. ¶ 152; Prosecutor v. Zdravko Tolimir. IT-05-88/2-T. *Supra* note 153. ¶ 698.

[1869] Prosecutor v. Dragoljub Kunarac *et al.* IT-96-23/1-T. *Supra* note 84. ¶ 416; Prosecutor v. Dragoljub Kunarac *et al.* IT-96-23/1-A. *Supra* note 85. ¶ 86; Prosecutor v. Mitar Vasiljević. IT-98-32-T. *Supra* note 117. ¶ 29; Prosecutor v. Blagoje Simić *et al.* IT-95-9-T. *Supra* note 78. ¶ 39; Prosecutor v. Radoslav Brđanin. IT-99-36-T. *Supra* note 130. ¶ 131; Prosecutor v. Vidoje Blagojević, Dragan Jokić. IT-02-60-T. *Supra* note

defined by the ICTY, in *Prosecutor v. Momčilo Krajišnik*, as "a resort to armed force between States or protracted armed violence between governmental authorities and organized armed groups or between such groups within a state."[1872] The armed conflict requirement is proved by demonstrating that "*there was*" an armed conflict "at the relevant time and place."[1873] [1874]

It is a mandatory element of crimes against humanity that the acts of the accused must be part of the *attack* against the civilian population."[1875] [1876] However, the underlying acts of the perpetrator "need not be

---

147. ¶ 543; Prosecutor v. Mile Mrkšić *et al.* IT-95-13/1. *Supra* note 108. ¶ 436; Prosecutor v. Nikola Šainović *et al.* IT-05-87-T, vol. 1. *Supra* note 125. ¶ 144; Prosecutor v. Ante Gotovina *et al.* IT-06-90-T, vol. I. *Supra* note 76. ¶ 1702; Prosecutor v. Momčilo Perišić. IT-04-81-T. *Supra* note 123. ¶ 82; Prosecutor v. Zdravko Tolimir. IT-05-88/2-T. *Supra* note 153. ¶ 693; Prosecutor v. Mićo Stanišić, Stojan Župljanin. IT-08-91-T, vol. 1. *Supra* note 102. ¶ 24; Prosecutor v. Radovan Karadžić. IT-95-5/18-T, vol. I. *Supra* note 134. ¶ 473; Prosecutor v. Ratko Mladić. IT-09-92-T, vol. III. *Supra* note 137. ¶ 3024.

[1870] Prosecutor v. Germain Katanga. ICC-01/04-01/07. *Supra* note 333. ¶ 1101; Prosecutor v. Jean-Pierre Bemba Gombo. ICC-01/05-01/08. *Supra* note 335. ¶¶ 149, 151; Prosecutor v. Bosco Ntaganda. ICC-01/04-02/06. *Supra* note 328. ¶ 662.

[1871] Prosecutor v. Fofana, Kondewa. SCSL-04-14-T. *Supra* note 281. ¶ 111; Prosecutor v. Sesay, Kallon and Gbao. SCSL-04-15-T. *Supra* note 268. ¶ 77; Prosecutor v. Taylor. SCSL-03-01-T. *Supra* note 270. ¶ 506.

[1872] Prosecutor v. Momčilo Krajišnik. IT-00-39-T. *Supra* note 121. ¶ 704.

[1873] *Ibidem.*

[1874] See also: Prosecutor v. Duško Tadić. IT-94-1-A. *Supra* note 90. ¶¶ 249, 251; Prosecutor v. Dragoljub Kunarac *et al.* IT-96-23/1-A. *Supra* note 85. ¶ 86.

[1875] Prosecutor v. Sesay, Kallon and Gbao. SCSL-04-15-T. *Supra* note 268. ¶ 89.

[1876] For the SCSL Trial Chamber, "the requirement that the acts of the Accused must be part of the attack is satisfied by the commission of an act which, by its nature or consequences, is objectively part of the attack. This is established if the alleged crimes were related to the attack on a civilian population, but need not have been committed in the midst of that attack. A crime which is committed before or after the main attack or away from it could still, if sufficiently connected, be part of that attack. However, it must not be an isolated act. A crime would be regarded as an 'isolated act' when it is so far removed from that attack that, having considered the context and circumstances in which it was committed, it cannot reasonably be said to have been part of the attack." (*Ibidem.*)

committed in the midst of that attack."[1877][1878][1879] According to the ICTY Trial Chamber, in *Prosecutor v. Milomir Stakić*, and to the SCSL, in *Brima*[1880] and *Sesay*,[1881] an attack, by its nature, can "precede, outlast, or continue during the armed conflict, but it need not be part of it," and "is not limited to the use of armed force; it encompasses any mistreatment of the civilian population."[1882][1883][1884][1885] Accordingly, an underlying act "that is committed before or after the main attack against the civilian population or away from it could still, if sufficiently connected, be part of that attack."[1886][1887]

---

[1877] Prosecutor v. Dragoljub Kunarac *et al.* IT-96-23/1-A. *Supra* note 85. ¶ 100; Prosecutor v. Blagoje Simić *et al.* IT-95-9-T. *Supra* note 78. ¶¶ 39, 41; Prosecutor v. Mile Mrkšić *et al.* IT-95-13/1. *Supra* note 108. ¶ 436; Prosecutor v. Nikola Šainović *et al.* IT-05-87-T, vol. 1. *Supra* note 125. ¶¶ 144, 152; Prosecutor v. Ante Gotovina *et al.* IT-06-90-T, vol. I. *Supra* note 76. ¶ 1706; Prosecutor v. Mićo Stanišić, Stojan Župljanin. IT-08-91-T, vol. 1. *Supra* note 102. ¶ 29; Prosecutor v. Jadranko Prlić, *et al.* IT-04-74-T, vol. I. *Supra* note 99. ¶ 43; Prosecutor v. Radovan Karadžić. IT-95-5/18-T, vol. I. *Supra* note 134. ¶ 478; Prosecutor v. Ratko Mladić. IT-09-92-T, vol. III. *Supra* note 137. ¶ 3028.

[1878] Prosecutor v. Sesay, Kallon and Gbao. SCSL-04-15-T. *Supra* note 268. ¶ 89.

[1879] Prosecutor v. Clément Kayishema and Ruzindana. ICTR 95-1-T. *Supra* note 209. ¶ 127.

[1880] Prosecutor v. Brima, Kamara, Kanu. SCSL-04-16-T. *Supra* note 280. ¶ 214.

[1881] Prosecutor v. Sesay, Kallon and Gbao. SCSL-04-15-T. *Supra* note 268. ¶ 77.

[1882] Prosecutor v. Milomir Stakić. IT-97-24-T. *Supra* note 109. ¶ 623.

[1883] See also: Prosecutor v. Goran Jelisić., IT-95-10-A. *Supra* note 98. ¶ 141; Prosecutor v. Dragoljub Kunarac *et al.* IT-96-23/1-A. *Supra* note 85. ¶ 86; Prosecutor v. Mitar Vasiljević. IT-98-32-T. *Supra* note 117. ¶ 30; Prosecutor v. Vidoje Blagojević, Dragan Jokić. IT-02-60-T. *Supra* note 147. ¶ 543; Prosecutor v. Nikola Šainović *et al.* IT-05-87-T, vol. 1. *Supra* note 125. ¶ 144; Prosecutor v. Ante Gotovina *et al.* IT-06-90-T, vol. I. *Supra* note 76. ¶ 1702; Prosecutor v. Momčilo Perišić. IT-04-81-T. *Supra* note 123. ¶ 82; Prosecutor v. Zdravko Tolimir. IT-05-88/2-T. *Supra* note 153. ¶ 693; Prosecutor v. Mićo Stanišić, Stojan Župljanin. IT-08-91-T, vol. 1. *Supra* note 102. ¶ 24; Prosecutor v. Jovica Stanišić and Franko Simatović. IT-03-69-T, vol. I. *Supra* note 101. ¶ 962; Prosecutor v. Radovan Karadžić. IT-95-5/18-T, vol. I. *Supra* note 134. ¶ 473; Prosecutor v. Ratko Mladić. IT-09-92-T, vol. III. *Supra* note 137. ¶ 3024.

[1884] See also: Prosecutor v. Brima, Kamara, Kanu. SCSL-04-16-T. *Supra* note 280. ¶ 214; Prosecutor v. Fofana, Kondewa. SCSL-04-14-T. *Supra* note 281. ¶ 111; Prosecutor v. Sesay, Kallon and Gbao. SCSL-04-15-T. *Supra* note 268. ¶ 77.

[1885] "An armed conflict is understood to continue beyond the cessation of hostilities, until a general conclusion of peace is reached, or, in the case of internal conflicts, a peaceful settlement is achieved." (Prosecutor v. Momčilo Krajišnik. IT-00-39-T. *Supra* note 121. ¶ 704).

[1886] Prosecutor v. Dragoljub Kunarac *et al.* IT-96-23/1-A. *Supra* note 85. ¶ 100. See also: Prosecutor v. Nikola Šainović *et al.* IT-05-87-T, vol. 1. *Supra* note 125. ¶ 152; Prosecutor v. Momčilo Perišić. IT-04-81-T. *Supra* note 123. ¶ 87; Prosecutor v. Jadranko Prlić, *et al.* IT-04-74-T, vol. I. *Supra* note 99. ¶ 43.

Similarly, it is not necessary that the accused perpetrates numerous acts so that they may bear international criminal responsibility for their conduct.[1888] A single act, if committed in a "context of a widespread or systematic attack upon a civilian population," may trigger "individual criminal liability upon the perpetrator."[1889]

In *Prosecutor v. Vidoje Blagojević, Dragan Jokić,* and *Prosecutor v. Dragoljub Kunarac,* the ICTY stated that the acts of the accused and the attack on the civilian population must be connected by a *nexus* consistent of two elements: (i) "the commission of an act which, by its nature or consequences, is objectively part of the attack"; and (ii) "knowledge on the part of the accused that there is an attack on the civilian population and that his act is part thereof."[1890] [1891] Such nexus is required "in circumstances where a crime is not entirely temporally and geographically connected to the attack."[1892] It is not necessary, however, proof that "the victims are linked to any particular side of the armed conflict"[1893] or that "the acts were committed in the midst of the attack," "provided that they are sufficiently connected therewith."[1894] [1895]

In determining whether the requisite nexus exists, an objective assessment must be conducted on a case-by-case basis.[1896] [1897] Such assessment

---

[1887]  Prosecutor v. Sesay, Kallon and Gbao. SCSL-04-15-T. *Supra* note 268. ¶ 89.
[1888]  Prosecutor v. Brima, Kamara, Kanu. SCSL-04-16-T. *Supra* note 280. ¶ 215.
[1889]  *Ibidem.*
[1890]  Prosecutor v. Dragoljub Kunarac *et al.* IT-96-23/1-A. *Supra* note 85. ¶ 99; Prosecutor v. Vidoje Blagojević, Dragan Jokić. IT-02-60-T. *Supra* note 147. ¶ 547.
[1891]  The SCSL Trial Chamber considered that "although this nexus depends on the factual circumstances of each case, reliable indicia of a nexus include the similarities between the perpetrator's acts and the acts occurring within the attack; the nature of the events and circumstances surrounding the perpetrator's acts; the temporal and geographic proximity of the perpetrator's acts with the attack; and the nature and extent of the perpetrator's knowledge of the attack when he commits the acts." (Prosecutor v. Brima, Kamara, Kanu. SCSL-04-16-T. *Supra* note 280. ¶ 220).
[1892]  Prosecutor v. Zdravko Tolimir. IT-05-88/2-T. *Supra* note 153. ¶ 699.
[1893]  Prosecutor v. Vidoje Blagojević, Dragan Jokić. IT-02-60-T. *Supra* note 147. ¶ 544.
[1894]  "The acts of the accused must be part of the attack against the civilian population, but they need not be committed in the midst of that attack. A crime which is committed before or after the main attack against the civilian population or away from it could still, if sufficiently connected, be part of that attack." (Prosecutor v. Dragoljub Kunarac *et al.* IT-96-23/1-A. *Supra* note 85. ¶ 100).
[1895]  See also: Prosecutor v. Dragoljub Kunarac *et al.* IT-96-23/1-A. *Supra* note 85. ¶ 96; Prosecutor v. Milan Lukić, Sredoje Lukić. IT-98-32/1-T. *Supra* note 104. ¶ 876.
[1896]  Prosecutor v. Jean-Pierre Bemba Gombo. ICC-01/05-01/08. *Supra* note 335. ¶ 165.
[1897]  See also: Prosecutor v. Zdravko Tolimir. IT-05-88/2-T. *Supra* note 153. ¶ 699.

might consider the following elements: 1) "the commission of an act which, by its nature or consequences, is objectively part of the attack,"[1898] [1899] and 2) "knowledge on the part of the accused that there is an attack on the civilian population and that his act is part thereof."[1900] [1901] If an act is committed in a clearly different context "and circumstances from other acts that occur during an attack," such act is regarded as an *isolated* act and falls outside the scope of application of the law of crimes against humanity.[1902] [1903] [1904] An act would be regarded as *isolated* "when it is so far removed from that attack that, having considered the context and circumstances in which it was committed, it cannot reasonably be said to have been part of the attack."[1905] [1906] [1907]

## 3.2.1.2. Directed against any civilian population

In customary international law, "there is an absolute prohibition against targeting civilians," irrespective of whether such targeting is committed in an armed conflict of international or internal character.[1908] [1909] [1910] A "ci-

---

[1898]  Prosecutor v. Vidoje Blagojević, Dragan Jokić. IT-02-60-T. *Supra* note 147. ¶ 547.

[1899]  See also: Prosecutor v. Dragoljub Kunarac *et al.* IT-96-23/1-A. *Supra* note 85. ¶ 99.

[1900]  Prosecutor v. Mitar Vasiljević. IT-98-32-T. *Supra* note 117. ¶ 32.

[1901]  See also: Prosecutor v. Dragoljub Kunarac *et al.* IT-96-23/1-T. *Supra* note 84. ¶ 418.

[1902]  Prosecutor v. Jean-Pierre Bemba Gombo. ICC-01/05-01/08. *Supra* note 335. ¶ 165.

[1903]  See also: Prosecutor v. Dragoljub Kunarac *et al.* IT-96-23/1-A. *Supra* note 85. ¶ 100; Prosecutor v. Vidoje Blagojević, Dragan Jokić. IT-02-60-T. *Supra* note 147. ¶ 547; Prosecutor v. Zdravko Tolimir. IT-05-88/2-T. *Supra* note 153. ¶ 699.

[1904]  See also: Prosecutor v. Sesay, Kallon and Gbao. SCSL-04-15-T. *Supra* note 268. ¶ 89.

[1905]  *Ibidem.*

[1906]  See also: Prosecutor v. Fofana, Kondewa. SCSL-04-14-T. *Supra* note 281. ¶ 120.

[1907]  See also: Prosecutor v. Dragoljub Kunarac *et al.* IT-96-23/1-A. *Supra* note 85. ¶ 100; Prosecutor v. Blagoje Simić *et al.* IT-95-9-T. *Supra* note 78. ¶ 41; Prosecutor v. Vidoje Blagojević, Dragan Jokić. IT-02-60-T. *Supra* note 147. ¶ 547; Prosecutor v. Momčilo Krajišnik. IT-00-39-T. *Supra* note 121. ¶ 706; Prosecutor v. Nikola Šainović *et al.* IT-05-87-T, vol. 1. *Supra* note 125. ¶ 152; Prosecutor v. Jadranko Prlić, *et al.* IT-04-74-T, vol. I. *Supra* note 99. ¶ 43.

[1908]  Prosecutor v. Brima, Kamara, Kanu. SCSL-04-16-T. *Supra* note 280. ¶ 216.

[1909]  Prosecutor v. Jean-Paul Akayesu. ICTR-96-4-T. *Supra* note 203. ¶ 565.

[1910]  The United Nations Convention on the Non-Applicability of Statutory Limitations to War Crimes and Crimes Against Humanity (1968), provides, in Article I, that "no statutory limitation shall apply to crimes against humanity, irrespective of the date of their commission, [...] whether committed in time of war or in time of peace as they are defined in the Charter of the International Military Tribunal, Nürnberg, of 8 August 1945 and confirmed by resolutions 3 (I) of 13 February 1946 and 95 (I) of 11 December 1946 of the General Assembly of the United Nations..."

vilian" population, for the purposes of crimes against humanity, is narrowly regarded as such if it is "predominantly civilian in nature" – the *principle of distinction*.[1911] [1912] However, "there is no numerical rule clearly denoting the point at which a population loses its civilian character."[1913]

The definition of a civilian, "as opposed to members of armed forces and other legitimate combatants,"[1914] [1915] has been expansively and broadly interpreted. It generally includes "not only civilians in the ordinary and strict sense of the term, but all persons who have taken no active part in the hostilities, or are no longer doing so,"[1916] [1917] [1918] "including "members of armed forces who have laid down their arms and those placed *hors de combat* by sickness, wounds, detention, or any other cause."[1919] [1920] [1921] What matters the most in analyzing whether a person stands as a civilian is "the specific situation of the victim at the moment the crimes were committed, rather than his status."[1922] International criminal courts have continuously stated that "the presence of isolated non-civilians among [the targeted] population does not deprive that population itself of its civilian character,"[1923] as long as the population is "predominantly civilian."[1924] [1925] [1926] [1927] [1928]

---

(G. A. Res. 2391, Convention on the Non-Applicability of Statutory Limitations to War Crimes and Crimes Against Humanity, U.N. Doc. A/RES/2391(XXIII) (Nov. 26, 1968).

[1911] Prosecutor v. Vidoje Blagojević, Dragan Jokić. IT-02-60-T. *Supra* note 147. ¶ 544; Prosecutor v. Momčilo Krajišnik. IT-00-39-T. *Supra* note 121. ¶ 706.

[1912] Prosecutor v. Brima, Kamara, Kanu. SCSL-04-16-T. *Supra* note 280. ¶¶ 216, 218–219; Prosecutor v. Sesay, Kallon and Gbao. SCSL-04-15-T. *Supra* note 268. ¶ 83.

[1913] Prosecutor v. Nikola Šainović *et al.* IT-05-87-T, vol. 1. *Supra* note 125. ¶ 148.

[1914] Prosecutor v. Jean-Pierre Bemba Gombo. ICC-01/05-01/08. *Supra* note 334. ¶ 78.

[1915] See also: Prosecutor v. Jovica Stanišić and Franko Simatović. IT-03-69-T, vol. I. *Supra* note 101. ¶ 965.

[1916] Prosecutor v. Brima, Kamara, Kanu. SCSL-04-16-T. *Supra* note 280. ¶ 216.

[1917] See also: Prosecutor v. Duško Tadic. IT-94-1-A. *Supra* note 90. ¶ 248; Prosecutor v. Momčilo Krajišnik. IT-00-39-T. *Supra* note 121. ¶ 706; Prosecutor v. Jovica Stanišić and Franko Simatović. IT-03-69-T, vol. I. *Supra* note 101. ¶ 965.

[1918] See also: Prosecutor v. Jean-Paul Akayesu. ICTR-96-4-T. *Supra* note 203. ¶ 582.

[1919] Prosecutor v. Vidoje Blagojević, Dragan Jokić. IT-02-60-T. *Supra* note 147. ¶ 544.

[1920] In International Humanitarian Law, a civilian is regarded as a person under the protection of Geneva Convention, Common Article 3, and Additional Protocol II. (Prosecutor v. Brima, Kamara, Kanu. SCSL-04-16-T. *Supra* note 280. ¶ 218).

[1921] See also: Prosecutor v. Jean-Paul Akayesu. ICTR-96-4-T. *Supra* note 203. ¶ 582; Prosecutor v. Momčilo Krajišnik. IT-00-39-T. *Supra* note 121. ¶ 706; Prosecutor v. Brima, Kamara, Kanu. SCSL-04-16-T. *Supra* note 280. ¶ 216.

[1922] Prosecutor v. Tihomir Blaškić. IT-95-14-T. *Supra* note 143. ¶ 215.

[1923] Prosecutor v. Jadranko Prlić, *et al.* IT-04-74-T, vol. I. *Supra* note 99. ¶ 38.

The expression "directed against" requires that, in the context of a crime against humanity, the civilian population, which is subjected to the attack, must be the *primary* object of the attack rather than an *incidental* victim of the attack.[1929] [1930] [1931] [1932] [1933] [1934] To determine "whether the attack may be said to have been *so directed*," international criminal case-law has identified a non-exhaustive list of relevant factors, *inter alia* 1) the "means and method used in the course of the attack;" 2) the number of the victims; 3) the status of the victims; 4) the "discriminatory nature of the attack;" 5) the "nature of the crimes committed in its course;" 6) the "resistance to

---

[1924]  Prosecutor v. Goran Jelisić., IT-95-10-A. *Supra* note 98. ¶ 143.

[1925]  See also: Prosecutor v. Germain Katanga. ICC-01/04-01/07. *Supra* note 333. ¶ 1105; Prosecutor v. Jean-Pierre Bemba Gombo. ICC-01/05-01/08. *Supra* note 335. ¶ 153; Prosecutor v. Bosco Ntaganda. ICC-01/04-02/06. *Supra* note 328. ¶ 668.

[1926]  See also: Prosecutor v. Duško Tadic. IT-94-1-T. *Supra* note 89. ¶ 638; Prosecutor v. Tihomir Blaškić. IT-95-14-T. *Supra* note 143. ¶ 211; Prosecutor v. Dragoljub Kunarac *et al.* IT-96-23/1-T. *Supra* note 84. ¶ 425; Prosecutor v. Dario Kordić and Mario Čerkez. IT-95-14/2-T. *Supra* note 80. ¶ 180; Prosecutor v. Blagoje Simić *et al.* IT-95-9-T. *Supra* note 78. ¶ 42; Prosecutor v. Radoslav Brđanin. IT-99-36-T. *Supra* note 130. ¶ 134; Prosecutor v. Momčilo Krajišnik. IT-00-39-T. *Supra* note 121. ¶ 706; Prosecutor v. Mile Mrkšić *et al.* IT-95-13/1. *Supra* note 108. ¶ 453; Prosecutor v. Momčilo Perišić. IT-04-81-T. *Supra* note 123. ¶ 84; Prosecutor v. Zdravko Tolimir. IT-05-88/2-T. *Supra* note 153. ¶ 696; Prosecutor v. Radovan Karadžić. IT-95-5/18-T, vol. I. *Supra* note 134. ¶ 474.

[1927]  See also: Prosecutor v. Jean-Paul Akayesu. ICTR-96-4-T. *Supra* note 203. ¶ 582; Prosecutor v. Clément Kayishema and Ruzindana. ICTR 95-1-T. *Supra* note 209. ¶ 128; Prosecutor v. Sylvestre Gacumbitsi. ICTR-2001-64-T. *Supra* note 228. ¶ 300; Prosecutor v. Mikaeli Muhimana. ICTR-95-1B-T. *Supra* note 214. ¶ 528.

[1928]  See also: Prosecutor v. Brima, Kamara, Kanu. SCSL-04-16-T. *Supra* note 280. ¶¶ 216, 218; Prosecutor v. Fofana, Kondewa. SCSL-04-14-T. *Supra* note 281. ¶ 117; Prosecutor v. Sesay, Kallon and Gbao. SCSL-04-15-T. *Supra* note 268. ¶ 83.

[1929]  Prosecutor v. Dragoljub Kunarac *et al.* IT-96-23/1-T. *Supra* note 84. ¶ 421; Prosecutor v. Goran Jelisić., IT-95-10-A. *Supra* note 98. ¶ 142; Prosecutor v. Dragoljub Kunarac *et al.* IT-96-23/1-A. *Supra* note 85. ¶¶ 91-92; Prosecutor v. Mitar Vasiljević. IT-98-32-T. *Supra* note 117. ¶ 33; Prosecutor v. Blagoje Simić *et al.* IT-95-9-T. *Supra* note 78. ¶ 42; Prosecutor v. Radoslav Brđanin. IT-99-36-T. *Supra* note 130. ¶ 134; Prosecutor v. Momčilo Krajišnik. IT-00-39-T. *Supra* note 121. ¶ 706; Prosecutor v. Mile Mrkšić *et al.* IT-95-13/1. *Supra* note 108. ¶ 440; Prosecutor v. Nikola Šainović *et al.* IT-05-87-T, vol. 1. *Supra* note 125. ¶ 149; Prosecutor v. Ante Gotovina *et al.* IT-06-90-T, vol. I. *Supra* note 76. ¶ 1704; Prosecutor v. Momčilo Perišić. IT-04-81-T. *Supra* note 123. ¶ 83; Prosecutor v. Zdravko Tolimir. IT-05-88/2-T. *Supra* note 153. ¶ 694; Prosecutor v. Jadranko Prlić, *et al.* IT-04-74-T, vol. I. *Supra* note 99. ¶ 36; Prosecutor v. Jovica Stanišić and Franko Simatović. IT-03-69-T, vol. I. *Supra* note 101. ¶ 964; Prosecutor v. Ratko Mladić. IT-09-92-T, vol. III. *Supra* note 137. ¶ 3026.

[1930]  See also: Prosecutor v. Sylvestre Gacumbitsi. ICTR-2001-64-T. *Supra* note 228. ¶ 300; Prosecutor v. Mikaeli Muhimana. ICTR-95-1B-T. *Supra* note 214. ¶ 528.

the assailants at the time;" and 7) the "extent to which the attacking force may be said to have complied or attempted to comply with the precautionary requirement of the laws of war."[1935] [1936] [1937]

Consequentially, it is a legal constituent of the criminal conduct proof that the attack was directed against a civilian population even when the attack 1) did not target the entire population of the geographical entity; or is 2) circumscribed only to a specific geographical area, rather than against the whole territory under consideration.[1938] [1939] [1940] Therefore, the consideration of whether an attack is widespread or systematic is essentially a "relative exercise" because the civilian population attacked by the perpetrator must always be assessed.[1941]

---

[1931] Prosecutor v. Brima, Kamara, Kanu. SCSL-04-16-T. *Supra* note 280. ¶ 216; Prosecutor v. Taylor. SCSL-03-01-T. *Supra* note 270. ¶ 507.

[1932] See also: Prosecutor v. Radovan Karadžić. IT-95-5/18-T, vol. I. *Supra* note 134. ¶ 475.

[1933] See also: Prosecutor v. Germain Katanga. ICC-01/04-01/07. *Supra* note 333. ¶ 1104; Prosecutor v. Jean-Pierre Bemba Gombo. ICC-01/05-01/08. *Supra* note 335. ¶ 154; Prosecutor v. Bosco Ntaganda. ICC-01/04-02/06. *Supra* note 328. ¶ 668.

[1934] See also: Prosecutor v. Sesay, Kallon and Gbao. SCSL-04-15-T. *Supra* note 268. ¶ 80.

[1935] Prosecutor v. Goran Jelisić., IT-95-10-A. *Supra* note 98. ¶ 142.

[1936] See also: Prosecutor v. Dragoljub Kunarac *et al.* IT-96-23/1-A. *Supra* note 85. ¶ 91; Prosecutor v. Radoslav Brđanin. IT-99-36-T. *Supra* note 130. ¶ 134; Prosecutor v. Mile Mrkšić *et al.* IT-95-13/1. *Supra* note 108. ¶ 440; Prosecutor v. Zdravko Tolimir. IT-05-88/2-T. *Supra* note 153. ¶ 694; Prosecutor v. Jadranko Prlić, *et al.* IT-04-74-T, vol. I. *Supra* note 99. ¶¶ 36, 38; Prosecutor v. Radovan Karadžić. IT-95-5/18-T, vol. I. *Supra* note 134. ¶ 475.

[1937] See also: Prosecutor v. Brima, Kamara, Kanu. SCSL-04-16-T. *Supra* note 280. ¶ 216.

[1938] Prosecutor v. Dragoljub Kunarac *et al.* IT-96-23/1-A. *Supra* note 85. ¶¶ 91, 98; Prosecutor v. Milomir Stakić. IT-97-24-T. *Supra* note 109. ¶ 624; Prosecutor v. Momčilo Krajišnik. IT-00-39-T. *Supra* note 121. ¶¶ 704, 706; Prosecutor v. Milan Lukić, Sredoje Lukić. IT-98-32/1-T. *Supra* note 104. ¶ 874.

[1939] "The use of the word *population* does not mean that the entire population of the geographical entity in which the attack is taking place must have been subjected to that attack. It is sufficient to show that enough individuals were targeted in the course of the attack, or that they were targeted in such a way as to satisfy the Chamber that the attack was in fact directed against a civilian *population*, rather than against a limited and randomly selected number of individuals." (Prosecutor v. Dragoljub Kunarac *et al.* IT-96-23/1-A. *Supra* note 85. ¶ 90).

[1940] "[i]t is sufficient to show that enough individuals were targeted in the course of the attack, or that they were targeted in such a way as to satisfy the Chamber that the attack was directed against a civilian 'population', rather than against a limited and randomly selected number of individuals." (Prosecutor v. Milomir Stakić. IT-97-24-T. *Supra* note 109. ¶ 624).

[1941] Prosecutor v. Dragoljub Kunarac *et al.* IT-96-23/1-A. *Supra* note 85. ¶ 95.

The term "population" "does not mean that the entire population of the geographical entity in which the attack is taking place must have been subjected to that attack."[1942] [1943] [1944] [1945] [1946] Customary international law accepts that "it is sufficient to show that enough individuals were targeted in the course of the attack, or that they were targeted in such a way as to satisfy (...) that the attack was *in fact* directed against a civilian "population."[1947] [1948] [1949] Such a jurisprudential approach requires evidence that the individuals targeted to be attacked were not *arbitrarily selected*.[1950] [1951] [1952] The term "of any sort" expresses the fact that the victims' nationality is irrelevant to the verification of the occurrence of a crime against humanity.[1953] The word "any" "makes it clear that crimes against humanity can be committed against civilians of the same nationality as the perpetrator or those who are stateless, as well as those of a different nationality."[1954]

### 3.2.1.3. Widespread or systematic

The Rome Statute of the International Criminal Court asserts that a "crime against humanity means any [...] act[.] when committed as a part of a widespread or systematic attack directed against any civilian population, with

---

[1942] Prosecutor v. Dragoljub Kunarac *et al.* IT-96-23/1-T. *Supra* note 84. ¶ 424.

[1943] See also: Prosecutor v. Paul Bisengimana. ICTR-00-60-T. *Supra* note 218. ¶ 51; Prosecutor v. Momčilo Krajišnik. IT-00-39-T. *Supra* note 121. ¶ 706; Prosecutor v. Zdravko Tolimir. IT-05-88/2-T. *Supra* note 153. ¶ 696.

[1944] See also: Prosecutor v. Brima, Kamara, Kanu. SCSL-04-16-T. *Supra* note 280. ¶ 217; Prosecutor v. Fofana, Kondewa. SCSL-04-14-T. *Supra* note 281. ¶ 119; Prosecutor v. Sesay, Kallon and Gbao. SCSL-04-15-T. *Supra* note 268. ¶ 85.

[1945] See also: Prosecutor v. Jean-Pierre Bemba Gombo. ICC-01/05-01/08. *Supra* note 334. ¶ 77; Prosecutor v. Germain Katanga. ICC-01/04-01/07. *Supra* note 333. ¶ 1105.

[1946] See also: Prosecutor v. Jean de Dieu Kamuhanda. ICTR-95-54A-T. *Supra* note 200. ¶ 670.

[1947] Prosecutor v. Mitar Vasiljević. IT-98-32-T. *Supra* note 117. ¶ 34.

[1948] See also: Prosecutor v. Jadranko Prlić, *et al.* IT-04-74-T, vol. I. *Supra* note 99. ¶ 37.

[1949] See also: Prosecutor v. Ante Gotovina *et al.* IT-06-90-T, vol. I. *Supra* note 76. ¶ 1704.

[1950] Prosecutor v. Milomir Stakić. IT-97-24-T. *Supra* note 109.

[1951] See also: Prosecutor v. Goran Jelisić., IT-95-10-A. *Supra* note 98. ¶ 143; Prosecutor v. Radoslav Brđanin. IT-99-36-T. *Supra* note 130. ¶ 134; Prosecutor v. Momčilo Perišić. IT-04-81-T. *Supra* note 123. ¶ 83; Prosecutor v. Jovica Stanišić and Franko Simatović. IT-03-69-T, vol. I. *Supra* note 101. ¶ 964; Prosecutor v. Radovan Karadžić. IT-95-5/18-T, vol. I. *Supra* note 134. ¶ 475.

[1952] See also: Prosecutor v. Taylor. SCSL-03-01-T. *Supra* note 270. ¶ 507.

[1953] Prosecutor v. Mile Mrkšić *et al.* IT-95-13/1. *Supra* note 108. ¶ 441; Prosecutor v. Jadranko Prlić, *et al.* IT-04-74-T, vol. I. *Supra* note 99. ¶ 39.

[1954] Prosecutor v. Duško Tadic. IT-94-1-T. *Supra* note 89. ¶ 635.

knowledge of the attack."[1955] [1956] Such attacks may target civilians on national, political, ethnic, racial, or religious grounds.[1957] The ICTR, the ICTY, and the SCSL consider that the legal requirement "widespread" or "systematic" is disjunctive/alternative rather than cumulative.[1958] This means that only one prong of the legal requirement suffices for the legal characterization of the crime.[1959] [1960] [1961] Importantly, international criminal tri-

---

[1955] Rome Statue of the International Criminal Court. Art. 7. This verbatim is quite similar to almost all statues of international criminal courts, e.g., the Statue of the ICTY, Art. 5; Statue of the ICTR, Art. 3; Regulation No. 2000/15, s.5 East Timor; Statue of the Special Court for Sierra Leone, Art. 2; Statue of the Iraqi Special Tribunal, Art. 12.

[1956] Prosecutor v. Emmanuel Rukundo. ICTR-2001-70-T. *Supra* note 179. ¶ 578; Prosecutor v. Hormisdas Nsengimana, Case No. ICTR-01-69-T, (Nov. 17, 2009). ¶¶ 843, 845; Prosecutor v. Jean-Baptiste Gatete. ICTR-2000-61-T. *Supra* note 195. ¶ 631.

[1957] Prosecutor v. Jean-Paul Akayesu. ICTR-96-4-T. *Supra* note 203. ¶ 579; Prosecutor v. Yussuf Munyakazi. ICTR-97-36A-T. *Supra* note 236. ¶ 503; Prosecutor v. Augustin Ndindiliyimana *et al.* ICTR-00-56-T. *Supra* note 163. ¶ 2087.

[1958] Prosecutor v. Dragoljub Kunarac *et al.* IT-96-23/1-A. *Supra* note 85. ¶¶ 93, 97–98; Prosecutor v. Brima, Kamara, Kanu. SCSL-04-16-T. *Supra* note 280. ¶¶ 214–215; Prosecutor v. Emmanuel Rukundo. ICTR-2001-70-T. *Supra* note 179. ¶ 578; Prosecutor v. Sesay, Kallon and Gbao. SCSL-04-15-T. *Supra* note 268. ¶ 78; Prosecutor v. Milan Lukić, Sredoje Lukić. IT-98-32/1-T. *Supra* note 104. ¶ 875; Prosecutor v. Hormisdas Nsengimana, Case No. ICTR-01-69-T, (Nov. 17, 2009). ¶ 843; Prosecutor v. Yussuf Munyakazi. ICTR-97-36A-T. *Supra* note 236. ¶ 503; Prosecutor v. Gaspard Kanyarukiga. ICTR-2002-78-T. *Supra* note 187. ¶ 657; Prosecutor v. Augustin Ndindiliyimana *et al.* ICTR-00-56-T. *Supra* note 163. ¶ 2087; Prosecutor v. Jean-Baptiste Gatete. ICTR-2000-61-T. *Supra* note 195. ¶ 631.

[1959] Prosecutor v. Brima, Kamara, Kanu. SCSL-04-16-T. *Supra* note 280. ¶ 215; Prosecutor v. Fofana, Kondewa. SCSL-04-14-T. *Supra* note 281. ¶ 112; Prosecutor v. Sesay, Kallon and Gbao. SCSL-04-15-T. *Supra* note 268. ¶ 78; Prosecutor v. Taylor. SCSL-03-01-T. *Supra* note 270. ¶ 511; Prosecutor v. Jean-Pierre Bemba Gombo. ICC-01/05-01/08. *Supra* note 335. ¶ 162.

[1960] Prosecutor v. Dragoljub Kunarac *et al.* IT-96-23/1-A. *Supra* note 85. ¶¶ 93, 97; Prosecutor v. Blagoje Simić *et al.* IT-95-9-T. *Supra* note 78. ¶ 43; Prosecutor v. Radoslav Brđanin. IT-99-36-T. *Supra* note 130. ¶ 135; Prosecutor v. Dragomir Milošević. IT-98-29/1-T. *Supra* note 86. ¶ 925; Prosecutor v. Nikola Šainović *et al.* IT-05-87-T, vol. 1. *Supra* note 125. ¶ 150; Prosecutor v. Zdravko Tolimir. IT-05-88/2-T. *Supra* note 153. ¶ 698; Prosecutor v. Mićo Stanišić, Stojan Župljanin. IT-08-91-T, vol. 1. *Supra* note 102. ¶ 28; Prosecutor v. Jadranko Prlić, *et al.* IT-04-74-T, vol. I. *Supra* note 99. ¶ 41; Prosecutor v. Radovan Karadžić. IT-95-5/18-T, vol. I. *Supra* note 134. ¶ 477.

[1961] Prosecutor v. Jean-Paul Akayesu. ICTR-96-4-T. *Supra* note 203. ¶ 579; Prosecutor v. Clément Kayishema and Ruzindana. ICTR 95-1-T. *Supra* note 209. ¶ 123; Prosecutor v. Elizaphan and Gérard Ntakirutimana. ICTR-96-10 & ICTR-96-17-T. *Supra* note 175. ¶ 804; Prosecutor v. Laurent Semanza. ICTR-97-20-T. *Supra* note 211. ¶ 328; Prosecutor v. Jean de Dieu Kamuhanda. ICTR-95-54A-T. *Supra* note 200. ¶ 662; Pro-

bunals require that only the attack, "not the individual acts of the accused, must be widespread or systematic."[1962] [1963] [1964]

The term "widespread" refers directly to 1) the massive, "large-scale nature" of the attack (*extraordinary* magnitude); 2) the relative number of the victims, or 3) "the cumulative effect of a series of inhumane acts or the singular effect of an inhumane act of extraordinary magnitude."[1965] [1966] [1967] [1968]

secutor v. Paul Bisengimana. ICTR-00-60-T. *Supra* note 218. ¶ 43; Prosecutor v. Théoneste Bagosora *et al.* ICTR-98-41-T. *Supra* note 234. ¶ 2165; Prosecutor v. Tharcisse Renzaho. ICTR-97-31-T. *Supra* note 232. ¶ 782; Prosecutor v. Ephrem Setako. ICTR-04-81-T. *Supra* note 181. ¶ 476; Prosecutor v. Yussuf Munyakazi. ICTR-97-36A-T. *Supra* note 236. ¶ 503; Prosecutor v. Gaspard Kanyarukiga. ICTR-2002-78-T. *Supra* note 187. ¶ 657; Prosecutor v. Ildephonse Hategekimana. ICTR-00-55B-T. *Supra* note 197. ¶ 700; Prosecutor v. Jean-Baptiste Gatete. ICTR-2000-61-T. *Supra* note 195. ¶ 631; Prosecutor v. Grégoire Ndahimana. ICTR-01-68-T. *Supra* note 191. ¶ 835; Prosecutor v. Édouard Karemera *et al.* ICTR-98-44-T. *Supra* note 172. ¶ 1674.

[1962] Prosecutor v. Dragoljub Kunarac *et al.* IT-96-23/1-T. *Supra* note 84. ¶ 431.

[1963] See also: Prosecutor v. Dragoljub Kunarac *et al.* IT-96-23/1-A. *Supra* note 85. ¶ 96; Prosecutor v. Blagoje Simić *et al.* IT-95-9-T. *Supra* note 78. ¶ 43; Prosecutor v. Tihomir Blaškić. IT-95-14-A. *Supra* note 144. ¶ 101; Prosecutor v. Radoslav Brđanin. IT-99-36-T. *Supra* note 130. ¶ 135; Prosecutor v. Dario Kordić and Mario Čerkez. IT-95-14/2-A. *Supra* note 80. ¶ 94; Prosecutor v. Nikola Šainović *et al.* IT-05-87-T, vol. 1. *Supra* note 125. ¶ 150; Prosecutor v. Jadranko Prlić, *et al.* IT-04-74-T, vol. I. *Supra* note 99. ¶ 42.

[1964] See also: Prosecutor v. Fofana, Kondewa. SCSL-04-14-T. *Supra* note 281. ¶ 120; Prosecutor v. Sesay, Kallon and Gbao. SCSL-04-15-T. *Supra* note 268. ¶ 89.

[1965] Prosecutor v. Dragoljub Kunarac *et al.* IT-96-23/1-A. *Supra* note 85. ¶¶ 94–95.

[1966] See also: Prosecutor v. Tihomir Blaškić. IT-95-14-T. *Supra* note 143. ¶ 206; Prosecutor v. Dragoljub Kunarac *et al.* IT-96-23/1-T. *Supra* note 84. ¶ 428; Prosecutor v. Goran Jelisić., IT-95-10-A. *Supra* note 98. ¶ 146; Prosecutor v. Mitar Vasiljević. IT-98-32-T. *Supra* note 117. ¶ 35; Prosecutor v. Milomir Stakić. IT-97-24-T. *Supra* note 109. ¶ 625; Prosecutor v. Blagoje Simić *et al.* IT-95-9-T. *Supra* note 78. ¶ 43; Prosecutor v. Tihomir Blaškić. IT-95-14-A. *Supra* note 144. ¶ 101; Prosecutor v. Radoslav Brđanin. IT-99-36-T. *Supra* note 130. ¶ 135; Prosecutor v. Dario Kordić and Mario Čerkez. IT-95-14/2-A. *Supra* note 80. ¶ 94; Prosecutor v. Vidoje Blagojević, Dragan Jokić. IT-02-60-T. *Supra* note 147. ¶ 545; Prosecutor v. Momčilo Krajišnik. IT-00-39-T. *Supra* note 121. ¶ 706; Prosecutor v. Dragomir Milošević. IT-98-29/1-T. *Supra* note 86. ¶ 925; Prosecutor v. Nikola Šainović *et al.* IT-05-87-T, vol. 1. *Supra* note 125. ¶ 150; Prosecutor v. Milan Lukić, Sredoje Lukić. IT-98-32/1-T. *Supra* note 104. ¶ 875; Prosecutor v. Ante Gotovina *et al.* IT-06-90-T, vol. I. *Supra* note 76. ¶ 1703; Prosecutor v. Momčilo Perišić. IT-04-81-T. *Supra* note 123. ¶ 86; Prosecutor v. Zdravko Tolimir. IT-05-88/2-T. *Supra* note 153. ¶ 698; Prosecutor v. Mićo Stanišić, Stojan Župljanin. IT-08-91-T, vol. 1. *Supra* note 102. ¶ 28; Prosecutor v. Jadranko Prlić, *et al.* IT-04-74-T, vol. I. *Supra* note 99. ¶ 41; Prosecutor v. Jovica Stanišić and Franko Simatović. IT-03-69-T, vol. I. *Supra* note 101. ¶ 963; Prosecutor v. Radovan Karadžić.

The term "systematic" has been conceived as encompassing multiple alternative elements, meaning that the act of violence (or the acts) perpetrated against a civilian population is (are) organized/methodical in its nature, follows a similar, regular, and deliberate pattern of criminal conduct, recurs non-accidentally, takes place on a regular basis, results "in continuous acts of commission," usually perpetrated in the furtherance of a common policy or ideology, and being improbable that such act/acts occur randomly.[1969] [1970] [1971] [1972] International case-law has also understood that, in many factual circumstances, the term "systematic" implicates that high-

---

IT-95-5/18-T, vol. I. *Supra* note 134. ¶ 477; Prosecutor v. Ratko Mladić. IT-09-92-T, vol. III. *Supra* note 137. ¶ 3025.

[1967] See also: Prosecutor v. Jean-Paul Akayesu. ICTR-96-4-T. *Supra* note 203. ¶ 580; Prosecutor v. Clément Kayishema and Ruzindana. ICTR 95-1-T. *Supra* note 209. ¶ 123; Prosecutor v. Elizaphan and Gérard Ntakirutimana. ICTR-96-10 & ICTR-96-17-T. *Supra* note 175. ¶ 804; Prosecutor v. Sylvestre Gacumbitsi. ICTR-2001-64-T. *Supra* note 228. ¶ 299; Prosecutor v. Mikaeli Muhimana. ICTR-95-1B-T. *Supra* note 214. ¶ 527; Prosecutor v. Théoneste Bagosora *et al.* ICTR-98-41-T. *Supra* note 234. ¶ 2165; Prosecutor v. Emmanuel Rukundo. ICTR-2001-70-T. *Supra* note 179. ¶ 578; Prosecutor v. Tharcisse Renzaho. ICTR-97-31-T. *Supra* note 232. ¶ 782; Prosecutor v. Hormisdas Nsengimana, Case No. ICTR-01-69-T, (Nov. 17, 2009). ¶ 843; Prosecutor v. Ephrem Setako. ICTR-04-81-T. *Supra* note 181. ¶ 476; Prosecutor v. Yussuf Munyakazi. ICTR-97-36A-T. *Supra* note 236. ¶ 503; Prosecutor v. Gaspard Kanyarukiga. ICTR-2002-78-T. *Supra* note 187. ¶ 657; Prosecutor v. Ildephonse Hategekimana. ICTR-00-55B-T. *Supra* note 197. ¶ 700; Prosecutor v. Jean-Baptiste Gatete. ICTR-2000-61-T. *Supra* note 195. ¶ 631; Prosecutor v. Augustin Ndindiliyimana *et al.* ICTR-00-56-T. *Supra* note 163. ¶ 2087; Prosecutor v. Pauline Nyiramasuhuko *et al.* ICTR-98-42-T. *Supra* note 219. ¶ 6040; Prosecutor v. Grégoire Ndahimana. ICTR-01-68-T. *Supra* note 191. ¶ 835; Prosecutor v. Callixte Nzabonimana. ICTR-98-44D-T. *Supra* note 168. ¶ 1777; Prosecutor v. Ildéphonse Nizeyimana. ICTR-2000-55C-T. *Supra* note 198. ¶ 1542.

[1968] See also: Prosecutor v. Brima, Kamara, Kanu. SCSL-04-16-T. *Supra* note 280. ¶ 215; Prosecutor v. Sesay, Kallon and Gbao. SCSL-04-15-T. *Supra* note 268. ¶ 78.

[1969] Prosecutor v. Elizaphan and Gérard Ntakirutimana. ICTR-96-10 & ICTR-96-17-T. *Supra* note 175. ¶ 804; Prosecutor v. Théoneste Bagosora *et al.* ICTR-98-41-T. *Supra* note 234. ¶ 2165; Prosecutor v. Tharcisse Renzaho. ICTR-97-31-T. *Supra* note 232. ¶ 782; Prosecutor v. Ephrem Setako. ICTR-04-81-T. *Supra* note 181. ¶ 476; Prosecutor v. Yussuf Munyakazi. ICTR-97-36A-T. *Supra* note 236. ¶ 503; Prosecutor v. Gaspard Kanyarukiga. ICTR-2002-78-T. *Supra* note 187. ¶ 657; Prosecutor v. Ildephonse Hategekimana. ICTR-00-55B-T. *Supra* note 197. ¶ 700; Prosecutor v. Jean-Baptiste Gatete. ICTR-2000-61-T. *Supra* note 195. ¶ 631; Prosecutor v. Pauline Nyiramasuhuko *et al.* ICTR-98-42-T. *Supra* note 219. ¶ 6040; Prosecutor v. Grégoire Ndahimana. ICTR-01-68-T. *Supra* note 191. ¶ 835; Prosecutor v. Callixte Nzabonimana. ICTR-98-44D-T. *Supra* note 168. ¶ 1777; Prosecutor v. Ildéphonse Nizeyimana. ICTR-2000-55C-T. *Supra* note 198. ¶ 1542.

level political and military authorities are involved in the planning or per-petration of the systematic attack. Or even that significant private or pub-lic resources (military or not) have been used in an attack.[1973] [1974] Also, "sys-tematic" might denote the existence of a pre-conceived plan or policy, whether formalized or not. However, proof of the existence of a plan does not constitute an element of the crime against humanity.[1975]

The assessment of whether the attack is widespread or systematic in practice is, in essence, a relative exercise always conducted on a case-by-case basis,[1976] "because it depends upon the civilian population that was attacked."[1977] [1978] It is "neither exclusively quantitative nor geo-graphical, but must be carried out based on all the relevant facts of the

---

[1970] Prosecutor v. Dragoljub Kunarac *et al.* IT-96-23/1-T. *Supra* note 84. ¶ 429; Prosecu-tor v. Goran Jelisić., IT-95-10-A. *Supra* note 98. ¶ 146; Prosecutor v. Dragoljub Kuna-rac *et al.* IT-96-23/1-A. *Supra* note 85. ¶ 94; Prosecutor v. Mitar Vasiljević. IT-98-32-T. *Supra* note 117. ¶ 35; Prosecutor v. Blagoje Simić *et al.* IT-95-9-T. *Supra* note 78. ¶ 43; Prosecutor v. Tihomir Blaškić. IT-95-14-A. *Supra* note 144. ¶ 101; Prosecutor v. Radoslav Brđanin. IT-99-36-T. *Supra* note 130. ¶ 135; Prosecutor v. Vidoje Blago-jević, Dragan Jokić. IT-02-60-T. *Supra* note 147. ¶ 545; Prosecutor v. Momčilo Kraj-išnik. IT-00-39-T. *Supra* note 121. ¶ 706; Prosecutor v. Dragomir Milošević. IT-98-29/1-T. *Supra* note 86. ¶ 925; Prosecutor v. Nikola Šainović *et al.* IT-05-87-T, vol. 1. *Supra* note 125. ¶ 150; Prosecutor v. Ante Gotovina *et al.* IT-06-90-T, vol. I. *Supra* note 76. ¶ 1703; Prosecutor v. Momčilo Perišić. IT-04-81-T. *Supra* note 123. ¶ 86; Prosecutor v. Zdravko Tolimir. IT-05-88/2-T. *Supra* note 153. ¶ 698; Prosecutor v. Mićo Stanišić, Stojan Župljanin. IT-08-91-T, vol. 1. *Supra* note 102. ¶ 28; Prosecutor v. Jadranko Prlić, *et al.* IT-04-74-T, vol. I. *Supra* note 99. ¶ 41; Prosecutor v. Jovica Stanišić and Franko Simatović. IT-03-69-T, vol. I. *Supra* note 101. ¶ 963; Prosecutor v. Radovan Karadžić. IT-95-5/18-T, vol. I. *Supra* note 134. ¶ 477; Prosecutor v. Ratko Mladić. IT-09-92-T, vol. III. *Supra* note 137. ¶ 3025.

[1971] Prosecutor v. Brima, Kamara, Kanu. SCSL-04-16-T. *Supra* note 280. ¶ 215; Prosecu-tor v. Sesay, Kallon and Gbao. SCSL-04-15-T. *Supra* note 268. ¶ 78; Prosecutor v. Taylor. SCSL-03-01-T. *Supra* note 270. ¶ 511.

[1972] Prosecutor v. Germain Katanga. ICC-01/04-01/07. *Supra* note 332. ¶ 397; Prosecu-tor v. Bosco Ntaganda. ICC-01/04-02/06. *Supra* note 328. ¶ 692.

[1973] Prosecutor v. Tihomir Blaškić. IT-95-14-T. *Supra* note 143. ¶ 203.

[1974] See also: Prosecutor v. Jean-Paul Akayesu. ICTR-96-4-T. *Supra* note 203. ¶ 580.

[1975] Prosecutor v. Sylvestre Gacumbitsi. ICTR-2001-64-T. *Supra* note 228. ¶ 299; Prose-cutor v. Mikaeli Muhimana. ICTR-95-1B-T. *Supra* note 214. ¶ 527.

[1976] Prosecutor v. Dragoljub Kunarac *et al.* IT-96-23/1-T. *Supra* note 84. ¶ 430; Prosecu-tor v. Dragoljub Kunarac *et al.* IT-96-23/1-A. *Supra* note 85. ¶ 95; Prosecutor v. Ni-kola Šainović *et al.* IT-05-87-T, vol. 1. *Supra* note 125. ¶ 151; Prosecutor v. Radovan Karadžić. IT-95-5/18-T, vol. I. *Supra* note 134. ¶ 477.

[1977] Prosecutor v. Nikola Šainović *et al.* IT-05-87-T, vol. 1. *Supra* note 125. ¶ 151.

[1978] See also: Prosecutor v. Goran Jelisić., IT-95-10-A. *Supra* note 98. ¶ 146; Prosecutor v. Dragomir Milošević. IT-98-29/1-T. *Supra* note 86. ¶ 926.

case."[1979] [1980] Notably, the International Criminal Law jurisprudence provides a non-exhaustive list of factors in considering whether an attack meets both "widespread" or "systematic" requirements of a crime against humanity: (i) "the (discriminatory) nature of the acts committed in its course;" (ii) "the status and the number of victims"; (iii) the means, methods, resources employed in the attacks; (iv) "the consequences of the attack upon the targeted population"; (v) "the possible participation of officials or authorities or any identifiable patterns of crimes."[1981] For instance, the ICTY considered that the widespread and systematic attack by Serbian police/military against the Bosnian Muslims and Bosnian Croats clearly targeted a civilian population with specific discriminatory measures on the basis of the victims' membership in a group.[1982]

## 3.2.2. Prohibited acts

### 3.2.2.1. Actus reus

The Statute of the International Criminal Court defines that, for the jurisdictional purposes of the Court and in respect of the principle of legality, any of the following acts may constitute a crime against humanity, "when committed as part of a widespread or systematic attack directed against any civilian population, with knowledge of the attack:"[1983]

"(a) Murder;
(b) Extermination;
(c) Enslavement;
(d) Deportation or forcible transfer of population;
(e) Imprisonment or other severe deprivation of physical liberty in violation

---

[1979] Prosecutor v. Bosco Ntaganda. ICC-01/04-02/06. *Supra* note 328. ¶ 691.

[1980] See also: Prosecutor v. Jean-Pierre Bemba Gombo. ICC-01/05-01/08. *Supra* note 335. ¶ 163.

[1981] Prosecutor v. Dragoljub Kunarac *et al.* IT-96-23/1-A. *Supra* note 85. ¶¶ 91, 95; Prosecutor v. Milomir Stakić. IT-97-24-T. *Supra* note 109. ¶ 625; Prosecutor v. Vidoje Blagojević, Dragan Jokić. IT-02-60-T. *Supra* note 147. ¶ 546; Prosecutor v. Milan Lukić, Sredoje Lukić. IT-98-32/1-T. *Supra* note 104. ¶ 875.

[1982] Prosecutor v. Dragoljub Kunarac *et al.* IT-96-23/1-A. *Supra* note 85. ¶¶ 92, 97, 101; Prosecutor v. Vidoje Blagojević, Dragan Jokić. IT-02-60-T. *Supra* note 147. ¶ 552; Prosecutor v. Momčilo Krajišnik. IT-00-39-T. *Supra* note 121. ¶ 787; Prosecutor v. Radoslav Brđanin. IT-99-36-A. *Supra* note 131. ¶ 257; Prosecutor v. Milan Lukić, Sredoje Lukić. IT-98-32/1-T. *Supra* note 104. ¶ 895; Prosecutor v. Radovan Karadžić. IT-95-5/18-T, vol. 1. *Supra* note 134. ¶¶ 2517, 2529, 2569.

[1983] United Nations. Rome Statute (July 17, 1998) 2187 UNTS 38544. Art. 7.

of fundamental rules of international law;

(f) Torture;

(g) Rape, sexual slavery, enforced prostitution, forced pregnancy, enforced sterilization, or any other form of sexual violence of comparable gravity;

(h) Persecution of any identifiable group, or collectively on political, racial, national, ethnic, cultural, religious, gender as defined in paragraph 3, or other grounds that are universally recognized as impermissible under international law, in connection with any act referred to in this paragraph or any crime within the jurisdiction of the court;

(i) Enforced disappearance of persons;

(j) The crime of apartheid;

(k) Other inhumane acts of a similar character intentionally causing great suffering, or serious injury to body or to mental or physical health."[1984]

For the purposes of this book in assessing ISIL/DAESH acts against Christians in Iraq, the author selected and explored only the perpetrators' *actus reus* that could be proven beyond a reasonable doubt, having considered the evidence and *indicia* demonstrated in a myriad of reports. Some of these acts are of much interest to assist in the assessment of whether ISIL/DAESH's conducts and omissions towards Christians in Iraq constitute genocide or persecution, as a crime against humanity: extermination (Art. 7, I, c), torture (Art. 7, I, f), persecution (Art. 7, I, h), and "other inhumane acts of a similar character intentionally causing great suffering, or serious injury to the body or to mental or physical health" (Art. 7, I, k).[1985]

### 3.2.2.2. Is there a policy element?

A significant jurisprudential and academic debate refers to the necessity – or not – of a policy element in crimes against humanity.[1986] In other words, the controversy resides in whether the existence of a pre-conceived plan is a *sine qua non* element for establishing the required *dolus specialis* of crimes against humanity.[1987] While the Rome Statute and the ICTR Statute seek an organizational policy behind a State attack,[1988] the jurisprudence of both the SCSL and ICTY sustains that the existence of a plan or policy behind the attack "is not a distinct legal element [of a crime against hu-

---

[1984] *Ibidem.*

[1985] *Ibidem.*

[1986] M. Cherif Bassiouni. *Supra* note 316. p. 26.

[1987] Prosecutor v. Georges Anderson Nderubumwe Rutaganda. ICTR-96-3-A. *Supra* note 189. ¶ 525.

[1988] United Nations. Rome Statute (July 17, 1998) 2187 UNTS 38544. Article 7.2.a.

manity]" and need not be proven.[1989] [1990] [1991] Customary international law sustains that if such a plan exists, it "need not necessarily be declared expressly or even stated clearly and precisely."[1992] [1993] However, proving the existence of such a plan may be "evidentially relevant, in that it may be useful in establishing that the attack was directed against a civilian population and that it was widespread or systematic."[1994] [1995] [1996] [1997]

In *Musema*, the ICTR Appeals Chamber approached the issue, considering that "there must exist some form of preconceived plan or policy [prior to any attack]." The Court had a similar approach in *Akayesu*[1998] and in *Rutaganda*.[1999] In 1996, the International Law Commission considered that the definition of crimes against humanity "established the two general conditions which must be met for one of the prohibited acts to qualify as a crime against humanity." For the ILC, the first condition "required that the act [be] 'committed in a systematic manner or on a large scale.'". The ILC explained that this first condition "consisted of two alternative require-

---

[1989]  Prosecutor v. Ratko Mladić. IT-09-92-T, vol. III. *Supra* note 137. ¶ 3025.

[1990]  See also: Prosecutor v. Dragoljub Kunarac *et al.* IT-96-23/1-A. *Supra* note 85. ¶ 98; Prosecutor v. Mitar Vasiljević. IT-98-32-T. *Supra* note 117. ¶ 36; Prosecutor v. Tihomir Blaškić. IT-95-14-A. *Supra* note 144. ¶ 126; Prosecutor v. Radoslav Brđanin. IT-99-36-T. *Supra* note 130. ¶ 137; Prosecutor v. Ante Gotovina *et al.* IT-06-90-T, vol. I. *Supra* note 76. ¶ 1703; Prosecutor v. Jovica Stanišić and Franko Simatović. IT-03-69-T, vol. I. *Supra* note 101. ¶ 963; Prosecutor v. Radovan Karadžić. IT-95-5/18-T, vol. I. *Supra* note 134. ¶ 477.

[1991]  See also: Prosecutor v. Jean-Paul Akayesu. ICTR-96-4-T. *Supra* note 203. ¶ 580; Prosecutor v. Sylvestre Gacumbitsi. ICTR-2001-64-T. *Supra* note 228. ¶ 299.

[1992]  Prosecutor v. Tihomir Blaškić. IT-95-14-T. *Supra* note 143. ¶ 204.

[1993]  See also: Prosecutor v. Duško Tadic. IT-94-1-T. *Supra* note 89. ¶ 653.

[1994]  Prosecutor v. Sylvestre Gacumbitsi. ICTR-2001-64-T. *Supra* note 228. ¶ 299.

[1995]  See also: Prosecutor v. Mikaeli Muhimana. ICTR-95-1B-T. *Supra* note 214. ¶ 527.

[1996]  See also: Prosecutor v. Brima, Kamara, Kanu. SCSL-04-16-T. *Supra* note 280. ¶ 215; Prosecutor v. Fofana, Kondewa. SCSL-04-14-T. *Supra* note 281. ¶ 113; Prosecutor v. Sesay, Kallon and Gbao. SCSL-04-15-T. *Supra* note 268. ¶ 79.

[1997]  See also: Prosecutor v. Blagoje Simić *et al.* IT-95-9-T. *Supra* note 78. ¶ 44; Prosecutor v. Momčilo Krajišnik. IT-00-39-T. *Supra* note 121. ¶ 706; Prosecutor v. Nikola Šainović *et al.* IT-05-87-T, vol. 1. *Supra* note 125. ¶ 151; Prosecutor v. Zdravko Tolimir. IT-05-88/2-T. *Supra* note 153. ¶ 698; Prosecutor v. Jadranko Prlić, *et al.* IT-04-74-T, vol. I. *Supra* note 99. ¶ 44.

[1998]  The ICTR Trial Chamber established in *Akayesu* that "there is no requirement that this policy must be adopted formally as the policy of a state. There must however be some kind of preconceived plan or policy." (Prosecutor v. Jean-Paul Akayesu. ICTR-96-4-T. *Supra* note 203. ¶ 580.

[1999]  Prosecutor v. Georges Anderson Nderubumwe Rutaganda. ICTR-96-3-A. *Supra* note 189. ¶¶ 521–531.

ments." The first alternative for the ILC, "required that the inhumane acts be 'committed in a systematic manner' meaning pursuant of a preconceived plan or policy."[2000]

The ICTY and the SCSL jurisprudence have an understanding that the definition of crimes against humanity in customary international law had no explicit requirement of a plan or policy.[2001] For instance, in *Kunarac*, the ICTY Appeals Chamber stated that:

> "Contrary to the Appellants' submissions, neither the attack nor the acts of the accused needs to be supported by any form of 'policy" or "plan.' There was nothing in the Statute or in customary international law at the time of the alleged acts which required proof of the existence of a plan or policy to commit these crimes."[2002]

Under this *rationale,* the Appeals Chamber considered that to prove these elements – *widespread* or *systematic* – it is not necessary

> "to show that they were the result of the existence of a policy or plan. It may be useful in establishing that the attack was directed against a civilian population and that it was widespread or systematic (especially the latter) to show that there was, in fact, a policy or plan, but it may be possible to prove these things by reference to other matters."[2003]

Thus, the ICTY Appeals Chamber concluded that "the existence of a policy or plan may be evidentially relevant, but it is not a legal element of the crime."[2004] In *Sesay, Kallon and Gbao*, the SCSL explicitly acknowledged that the existence of a policy or plan "is not a separate legal requirement of crimes against humanity."[2005] The SCSL had the same approach in *Prosecutor v. Brima, Kamara, Kanu.*[2006]

---

[2000]  U.N. Doc. A/51/10 (May 6, 1996 – July 26, 1996). p. 47. ¶ 3.

[2001]  M. Cherif Bassiouni. *Supra* note 316. p. 26.

[2002]  Prosecutor v. Dragoljub Kunarac *et al.* IT-96-23/1-A. *Supra* note 85. ¶ 98.

[2003]  *Ibidem.*

[2004]  *Ibidem.*

[2005]  "The existence of a policy or plan, or that the crimes were supported by a policy or plan to carry them out, may be evidentially relevant to establish the widespread or systematic nature of the attack and that it was directed against a civilian population, but it is not a separate legal requirement of crimes against humanity. Furthermore, the Chamber is of the view that customary international law does not presuppose a discriminatory or persecutory intent for all crimes against humanity." (Prosecutor v. Sesay, Kallon and Gbao. SCSL-04-15-T. *Supra* note 268. ¶ 79).

[2006]  Prosecutor v. Brima, Kamara, Kanu. SCSL-04-16-T. *Supra* note 280. ¶ 215.

In *Bemba Gombo,* the ICC Pre-Trial Chamber further considered that such an organized *plan* might be conceived by a myriad of entities and organizations and not only state actors. Consequentially, according to this *rationale*, private organizations, such as terrorist organizations, may commit *directed* and *organized* attacks against a civilian population.[2007] In the same vein, Customary International Criminal Law conceives that "crimes against humanity can be committed on behalf of entities exercising *de facto* control over a particular territory but without international recognition or formal status of a *de jure* state, or by a terrorist group or organization."[2008]

Given that the present book deals with conducts perpetrated by an armed terrorist group rather than a State, both the Rome Statute and customary international law assert the crucial importance of a demonstration of a plan or policy behind the unlawful acts committed by the organization (non-state actor) in the course of an attack.[2009] The *plan* from a non-state actor can be deduced from the occurrence of a series of events, *inter alia*:

1) the "general historical circumstances and the overall political background against which the criminal acts are set;"[2010]
2) the "establishment and implementation of autonomous political structures at any level of authority in a given territory;"[2011]
3) the "general content of a political programme [*sic*], as it appears in the writings and speeches of its authors;"[2012]
4) the existence of media propaganda:[2013] "statements, instructions or documentation attributable to [...] the organization condoning or encouraging the commission of crimes;"[2014]
5) indications that the attack against the civilian population was "planned, directed or organized;"[2015]
6) the "appointment of commanders and divisional commanders responsible for the operations on the field;"[2016]

---

[2007] Prosecutor v. Jean-Pierre Bemba Gombo. ICC-01/05-01/08. *Supra* note 334. ¶ 81.
[2008] Prosecutor v. Duško Tadic. IT-94-1-T. *Supra* note 89. ¶ 654.
[2009] Prosecutor v. Bosco Ntaganda. ICC-01/04-02/06. *Supra* note 328. ¶ 675.
[2010] Prosecutor v. Tihomir Blaškić. IT-95-14-T. *Supra* note 143. ¶ 204.
[2011] *Ibidem.*
[2012] *Ibidem.*
[2013] *Ibidem.*
[2014] Prosecutor v. Jean-Pierre Bemba Gombo. ICC-01/05-01/08. *Supra* note 335. ¶ 160.
[2015] *Ibidem.*
[2016] Prosecutor v. William Samoei Ruto *et al.* ICC-01/09-01/11. *Supra* note 344. ¶ 219.

7) the "production of maps marking areas;"[2017]
8) the "purchase of weapons as well as of material to produce crude weapons and their storage before the attack;"[2018]
9) the "transportation of the perpetrators to and from the target locations;"[2019]
10) the "use of public or private resources to further the policy;"[2020]
11) the "use of various means of communication, including radio networks, with trained radio operators, and satellite communication;"[2021]
12) the existence of "discriminatory measures, whether administrative or other (banking restrictions, laissez-passer);"[2022]
13) the "scale of the acts of violence perpetrated – in particular, murders and other physical acts of violence, rape, arbitrary imprisonment, deportations, and expulsions or the destruction of non-military property, in particular, sacral sites;"[2023]
14) the "establishment of a stipendiary scheme and a rewarding mechanism to motivate the perpetrators to kill and displace the largest number of persons belonging to the target communities as well as to destroy their properties;"[2024]
15) the existence of an underlying motivation for the attack;[2025]
16) the recurrence of a pattern of violence[2026] temporally and geographically repeated;[2027] and
17) "alterations to the composition of populations as a result of the attack."[2028]

### 3.2.2.3. Extermination

The crime of extermination is the intentional – *mens rea* – act of killing on a massive/large scale or indirectly subjecting "a large number of people to

---

[2017] *Ibidem.*
[2018] *Ibidem.*
[2019] *Ibidem.*
[2020] Prosecutor v. Jean-Pierre Bemba Gombo. ICC-01/05-01/08. *Supra* note 335. ¶ 160.
[2021] Prosecutor v. Bosco Ntaganda. ICC-01/04-02/06. *Supra* note 328. ¶ 679.
[2022] Prosecutor v. Tihomir Blaškić. IT-95-14-T. *Supra* note 143. ¶ 204.
[2023] *Ibidem.*
[2024] Prosecutor v. William Samoei Ruto *et al.* ICC-01/09-01/11. *Supra* note 344. ¶ 219.
[2025] Prosecutor v. Jean-Pierre Bemba Gombo. ICC-01/05-01/08. *Supra* note 335. ¶ 160.
[2026] *Ibidem.*
[2027] Prosecutor v. Tihomir Blaškić. IT-95-14-T. *Supra* note 143. ¶ 204.
[2028] *Ibidem.*

conditions of living that would lead to their death in a widespread or systematic manner."[2029] [2030] Although such a legal typification does not imply or require that a numerical minimum must be reached (no numerical threshold), "extermination differs from murder in that it requires an element of mass destruction."[2031] [2032] It is a crime "which by its very nature is directed against a group of individuals."[2033] [2034] According to ICTY's cases of *Prosecutor v. Momčilo Krajišnik* and *Prosecutor v. Vidoje Blagojević*, the assessment of whether a certain number of victims is considered "large" – scale/numerical minimum – is made on a case-by-case basis, in light of the proven facts and considering "all the relevant factors."[2035] Notably, in Prosecutor v. Emmanuel Rukundo, the ICTR Trial Chamber considered that "the Prosecution is not required to name the victims."[2036]

The *mens rea* of extermination, through act or omission, consists of 1) the *intent* to kill persons or to cause serious bodily injury on a large scale or 2) the *intent* to systematically create conditions of life for a widespread number of people that would cause their deaths.[2037] The *actus reus* of exter-

---

[2029]  Prosecutor v. François Karera. ICTR-01-74-T. *Supra* note 184. ¶ 552. See also: Prosecutor v. Emmanuel Rukundo. ICTR-2001-70-T. *Supra* note 179. ¶ 586; Prosecutor v. Ephrem Setako. ICTR-04-81-T. *Supra* note 181. ¶ 480; Prosecutor v. Yussuf Munyakazi. ICTR-97-36A-T. *Supra* note 236. ¶ 506; Prosecutor v. Gaspard Kanyarukiga. ICTR-2002-78-T. *Supra* note 187. ¶¶ 658, 665; Prosecutor v. Jean-Baptiste Gatete. ICTR-2000-61-T. *Supra* note 195. ¶¶ 642–643, Count IV, Disposition);Prosecutor v. Pauline Nyiramasuhuko *et al.* ICTR-98-42-A. *Supra* note 220. ¶ 2123.

[2030]  See also: Prosecutor v. Brima, Kamara, Kanu. SCSL-04-16-T. *Supra* note 280. ¶ 685.

[2031]  Prosecutor v. Milomir Stakić. IT-97-24-A. *Supra* note 110. ¶ 260.

[2032]  See also: Prosecutor v. Jean-Paul Akayesu. ICTR-96-4-T. *Supra* note 203. ¶ 591; Prosecutor v. Musema. ICTR-96-13-A. *Supra* note 216. ¶ 217; Prosecutor v. François Karera. ICTR-01-74-T. *Supra* note 184. ¶ 552;Prosecutor v. Emmanuel Rukundo. ICTR-2001-70-T. *Supra* note 179. ¶ 586; Prosecutor v. Milan Lukić, Sredoje Lukić. IT-98-32/1-T. *Supra* note 104. ¶ 938; Prosecutor v. Gaspard Kanyarukiga. ICTR-2002-78-T. *Supra* note 187. ¶ 658; Prosecutor v. Pauline Nyiramasuhuko *et al.* ICTR-98-42-A. *Supra* note 220. ¶ 2123.

[2033]  Prosecutor v. Jean-Paul Akayesu. ICTR-96-4-T. *Supra* note 203. ¶ 591.

[2034]  See also: Prosecutor v. Musema. ICTR-96-13-A. *Supra* note 216. ¶ 217; Prosecutor v. Ephrem Setako. ICTR-04-81-T. *Supra* note 181. ¶ 480; Prosecutor v. Yussuf Munyakazi. ICTR-97-36A-T. *Supra* note 236. ¶ 506.

[2035]  Prosecutor v. Vidoje Blagojević, Dragan Jokić. IT-02-60-T. *Supra* note 147. ¶ 573; Prosecutor v. Momčilo Krajišnik. IT-00-39-T. *Supra* note 121. ¶ 716; Prosecutor v. Milan Lukić, Sredoje Lukić. IT-98-32/1-T. *Supra* note 104. ¶ 938.

[2036]  Prosecutor v. Emmanuel Rukundo. ICTR-2001-70-T. *Supra* note 179. ¶ 586

[2037]  Prosecutor v. Vidoje Blagojević, Dragan Jokić. IT-02-60-T. *Supra* note 147. ¶¶ 572, 574; Prosecutor v. Milomir Stakić. IT-97-24-A. *Supra* note 110. ¶¶ 259–260; Prosecutor v. Milan Lukić, Sredoje Lukić. IT-98-32/1-T. *Supra* note 104. ¶ 939.

mination consists of any *act* or *omission* that, directly or indirectly, leads to the death of a large number of persons – massive scale.[2038] [2039]

The ICTR Chamber defined the essential elements/requirements of extermination as constituting a crime against humanity: 1) "the accused or his subordinate participated in the (widespread or systematic) killing of certain (...) described persons" or "in subjecting a widespread number of people or systematically subjecting a number of people to conditions of living that would inevitably lead to death"; 2) "the act or omission was unlawful and intentional"; 3) "the unlawful act or omission must be part of a widespread or systematic attack"; 4) "the attack must be against the civilian population"; 5) "the attack must be on discriminatory grounds, namely: national, political, ethnic, racial, or religious grounds."[2040] [2041]

It is also a requirement of the crime of extermination that the perpetrators "must (...) known of the vast scheme of collective murder" and manifested their will "to take part therein."[2042] The existence of a *plan* or a *policy* does not constitute a formal requirement of the crime of persecution as a crime against humanity. However, when such a plan or policy exists, it may provide evidence to verify the occurrence of the extermination crime.[2043] In contrast, in Prosecutor v. Vidoje Blagojević, Dragan Jokić, the ICTY Trial Chamber did not consider "the existence of a "vast scheme of collective murder" or "vast murderous enterprise" as a separate element of the crime nor as an additional layer of the *mens rea* required for the commission of the crime."[2044]

---

[2038] In this regard, the ICTY concluded that "the offender must intend to kill, to inflict grievous bodily harm, or to inflict serious injury, in the reasonable knowledge that such act or omission is likely to cause death, or otherwise intends to participate in the elimination of a number of individuals, in the knowledge that his action is part of a vast murderous enterprise in which a large number of individuals are systematically marked for killing or killed." (Prosecutor v. Mitar Vasiljević. IT-98-32-T. *Supra* note 117. ¶ 229).

[2039] See also: Prosecutor v. Vidoje Blagojević, Dragan Jokić. IT-02-60-T. *Supra* note 147. ¶¶ 572–573; Prosecutor v. Momčilo Krajišnik. IT-00-39-T. *Supra* note 121. ¶ 716; Prosecutor v. Milan Lukić, Sredoje Lukić. IT-98-32/1-T. *Supra* note 104. ¶ 937.

[2040] Prosecutor v. Jean-Paul Akayesu. ICTR-96-4-T. *Supra* note 203. ¶¶ 591–592. See also: Prosecutor v. Musema. ICTR-96-13-A. *Supra* note 216. ¶ 217; Prosecutor v. François Karera. ICTR-01-74-T. *Supra* note 184. ¶ 552; Prosecutor v. Emmanuel Rukundo. ICTR-2001-70-T. *Supra* note 179. ¶ 586.

[2041] The SCSL has a similar set of requirements. See, for example: Prosecutor v. Brima, Kamara, Kanu. SCSL-04-16-T. *Supra* note 280. ¶¶ 684–685.

[2042] Prosecutor v. Mitar Vasiljević. IT-98-32-T. *Supra* note 117. ¶¶ 228–229; Prosecutor v. Vidoje Blagojević, Dragan Jokić. IT-02-60-T. *Supra* note 147. ¶ 575.

[2043] Prosecutor v. Vidoje Blagojević, Dragan Jokić. IT-02-60-T. *Supra* note 147. ¶ 576.

[2044] *Ibidem.*

## 3.2.2.4. Torture

For the purposes and requirements of International Criminal Law, the essential elements of torture, prohibited at all times under customary international law,[2045] may be defined as: (i) "The perpetrator must intentionally inflict severe physical or mental pain or suffering upon the victim for one or more of the following purposes": (a) "to obtain information or a confession from the victim or a third person"; (b) "to punish the victim or a third person for an act committed or suspected of having been committed by either of them"; (c) "for the purpose of intimidating or coercing the victim or the third person"; (d) "for any reason based on discrimination of any kind."[2046] [2047] (ii) "The perpetrator was himself an official, or acted at the instigation of, or with the consent or acquiescence of, an official or person acting in an official capacity."[2048] [2049]

If, in addition to these essential elements, the following further elements are satisfied, torture may be considered as a crime against humanity: (a) "torture must be perpetrated as part of a widespread or systematic attack"; (b) "the attack must be against the civilian population"; (c) "the attack must be launched on discriminatory grounds, namely: national, ethnic, racial, religious and political grounds."[2050]

Three critical aspects must be observed concerning the essential elements/requirements of torture under International Criminal Law: Firstly) The *underlying prohibited purpose* behind the mistreating offense of torture need not be the *exclusive*, the *predominant*, or the *sole purpose* of the perpetrators in committing the crime; Secondly) There is no jurisprudential requirement that the underlying purpose of torturing the victim bears an illegitimate purpose; Thirdly) By definition, reflected by customary international law, torture cannot be committed by individuals acting in a private capacity, that is, the conduct must be committed by individuals acting in an official capacity – public official requirement.[2051]

Inflicting severe pain or suffering is a constitutive element of the crime of torture – implicit *substantial gravity* requirement/threshold –, although there is no dispositive list in customary international law – "exhaustive

---

[2045] Prosecutor v. Jean-Paul Akayesu. ICTR-96-4-T. *Supra* note 203. ¶ 594.
[2046] Prosecutor v. Milorad Krnojelac. IT-97-25-T. *Supra* note 111. ¶¶ 184–185, 241.
[2047] Prosecutor v. Jean-Paul Akayesu. ICTR-96-4-T. *Supra* note 203. ¶¶ 593, 594.
[2048] *Idem.* ¶ 594.
[2049] See also: *Idem.* ¶ 593.
[2050] *Idem.* ¶¶ 593, 595.
[2051] Prosecutor v. Milorad Krnojelac. IT-97-25-T. *Supra* note 111. ¶¶ 184, 186, 241; Prosecutor v. Dragoljub Kunarac *et al.* IT-96-23/1-A. *Supra* note 85. ¶ 146.

classification" – of which underlying acts suffice the "severity test."[2052] The assessment of the degree of severity of the *visible* physical or mental pain/suffering charged as torture must follow a holistic approach considering all the circumstances of the case as a whole.[2053] [2054] These circumstances include: 1) the nature of the pain inflicted on the victims; 2) the general context in which the torture was perpetrated; 3) the severity of the inflicted pain; 4) the premeditation of torture; 5) the authorities' institutionalization of torture; 6) the victim's physical/organic condition; 7) the nature of the torturing methods; 8) the prolonged period of time to which a victim was subjected to torture; 9) whether the victim was subjected to the same form/manner of torture or to different torturing methods; and 10) the superiority position of the perpetrator.[2055] Particular forms of violence, such as rape, imply/establish *per se* severe pain or suffering, whether physical or mental, as required by the definition/characterization of the crime of torture, even when absent a medical certificate.[2056] [2057]

## 3.2.2.5. Persecution

The Rome Statute defines persecution as the "intentional and severe deprivation of fundamental rights contrary to international law by reason of the identity of the group or collectivity."[2058] The crime of persecution, as a

---

[2052] Prosecutor v. Dragoljub Kunarac *et al.* IT-96-23/1-A. *Supra* note 85. ¶ 149. See also: Prosecutor v. Radoslav Brđanin. IT-99-36-A. *Supra* note 131. ¶¶ 240, 251.

[2053] Prosecutor v. Milorad Krnojelac. IT-97-25-T. *Supra* note 111. ¶¶ 181–182, 219, 241; Prosecutor v. Dragoljub Kunarac *et al.* IT-96-23/1-A. *Supra* note 85. ¶ 149.

[2054] The Convention against Torture's drafting history makes clear that "severe pain or suffering is not synonymous with extreme pain or suffering, and that the latter is a more intense level of pain and suffering – one that might come closer to pain ... equivalent in intensity to the pain accompanying serious physical injury, such as organ failure, impairment of bodily function, or even death – not required by the Convention against Torture." (Prosecutor v. Radoslav Brđanin. IT-99-36-A. *Supra* note 131. ¶ 240, 251).

[2055] Prosecutor v. Milorad Krnojelac. IT-97-25-T. *Supra* note 111. ¶ 182.

[2056] Prosecutor v. Dragoljub Kunarac *et al.* IT-96-23/1-A. *Supra* note 85. ¶¶ 150–151.

[2057] It is important to mention that, for the purposes of International Criminal Law, "solitary confinement is not, in and of itself, a form of torture. However, in view of its strictness, its duration, and the object pursued, solitary confinement could cause great physical or mental suffering of the sort envisaged by this offence. To the extent that the confinement of the victim can be shown to pursue one of the prohibited purposes of torture and to have caused the victim severe pain or suffering, the act of putting or keeping someone in solitary confinement may amount to torture." (Prosecutor v. Milorad Krnojelac. IT-97-25-T. *Supra* note 111. ¶ 183).

[2058] United Nations. Rome Statute (July 17, 1998) 2187 UNTS 38544. Article 7.2.g.

crime against humanity, consists of an act or omission which 1) "discriminates in fact and denies or infringes upon a fundamental right laid down in international customary or treaty law (the actus reus);" and 2) is "carried out deliberately with the intention to discriminate on one of the listed grounds," specifically race, religion, ethnicity or politics (the *mens rea*).[2059] [2060] [2061]

In *Tadic*, the ICTY Trial Chamber established the three basic requirements for the crime of persecution: (1) "the occurrence of a discriminatory act or omission"; (2) "a discriminatory basis for that act or omission on one of the listed grounds, specifically race, religion or politics"; and (3) "the intent to cause, and a resulting infringement of an individual's enjoyment of a basic or fundamental right."[2062] [2063] Although the occurrence of such discriminatory acts or omissions is generally part of discriminatory policies or governmental practices – or are supported by them –, the existence of such policies does not constitute a requirement for the crime of perse-

---

[2059] Prosecutor v. Zoran Kupreškić, et al. IT-95-16-T. *Supra* note 156. ¶ 627. See also: Prosecutor v. Miroslav Kvočka et al. IT-98-30/1-T. *Supra* note 114. ¶ 184; Prosecutor v. Milorad Krnojelac. IT-97-25-T. *Supra* note 111. ¶ 431; Prosecutor v. Mitar Vasiljević. IT-98-32-T. *Supra* note 117. ¶ 244; Prosecutor v. Mladen Naletilić, et al. IT-98-34-T. *Supra* note 119. ¶ 634; Prosecutor v. Milomir Stakić. IT-97-24-T. *Supra* note 109. ¶ 732; Prosecutor v. Blagoje Simić et al. IT-95-9-T. *Supra* note 78. ¶ 47; Prosecutor v. Tihomir Blaškić. IT-95-14-A. *Supra* note 144. ¶¶ 130-131; Prosecutor v. Radoslav Brđanin. IT-99-36-T. *Supra* note 130. ¶ 992; Prosecutor v. Dario Kordić and Mario Čerkez. IT-95-14/2-A. *Supra* note 80. ¶ 101; Prosecutor v. Vidoje Blagojević, Dragan Jokić. IT-02-60-T. *Supra* note 147. ¶ 579; Prosecutor v. Miroslav Kvočka et al. IT-98-30/1-A. *Supra* note 115. ¶¶ 320, 323; Prosecutor v. Miroslav Deronjić. IT-02-61-A. *Supra* note 113. ¶ 109; Prosecutor v. Momčilo Krajišnik. IT-00-39-T. *Supra* note 121. ¶ 734; Prosecutor v. Vujadin Popović et al. IT-05-88-T. *Supra* note 150. ¶ 964; Prosecutor v. Ante Gotovina et al. IT-06-90-T, vol. I. *Supra* note 76. ¶ 1802; Prosecutor v. Momčilo Perišić. IT-04-81-T. *Supra* note 123. ¶ 118; Prosecutor v. Zdravko Tolimir. IT-05-88/2-T. *Supra* note 153. ¶ 846; Prosecutor v. Mićo Stanišić, Stojan Župljanin. IT-08-91-T, vol. 1. *Supra* note 102. ¶ 66; Prosecutor v. Jadranko Prlić, et al. IT-04-74-T, vol. I. *Supra* note 99. ¶ 72; Prosecutor v. Jovica Stanišić and Franko Simatović. IT-03-69-T, vol. I. *Supra* note 101. ¶ 1238; Prosecutor v. Vlastimir Đorđević. IT-05-87/1-A. *Supra* note 149. ¶¶ 557–558; Prosecutor v. Radovan Karadžić. IT-95-5/18-T, vol. I. *Supra* note 134. ¶ 497.

[2060] Prosecutor v. Simon Bikindi. ICTR-01-72-T. *Supra* note 226. ¶ 435; Prosecutor v. Théoneste Bagosora et al. ICTR-98-41-T. *Supra* note 234. ¶ 2208; Prosecutor v. Pauline Nyiramasuhuko et al. ICTR-98-42-A. *Supra* note 220. ¶ 2138.

[2061] Prosecutor v. Bosco Ntaganda. ICC-01/04-02/06. *Supra* note 328. ¶ 988.

[2062] Prosecutor v. Duško Tadic. IT-94-1-T. *Supra* note 89. ¶ 715.

[2063] See also: Prosecutor v. Jean-Paul Akayesu. ICTR-96-4-T. *Supra* note 203. ¶ 583; Prosecutor v. Jean-Paul Akayesu. ICTR-96-4-A. *Supra* note 204. ¶ 464; Prosecutor v. Pauline Nyiramasuhuko et al. ICTR-98-42-A. *Supra* note 220. ¶ 2138.

cution.[2064] Ultimately, what matters in the course of the persecutory acts/omissions is the "intent to discriminate."[2065]

The Elements of Crimes of the International Criminal Court establishes six constitutive bases for the crime against humanity of persecution as follows:

"1. The perpetrator severely deprived, contrary to international law, one or more persons of fundamental rights.

2. The perpetrator targeted such person or persons by reason of the identity of a group or collectivity or targeted the group or collectivity as such.

3. Such targeting was based on political, racial, national, ethnic, cultural, religious, gender as defined in article 7, paragraph 3, of the Statute, or other grounds that are universally recognized as impermissible under international law.[2066]

4. The conduct was committed in connection with any act referred to in article 7, paragraph 1, of the Statute or any crime within the jurisdiction of the Court.[2067]

5. The conduct was committed as part of a widespread or systematic attack directed against a civilian population.

6. The perpetrator knew that the conduct was part of or intended the conduct to be part of a widespread or systematic attack directed against a civilian population."[2068]

The crime of persecution is a unique type of crime against humanity because it requires a specific discriminatory intent with a cumulative effect.[2069] This

---

[2064] Prosecutor v. Dario Kordić and Mario Čerkez. IT-95-14/2-T. *Supra* note 80. ¶ 211; Prosecutor v. Vidoje Blagojević, Dragan Jokić. IT-02-60-T. *Supra* note 147. ¶ 582; Prosecutor v. Milan Lukić, Sredoje Lukić. IT-98-32/1-T. *Supra* note 104. ¶ 994; Prosecutor v. Vujadin Popović *et al.* IT-05-88-T. *Supra* note 150. ¶ 967.

[2065] Prosecutor v. Dario Kordić and Mario Čerkez. IT-95-14/2-T. *Supra* note 80. ¶¶ 211, 213.

[2066] "For the purpose of this Statute, it is understood that the term "gender" refers to the two sexes, male and female, within the context of society [...]." United Nations. Rome Statute (July 17, 1998) 2187 UNTS 38544. Article 7.3.

[2067] "For the purpose of this Statute, "crime against humanity" means any of the following acts when committed as part of a widespread or systematic attack directed against any civilian population, with knowledge of the attack." *Idem.* Article 7.1.

[2068] International Criminal Court (ICC), Elements of Crimes, 2013. Reproduced from the Official Records of the Assembly of States Parties to the Rome Statute of the International Criminal Court, First session, New York, 3–10 September 2002, part II.B. The Elements of Crimes adopted at the 2010 Review Conference. Article 7.1.h.

[2069] Prosecutor v. Dario Kordić and Mario Čerkez. IT-95-14/2-T. *Supra* note 80. ¶¶ 189, 199, 212; Prosecutor v. Mitar Vasiljević. IT-98-32-T. *Supra* note 117. ¶ 248.

means that, in addition to fulfilling the general requirements of a crime against humanity, the perpetrator's acts must be carried on discriminatory grounds – the victim of the widespread or systematic attack is targeted by virtue of their membership to a political, racial, or religious group. Such a cumulative effect makes the definition of the crime of persecution *mens rea* a "complex task."[2070] Although the term "persecution" is frequently used to describe a series of acts, a single act may constitute persecution 1) If it discriminates in fact; 2) If "committed within the appropriate context," with the requisite knowledge; and 3) if it is "carried out deliberately with the intent to discriminate on a prohibited ground."[2071] [2072]

When prosecuting persecution as a crime against humanity, observance of the principle of legality – *nullum crimen sine lege* – must be strictly respected. This requires that, in factual cases, the underlying acts committed by the perpetrator bear a *specific* discriminatory intent – *in fact* persecutory – rather than a general/broad intent to discriminate – persecution *in general*.[2073] The verification of such discriminatory intent may be directly assessed or inferred from the surrounding political, racial, or religious circumstances and discriminatory acts of the accused.[2074]

International criminal case-law has already extensively stressed that neither international treaty law nor customary international law provides

---

[2070] Prosecutor v. Dario Kordić and Mario Čerkez. IT-95-14/2-T. *Supra* note 80. ¶ 211; Prosecutor v. Momčilo Krajišnik. IT-00-39-T. *Supra* note 121. ¶ 747.

[2071] Prosecutor v. Jadranko Prlić, *et al.* IT-04-74-T, vol. I. *Supra* note 99. ¶ 74.

[2072] See also: Prosecutor v. Zoran Kupreškić, *et al.* IT-95-16-T. *Supra* note 156. ¶ 624; Prosecutor v. Milorad Krnojelac. IT-97-25-T. *Supra* note 111. ¶ 433; Prosecutor v. Mitar Vasiljević. IT-98-32-T. *Supra* note 117. ¶ 246; Prosecutor v. Blagoje Simić *et al.* IT-95-9-T. *Supra* note 78. ¶ 50; Prosecutor v. Tihomir Blaškić. IT-95-14-A. *Supra* note 144. ¶¶ 135, 162; Prosecutor v. Radoslav Brđanin. IT-99-36-T. *Supra* note 130. ¶ 994; Prosecutor v. Dario Kordić and Mario Čerkez. IT-95-14/2-A. *Supra* note 80. ¶ 102; Prosecutor v. Vidoje Blagojević, Dragan Jokić. IT-02-60-T. *Supra* note 147. ¶ 582; Prosecutor v. Miroslav Deronjić. IT-02-61-A. *Supra* note 113. ¶ 108; Prosecutor v. Nikola Šainović *et al.* IT-05-87-T, vol. 1. *Supra* note 125. ¶ 179; Prosecutor v. Vujadin Popović *et al.* IT-05-88-T. *Supra* note 150. ¶ 965; Prosecutor v. Zdravko Tolimir. IT-05-88/2-T. *Supra* note 153. ¶ 847; Prosecutor v. Mićo Stanišić, Stojan Župljanin. IT-08-91-T, vol. 1. *Supra* note 102. ¶ 68.

[2073] Prosecutor v. Dario Kordić and Mario Čerkez. IT-95-14/2-T. *Supra* note 80. ¶¶ 192, 195, 202, 211; Prosecutor v. Mitar Vasiljević. IT-98-32-T. *Supra* note 117. ¶¶ 246, 249; Prosecutor v. Radoslav Brđanin. IT-99-36-T. *Supra* note 130. ¶ 994.

[2074] Prosecutor v. Radoslav Brđanin. IT-99-36-T. *Supra* note 130. ¶ 997; Prosecutor v. Dario Kordić and Mario Čerkez. IT-95-14/2-A. *Supra* note 80. ¶ 674; Prosecutor v. Vidoje Blagojević, Dragan Jokić. IT-02-60-T. *Supra* note 147. ¶ 584; Prosecutor v. Mladen Naletilić *et al.* IT-98-34-T. *Supra* note 120. ¶ 146; Prosecutor v. Vujadin Popović *et al.* IT-05-88-T. *Supra* note 150. ¶ 969.

a "comprehensive list of illegal acts encompassed by the charge of persecution."[2075] [2076] The grounds listed in various international criminal statutes consist of a *numerus apertus* list.[2077] Thus, persecution as a crime
against humanity may assume "different inhuman forms" and encompass
a variety of acts of physical and mental harm that are not explicitly mentioned in treaty law as long as such acts are committed on discriminatory
grounds.[2078] Therefore, the crime of persecution is regarded by customary
International Criminal Law as an "umbrella crime."[2079] [2080]

However, in observance of the commands of strict legality – *nullum
crimen, nulla poena sine lege* –, not every persecutory "act or omission denying a fundamental human right is serious enough to constitute a crime
against humanity."[2081] [2082] [2083] It is settled jurisprudence that the underlying

---

[2075]   Prosecutor v. Dario Kordić and Mario Čerkez. IT-95-14/2-T. *Supra* note 80. ¶ 192.

[2076]   See also: Prosecutor v. Duško Tadic. IT-94-1-T. *Supra* note 89. ¶ 712; Prosecutor v.
Milorad Krnojelac. IT-97-25-T. *Supra* note 111. ¶ 433; Prosecutor v. Radoslav
Brđanin. IT-99-36-T. *Supra* note 130. ¶ 994; Prosecutor v. Vujadin Popović *et al.* IT-
05-88-T. *Supra* note 150. ¶ 965.

[2077]   Prosecutor v. Duško Tadic. IT-94-1-T. *Supra* note 89. ¶ 712.

[2078]   Prosecutor v. Duško Tadic. IT-94-1-T. *Supra* note 89. ¶¶ 703, 707–708, 710–711;
Prosecutor v. Zoran Kupreškić, *et al.* IT-95-16-T. *Supra* note 156. ¶ 608; Prosecutor
v. Tihomir Blaškić. IT-95-14-T. *Supra* note 143. ¶ 218; Prosecutor v. Dario Kordić
and Mario Čerkez. IT-95-14/2-T. *Supra* note 80. ¶¶ 193-194, 208; Prosecutor v. Milorad Krnojelac. IT-97-25-T. *Supra* note 111. ¶ 433; Prosecutor v. Mitar Vasiljević.
IT-98-32-T. *Supra* note 117. ¶ 246; Prosecutor v. Milomir Stakić. IT-97-24-T. *Supra*
note 109. ¶ 735; Prosecutor v. Radoslav Brđanin. IT-99-36-T. *Supra* note 130. ¶ 994;
Prosecutor v. Momčilo Perišić. IT-04-81-T. *Supra* note 123. ¶ 119; Prosecutor v.
Zdravko Tolimir. IT-05-88/2-T. *Supra* note 153. ¶ 847.

[2079]   Prosecutor v. Predrag Banović. IT-02-65/1-S. *Supra* note 127. ¶ 38.

[2080]   See also: Prosecutor v. Zoran Kupreškić, *et al.* IT-95-16-T. *Supra* note 156. ¶ 8; Prosecutor v. Vidoje Blagojević, Dragan Jokić. IT-02-60-T. *Supra* note 147. ¶ 581; Prosecutor v. Vujadin Popović *et al.* IT-05-88-T. *Supra* note 150. ¶ 965; Prosecutor v. Mićo
Stanišić, Stojan Župljanin. IT-08-91-T, vol. 1. *Supra* note 102. ¶ 67.

[2081]   Prosecutor v. Milorad Krnojelac. IT-97-25-T. *Supra* note 111. ¶ 434.

[2082]   See also: Prosecutor v. Jean-Pierre Bemba Gombo. ICC-01/05-01/08. *Supra* note
335. ¶ 83.

[2083]   See also: Prosecutor v. Mitar Vasiljević. IT-98-32-T. *Supra* note 117. ¶ 246; Prosecutor v. Milomir Stakić. IT-97-24-T. *Supra* note 109. ¶ 735; Prosecutor v. Blagoje Simić
*et al.* IT-95-9-T. *Supra* note 78. ¶¶ 48, 50; Prosecutor v. Tihomir Blaškić. IT-95-14-A.
*Supra* note 144. ¶ 140; Prosecutor v. Radoslav Brđanin. IT-99-36-T. *Supra* note 130.
¶ 995; Prosecutor v. Vidoje Blagojević, Dragan Jokić. IT-02-60-T. *Supra* note 147. ¶
580; Prosecutor v. Momčilo Krajišnik. IT-00-39-T. *Supra* note 121. ¶ 735; Prosecutor
v. Nikola Šainović *et al.* IT-05-87-T, vol. 1. *Supra* note 125. ¶ 178; Prosecutor v. Vujadin Popović *et al.* IT-05-88-T. *Supra* note 150. ¶ 966; Prosecutor v. Ante Gotovina *et
al.* IT-06-90-T, vol. I. *Supra* note 76. ¶ 1803; Prosecutor v. Zdravko Tolimir. IT-05-

persecutory act(s) or omission(s), considered in isolation or in conjunction with other acts, must satisfy a severity test/requirement by demonstrating that they have "the same level of gravity as the other crimes against humanity" enumerated in the *caput* of the article that defines these crimes.[2084] The test of equal gravity requires that the underlying persecutory act or omission comprises a "gross or blatant denial of a fundamental right" "laid down in international customary or treaty law."[2085] The determination of whether such act(s) or omission(s) meets the *test* must always be analyzed on a case-by-case basis, taking into consideration their cumulative effect in context.[2086]

In customary International Criminal Law, several underlying acts have already been charged as persecution as a crime against humanity. For instance, murder; physical abuse and torture; psychological abuse and harassment; rape and other acts of sexual violence; terrorizing the civilian population with acts or threats of violence; forcing victims to live under inhumane conditions; the removal of civilians from their homes or the for-

---

88/2-T. *Supra* note 153. ¶ 848; Prosecutor v. Jovica Stanišić and Franko Simatović. IT-03-69-T, vol. I. *Supra* note 101. ¶ 1239.

[2084] Prosecutor v. Zoran Kupreškić, *et al.* IT-95-16-T. *Supra* note 156. ¶¶ 619, 621. See also: Prosecutor v. Miroslav Kvočka *et al.* IT-98-30/1-T. *Supra* note 114. ¶ 185; Prosecutor v. Milorad Krnojelac. IT-97-25-T. *Supra* note 111. ¶ 434; Prosecutor v. Mitar Vasiljević. IT-98-32-T. *Supra* note 117. ¶¶ 247, 251; Prosecutor v. Milomir Stakić. IT-97-24-T. *Supra* note 109. ¶ 736; Prosecutor v. Blagoje Simić *et al.* IT-95-9-T. *Supra* note 78. ¶ 48; Prosecutor v. Radoslav Brđanin. IT-99-36-T. *Supra* note 130. ¶ 995; Prosecutor v. Miroslav Kvočka *et al.* IT-98-30/1-A. *Supra* note 115. ¶ 321; Prosecutor v. Momčilo Krajišnik. IT-00-39-T. *Supra* note 121. ¶ 735; Prosecutor v. Radoslav Brđanin. IT-99-36-A. *Supra* note 131. ¶ 296; Prosecutor v. Nikola Šainović *et al.* IT-05-87-T, vol. 1. *Supra* note 125. ¶¶ 178–179, 193; Prosecutor v. Vujadin Popović *et al.* IT-05-88-T. *Supra* note 150. ¶ 966; Prosecutor v. Mićo Stanišić, Stojan Župljanin. IT-08-91-T, vol. 1. *Supra* note 102. ¶ 70; Prosecutor v. Jadranko Prlić, *et al.* IT-04-74-T, vol. I. *Supra* note 99. ¶ 75; Prosecutor v. Jovica Stanišić and Franko Simatović. IT-03-69-T, vol. I. *Supra* note 101. ¶ 1239; Prosecutor v. Radovan Karadžić. IT-95-5/18-T, vol. I. *Supra* note 134. ¶ 499.

[2085] Prosecutor v. Zdravko Tolimir. IT-05-88/2-T. *Supra* note 153. ¶ 848.

[2086] Prosecutor v. Zoran Kupreškić, *et al.* IT-95-16-T. *Supra* note 156. ¶ 622; Prosecutor v. Miroslav Kvočka *et al.* IT-98-30/1-T. *Supra* note 114. ¶ 185; Prosecutor v. Mitar Vasiljević. IT-98-32-T. *Supra* note 117. ¶¶ 247, 250; Prosecutor v. Laurent Semanza. ICTR-97-20-T. *Supra* note 211. ¶ 344; Prosecutor v. Blagoje Simić *et al.* IT-95-9-T. *Supra* note 78. ¶ 48; Prosecutor v. Radoslav Brđanin. IT-99-36-T. *Supra* note 130. ¶ 995; Prosecutor v. Miroslav Kvočka *et al.* IT-98-30/1-A. *Supra* note 115. ¶ 321; Prosecutor v. Vujadin Popović *et al.* IT-05-88-T. *Supra* note 150. ¶ 965; Prosecutor v. Mićo Stanišić, Stojan Župljanin. IT-08-91-T, vol. 1. *Supra* note 102. ¶ 70; Prosecutor v. Jadranko Prlić, *et al.* IT-04-74-T, vol. I. *Supra* note 99. ¶ 75.

cible transfer/deportation of victims; separation of the men from the women and children; enforced disappearance; unlawful detention or cruel or inhumane treatment in custody facilities; forced labor; use of victims as human shields; the destruction, appropriation, plunder, confiscation, or destruction of personal property with discriminatory intent; the intentional destruction of places of worship; the establishment of restraining and discriminatory policies in disrespect of international human rights norms, such as restrictions on freedom of movement, use of economic measures against the civilian population, denial of employment, dismissal *en masse,* the arbitrary searches of homes in violation of the right to privacy, the denial of the right to a fair trial, and restrictions on the equal access to public services.[2087] [2088] [2089] [2090]

---

[2087] Prosecutor v. Duško Tadic. IT-94-1-T. *Supra* note 89. ¶ 708; Prosecutor v. Zoran Kupreškić, *et al.* IT-95-16-T. *Supra* note 156. ¶¶ 628–631; Prosecutor v. Tihomir Blaškić. IT-95-14-T. *Supra* note 143. ¶ 218; Prosecutor v. Dario Kordić and Mario Čerkez. IT-95-14/2-T. *Supra* note 80. ¶¶ 203–207; Prosecutor v. Miroslav Kvočka *et al.* IT-98-30/1-T. *Supra* note 114. ¶¶ 190–192; Prosecutor v. Milorad Krnojelac. IT-97-25-T. *Supra* note 111. ¶¶ 182–183, 440–443, 466–485, 748–749, 807–809; Prosecutor v. Mitar Vasiljević. IT-98-32-T. *Supra* note 117. ¶ 250; Prosecutor v. Mladen Naletilić, *et al.* IT-98-34-T. *Supra* note 119. ¶ 632; Prosecutor v. Tihomir Blaškić. IT-95-14-A. *Supra* note 144. ¶¶ 143–145, 149–153, 159; Prosecutor v. Radoslav Brđanin. IT-99-36-T. *Supra* note 130. ¶¶ 1001–1020, 1023, 1025, 1029, 1031–1041; Prosecutor v. Dario Kordić and Mario Čerkez. IT-95-14/2-A. *Supra* note 80. ¶¶ 104, 106–108; Prosecutor v. Vidoje Blagojević, Dragan Jokić. IT-02-60-T. *Supra* note 147. ¶¶ 585–591, 594–602, 606–608, 611, 614, 616–621; Prosecutor v. Miroslav Kvočka *et al.* IT-98-30/1-A. *Supra* note 115. ¶¶ 190, 323, 326–327, 329–334; Prosecutor v. Momčilo Krajišnik. IT-00-39-T. *Supra* note 121. ¶¶ 736, 742–747, 751–752, 754, 758, 760–761, 763–764, 768–772, 778, 780–783, 792–794, 796, 805–806, 812–814, 816–819, 821–828, 834–840; Prosecutor v. Nikola Šainović *et al.* IT-05-87-T, vol. 1. *Supra* note 125. ¶¶ 182–192, 205–206, 210; Prosecutor v. Vujadin Popović *et al.* IT-05-88-T. *Supra* note 150. ¶¶ 963, 971–975, 978–980, 988–989, 990–991, 994–999, 1002–1003; Prosecutor v. Ante Gotovina *et al.* IT-06-90-T, vol. I. *Supra* note 76. ¶¶ 1804–1808, 1811–1812, 1814–1815, 1817, 1821, 1823, 1826–1829, 1836–1839, 1842, 1846–1855, 1860–1863, 1876, 1881, 1890; Prosecutor v. Momčilo Perišić. IT-04-81-T. *Supra* note 123. ¶¶ 117, 120; Prosecutor v. Zdravko Tolimir. IT-05-88/2-T. *Supra* note 153. ¶¶ 845, 851, 856–857, 859–860, 861–863, 869, 878–881; Prosecutor v. Mićo Stanišić, Stojan Župljanin. IT-08-91-T, vol. 1. *Supra* note 102. ¶¶ 71–72, 76–82, 85–86, 91–92; Prosecutor v. Jovica Stanišić and Franko Simatović. IT-03-69-T, vol. I. *Supra* note 101. ¶¶ 1240–1241, 1243–1248; Prosecutor v. Vlastimir Đorđević. IT-05-87/1-A. *Supra* note 149. ¶¶ 553, 559; Prosecutor v. Radovan Karadžić. IT-95-5/18-T, vol. I. *Supra* note 134. ¶¶ 496, 501–502, 503–504, 521–526, 529, 531, 535–536, 1042, 1097, 2063, 2117.

[2088] Prosecutor v. Simon Bikindi. ICTR-01-72-T. *Supra* note 226. ¶ 392.

[2089] Prosecutor v. Francis Kirimi Muthaura *et al.* ICC-01/09-02/11. *Supra* note 331. ¶¶ 281, 283.

It is important to note that some appropriation/destruction of private property can be regarded as lawful – as a general exception to the rules of the International Humanitarian Law – when it is "rendered absolutely necessary by military operations."[2091] [2092] However, confiscation, plunder or comprehensive destruction of private houses may constitute persecution if committed on discriminatory grounds against a legally protected group.[2093] In *Prosecutor v. Momčilo Krajišnik*, the ICTY Trial Chamber considered that an act of plunder/destruction of property, "carried out on discriminatory grounds," may constitute the crime of persecution, as a crime against humanity, even when it does not cause a *severe impact* on the victim, when considered in conjunction with the "nature and extent of the (acts of) destruction," and with the "general constituent elements of crimes against humanity."[2094] [2095] The "economic and emotional value of the property" and the impact on the victims of the wanton appropriation and destruction of their indispensable and vital property – whether "severe enough" – constitutes a decisive factor for the determination of a crime against humanity.[2096]

For an attack to constitute persecution as a crime against humanity, the underlying act or omission "must have been carried out deliberately,"

---

[2090]  "It is not necessary that the victim of the crime of persecution be a member of the group against whom the perpetrator of the crime intended to discriminate." (Prosecutor v. Radoslav Brđanin. IT-99-36-T. *Supra* note 130. ¶ 993).

[2091]  Prosecutor v. Momčilo Krajišnik. IT-00-39-T. *Supra* note 121. ¶¶ 769, 776; Prosecutor v. Radovan Karadžić. IT-95-5/18-T, vol. 1. *Supra* note 134. ¶ 2550.

[2092]  See also: Prosecutor v. Vidoje Blagojević, Dragan Jokić. IT-02-60-T. *Supra* note 147. ¶ 593.

[2093]  Prosecutor v. Vidoje Blagojević, Dragan Jokić. IT-02-60-T. *Supra* note 147. ¶ 594; Prosecutor v. Momčilo Krajišnik. IT-00-39-T. *Supra* note 121. ¶¶ 773, 823–824, 827, 829; Prosecutor v. Radovan Karadžić. IT-95-5/18-T, vol. 1. *Supra* note 134. ¶ 2555.

[2094]  Plunder encompasses "all forms of unlawful appropriation of property in armed conflict for which individual responsibility attaches under international law, including those acts traditionally described as 'pillage'". (...) Plunder acts of appropriation include "both widespread and systematized acts of dispossession and acquisition of property in violation of the rights of the owners and isolated acts of theft or plunder by individuals for their private gain." (Prosecutor v. Milomir Stakić. IT-97-24-T. *Supra* note 109. ¶ 762).

[2095]  Prosecutor v. Vidoje Blagojević, Dragan Jokić. IT-02-60-T. *Supra* note 147. ¶ 594; Prosecutor v. Momčilo Krajišnik. IT-00-39-T. *Supra* note 121. ¶¶ 768, 771–772, 774–775, 778–779, 824, 828; Prosecutor v. Radovan Karadžić. IT-95-5/18-T, vol. 1. *Supra* note 134. ¶ 2547.

[2096]  Prosecutor v. Vidoje Blagojević, Dragan Jokić. IT-02-60-T. *Supra* note 147. ¶ 594; Prosecutor v. Momčilo Krajišnik. IT-00-39-T. *Supra* note 121. ¶¶ 774, 824; Prosecutor v. Radovan Karadžić. IT-95-5/18-T, vol. 1. *Supra* note 134. ¶ 2557.

with the *intent* to discriminate on political, racial, ethnic, or religious grounds – *dolus specialis*.[2097] [2098] Relevantly, international criminal case-law has already stressed on numerous occasions that "there is no requirement in law that the actor possesses a "persecutory intent" over and above a discriminatory intent."[2099] [2100] What ultimately matters is that the perpetrator "must consciously intend to discriminate."[2101] [2102]

Therefore, the *mens rea* for persecution requires proof beyond a reasonable doubt of the "specific intent to cause injury to a human being because he belongs to a particular community or group."[2103] [2104] The context, objective facts, and surrounding circumstances in which the persecutory acts or omissions of the accused took place may corroborate the existence of discriminatory intent by *inference*. However, such intent cannot be inferred *directly* and *solely* "from the overall discriminatory nature of an attack characterized as a crime against humanity."[2105] [2106]

---

[2097] Prosecutor v. Nikola Šainović *et al.* IT-05-87-T, vol. 1. *Supra* note 125. ¶ 180.

[2098] See also: Prosecutor v. Zoran Kupreškić, *et al.* IT-95-16-T. *Supra* note 156. ¶ 607; Prosecutor v. Dario Kordić and Mario Čerkez. IT-95-14/2-T. *Supra* note 80. ¶¶ 211–213; Prosecutor v. Miroslav Kvočka *et al.* IT-98-30/1-T. *Supra* note 114. ¶ 194; Prosecutor v. Milorad Krnojelac. IT-97-25-T. *Supra* note 111. ¶ 435; Prosecutor v. Mitar Vasiljević. IT-98-32-T. *Supra* note 117. ¶ 248; Prosecutor v. Mladen Naletilić, *et al.* IT-98-34-T. *Supra* note 119. ¶ 638; Prosecutor v. Laurent Semanza. ICTR-97-20-T. *Supra* note 211. ¶ 350; Prosecutor v. Milomir Stakić. IT-97-24-T. *Supra* note 109. ¶¶ 737–738; Prosecutor v. Tihomir Blaškić. IT-95-14-A. *Supra* note 144. ¶ 164; Prosecutor v. Radoslav Brđanin. IT-99-36-T. *Supra* note 130. ¶ 1050; Prosecutor v. Dario Kordić and Mario Čerkez. IT-95-14/2-A. *Supra* note 80. ¶¶ 110, 674; Prosecutor v. Vidoje Blagojević, Dragan Jokić. IT-02-60-T. *Supra* note 147. ¶ 583; Prosecutor v. Miroslav Kvočka *et al.* IT-98-30/1-A. *Supra* note 115. ¶¶ 343, 346; Prosecutor v. Vujadin Popović *et al.* IT-05-88-T. *Supra* note 150. ¶¶ 967–969; Prosecutor v. Zdravko Tolimir. IT-05-88/2-T. *Supra* note 153. ¶ 849; Prosecutor v. Mićo Stanišić, Stojan Župljanin. IT-08-91-T, vol. 1. *Supra* note 102. ¶ 68; Prosecutor v. Jadranko Prlić, *et al.* IT-04-74-T, vol. I. *Supra* note 99. ¶ 76; Prosecutor v. Radovan Karadžić. IT-95-5/18-T, vol. I. *Supra* note 134. ¶¶ 498, 500; Prosecutor v. Vojislav Šešelj. IT-03-67-T, vol. 1. *Supra* note 145. p. 188/62399 BISa -187/62399 BISa.

[2099] Prosecutor v. Dario Kordić and Mario Čerkez. IT-95-14/2-A. *Supra* note 80. ¶ 111.

[2100] See also: Prosecutor v. Tihomir Blaškić. IT-95-14-A. *Supra* note 144. ¶ 165; Prosecutor v. Momčilo Perišić. IT-04-81-T. *Supra* note 123. ¶ 121.

[2101] Prosecutor v. Blagoje Simić *et al.* IT-95-9-T. *Supra* note 78. ¶ 51.

[2102] See also: Prosecutor v. Tihomir Blaškić. IT-95-14-T. *Supra* note 143. ¶ 244; Prosecutor v. Radoslav Brđanin. IT-99-36-T. *Supra* note 130. ¶ 996; Prosecutor v. Zdravko Tolimir. IT-05-88/2-T. *Supra* note 153. ¶ 850.

[2103] Prosecutor v. Dario Kordić and Mario Čerkez. IT-95-14/2-A. *Supra* note 80. ¶ 111.

[2104] See also: Prosecutor v. Radovan Karadžić. IT-95-5/18-T, vol. I. *Supra* note 134. ¶ 500.

[2105] Prosecutor v. Jadranko Prlić, *et al.* IT-04-74-T, vol. I. *Supra* note 99. ¶ 76.

In *Prosecutor v. Dario Kordić and Mario Čerkez*, the ICTY Trial Chamber attested that the requirement of a mental element – *mens rea* – of the crime of persecution is higher than for other types of ordinary crimes against humanity.[2107] It requires evidence that the perpetrator deliberately/consciously (*dolus specialis*) acted with the specific intent to "discriminate on political, racial or religious grounds," denying or infringing fundamental rights safeguarded by international customary or treaty law, with the "knowledge of the context of a widespread or systematic attack directed against a civilian population," through the perpetration of the underlying acts – *actus reus*.[2108]

The "discriminatory *intent*" (*dolus specialis*) – on political, racial, or religious grounds – in the conduct/attack of the perpetrators of persecution, as a crime against humanity, constitutes a particular *materially distinct/distinguishable element* – rather than *general intent*.[2109] Evidence of this element is not by itself sufficient.[2110] The specific charges of persecution must be related to the conscious discriminatory intent of the accused.[2111]

---

[2106] See also: Prosecutor v. Tihomir Blaškić. IT-95-14-A. *Supra* note 144. ¶ 164; Prosecutor v. Dario Kordić and Mario Čerkez. IT-95-14/2-A. *Supra* note 80. ¶¶ 110, 674; Prosecutor v. Vidoje Blagojević, Dragan Jokić. IT-02-60-T. *Supra* note 147. ¶ 584; Prosecutor v. Miroslav Kvočka *et al.* IT-98-30/1-A. *Supra* note 115. ¶ 366; Prosecutor v. Théoneste Bagosora *et al.* ICTR-98-41-T. *Supra* note 234. ¶ 2208; Prosecutor v. Nikola Šainović *et al.* IT-05-87-T, vol. 1. *Supra* note 125. ¶ 180; Prosecutor v. Vujadin Popović *et al.* IT-05-88-T. *Supra* note 150. ¶ 969; Prosecutor v. Momčilo Perišić. IT-04-81-T. *Supra* note 123. ¶ 122; Prosecutor v. Zdravko Tolimir. IT-05-88/2-T. *Supra* note 153. ¶ 850; Prosecutor v. Mićo Stanišić, Stojan Župljanin. IT-08-91-T, vol. 1. *Supra* note 102. ¶ 69.

[2107] Prosecutor v. Dario Kordić and Mario Čerkez. IT-95-14/2-T. *Supra* note 80. ¶ 213.

[2108] Prosecutor v. Dario Kordić and Mario Čerkez. IT-95-14/2-T. *Supra* note 80. ¶¶ 195, 203, 211. See also: Prosecutor v. Mitar Vasiljević. IT-98-32-T. *Supra* note 117. ¶ 244; Prosecutor v. Radoslav Brđanin. IT-99-36-T. *Supra* note 130. ¶¶ 992–993; Prosecutor v. Dario Kordić and Mario Čerkez. IT-95-14/2-A. *Supra* note 80. ¶ 674; Prosecutor v. Vidoje Blagojević, Dragan Jokić. IT-02-60-T. *Supra* note 147. ¶ 579; Prosecutor v. Momčilo Krajišnik. IT-00-39-T. *Supra* note 121. ¶ 734; Prosecutor v. Milan Lukić, Sredoje Lukić. IT-98-32/1-T. *Supra* note 104. ¶ 994; Prosecutor v. Vujadin Popović *et al.* IT-05-88-T. *Supra* note 150. ¶ 967; Prosecutor v. Vujadin Popović *et al.* IT-05-88-A. *Supra* note 151. ¶ 761.

[2109] Prosecutor v. Dario Kordić and Mario Čerkez. IT-95-14/2-T. *Supra* note 80. ¶ 212; Prosecutor v. Mitar Vasiljević. IT-98-32-T. *Supra* note 117. ¶ 267; Prosecutor v. Vidoje Blagojević, Dragan Jokić. IT-02-60-T. *Supra* note 147. ¶ 583; Prosecutor v. Vujadin Popović *et al.* IT-05-88-T. *Supra* note 150. ¶ 968.

[2110] Prosecutor v. Mitar Vasiljević. IT-98-32-T. *Supra* note 117. ¶¶ 245, 248–249.

[2111] Prosecutor v. Vidoje Blagojević, Dragan Jokić. IT-02-60-T. *Supra* note 147. ¶ 584.

Although there is no comprehensive cataloged list of physical and mental harm perpetrated in persecution, "not every persecutory act or omission is serious enough to constitute a crime against humanity."[2112] The underlying commissive or omissive acts of physical and mental harm that may constitute persecution, as a crime against humanity, may assume diversified forms and encompass acts not listed in the statutory norms of International Criminal Law.[2113] The crucial point of identifying an act of persecution resides in the fact that, under customary International Criminal Law, "the act or omission must, in fact, have discriminatory consequences rather than merely be done with discriminatory intent."[2114]

In *Prosecutor v. Momčilo Krajišnik*, for example, the ICTY Trial Chamber concluded that "acts imposing restrictive and discriminatory measures against Muslims and Croats constitute persecution as a crime against humanity."[2115] In *Prosecutor v. Radovan Karadžić*, the Chamber asserted that the use of persons as human shields, "carried out on discriminatory grounds," constitutes the crime of persecution as a crime against humanity.[2116] It also concluded that the "destruction of sacred sites carried out on discriminatory grounds [– not justified by military necessity –], and for which the general elements of crimes against humanity are fulfilled" "amounts to an attack on the very religious identity of a people," and, as such, "constitutes the crime of persecution."[2117]

---

[2112] Prosecutor v. Dario Kordić and Mario Čerkez. IT-95-14/2-T. *Supra* note 80. ¶¶ 192, 196. See also: Prosecutor v. Mitar Vasiljević. IT-98-32-T. *Supra* note 117. ¶ 246; Prosecutor v. Radoslav Brđanin. IT-99-36-T. *Supra* note 130. ¶ 994–995; Prosecutor v. Vidoje Blagojević, Dragan Jokić. IT-02-60-T. *Supra* note 147. ¶ 580; Prosecutor v. Vujadin Popović *et al.* IT-05-88-T. *Supra* note 150. ¶ 965;Prosecutor v. Vujadin Popović *et al.* IT-05-88-A. *Supra* note 151. ¶ 761.

[2113] Prosecutor v. Dario Kordić and Mario Čerkez. IT-95-14/2-T. *Supra* note 80. ¶ 192; Prosecutor v. Mitar Vasiljević. IT-98-32-T. *Supra* note 117. ¶ 246; Prosecutor v. Radoslav Brđanin. IT-99-36-T. *Supra* note 130. ¶ 994; Prosecutor v. Vujadin Popović *et al.* IT-05-88-T. *Supra* note 150. ¶ 965.

[2114] Prosecutor v. Dario Kordić and Mario Čerkez. IT-95-14/2-T. *Supra* note 80. ¶ 204. See also: Prosecutor v. Mitar Vasiljević. IT-98-32-T. *Supra* note 117. ¶ 245; Prosecutor v. Vidoje Blagojević, Dragan Jokić. IT-02-60-T. *Supra* note 147. ¶ 583; Prosecutor v. Vujadin Popović *et al.* IT-05-88-T. *Supra* note 150. ¶ 969.

[2115] Prosecutor v. Momčilo Krajišnik. IT-00-39-T. *Supra* note 121. ¶ 790; Prosecutor v. Radovan Karadžić. IT-95-5/18-T, vol. 1. *Supra* note 134. ¶ 2570.

[2116] Prosecutor v. Momčilo Krajišnik. IT-00-39-T. *Supra* note 121. ¶ 764; Prosecutor v. Radovan Karadžić. IT-95-5/18-T, vol. 1. *Supra* note 134. ¶¶ 2535, 2538.

[2117] Prosecutor v. Milomir Stakić. IT-97-24-T. *Supra* note 109. ¶¶ 768, 813. See also: Prosecutor v. Momčilo Krajišnik. IT-00-39-T. *Supra* note 121. ¶¶ 781, 783, 840; Prosecutor v. Radovan Karadžić. IT-95-5/18-T, vol. 1. *Supra* note 134. ¶ 2554.

Throughout its jurisprudence, the ICTY considered that some practices of the Serbian forces "repeated time and time again against the Muslim population" could constitute persecution as a crime against humanity.[2118] For instance, the shelling of Bosnian Muslim neighborhoods, restrictions on Muslims' freedom of movement, the searching of Muslim households, the appropriation/plunder of property, money, and other items, the setting on fire of Bosnian Muslim houses, and multiple accounts of Muslim women being raped.[2119] Therefore, the consideration as to whether a certain underlying discriminatory act or omission – or a series of acts/omissions – may amount to persecution is assessed "not in isolation," but rather upon a case-by-case basis, examining their context and considering their cumulative effect.[2120]

Numerous international legal instruments, as well as Customary International Criminal Law, assert that cruel and inhumane treatment may also constitute an act of persecution as a crime against humanity.[2121] Considering them all together, "cruel and inhumane treatment" is defined as "an intentional act or omission, which causes serious mental harm, physical suffering or injury, or which constitutes a serious attack on human dignity."[2122] The seriousness of such harm must present "more than a short-term or temporary effect on the victim," although it "does not need to be permanent and irremediable."[2123] The seriousness of such harm is comprehended by considering different factors, acts, or omissions of "equal"/ "sufficient gravity,"[2124] including: "the nature of the act or omission, the context in which it occurs, its duration and repetition, its physical and

---

[2118] Prosecutor v. Momčilo Krajišnik. IT-00-39-T. *Supra* note 121. ¶¶ 789, 814; Prosecutor v. Milan Lukić, Sredoje Lukić. IT-98-32/1-T. *Supra* note 104. ¶ 892.

[2119] Prosecutor v. Momčilo Krajišnik. IT-00-39-T. *Supra* note 121. ¶¶ 784, 787, 789; Prosecutor v. Milan Lukić, Sredoje Lukić. IT-98-32/1-T. *Supra* note 104. ¶ 892; Prosecutor v. Radovan Karadžić. IT-95-5/18-T, vol. 1. *Supra* note 134. ¶ 967–968, 970.

[2120] Prosecutor v. Dario Kordić and Mario Čerkez. IT-95-14/2-T. *Supra* note 80. ¶ 199; Prosecutor v. Mitar Vasiljević. IT-98-32-T. *Supra* note 117. ¶¶ 247, 249; Prosecutor v. Vidoje Blagojević, Dragan Jokić. IT-02-60-T. *Supra* note 147. ¶¶ 582, 584; Prosecutor v. Vujadin Popović *et al.* IT-05-88-T. *Supra* note 150. ¶¶ 965, 969.

[2121] Prosecutor v. Mitar Vasiljević. IT-98-32-T. *Supra* note 117. ¶ 267; Prosecutor v. Vidoje Blagojević, Dragan Jokić. IT-02-60-T. *Supra* note 147. ¶ 587; Prosecutor v. Radovan Karadžić. IT-95-5/18-T, vol. 1. *Supra* note 134. ¶ 2518.

[2122] Prosecutor v. Vidoje Blagojević, Dragan Jokić. IT-02-60-T. *Supra* note 147. ¶ 586.

[2123] *Ibidem.*

[2124] Prosecutor v. Dario Kordić and Mario Čerkez. IT-95-14/2-T. *Supra* note 80. ¶¶ 196, 201; Prosecutor v. Mitar Vasiljević. IT-98-32-T. *Supra* note 117. ¶ 247; Prosecutor v. Vidoje Blagojević, Dragan Jokić. IT-02-60-T. *Supra* note 147. ¶¶ 580, 587; Prosecutor v. Vujadin Popović *et al.* IT-05-88-T. *Supra* note 150. ¶ 966.

mental effects on the victim and, in some instances, the personal circumstances of the victim, including age, gender, and health."[2125]

Although persecutory acts or omissions are, in practice, commonly backed by a discriminatory policy, or at least supported by "a patterned discriminatory practice," the existence of such a policy does not constitute a legal requirement of the crime of persecution as a crime against humanity.[2126] Therefore, "it is not necessary that the accused have participated in the formulation of such policy or such practice by the governing authority."[2127] [2128] On the contrary, the Rome Statute in Article 7.2.a expressly asserts that an attack "directed against any civilian population" can only take place "pursuant to or in furtherance of a State or organizational policy [non-state actor] to commit such attack."

The discriminatory mens rea "must relate to the specific act or omission underlying the charge of persecution as opposed to the attack in general, notwithstanding the fact that the attack may also in practice have a discriminatory aspect."[2129] The final aim of the perpetrator must be removing from society – or "even from humanity itself" –[2130] persons "defined by the perpetrator," or subjectively perceived by the victims themselves, as belonging to legally protected groups, by "singling out and attacking certain individuals on discriminatory grounds."[2131] [2132] [2133]

While formulating the course of attack, only the perpetrator possesses the subjective perception of whether the victims are affiliated – or not – to a group that they want to discriminate against, through the commission of

---

[2125] Prosecutor v. Vidoje Blagojević, Dragan Jokić. IT-02-60-T. *Supra* note 147. ¶ 586.

[2126] Prosecutor v. Mitar Vasiljević. IT-98-32-T. *Supra* note 117. ¶ 248. See also: Prosecutor v. Milomir Stakić. IT-97-24-T. *Supra* note 109. ¶ 739; Prosecutor v. Radoslav Brđanin. IT-99-36-T. *Supra* note 130. ¶ 996; Prosecutor v. Vidoje Blagojević, Dragan Jokić. IT-02-60-T. *Supra* note 147. ¶ 582; Prosecutor v. Vujadin Popović *et al.* IT-05-88-T. *Supra* note 150. ¶ 967; Prosecutor v. Mićo Stanišić, Stojan Župljanin. IT-08-91-T, vol. 1. *Supra* note 102. ¶ 69; Prosecutor v. Radovan Karadžić. IT-95-5/18-T, vol. I. *Supra* note 134. ¶ 500

[2127] Prosecutor v. Jadranko Prlić, *et al.* IT-04-74-T, vol. I. *Supra* note 99. ¶ 76.

[2128] See also: Prosecutor v. Zoran Kupreškić, *et al.* IT-95-16-T. *Supra* note 156. ¶ 625; Prosecutor v. Milorad Krnojelac. IT-97-25-T. *Supra* note 111. ¶ 435; Prosecutor v. Blagoje Simić *et al.* IT-95-9-T. *Supra* note 78. ¶ 51.

[2129] Prosecutor v. Blagoje Simić *et al.* IT-95-9-T. *Supra* note 78. ¶ 51.

[2130] Prosecutor v. Dario Kordić and Mario Čerkez. IT-95-14/2-T. *Supra* note 80. ¶ 214.

[2131] Prosecutor v. Bosco Ntaganda. ICC-01/04-02/06. *Supra* note 328. ¶¶ 1009–1010.

[2132] Prosecutor v. Dario Kordić and Mario Čerkez. IT-95-14/2-T. *Supra* note 80. ¶ 214; Prosecutor v. Mladen Naletilić, *et al.* IT-98-34-T. *Supra* note 119. ¶ 636; Prosecutor v. Milomir Stakić. IT-97-24-T. *Supra* note 109. ¶ 734.

[2133] Prosecutor v. Dario Kordić and Mario Čerkez. IT-95-14/2-T. *Supra* note 80. ¶ 214.

impermissible acts under International Law. This means that "the targeted victims have no influence on the [perpetrators'] definition of their status."[2134] Therefore, the sole perpetrator's awareness of the existence of an attack is not sufficient to prove that "he is, in fact, acting in a way that is discriminatory."[2135]

Importantly, however, international criminal case-law considers that discriminatory intent by itself does not suffice all the legal requirements of the crime of persecution as a crime against humanity.[2136] The perpetrator's act(s) or omission(s) must, *in fact,* have discriminatory – *in fact* persecutory – consequences.[2137] Therefore, "the *mens rea* requirement for persecution is higher than for ordinary crimes against humanity [although lower than for genocide]."[2138] [2139] The prosecutorial judicial proceedings must prove the "accused's [distinguishable] intent to harm the victim on the basis of his or her affiliation with a particular group (*proof of intent*),"[2140] rather than proving the means employed by the perpetrator to achieve the attack against the victims – proof of *specificity.*[2141]

In this particular, taking the *mens rea* into consideration, persecution and genocide belong to a specific group of crimes – same *genus* –in which what matters is the intent to discriminate persons on account of their ethnic, racial, or religious characteristics ("as well as, in the case of persecution, their political affiliation"),[2142] being genocide considered as "an extreme and most inhuman form of persecution."[2143] [2144] However, while in

---

[2134]  Prosecutor v. Milomir Stakić. IT-97-24-T. *Supra* note 109. ¶ 734.

[2135]  Prosecutor v. Milorad Krnojelac. IT-97-25-T. *Supra* note 111. ¶ 435.

[2136]  Prosecutor v. Mitar Vasiljević. IT-98-32-T. *Supra* note 117. ¶ 245; Prosecutor v. Vidoje Blagojević, Dragan Jokić. IT-02-60-T. *Supra* note 147. ¶ 583; Prosecutor v. Jadranko Prlić, *et al.* IT-04-74-T, vol. I. *Supra* note 99. ¶ 73.

[2137]  Prosecutor v. Milorad Krnojelac. IT-97-25-T. *Supra* note 111. ¶¶ 432, 436; Prosecutor v. Mitar Vasiljević. IT-98-32-T. *Supra* note 117. ¶¶ 245, 249; Prosecutor v. Milomir Stakić. IT-97-24-T. *Supra* note 109. ¶ 733; Prosecutor v. Radoslav Brđanin. IT-99-36-T. *Supra* note 130. ¶¶ 993, 1050; Prosecutor v. Vidoje Blagojević, Dragan Jokić. IT-02-60-T. *Supra* note 147. ¶ 583; Prosecutor v. Nikola Šainović *et al.* IT-05-87-T, vol. 1. *Supra* note 125. ¶ 177; Prosecutor v. Radovan Karadžić. IT-95-5/18-T, vol. I. *Supra* note 134. ¶ 498.

[2138]  Prosecutor v. Dario Kordić and Mario Čerkez. IT-95-14/2-T. *Supra* note 80. ¶ 213.

[2139]  See also: Prosecutor v. Zoran Kupreškić, *et al.* IT-95-16-T. *Supra* note 156. ¶ 636.

[2140]  Prosecutor v. Zdravko Tolimir. IT-05-88/2-T. *Supra* note 153. ¶ 849.

[2141]  Prosecutor v. Dario Kordić and Mario Čerkez. IT-95-14/2-T. *Supra* note 80. ¶ 212.

[2142]  Prosecutor v. Zoran Kupreškić, *et al.* IT-95-16-T. *Supra* note 156. ¶ 636. See also: Prosecutor v. Vojislav Šešelj. IT-03-67-T, vol. 1. *Supra* note 145. p. 188/62399 BISa - 187/62399 BISa.

[2143]  Prosecutor v. Zoran Kupreškić, *et al.* IT-95-16-T. *Supra* note 156. ¶ 636.

persecution cases the "discriminatory intent can take multifarious forms and manifest itself in a plurality of inhumane acts, including murder," in genocide cases, "intent must be accompanied by the intention to destroy, in whole or in part, the group [as such]."[2145] [2146]

## 3.2.2.6. Other inhumane acts of a similar character

The *mens rea* of the crime of inhumane treatment requires either evidence of *commissive* conduct, meaning that "the perpetrators either had the intention to inflict *serious* mental and physical harm," or evidence of *omissive* conduct, meaning that the perpetrators "knew that their acts or omissions [were] likely to cause serious mental or physical suffering or injury, or a serious attack on human dignity, and was reckless as to that result."[2147] [2148] Once there is evidence of the plausibility and seriousness of the inhumane acts suffered by the victims, there is no requirement that the mental or physical suffering has long-lasting effects, although this may be relevant to assess the seriousness of the inhumane act.[2149]

To assess the *seriousness* of inhumane treatment, it is necessary to consider the circumstances on a case-by-case basis, such as: 1) the systematic manner as well as the large scale of the acts; 2) the nature of the act or omission; 3) the general context in which the violation occurred; 4) the duration and repetition of the act/omission; 5) the particular circumstances of the victim, such as age, gender and general conditions of health; 6) the physical and mental consequences on the victim, as well as 7) whether the victims suffered from *inhuman living conditions*.[2150]

In *Prosecutor v. Momčilo Krajišnik*, the ICTY Trial chamber considered the concept of "inhuman living conditions" as a subcategory of the crime of

---

[2144] See also: Prosecutor v. Vojislav Šešelj. IT-03-67-T, vol. 1. *Supra* note 145. p. 188/62399 BISa -187/62399 BISa.

[2145] Prosecutor v. Vojislav Šešelj. IT-03-67-T, vol. 1. *Supra* note 145. p. 188/62399 BISa - 187/62399 BISa.

[2146] See also: Prosecutor v. Zoran Kupreškić, *et al.* IT-95-16-T. *Supra* note 156. ¶ 636; Prosecutor v. Vujadin Popović *et al.* IT-05-88-T. *Supra* note 150. ¶ 968; Prosecutor v. Momčilo Perišić. IT-04-81-T. *Supra* note 123. ¶ 121.

[2147] Prosecutor v. Mitar Vasiljević. IT-98-32-T. *Supra* note 117. ¶ 236. See also: Prosecutor v. Momčilo Krajišnik. IT-00-39-T. *Supra* note 121. ¶¶ 746, 803; Prosecutor v. Milan Lukić, Sredoje Lukić. IT-98-32/1-T. *Supra* note 104. ¶¶ 957, 961–962.

[2148] See also: Prosecutor v. Brima, Kamara, Kanu. SCSL-04-16-T. *Supra* note 280. ¶ 698; Prosecutor v. Brima, Kamara, Kanu. SCSL-04-16-A. *Supra* note 284. ¶ 198.

[2149] Prosecutor v. Milorad Krnojelac. IT-97-25-T. *Supra* note 111. ¶ 144; Prosecutor v. Mitar Vasiljević. IT-98-32-T. *Supra* note 117. ¶ 235; Prosecutor v. Milan Lukić, Sredoje Lukić. IT-98-32/1-T. *Supra* note 104. ¶¶ 957, 961.

cruel or inhumane treatment."[2151] International Criminal Law jurisprudence recognizes that the subcategory of "inhumane living conditions" can be manifested in numerous ways, such as submitting persons to: starvation rations, extreme weight loss, lack of drinkable water, lack of hygienic sanitation facilities, lack of adequate accommodation or shelter, lack of medical care, heatstroke, mutilations, severe beatings on a regular basis, serious mental injuries, evacuations, preventing persons from receiving visits in detention centers, subjecting victims to electric shocks, exposing them to an "intimidating atmosphere marked by panic, fear, and despair," as well as burning babies, women and elderly persons to death.[2152]

### 3.2.3. Mental element – Mens rea

The *mens rea* for crimes against humanity requires a specific mental state in the perpetrator. The perpetrator of the attack(s) must have knowledge – *awareness* – that 1) there is an attack against a civilian population and that 1) their act(s) "constitute part of a widespread or systematic attack directed against this civilian population."[2153] [2154] [2155] The concept of knowledge in this context means that "the perpetrator understands the overall context and characteristics in which their acts took place." However, "this stipulation does not entail or require precise or detailed knowledge of the attack."[2156] [2157] [2158]

---

[2150]  Prosecutor v. Dario Kordić and Mario Čerkez. IT-95-14/2-T. *Supra* note 80. ¶ 269; Prosecutor v. Milan Lukić, Sredoje Lukić. IT-98-32/1-T. *Supra* note 104. ¶¶ 957, 960–961.

[2151]  Prosecutor v. Momčilo Krajišnik. IT-00-39-T. *Supra* note 121. ¶ 756.

[2152]  Prosecutor v. Dario Kordić and Mario Čerkez. IT-95-14/2-T. *Supra* note 80. ¶ 270; Prosecutor v. Momčilo Krajišnik. IT-00-39-T. *Supra* note 121. ¶¶ 720, 755, 795–796, 798; Prosecutor v. Milan Lukić, Sredoje Lukić. IT-98-32/1-T. *Supra* note 104. ¶¶ 392, 667; Prosecutor v. Vujadin Popović *et al.* IT-05-88-A. *Supra* note 151. ¶ 752.

[2153]  Prosecutor v. Dragoljub Kunarac *et al.* IT-96-23/1-A. *Supra* note 85. ¶ 102. See also: Prosecutor v. Vidoje Blagojević, Dragan Jokić. IT-02-60-T. *Supra* note 147. ¶ 548; Prosecutor v. Emmanuel Rukundo. ICTR-2001-70-T. *Supra* note 179. ¶ 578; Prosecutor v. Tharcisse Renzaho. ICTR-97-31-T. *Supra* note 232. ¶ 783; Prosecutor v. Milan Lukić, Sredoje Lukić. IT-98-32/1-T. *Supra* note 104. ¶ 877.

[2154]  Prosecutor v. Hormisdas Nsengimana, Case No. ICTR-01-69-T, (Nov. 17, 2009). ¶ 844. See also: Prosecutor v. Gaspard Kanyarukiga. ICTR-2002-78-T. *Supra* note 187. ¶¶ 645, 651, 657; Prosecutor v. Jean-Baptiste Gatete. ICTR-2000-61-T. *Supra* note 195. ¶ 632; Prosecutor v. Augustin Ndindiliyimana *et al.* ICTR-00-56-T. *Supra* note 163. ¶ 2088.

[2155]  See also: Prosecutor v. Brima, Kamara, Kanu. SCSL-04-16-T. *Supra* note 280. ¶¶ 220–221.

Although the offender need not know the details or the full context of the attack(s),[2159] the Prosecution is required to "show that the accused either knew or had reason to know that his acts comprised part of the attack" and that the accused "understand[s] the overall context in which his acts took place."[2160] For the international criminal case-law, "knowledge of certain events, not necessarily every individual attack, is sufficient to warrant the conclusion that the perpetrator had notice of the wider context and nature of the crimes."[2161] The jurisprudence has sustained that evidence of knowledge is determined on a case-by-case basis.[2162]

In other words, the perpetrator must know that their acts are part of or fit into such a pattern of widespread or systematic attack(s) directed against a civilian population.[2163] [2164] The prosecutor must demonstrate that

---

[2156]  Prosecutor v. Jean-Pierre Bemba Gombo. ICC-01/05-01/08. *Supra* note 334. ¶ 88. See also: Prosecutor v. Germain Katanga. ICC-01/04-01/07. *Supra* note 333. ¶ 1125; Prosecutor v. Jean-Pierre Bemba Gombo. ICC-01/05-01/08. *Supra* note 335. ¶ 167.

[2157]  See also: Prosecutor v. Brima, Kamara, Kanu. SCSL-04-16-T. *Supra* note 280. ¶ 221; Prosecutor v. Fofana, Kondewa. SCSL-04-14-T. *Supra* note 281. ¶ 121; Prosecutor v. Sesay, Kallon and Gbao. SCSL-04-15-T. *Supra* note 268. ¶ 90; Prosecutor v. Taylor. SCSL-03-01-T. *Supra* note 270. ¶¶ 513, 515.

[2158]  Prosecutor v. Dragoljub Kunarac *et al.* IT-96-23/1-T. *Supra* note 84. ¶ 434; Prosecutor v. Goran Jelisić., IT-95-10-A. *Supra* note 98. ¶ 148; Prosecutor v. Blagoje Simić *et al.* IT-95-9-T. *Supra* note 78. ¶ 45; Prosecutor v. Vidoje Blagojević, Dragan Jokić. IT-02-60-T. *Supra* note 147. ¶ 548; Prosecutor v. Momčilo Krajišnik. IT-00-39-T. *Supra* note 121. ¶ 706; Prosecutor v. Mile Mrkšić *et al.* IT-95-13/1. *Supra* note 108. ¶ 439; Prosecutor v. Dragomir Milošević. IT-98-29/1-T. *Supra* note 86. ¶ 929; Prosecutor v. Ante Gotovina *et al.* IT-06-90-T, vol. I. *Supra* note 76. ¶ 1707; Prosecutor v. Momčilo Perišić. IT-04-81-T. *Supra* note 123. ¶ 88; Prosecutor v. Mićo Stanišić, Stojan Župljanin. IT-08-91-T, vol. 1. *Supra* note 102. ¶ 30; Prosecutor v. Jovica Stanišić and Franko Simatović. IT-03-69-T, vol. I. *Supra* note 101. ¶ 966; Prosecutor v. Radovan Karadžić. IT-95-5/18-T, vol. I. *Supra* note 134. ¶ 479; Prosecutor v. Ratko Mladić. IT-09-92-T, vol. III. *Supra* note 137. ¶ 3029.

[2159]  In *Brima, Kamara, Kanu*, the SCSL established that "the accused need not know the details of the attack or approve of the context in which his or her acts occur; the accused merely needs to understand the overall context in which his or her acts took place.390 The motives for the accused's participation in the attack are irrelevant; the accused need only know that his or her acts are parts thereof." (Prosecutor v. Brima, Kamara, Kanu. SCSL-04-16-T. *Supra* note 280. ¶ 222).

[2160]  Prosecutor v. Sesay, Kallon and Gbao. SCSL-04-15-T. *Supra* note 268. ¶ 90.

[2161]  Prosecutor v. Dragomir Milošević. IT-98-29/1-T. *Supra* note 86. ¶ 929.

[2162]  Prosecutor v. Brima, Kamara, Kanu. SCSL-04-16-T. *Supra* note 280. ¶ 221; Prosecutor v. Sesay, Kallon and Gbao. SCSL-04-15-T. *Supra* note 268. ¶ 90; Prosecutor v. Taylor. SCSL-03-01-T. *Supra* note 270. ¶ 515.

[2163]  Prosecutor v. Momčilo Krajišnik. IT-00-39-T. *Supra* note 121. ¶ 706; Prosecutor v. Milan Lukić, Sredoje Lukić. IT-98-32/1-T. *Supra* note 104. ¶ 877.

the perpetrator acted with such knowledge – *awareness* – or, at least, show that the accused knew the risks of his actions and took the risks."[2165] However, it is not necessary that the accused possesses detailed knowledge of the attack or that they have approved "the context in which his acts occurred."[2166] [2167] When absent proof of detailed knowledge of the attack, the perpetrator's *means rea* "may be inferred from the circumstances."[2168]

Importantly, Customary International Law does not require "that the accused shares the purpose or goal behind the attack."[2169] "It is sufficient that through [their] acts or function the accused knowingly participated in the attack."[2170] The reasons/motives/purpose/goal of the accused of taking part in the attack against a civilian population are not relevant,[2171] [2172] that is, an attacker may "commit a crime against humanity for purely personal reasons"[2173] [2174] In *Prosecutor v. Milan Lukić, Sredoje Lukić*, the ICTY concluded that when the perpetrator *understands* "the overall context in which his acts took place," this is sufficient to meet the legal requirements of the crime against humanity.[2175]

---

[2164] With respect to the *mens rea*, the ICTR considers that "the perpetrator must have acted with knowledge of the broader context and knowledge that his acts formed part of the attack..." (Prosecutor v. Yussuf Munyakazi. ICTR-97-36A-T. *Supra* note 236. ¶ 504).

[2165] Prosecutor v. Dragoljub Kunarac *et al.* IT-96-23/1-A. *Supra* note 85. ¶ 102.

[2166] Prosecutor v. Momčilo Krajišnik. IT-00-39-T. *Supra* note 121. ¶ 706; Prosecutor v. Milan Lukić, Sredoje Lukić. IT-98-32/1-T. *Supra* note 104. ¶ 877.

[2167] Prosecutor v. Brima, Kamara, Kanu. SCSL-04-16-T. *Supra* note 280. ¶ 222.

[2168] Prosecutor v. Milan Lukić, Sredoje Lukić. IT-98-32/1-T. *Supra* note 104. ¶ 900.

[2169] Prosecutor v. Goran Jelisić., IT-95-10-A. *Supra* note 98. ¶ 148.

[2170] *Ibidem.*

[2171] Prosecutor v. Dragoljub Kunarac *et al.* IT-96-23/1-T. *Supra* note 84. ¶ 433; Prosecutor v. Dragoljub Kunarac *et al.* IT-96-23/1-A. *Supra* note 85. ¶ 103; Prosecutor v. Mitar Vasiljević. IT-98-32-T. *Supra* note 117. ¶ 37; Prosecutor v. Radoslav Brđanin. IT-99-36-T. *Supra* note 130. ¶ 138; Prosecutor v. Momčilo Krajišnik. IT-00-39-T. *Supra* note 121. ¶ 706; Prosecutor v. Zdravko Tolimir. IT-05-88/2-T. *Supra* note 153. ¶ 700; Prosecutor v. Mićo Stanišić, Stojan Župljanin. IT-08-91-T, vol. 1. *Supra* note 102. ¶ 30; Prosecutor v. Radovan Karadžić. IT-95-5/18-T, vol. I. *Supra* note 134. ¶ 479.

[2172] Prosecutor v. Fofana, Kondewa. SCSL-04-14-T. *Supra* note 281. ¶ 121; Prosecutor v. Sesay, Kallon and Gbao. SCSL-04-15-T. *Supra* note 268. ¶ 90; Prosecutor v. Taylor. SCSL-03-01-T. *Supra* note 270. ¶ 513.

[2173] Prosecutor v. Momčilo Krajišnik. IT-00-39-T. *Supra* note 121. ¶ 706.

[2174] See also: Prosecutor v. Mićo Stanišić, Stojan Župljanin. IT-08-91-T, vol. 1. *Supra* note 102. ¶ 30.

[2175] Prosecutor v. Brima, Kamara, Kanu. SCSL-04-16-T. *Supra* note 280. ¶ 222; Prosecutor v. Milan Lukić, Sredoje Lukić. IT-98-32/1-T. *Supra* note 104. ¶ 877.

*Chart of United Nations documents cited in Chapter 3 – Chronological order*

## 1986

U.N. Doc. A/CN.4/398 (March 11, 1986).
Rep. of the Special Rapporteur on the Draft Code of Offences against the Peace and Security of Mankind, by Doudou Thiam.

## 1989

U.N. Doc. A/CN.4/SER.A/1989/Add.l (Part 2) (1989).
United Nations, Report of the Commission to the General Assembly on the work of its forty-first session, Yearbook of the International Law Commission, Vol. II.

## 1996

U.N. Doc. A/51/10 (May 6, 1996 – July 26, 1996).
United Nations, Report of the International Law Commission on the Work of its Forty-Eighth Session, Yearbook of the International Law Commission, Vol. II(2).

U.N. Doc. A/CN.4/SER.A/1996/Add.l (Part 2) (1996).
United Nations, Report of the Commission to the General Assembly on the work of its forty-eighth session, Yearbook of the International Law Commission, Vol. II, UN Doc. A/CN.4/SER.A/1996/Add.l (Part 2).

## 2005

U.N. Doc. S/2005/60 (Feb. 1, 2005).
Rep. of the International Commission of Inquiry on Darfur to the Secretary-General Pursuant to Security Council Resolution 1564 (2004).

## 2015

U.N. Doc. A/HRC/28/18 (March 27, 2015).
Rep. of the Office of the United Nations High Commissioner for Human Rights, submitted to the Human Rights Council, Human Rights Situation in Iraq in the Light of Abuses Committed by The so Called Islamic State in Iraq and The Levant and Associated Groups.

## 2017

U.N. Doc. A/HRC/34/53/Add.1 (Jan. 9, 2017).
Rep. of the Special Rapporteur on Minority Issues, submitted to the Human Rights Council concerning her mission to Iraq.

## 2018

U.N. Docs. S/2018/1031 (Nov. 16, 2018).
Rep. of the Special Adviser and Head of the U. N. Investigative Team to Promote Accountability for Crimes Committed by Da'esh/Islamic State in Iraq and the Levant submitted to the S.C, First report of the Special Adviser and Head of the United Nations Investigative Team to Promote Accountability for Crimes Committed by Da'esh/Islamic State in Iraq and the Levant.

## 2019

U.N. Doc. S/2019/407 (May 17, 2019).
Rep. of the Special Adviser and Head of the U. N. Investigative Team to Promote Accountability for Crimes Committed by Da'esh/Islamic State in Iraq and the Levant submitted to the S.C, Second report of the Special Adviser and Head of the United Nations Investigative Team to Promote Accountability for Crimes Committed by Da'esh/Islamic State in Iraq and the Levant.

U.N. Doc. S/2019/878 (Nov. 13, 2019).
Rep. of the Special Adviser and Head of the U. N. Investigative Team to Promote Accountability for Crimes Committed by Da'esh/Islamic State in Iraq and the Levant submitted to the S.C, Third report of the Special Adviser and Head of the United Nations Investigative Team to Promote Accountability for Crimes Committed by Da'esh/Islamic State in Iraq and the Levant.

## 2020

U.N. Doc. S/2020/386 (May 11, 2020)
Rep. of the Special Adviser and Head of the U. N. Investigative Team to Promote Accountability for Crimes Committed by Da'esh/Islamic State in Iraq and the Levant submitted to the S.C, Fourth report of the Special Adviser and Head of the United Nations Investigative Team to Promote Accountability for Crimes Committed by Da'esh/Islamic State in Iraq and the Levant.

U.N. Doc. S/2020/1107 (Nov. 11, 2020).

Rep. of the Special Adviser and Head of the U. N. Investigative Team to Promote Accountability for Crimes Committed by Da'esh/Islamic State in Iraq and the Levant submitted to the S.C, Fifth report of the Special Adviser and Head of the United Nations Investigative Team to Promote Accountability for Crimes Committed by Da'esh/Islamic State in Iraq and the Levant.

# 4. Legal assessment of ISIL/DAESH violations of International Human Rights Law, International Humanitarian Law, and International Criminal Law against Christians in Iraq

In areas under its control in Iraq, ISIL/DAESH engaged in multiple criminal acts and omissions against Christians. This chapter assesses whether the perpetrators' *actus reus* and *mens rea* fall under the definition of genocide, as prescribed by the Rome Statute,[2176] or fall under the crime of persecution, as a crime against humanity, as defined in the Rome Statute – the *test of equal gravity*.[2177] To perform this assessment, ISIL/DAESH violations of international human rights, humanitarian and criminal law will be grouped in seven different categories in this chapter, as follows:

1) **Physical and mental harm** – ISIL/DAESH fighters intentionally and deliberately committed the following crimes and violations against Christians in Iraq: targeted killings; mass summary killings, and other unlawful killings, through the extensive recourse to beheadings, burning victims alive in caskets, crucifixions, shootings, slaughtering, and burnings; causing serious bodily or mental harm, through the expedient of torture, violent beatings, extreme physical abuse, and other inhuman and degrading treatments; rape and other forms of sexual violence; sexual enslavement, and sex trafficking committed against hundreds of Christian women and girls; forced marriage and the resulting pregnancies and abortions; persecution, imposition of measures intended to prevent births.[2178] [2179] [2180]

---

[2176] United Nations. Rome Statute (July 17, 1998) 2187 UNTS 38544. Article 6.

[2177] *Idem.* Article 7.1.a-k.

[2178] UNAMI (Nov. 6, 2018). p. 4.

[2179] U.N. Doc. S/2014/774 (Oct. 31, 2014). ¶ 46; U.N. Doc. A/HRC/28/18 (March 27, 2015). ¶ 76; U.N. Doc. S/2016/92 (Jan. 29, 2016). ¶ 9; U.N. Doc. S/2016/897 (Oct. 25, 2016). ¶ 52; U.N. Doc. CCPR/C/IRQ/CO/5/Add.1 (Aug. 18, 2017). ¶¶ 2–4; U.N. Doc. CERD/C/IRQ/22-25 (Nov. 22, 2017). ¶¶ 15–16; U.N. Doc. CEDAW/C/IRQ/7 (Aug. 15, 2018). ¶¶ 9–10; U.N. Doc. A/HRC/39/NGO/X (Aug. 23, 2018). p. 3; U.N. Doc. CED/C/IRQ/AI/1 (Aug. 1, 2019). ¶¶ 43–45; U.N. Doc. CAT/C/IRQ/2 (Aug. 20, 2019). ¶¶ 52–53; U.N. Doc. A/HRC/44/41/Add.1 (May 13, 2020). ¶ 54.

[2180] S.C. Res. 2379 (Sept. 21, 2017). Preamble.

[2181] [2182] [2183] In addition, there is conclusive evidence that ISIL/DAESH deployed members of Christian minorities as human shields and separated Christian children from their families, forcibly transferring them to other groups.[2184] [2185]

**2) Use of economic measures against the civilian population** – ISIL/DAESH systematically and extensively committed economic-related violations against Christians in Iraq and barred them from working at public sector jobs and receiving wage stipends.[2186] [2187]

**3) Attacks against property of sacred religious relevance** – In hundreds of instances, ISIL/DAESH deliberately destroyed – partially or entirely – Christian churches, shrines, monasteries, places of Christian worship, and

---

[2181]  Eur. Parl., Situation in Iraq and Syria and the IS Offensive Including the Persecution of Minorities, Resolution, P8_TA(2014)0027 (Sept. 18, 2014). ¶ C; Eur. Parl., Humanitarian Crisis in Iraq and Syria, in Particular in the IS Context, Resolution, P8_TA(2015)0040 (Feb. 12, 2015). ¶ G; Eur. Parl. Plenary sitting. Joint Motion for a Resolution Pursuant to Rule 123(2) and (4), of the Rules of Procedure. Systematic Mass Murder of Religious Minorities by The So-called ISIS/Daesh 2014–2019. (Feb. 3, 2016). ¶ B; Eur. Parl., Systematic mass murder of religious minorities by ISIS, Resolution, P8_TA(2016)0051 (Feb. 4, 2016). ¶ B; Eur. Parl., Prosecuting and Punishing the Crimes Against Humanity or Even Possible Genocide Committed by Daesh, Report, Doc. No. 14402 (Sept. 22, 2017). ¶¶ 3, 3.2, 16, 21; Eur. Parl., Prosecuting and Punishing the Crimes Against Humanity or Even Possible Genocide Committed by Daesh, Resolution 2190 (2017). ¶ 3.2; Eur. Parl., Prosecuting and Punishing the Crimes Against Humanity or Even Possible Genocide Committed by Daesh, Compendium of Amendments, Doc. No. 14402 (Oct. 11, 2017). ¶ 3.2.
[2182]  H.R.Con.Res. 75, 114th Cong. (Sept. 9, 2015). p. 2; 163 Cong. Rec. H5368 (daily ed. June 29, 2017) (statement of Rep. Ted Poe). p. H5369.
[2183]  UK Parliament, Genocide in Syria and Iraq, Early Day Motion, Sponsored by Robert Flello (Jan. 26, 2016).
[2184]  Eur. Parl., Prosecuting and Punishing the Crimes Against Humanity or Even Possible Genocide Committed by Daesh, Resolution 2190 (2017). ¶ 3.2. Eur. Parl., Prosecuting and Punishing the Crimes Against Humanity or Even Possible Genocide Committed by Daesh, Report, Doc. No. 14402 (Sept. 22, 2017). ¶ 3.2, 16, 21; Eur. Parl., Prosecuting and Punishing the Crimes Against Humanity or Even Possible Genocide Committed by Daesh, Compendium of Amendments, Doc. No. 14402 (Oct. 11, 2017). ¶ 3.2.
[2185]  U.N. Doc. CAT/C/IRQ/2 (Aug. 20, 2019). ¶ 53.
[2186]  U.N. Doc. CEDAW/C/IRQ/7 (Aug. 15, 2018). ¶ 10. See also: U.N. Doc. CED/C/IRQ/AI/1 (Aug. 1, 2019). ¶ 44; U.N. Doc. CAT/C/IRQ/2 (Aug. 20, 2019). ¶ 53.
[2187]  H. Res. House Foreign Affairs Subcommittees on Africa, Global Health, Global Human Rights and International Organizations and the Middle East and North Africa. Testimony of Assistant Secretary Tom Malinowski (Sept. 10, 2014).

religious monuments in Iraq.[2188] [2189] [2190] [2191] [2192] [2193] Areas of immense religious importance for Christians were burned, exploded, targeted with rocket-propelled grenades, or demolished with bulldozers, particularly in Mosul, Qaraqosh, Baqofa, Al-Nimrod, Karemlash, Bartella, Telkeppe, Bashiqa, Bahzani, Batnaya, and Teleskof.[2194] [2195] [2196] ISIL/DAESH mainly targeted ancient/historic churches and cathedrals,[2197] "eradicating all physical traces of the 2,000-year-old history of Christianity from the [Iraqi] towns

---

[2188] UNAMI (July 6, 2014 – Sept. 10, 2014). p. 9.

[2189] U.N. Doc. A/HRC/RES/S-22/1 (Sept. 3, 2014). p. 2; U.N. Doc. S/2014/774 (Oct. 31, 2014). ¶ 46; U.N. Doc. A/HRC/28/18 (March 27, 2015). ¶ 22; U.N. Doc. CCPR/C/IRQ/CO/5/Add.1 (Aug. 18, 2017). ¶ 3; U.N. Doc. CERD/C/IRQ/22-25 (Nov. 22, 2017). ¶ 15; U.N. Doc. CEDAW/C/IRQ/7 (Aug. 15, 2018). ¶ 10; U.N. Doc. A/HRC/39/NGO/X (Aug. 23, 2018). p. 3; U.N. Doc. CED/C/IRQ/AI/1 (Aug. 1, 2019). ¶ 44; U.N. Doc. CAT/C/IRQ/2 (Aug. 20, 2019). ¶ 53.

[2190] S.C. Res. 2367 (July 14, 2017). preamble.

[2191] Eur. Parl., Situation in Iraq, Resolution, P8_TA(2014)0011 (Jul. 17, 2014). ¶ B; Eur. Parl., Situation in Iraq and Syria and the IS Offensive Including the Persecution of Minorities, Resolution, P8_TA(2014)0027 (Sept. 18, 2014). ¶ C; Eur. Parl., Humanitarian Crisis in Iraq and Syria, in Particular in the IS Context, Resolution, P8_TA(2015)0040 (Feb. 12, 2015). ¶ D; Eur. Parl. Plenary sitting. Joint Motion for a Resolution Pursuant to Rule 123(2) and (4), of the Rules of Procedure. Systematic Mass Murder of Religious Minorities by The So-called ISIS/Daesh 2014–2019. (Feb. 3, 2016). ¶ B.

[2192] U.S. Dep't of State, Bureau of Democracy, H.R. and Lab., International Religious Freedom Report (2017). p. 164.

[2193] Iraq: ISIS Abducting, Killing, Expelling Minorities. Armed Group Targeting Christian Nuns, Turkmen, Shabaks, Yazidis, HUMAN RIGHTS WATCH (Jul. 19, 2014); *No Way Home: Iraq's Minorities on the Verge of Disappearance,* CEASEFIRE CENTRE FOR CIVILIAN RIGHTS, Jul. 2016. pp. 13, 43; AMNESTY INTERNATIONAL. *Supra* note 495. p. 15; Life after ISIS: New challenges to Christianity in Iraq. Results from ACN's survey of Christians in the liberated Nineveh Plains, AID TO THE CHURCH IN NEED – ACN INTERNATIONAL, June 2020. p. 29.

[2194] UNAMI (May 1, 2015 – Oct. 31, 2015). p. 16.

[2195] U.S. Dep't of State, Bureau of Democracy, H.R. and Lab., International Religious Freedom Report (2017). p. 164.

[2196] HUMAN RIGHTS WATCH (Jul. 19, 2014). *Supra* note 2193; Nina Shea, *Falling For ISIS Propaganda About Christians,* THE HUDSON INSTITUTE, July 21, 2016; CEASEFIRE CENTRE FOR CIVILIAN RIGHTS (Jul. 2016). *Supra* note 2193. p. 43; SHLOMO ORGANIZATION FOR DOCUMENTATION, Gregory Stanton, Elisa Yuden von Furkin, Irina Victoria Massimino & Jan Vermon (2017). pp. 69–83).

[2197] 163 Cong. Rec. H5368 (daily ed. June 29, 2017) (statement of Rep. Ted Poe). p. H5369; Eur. Parl., Prosecuting and Punishing the Crimes Against Humanity or Even Possible Genocide Committed by Daesh, Report, Doc. No. 14402 (Sept. 22, 2017). ¶ 21.

the faithful left behind,"[2198] for example, the destruction of the tomb of the eighth century BC Old Testament Prophet Jonah, the destruction of the 1,400-year-old Iraq's oldest Christian monastery – St Elijah's monastery, in Mosul –, and the destruction of the 1,000-year-old church of the Mother of Perpetual Help, also in Mosul.[2199 2200 2201]

As a common practice, ISIL/DAESH used to remove church crosses and replace them with ISIL/DAESH black flags.[2202] Also, ISIL/DAESH generally looted these sacred sites before destroying them. The fighters used to sell priceless artifacts, ancient manuscripts, books, and texts through illegal markets.[2203] ISIL/DAESH also destroyed Christian cemeteries, demolished graves and burial sites,[2204] and played with the corpses therein, particularly in Bartella, Qaraqosh, Telkeppe, and Bashiqa.[2205] Assuming that gold had been buried alongside the bodies of their victims, ISIL/DAESH militants inspected corpses to search for valuable items.[2206] After inspections, the militants used to leave the bodies exposed to the open air.[2207] In some instances, ISIL/DAESH fighters decided not to destroy the religious sites and use them for other purposes, such as converting churches into mosques or turning them into military bases or administrative buildings.[2208 2209 2210 2211]

---

[2198] Ronald Rychlak & Jane Adolphe eds., *Supra* note 429. pp. 43–44.

[2199] U.N. Doc. A/HRC/39/NGO/X (Aug. 23, 2018). p. 3.

[2200] 163 Cong. Rec. H5368 (daily ed. June 29, 2017) (statement of Rep. Ted Poe). p. H5369.

[2201] Ronald Rychlak & Jane Adolphe eds. *Supra* note 429. pp. 43–44.

[2202] UNAMI (Dec. 11, 2014 – Apr. 30, 2015). p. 19.

[2203] H. Res. House Foreign Affairs Subcommittees on Africa, Global Health, Global Human Rights and International Organizations and the Middle East and North Africa. Testimony of Assistant Secretary Tom Malinowski (Sept. 10, 2014); CEASEFIRE CENTRE FOR CIVILIAN RIGHTS (Jul. 2016). *Supra* note 2193. p. 43; Eur. Parl., Prosecuting and Punishing the Crimes Against Humanity or Even Possible Genocide Committed by Daesh, Report, Doc. No. 14402 (Sept. 22, 2017). ¶ 21.

[2204] U.S. Dep't of State, Bureau of Democracy, H.R. and Lab., International Religious Freedom Report (2017). p. 164

[2205] Ronald Rychlak & Jane Adolphe eds. *Supra* note 429. p. 43.

[2206] ACN INTERNATIONAL (June 2020). *Supra* note 2193. p. 28.

[2207] *Ibidem.*

[2208] UNAMI (July 6, 2014 – Sept. 10, 2014). p. 12.

[2209] H. Res. House Foreign Affairs Subcommittees on Africa, Global Health, Global Human Rights and International Organizations and the Middle East and North Africa. Testimony of Assistant Secretary Tom Malinowski (Sept. 10, 2014).

[2210] U.S. Dep't of State, Bureau of Democracy, H.R. and Lab., International Religious Freedom Report (2017). p. 164.

[2211] Ronald Rychlak & Jane Adolphe eds. *Supra* note 429. p. 43.

**4) Infringements upon the right to physical liberty and security–** Several documents indicate that ISIL/DAESH sold (slave trading), enslaved (enslavement), trafficked (human trafficking), and smuggled (smuggling) several Christian women and girls on the basis of their professing Christianity. ISIL/DAESH committed hundreds of abductions, kidnappings, and hostage-takings of members of the Christian community in Iraq, including the deliberate kidnappings of priests and nuns.[2212] [2213] [2214] [2215] [2216] ISIL/DAESH caused the forced migration and displacement of thousands of Christians in Iraq on the basis of religious persecution.[2217] [2218] [2219] [2220] ISIL/DAESH unlawfully detained, imprisoned, or committed enforced disappearances of Christians.[2221] [2222] [2223] Also, on the basis of religious dis-

---

[2212] UNAMI (July 6, 2014 – Sept. 10, 2014). p. 12; UNAMI (Nov. 6, 2018). p. 4.

[2213] U.N. Doc. S/2014/774 (Oct. 31, 2014). ¶ 46; U.N. Doc. A/HRC/28/18 (March 27, 2015). ¶ 76; U.N. Doc. S/2016/897 (Oct. 25, 2016). ¶ 52; U.N. Doc. CCPR/C/IRQ/CO/5/Add.1 (Aug. 18, 2017). ¶ 2; U.N. Doc. CERD/C/IRQ/22-25 (Nov. 22, 2017). ¶ 15; U.N. Doc. CEDAW/C/IRQ/7 (Aug. 15, 2018). ¶¶ 9–10; U.N. Doc. A/HRC/39/NGO/X (Aug. 23, 2018). p. 3; U.N. Doc. CED/C/IRQ/AI/1 (Aug. 1, 2019). ¶¶ 43–44; U.N. Doc. CAT/C/IRQ/2 (Aug. 20, 2019). ¶¶ 52–53.

[2214] Eur. Parl., Situation in Iraq and Syria and the IS Offensive Including the Persecution of Minorities, Resolution, P8_TA(2014)0027 (Sept. 18, 2014). ¶ C; Eur. Parl., Humanitarian Crisis in Iraq and Syria, in Particular in the IS Context, Resolution, P8_TA(2015)0040 (Feb. 12, 2015). ¶ G; Eur. Parl. Plenary sitting. Joint Motion for a Resolution Pursuant to Rule 123(2) and (4), of the Rules of Procedure. Systematic Mass Murder of Religious Minorities by The So-called ISIS/Daesh 2014–2019. (Feb. 3, 2016). ¶¶ B, H; Eur. Parl., Systematic mass murder of religious minorities by ISIS, Resolution, P8_TA(2016)0051 (Feb. 4, 2016). ¶¶ B, I; Eur. Parl., Prosecuting and Punishing the Crimes Against Humanity or Even Possible Genocide Committed by Daesh, Report, Doc. No. 14402 (Sept. 22, 2017). ¶¶ 16, 21.

[2215] S.C. Res. 2379 (Sept. 21, 2017). Preamble.

[2216] HUMAN RIGHTS WATCH (Jul. 19, 2014). *Supra* note 2193; "Our Generation is Gone": The Islamic State's Targeting of Iraqi Minorities in Ninewa. Bearing Witness Trip Report, Naomi Kikoler, UNITED STATES HOLOCAUST MEMORIAL MUSEUM (2015). p. 18; AMNESTY INTERNATIONAL. *Supra* note 495. p. 15; ACN INTERNATIONAL (June 2020). *Supra* note 2193. p. 26.

[2217] U.N. Doc. A/HRC/28/18 (March 27, 2015). ¶ 76; U.N. Doc. CCPR/C/IRQ/CO/5/Add.1 (Aug. 18, 2017). ¶ 3; U.N. Doc. CERD/C/IRQ/22-25 (Nov. 22, 2017). ¶ 15; U.N. Doc. CEDAW/C/IRQ/7 (Aug. 15, 2018). ¶ 10; U.N. Doc. CED/C/IRQ/AI/1 (Aug. 1, 2019). ¶ 44; U.N. Doc. CAT/C/IRQ/2 (Aug. 20, 2019). ¶¶ 21, 53; U.N. Doc. A/HRC/44/41/Add.1 (May 13, 2020). ¶ 30.

[2218] H.R.Con.Res. 75, 114th Cong. (Sept. 9, 2015). p. 2.

[2219] Eur. Parl., Prosecuting and Punishing the Crimes Against Humanity or Even Possible Genocide Committed by Daesh, Report, Doc. No. 14402 (Sept. 22, 2017). ¶ 16.

[2220] UNITED STATES HOLOCAUST MEMORIAL MUSEUM (2015). *Supra* note 2216. p. 18.

[2221] UNAMI (July 6, 2014 – Sept. 10, 2014). p. 12; UNAMI (Nov. 6, 2018). p. 4.

crimination, ISIL/DAESH recruited and used children, including for purposes of suicide bombings.[2224] [2225] [2226] [2227]

5) Infringements upon the right to privacy, and deprivation, destruction, and plunder of private property – ISIL/DAESH fighters, on the basis of religious persecution, deliberately invaded the privacy of Christians in Iraq through unlawful searches, lootings, destructions, extorsions, confiscations, appropriations and selling/trading of their homes, personal property, valuables, belongings, civilian infrastructure, and businesses.[2228] [2229] [2230] [2231] [2232]

## 6) The imposition and maintenance of other restrictive and discriminatory measures involving denial of fundamental rights – Based on reli-

---

[2222] U.N. Doc. A/HRC/28/18 (March 27, 2015). ¶ 76; U.N. Doc. CAT/C/IRQ/2 (Aug. 20, 2019). ¶ 53.

[2223] Eur. Parl., Systematic mass murder of religious minorities by ISIS, Resolution, P8_TA(2016)0051 (Feb. 4, 2016). ¶ I.

[2224] U.N. Doc. S/2014/774 (Oct. 31, 2014). ¶ 46; U.N. Doc. CCPR/C/IRQ/CO/5/Add.1 (Aug. 18, 2017). ¶ 2; U.N. Doc. CERD/C/IRQ/22-25 (Nov. 22, 2017). ¶ 15; U.N. Doc. CEDAW/C/IRQ/7 (Aug. 15, 2018). ¶ 9; U.N. Doc. CED/C/IRQ/AI/1 (Aug. 1, 2019). ¶ 43; U.N. Doc. CAT/C/IRQ/2 (Aug. 20, 2019). ¶ 52.

[2225] S.C. Res. 2379 (Sept. 21, 2017). Preamble.

[2226] Eur. Parl., Situation in Iraq and Syria and the IS Offensive Including the Persecution of Minorities, Resolution, P8_TA(2014)0027 (Sept. 18, 2014). ¶ C; Eur. Parl., Humanitarian Crisis in Iraq and Syria, in Particular in the IS Context, Resolution, P8_TA(2015)0040 (Feb. 12, 2015). ¶ G; Eur. Parl. Plenary sitting. Joint Motion for a Resolution Pursuant to Rule 123(2) and (4), of the Rules of Procedure. Systematic Mass Murder of Religious Minorities by The So-called ISIS/Daesh 2014–2019. (Feb. 3, 2016). ¶ B; Eur. Parl., Systematic mass murder of religious minorities by ISIS, Resolution, P8_TA(2016)0051 (Feb. 4, 2016). ¶ B.

[2227] AMNESTY INTERNATIONAL. *Supra* note 495. p. 15.

[2228] UNAMI (July 6, 2014 – Sept. 10, 2014). pp. 11–12; UNAMI (Dec. 11, 2014 – Apr. 30, 2015). p. 21; UNAMI (May 1, 2015 – Oct. 31, 2015). p. 15.

[2229] U.N. Doc. A/HRC/28/18 (March 27, 2015). ¶ 21; U.N. Doc. A/HRC/34/53/Add.1 (Jan. 9, 2017). ¶ 32.

[2230] Eur. Parl. Plenary sitting. Joint Motion for a Resolution Pursuant to Rule 123(2) and (4), of the Rules of Procedure. Systematic Mass Murder of Religious Minorities by The So-called ISIS/Daesh 2014–2019. (Feb. 3, 2016). ¶¶ B, H; Eur. Parl., Systematic mass murder of religious minorities by ISIS, Resolution, P8_TA(2016)0051 (Feb. 4, 2016). ¶ H; Eur. Parl., Prosecuting and Punishing the Crimes Against Humanity or Even Possible Genocide Committed by Daesh, Report, Doc. No. 14402 (Sept. 22, 2017). ¶¶ 4, 21.

[2231] U.S. Dep't of State, Bureau of Democracy, H.R. and Lab., International Religious Freedom Report (2017). p. 164.

[2232] HUMAN RIGHTS WATCH (Jul. 19, 2014). *Supra* note 2193; THE HUDSON INSTITUTE (July 21, 2016). *Supra* note 2196.; AMNESTY INTERNATIONAL. *Supra* note 495. p. 15.

gious discrimination, ISIL/DAESH fighters compelled members of the Christian community to either 1) convert to Islam; 2) "pay a tax historically levied on non-Muslims known as the *jizya* (*jiziye; jezyah*) [toleration tax];" 3) leave their home cities/villages or 4) or face summary killings – *death by sword*.[2233] [2234] [2235] [2236] Besides, through the establishment of self-appointed *sharia* courts, ISIL/DAESH denied Christians in Iraq the right to judicial process by sentencing them to death without any formal accusation, right to proper defense, right to equality of arms, or respect to legality.[2237]

**7) Other violations of International Humanitarian Law** – ISIL/DAESH fighters intentionally and deliberately committed the following crimes and violations against Christians in Iraq: ISIL/DAESH deprived Christians of humanitarian assistance through the closing of humanitarian corridors for international missions or through the reported confiscation of identification cards, passports, and financial records of those attempting to flee, which jeopardized the resettlement and access to health treatment of Christian families.[2238] [2239] ISIL/DAESH fighters also killed or attempted to kill Christians trying to escape from Iraq.[2240] ISIL/DAESH deprived Christians of their right to housing through the expropriation, looting, seizing, and destruction of homes owned by members of the Christian group in Iraq.[2241] ISIL/DAESH fighters systematically looted personal and indispensable food items from Christians and deliberately denied them the right to

---

[2233]  UNAMI (July 6, 2014 – Sept. 10, 2014). p. 12.

[2234]  U.N. Doc. S/2014/774 (Oct. 31, 2014). ¶ 47; U.N. Doc. A/HRC/30/66 (July 27, 2015). ¶ 48; U.N. Doc. CCPR/C/IRQ/CO/5/Add.1 (Aug. 18, 2017). ¶ 2; U.N. Doc. CERD/C/IRQ/22-25 (Nov. 22, 2017). ¶ 15; U.N. Doc. CEDAW/C/IRQ/7 (Aug. 15, 2018). ¶ 9; U.N. Doc. A/HRC/39/NGO/X (Aug. 23, 2018). p. 3; U.N. Doc. CED/C/IRQ/AI/1 (Aug. 1, 2019). ¶ 43; U.N. Doc. CAT/C/IRQ/2 (Aug. 20, 2019). ¶ 52.

[2235]  Eur. Parl., Systematic mass murder of religious minorities by ISIS, Resolution, P8_TA(2016)0051 (Feb. 4, 2016). ¶ B.

[2236]  AMNESTY INTERNATIONAL. *Supra* note 495. p. 15; HUMAN RIGHTS WATCH. (December 2017). p. 16.

[2237]  UNAMI (Dec. 11, 2014 – Apr. 30, 2015). p. 21.

[2238]  U.N. Doc. A/HRC/28/18 (March 27, 2015). ¶ 22; U.S. Dep't of State, Bureau of Democracy, H.R. and Lab., International Religious Freedom Report (2017). p. 164.

[2239]  ACN INTERNATIONAL (June 2020). *Supra* note 2193. p. 28.

[2240]  U.S. Dep't of State, Bureau of Democracy, H.R. and Lab., International Religious Freedom Report (2017). p. 164

[2241]  UNAMI (Dec. 11, 2014 – Apr. 30, 2015). p. 21; U.S. Dep't of State, Bureau of Democracy, H.R. and Lab., International Religious Freedom Report (2017). p. 164; ACN INTERNATIONAL (June 2020). *Supra* note 2193. p. 28.

proper medical care.[2242] [2243] Some Christians who remained in their villages and towns reported that ISIL/DAESH had interrupted the electricity and water supply to their areas.[2244] Others claimed that ISIL/DAESH demanded "the payment of protection money, while others faced forced conversion or execution if they failed to comply with [ISIL/DAESH] demands."[2245]

## 4.1. Legal assessment of whether ISIL/DAESH acts and omissions against Christians in Iraq fall under the classification of the crime of genocide

It is incontrovertible that the group of individuals that profess the Christian faith in Iraq is a group protected from genocide by international law, as prescribed in the Genocide Convention and the Rome Statute. It is also indisputable that ISIL/DAESH perpetrated some objective elements of the crime of genocide against this group in Iraq – material acts/actus reus. For instance, "killing members of the group," "causing serious bodily harm to the members of the group," and "forcibly transferring children of the group to another group."[2246]

Besides, it is unquestionable that the suffering that ISIL/DAESH fighters inflicted on Christians in Iraq was horrific and caused a long-lasting physical and psychological impact on the victims. ISIL/DAESH actions also led to the Christians' displacement in IDP (Internally Displaced Persons) and refugee camps locally and across borders, and, ultimately, contributed to the partial destruction of the group in Iraq, particularly in the Ninewa Plains. Many of the survivors could not have a normal and constructive life. The totality of the available evidence is sufficient to sustain that ISIL/DAESH targeted Christians in Iraq based on religious discrimination. However, the question to be discussed in this section is whether, taking together the circumstantial evidence, one can legitimately and sufficiently draw a reasonable inference that these discriminatory acts suffice to prove intent – mens rea – to destroy a group as a separate, distinct entity.

---

[2242] UNAMI (July 6, 2014 – Sept. 10, 2014). p. 11; U.N. Doc. CEDAW/C/IRQ/7 (Aug. 15, 2018). ¶ 10; U.N. Doc. CED/C/IRQ/AI/1 (Aug. 1, 2019). ¶ 44; U.N. Doc. CAT/C/IRQ/2 (Aug. 20, 2019). ¶ 53.

[2243] ACN INTERNATIONAL (June 2020). *Supra* note 2193. p. 28.

[2244] UNAMI (July 6, 2014 – Sept. 10, 2014). p. 12

[2245] U.N. Doc. A/HRC/34/53/Add.1 (Jan. 9, 2017). ¶ 32.

[2246] United Nations. Rome Statute (July 17, 1998) 2187 UNTS 38544. Article 6.

## 4.1.1. Destroy as such: Was there a genocidal intent?

Some elements could be indicative of ISIL/DAESH fighters' genocidal intent. Among these elements, ISIL/DAESH public declarations against Christians; the several ultimatums that Christians should leave the Ninewa plains – or to be else killed –; the material nature of the violations of international human rights; the egregious acts of physical and mental torture; the extensive perpetration of rape and other forms of sexual abuse against Christian women and children; the deportations; and the separation of children from their parents.

Nevertheless, other aspects of ISIL/DAESH fighters' conduct indicate a lack of genocidal intent. The existing circumstantial evidence demonstrates that ISIL/DAESH fighters intended to religiously persecute, disperse, submit, weaken – and eventually destroy – all those who disagreed with the group's own interpretation of Islam and harsh interpretation of Sharia law,[2247] all those who did not conform to its *takfiri* doctrine,[2248] including Christians, but also Yazidis, Shias, and Sunnis, Shabak, Sabeans, Kaka'es, and Turkmen.[2249][2250][2251][2252][2253] The existing evidence shows that ISIL/DAESH systematically targeted religious and ethnic minority groups who refused to subscribe and pledge allegiance to its extremist and triumphalist ideology, those who the terrorist group considered "infidels" or "heretics," those who refused to "repent" from not being Muslims.[2254][2255][2256][2257] Several documents from the European Parliament, for

---

[2247] Eur. Parl., Prosecuting and Punishing the Crimes Against Humanity or Even Possible Genocide Committed by Daesh, Compendium of Amendments, Doc. No. 14402 (Oct. 11, 2017). ¶ 4.

[2248] U.N. Doc. A/HRC/30/66 (July 27, 2015). ¶ 48.

[2249] U.N. Doc. A/HRC/28/18 (March 27, 2015). ¶ 16; U.N. Doc. S/2016/92 (Jan. 29, 2016). ¶ 9; U.N. Doc. A/HRC/34/53/Add.1 (Jan. 9, 2017). p. 1, ¶ 61.

[2250] UNAMI (Dec. 11, 2014 – Apr. 30, 2015). pp. 19–20.

[2251] H.R.Con.Res. 75, 114th Cong. (Sept. 9, 2015). pp. 1–2; S. 2377, 114th Cong. (Dec. 9, 2015). p. 9; U.S. Dep't of State, Bureau of Democracy, H.R. and Lab., International Religious Freedom Report (2017). p. 162; H.R.Con.Res. 75, 114th Cong. (Mar. 15, 2016). p. 2; H. Res. 1117, 115th Cong. (Oct. 5, 2018). p. 2.

[2252] Eur. Parl., Prosecuting and Punishing the Crimes Against Humanity or Even Possible Genocide Committed by Daesh, Report, Doc. No. 14402 (Sept. 22, 2017). ¶¶ 4, 16.

[2253] AMNESTY INTERNATIONAL. *Supra* note 495. p. 15.

[2254] U.N. Doc. A/HRC/28/18 (March 27, 2015). ¶ 29; U.N. Doc. S/2016/92 (Jan. 29, 2016). ¶ 9; U.N. Doc. A/HRC/34/53/Add.1 (Jan. 9, 2017). ¶ 7.

[2255] U.S. Dep't of State, Bureau of Democracy, H.R. and Lab., International Religious Freedom Report (2017). p. 162.

example, account for ISIL/DAESH's attempts to "complete a religious cleansing in the region"[2258] by exterminating "any religious minorities from the areas under its control."[2259]

Thus, ISIL/DAESH did target and persecute Christians because of their affiliation or perceived affiliation to a religious group,[2260] but not with the exclusive genocidal intent to destroy this group *exclusively* because they were Christians – destroy them as a separate, distinct entity *as such*. Importantly, in *Prosecutor v. Radoslav Brđanin*, the ICTY, making considerations about genocidal acts committed against both Bosnian Muslims as well as Bosnian Croats in the Former Yugoslavia, concluded that a perpetrator might target *at the same time* more than one protected group, provided that the elements of the crime of genocide are considered in relation to each group separately.[2261]

The crucial point of consideration here is not whether ISIL/DAESH could target Christians and other religious and ethnic groups for genocide *simultaneously* in Iraq. Instead, the *crux* is whether the terrorist group fighters harbored a distinct, unique, separate, and, importantly, *positive* genocidal intent for each group. Customary International Law "has a long-standing rule that groups, in genocide offenses, must be defined by their *positive* characteristics" — as belonging to/or as possessing the characteristics of a national, ethnical, racial, or religious group — rather than by their *negative* characteristics (by exclusion) – that is, not possessing a specific *distinct* identity.[2262]

In *Goran Jelisić*, the ICTY defined that "a *positive* approach would consist of the perpetrators of the crime distinguishing a group by the characteristics which they deem to be particular to a national, ethnical, racial or religious group."[2263] In contrast, a *negative* approach "would consist of identifying individuals as not being part of the group to which the perpetrators

---

[2256]  Robert Manne. *Supra* note 437. p. 76.

[2257]  AMNESTY INTERNATIONAL. *Supra* note 495. p. 15.

[2258]  Eur. Parl., Situation in Iraq and Syria and the IS Offensive Including the Persecution of Minorities, Resolution, P8_TA(2014)0027 (Sept. 18, 2014). ¶ 4; Eur. Parl., Humanitarian Crisis in Iraq and Syria, in Particular in the IS Context, Resolution, P8_TA(2015)0040 (Feb. 12, 2015). ¶ G.

[2259]  Eur. Parl., Recent Attacks and Abductions by ISIS/Da'esh in the Middle East, Notably of Assyrians, Resolution, P8_TA(2015)0071 (Mar. 12, 2015). ¶ 2.

[2260]  U.N. Doc. A/HRC/28/18 (March 27, 2015). ¶ 16.

[2261]  Prosecutor v. Radoslav Brđanin. IT-99-36-T. *Supra* note 130. ¶ 735.

[2262]  Prosecutor v. Radoslav Brđanin. IT-99-36-T. *Supra* note 130. ¶ 685; Prosecutor v. Vujadin Popović *et al.* IT-05-88-T. *Supra* note 150. ¶ 809.

[2263]  Prosecutor v. Goran Jelisić. IT-95-10-T. *Supra* note 97. ¶ 71.

of the crime consider that they themselves belong and which to them displays specific national, ethnical, racial or religious characteristics."[2264] In *Popović*, the ICTY characterized a *negatively defined group* as, for example, "all *non-Serbs* in a particular region."[2265]

In *Stakić*, the ICTY Appeals Chamber considered that "the drafting history of the Genocide Convention (...) was meant to incorporate an understanding [that is] incompatible with the negative definition of target groups."[2266] [2267] [2268] In *Bosnia and Herzegovina v. Serbia and Montenegro*, the ICJ recalled that "the essence of the intent is to destroy the protected group, in whole or in part, as such. It is a group which must have particular positive characteristics — national, ethnical, racial or religious — and not the lack of them."[2269]

Accordingly, the ICJ concluded that it should "deal with the matter on the basis that the targeted group must in law be defined positively, and thus not negatively as the "non-Serb" population."[2270] Importantly, in *Prosecutor v. Radoslav Brđanin*, the ICTY considered that when more than one group is targeted at the same time, a *positive* genocidal intent "must be considered in relation to each group separately."[2271]

Bearing that in mind, there is no evidence to date that ISIL *positively* wanted to destroy, in whole or in part, the group of Christians, the group of Yazidis, the group of Shias, the group of Sunnis, the group of Shabaks, the group of Sabeans, the group of Kaka'es, and the group of Turkmens in Iraq as *distinct* entities (*as such*), *solely* and *exclusively* for their belonging/affiliation to these groups – genocidal *mens rea*. Rather, the existing evidence to date only supports the hypothesis that ISIL wanted to destroy in Iraq every group that *did not belong* to their own concept of an Islamic religious group (*negative* approach).

---

[2264] *Ibidem.*

[2265] "A negatively defined group — for example all "non-Serbs" in a particular region— thus does not meet the definition." (Prosecutor v. Vujadin Popović *et al.* IT-05-88-T. *Supra* note 150. ¶ 809).

[2266] Prosecutor v. Milomir Stakić. IT-97-24-A. *Supra* note 110. ¶ 22.

[2267] For the ICTY, "given that negatively defined groups lack specific characteristics, defining groups by reference to a negative would run counter to the intent of the Genocide Convention's drafters." (Prosecutor v. Milomir Stakić. IT-97-24-A. *Supra* note 110. ¶ 22).

[2268] See also: Prosecutor v. Radoslav Brđanin. IT-99-36-T. *Supra* note 130. ¶¶ 686, 735.

[2269] Application of the Convention on the Prevention and Punishment of the Crime of Genocide (Bosnia and Herzegovina v. Serbia and Montenegro), Judgement, 2007, I.C.J. 43 (Feb. 26). ¶ 193

[2270] *Idem.* ¶ 196

[2271] Prosecutor v. Radoslav Brđanin. IT-99-36-T. *Supra* note 130. ¶ 686.

In one significant instance, the European Parliament concluded that "Daesh commit[ted] crimes against the population at large."[2272] The Parliament, however, stated that there was "no evidence that this [was] done with the specific intent necessary to classify these [...] crimes as genocide [against Christians]."[2273] Thus, the existing evidence concerning ISIL/DAESH atrocities against Christians in Iraq, however, is not, at least to this date, sufficient to prove, beyond a reasonable doubt, that the only possible inference about the perpetrators' mens rea may lead to individual criminal responsibility for genocide.

## 4.1.2. Jizya protection tax

Another element that tends to show ISIL/DAESH's lack of genocidal intent can be seen in the controversial payment of *Jizya* (toleration/protection tax) that Christians paid to ISIL/DAESH fighters. In Mosul, ISIL/DAESH threatened Christians with "death by sword" or expulsion from their houses unless they converted to Islam or paid a fine – *Jizya*.[2274] [2275] [2276] *Jizya* constituted a tax granted to the "People of the Book" – how Christians are regarded in the *Quran* – in Islam's early origins.[2277] Those who paid the tax could save their lives and be set free. Nevertheless, ISIL/DAESH did not offer such a "merciful" tax to other minority groups in Iraq.

The controversy related to the payment of *Jizya* lies on two grounds: Firstly, according to ISIL/DAESH itself, through the wording of their Caliph Abu Omar al-Baghdadi, "Christians no longer qualify for the historical protection offered by Islamic law;"[2278] Secondly, it is argued that the term "*jizya*," as used by ISIL/DAESH fighters, has no comparison with the his-

---

[2272] Eur. Parl., Prosecuting and Punishing the Crimes Against Humanity or Even Possible Genocide Committed by Daesh, Report, Doc. No. 14402 (Sept. 22, 2017). ¶ 16.

[2273] *Ibidem*. Later in 2018, the Parliament issued several statements considering that the crimes perpetrated by ISIL/DAESH against Christians could be classified as genocide, without, however, presenting any new factual circumstances and evidence.

[2274] UNAMI (Dec. 11, 2014 – April 30, 2015). p. 20.

[2275] U.N. Doc. A/HRC/S-22/NGO/8 (Aug. 29, 2014). p.3; U.N. Doc. S/2014/774 (Oct. 31, 2014). ¶ 47; U.N. Doc. A/HRC/28/18 (March 27, 2015). ¶ 21; U.N. Doc. A/HRC/30/66 (July 27, 2015). ¶ 48; U.N. Doc. A/HRC/34/53/Add.1 (Jan. 9, 2017). ¶ 8.

[2276] Hamdi Alkhshali & Joshua Berlinger, *Facing Fines, Conversion or Death, Christian Families Flee Mosul,* CNN, July 20, 2014; AMNESTY INTERNATIONAL. *Supra* note 495. p. 15; HUMAN RIGHTS WATCH. (December 2017). p. 16.

[2277] KNIGHTS OF COLUMBUS. *Supra* note 409. p. 12; THE HUDSON INSTITUTE (July 21, 2016). *Supra* note 2196.. p. 19.

[2278] KNIGHTS OF COLUMBUS. *Supra* note 409. pp. 12–13.

toric tax granted to the "People of the Book."[2279] Some evidence shows that even when Christians paid the amounts, ISIL/DAESH murdered, kidnapped, enslaved, and raped them. Fighters destroyed properties belonging to Christians and punished those who gathered for worship meetings.[2280] Allegedly, for ISIL/DAESH, *"Jizya"* taxes constituted "simply extortion and ransom payments that at most provided temporary protection from attacks."[2281]

However, the pieces of evidence that show that *Jizya* turned to *extortion* only – and no longer *protection* – are scarce. Most of the existing evidence indicates that ISIL/DAESH did not attack those who made payments to ISIL/DAESH fighters during 2014-2015. Obviously, the concession of such payment does not mean that ISIL/DAESH fighters recognized Christians' right to exist as a group. At the root of the interpretation of what *Jizya* constituted in Iraq lies the assumption that the brutal acts of violence against Christians were not directed against them *exclusively*. Therefore, the existing evidence on *Jizya* does not support the assumption that ISIL/DAESH had the *mens rea* to destroy Christians in Iraq as a group – *as such*.[2282]

### 4.1.3. Beyond a reasonable doubt

Both the ICTY and the ICTR concur that the existing evidence presented in a criminal case must demonstrate beyond a reasonable doubt that the only possible inference about the perpetrators' mens rea is one that leads to individual criminal responsibility for genocide.[2283] [2284] Nevertheless, comprehensive documentation of the crimes committed by ISIL/DAESH against Christians is still lacking.[2285] Lack of access to conflict-affected areas, the fear of the Christian families in reporting crimes, and other security and administrative concerns seriously impeded the documentation of cases leading to a conclusion that genocide was committed against Christians.[2286] [2287] Thus, the exact figures and the clarifi-

---

[2279] THE HUDSON INSTITUTE (July 21, 2016). *Supra* note 2196. p. 19.

[2280] *Idem.* p. 4.

[2281] *Idem.* pp. 3–4.

[2282] KNIGHTS OF COLUMBUS. *Supra* note 409. p. 11.

[2283] Prosecutor v. Zdravko Tolimir. IT-05-88/2-T. *Supra* note 153. ¶¶ 750–759.

[2284] Prosecutor v. Callixte Nzabonimana. ICTR-98-44D-T. *Supra* note 168. ¶ 1715.

[2285] THE HUDSON INSTITUTE (August 2016). *Supra* note 410. p. 1; UNITED STATES HOLOCAUST MEMORIAL MUSEUM (2015). *Supra* note 2216. p. 3.

[2286] U.N. Doc. A/69/926–S/2015/409 (June 5, 2015). ¶ 77; U.N. Doc. S/2015/852 (Nov. 9, 2015). ¶ 5.

cation of the atrocities committed on the basis of religious discrimination remain unclear.[2288]

To this date, the Investigative Team[2289] produced five reports with updates on the investigation measures and findings on the crimes committed by ISIL/DAESH in Iraq against religious minorities.[2290] They all mention the "efforts" to "uncover the truth." Some of them point to conduct that leads to the conclusion of the perpetration of the crime of persecution, as the reader can see in section 6.3. However, none of them brought a detailed account of facts or disclosed evidence descriptively and conclusively to permit a conclusive legal finding that ISIL/DAESH members perpetrated genocide against Christians in Iraq. Therefore, the existing evidence to this date does not meet the necessary legal standards of admissibility of a genocide conviction for ISIL/DAESH fighters in Iraq.

## 4.2. Legal assessment of whether the definition of persecution, as a crime against humanity, is satisfied in ISIL/DAESH conduct in Iraq

The Elements of Crimes of the International Criminal Court establishes six constitutive bases for the crime against humanity of persecution.[2291] Five of them concern the *actus reus* of the crime of persecution, as follows:

"1. The perpetrator severely deprived, contrary to international law, one or more persons of fundamental rights.

2. The perpetrator targeted such person or persons by reason of the identity of a group or collectivity or targeted the group or collectivity as such.

3. Such targeting was based on political, racial, national, ethnic, cultural, religious, gender as defined in article 7, paragraph 3, of the Statute, or other grounds that are universally recognized as impermissible under international law.

---

[2287] Eur. Parl., Prosecuting and Punishing the Crimes Against Humanity or Even Possible Genocide Committed by Daesh, Report, Doc. No. 14402 (Sept. 22, 2017). ¶ 42.

[2288] U.N. Doc. A/HRC/34/53/Add.1 (Jan. 9, 2017). ¶ 63.

[2289] The "Investigative Team to support Iraqi efforts to prosecute ISIL/DAESH fighters." Please, refer to section: 1.1.5. International efforts to hold ISIL/DAESH terrorist fighters accountable.

[2290] U.N. Docs. S/2018/1031 (Nov. 16, 2018), S/2019/407 (May 17, 2019), S/2019/878 (Nov. 13, 2019), S/2020/386 (May 11, 2020), and S/2020/1107 (Nov. 11, 2020).

[2291] International Criminal Court (ICC), Elements of Crimes, 2013. *Supra* note 2068. Article 7.1.h.

4. The conduct was committed in connection with any act referred to in article 7, paragraph 1, of the Statute or any crime within the jurisdiction of the Court.

5. The conduct was committed as part of a widespread or systematic attack directed against a civilian population."[2292]

As it will be argued in the next sections, ISIL/DAESH acts and omissions against Christians in Iraq meet all these five constitutive bases. One of these Elements of Crimes exclusively concerns the assessment of whether an *intent* to discriminate on the grounds of religion (*mens rea*) falls within the definition established in Article 7.1.h of the Rome Statute:[2293] "6. The perpetrator knew that the conduct was part of or intended the conduct to be part of a widespread or systematic attack directed against a civilian population."[2294]

## 4.2.1. Widespread attacks

Numerous factual circumstances sustain the conclusion that ISIL/DAESH's acts and omissions perpetrated against Christians in Iraq were widespread, as follows: 1) the fact that ISIL/DAESH took administrative and military control of many parts of Iraq, ruling an area larger than the United Kingdom, including the complete seizing and/or storming and attacking of areas, cities and villages predominantly inhabited by Christians, in particular Mosul, Ninewa, Bashiqa, Bartella, Tel Keif, Shirkhan, districts around Makhmour, the region of Zummar, Mount Sinjar, parts of Salah al-Din Governorate, Al-Hamdaniya (Qaraqosh), and numerous villages in Kirkuk and Diyala Governorates; 2) the explicit targeted killing of tens of thousands of Christians; 3) the fact that an estimated "200,000 Christians and members of other ethnic and religious groups" were displaced by force from areas taken over by ISIL/DAESH, "in fear of ISIL/DAESH threats when they were given the choice to pay a tax, convert or leave;"[2295] 4) the sweeping scale of the cruel acts by ISIL/DAESH fighters, financially extorting members of the Christian community trying to flee from Iraq; 5) the widespread seizing, appropriation, looting of houses, belongings, and properties owned by Christians in Iraq; 6) the large-scale sexual abuse of Christian children; and 7) the abduction, and/or recruitment and use of Christian children in large

---

[2292] *Idem.* Article 7.1.h.
[2293] United Nations. Rome Statute (July 17, 1998) 2187 UNTS 38544. Article 7.1.h.
[2294] International Criminal Court (ICC), Elements of Crimes, 2013. *Supra* note 2068. Article 7.1.h.
[2295] U.N. Doc. A/HRC/28/18 (March 27, 2015). ¶ 21.

numbers, particularly in areas of Sinjar, and Zummar in Ninewa Governorate.[2296] [2297] [2298] [2299] [2300]

It is also documented that ISIL/DAESH also committed other atrocious acts against Christians in Iraq in a *widespread* manner: mass murder; beatings; torture; assault; imprisonment; crucifixions; beheadings; and other inhuman and degrading treatment; extermination, and systematic 'cleansing;' abduction/kidnappings; deprivation of liberty; enslavement; human trafficking; hostage-taking; use of persons as human shields or for suicide bombing; forced marriage; the kidnapping of children; separation of Christian children from their mothers; forcibly transferring them to another group; and other violent acts seeking to destroy/eradicate/exterminate their entire community of Christians in Iraq.[2301] [2302]

---

[2296] U.N. Doc. S/2014/774 (Oct. 31, 2014). ¶ 46; U.N. Doc. A/HRC/28/18 (March 27, 2015). ¶¶ 21–22, 76; U.N. Doc. A/69/926–S/2015/409 (June 5, 2015). ¶ 77; U.N. Doc. A/HRC/30/66 (July 27, 2015). ¶¶ 37, 48; U.N. Doc. S/2015/852 (Nov. 9, 2015). ¶¶ 5, 10; U.N. Doc. A/HRC/34/53/Add.1 (Jan. 9, 2017). ¶ 8; U.N. Doc. CCPR/C/IRQ/CO/5/Add.1 (Aug. 18, 2017). ¶ 4; S.C. Res. 2379 (Sept. 21, 2017). preamble; U.N. Doc. CERD/C/IRQ/22-25 (Nov. 22, 2017). ¶ 16; U.N. Doc. CEDAW/C/IRQ/7 (Aug. 15, 2018). ¶ 8; U.N. Doc. A/HRC/39/NGO/X (Aug. 23, 2018). p. 3; U.N. Doc. CED/C/IRQ/AI/1 (Aug. 1, 2019). ¶¶ 42, 45; U.N. Doc. CAT/C/IRQ/2 (Aug. 20, 2019). ¶ 52; S.C. Res. 2490 (Sept. 20, 2019). preamble; U.N. Doc. S/2019/761 (Sept. 20, 2019). Preamble; U.N. Doc. S/2019/984 (Dec. 23, 2019). ¶ 60; U.N. Doc. CAT/C/IRQ/FCO/1 (June 15, 2020). ¶ 2.

[2297] UNAMI (July 6, 2014 – Sept. 10, 2014). p. 12; UNAMI (Dec. 11, 2014 – Apr. 30, 2015). pp. 19–20.

[2298] Eur. Parl., Report, Funding of the Terrorist Group Daesh: Lessons Learned, Doc. No. 14510 (Mar. 12, 2018). ¶ 4.

[2299] 164 Cong. Rec. H9600 (daily ed. Nov. 27, 2018) (statement of Rep. Christopher H. Smith). p. H9603.

[2300] UNITED STATES HOLOCAUST MEMORIAL MUSEUM (2015). *Supra* note 2216. pp. 3, 12, 18; *What ISIS Really Wants*, THE ATLANTIC, March 2015; CEASEFIRE CENTRE FOR CIVILIAN RIGHTS (Jul. 2016). *Supra* note 2193. p. 13.

[2301] Eur. Parl., Threats Against Humanity Posed by the Terrorist Group Known as "IS": Violence Against Christians and Other Religious or Ethnic Communities (Final version), Doc. No. 13618 (Sept. 30, 2014). ¶ 7; Eur. Parl., Systematic Mass Murder of Religious Minorities by the so-called 'ISIS/Daesh' (2016/2529(RSP)), Resolution (Feb. 4, 2016). b, ¶ 1; Eur. Parl., Situation in Northern Iraq/Mosul (TA(2016)0422), Resolution (Oct. 27, 2016). d; Eur. Parl., Prosecuting and Punishing the Crimes Against Humanity or Even Possible Genocide Committed by Daesh, Resolution 2190 (2017). ¶ 3.2; Eur. Parl., Prosecuting and Punishing the Crimes Against Humanity or Even Possible Genocide Committed by Daesh, Report, Doc. No. 14402 (Sept. 22, 2017). ¶ 3; 3.2; 21; Eur. Parl., Prosecuting and Punishing the Crimes Against Humanity or Even Possible Genocide Committed by Daesh, Compendium of Amendments, Doc. No. 14402 (Oct. 11, 2017). ¶¶ 3, 3.2; Eur. Parl., Annual Report

## 4.2.2. Systematic attacks

Beyond any reasonable doubt, the human rights and humanitarian violations perpetrated by ISIL/DAESH against Christians in Iraq were systematic and displayed an unequivocal organizational policy of brutal, violent,
murderous, radical, and extremist ideology.[2303] [2304] Information provided
by multiple sources demonstrates that ISIL/DAESH furthered a *calculated*
pattern of widespread murder, barbarism, domination, massive deportations, humiliation, recruitment, and use of children, countless rapes and
acts of sexual abuse, systematic abduction and enslavement of Christian
women and girls, and administrative, infrastructural, exploitive, and fiscal
control of vast areas of the Iraqi territory (taxes, oil extraction, security,
and education). These acts were perpetrated through a gradual weakening
of the Christian population in a process construed to "suppress, permanently expel or destroy th[is] communit[y] within areas under the control
of ISIL/DAESH."[2305] [2306] [2307]

ISIL/DAESH systematically persecuted Christians in Iraq for opposing
the terrorist group's extreme ideology and *Takfiri* doctrines: ISIL/DAESH
fighters systematically sentenced Christians to death, accusing them of
blasphemy, apostasy, and "infidelity." In addition, different reports indi-

---

on Human Rights and Democracy in the World 2016 and the European Union's
Policy on the Matter (2017/2122(INI)), Resolution (Dec. 13, 2017). ¶ 36; Eur. Parl.,
Systematic Mass Murder of Religious Minorities by the so-called 'ISIS/Daesh'
(2016/2529(RSP)), Resolution (Feb. 4, 2016).

[2302] H.R.Con.Res. 75, 114th Cong. (Mar. 15, 2016). p. 2; 163 Cong. Rec. H4632 (daily ed.
June 6, 2017) (statement of Rep. Edward Royce). p. H4633; 163 Cong. Rec. H5368
(daily ed. June 29, 2017) (statement of Rep. Ted Poe). p. H5369; H.R. 407, 115th
Cong. (Dec. 12, 2017). Preamble; H.R. 390, 115th Cong. (Nov. 29, 2018). Drafting. Sec.
2. Findings. ¶ 3; 165 Cong. Rec. H349 (daily ed. Jan. 9, 2019) (statement of Rep. Jeff
Fortenberry). p. H351; 165 Cong. Rec. H2350 (daily ed. Mar. 5, 2019) (statement of
Rep. Jeff Fortenberry). p. H2350; H. Res. 259, 116th Cong. (Mar. 27, 2019). p. 2.

[2303] U.N. Doc. S/2014/774 (Oct. 31, 2014). ¶ 46; U.N. Doc. S/PV.7316 (Nov. 19, 2014). p.
26; U.N. Doc. S/2016/92 (Jan. 29, 2016). ¶ 9; S.C. Res. 2379 (Sept. 21, 2017). preamble;
S.C. Res. 2490 (Sept. 20, 2019). Preamble; U.N. Doc. S/2019/761 (Sept. 20, 2019). Preamble; U.N. Doc. S/2019/984 (Dec. 23, 2019). ¶ 60.

[2304] UNITED STATES HOLOCAUST MEMORIAL MUSEUM (2015). *Supra* note 2216. p. 18.

[2305] U.N. Doc. A/HRC/28/18 (March 27, 2015). ¶ 76. See also: U.N. Doc. A/HRC/30/66
(July 27, 2015). ¶¶ 37, 48; U.N. Doc. A/HRC/34/53/Add.1 (Jan. 9, 2017). ¶ 8; S.C. Res.
2367 (July 14, 2017). Preamble; U.N. Doc. CEDAW/C/IRQ/7 (Aug. 15, 2018). ¶ 13;
U.N. Doc. A/HRC/39/NGO/X (Aug. 23, 2018). p. 3.

[2306] Eur. Parl., Report, Funding of the Terrorist Group Daesh: Lessons Learned, Doc. No.
14510 (Mar. 12, 2018). ¶ 4.

[2307] H.R.Con.Res. 75, 114th Cong. (Sept. 9, 2015). p. 2.

cated that, in pursuing their campaign to destroy Christians in Iraq, ISIL/DAESH fighters systematically chose both extremely efficient methods of direct physical destruction of lives, as well as *slow death* methods.[2308 2309 2310]

Some of these efficient methods included: mass and individual killings, executions by, *inter alia*, hanging, stoning, drowning, throwing persons off buildings, beheadings, crucifixions, shootings, burnings, and other forms of murder. While *slow death* methods included: taking of hostages, use of persons as human shields, torture, beatings, mutilation, amputation, rape, extensive violence, inhuman and degrading treatment causing serious bodily or mental harm, sexual slavery, and abuse of women and girls, abductions, enforced disappearances, intentional displacement of the Christian population, separation of children from their mothers, systematic destruction of Christian places of worship, and forced conversions.[2311 2312 2313 2314 2315]

### 4.2.3. In fact discriminatory

ISIL/DAESH persecutory acts and omissions not only displayed a discriminatory policy. Importantly, these acts resulted in multiple discriminatory consequences for the Christian community in Iraq. According to reliable sources, the population of Christians in Iraq is thought to have

---

[2308] IRQ 4/2014 (July 24, 2014). p. 2; U.N. Doc. S/2014/774 (Oct. 31, 2014). ¶ 49; U.N. Doc. A/HRC/30/66 (July 27, 2015). ¶¶ 19, 48; U.N. Doc. S/2016/77 (Jan. 26, 2016). ¶ 49; U.N. Doc. S/2016/897 (Oct. 25, 2016). ¶ 45; U.N. Doc. S/2016/92 (Jan. 29, 2016). ¶ 9; U.N. Doc. A/HRC/38/44/Add.1 (June 20, 2018). ¶ 26.

[2309] UNAMI (June 5 – July 5, 2014). p. 13; UNAMI (May 1, 2015 – Oct. 31, 2015). pp. 8, 11.

[2310] AMNESTY INTERNATIONAL. *Supra* note 495.

[2311] U.N. Doc. A/HRC/28/18 (March 27, 2015). ¶ 78; U.N. Doc. A/69/926–S/2015/409 (June 5, 2015). ¶ 71; S.C. Res. 2379 (Sept. 21, 2017). ¶ 1; U.N. Doc. A/HRC/38/44/Add.1 (June 20, 2018). ¶¶ 23, 25, 28, 73; U.N. Doc. S/2018/677 (July 9, 2018). p.3; U.N. Doc. S/PV.8324 (Aug. 8, 2018). p.3; U.N. Doc. CEDAW/C/IRQ/7 (Aug. 15, 2018). ¶ 9; U.N. Doc. A/73/347 (Aug. 28, 2018). ¶ 9.

[2312] Eur. Parl., Systematic Mass Murder of Religious Minorities by the so-called 'ISIS/Daesh' (2016/2529(RSP)), Resolution (Feb. 4, 2016). p. 35/79. H; Eur. Parl., Prosecuting and Punishing the Crimes Against Humanity or Even Possible Genocide Committed by Daesh, Resolution 2190 (2017). ¶¶ 3; 3.1; 4.

[2313] U.S. Dep't of State, Department Press, Remarks by Secretary of State John Kerry (Mar. 17, 2016).

[2314] UK Parliament, Genocide in Syria and Iraq, Early Day Motion, Sponsored by Robert Flello (Jan. 26, 2016).

[2315] Michelle Nichols, Iraq Tells United Nations That Islamic State Committed Genocide, REUTERS, Feb. 17, 2015; Anugrah Kumar, ISIS Burns Christians Alive in Locked Caskets, Escaped Prisoner Reveals, CHRISTIAN POST, Jan. 6, 2016.

severely declined through forced displacement since the rise of ISIL/DAESH in locations highly inhabited by this religious group, particularly in the Ninewa plains. With the advancement of ISIL/DAESH warfare and the terrorist group's deliberate intent to persecute on religious grounds, thousands of Christians fled from Al-Hamdaniya, Bashiqa, Bartella, Tel Keif to other towns and villages in Iraq or other countries, "in fear of ISIL/DAESH threats when they were given the choice to pay a tax, convert or leave."[2316] [2317] [2318] [2319] In Mosul, on the night of 6 August 2014 alone, almost 150,000 (one hundred fifty thousand) persons who professed the Christian faith fled the advance of ISIL/DAESH.[2320] The disabled, the elderly, or the impoverished victims could not leave to seek "shelter with relatives and community members" in other locations.[2321]

It is documented through multiple sources that ISIL/DAESH has seized the houses and properties of Christians in Mosul. At the checkpoints, many Christians who were fleeing their villages "reported having their possessions stripped from them" or that ISIL/DAESH fighters physically or sexually assaulted them." Countless families have not been able to return. The suffering deliberately caused by ISIL/DAESH fighters took a tremendous toll on the physical and mental health of Christians in the Iraqi territory.[2322] [2323] [2324] Therefore, ISIL/DAESH fighters' acts and omissions were *in fact* persecutory and fall under the classification of the crime of persecution, as a crime against humanity, under Article 7.1.h of the Rome Statute.[2325]

---

[2316] U.N. Doc. A/HRC/28/18 (March 27, 2015). ¶ 21; U.N. Doc. A/HRC/34/53/Add.1 (Jan. 9, 2017). ¶ 32.

[2317] UNAMI (July 6, 2014 – Sept. 10, 2014). p. 12.

[2318] U.S. Dep't of State, Bureau of Democracy, H.R. and Lab., International Religious Freedom Report (2017). p. 164; 163 Cong. Rec. H5368 (daily ed. June 29, 2017) (statement of Rep. Ted Poe). p. H5369.

[2319] THE HUDSON INSTITUTE (July 21, 2016). *Supra* note 2196..

[2320] U.S. Dep't of State, Bureau of Democracy, H.R. and Lab., International Religious Freedom Report (2017). p. 164.

[2321] UNAMI (July 6, 2014 – Sept. 10, 2014). p. 12.

[2322] U.N. Doc. A/HRC/28/18 (March 27, 2015). ¶ 21; U.N. Doc. CAT/C/IRQ/2 (Aug. 20, 2019). ¶ 53.

[2323] UNAMI (July 6, 2014 – Sept. 10, 2014). p. 12.

[2324] U.S. Dep't of State, Bureau of Democracy, H.R. and Lab., International Religious Freedom Report (2017). p. 164.

[2325] United Nations. Rome Statute (July 17, 1998) 2187 UNTS 38544.

## 4.2.4. Mens rea

ISIL/DAESH carried out all the underlying persecutory acts and omissions against Christians in Iraq in a deliberate/not incidental manner. ISIL/DAESH clearly displayed the particular intent to discriminate and target Christians on religious grounds – religious persecution *dolus specialis*, subjecting them to a systematic and widespread policy of multiple and egregious violations of international human rights, humanitarian and criminal law (discriminatory policy – Article 7.1.h.5, Elements of Crimes[2326]).[2327] [2328] [2329] [2330] [2331] [2332] In other words, from mid-2014 until December 2017, ISIL/DAESH intentionally persecuted individuals on the basis of their religious – Christian – identity within ISIL/DAESH areas of control in Iraq (Article 7.1.h.6, Elements of Crimes[2333]), with the knowledge that such "conduct was part of or intended the conduct to be part of a widespread or systematic attack directed against a civilian population" (Article 7.1.h.6, Elements of Crimes[2334]).[2335] [2336]

---

[2326] International Criminal Court (ICC), Elements of Crimes, 2013. *Supra* note 2068. Article 7.1.h.5.

[2327] U.N. Doc. A/HRC/RES/S-22/1 (Sept. 3, 2014). pp. 1–2; U.N. Doc. S/2014/774 (Oct. 31, 2014). ¶ 47; U.N. Doc. A/HRC/30/66 (July 27, 2015). ¶ 48; U.N. Doc. S/2016/897 (Oct. 25, 2016). ¶ 52; S.C. Res. 2367 (July 14, 2017). Preamble; U.N. Doc. CEDAW/C/IRQ/7 (Aug. 15, 2018). ¶ 10; U.N. Doc. CED/C/IRQ/AI/1 (Aug. 1, 2019). ¶ 44; U.N. Doc. CAT/C/IRQ/2 (Aug. 20, 2019). ¶ 53.

[2328] UNAMI (Nov. 6, 2018). p. 4.

[2329] Eur. Parl., Situation in Iraq and Syria and the IS Offensive Including the Persecution of Minorities, Resolution, P8_TA(2014)0027 (Sept. 18, 2014). ¶ C; Eur. Parl., Iraq: Kidnapping and Mistreatment of Women, Resolution, P8_TA(2014)0066 (Nov. 27, 2014). ¶ C; Eur. Parl., Humanitarian Crisis in Iraq and Syria, in Particular in the IS Context, Resolution, P8_TA(2015)0040 (Feb. 12, 2015). ¶ G; Eur. Parl. Plenary sitting. Joint Motion for a Resolution Pursuant to Rule 123(2) and (4), of the Rules of Procedure. Systematic Mass Murder of Religious Minorities by The So-called ISIS/Daesh 2014–2019. (Feb. 3, 2016). ¶¶ 1, B.

[2330] H. Res. House Foreign Affairs Subcommittees on Africa, Global Health, Global Human Rights and International Organizations and the Middle East and North Africa. Testimony of Assistant Secretary Tom Malinowski (Sept. 10, 2014).

[2331] UK Parliament, Genocide in Syria and Iraq, Early Day Motion, Sponsored by Robert Flello (Jan. 26, 2016).

[2332] CEASEFIRE CENTRE FOR CIVILIAN RIGHTS (Jul. 2016). *Supra* note 2193. p. 43; AMNESTY INTERNATIONAL. *Supra* note 495. p. 15; HUMAN RIGHTS WATCH. (December 2017). p. 16; ACN INTERNATIONAL (June 2020). *Supra* note 2193. p. 26.

[2333] International Criminal Court (ICC), Elements of Crimes, 2013. *Supra* note 2068. Article 7.1.h.6.

[2334] *Ibidem.*

ISIL/DAESH aimed to severely deprive the Christian community of their fundamental rights and to finally suppress, permanently expel or exterminate from the Iraqi society – and from humanity itself – persons defined by the terrorist group as Christians, which shows that such conducts were committed in connection with the acts referred to in Article 7.1.h of the Rome Statute.[2337] [2338] [2339] [2340] Several instances of the United Nations protective umbrella of human rights explicitly recognized that such aim was perpetrated in a deliberate/intentional manner, for instance, the U.N. Secretary-General,[2341] the Office of the United Nations High Commissioner for Human Rights,[2342] the Human Rights Council,[2343] the Committee on the Elimination of Racial Discrimination,[2344] the Committee on the Elimination of Discrimination against Women,[2345] the Human Rights Committee,[2346] the Committee on Enforced Disappearances,[2347] and the Special Rapporteur on Minority Issues.[2348]

It is demonstrated that ISIL/DAESH issued several declarations, statements of doctrine and policies encompassing the destruction of Christians.[2349] In these public statements, ISIL/DAESH fighters deliberately

---

[2335] U.N. Doc. A/HRC/RES/S-22/1 (Sept. 3, 2014). pp. 1–2.

[2336] UNAMI (Dec. 11, 2014 – Apr. 30, 2015). p. i.

[2337] United Nations. Rome Statute (July 17, 1998) 2187 UNTS 38544. Article 7.1.h.

[2338] Eur. Parl. Plenary sitting. Joint Motion for a Resolution Pursuant to Rule 123(2) and (4), of the Rules of Procedure. Systematic Mass Murder of Religious Minorities by The So-called ISIS/Daesh 2014–2019. (Feb. 3, 2016). ¶ 1.

[2339] UNAMI (July 6, 2014 – Sept. 10, 2014). p. 11; UNAMI (Dec. 11, 2014 – Apr. 30, 2015). p. i; UNAMI (May 1, 2015 – Oct. 31, 2015). p. 19; U.N. Doc. A/HRC/30/66 (July 27, 2015). ¶ 48; UNAMI (Nov. 6, 2018). p. 4.

[2340] Comparatively: Prosecutor v. Dario Kordić and Mario Čerkez. IT-95-14/2-T. *Supra* note 80. ¶ 214.

[2341] U.N. Doc. S/2014/774 (Oct. 31, 2014). ¶ 46; U.N. Doc. S/2019/984 (Dec. 23, 2019). ¶ 60.

[2342] U.N. Doc. A/HRC/28/18 (March 27, 2015). ¶ 16; U.N. Doc. A/HRC/30/66 (July 27, 2015). ¶ 48.

[2343] U.N. Doc. A/HRC/RES/S-22/1 (Sept. 3, 2014). pp. 1–2.

[2344] U.N. Doc. CERD/C/IRQ/22-25 (Nov. 22, 2017). ¶¶ 15–16.

[2345] U.N. Doc. CEDAW/C/IRQ/7 (Aug. 15, 2018). ¶ 11.

[2346] U.N. Doc. CCPR/C/IRQ/CO/5/Add.1 (Aug. 18, 2017). ¶¶ 1, 3–4.

[2347] U.N. Doc. CED/C/IRQ/AI/1 (Aug. 1, 2019). ¶ 45.

[2348] U.N. Doc. A/HRC/34/53/Add.1 (Jan. 9, 2017). ¶ 61.

[2349] Eur. Parl., Prosecuting and Punishing the Crimes Against Humanity or Even Possible Genocide Committed by Daesh, Resolution 2190 (2017). ¶ 4; Eur. Parl., Prosecuting and Punishing the Crimes Against Humanity or Even Possible Genocide Committed by Daesh, Report, Doc. No. 14402 (Sept. 22, 2017). ¶¶ 4, 21; Eur. Parl., Prosecuting and Punishing the Crimes Against Humanity or Even Possible Geno-

compelled members of Christian communities, including young children, to either 1) convert to Islam, 2) pay a fine – in accordance with Sharia Law – *jizyah* –,3) face expulsion, or 4) face summary killings – "death by the sword.[2350] [2351] [2352] [2353] Children were reportedly being beheaded by ISIL/DAESH members for refusing to convert to Islam.[2354] These orders were announced publicly in leaflets and in all the mosques' loudspeakers during Friday's prayers, which demonstrates again that ISIL/DAESH fighters were fully aware of the atrocities deliberately committed against Christians.[2355]

Therefore, it is incontrovertible that ISIL/DAESH targeted Christians in Iraq on the basis of religious discrimination. It is also incontrovertible that the available evidence contains some objective elements (material acts/*actus reus*) that could be indicative of ISIL/DAESH fighters' genocidal intent against Christians. Nevertheless, there is not enough evidence to date that ISIL/DAESH harbored a distinct, unique, separate, and positive genocidal intent to destroy, in whole or in part, the group of Christians in Iraq solely and exclusively for their belonging/affiliation to this group – genocidal *mens rea* (as such). In this case, genocidal intent is not the only possible

---

cide Committed by Daesh, Compendium of Amendments, Doc. No. 14402 (Oct. 11, 2017). ¶ 4.

[2350] U.N. Doc. A/HRC/S-22/NGO/8 (Aug. 29, 2014). p.3; U.N. Doc. A/HRC/RES/S-22/1 (Sept. 3, 2014). p.1; U.N. Doc. A/HRC/28/18 (March 27, 2015). ¶ 21; U.N. Doc. A/HRC/34/53/Add.1 (Jan. 9, 2017). ¶ 32.

[2351] UNAMI (July 6, 2014 – Sept. 10, 2014). p.11; UNAMI (Dec. 11, 2014 – Apr. 30, 2015). p.21.

[2352] AMNESTY INTERNATIONAL. *Supra* note 495. p. 15; HUMAN RIGHTS WATCH. (December 2017). p. 16.

[2353] Hamdi Alkhshali & Joshua Berlinger, *Facing Fines, Conversion or Death, Christian Families Flee Mosul,* CNN, July 20, 2014; Eleftheriou-Smith, Loulla-Mae. The Independent: British 'Vicar of Baghdad' claims Isis beheaded four children for refusing to convert to Islam. December 8, 2014; Jane Corbin, *Could Christianity Be Driven From Middle East?* BBC, April 15, 2015; Moni Basu, *Being Christian in Iraq after ISIS: In Biblical Lands of Iraq, Christianity in Peril After ISIS,* CNN, Nov. 21, 2016; Perry Chiaramonte & Hollie McKay, *Iraqi Christians Forced to Flee Homes Again After Skirmishes Between Kurds and Central Government,* FOX NEWS, Oct. 24, 2017; Myers, Russell. The Mirror: ISIS behead four children in Iraq after they refuse to convert to Islam. December 8, 2017; Hollie McKay, *Life After ISIS: Christians Say They Can't Go Home Without International Protection,* FOX NEWS, Dec. 14, 2017.

[2354] Loulla-Mae Eleftheriou-Smith, *British 'Vicar of Baghdad' Claims Isis Beheaded Four Children For Refusing to Convert to Islam,* THE INDEPENDENT, Dec. 8, 2014; Russell Myers, *ISIS Behead Four Children in Iraq After They Refuse to Convert to Islam,* THE MIRROR, Dec. 8, 2017.

[2355] UNAMI (July 6, 2014 – Sept. 10, 2014). p.11.

inference about the perpetrators' *mens rea* (positive approach). This means that the existing evidence does not meet the necessary legal standards of admissibility of a genocide conviction for ISIL/DAESH – beyond a reasonable doubt requirement.

On the other hand, the existing evidence shows that ISIL/DAESH aimed to severely *deprive* the Christian community of their *fundamental rights* in Iraq in a persecutory fashion. Unquestionably, such deprivation of rights was horrific and caused a long-lasting physical and psychological impact on the victims. Moreover, numerous factual circumstances indicate that the underlying persecutory acts and omissions perpetrated by ISIL/DAESH against Christians in Iraq were *systematic* and *widespread*. Importantly, these acts resulted in multiple *discriminatory consequences*, inflicting horrific and long-lasting physical and psychological impacts on the victims. Consequently, these acts and omissions fall under the crime of persecution, as a crime against humanity, as defined in the Rome Statute – the test of *equal gravity*.

*Chart of United Nations documents cited in Chapter 4 – Chronological order*

**2005**

U.N. Doc. A/60/335 (Sept. 7, 2005).
Rep. of the Special Representative of the Secretary-General for Children and Armed Conflict, addressed to the G.A. on its Sixtieth session.

**2006**

U.N. Doc. A/61/529–S/2006/826 (Oct. 26, 2006).
Rep. of the Special Representative of the Secretary-General for Children and Armed Conflict, addressed to the G.A. on its Sixty-first session.

**2007**

U.N. Doc. A/62/609–S/2007/757 (Dec. 21, 2007).
Rep. of the Special Representative of the Secretary-General for Children and Armed Conflict, addressed to the G.A. on its Sixty-second session.

**2009**

U.N. Doc. A/63/785–S/2009/158 (Mar. 26, 2009).
Rep. of the Special Representative of the Secretary-General for Children and Armed Conflict, addressed to the G.A. on its Sixty-third session.

## 2010

U.N. Doc. A/64/742–S/2010/181 (Apr. 13, 2010).
Rep. of the Special Representative of the Secretary-General for Children and Armed Conflict, addressed to the G.A. on its Sixty-fourth session.

## 2011

U.N. Doc. A/65/820–S/2011/250 (Apr. 23, 2011).
Rep. of the Special Representative of the Secretary-General for Children and Armed Conflict, addressed to the G.A. on its Sixty-fifth session.

U.N. Doc. S/2011/366 (June 15, 2011).
Rep. of the U.N. Secretary-General submitted to the S.C, pursuant to *Children and Armed Conflict in Iraq*.

U.N. Doc. S/AC.51/2011/6 (Oct. 3, 2011).
Rep. of the S.C. Working Group on Children and Armed Conflict, Conclusions on Children and Armed Conflict *in Iraq*.

## 2012

U.N. Doc. A/66/782–S/2012/261 (Apr. 6, 2012).
U.N. Secretary-General, *Children and Armed Conflict*.

U.N. Doc. CRC/C/OPAC/IRQ/1 (May 9, 2012).
Rep. of the Committee on the Rights of the Child, Consideration of reports submitted by States parties under article 8, paragraph 1, of the Optional Protocol to the Convention on the Rights of the Child on the involvement of children in armed conflict Initial reports of States parties due in 2010 Iraq.

## 2013

U.N. Doc. A/67/845–S/2013/245 (May 15, 2013).
U.N. Secretary-General, *Children and Armed Conflict*.

## 2014

U.N. Doc. A/68/878–S/2014/339 (May 15, 2014).
U.N. Secretary-General, *Children and Armed Conflict*.

U.N. Doc. S/2014/485 (July 11, 2014).
Rep. of the U.N. Secretary-General submitted to the S.C, pursuant to *Paragraph 6 of Rresolution 2110 (2013)*.

IRQ 4/2014 (July 24, 2014).
Office of the United Nations High Commissioner for Human Rights, Internal Communication Clearance Form, UA.

U.N. Doc. A/69/212 (July 31, 2014).
Rep. of the Special Representative of the Secretary-General for Children and Armed Conflict, addressed to the G.A. on its Sixty-eighth session.

U.N. Doc. A/HRC/S-22/NGO/8 (Aug. 29, 2014).
U.N. Human Rights Council, Written Statement Submitted by the European Centre for Law and Justice, A Non-Governmental Organization in Special Consultative Status.

U.N. Doc. A/69/53/Add.1 (Sept. 1, 2014).
Rep. of the Human Rights Council.

U.N. Doc. A/HRC/RES/S-22/1 (Sept. 3, 2014).
Human Rights Council Res. S-22/1.

U.N. Doc. S/2014/774 (Oct. 31, 2014).
Rep. of the U.N. Secretary-General submitted to the S.C, pursuant to paragraph 6 or Res. 2169 (2014).

U.N. Doc. S/PV.7316 (Nov. 19, 2014).
S. C. Threats to International Peace and Security Caused by Terrorist Acts, 7316th meeting.

U.N. Doc. A/HRC/28/14 (Dec. 12, 2014).
Human Rights Council. Report of the Working Group on the Universal Periodic Review: Iraq. U.N. Doc.

## 2015

U.N. Doc. S/2015/82 (Feb. 2, 2015).
Rep. of the U.N. Secretary-General submitted to the S.C, pursuant to *Paragraph 6 or Res. 2169 (2014)*.

U.N. Doc. CRC/C/IRQ/CO/2-4 (March 3, 2015).
Committee on the Rights of the Child, Concluding observations on the combined second to fourth periodic reports of Iraq.

U.N. Doc. A/HRC/28/18 (March 27, 2015).
Rep. of the Office of the United Nations High Commissioner for Human Rights, submitted to the Human Rights Council, *Human Rights Situation in Iraq in the Light of Abuses Committed by The so Called Islamic State in Iraq and The Levant and Associated Groups.*

U.N. Doc. A/HRC/RES/28/32 (April 8, 2015).
Human Rights Council Res. 28/32.

U.N. Doc. A/69/926–S/2015/409 (June 5, 2015).
U.N. Secretary-General, *Children and Armed Conflict.*

U.N. Doc. A/HRC/29/NGO/95 (June 10, 2015).
U.N. Human Rights Council, Written Statement Submitted by the Al-khoei Foundation, A Non-Governmental Organization in Special Consultative Status.

U.N. Doc. S/2015/530 (July 13, 2015).
Rep. of the U.N. Secretary-General submitted to the S.C, pursuant to *Paragraph 6 or Res. 2169 (2014).*

U.N. Doc. A/HRC/30/66 (July 27, 2015).
Rep. of the Office of the United Nations High Commissioner for Human Rights, submitted to the Human Rights Council, Technical Assistance Provided to Assist in The Promotion and Protection of Human Rights in Iraq.

U.N. Doc. A/HRC/30/NGO/116 (Sept. 8, 2015).
U.N. Human Rights Council, Written statement submitted by the International Youth and Student Movement for the United Nations, A Non-Governmental Organization in Special Consultative Status.

U.N. Doc. S/2015/739 (Sept. 25, 2015).
U.N. Chair of the S.C., Letter dated 25 September 2015 from the Chair of the Security Council Committee pursuant to resolutions 1267 (1999) and 1989 (2011) concerning Al-Qaida and associated individuals and entities addressed to the President of the Security Council.

U.N. Doc. S/2015/852 (Nov. 9, 2015).
Rep. of the U.N. Secretary-General submitted to the S.C, pursuant to *Children and Armed Conflict in Iraq*.

U.N. Doc. S/PV.7556 (Nov. 11, 2015).
Rep. of the U.N. Secretary-General submitted to the S.C, pursuant to *Res. 2233 (2015)*.

U.N. Doc. S/2015/975 (Dec. 29, 2015).
U.N. Chair of the S.C., Letter dated 15 December 2015 from the Chair of the Security Council Committee established pursuant to resolution 1373 (2001) concerning counter-terrorism addressed to the President of the Security Council.

## 2016

U.N. Doc. S/2016/77 (Jan. 26, 2016).
Rep. of the U.N. Secretary-General submitted to the S.C, pursuant to paragraph 7 or Res. 2233 (2015).

U.N. Doc. S/2016/92 (Jan. 29, 2016).
Rep. of the U.N. Secretary-General submitted to the S.C, pursuant to the Threat Posed by ISIL/DAESH (Da'esh) to International Peace and Security.

U.N. Doc. A/HRC/32/35/Add.1 (April 5, 2016).
U.N. Human Rights Council, Report of the Special Rapporteur on the Human Rights of Internally Displaced Persons, Chaloka Beyani, Visit to Iraq.

U.N. Doc. S/2016/361 (Apr. 20, 2016).
Rep. of the U.N. Secretary-General submitted to the S.C, on *Conflict-Related Sexual Violence*.

U.N. Doc. A/70/836–S/2016/360 (Apr. 20, 2016).
U.N. Secretary-General, *Children and Armed Conflict*.

U.N. Doc. A/HRC/41/46 (Abr. 23, 2019).
Rep. of the Special Rapporteur on Trafficking in persons, especially women and children, Maria Grazia Giammarinaro, submitted to the Human Rights Council.

U.N. Doc. S/2016/396 (Apr. 27, 2016).
Rep. of the U.N. Secretary-General submitted to the S.C, pursuant to *Paragraph 7 or Res. 2233 (2015)*.

U.N. Doc. S/2016/592 (July 5, 2016).
Rep. of the U.N. Secretary-General submitted to the S.C, pursuant to the *Paragraph 7 of Res. 2233 (2015)*,

U.N. Doc. S/2015/739 (July 19, 2016).
U.N. Chair of the S.C., Letter dated 25 September 2015 from the Chair of the Security Council Committee pursuant to resolutions 1267 (1999) and 1989 (2011) concerning Al-Qaida and associated individuals and entities addressed to the President of the Security Council.

U.N. Doc. A/71/205 (July 25, 2016).
Rep. of the Special Representative of the Secretary-General for Children and Armed Conflict, addressed to the G.A. on its Seventy-first session.

U.N. Doc. A/71/303 (Aug. 5, 2016).
Rep. of the Special Rapporteur on Trafficking in persons, especially women and children, Maria Grazia Giammarinaro, submitted to the Human Rights Council concerning her mission to Iraq.

U.N. Doc. S/AC.51/2016/2 (Aug. 18, 2016).
Rep. of the S.C. Working Group on Children and Armed Conflict, *Conclusions on Children and Armed Conflict in Iraq*.

U.N. Doc. S/2016/897 (Oct. 25, 2016). ¶ 52.
Rep. of the U.N. Secretary-General submitted to the S.C, pursuant to the implementation of Res. 2299 (2016).

U.N. Doc. S/2016/949 (Nov. 10, 2016).
Rep. of the U.N. Secretary-General submitted to the S.C, pursuant to the *Implementation of Measures to Counter Trafficking in Persons*.

U.N. Doc. S/2016/1090 (Dec. 21, 2016).
U.N. Chair of the S.C., Letter dated 20 December 2016 from the Secretary-General addressed to the President of the Security Council.

**2017**

U.N. Doc. A/HRC/34/53/Add.1 (Jan. 9, 2017).
Rep. of the Special Rapporteur on Minority Issues, submitted to the Human Rights Council concerning her mission to Iraq.

U.N. Doc. A/HRC/34/50 (Jan. 17, 2017).
U.N. Human Rights Council, Report of the Special Rapporteur on freedom of religion and belief, U.N. Doc. A/HRC/34/50 (Jan. 17, 2017).

U.N. Doc. S/2017/75 (Jan. 26, 2017).
Rep. of the U.N. Secretary-General submitted to the S.C, pursuant to *the Implementation of Res. 2299 (2016)*.

U.N. Doc. A/72/164 (July 18, 2017).
Joint Rep. of the Special Rapporteur on the sale and sexual exploitation of children, including child prostitution, child pornography and other child sexual abuse material and the Special Rapporteur on trafficking in persons, especially women and children.

U.N. Doc. S/2017/573 (Aug. 7, 2017).
U.N. Chair of the S.C., Letter dated 7 August 2017 from the Chair of the Security Council Committee pursuant to resolutions 1267 (1999), 1989 (2011) and 2253 (2015) concerning Islamic State in Iraq and the Levant (Da'esh), Al-Qaida and associated individuals, groups, undertakings and entities addressed to the President of the Security Council.

U.N. Doc. S/2018/773 (Aug. 17, 2017).
U.N. Secretary-General, Letter dated Aug. 15, 2018 from the Secretary-General addressed to the President of the Security Council

U.N. Doc. CCPR/C/IRQ/CO/5/Add.1 (Aug. 18, 2017).
Rep. of the Human Rights Committee, Concluding Observations on the Fifth Periodic Report of Iraq.

U.N. Doc. A/HRC/39/NGO/X (Aug. 23, 2018).
U.N. Human Rights Council, Written Statement Submitted by the European Centre for Law and Justice, A Non-Governmental Organization in Special Consultative Status, Request that the U.N. Recognize ISIS Atrocities Against Christians and Other Religious and Ethnic Minorities as Genocide and Take Immediate Appropriate Action.

U.N. Doc. A/72/361–S/2017/821 (Aug. 24, 2017).
U.N. Secretary-General, *Children and Armed Conflict.*

U.N. Doc. A/72/53/Add.1 (Sept. 29, 2017).
Rep. of the Human Rights Council.

U.N. Doc. S/2017/881 (Oct. 19, 2017).
Rep. of the U.N. Secretary-General submitted to the S.C, pursuant to *Res. 2367 (2017).*

U.N. Doc. S/2017/939 (Nov. 10, 2017).
Rep. of the U.N. Secretary-General submitted to the S.C, pursuant *Trafficking in Persons in Armed Conflict,* according to the S. C. Res. 2331 (2016).

U.N. Doc. CERD/C/IRQ/22-25 (Nov. 22, 2017).
Rep. of the Committee on the Elimination of Racial Discrimination, Combined Twenty-Second to Twenty-Fifth Periodic Reports Submitted by Iraq Under Article 9 of the Convention.

U.N. Doc. S/2017/966 (2017).
U.N. Secretary-General, Letter dated Nov. 15, 2017 from the Secretary-General addressed to the President of the Security Council.

## 2018

U.N. Doc. S/2018/42 (Jan. 17, 2018).
Rep. of the U.N. Secretary-General submitted to the S.C, pursuant to *Res. 2367 (2017).*

U.N. Doc. S/2018/80 (Jan. 31, 2018).
Rep. of the U.N. Secretary-General submitted to the S.C, pursuant to the *Threat Posed by ISIL/DAESH (Da'esh) to International Peace and Security.*

U.N. Doc. S/2018/118 (Feb. 14, 2018).
U.N. Chair of the S.C., Letter dated 9 February 2018 from the Secretary-General addressed to the President of the Security Council.

U.N. Doc. S/2018/14/Rev.1 (Feb. 27, 2018).
U.N. Chair of the S.C., Letter dated 17 January 2018 from the Chair of the Security Council Committee pursuant to resolutions 1267 (1999), 1989 (2011), and 2253 (2015) concerning Islamic State in Iraq and the Levant

(Da'esh), Al-Qaida and associated individuals, groups, undertakings and entities addressed to the President of the Security Council.

U.N. Doc. S/2018/359 (Apr. 17, 2018).
Rep. of the U.N. Secretary-General submitted to the S.C, pursuant to *Res. 2367 (2017)*.

U.N. Doc. A/72/865–S/2018/465 (May 16, 2018).
U.N. Secretary-General, *Children and Armed Conflict.*

U.N. Doc. A/HRC/38/44/Add.1 (June 20, 2018).
Rep. of the Special Rapporteur on Extrajudicial, Summary or Arbitrary Executions, submitted to the Human Rights Council concerning her mission to Iraq.

U.N. Doc. S/2018/677 (July 9, 2018).
Rep. of the U.N. Secretary-General submitted to the S.C, pursuant to the implementation of Res. 2367 (2017).

U.N. Doc. S/2018/705 (July 27, 2018).
U.N. Chair of the S.C., United Nations. Security Council. Letter dated July 16, 2018 from the Chair of the Security Council addressed to the President of the Security Council pursuant to resolutions 1267 (1999), 1989 (2011) and 2253 (2015) concerning Islamic State in Iraq and the Levant.

U.N. Doc. S/PV.8324 (Aug. 8, 2018).
Rep. of the U.N. Secretary-General submitted to the S.C, *The Situation Concerning Iraq,* pursuant to Res. 2367 (2017).

U.N. Doc. CEDAW/C/IRQ/7 (Aug. 15, 2018).
Rep. of the Committee on the Elimination of Discrimination against Women, Seventh Periodic Report Submitted by Iraq Under Article 18 of the Convention.

U.N. Doc. S/2018/770 (August 16, 2018).
Rep. of the U.N. Secretary-General submitted to the S.C, pursuant to the *Threat Posed by ISIL/DAESH (Da'esh) to International Peace and Security.*

U.N. Doc. A/HRC/39/NGO/X (Aug. 23, 2018).
U.N. Human Rights Council, Written Statement Submitted by the European Centre for Law and Justice, A Non-Governmental Organization in Special Consultative Status, Request that the U.N. Recognize ISIS Atrocities

Against Christians and Other Religious and Ethnic Minorities as Genocide and Take Immediate Appropriate Action.

U.N. Doc. A/73/347 (Aug. 28, 2018).
U.N. Secretary-General, *Effects of terrorism on the enjoyment of human rights.*

U.N. Doc. A/73/53/Add.1 (Sept. 28, 2018).
Rep. of the Human Rights Council.

U.N. Doc. S/2018/975 (Oct. 31, 2018).
Rep. of the U.N. Secretary-General submitted to the S.C, pursuant to the *Implementation of Res. 2421 (2018).*

U.N. Doc. A/73/352/Add.6 (Oct. 2018).
U.N. Secretary-General, *United Nations Investigative Team to Promote Accountability for Crimes Committed by Da'esh/Islamic State in Iraq and the Levant.*

U.N. Doc. S/2018/1031 (Nov. 16, 2018).
Rep. of the Special Adviser and Head of the U. N. Investigative Team to Promote Accountability for Crimes Committed by Da'esh/Islamic State in Iraq and the Levant submitted to the S.C, First report of the Special Adviser and Head of the United Nations Investigative Team to Promote Accountability for Crimes Committed by Da'esh/Islamic State in Iraq and the Levant.

U.N. Doc. S/2018/770 (2018)
Rep. of the U.N. Secretary-General submitted to the S.C, pursuant to the *Threat Posed by ISIL/DAESH (Da'esh) to International Peace and Security.*

## 2019

U.N. Doc. S/2019/101 (Feb. 1, 2019).
Rep. of the U.N. Secretary-General submitted to the S.C, on the *Implementation of resolution 2421 (2018).*

U.N. Doc. S/2019/103 (Feb. 1, 2019).
Rep. of the U.N. Secretary-General submitted to the S.C, pursuant to the *Threat Posed by ISIL/DAESH (Da'esh) to International Peace and Security.*

U.N. Doc. S/2019/365 (May 2, 2019).
Rep. of the U.N. Secretary-General submitted to the S.C, pursuant to the *Implementation of Res. 2421 (2018).*

U.N. Doc. S/2019/407 (May 17, 2019).
Rep. of the Special Adviser and Head of the U. N. Investigative Team to Promote Accountability for Crimes Committed by Da'esh/Islamic State in Iraq and the Levant submitted to the S.C, Second report of the Special Adviser and Head of the United Nations Investigative Team to Promote Accountability for Crimes Committed by Da'esh/Islamic State in Iraq and the Levant.

U.N. Doc. A/73/907–S/2019/509 (June 20, 2019).
U.N. Secretary-General, *Children and Armed Conflict*.

U.N. Doc. S/2019/570 (July 15, 2019).
U.N. Chair of the S.C., Letter dated 15 July 2019 from the Chair of the Security Council Committee pursuant to resolutions 1267 (1999), 1989 (2011) and 2253 (2015) concerning Islamic State in Iraq and the Levant (Da'esh), Al-Qaida and associated individuals, groups, undertakings and entities addressed to the President of the Security Council.

U.N. Doc. CED/C/IRQ/AI/1 (Aug. 1, 2019).
Committee on Enforced Disappearances, Additional Information Submitted by Iraq Under Article 29 (4) of the Convention.

U.N. Doc. CAT/C/IRQ/2 (Aug. 20, 2019).
Committee Against Torture, Second Periodic Report Submitted by Iraq Under Article 19 of the Convention, Due in 2019.

U.N. Doc. S/2019/878 (Nov. 13, 2019).
Rep. of the Special Adviser and Head of the U. N. Investigative Team to Promote Accountability for Crimes Committed by Da'esh/Islamic State in Iraq and the Levant submitted to the S.C, Third report of the Special Adviser and Head of the United Nations Investigative Team to Promote Accountability for Crimes Committed by Da'esh/Islamic State in Iraq and the Levant.

U.N. Doc. S/2019/903 (Nov. 22, 2019).
Rep. of the U.N. Secretary-General submitted to the S.C, on the *Implementation of resolution 2470 (2019)*.

U.N. Doc. S/2019/984 (Dec. 23, 2019).
Rep. of the U.N. Secretary-General submitted to the S.C, pursuant to *Children and Armed Conflict in Iraq*.

**2020**

U.N. Doc. S/2020/53 (Jan. 20, 2020).
U.N. Chair of the S.C., Letter dated 20 January 2020 from the Chair of the Security Council Committee pursuant to resolutions 1267 (1999), 1989 (2011) and 2253 (2015) concerning Islamic State in Iraq and the Levant (Da'esh), Al-Qaida and associated individuals, groups, undertakings and entities addressed to the President of the Security Council.

U.N. Doc. S/2020/140 (Feb. 21, 2020).
Rep. of the U.N. Secretary-General submitted to the S.C, on the *Implementation of resolution 2470 (2019)*.

U.N. Doc. S/2020/363 (May 6, 2020).
Rep. of the U.N. Secretary-General submitted to the S.C, on the *Implementation of resolution 2470 (2019)*.

U.N. Doc. S/2020/386 (May 11, 2020).
Rep. of the Special Adviser and Head of the U. N. Investigative Team to Promote Accountability for Crimes Committed by Da'esh/Islamic State in Iraq and the Levant submitted to the S.C, Fourth report of the Special Adviser and Head of the United Nations Investigative Team to Promote Accountability for Crimes Committed by Da'esh/Islamic State in Iraq and the Levant.

U.N. Doc. A/74/845–S/2020/525 (June 9, 2020).
Rep. of the U.N. Secretary-General submitted to the S.C, on *Children and Armed Conflict*.

U.N. Doc. A/HRC/44/41/Add.1 (May 13, 2020).
U.N. Human Rights Council, Report of the Special Rapporteur on the Human Rights of Internally Displaced Persons, Cecilia Jimenez-Damary, Visit to Iraq.

U.N. Doc. CAT/C/IRQ/FCO/1 (June 15, 2020).
Committee Against Torture, Information Received From Iraq on Follow-up to the Concluding Observations on Its Initial Report.

U.N. Doc. A/HRC/44/NGO/115 (June 30, 2020).
U.N. Human Rights Council, Written Statement Submitted by the Society for Threatened Peoples, A Non-Governmental Organization in Special Consultative Status

U.N. Doc. S/2020/717 (July 23, 2020).
U.N. Chair of the S.C., Letter dated 16 July 2020 from the Chair of the Security Council Committee pursuant to resolutions 1267 (1999), 1989 (2011) and 2253 (2015) concerning Islamic State in Iraq and the Levant (Da'esh), Al-Qaida and associated individuals, groups, undertakings and entities addressed to the President of the Security Council

*Chart of documents from the United Nations Assistance Mission for Iraq (UNAMI) – Chronological order*

## 2014

July 6, 2014 – Sept. 10, 2014.
UNAMI, Protection of Civilians in the Armed Conflict in Iraq.

Sept. 11, 2014 – Dec. 10, 2014.
UNAMI, Protection of Civilians in the Armed Conflict in Iraq.

Dec. 11, 2014 – April 30, 2015.
UNAMI, Protection of Civilians in the Armed Conflict in Iraq.

## 2015

May 1, 2015 – Oct. 31, 2015.
UNAMI, Protection of Civilians in the Armed Conflict in Iraq.

## 2016

Aug. 2016.
UNAMI, Report: A Call for Accountability and Protection: Yezidi Survivors of Atrocities Committed by ISIL/DAESH.

Aug. 2016.
UNAMI, Report: A Call for Accountability and Protection: Yezidi Survivors of Atrocities Committed by ISIL/DAESH.

## 2018

Nov. 6, 2018.
UNAMI, Unearthing Atrocities: Mass Graves in territory formerly controlled by ISIL/DAESH.

## 2020

Jan. 2020.
UNAMI, Human Rights in the Administration of Justice in Iraq: Trials under the anti-terrorism laws and implications for justice, accountability and social cohesion in the aftermath of ISIL/DAESH.

# Conclusion

The main goal of this book was to determine the legal nature, typification, and criminal responsibility of the acts perpetrated against Christians in Iraq by the terrorist group ISIL/DAESH. The first hypothesis and tentative main research question considered by the author back in February 2019 was "whether the reported actions of ISIL/DAESH fighters against Christians in Iraq, during the ISIL/DAESH regime, might amount to the crime of genocide, under the categorization of Article II of the 1948 Genocide Convention." Four tentative sub-research questions were also assessed: 1) "Do ISIL/DAESH actions amount to genocide? In particular, can genocidal *mens rea* be proved? "2) "Can genocide be perpetrated by members of terrorist groups?" 3) "Does the labeling of an armed group as a "terrorist group" modify the activities of such group under the International Criminal Law regime?" 4) What happened to the *jus cogens* obligation to prevent genocide in Iraq?"

Later, the author abandoned sub-question number 4 because he understood that it would excessively broaden the scope of the book and shift the legal focus to issues related to the field of international relations and international politics. The theoretical answer to question 2 was easily in the affirmative. In addition, the author understood that the definition of ISIL/DAESH members as terrorists or not was not decisive in the legal qualification of their crimes. As a result, the final focus was devoted to 1) the legal elements of the crime of genocide and crimes against humanity; 2) the factual findings respective to the crimes committed by ISIL/DAESH, and 3) the subsumption of those acts under the existing law.

In an academic attempt to address the main research question, the author explored a vast body of literature in the introductory chapter (Introduction, section D), employing triangulation methods described in Introduction, section E, both quantitatively and qualitatively. One hundred and thirty books and seventy-five papers gave substratum for the discussion of the material law of genocide, crimes against humanity, and persecution as a crime against humanity. Although the literature on the general aspects of genocide and crimes against humanity encountered was substantial, the literature of the International Criminal Law scholarship was very deficient in works that analyzed the specific issue of whether the ISIL/DAESH persecution of Christians in Iraq, from 2014 to early 2017, constituted genocide, within the meaning and scope of the 1948 Genocide Convention, or persecution, within the meaning of the 1998 Rome Statute. The author found that many pieces of work addressed the issue, but only incidentally. However, these works explored the general aspects and the machinery of ISIL/DAESH and its threat to global security rather than the risks that ISIL/DAESH directly posed for Christians in Iraq.

In chapter 1, the author provided the reader with a detailed, methodical, and scrutinized account of the major criminal acts that ISIL/DAESH perpetrated against civilians in Iraq, focusing on the violations against Christians. The overall consideration and analysis of the circumstantial evidence pertaining to the violations perpetrated by ISIL/DAESH against Christians in Iraq were supported by one hundred and seventy-five documents from the United Nations umbrella, fifty-five newspaper articles, forty-six documents from the U.S. (U.S. Congress, U.S. Federal Government, U.S. Department of State and the White House), twenty-two documents from the European Parliament/Council of Europe, and several documents from states and state organizations such as the North Atlantic Treaty Organization (NATO).

Here, the author demonstrated that ISIL/DAESH violations of international law against Christians were multidimensional and multifaceted: 1) Physical and mental harm; 2) Violation of rights of International Humanitarian Law; 3) Use of economic measures against the civilian population; 4) Attacks against property of sacred religious relevance; 5) Infringements of individual freedom; 6) Infringements of the right to privacy, and deprivation, destruction, and plunder of private property; and 7) The imposition and maintenance of other restrictive and discriminatory measures involving denial of fundamental rights.

In chapters 2 and 3, the author explored, appraised, and legally assessed the factual matrix of human rights and humanitarian law violations contained in the case-law from the Nuremberg, the ICTR, the ICTY, the SCSL, and the ICC tribunals. Over three hundred decisions concerning more than two hundred cases from these criminal courts were thoroughly read in three stages of reading: on the writing of the Literature Review (Introduction, section D), through the writing of the factual matrix (Chapter 2), and finally, during the preparation of Chapters 3 and 4. In this process, two hundred and six decisions concerning one hundred and thirty-six cases were meticulously scrutinized, divided and separated into different topics, and grouped following the themes of each chapter.

In chapter 4, the author attempted to find, dissect, interpret, demonstrate, and legally assess ISIL/DAESH fighters' intent behind the underlying criminal acts against Christians. Thus, in this chapter, the author attempted to determine whether the *actus reus* and the perpetrators' *mens rea* behind these conducts fall under the definition of genocide, as prescribed by the

Rome Statute, or fall under the crime of persecution, as a crime against humanity, as defined in the Rome Statute – the test of equal gravity.

The author of this book encountered many limitations when trying to assess ISIL/DAESH's intent behind their acts/omissions. The most important limitation lies in the extreme risk of collecting data, evidence, and interviewing surviving victims or the families of deceased victims. The main challenges were:

1) Due to security concerns, access to different parts of Iraq was restricted until ISIL/DAESH's defeat in December 2017. Despite ISIL/DAESH's defeat, the terrorist group reportedly continued to attempt isolated attacks against civilians and security forces, particularly in the Baghdad region. There were several reports of active foreign terrorist fighters searching for children for the purpose of trafficking and sexual slavery;

2) Most of the humanitarian advocacy agencies placed in the Autonomous Administration in Northern Iraq lack official access permits to the areas affected by the conflict in the northern areas of Mosul. This compromised the reporting and documentation of possible cases of genocide/persecution, as it limited the analysis and sampling in several ways;

3) Owing to the fear of police involvement with armed groups, several families of victims were reluctant to report violations of rights to the Iraqi national police authorities.

Another challenge lies in the fact that many local NGOs presented their reports to the public with an already established presumption that the conduct of ISIL/DAESH against Christians in Iraq constituted genocide instead of simply presenting the facts and considering that different legal interpretations were possible. The *Knights of Columbus* Report, for example, made no attempt to differentiate between genocide or persecution as a crime against humanity. Considering the limited size of this sample, the author considered the need to exercise caution in legally interpreting the facts revealed in the reports that were the object of the literature review for this book.

Christians in Iraq are a group of individuals who share the "same religion, denomination or mode of worship," as defined in *Akayesu* (ICTR-96-4-T, judgement, (Sept. 2, 1998). ¶ 515). For this reason, the author considered it incontrovertible that the group of individuals who profess the Christian faith in Iraq is protected from genocide by international law, as prescribed in the Genocide Convention and the Rome Statute.

With the amount of evidence found, it was also indisputable that ISIL/DAESH perpetrated some objective elements of the crime of genocide against this group in Iraq – material acts/*actus reus*. For instance, "killing members of the group," "causing serious bodily harm to the members of the group," and "forcibly transferring children of the group to another group." (Rome Statute, Article 6).

Returning to the hypothesis/question posed at the beginning of this study, the author needed to assess whether, considering all the circumstantial evidence, one could legitimately and sufficiently draw a reasonable inference that these discriminatory acts suffice to prove intent – *mens rea* – to destroy a group, as a separate, distinct entity. The evidence showed that some elements could be indicative of ISIL/DAESH fighters' genocidal intent, *e.g.*, the several ultimatums that Christians should leave the Ninewa plains – or to be else killed – and the material nature of the violations of international human rights. Nevertheless, other important aspects of ISIL/DAESH fighters' conduct indicated a lack of genocidal intent, such as the possibility of Christians in Iraq paying a tax to ISIL/DAESH members so they could be protected from being killed.

The threshold to prove genocidal intent in International Criminal Law is extremely high. The existing evidence showed that ISIL/DAESH systematically targeted and persecuted Christians because of their affiliation or perceived affiliation to a religious group, but not with the exclusive genocidal intent to destroy this group exclusively because they were Christians – thus destroying them as a *separate, distinct* entity *as such*. Therefore, the existing circumstantial evidence concerning ISIL/DAESH atrocities against Christians in Iraq was not, at least to this date, sufficient to prove, beyond a reasonable doubt, that the only possible inference about the perpetrators' *mens rea* may lead to individual criminal responsibility for genocide.

In addition, the existing circumstantial evidence demonstrated that ISIL/DAESH fighters intended to persecute, disperse, submit, weaken – and eventually destroy for religious reasons – all of those who disagreed with the group's own interpretation of Islam and harsh interpretation of Sharia law, all of those who did not conform to its *takfiri* doctrine (*negative* approach), including Christians, but also Yazidis, Shias, and Sunnis, Shabak, Sabeans, Kaka'es, and Turkmen. The existing evidence shows that ISIL/DAESH systematically targeted religious and ethnic minority groups who refused to subscribe and pledge allegiance to its extremist and triumphalist ideology, those who the terrorist group considered "infidels" or "heretics," those who refused to "repent" for not being Muslims.

Whilst this study did not confirm genocidal intent, it did satisfactorily substantiate the threshold for other egregious international crimes.

Therefore, almost eighteen months after the author set the tentative hypothesis and research questions of this present book, he elaborated a second and final research question for the concluding writings of this extensive work: "Whether the existing evidence of crimes against Christians in Iraq, by members of the ISIL/DAESH (2014-2017) may amount to the crime of genocide, or if not, to crimes against humanity."

Although the evidence did not substantiate ISIL/DAESH's intent to destroy Christians as such in Iraq beyond a reasonable doubt, it satisfactorily demonstrated that ISIL/DAESH intended to persecute the group as one of the modalities of crimes against humanity. In *Radovan Karadžić* and *Pauline Nyiramasuhuko et al*, the ICTY and the ICTR, respectively, defined that the crime of persecution, as a crime against humanity, consisted of an act or omission which 1) "discriminates in fact and denies or infringes upon a fundamental right laid down in international customary or treaty law (the *actus reus*);" and 2) is "carried out deliberately with the intention to discriminate on one of the listed grounds," specifically race, religion, ethnicity or politics (the *mens rea*) (Respectively: IT-95-5/18-T, judgement, vol. I, (March 24, 2016). ¶ 497; ICTR-98-42-A, judgement, (Dec. 14, 2015). ¶ 2138).

ISIL/DAESH carried out all the underlying persecutory acts and omissions against Christians in Iraq in a deliberate/not incidental manner. Even with limited evidence, it was apparent that ISIL/DAESH displayed the particular intent to discriminate and target Christians on religious grounds – religious persecution *dolus specialis*, subjecting them to a systematic and widespread policy of multiple and egregious violations of international human rights, humanitarian and criminal law (discriminatory policy – Article 7.1.h.5, Elements of Crimes). This book could satisfactorily demonstrate that, from mid-2014 until December of 2017, ISIL/DAESH intentionally persecuted individuals on the basis of their religious identity – Christians – within ISIL/DAESH areas of control in Iraq (Article 7.1.h.6, ICC Elements of Crimes), with the knowledge that such "conduct was part of or intended the conduct to be part of a widespread or systematic attack directed against a civilian population" (Article 7.1.h.6, ICC Elements of Crimes).

ISIL/DAESH aimed to severely deprive the Christian community of their fundamental rights and to finally suppress, permanently expel or exterminate from the Iraqi society – and from humanity itself – persons defined by the terrorist group as Christians. This shows that such conduct was committed in connection with the acts referred to in Article 7.1.h of the Rome Statute. ISIL/DAESH's persecutory acts and omissions not only displayed a discriminatory policy but, importantly, they caused multiple discriminatory consequences on the Christian community in Iraq. These acts were in fact persecutory. Therefore, this book concludes that ISIL/DAESH fighters' acts and omissions against Christians in Iraq fall under the classification of persecution, as a crime against humanity, under Article 7.1.h of the Rome Statute.

Although from a material standpoint, the general public perceives nuances and gradations between genocide and crimes against humanity – *material seriousness* –, the author firmly believes that both forms of crimes are on an equal footing – they possess the same gravity. It is true that from a *juridical seriousness* standpoint, the legal consequences might be different depending on the penalties that each juridical system or each society determines. But this is different from presuming that genocide is legally more serious than persecution, as a crime against humanity. After all, the Rome Statute, which guided the writing of this book, establishes no juridical ranking between these two crimes. Article 77 subjects perpetrators of genocide and crimes against humanity to the same penalties.

Prosecuting the ISIL/DAESH members has the potential of establishing retribution and deterrence, meaning that the whole international community clearly condemns the atrocities perpetrated by the group and believes that, through criminal responsibilization, others will be discouraged and dissuaded from committing similar crimes in the future. Besides, assuring that ISIL/DAESH terrorist fighters are held responsible for their crimes against Christians in Iraq has the power to secure that all the peripheral aspects of the criminal responsibilization will be safeguarded, for instance: mitigating the circumstances and consequences of the criminal acts; promoting the rule of law through the eradication of the culture of impunity and the realization that wrongdoings are not tolerated; restoring and maintaining peace; promoting national reconciliation; and, ultimately, protecting the society as a whole from crimes that threaten humanity.

Nevertheless, the path that leads to the criminal identification and responsibilization of ISIL/DAESH fighters and the identification of all their victims is complex, time-consuming, intricate, multiphasic, and dependent on the cooperation and partnership of several local and international actors. Alternatives to holding the perpetrators responsible exist, but they are extremely challenging in many aspects. Critically, Iraq is not signatory to the Rome Statute of the International Criminal Court, whose material jurisdiction comprises genocide and crimes against humanity. Consequently, the Court has no automatic jurisdiction over situations that take place on Iraqi territory.

Here, the author demonstrates three possible solutions to overcome the legal obstacles for the ICC to exercise its jurisdiction in relation to situations in Iraq:

Firstly, although unrealistic, Iraq could ratify the Rome Statute in 2021 and grant the ICC retroactive *ratione temporis* jurisdiction over the crimes that took place on Iraqi territory before 2021 and after July 1, 2002 (when the Statute entered into power), through an explicit declaration lodged with the ICC Registrar, following Articles 11.2 and 12.3. After that, the Prosecutor could trigger the proceedings *proprio motu* – Article 13.c and 15.1 – or Iraq itself could refer the situation to the Prosecutor, following Articles 13.a and 14.1.

Secondly, following Article 13.b of the Rome Statute, the Security Council could pass a resolution, under the authority of Chapter VII of the U.N. Charter, referring the situation in Iraq to the ICC Prosecutor, granting him/her the power to investigate crimes of genocide and crimes against humanity that took place on Iraqi territory. Considering that China and Russia exercised their veto power four times in the Security Council to prevent the ICC Prosecutor from exercising jurisdiction over the crimes on Syrian territory – where ISIL/DAESH also committed atrocious violations of International Criminal Law in the same period as in Iraq – it is very unlikely that China and Russia would act differently now regarding the situation in Iraq.

Thirdly, following Article 12.2.b of the Rome Statute, the ICC Prosecutor, using the powers granted by Articles 13.c and 15.1, could decide to investigate and prosecute the ISIL/DAESH foreign terrorist fighters in Iraq, who are nationals of states that have ratified/acceded (to) the Rome Statute and have granted jurisdictional powers to the ICC. This solution would bring important practical contributions, namely: 1) It would help in the collecting and preservation of forensic materials and documentary evidence according to international standards; 2) It would help in the identification, hearing, and protection of witnesses; 3) It would promote domestic and international accountability of wrongdoings; and, ultimately, 4) It would serve the interests of justice and promote peace.

As an alternative path to hold ISIL/DAESH fighters accountable for their violations of International Criminal Law, the author presents here three possible solutions that are not dependent on the ICC:

Firstly, the U.N. Security Council could establish an *ad hoc* tribunal to investigate and prosecute the crimes perpetrated by ISIL/DAESH fighters in Iraq. This solution would require two former special courts such as: 1) the Special Court for Sierra Leone, created upon request of the president of the country, through S.C. Resolution 1315, on August 14, 2000, and established on January 16, 2002, through a special agreement between the local Government and the U.N. Secretary-General; and 2) the Special Tribunal for Lebanon, which resulted from the agreement between the

United Nations and the Lebanese Republic, through S.C. Resolution 1757, from May 30, 2007. Alternatively, the United Nations, through an agreement with the local Iraqi Government, could establish a special hybrid judicial mechanism, composed of Iraqi and international judges/experts, like the Extraordinary Chambers in the Courts of Cambodia, which resulted from an agreement between the United Nations and the Government of Cambodia on May 13, 2003 (U.N. General Assembly Resolution 57/228B). Regarding legality and typicity, either model would bring charges only if materially based on *jus cogens* norms or Customary International Criminal Law.

These models would strengthen the capacity of Iraqi authorities and would be more assertive concerning the factual circumstances of the violations perpetrated by ISIL/DAESH in Iraq. Nevertheless, aspects like the (im)partiality of national prosecutors and judges and the extremely high financial costs of such models pose serious challenges in their availability.

Secondly, Iraqi domestic judicial authorities have been unable to prosecute most of ISIL/DAESH's atrocious acts due to its courts' lack of material jurisdiction, once genocide and crimes against humanity are not typified as such under Iraqi law. Nevertheless, the primary responsibility to investigate and prosecute such violations rests, in the first place, on the state where these violations occurred. Therefore, the international community should, at the same time, press and assist local judicial authorities to investigate and prosecute the individual underlying acts behind the ISIL/DAESH fighters' genocidal or persecutory acts against religious minorities in Iraq, for example, murder and torture.

Thirdly, In *ultima ratio*, universal jurisdiction in relation to returnees from Iraq should be exercised. In virtue of the atrocious nature of some crimes, e.g., genocide and crimes against humanity, states are called to exercise their obligation, under international law, to investigate, prosecute, and bring to justice the perpetrators of such crimes irrespective of where they have been committed, on the basis of the principle of *aut dedere, aut judicare*, when appropriate. In relation specifically to ISIL/DAESH returnees, states should work on the operational level to 1) deny them safe havens; and 2) investigate, prosecute, and apprehend them, if convicted, following the dictates of the rule of law and due process. In this case, the international community should encourage Iraq's judicial authorities to cooperate to disclose and share the relevant evidence for the specific cases.

Holding ISIL/DAESH's fighters accountable for their crimes is crucial, but this consists of only a segmented part towards national reconciliation. The **road** that leads to justice and peace in Iraq is long and challenging but possible. It starts with the recognition that ISIL/DAESH created an environment of deleterious effect on the enjoyment of fundamental freedoms and human dignity and imposed severe threats to the full enjoyment and exercise of human rights in Iraq. ISIL/DAESH's violations of International Humanitarian Law and International Criminal Law have had a devastating humanitarian impact on the civilian population, particularly on religious and ethnic groups. The crimes perpetrated by the terrorist group constituted a violation of the very human right of freedom from fear and the right to enjoy peace. Ultimately, these crimes represented an attack against all of humanity. Multifold actions are necessary for Iraqi society to cope with such atrocious violations of rights.

The **road** must lead to the victims. The international community should partner with Iraq's public authorities to provide the ISIL/DAESH's surviving victims and victims' families with support, assistance, and coping mechanisms – judicial, psychological, financial, or of other nature. This would help them to rebuild their lives, lessening the conditions conducive to anger and revenge. Iraq's authorities should: 1) provide ISIL/DAESH victims with the necessary conditions for compensation, protection, humanization, remembrance, international solidarity, dignity, truth, and respect, in accordance with Public International Law, International Human Rights Law, and International Refugee Law; and 2) recognize that victims have a substantial role in countering extremist ideologies, prejudice, discrimination, thus ultimately avoiding future atrocities.

The **road** to preventing ISIL/DAESH from perpetrating genocide and crimes against humanity in Iraq also depends on national authorities, academicians, politicians, the civil society, religious leaders, and leaders of ethnical groups creating, promoting, and maintaining a culture of: 1) interfaith tolerance, and combat of all sorts of religious discrimination, religious exclusion, and religious persecution; and 2) intercultural, inter-civilizational, and inter-ethnical tolerance, dialogue and understanding; and 3) education for peace and justice, nationally, regionally and globally.

The international community should partner with Iraq's authorities to take national, bilateral, regional, and international measures to prevent and combat the transboundary recruitment of foreign terrorist fighters to the region. In this partnership, states should: 1) take cooperative and collaborative actions to impede ISIL/DAESH from making use of technologies, communications, social media, and other virtual sources to recruit their fighters, including the recruitment of lone terrorists in several parts of the world; 2) share their border control information and profile databases concerning persons with proven links with the ISIL/DAESH network; 3) expand the inclusion of new ISIL/DAESH terrorist foreign fighters in the International Criminal Police Organization (INTERPOL)'s Special Notices; and 4) take full consideration of the United Nations' mechanisms and instruments on the prevention and combat of international recruitment of terrorist fighters. In cooperation with Iraq, states should pay special attention to returning ISIL/DAESH terrorist fighters – *"blowback effect"* – to prevent them from spreading terrorist propaganda and promoting extreme violence upon return to their home countries.

With the cooperation of states and international organisms, such as the U.N. Security Council, Iraq's law enforcement authorities should work together in taking urgent, forceful, effective, and decisive joint actions to prevent active and passive financial support to the ISIL/DAESH network in Iraq. Among main measures that should be put into practice, the author indicates: 1) freezing all ISIL/DAESH network funds and financial assets; 2) working to prevent ISIL/DAESH from collecting external donations internationally; 3) preventing ISIL/DAESH from performing, directly or indirectly, any commercial or financial transaction in Iraq; and 4) denying safe haven to all of those engaged in the financing of ISIL/DAESH and prosecuting the perpetrators or extraditing them, in accordance with the principle of *aut dedere, aut judicare*. The international community should also encourage the Security Council to enact or maintain other specific target sanctions on individuals with proven criminal links with the ISIL/DAESH network in Iraq, namely travel ban, arms embargo, listing criteria, and reporting measures.

Iraq, in cooperation with the international community, must also address other critical underlying conditions that contributed to ISIL/DAESH's actions in the region: 1) structural causes: rule of law deficiencies, lack of an effective criminal justice system, weak governance, political instability, government corruption, police collusion, general violations of human rights while combating terrorism, prolonged unresolved territorial and international military conflicts that create domestic and external political tensions, arms trafficking in the region, and porous state borders with neighbors; 2) socio-economic: extreme poverty of more than thirty percent of the population, socio-economic marginalization, lack of sustained economic growth, inefficient sustainable development, and high rates of youth unemployment; 3) civil-political: political exclusion, lack of pluralism, and religious discrimination.

The **road** that leads to justice and peace in Iraq has no end. The Latin-American filmmaker Fernando Birri once said: "Utopia lies at the horizon. When I draw nearer by two steps, it retreats two steps. If I proceed ten steps forward, it swiftly slips ten steps ahead. No matter how far I go, I can never reach it." If one desires to achieve justice and peace in Iraq, one must focus on justice on the horizon. The more Iraq walks towards justice, the more peace can be found along the way. There will always be more justice to be established on the horizon. There will always be more peace to be found along the way.

The author believes that the clear picture of what happened to Christians in Iraq during the ISIL/DAESH regime is still incomplete. Future fieldwork from international agencies, NGOs, states, international organizations, and academicians should concentrate on Iraq's areas where ISIL/DAESH's conduct was not investigated due to security and administrative concerns. More research is needed to better understand the character and the legal nature behind ISIL/DAESH's intent in persecuting Christians. The author hopes that, as more families of victims and surviving victims themselves are identified, heard, and offered protection, more legal elements could substantiate allegations of genocide. The overall process of reading and scrutinizing hundreds of books, papers, reports, caselaw, and other types of documents and writing this book took more than four thousand hours. Notwithstanding the limitations of this study, its findings make several contributions to the current literature on genocide and persecution as a crime against humanity. The author sincerely hopes that this research will extend the public knowledge on the atrocities suffered by Christians in Iraq and serve as a base for future studies, documentation, investigation, prosecution, and punishment of ISIL/DAESH terrorist fighters.

# References

*References made according to The Bluebook, 20<sup>th</sup> edition.*

## 1. Books and book chapters

### 1.1. Books and book chapters on International Law, International Criminal Law, and ISIL/DAESH crimes – Alphabetic order

Adam Jones, Genocide: A Comprehensive Introduction (Routledge, 2006).

Adam Jones ed., Genocide, War Crimes, and the West: History and Complicity (Palgrave, 2004).

Alexander Boraine, Retributive Justice and Restorative Justice: Contradictory or Complimentary? *in* Genocide and Accountability: Three Public Lectures by Simone Veil, Geoffrey Nice, Alex Boraine 39-52 (Nanci Adler ed., Vossiuspers UvA, 2004).

Alexander Zahar & Göran Sluiter, International Criminal Law: A Critical Introduction (Oxford University Press, 2007).

Alex Odora-Obote, Investigations and Case Selection in the ICTR *in* The Elgar Companion to the International Criminal Tribunal for Rwanda 235-264 (Anne-Marie de Brouwer & Alette Smeulers eds., Edward Elgar Publishing, 2016).

Anne-Marie de Brouwer & Alette Smeulers eds., The Elgar Companion to the International Criminal Tribunal for Rwanda (Edward Elgar Publishing, 2016).

Andrew Hosken, Empire of Fear: Inside the Islamic State (One World Publications, 2015).

Antonio Cassese, International Criminal Law (Oxford University Press, 2013).

Antonio Cassese, The Human Dimension of International Law: Selected Papers (Oxford University Press, 2008).

Aram A. Schvey, Striving for Accountability in the Former Yugoslavia *in* Accountability for Atrocities: National and International Responses 39-85 (Jane E. Stromseth ed., Transnational Publishers Inc: Ardsley, 2003).

Aisling O'Sullivan, Universal Jurisdiction in International Criminal Law: The Debate and the Battle for Hegemony (Routledge, 2017).

Barbora Holá & Alette Smeulers, Rwanda and the ICTR: facts and figures *in* The Elgar Companion to the International Criminal Tribunal for Rwanda 44-75 (Anne-Marie de Brouwer & Alette Smeulers eds., Edward Elgar Publishing, 2016).

Benjamin N. Schiff, Building the International Criminal Court (Cambridge University Press, 2008).

Ben Saul, Research Handbook on International Law and Terrorism (Edward Elgar, 2014).

Ben Saul, Terrorism: Documents in International Law (Hart Publishing, 2012).

Ianin Cameron, Jurisdiction and admissibility issues under the ICC Statute *in* The Permanent International Criminal Court: Legal and Policy Issues 65-94 (Dominic McGoldrick & Eric Donnelly eds., Hart Publishing, 2004).

Carla Ferstman, Mariana Goetz & Alan Stephens eds., Reparations for Victims of Genocide, War Crimes and Crimes against Humanity Systems in Place and Systems in the Making (Martinus Nijhoff Publishers, 2009).

Carsten Stahn ed., The Law and Practice of the International Criminal Court (Oxford University Press, 2015).

Christine Byron, The Crime of Genocide *in* The Permanent International Criminal Court: Legal and Policy Issues 143-177 (Dominic McGoldrick & Eric Donnelly eds., Hart Publishing, 2004).

Christoph J. M. Safferling, Towards an International Criminal Procedure (Oxford University Press, 2007).

Christopher K. Hall, Joseph Powderly & Niamh Hayes, Article 7. Crimes Against Humanity *in* The Rome Statute of the International Criminal Court: A Commentary 144-294 (Otto Triffterer & Kai Ambos eds., Hart Publishing, 3d ed. 2016).

Ciara Damgaard, Individual Criminal Responsibility for Core International Crimes: Selected Pertinent Issues (Springer, 2008).

Claudia Card & Armen T. Marsoobian eds., Genocide's Aftermath: Responsibility and Repair (Blackwell Pub., 2007).

Claus Kreß, The ICC's First Encounter with the Crime of Genocide: The Case against Al Bashir *in* The Law and Practice of the International Criminal Court 669-704 (Carsten Stahn ed., Oxford University Press, 2015).

Daniel Silander, Don Wallace & John Janzekovic eds. International Organizations and the rise of ISIL/DAESH: Global Responses to Human Security Threats (Routledge, 2017).

David A Tallman, Universal Jurisdiction: Lessons From Belgium's Experience *in* Accountability for Atrocities: National and International Responses 375-409 (Jane E. Stromseth ed., Transnational Publishers Inc: Ardsley, 2003).

Diane F. Orentlicher, Universal Jurisdiction: A Pragmatic Strategy in Pursuit of a Moralist's Vision *in* The Theory and Practice of International Criminal Law Essays in Honor of M. Cherif Bassiouni 127-154 (Leila Nadya Sadat & Michael P. Scharf eds., Martinus Nijhoff Publishers, 2008).

Dinah L. Shelton, Encyclopedia of Genocide and Crimes Against Humanity (Thomson Gale, v. 1, 2005).

Dinah L. Shelton, Encyclopedia of Genocide and Crimes Against Humanity (Thomson Gale, v. 2, 2005).

Dinah L. Shelton, Encyclopedia of Genocide and Crimes Against Humanity (Thomson Gale, v. 3, 2005).

Dominic McGoldrick & Eric Donnelly eds., The Permanent International Criminal Court: Legal and Policy Issues (Hart Publishing, 2004).

Dominic McGoldrick, Criminal Trials Before International Tribunals: Legality and Legitimacy *in* The Permanent International Criminal Court: Legal and Policy Issues 9-46 (Dominic McGoldrick & Eric Donnelly eds., Hart Publishing, 2004).

Donald Bloxham & A. Dirk Moses eds., The Oxford Handbook of Genocide Studies (Oxford University Press, 2010).

Douglas Irvin-Erickson, Raphaël Lemkin and the Concept of Genocide (University of Pennsylvania Press, 2017).

E. Van. Sliedregt, The Criminal Responsibility of Individuals for Violations of International Humanitarian Law (Asser Press, 2003).

Fabricio Guariglia and Emeric Rogier, The Selection of Situations and Cases by the OTP of the ICC *in* The Law and Practice of the International Criminal Court 350-364 (Carsten Stahn ed., Oxford University Press, 2015).

Fawaz A. Gerges, ISIS: A History (Princeton University Press, 2016).

Fred Grünfeld & Anke Huijboom, The Failure to Prevent Genocide in Rwanda: The Role of Bystanders (Martinus Nijhoff Publishers, 2007).

Geert-Jan Alexander Knoops, Defenses in Contemporary International Criminal Law (Martinus Nijhoff, 2d ed. 2008).

Gérard Prunier, Darfur: Genocidal Theory and Practical Atrocities *in* Confronting genocide 45-56 (René Provost & Payam Akhavan eds., Springer, 2011).

Gerhard Werle & Florian Jessberger, Principles of International Criminal Law (Oxford University Press, 2014).

Gideon Boas, James L. Bischoff & Natalie L. Reid, International Criminal Law Practitioner Library, Vol. I, Forms of Responsibility in International Criminal Law (Cambridge University Press, 2007).

Gideon Boas, James L. Bischoff & Natalie L. Reid, International Criminal Law Practitioner Library, Vol. II, Elements of Crime under International Criminal Law (Cambridge University Press, 2009).

Gideon Boas et al, International Criminal Law Practitioner Library, Volume III: International Criminal Procedure (Cambridge university Press, 2011).

Gregor Noll, Theorizing Jurisdiction *in* The Oxford Handbook of the Theory of International Law 600-617 (Anne Oford & Florian Hoffmann eds., Oxford University Press, 2016).

Guénaël Mettraux, International Crimes and the *Ad Hoc* Tribunals, (Oxford University Press, 2006).

Harmen Van Der Wilt et al eds., The Genocide Convention: The Legacy of 60 Years (Martinus Nijhoff Publishers, 2012).

Helen Hintjens, The Creation of the ICTR *in* The Elgar Companion to the International Criminal Tribunal for Rwanda 15-43 (Anne-Marie de Brouwer & Alette Smeulers eds., Edward Elgar Publishing, 2016).

Herbert R. Reginbogin & Christoph J. M. Safferling eds., The Nuremberg Trials International Criminal Law Since 1945 60th Anniversary International Conference (K.G. Saur, 2006).

Hirad Abtahi & Philippa Webb, The Genocide Convention: The Travaux Préparatoires, Volume 2 (Martinus Nijhoff Publishers, 2008).

Hisakazu Fujita, The Tokyo Trial Revisited *in* The Legal Regime of the International Criminal Court: Essays in Honour of Professor Igor Blishchenko 23-49 (Martinus Nijhoff Publishers, 2009).

Jack Donnelly, Genocide and humanitarian intervention *in* Genocide and Human Rights 385-401 (Mark Lattimer ed., Ashgate Publishing Limited, 2007).

Jackson Maogoto, Early Efforts to Establish an International Criminal Court *in* The Legal Regime of the International Criminal Court: Essays in Honour of Professor Igor Blishchenko 3-22 (Martinus Nijhoff Publishers, 2009).

Jackson Maogoto, The Experience of the Ad Hoc Tribunals for the Former Yugoslavia and Rwanda *in* The Legal Regime of the International Criminal Court: Essays in Honour of Professor Igor Blishchenko 63-74 (Martinus Nijhoff Publishers, 2009).

Jacqes Semelin, Purify and Destroy: The Political Uses of Massacre and Genocide (Columbia University Press, 2007).

Jane E. Stromseth, Challenges in the Pursuit of Accountability *in* Accountability for Atrocities: National and International Responses 1-36 (Jane E. Stromseth ed., Transnational Publishers Inc: Ardsley, 2003).

Jason Strain & Elizabeth Keyes, Accountability in the Aftermath of Rwanda's Genocide *in* Accountability for Atrocities: National and International Responses 87-133 (Jane E. Stromseth ed., Transnational Publishers Inc: Ardsley, 2003).

Janzekovic, John. The Rise of the Islamic State of Iraq and the Levant *in* International Organizations and the Rise of ISIL/DAESH: Global Responses to Human Security Threats 9-57 (Daniel Silander, Don Wallace & John Janzekovic eds., Routledge, 2017).

John B. Quigley, The Genocide Convention: An International Law Analysis (Ashgate, 2006).

Jonathan I. Charney, Anticipatory Humanitarian Intervention in Kosovo *in* Genocide and Human Rights 403-426 (Mark Lattimer ed., Ashgate Publishing Limited, 2007).

José Doria, Hans-Peter Gasser & M. Cherif Bassiouni eds., The Legal Regime of the International Criminal Court: Essays in Honour of Professor Igor Blishchenko (Martinus Nijhoff Publishers, 2009).

Juan E. Méndez, Accountability for Past Abuses *in* Genocide and Human Rights 429-456 (Mark Lattimer ed., Ashgate Publishing Limited, 2007).

Justice Hassan Bubacar Jallow, The ICTR's Elaboration of the Core International Crimes of Genocide, Crimes Against Humanity and War Crimes and Modes of Liability *in* The Elgar Companion to the International Criminal Tribunal for Rwanda 447-487 (Anne-Marie de Brouwer & Alette Smeulers eds., Edward Elgar Publishing, 2016).

Kai Ambos, Treatise on International Criminal Law, Volume I: Foundations and General Part (Oxford University Press, 2013).

Kai Ambos, Treatise on International Criminal Law, Volume II: The Crimes and Sentencing (Oxford University Press, 2014).

Kai Ambos & Stefanie Bock, Individual Criminal Responsibility in the ICTR *in* The Elgar Companion to the International Criminal Tribunal for Rwanda 202-231 (Anne-Marie de Brouwer & Alette Smeulers eds., Edward Elgar Publishing, 2016).

Kevin R. Gray, Evidence Before the ICC *in* The Permanent International Criminal Court: Legal and Policy Issues 287-313 (Dominic McGoldrick & Eric Donnelly eds., Hart Publishing, 2004).

Kevin Jon Heller, The Nuremberg Military Tribunals and the Origins of International Criminal Law (Oxford University Press, 2011)

Knut Dormann, Elements of War Crimes under the Rome Statute of the International Criminal Court: Sources and Commentary (with contributions by Louise Doswald-Beck & Robert Kolb) (Cambridge university press & International Committee of the Red Cross, 2004).

Krit Zeegers, International Criminal Tribunals and Human Rights: Adherence and Contextualization (Asser Press, 2016).

Kurt Jonassohn & Karin Solveig Björnson, Genocide and Gross Human Rights Violation in Comparative Perspective (Transaction Publishers, 1997).

Larry Charles Dembowski, The International Criminal Court: Complementarity *in* Accountability for Atrocities: National and International Responses 135-169 (Jane E. Stromseth ed., Transnational Publishers Inc: Ardsley, 2003).

Larry May, Crimes Against Humanity: A Normative Account (Cambridge University Press, 2005).

Lawrence Wright, The Terror Years: From Al-Qaeda to the Islamic State (Alfred A. Knopf, 2016).

Leila Nadya Sadat & Michael P. Scharf eds., The Theory and Practice of International Criminal Law Essays in Honor of M. Cherif Bassiouni (Martinus Nijhoff Publishers, 2008).

Raphael Lemkin, Genocide as a Crime Under International Law *in* Genocide and Human Rights 3-9 (Mark Lattimer ed., Ashgate Publishing Limited, 2007).

Liam Freeman, Islamic State & ISIS Crisis: An Examination (Nova Science Publishers, 2014).

Malcolm N. Shaw, International Law (Cambridge University Press, 2008).

Malcolm W. Nance, The Terrorists of Iraq: Inside the Strategy and Tactics of the Iraq Insurgency 2003 –2014 (Taylor & Francis, 2nd. ed. 2015).

Mark A. Drumbl, Reimagining Child Soldiers in International Law and Policy (Oxford University Press, 2012).

Mark Lattimer ed., Genocide and Human Rights (Ashgate Publishing Limited, 2007).

Martin Shaw, War and genocide: Organized Killing in Modern Societies (Polity Press, 2003).

Martin Shaw, What is Genocide? (Polity Press, 2007).

M. Cherif Bassiouni, Crimes Against Humanity: Historical Evolution and Contemporary Application (Cambridge University Press, 2011).

M. Cherif. Bassiouni, Introduction to International Criminal Law (Transnational Publishers Inc., 2003).

M. Cherif Bassiouni, The Legislative History of the International Criminal Court, Vol. 1 (Transnational Publishers Inc., 2005).

M. Cherif Bassiouni, The Legislative History of the International Criminal Court, Vol. 2 (Transnational Publishers Inc., 2005).

M. Cherif Bassiouni, The Legislative History of the International Criminal Court, Vol. 3 (Transnational Publishers Inc., 2005).

Mindy Belz, They Say We Are Infidels: On the Run From ISIS With Persecuted Christians in the Middle East (Tyndale House Publishers Inc., 2016).

Mohamed Elewa Badar and Sara Porro, Rethinking the Mental Elements in the Jurisprudence of the ICC in The Law and Practice of the International Criminal Court 649-668 (Carsten Stahn ed., Oxford University Press, 2015).

M. Patricia Marchak, Reigns of Terror (McGill-Queen's University Press, 2003).

Nanci Adler ed., Genocide and Accountability: Three Public Lectures by Simone Veil, Geoffrey Nice, Alex Boraine (Amsterdam University Press – Vossiuspers UvA, 2004).

Nasour Koursami, The 'Contextual Elements' of the Crime of Genocide (Asser Press, 2018).

Nicholas A. Jones, The Courts of Genocide: Politics and the Rule of Law in Rwanda and Arusha (Routledge, 2010).

Nina Bang-Jensen & Stefanie Frease, Creating the ADT: turning a Good Idea into Reality in Genocide in Darfur: Investigating the Atrocities in the Sudan 45-57 (Samuel Totten & Eric Markusen eds., Routledge, 2006).

Norman Geras, Crimes Against Humanity: Birth of a Concept (Manchester University Press, 2011).

Otto Triffterer & Kai Ambos eds., The Rome Statute of the International Criminal Court: A Commentary (Hart Publishing, 3d ed. 2016).

Patrick Cockburn, The Rise of Islamic State: ISIS and the New Sunni Revolution (Verso, 2015).

Payam Akhavan, Genocide in the ICTR *in* The Elgar Companion to the International Criminal Tribunal for Rwanda 79-109 (Anne-Marie de Brouwer & Alette Smeulers eds., Edward Elgar Publishing, 2016).

Payam Akhavan, Reducing Genocide to Law: Definition, Meaning, and the Ultimate Crime (Cambridge University Press, 2012).

Rachel Kerr, The International Criminal Tribunal for the Former Yugoslavia: An Exercise in Law, Politics, and Diplomacy (Oxford University Press, 2004).

Raffi Sarkissian, The Armenian Genocide: A Contextual View of the Crime and Politics of Denial *in* The Criminal Law of Genocide: International, Comparative and Contextual Aspects 3-15 (Ralph Henham & Paul Behrens eds., Ashgate Publishing Limited, 2007).

Ralph Henham & Paul Behrens eds., The Criminal Law of Genocide: International, Comparative and Contextual Aspects (Ashgate Publishing Limited, 2007).

Razaw Salihy, Terror and Torment: The Civilian Journey to Escape Iraq's War Against the "Islamic State" *in* Iraq After ISIS: The Challenges of Post-War Recovery 79-98 (Jacob Eriksson & Ahmed Khaleel eds., Palgrave Macmillan, 2019).

Robert Cryer, Håkan Friman, Darryl Robinson & Elizabeth Wilmshurst, An introduction to International Criminal Law and Procedure (Cambridge University Press, 3rd ed. 2014).

Robert Cryer, Prosecuting International Crimes: Selectivity and International Criminal Law Regime (Cambridge University Press, 2005).

Robert Dubler SC & Matthew Kalyk, Crimes Against Humanity in the 21st Century: Law, Practice and Threats to International Peace and Security (Brill/Nijhoff, 2018).

Robert Frau, The International Criminal Court and the Security Council: The International Criminal Court as a Political Tool? In The International Criminal Court in Turbulent Times 112-130 (Gerhard Werle & Andreas Zimmermann eds., Asser Press, 2019).

Robert Gellately & Ben Kiernan, The specter of Genocide: Mass Murder in Historical Perspective (Cambridge University Press, 2003).

Robert Manne, The Mind of the Islamic State: ISIS and the Ideology of the Caliphate (Prometheus Books, 2017).

Robert Spencer, The Complete Infidel's Guide to ISIS (Regnery Publishing, 2015).

Ronald Rychlak & Jane Adolphe eds., The Persecution and Genocide of Christians in the Middle East: Prevention, Prohibition & Prosecution (Angelico Press, 2017).

Sadi Cayci, Armenian Genocide Claims: A Contextual Version of the 1915 Incidents *in* The Criminal Law of Genocide: International, Comparative and Contextual Aspects 17-27 (Ralph Henham & Paul Behrens eds., Ashgate Publishing Limited, 2007).

Samuel Totten & Eric Markusen eds., Genocide in Darfur: Investigating the Atrocities in the Sudan (Routledge, 2006).

Simon Mabon & Ana Maria Kumarasamy, Da'ish, Stasis and Bare Life in Iraq *in* Iraq After ISIS: The Challenges of Post-War Recovery 9-28 (Jacob Eriksson & Ahmed Khaleel eds., Palgrave Macmillan, 2019).

Sonja C. Grover, Child Soldier Victims of Genocidal Forcible Transfer: Exonerating Child Soldiers Charged with Grave Conflict-related International Crimes (Springer, 2012).

Steven R. Ratner & Jason S. Abrams, Accountability for Human Rights Atrocities in International Law: Beyond the Nuremberg Legacy (Oxford University Press, 2001).

Thierry Cruvellier, Court of Remorse: Inside the International Criminal Tribunal for Rwanda, Translated by Chari Voss (University of Wisconsin Press, 2006).

Trevor Buck, International Child Law (Routledge, 2014).

Valeria Cetorelli & Ashraph, Sareta, A Demographic Documentation of ISIS's Attack on the Yazidi Village of Kocho (The London School of Economics and Political Science – LSE, 2019).

Victor Tsilonis, The Jurisdiction of the International Criminal Court (Springer, 2019).

Wallace, Don. International Criminal Court *in* International Organizations and the Rise of ISIL/DAESH: Global Responses to Human Security Threats 121-136 (Daniel Silander, Don Wallace & John Janzekovic eds., Routledge, 2017).

William A. Schabas, An Introduction to the International Criminal Court (Cambridge University Press, 2007).

William A. Schabas, Genocide in International Law: The Crime of Crimes (Cambridge University Press, 2009).

William A. Schabas, Has Genocide Been Committed in Darfur? The State Plan or Policy Element in the Crime of Genocide *in* The Criminal Law of Genocide: International, Comparative and Contextual Aspects 39-47 (Ralph Henham & Paul Behrens eds., Ashgate Publishing Limited, 2007).

William A. Schabas, Selecting Situations and Cases *in* The Law and Practice of the International Criminal Court 365-381 (Carsten Stahn ed., Oxford University Press, 2015).

William A. Schabas, The Law and Genocide 123-141 *in* The Oxford Handbook of Genocide Studies (Donald Bloxham & A. Dirk Moses eds., Oxford University Press, 2010).

William A. Schabas, The UN International Criminal Tribunals: The Former Yugoslavia, Rwanda and Sierra Leone (Cambridge University Press, 2006).

William Harris, Quicksilver War: Syria, Iraq and the Spiral of Conflict (Oxford University Press, 2018).

Władysław Czapliński, Jus Cogens, Obligations Erga Omnes and International Criminal Responsibility *in* The Legal Regime of the International Criminal Court: Essays in Honour of Professor Igor Blishchenko 403-420 (Martinus Nijhoff Publishers, 2009).

Yonah Alexander & Dean C. Alexander, The Islamic State: Combating the Caliphate Without Borders (Lexington Books, 2015).

Yuki Tanaka, Tim McCormack & Gerry Simpson eds., Beyond Victor's Justice? The Tokyo War Crimes Trial Revisited (Martinus Nijhoff Publishers, 2011).

Yusuf Aksar, Implementing International Humanitarian Law: From The Ad Hoc Tribunals to a Permanent International Criminal Court (Routledge, 2004).

## 1.2. Books and book chapters on research methodology – Alphabetic order

Alan Bryman, Social Research Methods (Oxford University Press, 4th. ed. 2012).

Bård A. Andreassen, Hans-Otto Sano & Siobhán McInerney-Lankford. Research Methods in Human Rights: A Handbook (Edward Elgar, 2017)

Desmond Thomas, The PhD Writing Handbook (Palgrave-Macmillan, 2016).

Jane Ritchie & Jane Lewis, Qualitative Research Practice: A Guide for Social Science Students and Researchers (Sage Publications Ltd., 2003).

John Biggam, Succeeding With Your Master's Dissertation: A Step-by-step Handbook (Open University-McGraw-Hill Education, 2015).

Keith F Punch, Developing Effective Research Proposals (Sage Publications Ltd., 2000).

Michael McConville & Wing Hong Chui eds., Research Methods for Law (Edinburgh University Press, 2007).

Patrick Dunleavy, Authoring a PhD: How to Plan, Praft, Write and Finish a Doctoral Thesis or Dissertation (Palgrave-Macmillan, 2003).

Ronald Dworkin, A New Philosophy for International Law. Lecciones y Ensayos, Nro. 93. 2014.pp. 283-291.

Sarah Nouwen, International Criminal Law: Theory all over the place *in* The Oxford Handbook of the Theory of International Law 738-762 (Anne Orford & Florian Hoffmann eds. Oxford University Press, 2016).

W. Lawrence Neuman, Social Research Methods: Qualitative and Quantitative Approaches (Pearson Education Limited, 7th. ed. 2014).

## 2. Papers from international journals

### 2.1. Papers on International Criminal Law – Alphabetic order by author

Adeno Addis, Genocide and Belonging: Processes of Imagining Communities, 38 U. Pa. J. Int'l L. 1041 (2017).

Alberto Costi, The 60th Anniversary of the Genocide Convention, 39 Victoria U. Wellington L. Rev. 831 (2009).

Ana Martin Beringola, Ensuring Protection of Child Soldiers from Sexual Violence: Relevance of the Ntaganda Decision on the Confirmation of Charges in Narrowing the Gap, 8 Amsterdam L.F. 58 (2016).

Andrea Bianchi, Security Council's Anti-Terror Resolutions and Their Implementation by Member States, 4 J. Int'l Crim. Just. 1044 (2006).

Andreas Zimmermann, Security Council and the Obligation to Prevent Genocide and War Crimes, The, 32 Polish Y.B. Int'l L. 307 (2012).

Awet Hailezgi Tefera, The Elements of Rape as a Crime of Genocide under International Criminal Law: Case Law Analysis, 2 Mekelle U. L.J. 35 (2014).

Ben Saul, Defending Terrorism: Justifications and Excuses for Terrorism in International Criminal Law, 25 Aust. YBIL 177 (2006).

Ben Saul, Definition of Terrorism in the UN Security Council: 1985-2004, 4 Chinese J. Int'l L. 141 (2005).

Caroline E. Nabity, It's Genocide, Now What: The Obligations of the United States under the Convention to Prevent and Punish Genocide Being Committed at the Hands of ISIS, 8 Creighton Int'l & Comp. L.J. 70 (2016).

Cassie Powell, You Have No God: An Analysis of the Prosecution of Genocidal Rape in International Criminal Law, 20 Rich. Pub. Int. L. Rev. 25 (2017).

Claus Kress, The Darfur Report and Genocidal Intent, 3 J. Int'l Crim. Just. 562 (2005).

Claus Kress, The International Court of Justice and the Elements of the Crime of Genocide, 18 Eur. J. Int'l L. 619 (2007).

Coman Kenny, Prosecuting Crimes of International Concern: Islamic State at the ICC, 33 Utrecht J. Int'l & Eur. L. 120 (2017).

Cory Kopitzke, Security Council Resolution 2178 (2014): An Ineffective Response to the Foreign Terrorist Fighter Phenomenon, 24 Ind. J. Global Legal Stud. 309 (2017).

Courtney McCausland, From Tolerance to Tactic: Understanding Rape in Armed Conflict as Genocide, 25 Mich. St. Int'l L. Rev. 149 (2017).

Cristina Martinez Squires, How the Law Should View Voluntary Child Soldiers: Does Terrorism Pose a Different Dilemma, 68 S.M.U. L. Rev. 567 (2015).

Daniela De Vito; Aisha Gill; Damien Short, Rape Characterised as Genocide, 10 SUR – Int'l J. on Hum Rts. 29 (2009).

Daniel J. Hickman, Terrorism as a Violation of the Law of Nations: Finally Overcoming the Definitional Problem, 29 Wis. Int'l L.J. 447 (2011).

David S. Koller; Miriam Eckenfels-Garcia, Using Targeted Sanctions to End Violations against Children in Armed Conflict, 33 B.U. Int'l L.J. 1 (2015).

Devrim Aydin, The Interpretation of Genocidal Intent under the Genocide Convention and the Jurisprudence of International Courts, 78 J. Crim. L. 423 (2014).

Diane F. Orentlicher, Settling Accounts: The Duty to Prosecute Human Rights Violations of a Prior Regime, 100 Yale L.J. 2537 (1991).

Erin Lafayette, The Prosecution of Child Soldiers: Balancing Accountability with Justice, 63 Syracuse L. Rev. 297 (2013).

Eric Osborne; Matthew Dowd; Ryan McBrearty, Intending the Worst: The Case of ISIS's Specific Intent to Destroy the Christians of Iraq, 46 Pepp. L. Rev. 545 (2019).

Frederic Gilles Sourgens, The End of Law: The ISIL/DAESH Case Study for a Comprehensive Theory of Lawlessness, 39 Fordham Int'l L.J. 355 (2015).

Gabor Kajtar, The Use of Force against ISIL/DAESH in Iraq and Syria – A Legal Battlefield, 34 Wis. Int'l L.J. 535 (2017).

George S. Jr. Yacoubian; Anna N. Astvatsaturova; Tracy M. Proietti, Iraq and the ICC: Should Iraq Nationals by Prosecuted for the Crime of Genocide before the International Criminal Court, 1 War Crimes Genocide & Crimes against Human. 47 (2005).

Hannibal Travis, Genocide, Counterinsurgency, and the Self-Defense of UN Member States before the International Criminal Court, 22 U.C. Davis J. Int'l L. & Pol'y 139 (2016).

Helene de Pooter, Obligation to Prevent Genocide: A Large Shell Yet to Be Filled, The, 17 Afr. Y.B. Int'l L. 287 (2009).

Henry T. Jr. King; Benjamin B. Ferencz; Whitney R. Harris, Origins of the Genocide Convention, 40 Case W. Res. J. Int'l L. 13 (2007).

Inger Skjelsbaek, Responsibility to Protect or Prevent: Victims and Perpetrators of Sexual Violence Crimes in Armed Conflicts, 4 Global Resp. Protect 154 (2012).

Jeffery R. Ray, Children, Armed Conflict, and Genocide: Applying the Law of Genocide to the Recruitment and Use of Children in Armed Conflict, 19 Barry L. Rev. 335 (2013).

Jennifer Balint, Genocide and Law: International and National Dimensions, 14 World Bull. 1 (1998).

Jeremy Sarkin; Carly Fowler, The Responsibility to Protect and the Duty to Prevent Genocide: Lessons to Be Learned from the Role of the International Community and the Media during the Rwandan Genocide and the Conflict in Former Yugoslavia, 33 Suffolk Transnat'l L. Rev. 35 (2010).

J. Le Roux; Yves Muhire, The Status of Acts of Sexual Violence in International Criminal Law, 22 S. Afr. J. Crim. Just. 69 (2009).

Johan D. van der Vyver, Prosecution and Punishment of the Crime of Genocide, 23 Fordham Int'l L.J. 286 (1999).

Kevin Jon Heller, What Is an International Crime: (A Revisionist History), 58 Harv. Int'l L.J. 353 (2017).

Kurt Mundorff, Other Peoples' Children: A Textual and Contextual Interpretation of the Genocide Convention, Article 2(e), 50 Harv. Int'l L.J. 61 (2009).

L. Edward Day; Margaret Vandiver; W. Richard Janikowski, Teaching the Ultimate Crime: Genocide and International Law in the Criminal Justice Curriculum, 14 J. Crim. Just. Educ. 119 (2003).

Leila Sadat Wexler, The Proposed Permanent International Criminal Court: An Appraisal, 29 Cornell Int'l L.J. 665 (1996).

Mark Gibney, Universal Duties: The Responsibility to Protect, the Duty to Prevent (Genocide) and Extraterritorial Human Rights Obligations, 3 Global Resp. Protect 123 (2011).

Marquise Houle, The Responsibility to Protect, Military Intervention and Genocide, 8 Int'l L. Y.B. 139 (2017-2018).

Martin M. Sychold, Ratification of the Genocide Convention: The Legal Effects in Light of Reservations and Objections, 8 Swiss. Rev. Int'l & Eur. L. 533 (1998).

Matthew Happold, Protecting Children in Armed Conflict: Harnessing the Security Council's Soft Power, 43 Isr. L. Rev. 360 (2010).

Matthew Lippman, The Convention on the Prevention and Punishment of the Crime of Genocide: Fifty Years Later, 15 Ariz. J. Int'l & Comp. L. 415 (1998).

Matthew Lippman, The Drafting of the 1948 Convention on the Prevention and Punishment of the Crime of Genocide, 3 B.U. Int'l L. J. 1 (1985).

M. Cherif Bassiouni, Former Yugoslavia: Investigating Violations of International Humanitarian Law and Establishing an International Criminal Tribunal, 18 Fordham Int'l L.J. 1191 (1995).

M. Cherif Bassiouni, The Time Has Come for an International Criminal Court, 1 Ind. Int'l & Comp. L. Rev. 1 (1991).

M. Cherif Bassiouni, Universal Jurisdiction for International Crimes: Historical Perspectives and Contemporary Practice, 42 Va. J. Int'l L. 81 (2001).

Megan Nobert, Children at War: The Criminal Responsibility of Child Soldiers, 2011 Pace Int'l L. Rev. Online Companion [v] (2011).

Milena Sterio, The Applicability of the Humanitarian Intervention Exception to the Middle Eastern Refugee Crisis: Why the International Community Should Intervene against ISIS, 38 Suffolk Transnat'l L. Rev. 325 (2015).

Nancy Amoury Combs, Deconstructing the Epistemic Challenges to Mass Atrocity Prosecutions, 75 Wash. & Lee L. Rev. 223 (2018).

Noelle Quenivet, Girl Soldiers and Participating in Hostilities, 16 Afr. J. Int'l & Comp. L. 219 (2008).

Nina H. B. Jorgensen, Child Soldiers and the Parameters of International Criminal Law, 11 Chinese J. Int'l L. 657 (2012).

Peter Margulies, Aftermath of an Unwise Decision: The U.N. Terrorist Sanctions Regime after Kadi II, 6 Amsterdam L.F. 51 (2014).

Peter Quayle, Unimaginable Evil: The Legislative of the Genocide Convention, 5 Int'l Crim. L. Rev. 363 (2005).

Philip Alston, The Darfur Commission as a Model for Future Responses to Crisis Situations, 3 J. Int'l Crim. Just. 600 (2005).

Radhika Jagtap, Defining International Terrorism: Formulation of a Universal Concept out of the Ideological Quagmires and Overlapping Approaches, 4 J. Phil. Int'l L. 56 (2013).

Reuven Young, Defining Terrorism: The Evolution of Terrorism as a Legal Concept in International Law and Its Influence on Definitions in Domestic Legislation, 29 B. C. Int'l & Comp. L. Rev. 23 (2006).

Sandrine Valentine, Trafficking of Child Soldiers: Expanding the United Nations Convention on the Rights of the Child and its Optional Protocol on the

Involvement of Children in Armed Conflict, 9 New Eng. J. Int'l & Comp. L. 109 (2003).

Sarah Hafen, Incentivizing Armed Non-State Actors to Comply with the Law: Protecting Children in Times of Armed Conflict, 2016 BYU L. Rev. 989 (2016).

Sarah Lesser, Early Non-Military Intervention to Prevent Atrocity Crimes, 10 Am. J. Mediation 84 (2017).

Sarah Myers Raben, The ISIS Eradication of Christians and Yazidis: Human Trafficking, Genocide, and the Missing International Efforts to Stop It, 15 Braz. J. Int'l L. 239 (2018).

Sarah Schwartz, Wartime Sexual Violence as More than Collateral Damage: Classifying Sexual Violence as Part of a Common Criminal Plan in International Criminal Law, 40 U.N.S.W.L.J. 57 (2017).

Serena Forlati, Legal Obligation to Prevent Genocide: Bosnia v. Serbia and beyond, The, 31 Polish Y.B. Int'l L. 189 (2011).

Shayna Rogers, Sexual Violence or Rape as a Constituent Act of Genocide: Lessons from the Ad Hoc Tribunals and a Prescription for the International Criminal Court, 48 Geo. Wash. Int'l L. Rev. 265 (2016).

Sherrie L. Russell-Brown, Rape as an Act of Genocide, 21 Berkeley J. Int'l L. 350 (2003).

William A. Schabas, Ethnic Cleansing and Genocide: Similarities and Distinctions, 3 Eur. Y.B. Minority Issues 109 (2003-2004).

William A. Schabas, Genocide and the International Court of Justice: Finally, a Duty to Prevent the Crime of Crimes, 4 Int'l Stud. J. 17 (2007).

William A. Schabas, Genocide Law in a Time of Transition: Recent Developments in the Law of Genocide, 61 Rutgers L. Rev. 161 (2008).

William A. Schabas, Is Terrorism a Crime against Humanity, 8 Int'l Peacekeeping 255 (2004).

William A. Schabas, National Courts Finally Begin to Prosecute Genocide, the Crime of Crimes, 1 J. Int'l Crim. Just. 39 (2003).

William A. Schabas, Origins of the Genocide Convention: From Nuremberg to Paris, 40 Case W. Res. J. Int'l L. 35 (2007).

William A. Schabas, Retroactive Application of the Genocide Convention, 4 U. St. Thomas J.L. & Pub. Pol'y 36 (2010).

William A. Schabas, Victor's Justice: Selecting Situations at the International Criminal Court, 43 J. Marshall L. Rev. 535 (2010).

Yuri Mantilla, ISIS's International Crimes and Jus Cogens Norms: The Protection of Human Rights in Times of Global Terrorism, 11 Liberty U. L. Rev. 451 (2016).

## 2.2. Papers on applied research methodology for genocide and/or international sex crimes studies – Alphabetic order

Alexander Laban Hinton, Critical genocide studies. Genocide Studies and Prevention International Journal. Article 3. Volume 7. 2012 Issue 1.

Anne-Marie De Brouwer, The Importance of Understanding Sexual Violence in Conflict for Investigation and Prosecution Purposes. 48 Cornell Int'l L.J. 639 (2015).

ai Ambos, Thematic investigations and prosecution of international sex crimes: Some critical comments from a theoretical and comparative perspective in International Sex Crimes. Morten Bergsmo (editor). Torkel Opsahl Academic E-Publisher. FICHL Publication. Series No. 13.

# 3. Documents from the United Nations – United Nations Official Documentation codes.

## 3.1. Treaties and declarations – Chronological Order

United Nations, Charter of the International Military Tribunal, annex to the agreement for the prosecution and punishment of the major war criminals of the European Axis ("London Agreement") (Aug. 8, 1945).

United Nations. Charter of the United Nations (Oct. 24, 1945). 1 UNTS XVI.

G. A. Res. 260 A (III), Convention on the Prevention and Punishment of the Crime of Genocide (Dec. 9, 1948).

G. A. Res. 217 (III) A, Universal Declaration of Human Rights (Dec. 10, 1948).

G. A. Res. 429 (V), Convention Relating to the Status of Refugees (July 28, 1951).

G. A. Res. 2200A (XXI), International Covenant on Civil and Political Rights (Dec. 16, 1966).

G.A. Res. 2198 (XXI), Protocol Relating to the Status of Refugees (Dec. 16, 1966).

G. A. Res. 2391, Convention on the Non-Applicability of Statutory Limitations to War Crimes and Crimes Against Humanity, U.N. Doc. A/RES/2391(XXIII) (Nov. 26, 1968).

United Nations, Vienna Convention on the Law of Treaties (May 23, 1969) 1155 UNTS 331.

G.A. Res. 30/3452, Declaration on the Protection of All Persons from Being Subjected to Torture and Other Cruel, Inhuman or Degrading (Dec. 9, 1975).

G.A. Res. 39/46, Convention Against Torture and Other Cruel, Inhuman or Degrading Treatment or Punishment (Dec. 10, 1984).

G.A. Res. 40/33, United Nations Standard Minimum Rules for the Administration of Juvenile Justice ("The Beijing Rules") (Nov. 29, 1985).

G.A. Res. 44/25, Convention on the Rights of the Child (Nov. 20, 1989).

G.A. Res. 45/113, United Nations Rules for the Protection of Juveniles Deprived of their Liberty (Dec. 14, 1990).

United Nations, Commission on Human Rights, Declaration on the Protection of All Persons from Enforced Disappearance, U.N. Doc. E/CN.4/RES/1992/29 (Feb. 28, 1992).

United Nations. Rome Statute (July 17, 1998) 2187 UNTS 38544.

U.N. Econ. & Soc. Res. 2005/20, Guidelines on Justice in Matters involving Child Victims and Witnesses of Crime, U.N. Doc. E/RES/2005/20 (July 22, 2005).

G.A. Res. 60/1, Responsibility to Protect, adopted following 2005 World Summit Outcome (Sept. 16, 2005).

G.A. Res. 61/177, International Convention for the Protection of All Persons from Enforced Disappearance (Dec. 20, 2006).

G.A. Res. 70/175, United Nations Standard Minimum Rules for the Treatment of Prisoners ("The Nelson Mandela Rules") (Jan. 8, 2016).

## 3.2. Documents from the United Nations General Assembly – Chronological Order

### 3.2.1. General Assembly reports

Rep. of the Working Group on a Draft Statute for An International Criminal Court, International Law Commission, U.N. Doc. A/CN.4/L.491/Rev.1 (July 8, 1994).

Rep. of the Expert of the Secretary-General, Ms. Graça Machel, *Impact of armed conflict on children*, U.N. Doc. A/51/306 (Aug. 26, 1996).

U.N. Secretary-General, *United Nations Assistance Mission for Iraq*. U.N. Doc. A/68/327/Add.5 (Oct. 18, 2013).

U.N. Secretary-General, *United Nations Assistance Mission for Iraq*, U.N. Doc. A/72/371/Add.10 (Mar. 9, 2018).

U.N. Secretary-General, *Trafficking in women and girls*, U.N. Doc. A/73/263 (July 27, 2018).

U.N. Secretary-General, *Effects of terrorism on the enjoyment of human rights*, U.N. Doc. A/73/347 (Aug. 28, 2018).

U.N. Secretary-General, *United Nations Assistance Mission for Iraq*, U.N. Doc. A/73/352/Add.5 (Oct. 10, 2018).

S/2018/1031, U.N. Doc. A/73/352/Add.6 (Oct. 2018).

3.2.2. Reports of the Secretary-General – Children and armed conflict

U.N. Secretary-General, *Children and Armed Conflict*, U.N. Doc. A/65/820–S/2011/250 (Apr. 23, 2011).

U.N. Secretary-General, *Children and Armed Conflict*, U.N. Doc. A/66/782–S/2012/261 (Apr. 6, 2012).

U.N. Secretary-General, *Children and Armed Conflict*, U.N. Doc. A/67/845–S/2013/245 (May 15, 2013).

U.N. Secretary-General, *Children and Armed Conflict*, U.N. Doc. A/68/878–S/2014/339 (May 15, 2014).

U.N. Secretary-General, *Children and Armed Conflict*, U.N. Doc. A/69/926–S/2015/409 (June 5, 2015).

U.N. Secretary-General, *Children and Armed Conflict*, U.N. Doc. A/70/836–S/2016/360 (Apr. 20, 2016).

U.N. Secretary-General, *Children and Armed Conflict*, U.N. Doc. A/72/361–S/2017/821 (Aug. 24, 2017).

U.N. Secretary-General, *Children and Armed Conflict*, U.N. Doc. A/72/865–S/2018/465 (May 16, 2018).

U.N. Secretary-General, *Children and Armed Conflict*, U.N. Doc. A/73/907–S/2019/509 (June 20, 2019).

## 3.2.3. Reports of the Special Representative of the Secretary-General for Children and Armed Conflict

Rep. of the Special Representative of the Secretary-General for Children and Armed Conflict, addressed to the G.A. on its Fifty-fifth session, U.N. Doc.A/55/442 (Oct. 3, 2000).

Rep. of the Special Representative of the Secretary-General for Children and Armed Conflict, addressed to the G.A. on its Fifty-ninth session, U.N. Doc.A/59/426 (Oct. 8, 2004).

Rep. of the Special Representative of the Secretary-General for Children and Armed Conflict, addressed to the G.A. on its Sixtieth session, U.N. Doc.A/60/335 (Sept. 7, 2005).

Rep. of the Special Representative of the Secretary-General for Children and Armed Conflict, addressed to the G.A. on its Sixty-first session, A/61/275 (Aug. 17, 2006).

Rep. of the Special Representative of the Secretary-General for Children and Armed Conflict, addressed to the G.A. on its Sixty-first session, U.N. Doc. A/61/529–S/2006/826 (Oct. 26, 2006).

Rep. of the Special Representative of the Secretary-General for Children and Armed Conflict, addressed to the G.A. on its Sixty-second session, U.N. Doc. A/62/228 (Aug. 13, 2007).

Rep. of the Special Representative of the Secretary-General for Children and Armed Conflict, addressed to the G.A. on its Sixty-second session, U.N. Doc. A/62/609–S/2007/757 (Dec. 21, 2007).

Rep. of the Special Representative of the Secretary-General for Children and Armed Conflict, addressed to the G.A. on its Sixty-third session, U.N. Doc. A/63/785–S/2009/158 (Mar. 26, 2009).

Rep. of the Special Representative of the Secretary-General for Children and Armed Conflict, addressed to the G.A. on its Sixty-third session, U.N. Doc.A/63/227 (Aug. 6, 2008).

Rep. of the Special Representative of the Secretary-General for Children and Armed Conflict, addressed to the G.A. on its Sixty-fourth session, U.N. Doc.A/64/254 (Aug. 6, 2009).

Rep. of the Special Representative of the Secretary-General for Children and Armed Conflict, addressed to the G.A. on its Sixty-fourth session, U.N. Doc. A/64/742–S/2010/181 (Apr. 13, 2010).

Rep. of the Special Representative of the Secretary-General for Children and Armed Conflict, addressed to the G.A. on its Sixty-fifth session, U.N. Doc. A/65/219 (Aug. 4, 2010).

Rep. of the Special Representative of the Secretary-General for Children and Armed Conflict, addressed to the G.A. on its Sixty-fifth session, U.N. Doc. A/65/820–S/2011/250 (Apr. 23, 2011).

Rep. of the Special Representative of the Secretary-General for Children and Armed Conflict, addressed to the G.A. on its Sixty-sixth session, U.N. Doc. A/66/256 (Aug. 3, 2011).

Rep. of the Special Representative of the Secretary-General for Children and Armed Conflict, addressed to the G.A. on its Sixty-eighth session, U.N. Doc. A/68/267 (Aug. 5, 2013).

Rep. of the Special Representative of the Secretary-General for Children and Armed Conflict, addressed to the G.A. on its Sixty-eighth session, U.N. Doc. A/69/212 (July 31, 2014).

Rep. of the Special Representative of the Secretary-General for Children and Armed Conflict, addressed to the G.A. on its Seventieth session, U.N. Doc. A/70/162 (July 20, 2015).

Rep. of the Special Representative of the Secretary-General for Children and Armed Conflict, addressed to the G.A. on its Seventy-first session, U.N. Doc. A/71/205 (July 25, 2016).

## 3.3. Documents from the United Nations Security Council – Chronological Order

### 3.3.1. Security Council Resolutions

S.C. Res. 827 (May 25, 1993).

S.C. Res. 955 (Nov. 8, 1994).

S.C. Res. 1830 (Aug. 7, 2008).

S.C. Res. 1859 (Dec. 22, 2008).

S.C. Res. 1883 (Aug. 7, 2009).

S.C. Res. 1936 (Aug. 5, 2010).

S.C. Res. 1966 (Dec. 22, 2010).

S.C. Res. 2001 (July 28, 2011).

S.C. Res. 2061 (July 25, 2012).

S.C. Res. 2063 (July 31, 2012).

S.C. Res. 2068 (Sept. 19, 2012).

S.C. Res. 2086 (Jan. 21, 2013).

S.C. Res. 2110 (July 24, 2013).

S.C. Res. 2121 (Oct. 10, 2013).

S.C. Res. 2139 (Feb. 22, 2014).

S.C. Res. 2143 (Mar. 7, 2014).

S.C. Res. 2165 (July 14, 2014).

S.C. Res. 2169 (July 30, 2014).

S.C. Res. 2170 (Aug. 15, 2014).

S.C. Res. 2185 (Nov. 20, 2014).

S.C. Res. 2187 (Nov. 25, 2014).

S.C. Res. 2199 (Feb. 12, 2015).

S.C. Res. 2220 (May 22, 2015).

S.C. Res. 2225 (June 18, 2015).

S.C. Res. 2233 (July 29, 2015).

S.C. Res. 2249 (Nov. 20, 2015).

S.C. Res. 2299 (July 25, 2016).

S.C. Res. 2331 (Dec. 20, 2016).

S.C. Res. 2367 (July 14, 2017).

S.C. Res. 2379 (Sept. 21, 2017).

S.C. Res. 2388 (Nov. 21, 2017).

S.C. Res. 2417 (May 24, 2018).

S.C. Res. 2421 (June 14, 2018).

S.C. Res. 2427 (July 9, 2018).

S.C. Res. 2490 (Sept. 20, 2019).

*3.3.2. Reports submitted by / transmitted by the Secretary-General to the Security Council*

Rep. of the International Commission of Inquiry on Darfur to the Secretary-General Pursuant to Security Council Resolution 1564 (2004), U.N. Doc. S/2005/60 (Feb. 1, 2005).

Rep. of the U.N. Secretary-General submitted to the S.C, pursuant to *Protection of Civilians in Armed Conflict*, U.N. Doc. S/2010/579 (Nov. 11, 2010).

Rep. of the U.N. Secretary-General submitted to the S.C, pursuant to *Small Arms*, U.N. Doc. S/2011/255 (Apr. 5, 2011).

Rep. of the U.N. Secretary-General submitted to the S.C, pursuant to *Children and Armed Conflict in Iraq*, U.N. Doc. S/2011/366 (June 15, 2011).

Rep. of the U.N. Secretary-General submitted to the S.C, pursuant to *Women and Peace and Security*, U.N. Doc. S/2011/598 (Sept. 29, 2011).

Rep. of the U.N. Secretary-General submitted to the S.C, pursuant to *Protection of Civilians in Armed Conflict*, U.N. Doc. S/2012/376 (May 22, 2012).

Rep. of the U.N. Secretary-General submitted to the S.C, pursuant to *Women and Peace and Security*, U.N. Doc. S/2012/732 (Oct. 2, 2012).

Rep. of the U.N. Secretary-General submitted to the S.C, pursuant to paragraph 6 of Res. 2061 (2012), U.N. Doc. S/2013/154 (March 12, 2013).

Rep. of the U.N. Secretary-General submitted to the S.C, pursuant to *Small Arms*, U.N. Doc. S/2013/503 (Aug. 22, 2013).

Rep. of the U.N. Secretary-General submitted to the S.C, pursuant to *Women and Peace and Security*, U.N. Doc. S/2013/525 (Sept. 4, 2013).

Rep. of the U.N. Secretary-General submitted to the S.C, on *Children and Armed Conflict in the Syrian Arab Republic*, U.N. Doc. S/2014/31 (Jan. 27, 2014).

Rep. of the U.N. Secretary-General submitted to the S.C, on *Conflict-Related Sexual Violence*, U.N. Doc. S/2014/181 (Mar. 13, 2014).

Rep. of the U.N. Secretary-General submitted to the S.C, pursuant to *Paragraph 6 of Rresolution 2110 (2013)*. U.N. Doc. S/2014/485 (July 11, 2014).

Rep. of the U.N. Secretary-General submitted to the S.C, pursuant to *Women and Peace and Security*, U.N. Doc. S/2014/693 (Sept. 23, 2014).

Rep. of the U.N. Secretary-General submitted to the S.C, pursuant to paragraph 6 or Res. 2169 (2014). U.N. Doc. S/2014/774 (Oct. 31, 2014).

Rep. of the U.N. Secretary-General submitted to the S.C, pursuant to *Paragraph 6 or Res. 2169 (2014)*. U.N. Doc. S/2015/82 (Feb. 2, 2015).

Rep. of the U.N. Secretary-General submitted to the S.C, pursuant to *Small Arms*, U.N. Doc. S/2015/289 (Apr. 27, 2015).

Rep. of the U.N. Secretary-General submitted to the S.C, pursuant to *Paragraph 6 or Res. 2169 (2014)*. U.N. Doc. S/2015/530 (July 13, 2015).

Rep. of the U.N. Secretary-General submitted to the S.C, pursuant to *Children and Armed Conflict in Iraq*, U.N. Doc. S/2015/852 (Nov. 9, 2015).

Rep. of the U.N. Secretary-General submitted to the S.C, pursuant to *Res. 2233 (2015)*, U.N. Doc. S/PV.7556 (Nov. 11, 2015).

Rep. of the U.N. Secretary-General submitted to the S.C, pursuant to *Paragraph 7 or Res. 2233 (2015)*. U.N. Doc. S/2016/77 (Jan. 26, 2016).

Rep. of the U.N. Secretary-General submitted to the S.C, pursuant to the *Threat Posed by ISIL/DAESH (Da'esh) to International Peace and Security*. U.N. Doc. S/2016/92 (Jan. 29, 2016).

Rep. of the U.N. Secretary-General submitted to the S.C, on *Conflict-Related Sexual Violence*, U.N. Doc. S/2016/361 (Apr. 20, 2016).

Rep. of the U.N. Secretary-General submitted to the S.C, pursuant to *Paragraph 7 or Res. 2233 (2015)*. U.N. Doc. S/2016/396 (Apr. 27, 2016).

Rep. of the U.N. Secretary-General submitted to the S.C, pursuant to *Protection of Civilians in Armed Conflict*, U.N. Doc. S/2016/447 (May 13, 2016).

Rep. of the U.N. Secretary-General submitted to the S.C, on *Conflict-Related Sexual Violence*, U.N. Doc. S/2016/361/Rev.1 (June 22, 2016).

Rep. of the U.N. Secretary-General submitted to the S.C, pursuant to the *Paragraph 7 of Res. 2233 (2015)*, U.N. Doc. S/2016/592 (July 5, 2016).

Rep. of the U.N. Secretary-General submitted to the S.C, pursuant to *Women and Peace and Security*, U.N. Doc. S/2016/822 (Sept. 29, 2016).

Rep. of the U.N. Secretary-General submitted to the S.C, pursuant to the *Implementation of Res. 2299 (2016)*. U.N. Doc. S/2016/897 (Oct. 25, 2016).

Rep. of the U.N. Secretary-General submitted to the S.C, pursuant to the *Implementation of Measures to Counter Trafficking in Persons*, U.N. Doc. S/2016/949 (Nov. 10, 2016).

Rep. of the U.N. Secretary-General submitted to the S.C, pursuant to *the Implementation of Res. 2299 (2016)*. U.N. Doc. S/2017/75 (Jan. 26, 2017).

Rep. of the U.N. Secretary-General submitted to the S.C, pursuant to *Res. 2367 (2017)*, U.N. Doc. S/2017/881 (Oct. 19, 2017).

Rep. of the U.N. Secretary-General submitted to the S.C, pursuant *Trafficking in Persons in Armed Conflict,* according to the S. C. Res. 2331 (2016), U.N. Doc. S/2017/939 (Nov. 10, 2017).

Rep. of the U.N. Secretary-General submitted to the S.C, pursuant to *Small Arms and Light Weapons*, U.N. Doc. S/2017/1025 (Dec. 6, 2017).

Rep. of the U.N. Secretary-General submitted to the S.C, pursuant to *Res. 2367 (2017)*, U.N. Doc. S/2018/42 (Jan. 17, 2018).

Rep. of the U.N. Secretary-General submitted to the S.C, pursuant to the *Threat Posed by ISIL/DAESH (Da'esh) to International Peace and Security.* U.N. Doc. S/2018/80 (Jan. 31, 2018).

Rep. of the U.N. Secretary-General submitted to the S.C, pursuant to *Res. 2367 (2017)*, U.N. Doc. S/2018/359 (Apr. 17, 2018).

Rep. of the U.N. Secretary-General submitted to the S.C, pursuant to *Protection of Civilians in Armed Conflict*, U.N. Doc. S/2018/462 (May 22, 2018).

Rep. of the U.N. Secretary-General submitted to the S.C, pursuant to the *Implementation of Res. 2367* (2017). U.N. Doc. S/2018/677 (July 9, 2018).

Rep. of the U.N. Secretary-General submitted to the S.C, *The Situation Concerning Iraq*, pursuant to Res. 2367 (2017), U.N. Doc. S/PV.8324 (Aug. 8, 2018).

Rep. of the U.N. Secretary-General submitted to the S.C, pursuant to the *Threat Posed by ISIL/DAESH (Da'esh) to International Peace and Security,* U.N. Doc. S/2018/770 (August 16, 2018).

Rep. of the U.N. Secretary-General submitted to the S.C, pursuant to the *Situation in the Middle East,* and the implementation of S. C. Res. 2139 (2014), 2165 (2014), 2191 (2014), 2258 (2015), 2332 (2016), 2393 (2017) and 2401 (2018) (S/2018/845), U.N. Doc. S/PV.8355 (Sept. 18, 2018).

Rep. of the U.N. Secretary-General submitted to the S.C, *The United Nations Assistance Mission for Iraq (UNAMI)*, pursuant to Res. 2299 (2016), U.N. Doc. S/2016/897 (Oct. 25, 2018).

Rep. of the U.N. Secretary-General submitted to the S.C, pursuant to the *Implementation of Res. 2421 (2018)*, U.N. Doc. S/2018/975 (Oct. 31, 2018).

Rep. of the U.N. Secretary-General submitted to the S.C, pursuant to the *Threat Posed by ISIL/DAESH (Da'esh) to International Peace and Security.* U.N. Doc. S/2019/103 (Feb. 1, 2019).

Rep. of the U.N. Secretary-General submitted to the S.C, on the *Implementation of resolution 2421 (2018)*, U.N. Doc. S/2019/101 (Feb. 1, 2019).

Rep. of the U.N. Secretary-General submitted to the S.C, pursuant to the *Implementation of Res. 2421 (2018)*, U.N. Doc. S/2019/365 (May 2, 2019).

Rep. of the U.N. Secretary-General submitted to the S.C, on the *Implementation of resolution 2470 (2019).* U.N. Doc. S/2019/903 (Nov. 22, 2019).

Rep. of the U.N. Secretary-General submitted to the S.C, pursuant to *Children and Armed Conflict in Iraq*, U.N. Doc. S/2019/984 (Dec. 23, 2019).

Rep. of the U.N. Secretary-General submitted to the S.C, on the *Implementation of resolution 2470 (2019).* U.N. Doc. S/2020/140 (Feb. 21, 2020).

Rep. of the U.N. Secretary-General submitted to the S.C, on the *Implementation of resolution 2470 (2019).* U.N. Doc. S/2020/363 (May 6, 2020).

Rep. of the U.N. Secretary-General submitted to the S.C, on *Children and Armed Conflict,* U.N. Doc. A/74/845–S/2020/525 (June 9, 2020).

### 3.3.4. Documents from the U. N. Security Council Investigative Team to Promote Accountability for Crimes Committed by Da'esh/Islamic State in Iraq

Rep. of the Special Adviser and Head of the U. N. Investigative Team to Promote Accountability for Crimes Committed by Da'esh/Islamic State in Iraq and the Levant submitted to the S.C, First report of the Special Adviser and Head of the United Nations Investigative Team to Promote Accountability for Crimes Committed by Da'esh/Islamic State in Iraq and the Levant, U.N. Doc. S/2018/1031 (Nov. 16, 2018).

Rep. of the Special Adviser and Head of the U. N. Investigative Team to Promote Accountability for Crimes Committed by Da'esh/Islamic State in Iraq and the Levant submitted to the S.C, Second report of the Special Adviser and Head of the United Nations Investigative Team to Promote Accountability for Crimes Committed by Da'esh/Islamic State in Iraq and the Levant, U.N. Doc. S/2019/407 (May 17, 2019).

Rep. of the Special Adviser and Head of the U. N. Investigative Team to Promote Accountability for Crimes Committed by Da'esh/Islamic State in Iraq and the Levant submitted to the S.C, Third report of the Special Adviser and Head of the United Nations Investigative Team to Promote Accountability for Crimes Committed by Da'esh/Islamic State in Iraq and the Levant, U.N. Doc. S/2019/878 (Nov. 13, 2019).

Rep. of the Special Adviser and Head of the U. N. Investigative Team to Promote Accountability for Crimes Committed by Da'esh/Islamic State in Iraq and the Levant submitted to the S.C, Fourth report of the Special Adviser and Head of the United Nations Investigative Team to Promote Accountability for Crimes Committed by Da'esh/Islamic State in Iraq and the Levant, U.N. Doc. S/2020/386 (May 11, 2020).

Rep. of the Special Adviser and Head of the U. N. Investigative Team to Promote Accountability for Crimes Committed by Da'esh/Islamic State in Iraq and the Levant submitted to the S.C, Fifth report of the Special Adviser and Head of the United Nations Investigative Team to Promote Accountability for Crimes Committed by Da'esh/Islamic State in Iraq and the Levant, U.N. Doc. S/2020/1107 (Nov. 11, 2020).

### 3.3.5. Other Security Council documents

Statute of the International Tribunal for the Prosecution of Persons Responsible for Serious Violations of International Humanitarian Law Committed in the Territory of the Former Yugoslavia since 1991, U.N. Doc. S/RES/827 (May 25, 1993).

S. C. Final Report of the Commission of Experts Established Pursuant to Security Council Resolution 780 (1992), U.N. Doc. S/1994/674 (May 27, 1994).

Statute of the International Criminal Tribunal for Rwanda, U.N. Doc. S/RES/955 (Nov. 8, 1994).

Rep. of the S.C. Working Group on Children and Armed Conflict, *Conclusions on Children and Armed Conflict in Iraq*, U.N. Doc. S/AC.51/2011/6 (Oct. 3, 2011).

S. C. Threats to International Peace and Security Caused by Terrorist Acts, 7316th meeting, U.N. Doc. S/PV.7316 (Nov. 19, 2014).

Rep. of the S.C. Working Group on Children and Armed Conflict, *Conclusions on Children and Armed Conflict in the Syrian Arab Republic*, U.N. Doc. S/AC.51/2014/4 (Nov. 26, 2014).

U.N. Chair of the S.C., Letter dated 15 December 2015 from the Chair of the Security Council Committee established pursuant to resolution 1373 (2001) concerning counter-terrorism addressed to the President of the Security Council, U.N. Doc. S/2015/975 (Dec. 29, 2015).

U.N. Chair of the S.C., Letter dated 25 September 2015 from the Chair of the Se-curity Council Committee pursuant to resolutions 1267 (1999) and 1989 (2011) concerning Al-Qaida and associated individuals and entities ad-dressed to the President of the Security Council, U.N. Doc. S/2015/739 (July 19, 2016).

Rep. of the S.C. Working Group on Children and Armed Conflict, *Conclusions on Children and Armed Conflict in Iraq*, U.N. Doc. S/AC.51/2016/2 (Aug. 18, 2016).

U.N. Chair of the S.C., Letter dated 20 December 2016 from the Secretary-General addressed to the President of the Security Council, U.N. Doc. S/2016/1090 (Dec. 21, 2016).

U.N. Chair of the S.C., Letter dated 7 August 2017 from the Chair of the Security Council Committee pursuant to resolutions 1267 (1999), 1989 (2011) and 2253 (2015) concerning Islamic State in Iraq and the Levant (Da'esh), Al-Qaida and associated individuals, groups, undertakings and entities ad-dressed to the President of the Security Council, U.N. Doc. S/2017/573 (Aug. 7, 2017).

Chargé d'affaires of the Permanent Mission of Iraq to the United Nations, Letter dated Aug. 14, 2017 from the Chargé d'affaires a.i. of the Permanent Mis-sion of Iraq to the United Nations addressed to the President of the Secu-rity Council, U.N. Doc. S/2017/710 (Aug. 16, 2017).

U.N. Secretary-General, Letter dated Nov. 15, 2017 from the Secretary-General addressed to the President of the Security Council, U.N. Doc. S/2017/966 (Nov. 20, 2017).

Statement by the President of the S.C., U.N. Doc. S/PRST/2017/21 (Oct. 31, 2017).

Rep. of the S.C., Monthly Forecast: Situation in Iraq, February 2018 (Jan. 31, 2018).

https://www.securitycouncilreport.org/monthly-forecast/2018-02/iraq_18.php

U.N. Chair of the S.C., Letter dated 9 February 2018 from the Secretary-General addressed to the President of the Security Council, U.N. Doc. S/2018/118 (Feb. 14, 2018).

U.N. Chair of the S.C., Letter dated 17 January 2018 from the Chair of the Security Council Committee pursuant to resolutions 1267 (1999), 1989 (2011), and 2253 (2015) concerning Islamic State in Iraq and the Levant (Da'esh), Al-Qaida and associated individuals, groups, undertakings and entities ad-dressed to the President of the Security Council, U.N. Doc. S/2018/14/Rev.1 (Feb. 27, 2018).

U.N. Chair of the S.C., United Nations. Security Council. Letter dated July 16, 2018 from the Chair of the Security Council addressed to the President of the

Security Council pursuant to resolutions 1267 (1999), 1989 (2011) and 2253 (2015) concerning Islamic State in Iraq and the Levant, U.N. Doc. S/2018/705 (July 27, 2018).

U.N. Secretary-General, Letter dated Aug. 15, 2018 from the Secretary-General addressed to the President of the Security Council, U.N. Doc. S/2018/773 (Aug. 17, 2017).

Rep. of the S.C., Monthly Forecast: Situation in Iraq, November 2018 (Oct. 30, 2018).

https://www.securitycouncilreport.org/monthly-forecast/2018-11/iraq_21.php

U.N. Chair of the S.C., Letter dated 15 July 2019 from the Chair of the Security Council Committee pursuant to resolutions 1267 (1999), 1989 (2011) and 2253 (2015) concerning Islamic State in Iraq and the Levant (Da'esh), Al-Qaida and associated individuals, groups, undertakings and entities addressed to the President of the Security Council, U.N. Doc. S/2019/570 (July 15, 2019).

S. C. Draft Resolution, U.N. Doc. S/2019/761 (Sept. 20, 2019).

S. C. Threats to International Peace and Security, 8675th meeting, U.N. Doc. S/PV.8675 (Nov. 26, 2019).

U.N. Chair of the S.C., Letter dated 20 January 2020 from the Chair of the Security Council Committee pursuant to resolutions 1267 (1999), 1989 (2011) and 2253 (2015) concerning Islamic State in Iraq and the Levant (Da'esh), Al-Qaida and associated individuals, groups, undertakings and entities addressed to the President of the Security Council, U.N. Doc. S/2020/53 (Jan. 20, 2020).

U.N. Chair of the S.C., Letter dated 16 July 2020 from the Chair of the Security Council Committee pursuant to resolutions 1267 (1999), 1989 (2011) and 2253 (2015) concerning Islamic State in Iraq and the Levant (Da'esh), Al-Qaida and associated individuals, groups, undertakings and entities addressed to the President of the Security Council, U.N. Doc. S/2020/717 (July 23, 2020).

## 3.4. Documents from the United Nations Human Rights Council – Chronological Order

U.N. Human Rights Council, Written Statement Submitted by the European Centre for Law and Justice, A Non-Governmental Organization in Special Consultative Status, U.N. Doc. A/HRC/S-22/NGO/8 (Aug. 29, 2014).

Rep. of the Human Rights Council, U.N. Doc. A/69/53/Add.1 (Sept. 1, 2014).

Human Rights Council Res. S-22/1, U.N. Doc. A/HRC/RES/S-22/1 (Sept. 3, 2014).

Human Rights Council. Report of the Working Group on the Universal Periodic Review: Iraq. U.N. Doc. A/HRC/28/14 (Dec. 12, 2014).

Rep. of the Office of the United Nations High Commissioner for Human Rights, submitted to the Human Rights Council, *Human Rights Situation in Iraq in the Light of Abuses Committed by The so Called Islamic State in Iraq and The Levant and Associated Groups*, U.N. Doc. A/HRC/28/18 (March 27, 2015).

U.N. Human Rights Council, Written Statement Submitted by the Al-khoei Foundation, A Non-Governmental Organization in Special Consultative Status, U.N. Doc. A/HRC/29/NGO/95 (June 10, 2015).

Rep. of the Office of the United Nations High Commissioner for Human Rights, submitted to the Human Rights Council, Technical Assistance Provided to Assist in The Promotion and Protection of Human Rights in Iraq, U.N. Doc. A/HRC/30/66 (July 27, 2015).

Human Rights Council Res. 28/32. U.N. Doc. A/HRC/RES/28/32 (April 8, 2015).

Rep. of the Human Rights Council, *"They Came to Destroy": ISIS Crimes Against the Yazidis"*, U.N. Doc. A/HRC/32/CRP.2 (June 15, 2016).

U.N. Human Rights Council, Written statement submitted by the International Youth and Student Movement for the United Nations, A Non-Governmental Organization in Special Consultative Status, U.N. Doc. A/HRC/30/NGO/116 (Sept. 8, 2015).

U.N. Human Rights Council, Report of the Special Rapporteur on the Human Rights of Internally Displaced Persons, Chaloka Beyani, Visit to Iraq, U.N. Doc. A/HRC/32/35/Add.1 (April 5, 2016).

Rep. of the Special Rapporteur on Trafficking in persons, especially women and children, Maria Grazia Giammarinaro, submitted to the Human Rights Council concerning her mission to Iraq, U.N. Doc. A/71/303 (Aug. 5, 2016).

Office of the United Nations High Commissioner for Human Rights, Press briefing note on Myanmar, Mosul and Syria, Spokesperson for the UN High Commissioner for Human Rights: Ravina Shamdasani (Nov. 29, 2016).

Rep. of the Special Rapporteur on Minority Issues, submitted to the Human Rights Council concerning her mission to Iraq, U.N. Doc. A/HRC/34/53/Add.1 (Jan. 9, 2017).

U.N. Human Rights Council, Report of the Special Rapporteur on freedom of religion and belief, U.N. Doc. A/HRC/34/50 (Jan. 17, 2017).

Joint Rep. of the Special Rapporteur on the sale and sexual exploitation of children, including child prostitution, child pornography and other child sexual abuse material and the Special Rapporteur on trafficking in persons, especially women and children, U.N. Doc. A/72/164 (July 18, 2017).

Rep. of the Human Rights Council, U.N. Doc. A/72/53/Add.1 (Sept. 29, 2017).

Rep. of the Special Rapporteur on Extrajudicial, Summary or Arbitrary Executions, submitted to the Human Rights Council concerning her mission to Iraq, U.N. Doc. A/HRC/38/44/Add.1 (June 20, 2018).

U.N. Human Rights Council, Written Statement Submitted by the European Centre for Law and Justice, A Non-Governmental Organization in Special Consultative Status, Request that the U.N. Recognize ISIS Atrocities Against Christians and Other Religious and Ethnic Minorities as Genocide and Take Immediate Appropriate Action, U.N. Doc. A/HRC/39/NGO/X (Aug. 23, 2018).

Rep. of the Human Rights Council, U.N. Doc. A/73/53/Add.1 (Sept. 28, 2018).

Rep. of the Special Rapporteur on Trafficking in persons, especially women and children, Maria Grazia Giammarinaro, submitted to the Human Rights Council, U.N. Doc. A/HRC/41/46 (Abr. 23, 2019).

U.N. Human Rights Council, Working Group on the Universal Periodic Review, Summary of Stakeholders' Submissions on Iraq, Report of the Office of the United Nations High Commissioner for Human Rights, U.N. Doc. A/HRC/WG.6/34/IRQ/3 (Aug. 19, 2019).

U.N. Human Rights Council, Report of the Special Rapporteur on the Human Rights of Internally Displaced Persons, Cecilia Jimenez-Damary, Visit to Iraq, U.N. Doc. A/HRC/44/41/Add.1 (May 13, 2020).

U.N. Human Rights Council, Written Statement Submitted by the Society for Threatened Peoples, A Non-Governmental Organization in Special Consultative Status, U.N. Doc. A/HRC/44/NGO/115 (June 30, 2020).

## 3.5. Other United Nations documents – Chronological Order

G. A. Res. 96(I), The Crime of Genocide, Fifty-fifth plenary meeting, U.N. Doc. A/RES/96 (Dec. 11, 1946).

Rep. of the Special Rapporteur on the Draft Code of Offences against the Peace and Security of Mankind, by Doudou Thiam, U.N. Doc. A/CN.4/398 (March 11, 1986).

United Nation, Report of the Commission to the General Assembly on the work of its forty-first session, Yearbook of the International Law Commission, Vol. II, UN Doc. A/CN.4/SER.A/1989/Add.l (Part 2) (1989).

United Nation, Report of the Commission to the General Assembly on the work of its forty-eighth session, Yearbook of the International Law Commission, Vol. II, U.N. Doc. A/CN.4/SER.A/1996/Add.l (Part 2) (1996).

United Nation, Report of the International Law Commission on the Work of its Forty-Eighth Session, Yearbook of the International Law Commission, Vol. II(2), UN Doc. A/51/10 (May 6, 1996 – July 26, 1996).

Rep. of the Preparatory Committee on the Establishment of an International Criminal Court, U.N. Doc. A/CONF.183/2/Add.1 (April 14, 1998).

Rep. of the Committee on the Rights of the Child, Consideration of reports submitted by States parties under article 8, paragraph 1, of the Optional Protocol to the Convention on the Rights of the Child on the involvement of children in armed conflict Initial reports of States parties due in 2010 Iraq, U.N. Doc. CRC/C/OPAC/IRQ/1 (May 9, 2012).

Rep. of the Committee on the Rights of the Child, Consideration of reports submitted by States parties under article 44 of the Convention Combined second to fourth periodic reports of States parties due in 2011 Iraq, U.N. Doc. CRC/C/IRQ/2-4 (Dec. 2, 2013).

Rep. of the Office of the United Nations High Commissioner for Human Rights, United Nations Assistance Mission for Iraq (UNAMI), Report on the Protection of Civilians in the Armed Conflict in Iraq (July 6, 2014 – Sept. 10, 2014),

https://www.ohchr.org/Documents/Countries/IQ/UNAMI_OHCHR_POC_Report_FINAL_6July_10September2014.pdf

Committee on the Rights of the Child, Concluding observations on the combined second to fourth periodic reports of Iraq, U.N. Doc. CRC/C/IRQ/CO/2-4 (March 3, 2015).

Rep. of the Office of the United Nations High Commissioner for Human Rights, United Nations Assistance Mission for Iraq (UNAMI), Report on the Protection of Civilians in the Armed Conflict in Iraq (Dec. 11, 2014 – Apr. 30, 2015).

https://www.ohchr.org/Documents/Countries/IQ/UNAMI_OHCHR_4th_POC Report-11Dec2014-30April2015.pdf

Rep. of the Office of the United Nations High Commissioner for Human Rights, United Nations Assistance Mission for Iraq (UNAMI), Report on the Protection of Civilians in the Armed Conflict in Iraq (May 1, 2015 – Oct. 31, 2015).

https://www.ohchr.org/Documents/Countries/IQ/UNAMIReport1May31October2015.pdf

Rep. of the Human Rights Committee, Concluding Observations on the Fifth Periodic Report of Iraq, U.N. Doc. CCPR/C/IRQ/CO/5/Add.1 (Aug. 18, 2017).

Rep. of the Committee on the Elimination of Racial Discrimination, Combined Twenty-Second to Twenty-Fifth Periodic Reports Submitted by Iraq Under Article 9 of the Convention, U.N. Doc. CERD/C/IRQ/22-25 (Nov. 22, 2017).

Rep. of the Committee on the Elimination of Discrimination against Women, Seventh Periodic Report Submitted by Iraq Under Article 18 of the Convention, U.N. Doc. CEDAW/C/IRQ/7 (Aug. 15, 2018).

Rep. of the Office of the United Nations High Commissioner for Human Rights, United Nations Assistance Mission for Iraq (UNAMI), "Unearthing Atrocities: Mass Graves in Territory Formerly Controlled by ISIL/DAESH," (Nov. 6, 2018).

Rep. of the Committee on the Elimination of Racial Discrimination, Concluding Observations on the Combined Twenty-Second to Twenty-Fifth Periodic Reports of Iraq, U.N. Doc. CERD/C/IRQ/22-25 (Jan. 11, 2019).

Committee on Enforced Disappearances, Additional Information Submitted by Iraq Under Article 29 (4) of the Convention, U.N. Doc. CED/C/IRQ/AI/1 (Aug. 1, 2019).

Committee Against Torture, Second Periodic Report Submitted by Iraq Under Article 19 of the Convention, Due in 2019, U.N. Doc. CAT/C/IRQ/2 (Aug. 20, 2019).

Committee Against Torture, Information Received From Iraq on Follow-up to the Concluding Observations on Its Initial Report, U.N. Doc. CAT/C/IRQ/FCO/1 (June 15, 2020).

## 3.6. United Nations International Courts

*3.6.1. International Criminal Tribunal for Rwanda – ICTR – Chronological order*

### International Residual Mechanism for Criminal Tribunals

Prosecutor v. Jean-Paul Akayesu, Case No. ICTR-96-4-T, judgement, (Sept. 2, 1998).

Prosecutor v. Jean Kambanda, Case No. ICTR-97-23, judgement and sentence, (Sept. 4, 1998).

Prosecutor v. Omar Serushago, Case No. ICTR-98-39-S, sentence, (Feb. 5, 1999).

Prosecutor v. Clément Kayishema and Ruzindana, Case No. ICTR 95-1-T, judgement, (May 21, 1999).

Prosecutor v. Georges Anderson Nderubumwe Rutaganda, Case No. ICTR-96-3-T, judgement, (Dec. 6, 1999).

Prosecutor v. Musema, Case No. ICTR-96-13-A, judgement and sentence, (Jan. 27, 2000).

Prosecutor v. Georges Ruggiu, Case No. ICTR-97-32-I, judgement and sentence, (June 1, 2000).

Prosecutor v. Clément Kayishema and Ruzindana, Case No. ICTR-95-1-A, judgement, (June 1, 2001).

Prosecutor v. Jean-Paul Akayesu, Case No. ICTR-96-4-A, judgement, (June 1, 2001).

Prosecutor v. Ignace Bagilishema, Case No. ICTR-95-1-A, judgement, (June 7, 2001).

Prosecutor v. Elizaphan and Gérard Ntakirutimana, Case No. ICTR- ICTR-96-10 & ICTR-96-17-T, judgement and sentence, (Feb. 21, 2003).

Prosecutor v. Laurent Semanza, Case No. ICTR-97-20-T, judgement and sentence, (May 15, 2003).

Prosecutor v. Georges Anderson Nderubumwe Rutaganda, Case No. ICTR-96-3-A, judgement, (May 26, 2003).

Prosecutor v. Juvénal Kajelijeli, Case No. ICTR-98-44A-T), judgement and sentence, (Dec. 1, 2003).

Prosecutor v. Ferdinand Nahimana et al, Case No. ICTR-99-52-T, judgement, (Dec. 3, 2003).

Prosecutor v. Jean de Dieu Kamuhanda, Case No. ICTR-95-54A-T, judgement, (Jan. 22, 2004).

Prosecutor v. André Ntagerura, Emmanuel Bagambiki, Samuel Imanishimwe, Case No. ICTR-99-46-T, judgement and sentence, (Feb. 25, 2004).

Prosecutor v. Sylvestre Gacumbitsi, Case No. ICTR-2001-64-T, judgement, (June 17, 2004).

Prosecutor v. Emmanuel Ndindabahizi, Case No. ICTR-2001-71-I, judgement and sentence, (July 15, 2004).

Prosecutor v. Elizaphan and Gérard Ntakirutimana, Case No. ICTR-96-10-A & ICTR-96-17-A, judgement, (Dec. 13, 2004).

Prosecutor v. Vincent Rutaganira, Case No. ICTR-95-1C-T, judgement and sentence, (March 14, 2005).

Prosecutor v. Mikaeli Muhimana, Case No. ICTR-95-1B-T, judgement and sentence, (April 28, 2005).

Jean de Dieu Kamuhanda v. Prosecutor, Case No. ICTR-95-54A-A, judgement, (Sept. 19, 2005).

Prosecutor v. Aloys Simba, Case No. ICTR-01-76-T, judgement and sentence, (Dec. 13, 2005).

Prosecutor v. Paul Bisengimana, Case No. ICTR-00-60-T, judgement and sentence, (Apr. 13, 2006).

Sylvestre Gacumbitsi v. Prosecutor, Case No. ICTR-2001-64-A, judgement, (July 7, 2006).

Prosecutor v. Jean Mpambara, Case No. ICTR-01-65-T, judgement, (Sept. 11, 2006).

Prosecutor v. Athanase Seromba, Case No. ICTR-2001-66-T, judgement, (Dec. 13, 2006).

Emmanuel Ndindabahizi v. Prosecutor, Case No. ICTR-01-71-A, judgement, (Jan. 16, 2007).

Mikaeli Muhimana v. Prosecutor, Case No. ICTR-95-1B-A, judgement, (May 21, 2007).

Prosecutor v. Joseph Nzabirinda, Case No. ICTR-2001-77-T, judgement and sentence, (Feb. 23, 2007).

Prosecutor v. Juvénal Rugambarara, Case No. ICTR-00-59-T, sentencing judgement, (Nov. 16, 2007).

Aloys Simba v. Prosecutor, Case No. ICTR-01-76-A, judgement, (Nov. 27, 2007).

Ferdinand Nahimana et al v. Prosecutor, Case No. ICTR-99-52-A, judgement, (Nov. 28, 2007).

Prosecutor v. François Karera, Case No. ICTR-01-74-T, Judgement and sentence, (Dec. 7, 2007).

Prosecutor v. GAA1, Case No. ICTR-07-90-R77-I, judgement and sentence, (Dec. 4, 2007).

Prosecutor v. Athanase Seromba, Case No. ICTR-2001-66-A, judgement, (March 12, 2008).

Tharcisse Muvunyi v. Prosecutor, Case No. ICTR-2000-55A-A, judgement, (August 29, 2008).

Prosecutor v. Siméon Nchamihigo, Case No. ICTR-01-63-T, judgement and sentence, (Nov. 12, 2008).

Prosecutor v. Simon Bikindi, Case No. ICTR-01-72-T, judgement, (Dec. 2, 2008).

Prosecutor v. Théoneste Bagosora, Gratien Kabiligi, Aloys Ntabakuze, Anatole Nsengiyumva, Case No. ICTR-98-41-T, judgement and sentence, (Dec. 18, 2008).

Prosecutor v. Protais Zigiranyirazo, Case No. ICTR-01-73-T, judgement, (Dec. 18, 2008).

François Karera v. Prosecutor, Case No. ICTR-01-74-A, judgement, (Feb. 2, 2009).

Prosecutor v. Emmanuel Rukundo, Case No. ICTR-2001-70-T, judgement, (Feb. 27, 2009).

Prosecutor v. Callixte Kalimanzira, Case No. ICTR-05-88-T, judgement, (June 22, 2009).

Prosecutor v. Léonidas Nshogoza, Case No. ICTR-07-91-T, judgement (July 7, 2009).

Prosecutor v. Tharcisse Renzaho, Case No. ICTR-97-31-T, judgement and sentence, (July 14, 2009).

Protais Zigiranyirazo v. Prosecutor, Case No. ICTR-01-73-A, judgement, (Nov. 16, 2009).

Prosecutor v. Michel Bagaragaza, Case No. ICTR-05-86-S, sentencing judgement, (Nov. 17, 2009).

Prosecutor v. Hormisdas Nsengimana, Case No. ICTR-01-69-T, judgement, (Nov. 17, 2009).

Prosecutor v. Tharcisse Muvunyi, Case No. ICTR-00-55A-T, judgement, (Feb. 11, 2010).

Prosecutor v. Ephrem Setako, Case No. ICTR-04-81-T, judgement and sentence, (Feb. 25, 2010).

Siméon Nchamihigo v. Prosecutor, Case No. ICTR-2001-63-A, judgement, (March 18, 2010).

Simon Bikindi v. Prosecutor, Case No. ICTR-01-72-A, judgement, (March 18, 2010).

Prosecutor v. Yussuf Munyakazi, Case No. ICTR-97-36A-T, judgement and sentence, (July 5, 2010).

Prosecutor v. Dominique Ntawukulilyayo, Case No. ICTR-05-82-T, judgement and sentence, (Aug. 3, 2010).

Emmanuel Rukundo v. Prosecutor, Case No. ICTR-2001-70-A, judgement, (Oct. 20, 2010).

Callixte Kalimanzira v. Prosecutor, Case No. ICTR-05-88-A, judgement, (Oct. 20, 2010).

Prosecutor v. Gaspard Kanyarukiga, Case No. ICTR-2002-78-T, judgement and sentence, (Nov. 1, 2010).

Prosecutor v. Ildephonse Hategekimana, Case No. ICTR-00-55B-T, judgement and sentence, (Dec. 6, 2010).

Prosecutor v. Jean-Baptiste Gatete, Case No. ICTR-2000-61-T, judgement and sentence, (March 31, 2011).

Tharcisse Renzaho v. Prosecutor, Case No. ICTR-97-31-A, judgement, (Apr. 1, 2011).

Prosecutor v. Augustin Ndindiliyimana, Augustin Bizimungu, François-Xavier Nzuwonemeye, Case No: ICTR-00-56-T, judgement and sentence, (May 17, 2011).

Prosecutor v. Pauline Nyiramasuhuko et al., Case No. ICTR-98-42-T, judgement and sentence, (June 24, 2011).

Prosecutor v. Yussuf Munyakazi, Case No. ICTR-97-36A-A, judgement, (Sept. 28, 2011).

Dominique Ntawukulilyayo v. Prosecutor, Case No. ICTR-05-82-A, judgement, (Dec. 14, 2011).

Prosecutor v. Grégoire Ndahimana, Case No. ICTR-01-68-T, judgement and sentence, (Dec. 30, 2011).

Prosecutor v. Édouard Karemera et al, Case No. ICTR-98-44-T, judgement and sentence, (Feb. 2, 2012).

Prosecutor v. Callixte Nzabonimana, Case No. ICTR-98-44D-T, judgement and sentence, (May 31, 2012).

Prosecutor v. Ildéphonse Nizeyimana, Case No. ICTR-2000-55C-T, judgement and sentence, (June 19, 2012).

Jean-Baptiste Gatete v. Prosecutor, Case No. ICTR-00-61-A, judgement, (Oct. 9, 2012).

Prosecutor v. Augustin Ngirabatware, Case No. ICTR-99-54-T, judgement and sentence, (Dec. 20, 2012).

Justin Mugenzi et al v. Prosecutor, Case No. ICTR-99-50-A, judgement, (Feb. 4, 2013).

Grégoire Ndahimana v. Prosecutor, Case No. ICTR-01-68-A, judgement, (Dec. 16, 2013).

Augustin Bizimungu v. Prosecutor, Case No. ICTR-00-56B-A, judgement, (June 30, 2014).

Eliézer Niyitegeka v. Prosecutor, Case No. ICTR-96-14-A, judgement, (July 9, 2014).

Édouard Karemera et al v. Prosecutor, Case No. ICTR-98-44-A, judgement, (Sept. 29, 2014).

Callixte Nzabonimana v. Prosecutor, Case No. ICTR-98-44D-A, judgement, (Sept. 29, 2014).

Augustin Ngirabatware v. Prosecutor, Case No. MICT-12-29, judgement, Dec. 18, 2014.

Prosecutor v. Pauline Nyiramasuhuko et al., Case No. ICTR-98-42-A, judgement, (Dec. 14, 2015).

### 3.6.2. International Criminal Tribunal for the former Yugoslavia – ICTY – Chronological order

#### International Residual Mechanism for Criminal Tribunals

Prosecutor v. Duško Tadic, Case No.: IT-94-1-T, opinion and judgement, (May 7, 1997).

Prosecutor v. Duško Tadic, Case No.: IT-94-1-A, judgement, (July 15, 1999).

Prosecutor v. Duško Tadic, Case No.: IT-94-1-T bis-R117, judgement, (Nov. 11, 1999).

Prosecutor v. Goran Jelisić., Case No. IT-95-10-T, judgement, (Dec. 14, 1999).

Prosecutor v. Zoran Kupreškić, Mirjan Kupreškić, Vlatko Kupreškić, Vladimir Šantić ("Vlado"), Stipo Alilovic ("BRKO"), Drago Josipović, Marinko Katava, Dragan Papić, Case No. IT-95-16-T, judgement, (Jan. 14, 2000).

Prosecutor v. Duško Tadic, Case No.: IT-94-1-Abis, judgement in sentencing appeals, (Jan. 26, 2000).

Prosecutor v. Duško Tadic, Case No.: IT-94-1-Abis, judgement in sentencing appeals, separate opinion of Judge Shahabuddeen (Jan. 26, 2000).

Prosecutor v. Tihomir Blaškić, Case No. IT-95-14-T, judgement, (Mar. 3, 2000).

Prosecutor v. Zlatko Aleksovski, Case No. IT-95-14/1-A, judgement, (Mar. 24, 2000).

Prosecutor v. Dragoljub Kunarac, Radomir Kovac and Zoran Vukovic, Case No. IT-96-23/1-T, judgement, (Feb. 22, 2001).

Prosecutor v. Dario Kordić and Mario Čerkez, Case No. IT-95-14/2-T, judgement, (Feb 26, 2001).

Prosecutor v. Goran Jelisić, Case No. IT-95-10-A, judgement, (July 5, 2001).

Prosecutor v. Stevan Todorović, Case No. IT-95-9/1-S, sentencing judgement, (July 31, 2001).

Prosecutor v. Radislav Krstić, Case No. IT-98-33-T, judgement, (Aug. 2, 2001).

Prosecutor v. Duško Sikirica, Damir Došen and Dragan Kolundžija, Case No. IT-95-8-T, judgement on defence motions to acquit, (Sept. 3, 2001).

Prosecutor v. Zoran Kupreškić, Mirjan Kupreškić, Vlatko Kupreškić, Vladimir Šantić ("Vlado"), Stipo Alilovic ("BRKO"), Drago Josipović, Marinko Katava, Dragan Papić, Case No. IT-95-16-A, judgement, (Oct. 23, 2001).

Prosecutor v. Miroslav Kvočka, Mlađo Radić, Dragoljub Prcač, Zoran Zigićand Milojica Kos, Case No. IT-98-30/1-T, judgement, (Nov. 2, 2001).

Prosecutor v. Milorad Krnojelac, Case No. IT-97-25-T, judgement, (Mar. 15, 2002).

Prosecutor v. Dragoljub Kunarac, Radomir Kovac and Zoran Vukovic, Case No. IT-96-23/1-A, judgement, (June 12, 2002).

Prosecutor v. Milan Simić, Case No. IT-95-9/2-S, sentencing judgement, (Oct. 17, 2002).

Prosecutor v. Mitar Vasiljević, Case No. IT-98-32-T, judgement, (Nov. 29, 2002).

Prosecutor v. Biljana Plavšić, Case No. IT-00-39 & 40/1, sentencing judgement, (Feb. 27, 2003).

Prosecutor v. Mladen Naletilić, a.k.a. "Tuta", and Vinko Martinović, a.k.a. "Štela", Case No. IT-98-34-T, judgement, (Mar. 31, 2003).

Prosecutor v. Milomir Stakić, Case No. IT-97-24-T, judgement, (July 31, 2003).

Prosecutor v. Milorad Krnojelac, Case No. IT-97-25-A, judgement, (Sept. 17, 2003).

Prosecutor v. Blagoje Simić, Miroslav Tadić and Simo Zarić, Case No. IT-95-9-T, judgement, (Oct. 17, 2003).

Prosecutor v. Predrag Banović, Case No. IT-02-65/1-S, sentencing judgement, (Oct. 28, 2003).

Prosecutor v. Stanislav Galić, Case No. IT-98-29-T, judgement and opinion, (Dec. 5, 2003).

Prosecutor v. Dragan Obrenović, Case No. IT-02-60/2-S, sentencing judgement, (Dec. 10, 2003).

Prosecutor v. Mitar Vasiljević, Case No. IT-98-32-A, judgement, (Feb. 25, 2004).

Prosecutor v. Ranko Češić, Case No. IT-95-10/1-S, sentencing judgement, (March 11, 2004).

Prosecutor v. Miodrag Jokić, Case No. IT-01-42/1-S, sentencing judgement, (March 18, 2004).

Prosecutor v. Darko Mrđa, Case No. IT-02-59-S, sentencing judgement, (March 31, 2004).

Prosecutor v. Radislav Krstić, Case No. IT-98-33-A, judgement, (Apr. 19, 2004).

Prosecutor v. Slobodan Milošević, Case No. IT-02-54-T, decision on motion for judgement of acquittal, (June 16, 2004).

Prosecutor v. Milan Babić, Case No. IT-03-72-S, sentencing judgement, (June 29, 2004).

Prosecutor v. Tihomir Blaškić, Case No. IT-95-14-A, judgement, (July 29, 2004).

Prosecutor v. Radoslav Brđanin, Case No. IT-99-36-T, judgement, (Sept. 1, 2004).

Prosecutor v. Dario Kordić and Mario Čerkez, Case No. IT-95-14/2-A, judgement, (Dec. 17, 2004).

Prosecutor v. Vidoje Blagojević, Dragan Jokić, Case No. IT-02-60-T, judgement, (Jan. 17, 2005).

Prosecutor v. Miroslav Kvočka, Mlađo Radić, Dragoljub Prcač, Zoran Zigićand Milojica Kos, Case No. IT-98-30/1-A, judgement, (Fev. 28, 2005).

Prosecutor v. Miroslav Deronjić, Case No. IT-02-61-A, judgement on sentencing appeal, (July 20, 2005).

Prosecutor v. Fatmir Limaj, Haradin Bala and Isak Musliu, Case No. IT-03-66-T, judgement, (Nov. 30, 2005).

Prosecutor v. Momir Nikolić, Case No. IT-02-60/1-A, judgement, (Mar. 8, 2006).

Prosecutor v. Milomir Stakić, Case No. IT-97-24-A, judgement, (Mar. 22, 2006).

Prosecutor v. Mladen Naletilić, a.k.a. "Tuta", and Vinko Martinović, a.k.a. "Štela", Case No. IT-98-34-A, judgement, (May 3, 2006).

Prosecutor v. Momčilo Krajišnik, Case No. IT-00-39-T, judgement, (Sept. 27, 2006).

Prosecutor v. Blagoje Simić, Miroslav Tadić and Simo Zarić, Case No. IT-95-9-A, judgement, (Nov. 28, 2006).

Prosecutor v. Stanislav Galić, Case No. IT-98-29-A, judgement, (Nov. 30, 2006).

Prosecutor v. Radoslav Brđanin, Case No. IT-99-36-A, judgement, (Apr. 3, 2007).

Prosecutor v. Vidoje Blagojević, Dragan Jokić, Case No. IT-02-60-A, judgement, (May 9, 2007).

Prosecutor v. Milan Martić, Case No. IT-95-11-T, judgement, (June 12, 2007).

Prosecutor v. Mile Mrkšić, Miroslav Radić and Veselin Šljivančanin, Case No. IT-95-13/1, judgement, (Sept. 27, 2007).

Prosecutor v. Sefer Halilović, Case No. IT-01-48-A, judgement, (Oct. 16, 2007).

Prosecutor v. Dragan Zelenović, Case No. IT-96-23/2-A, judgement on sentencing appeal, (Oct. 31, 2007).

Prosecutor v. Dragomir Milošević, Case No. IT-98-29/1-T, judgement, (Dec. 12, 2007).

Prosecutor v. Ramush Haradinaj, Idriz Balaj, and Lahi Brahimaj, Case No. IT-04-84-T, judgement, (Apr. 3, 2008).

Prosecutor v. Enver Hadžihasanović and Amir Kubura, Case No. IT-01-47-A, judgement, (Apr. 22, 2008).

Prosecutor v. Naser Orić, Case No. IT-03-68-A, judgement, (July 3, 2008).

Prosecutor v. Milan Martić, Case No. IT-95-11-A, judgement, (Oct. 8, 2008). CAH

Prosecutor v. Nikola Šainović, Nebojša Pavković, Vladimir Lazarević, Case No. IT-05-87-T, judgement, vol. 1, (Feb. 26, 2009).

Prosecutor v. Nikola Šainović, Nebojša Pavković, Vladimir Lazarević, Case No. IT-05-87-T, judgement, vol. 2, (Feb. 26, 2009).

Prosecutor v. Nikola Šainović, Nebojša Pavković, Vladimir Lazarević, Case No. IT-05-87-T, judgement, vol. 3, (Feb. 26, 2009).

Prosecutor v. Nikola Šainović, Nebojša Pavković, Vladimir Lazarević, Case No. IT-05-87-T, judgement, vol. 4, (Feb. 26, 2009).

Prosecutor v. Momčilo Krajišnik, Case No. IT-00-39-A, judgement, (March 17, 2009).

Prosecutor v. Milan Lukić, Sredoje Lukić, Case No. IT-98-32/1-T, judgement, (July 20, 2009).

Prosecutor v. Radovan Karadžić, Case No. IT-95-5/18-AR73.4, decision on Karadžić's appeal of trial chamber's decision on alleged Holbrooke Agreement, (Oct. 12, 2009).

Prosecutor v. Dragomir Milošević, Case No. IT-98-29/1-A, judgement, (Nov. 12, 2009).

Prosecutor v. Vujadin Popović et al., Case No. IT-05-88-T, judgement, (June 10, 2010).

Prosecutor v. Ante Gotovina, Ivan Čermak, and Mladen Markač, Case No. IT-06-90-T, judgement, vol. I, (April 15, 2011).

Prosecutor v. Ante Gotovina, Ivan Čermak, and Mladen Markač, Case No. IT-06-90-T, judgement, vol. II, (April 15, 2011).

Prosecutor v. Momčilo Perišić, Case No. IT-04-81-T, judgement, (Sept. 6, 2011).

Prosecutor v. Zdravko Tolimir, Case No. IT-05-88/2-T, judgement, (Dec. 12, 2012).

Prosecutor v. Mićo Stanišić, Stojan Župljanin, Case No. IT-08-91-T, judgement, vol. 1, (Mar. 27, 2013).

Prosecutor v. Mićo Stanišić, Stojan Župljanin, Case No. IT-08-91-T, judgement, vol. 2, (Mar. 27, 2013).

Prosecutor v. Mićo Stanišić, Stojan Župljanin, Case No. IT-08-91-T, judgement, vol. 3, (Mar. 27, 2013).

Prosecutor v. Jadranko Prlić, Bruno Stojić, Slobodan Praljak, Milivoj Petković, Valentin Ćorić & Berislav Pušić, Case No. IT-04-74-T, vol. I, (May 29, 2013).

Prosecutor v. Jadranko Prlić, Bruno Stojić, Slobodan Praljak, Milivoj Petković, Valentin Ćorić & Berislav Pušić, Case No. IT-04-74-T, vol. II, (May 29, 2013).

Prosecutor v. Jadranko Prlić, Bruno Stojić, Slobodan Praljak, Milivoj Petković, Valentin Ćorić & Berislav Pušić, Case No. IT-04-74-T, vol. III, (May 29, 2013).

Prosecutor v. Jadranko Prlić, Bruno Stojić, Slobodan Praljak, Milivoj Petković, Valentin Ćorić & Berislav Pušić, Case No. IT-04-74-T, vol. IV, (May 29, 2013).

Prosecutor v. Jadranko Prlić, Bruno Stojić, Slobodan Praljak, Milivoj Petković, Valentin Ćorić & Berislav Pušić, Case No. IT-04-74-T, vol. V, (May 29, 2013).

Prosecutor v. Jadranko Prlić, Bruno Stojić, Slobodan Praljak, Milivoj Petković, Valentin Ćorić & Berislav Pušić, Case No. IT-04-74-T, vol. VI, (May 29, 2013).

Prosecutor v. Jovica Stanišić and Franko Simatović, Case No. IT-03-69-T, judgement, vol. I, (May 30, 2013).

Prosecutor v. Jovica Stanišić and Franko Simatović, Case No. IT-03-69-T, judgement, vol. II, (May 30, 2013).

Prosecutor v. Radovan Karadžić, Case No. IT-95-5/18-AR98bis, judgement, (Jul. 13, 2013).

Prosecutor v. Nikola Šainović, Nebojša Pavković, Vladimir Lazarević, Case No. IT-05-87-A, judgement, (Jan. 23, 2014).

Prosecutor v. Vlastimir Đorđević, Case No. IT-05-87/1-A, judgement, (Jan. 27, 2014).

Prosecutor v. Vujadin Popović et al., Case No. IT-05-88-A, judgement, (Jan. 30, 2015).

Prosecutor v. Zdravko Tolimir, Case No. IT-05-88/2-A, judgement, (April 8, 2015).

Prosecutor v. Zdravko Tolimir, Case No. IT-05-88/2-A A172-1/2054bis, separate and partly dissenting opinion of Judge Antonetti, (Jul. 14, 2015).

Prosecutor v. Radovan Karadžić, Case No. IT-95-5/18-T, judgement, vol. I, (March 24, 2016).

Prosecutor v. Radovan Karadžić, Case No. IT-95-5/18-T, judgement, vol. II, (March 24, 2016).

Prosecutor v. Radovan Karadžić, Case No. IT-95-5/18-T, judgement, vol. III, (March 24, 2016).

Prosecutor v. Radovan Karadžić, Case No. IT-95-5/18-T, judgement, vol. IV, (March 24, 2016). P+G+CAH

Prosecutor v. Vojislav Šešelj, Case No. IT-03-67-T, judgement, vol. 1, (Mar. 31, 2016).

Prosecutor v. Vojislav Šešelj, Case No. IT-03-67-T, judgement, vol. 3, partially dissenting opinion of Judge Flavia Lattanzi – amended version, (Mar. 31, 2016).

Prosecutor v. Ratko Mladić, Case No. IT-09-92-T, judgement, vol. I, (Nov. 22, 2017).

Prosecutor v. Ratko Mladić, Case No. IT-09-92-T, judgement, vol. II, (Nov. 22, 2017).

Prosecutor v. Ratko Mladić, Case No. IT-09-92-T, judgement, vol. III, (Nov. 22, 2017).

Prosecutor v. Ratko Mladić, Case No. IT-09-92-T, judgement, vol. VI, (Nov. 22, 2017).

Prosecutor v. Ratko Mladić, Case No. IT-09-92-T, judgement, vol. V, (Nov. 22, 2017).

Prosecutor v. Jadranko Prlić, Bruno Stojić, Slobodan Praljak, Milivoj Petković, Valentin Ćorić & Berislav Pušić, Case No. IT-04-74-A, vol. I, (Nov. 29, 2017).

Prosecutor v. Jadranko Prlić, Bruno Stojić, Slobodan Praljak, Milivoj Petković, Valentin Ćorić & Berislav Pušić, Case No. IT-04-74-A, vol. II, (Nov. 29, 2017).

Prosecutor v. Jadranko Prlić, Bruno Stojić, Slobodan Praljak, Milivoj Petković, Valentin Ćorić & Berislav Pušić, Case No. IT-04-74-A, vol. III, (Nov. 29, 2017).

### 3.6.3. The Special Court for Sierra Leone – SCSL – Chronological order

Prosecutor v. Norman, Case No. SCSL-04-14-PT, motion to recuse judge Winter from deliberating in the preliminary motion on the recruitment of child soldiers, (March 24, 2004).

Prosecutor v. Sesay, Kallon, Gbao, Case No. SCSL-2004-15-PT, decision on prosecution request for leave to amend the indictment (May 6, 2004). (RUF case)

Prosecutor v. Norman, Case No. SCSL-04-14-PT, judge Winter's response to motion to recuse her from deliberating on the preliminary motion on the recruitment of child soldiers, (May 14, 2004).

Prosecutor v. Norman, Case No. SCSL-04-14, motion to recuse judge Winter from deliberating in the preliminary motion on the recruitment of child soldiers, (May 28, 2004).

Prosecutor v. Norman, Case No. SCSL-2004-14-AR72(E), decision on preliminary motion based on lack of jurisdiction (child recruitment), (May 31, 2004).

Prosecutor v. Sesay, Kallon and Gbao, Case No. SCSL-04-15-T, prosecution application for leave to amend indictment, (Feb. 20, 2006). (*RUF case*).

Prosecutor v. Sesay, Kallon and Gbao, Case No. SCSL-04-15-T, oral Rule 98 decision, transcript, (Oct. 25, 2006). (*RUF case*).

Prosecutor v. Brima, Kamara, Kanu, Case No. SCSL-04-16-T, judgement, (June 20, 2007 as revised on 19 July 2007). (*AFRC case*).

Prosecutor v. Fofana, Kondewa, Case No. SCSL-04-14-T, judgement (Aug. 2, 2007). (*CDF case*).

Prosecutor v. Fofana, Kondewa, Case No. SCSL-04-14-T, judgement, partially dissenting opinion of honorable justice Renate Winter (Aug. 2, 2007). (*CDF case*).

Prosecutor v. Brima, Kamara, Kanu, Case No. SCSL-04-16-A, judgement, (Feb. 22, 2008).

Prosecutor v. Fofana, Kondewa, Case No. SCSL-04-14-A, judgement (May 28, 2008). (*CDF case*).

Prosecutor v. Sesay, Kallon and Gbao, Case No. SCSL-04-15-T, judgement, (March 2, 2009). (*RUF case*).

Prosecutor v. Sesay, Kallon and Gbao, Case No. SCSL-04-15-T, sentencing judgement, (Apr. 8, 2009). (*RUF case*).

Prosecutor v. Taylor, Case No. SCSL-03-01-T, judgement, (May 18, 2012).

## 3.6.4. International Court of Justice – Chronological order

Reservations to Convention on the Prevention and Punishment of the Crime of Genocide, Advisory Opinion, 1951 I.C.J. 15 (May 28).

Application of the Convention on the Prevention and Punishment of the Crime of Genocide, Preliminary Objections, judgement, 1996 1. C. J. 595 (July 11, 1996).

Arrest Warrant of 11 April 2000 (Democratic Republic of the Congo v. Belgium), judgement, 2000, I.C.J. 3 (Feb. 14).

Application for Revision of the Judgement of 11 July 1996 in the Case concerning Application of the Convention on the Prevention and Punishment of the Crime of Genocide (Bosnia and Herzegovina v. Yugoslavia), preliminary objections (Yugoslavia v. Bosnia and Herzegovina), 2003, I.C.J. 7 (Feb. 3).

Application of the Convention on the Prevention and Punishment of the Crime of Genocide (Bosnia and Herzegovina v. Serbia and Montenegro), Judgement, 2007, I.C.J. 43 (Feb. 26).

Application of the Convention on the Prevention and Punishment of the Crime of Genocide (Croatia v. Serbia), judgement, 2008, I.C.J. 412 (Nov. 18).

Application of the Convention on the Prevention and Punishment of the Crime of Genocide (Croatia v. Serbia), 2015 I.C.J. 3 (Feb. 3).

## 4. International Criminal Court – Chronological order

International Criminal Court (ICC), Elements of Crimes, 2013. Reproduced from the Official Records of the Assembly of States Parties to the Rome Statute of the International Criminal Court, First session, New York, 3-10 September 2002, part II.B. The Elements of Crimes adopted at the 2010 Review Conference.

Prosecutor v. Thomas Lubanga Dyilo, Case No. ICC-01/04-01/06, decision on the confirmation of charges, (Jan. 29, 2007).

Prosecutor v. Ahmad Muhammad Harun ("Ahmad Harun") and Ali Muhammad Ali Abd-Al-Rahman ("Ali Kushayb"), Case No. ICC-02/05-01/07, decision on the prosecution application under Article 58(7) of the Rome Statute, (Apr. 27, 2007).

Prosecutor v. Thomas Lubanga Dyilo, Case No. ICC-01/04-01/06-1229-AnxA, written submissions of the United Nations Special Representative of the Secretary-General on Children and Armed Conflict submitted in application of Rule 103 of the Rules of Procedure and Evidence, (March 18, 2008).

Prosecutor v. Germain Katanga, Case No. ICC-01/04-01/07, decision on the confirmation of charges, (Sept. 30, 2008).

Prosecutor v. Thomas Lubanga Dyilo, Case No. ICC-01/04-01/06, redacted version of decision on "indirect victims," (Apr. 8, 2009).

Prosecutor v. Jean-Pierre Bemba Gombo, Case No. ICC-01/05-01/08, Decision Pursuant to Article 61(7)(a) and (b) of the Rome Statute on the charges of the Prosecutor against Jean-Pierre Bemba Gombo, (June 15, 2009).

Prosecutor v. Omar Hassan Ahmad Al Bashir, Case No. ICC-02/05-01/09, second decision on the prosecution's application for a warrant of arrest, (July 12, 2010).

Prosecutor v. Callixte Mbarushimana, Case No. ICC-01/04-01/10, decision on the confirmation of charges, (Dec. 16, 2011).

Prosecutor v. William Samoei Ruto, Henry Kiprono Kosgey and Joshua Arap Sang, Case No. ICC-01/09-01/11, decision on the confirmation of charges pursuant to Article 61(7)(a) and (b) of the Rome Statute, (Jan. 23, 2012).

Prosecutor v. Francis Kirimi Muthaura, Uhuru Muigai Kenyatta and Mohammed Hussein Ali, Case No. ICC-01/09-02/11, decision on the confirmation of charges pursuant to Article 61(7)(a) and (b) of the Rome Statute, (Jan. 23, 2012).

Prosecutor v. Thomas Lubanga Dyilo, Case No. ICC-01/04-01/06, judgement pursuant to Art. 74 of the Statute, (March 14, 2012).

Prosecutor v. Thomas Lubanga Dyilo, Case No. ICC-01/04-01/06, decision on sentence pursuant to Article 76 of the Statute, (July 10, 2012).

Prosecutor v. Thomas Lubanga Dyilo, Case No. ICC-01/04-01/06, separate and dissenting opinion of judge Odio Benito, trial judgement, (July 10, 2012).

Prosecutor v. Germain Katanga, Case No. ICC-01/04-01/07, judgement pursuant to article 74 of the Statute, (March 7, 2014).

Prosecutor v. Bosco Ntaganda, Case No. ICC-01/04-02/06, decision pursuant to Article 61(7)(a) and (b) of the Rome Statute, (June 9, 2014).

Prosecutor v. Thomas Lubanga Dyilo, Case No. ICC-01/04-01/06 A 5, judgement on the appeal of Mr. Thomas Lubanga Dyilo against his conviction, (Dec. 1, 2014).

Prosecutor v. Jean-Pierre Bemba Gombo, Case No. ICC-01/05-01/08, judgement pursuant to article 74 of the Statute, (March 21, 2016).

Prosecutor v. Bosco Ntaganda, Case No. ICC-01/04-02/06, judgement, (July 8, 2019).

Prosecutor v. Bosco Ntaganda, Case No. ICC-01/04-02/06, sentencing judgement, (Nov. 7, 2019).

## 5. International Military Tribunal – Nuremberg – Chronological order

United Nation, International Law Commission, Principles of International Law Recognized in the Charter of the Nürnberg Tribunal and in the Judgement of the Tribunal ("the Nuremberg Principles"), Yearbook of the International Law Commission, Vol. II (1950)

1 Trial of the Major War Criminals before the International Military Tribunal (1947).

United States of America v. Oswald Pohl, et al. Case 4 (Pohl case) (1947).

4 Trial of the Major War Criminals before the International Military Tribunal (1947).

5 Trial of the Major War Criminals before the International Military Tribunal (1947).

United States of America vs. Friedrich Flick et al. (1947).

United States of America v. Ulrich Greifelt, et al. (RuSHA case) (1947).

United States of America v. Carl Krauch, et al. Volume 8 (I.G. Farben case) (1947).

11 Trial of the Major War Criminals before the International Military Tribunal (1947).

30 Trial of the Major War Criminals before the International Military Tribunal (1948).

36 Trial of the Major War Criminals before the International Military Tribunal (1949).

## 6. European Court of Human Rights

Vasiliauskas v. Lithuania, App. No. 35343/05 (Eur. Ct. H.R. Oct. 20, 2015).

## 7. Inter-American Court of Human Rights – Chronological order

Chitay Nech et al. v Guatemala, Preliminary Objections, merits, reparations, and costs, Judgement, Inter-Am. Ct. H.R. (ser. C) No. 212, (May 25, 2010).

Río Negro Massacres v. Guatemala, Preliminary objection, merits, reparations and costs, Judgement, Inter-Am. Ct. H.R. (ser. C) No. 250 (Sept.4, 2012).

Gudiel Álvarez et al ("Diario Militar") v. Guatemala, Judgement, merits, reparations and costs, Inter-Am. Ct. H.R. (ser. C) No. 253 (Nov. 20, 2012).

## 8. Newspaper articles (website) – Alphabetic order by author

Adam Chandler, *How Meaningful Is the ISIS 'Genocide' Designation? A Look At the Implications of the State Department's Declaration About the Islamic State's Brutal Campaign in Iraq and Syria,* THE ATLANTIC, Mar. 19, 2016,

https://www.theatlantic.com/international/archive/2016/03/isis-genocide-designation/474414/

Amanda Holpuch, Harriet Sherwood & Owen Bowcott, John Kerry: Isis Is Committing Genocide in Syria and Iraq, says US House, THE GUARDIAN, Mar. 17, 2016, https://www.theguardian.com/world/2016/mar/17/john-kerry-isis-genocide-syria-iraq

Andrea Mitchell, Cassandra Vinograd, F. Brinley Bruton & Abigail Williams, Daesh Is Responsible For Genocide: Kerry: ISIS Is Committing Genocide Against Yazidis, Christians and Shiite Muslims, NBC NEWS, Mar. 17, 2016,

https://www.nbcnews.com/storyline/isis-terror/john-kerry-isis-committing-genocide-n540706

Anugrah Kumar, *ISIS Burns Christians Alive in Locked Caskets, Escaped Prisoner Reveals,* CHRISTIAN POST, Jan. 6, 2016,

https://www.christianpost.com/news/isis-burns-christians-alive-locked-cas kets-escaped-iraqi-soldier-islamic-state-prisoner-revels-154281/

Arabella Lang & Ben Smith, *Declaring Daesh Massacres' Genocide,* HOUSE OF COMMONS PUBLISHING HOUSE, Apr. 15, 2016,

researchbriefings.files.parliament.uk/documents/CBP-7561/CBP-7561.pdf

Bendaoudi Abdelillah, *After the "Almost 100 Percent" Defeat of ISIS, What About Its Ideology?* AL JAZEERA, May 8, 2018,

http://studies.aljazeera.net/en/reports/2018/05/100-percent-defeat-isis-ide ology-180508042421376.html

Bethan McKernan, *Raqqa's all: A Journey Into the Heart of Isis's Failed Caliphate,* THE INDEPENDENT, Oct. 28, 2017,

https://www.independent.co.uk/news/world/middle-east/raqqa-isis-capital-syria-liberate-islamic-state-caliphate-city-a8023801.html

Beth Van Schaack, *Iraq and Syria: Prospects for Accountability,* JUST SECU-RITY, Feb. 22, 2016,

https://www.justsecurity.org/29427/iraq-syria-prospects-accountability/

*Daesh Is Responsible for Genocide: Kerry: ISIS Is Committing Genocide Against Yazidis, Christians and Shiite Muslims,* NBCNEWS.COM, Mar. 17, 2016, https://www.nbcnews.com/storyline/isis-terror/john-kerry-isis-com mitting-genocide-n540706

*Death Toll on Shingal Mountain Rising by the Minute,* RUDAW.NET, Aug. 6, 2014,

http://www.rudaw.net/english/kurdistan/060820141

Dominic Evans, Iraq Calls For Air Power to Protect Antiquities, REUTERS, Mar. 8, 2015, https://www.reuters.com/article/us-mideast-crisis-iraq-hatra/ iraq-calls-for-air-power-to-protect-antiquities-idUSKBN0M4O0320150308

Eliza Griswold, Is this the end of Christianity in the Middle East? THE NEW YORK TIMES, July 22, 2015,

https://www.nytimes.com/2015/07/26/magazine/is-this-the-end-of-christia nity-in-the-middle-east.html

Ewelina U. Ochab, *Bringing Daesh to Justice – On the Road to Nowhere?* FORBES, Oct. 13, 2017,

https://www.forbes.com/sites/ewelinaochab/2017/10/13/bringing-daesh-to-justice-on-the-road-to-nowhere/#4f3b2ed84eea

Ewelina U. Ochab, *When We Fail to See the Warnings, We Fail to Prevent,* FORBES, Sept. 17, 2018,

https://www.forbes.com/sites/ewelinaochab/2018/09/17/when-we-fail-to-see-the-warnings-we-fail-to-prevent/#64b66b49c5cd

*Ex-Lebanon Leader: Christians Target of Genocide,* CBS.COM, Jan. 3, 2011, https://www.cbsnews.com/news/ex-lebanon-leader-christians-target-of-genocide/

*Fierce Clashes as Iraqi Forces Move on ISIL/DAESH-Held Tikrit,* ALJAZEERA.COM, Mar. 9, 2015,

https://www.aljazeera.com/news/2015/03/iraqi-forces-advance-ISIL/DAESH-held-tikrit-50308054623411.html

Hamdi Alkhshali & Joshua Berlinger, *Facing Fines, Conversion or Death, Christian Families Flee Mosul,* CNN, July 20, 2014,

https://edition.cnn.com/2014/07/19/world/meast/christians-flee-mosul-iraq/index.html

Harriet Sherwood, *Calls Grow to Label Attacks on Middle East Christians as Genocide,* THE GUARDIAN, Mar. 10, 2016,

https://www.theguardian.com/world/2016/mar/10/middle-east-christians-label-genocide-hillary-clinton-european-parliament

Hollie McKay, *Life After ISIS: Christians Say They Can't Go Home Without International Protection,* FOX NEWS, Dec. 14, 2017,

https://www.foxnews.com/world/life-after-isis-christians-say-they-cant-go-home-without-international-protection

*How the Islamic State Rose, Fell and Could Rise Again in the Maghreb,* CRISIS-GROUP.ORG, July 24, 2017,

https://www.crisisgroup.org/middle-east-north-africa/north-africa/178-how-islamic-state-rose-fell-and-could-rise-again-maghreb

*Iraqi Forces Retake Key Town of Al-Baghdadi From ISIL/DAESH,* ALJAZEERA.COM, Mar. 7, 2015,

https://www.aljazeera.com/news/2015/03/iraqi-forces-retake-al-baghdadi-ISIL/DAESH-150307050409010.html

Iraq's Oldest Christian Monastery Destroyed by Islamic State, BBC.COM, Jan. 20, 2016, https://www.bbc.com/news/world-middle-east-35360415

Isabel Coles, Kurdish Forces Attack Islamic State West of Kirkuk, REUTERS, Mar. 9, 2015, https://www.reuters.com/article/us-mideast-crisis-iraq-kir

kuk/kurdish-forces-attack-islamic-state-west-of-kirkuk-idUSKBN0
M50JY20150309

*Isis Has Destroyed Iraq's Oldest Christian Monastery, Satellite Images Confirm*, AS-
SOCIATED PRESS, Jan. 20, 2016,

https://www.theguardian.com/world/2016/jan/20/isis-has-destroyed-iraqs-
oldest-christian-monastery-satellite-images-confirm

*Islamic State Crisis: Iraqi Army Drives IS From Key Town*, BBC.COM, Mar. 7, 2015,
https://www.bbc.com/news/world-middle-east-31773357

*Islamic State: Key Iraqi Town Near US Training Base Falls to Jihadists*, BBC.COM,
Feb. 14, 2015,

https://www.bbc.com/news/world-middle-east-31449976

James Verini, *Surviving the Fall of ISIS: As Iraqi and Coalition Forces Invade Mosul, the Last ISIS Stronghold in Iraq, the Grim Details of the Extremist Group's
Rule Come to Light*, NATIONAL GEOGRAPHIC, Oct. 16, 2016,

https://news.nationalgeographic.com/2016/10/islamic-state-isis-iraq-mosul-
syria-offensive/

Jane Corbin, Could Christianity Be Driven From Middle East? BBC, April 15, 2015,
https://www.bbc.com/news/world-middle-east-32287806

Jason Burke, Rise and Fall of Isis: Its Dream of a Caliphate is Over, So What Now?
THE GUARDIAN, Oct. 21, 2017,

https://www.theguardian.com/world/2017/oct/21/isis-caliphate-islamic-state-
raqqa-iraq-islamistTheguardian

John Bingham, *ISIL/DAESH Attacks on Christians and Yazidis 'Genocide' Say
Peers*, THE TELEGRAPH, Feb. 23, 2016,

https://www.telegraph.co.uk/news/religion/12169130/ISIL/DAESH-attacks-
on-Christians-and-Yazidis-genocide-say-peers.html

John Hudson, *Obama Administration Declares Islamic State Genocide Against
Christians*, FOREIGN POLICY, Mar. 17, 2016,

https://foreignpolicy.com/2016/03/17/obama-administration-declares-islamic-
state-genocide-against-christians/

Life after ISIS: New challenges to Christianity in Iraq. Results from ACN's survey
of Christians in the liberated Nineveh Plains, AID TO THE CHURCH IN
NEED – ACN INTERNATIONAL, June 2020,

https://www.churchinneed.org/wp-content/uploads/2020/07/Report-on-Chris
tianity-in-northern-Iraq.pdf

Loulla-Mae Eleftheriou-Smith, *British 'Vicar of Baghdad' Claims Isis Beheaded Four Children For Refusing to Convert to Islam,* THE INDEPENDENT, Dec. 8, 2014,

https://www.independent.co.uk/news/world/middle-east/british-vicar-of-baghdad-claims-isis-beheaded-four-children-for-refusing-to-convert-to-islam-9911072.html

Mark Green, *Help Is On the Way for Middle Eastern Christians: Under President Trump's Orders, USAID is Directing Aid to Persecuted Communities in Iraq,* THE WALL STREET JOURNAL, June 13, 2018,

https://www.wsj.com/articles/help-is-on-the-way-for-middle-eastern-christians-1528931329

Martin Reardon, *The Real Threat of Foreign Fighters in Syria,* AL JAZEERA, Dec. 13, 2015,

https://www.aljazeera.com/indepth/opinion/2015/12/real-threat-foreign-fighters-syria-151213100618715.html

Michelle Nichols, *Iraq Tells United Nations That Islamic State Committed Genocide,* REUTERS, Feb. 17, 2015,

https://www.reuters.com/article/us-mideast-crisis-iraq-un-idUSKBN0LL1O020150217

Moni Basu, *Being Christian in Iraq after ISIS: In Biblical Lands of Iraq, Christianity in Peril After ISIS,* CNN, Nov. 21, 2016,

https://edition.cnn.com/2016/11/20/middleeast/iraq-christianity-peril/index.html

Jim Muir, 'Islamic State': Raqqa's Loss Seals Rapid Rise and Fall, BBC NEWS, Oct. 17, 2017, https://www.bbc.com/news/world-middle-east-35695648

Nick Gutteridge, ISIS Barbarity: How 100,000 Christians Fled Mosul In One Night, DAILY EXPRESS, Oct. 20, 2015,

https://www.express.co.uk/news/world/613149/ISIS-barbarity-100000-Christians-fled-Mosul-one-night

Nina Shea, *As We Work to Eradicate ISIS, Iraq's Christians, Yizidis Need Our Help Now More Than Ever,* FOX NEWS, Mar. 17, 2017,

https://www.foxnews.com/opinion/as-we-work-to-eradicate-isis-iraqs-christians-yizidis-need-our-help-now-more-than-ever

Nina Shea, *Falling For ISIS Propaganda About Christians,* THE HUDSON INSTITUTE, Jul. 21, 2016, https://www.hudson.org/research/12664-falling-for-isis-propaganda-about-christians

*No Way Home: Iraq's Minorities on the Verge of Disappearance,* CEASEFIRE CENTRE FOR CIVILIAN RIGHTS, Jul. 2016,

https://minorityrights.org/wp-content/uploads/2016/07/MRG_CFRep_Iraq_Aug16_UPD-2.pdf

Omar Al-Jawoshy & Tim Arango, *Iraqi Offensive to Retake Tikrit From ISIS Begins,* THE NEW YORK TIMES, Mar. 2, 2015,

https://www.nytimes.com/2015/03/03/world/middleeast/iraq-tikrit-isis.html

Patrick Wintour, *MPs Unanimously Declare Yazidis and Christians Victims of Isis Genocide: British Parliament Defies Government to Condemn Barbarity of Islamic State in Syria and Iraq,* THE GUARDIAN, April 20, 2016,

https://www.theguardian.com/politics/2016/apr/20/mps-unanimously-declare-yazidis-victims-of-isis-genocide

Perry Chiaramonte & Hollie McKay, Iraqi Christians Forced to Flee Homes Again After Skirmishes Between Kurds and Central Government, FOX NEWS, Oct. 24, 2017, https://www.foxnews.com/world/iraqi-christians-forced-to-flee-homes-again-after-skirmishes-between-kurds-and-central-government

Ranj Alaaldin, Victory in the Mosul Offensive Will Not Solve Iraq's Problems, THE GUARDIAN, Oct. 17, 2016,

https://www.theguardian.com/commentisfree/2016/oct/17/victory-isis-iraq-offensive-mosul

Richard Norton Taylor, *Up to 30,000 Foreign Fighters Have Hone to Syria and Iraq Since 2011,* THE GUARDIAN, Nov. 17, 2015,

https://www.theguardian.com/world/2015/nov/17/30000-foreign-fighters-syria--iraq-2014-terrorism-report

Robert A. Destro, Iraq's Christians And Us: Will time And Neglect Complete the Job That ISIS Began? FOX NEWS, Dec. 15, 2017,

https://www.foxnews.com/opinion/iraqs-christians-and-us-will-time-and-neglect-complete-the-job-that-isis-began

Russell Myers, ISIS Behead Four Children in Iraq After They Refuse to Convert to Islam, THE MIRROR, Dec. 8, 2017,

https://www.mirror.co.uk/news/world-news/isis-behead-four-children-iraq-4767241

*The Rise and Fall of ISIL/DAESH Explained,* ALJAZEERA.COM, June 20, 2017,
https://www.aljazeera.com/indepth/features/2017/06/rise-fall-ISIL/
DAESH-explained-170607085701484.html

*U.S. Decries ISIS 'Genocide' of Christians, Other Groups,* NBCNEWS.COM, August
15, 2017, https://www.nbcnews.com/news/us-news/u-s-decries-is
lamic-state-genocide-christians-other-groups-n792866

*What ISIS Really Wants,* THE ATLANTIC, March 2015,

https://www.theatlantic.com/magazine/archive/2015/03/what-isis-really-wa
nts/384980/

Willem Oosterveld & Theo Bloem, *The Rise and Fall of ISIS: From Evitability to
Inevitability,* THE HAGUE CENTRE FOR STRATEGIC STUDIES, Annual
Report 2016/2017,

https://hcss.nl/sites/default/files/files/reports/The%20Rise%20and%20Fall%
20of%20ISIS.pdf

Zack Beauchamp, *ISIS, a History: How the World's Worst Terror Group Came to
Be,* VOX, Nov. 19, 2015,

https://www.vox.com/2015/11/19/9760284/isis-history

Zvi Bar'el, *The Rise and Fall of ISIS: From Organization to State,* HAARETZ, Dec.
17, 2017,

https://www.haaretz.com/middle-east-news/isis/.premium.MAGAZINE-unin-
tended-alliances-boost-to-nationalism-and-toxic-legacy-the-rise-and-
fall-of-isis-1.5628624

# 9. US Documents – Chronological order

## 9.1. US Congress

H. Res. House Foreign Affairs Subcommittees on Africa, Global Health, Global
Human Rights and International Organizations and the Middle East and
North Africa. Testimony of Assistant Secretary Tom Malinowski (Sept. 10,
2014).

H.R.Con.Res. 75, 114th Cong. (Sept. 9, 2015).

H.R. 4017, 114th Cong. (Nov. 16, 2015).

S. 2377, 114th Cong. (Dec. 9, 2015).

H.R.Con.Res. 75, 114th Cong. (Mar. 15, 2016).

H.R.Con.Res. 41, 114th Cong. (July 18, 2016).

165 Cong. Rec. X 1.1/A: X/A (daily ed. Jan. 10, 2017) (statement of Rep. Christopher H. Smith).

163 Cong. Rec. H4632 (daily ed. June 6, 2017) (statement of Rep. Edward Royce).

163 Cong. Rec. H5368 (daily ed. June 29, 2017) (statement of Rep. Ted Poe).

163 Cong. Rec. E1315 (daily ed. Oct. 3, 2017) (statement of Rep. Christopher H. Smith).

H.R. 407, 115th Cong. (Dec. 12, 2017).

H. Res. 1117, 115th Cong. (Oct. 5, 2018).

164 Cong. Rec. S6876 (daily ed. Oct. 11, 2018) (statement of Rep. Mitch McConnell).

164 Cong. Rec. H9600 (daily ed. Nov. 27, 2018) (statement of Rep. Christopher H. Smith).

H.R. 390, 115th Cong. (Nov. 29, 2018).

164 Cong. Rec. E1606 – H.R. 390 (daily ed. Dec. 6, 2018) (statement of Rep. Anna G. Eshoo).

165 Cong. Rec. H349 (daily ed. Jan. 9, 2019) (statement of Rep. Jeff Fortenberry).

165 Cong. Rec. H2350 (daily ed. Mar. 5, 2019) (statement of Rep. Jeff Fortenberry).

H. Res. 259, 116th Cong. (Mar. 27, 2019).

## 9.2. U.S. Federal Government, the White house & the Department of State

U.S. Dep't of State, Bureau of Democracy, H.R. and Lab., International Religious Freedom Report (2016).

U.S. Dep't of State, Bureau of Democracy, H.R. and Lab., International Religious Freedom Report, Executive Summary, Iraq (2016).

U.S. Dep't of State, Office of the Legal Adviser, Digest of the United States Practice in International Law (2016).

The White House, Office of the Press Secretary, Press Briefing by Press Secretary Josh Earnest (Feb. 4, 2016).

U.S. Dep't of State, Department Press, Remarks by Secretary of State John Kerry (Mar. 17, 2016).

U.S. Commission on Security and Cooperation in Europe, the U.S. Helsinki Commission, Hearing, Atrocities in Iraq and Syria: Relief for Survivors and Accountability for Perpetrators (Sept. 22, 2016).

U.S. Dep't of State, Bureau of Democracy, H.R. and Lab., International Religious Freedom Report (2017).

U.S. Dep't of State, Bureau of Democracy, H.R. and Lab., International Religious Freedom Report, Executive Summary, Iraq (2017).

U.S. Dep't of State, Office of the Legal Adviser, Digest of the United States Practice in International Law (2017).

U.S. Dep't of State, Office of the Spokesperson, Department Press, Briefing by Mark C. Toner (Mar. 16, 2017).

U. S. Dep't of State, Bureau of Democracy, H.R. and Lab., Country Reports on Human Rights Practices: Iraq, 2016 (*errata,* Mar. 29, 2017).

U.S. Dep't of State, Department Press, Remarks by Special Presidential Envoy for the Global Coalition to Defeat ISIS Brett McGurk (June 22, 2017).

U. S. Dep't of State, Bureau of Counterterrorism, Country Reports on Terrorism 2016 (Jul. 2017).

U.S. Dep't of State, Department Press, Remarks by Special Presidential Envoy for the Global Coalition to Defeat ISIS Brett McGurk (July 8, 2017).

U.S. Dep't of State, Office of the Spokesperson, Department Press, Briefing by Heather Nauert (Jul. 11, 2017).

U.S. Dep't of State, Department Press, Remarks by Special Presidential Envoy for the Global Coalition to Defeat ISIS Brett McGurk (July 13, 2017).

U.S. Dep't of State, Office of the Spokesperson, Department Press, Briefing by Heather Nauert (Aug. 3, 2017).

U.S. Dep't of State, Office of the Spokesperson, Department Press, Briefing by Heather Nauert (Aug. 15, 2017).

U.S. Permanent Representative to the United Nations, Ambassador Nikki Haley, Explanation of Vote Following the Adoption of UN Security Council Resolution 2379 on Accountability for ISIS Atrocities (Sept. 21, 2017).

U.S. Dep't of State, Office of the Spokesperson, Department Press, Briefing by Heather Nauert (Oct. 24, 2017).

U.S. Dep't of State, Office of the Spokesperson, Department Press, Briefing by Heather Nauert (Oct. 26, 2017).

U.S. Dep't of State, Department Press, Special Briefing by Special Presidential Envoy for the Global Coalition to Defeat ISIS Brett McGurk (Dec. 21, 2017).

U.S. Dep't of State, Bureau of Democracy, H.R. and Lab., International Religious Freedom Report (2018).

U.S. Dep't of State, Bureau of Democracy, H.R. and Lab., International Religious Freedom Report, Executive Summary, Iraq (2018).

U. S. Department of State, Bureau of Democracy, H.R. and Lab., Country Reports on Human Rights Practices: Iraq, 2017 (Apr. 20, 2018).

U.S. Dep't of State, Department Press, Remarks by Special Presidential Envoy for the Global Coalition to Defeat ISIS Brett McGurk (June 26, 2018).

U.S. Dep't of State, Office of the Spokesperson, Department Press, Readout of USAID Administrator Green and Ambassador-at-Large for International Religious Freedom Samuel Brownback's Trip to Northern Iraq (July 5, 2018).

The White House, Report of the President of the USA Donald J. Trump, National Strategy for Countering Weapons of Mass Destruction (Dec. 2018).

U.S. Dep't of State, Bureau of Counterterrorism, Country Reports on Terrorism (2019).

## 10. Council of Europe and European Parliament

Eur. Parl., Situation in Iraq, Resolution, P8_TA(2014)0011 (Jul. 17, 2014).

Eur. Parl., Situation in Iraq and Syria and the IS Offensive Including the Persecution of Minorities, Resolution, P8_TA(2014)0027 (Sept. 18, 2014).

Eur. Parl., Iraq: Kidnapping and Mistreatment of Women, Resolution, P8_TA(2014)0066 (Nov. 27, 2014).

Eur. Parl., Humanitarian Crisis in Iraq and Syria, in Particular in the IS Context, Resolution, P8_TA(2015)0040 (Feb. 12, 2015).

Eur. Parl., Recent Attacks and Abductions by ISIS/Da'esh in the Middle East, Notably of Assyrians, Resolution, P8_TA(2015)0071 (Mar. 12, 2015).

Eur. Parl., Foreign fighters in Syria and Iraq, Resolution 2091 (2016).

Eur. Parl., Plenary sitting. Joint Motion for a Resolution Pursuant to Rule 123(2) and (4), of the Rules of Procedure. Systematic Mass Murder of Religious Minorities by The So-called ISIS/Daesh 2014-2019. (Feb. 3, 2016).

Eur. Parl., Systematic Mass Murder of Religious Minorities by The So-called 'ISIS/Daesh' (2016/2529(RSP)), Resolution (Feb. 4, 2016).

Eur. Parl., MEPs Call for Urgent Action to Protect Religious Minorities Against ISIS, Press Release (Feb. 4, 2016).

Eur. Parl., Systematic mass murder of religious minorities by ISIS, Resolution, P8_TA(2016)0051 (Feb. 4, 2016).

Eur. Parl., Situation in Northern Iraq/Mosul (TA(2016)0422), Resolution (Oct. 27, 2016).

Eur. Parl., Mass Graves in Iraq, Resolution, P8_TA(2016)0507 (Dec. 15, 2016).

Eur. Parl., Prosecuting and Punishing the Crimes Against Humanity or Even Possible Genocide Committed by Daesh, Resolution 2190 (2017).

Eur. Parl., EU priorities for the UN Human Rights Council Sessions in 2017 (2017/2598(RSP)), Resolution (Mar. 16, 2017).

Eur. Parl., Committee on Legal Affairs and Human Rights, Humanitarian Consequences of the Actions of the Terrorist Group Known as "Islamic State," Draft Resolution, Compendium of Amendments (Revised version), Doc. No. 13741 (Apr. 21, 2017).

Eur. Parl., Committee on Legal Affairs and Human Rights, Prosecuting and Punishing the Crimes Against Humanity or Even Possible Genocide Committed by Daesh, Report, Doc. No. 14402 (Sept. 22, 2017).

Eur. Parl., Committee on Legal Affairs and Human Rights, Threats Against Humanity Posed by the Terrorist Group Known as "IS": Violence Against Christians and Other Religious or Ethnic Communities, Compendium of Amendments (Final version), Doc. No. 13618 (Sept. 30, 2014).

Eur. Parl., Committee on Legal Affairs and Human Rights, Prosecuting and Punishing the Crimes Against Humanity or Even Possible Genocide Committed by Daesh, Compendium of Amendments, Doc. No. 14402 (Oct. 11, 2017).

Eur. Parl., Committee on Legal Affairs and Human Rights, Prosecuting and Punishing the Crimes Against Humanity or Even Possible Genocide Committed by Daesh, Text adopted by the Assembly on the 34th Sitting, Doc. No. 14402 (Oct. 12, 2017).

Eur. Parl., Annual Report on Human Rights and Democracy in the World 2016 and the European Union's Policy on the Matter (2017/2122(INI)), Resolution (Dec. 13, 2017).

Eur. Parl., Committee on Legal Affairs and Human Rights, Report, Funding of the Terrorist Group Daesh: Lessons Learned, Doc. No. 14510 (Mar. 12, 2018).

Eur. Parl., Committee of Ministers, Prosecuting Daesh Fighters for Genocide, Reply to Written Question No. 729, Doc. No. 14885 (May 3, 2019).

## 11. Reports from international non-governmental organizations – Alphabetic order

Caliphate in Decline: An Estimate of Islamic State's Financial Fortunes, THE INTERNATIONAL CENTRE FOR THE STUDY OF RADICALISATION (ICSR) (Feb. 17, 2018), https://icsr.info/wp-content/uploads/2017/02/ICSR-Report-Caliphate-in-Decline-An-Estimate-of-Islamic-States-Financial-Fortunes.pdf

Children and Transitional Justice: Truth-Telling, Accountability and Reconciliation, HUMAN RIGHTS PROGRAM AT HARVARD LAW SCHOOL, Sharanjeet

Parmar, Mindy Jane Roseman, Saudamini Siegrist & Teo Sowa Eds. (March 2010), http://www.hup.harvard.edu/catalog.php?isbn=9780979639548

Christians and ISIS in Iraq, SHLOMO ORGANIZATION FOR DOCUMENTATION, Gregory Stanton, Elisa Yuden von Furkin, Irina Victoria Massimino & Jan Vermon (2017), https://indefenseofchristians.org/wp-content/uploads/2018/05/Shlomo-Report-on-Christians-in-Iraq.pdf

Flawed Justice Report: Accountability for ISIS Crimes in Iraq, HUMAN RIGHTS WATCH (December 2017), https://www.hrw.org/report/2017/12/05/flawed-justice/accountability-isis-crimes-iraq

Genocide Against Christians in the Middle East: A Report Submitted to Secretary of State John Kerry by the Knights of Columbus and in Defense of Christians, KNIGHTS OF COLUMBUS, Observatory on intolerance and discrimination against Christians, Mar. 9, 2016),

https://www.intoleranceagainstchristians.eu/fileadmin/user_upload/reports/Genocide-report.pdf

Iraq: Barwana Massacre – Botched Investigation, Families Waiting for Justice, AMNESTY INTERNATIONAL (June 10, 2015), https://www.amnesty.org/en/documents/mde14/1812/2015/en/

Iraq: ISIS Abducting, Killing, Expelling Minorities. Armed Group Targeting Christian Nuns, Turkmen, Shabaks, Yazidis, HUMAN RIGHTS WATCH (Jul. 19, 2014), https://www.hrw.org/news/2014/07/19/iraq-isis-abducting-killing-expelling-minorities

ISIS is Committing Genocide, GENOCIDE WATCH (Oct. 14, 2015),

http://genocidewatch.net/2015/10/15/isis-is-committing-genocide-2/

The Condemned: Woman and Children Isolated, Trapped and Exploited in Iraq, AMNESTY INTERNATIONAL (Apr. 17, 2018). https://www.amnesty.org/en/documents/mde14/8196/2018/en/

"Our Generation is Gone": The Islamic State's Targeting of Iraqi Minorities in Ninewa. Bearing Witness Trip Report, Naomi Kikoler, UNITED STATES HOLOCAUST MEMORIAL MUSEUM (2015), https://www.ushmm.org/m/pdfs/Iraq-Bearing-Witness-Report-111215.pdf

Punished for Daesh's crimes: Displaced Iraqis Abused by Militias and Government Forces, AMNESTY INTERNATIONAL (Oct. 18, 2016), https://www.amnesty.org/en/documents/mde14/4962/2016/en/

Supplement to the International Protocol on the Documentation and Investigation of Sexual Violence in Conflict, Iraq: Guidance for Practitioners in Iraq, INSTITUTE FOR INTERNATIONAL CRIMINAL INVESTIGATIONS (IICI) (March 2018). https://iici.global/0.5.1/wp-content/uploads/2018/03/Iraq-IP2-Supplement_English_Online.pdf

The legal foundations of the Islamic State, THE BROOKINGS INSTITUTION, The Brookings Project on U.S. Relations with the Islamic World. Mara Revkin (July 2016). https://www.brookings.edu/wp-content/up loads/2016/07/Brookings-Analysis-Paper_Mara-Revkin_Web.pdf

The children of Islamic State, QUILLIAM INTERNATIONAL, Noman Benotman, Nikita Malik (March 2016), https://www.quilliaminternational.com/ shop/e-publications/the-children-of-islamic-state/

The ISIS Genocide of Middle Eastern Christian Minorities and Its *Jizya* Propaganda Ploy, THE HUDSON INSTITUTE, Center for Religious Freedom, Nina Shea (August 2016), http://www.aina.org/reports/ igmecmajpp.pdf

## 12. Documents from Governments – Chronological order

UK Parliament, Genocide in Syria and Iraq, Early Day Motion, Sponsored by Robert Flello (Jan. 26, 2016).

Huma Haider, The Persecution of Christians in the Middle East. University of Birmingham. London: Assets Publishing Service – UK Government. February 16, 2017.

Claire Mills, ISIS/Daesh: the military response in Iraq and Syria, HOUSE OF COMMONS PUBLISHING HOUSE, Mar. 8, 2017.

Permanent Mission of France to the United Nations, "The Fight Against Impunity for Atrocities: Bringing Daesh to Justice," Remarks by François Delattre, (Mar. 9, 2017).

France Ministry for Europe and Foreign Affairs, "Has Daesh been defeated?", France Diplomacy (Nov. 2019).

## 13. Documents from NATO – Chronological order

North Atlantic Treaty Organization (NATO) – NATO Public Diplomacy Division, "NATO Encyclopedia 2015" (Dec. 2015).

https://www.nato.int/nato_static_fl2014/assets/pdf/pdf_publications/201604 14_2015-nato-encyclopedia-eng.pdf

North Atlantic Treaty Organization (NATO) – The NATO Strategic Communications Centre of Excellence (NATO StratCom COE), "DAESH Information Campaign and its influence: Results of the Study" (Jan. 2016).

https://www.difesa.it/SMD_/CASD/IM/IASD/65sessioneordinaria/Documents/ DaeshInformationCampaignanditsInfluence.pdf

North Atlantic Treaty Organization (NATO) – NATO Public Diplomacy Division, "NATO Encyclopedia 2019" (Dec. 2019).

https://www.nato.int/nato_static_fl2014/assets/pdf/2020/1/pdf/2019-nato-encyclopedia-eng.pdf

North Atlantic Treaty Organization (NATO) – NATO Public Diplomacy Division, NATO Mission Iraq (NMI), "December 2019: Factsheet" (Dec. 2019).

https://www.nato.int/nato_static_fl2014/assets/pdf/pdf_2019_12/20191203_191203-factsheet-NMI-en.pdf

North Atlantic Treaty Organization (NATO) – NATO Public Diplomacy Division, The NATO Mission Iraq,

"Relations with Iraq: Factsheet" (Feb. 14, 2020).

https://www.nato.int/cps/en/natohq/topics_88247.htm

North Atlantic Treaty Organization (NATO) – NATO Public Diplomacy Division, "The NATO Mission Iraq" (Feb. 17, 2020).

https://www.nato.int/cps/en/natohq/topics_166936.htm

## 14. Other documents – Chronological order

Attorney General of the Government of Israel v. Adolph Eichmann, District Court of Jerusalem, Israel, Criminal Case No. 40/61, judgement (Dec. 12, 1961), The International Crimes Database, Asser Institute.

http://www.internationalcrimesdatabase.org/Case/192/Eichmann/

Organization of American States, Inter-American Convention on Forced Disappearance of Persons, June 9, 1994, 33 I.L.M. 1429.

Dabiq, Issue 1, Ramadan 1435 (July 2014), CLARION PROJECT,

https://clarionproject.org/docs/isis-ISIL/DAESH-islamic-state-magazine-Issue-1-the-return-of-khilafah.pdf

Dabiq, Issue 2, Ramadan 1435 (July 2014), CLARION PROJECT,

https://clarionproject.org/docs/isis-ISIL/DAESH-islamic-state-magazine-Issue-2-the-flood.pdf

Dabiq, Issue 3, Shawwal 1435 (July/August 2014), CLARION PROJECT,

https://clarionproject.org/docs/isis-ISIL/DAESH-islamic-state-magazine-Issue-3-the-call-to-hijrah.pdf

Dabiq, Issue 4, Dhul-Hijah 1435 (September 2014), CLARION PROJECT,

https://clarionproject.org/docs/islamic-state-isis-magazine-Issue-4-the-failed-crusade.pdf

Dabiq, Issue 5, Muharram 1436 (October 2014), CLARION PROJECT, https://clarionproject.org/docs/isis-ISIL/DAESH-islamic-state-magazine-issue-5-remaining-and-expanding.pdf

Dabiq, Issue 6, Rabi'Al-Awwal 1436 (December, 2014), CLARION PROJECT,

https://clarionproject.org/docs/isis-ISIL/DAESH-islamic-state-magazine-issue-6-al-qaeda-of-waziristan.pdf

Dabiq, Issue 7, Rabi 'Al Akhir 1436 (February, 2015), CLARION PROJECT,

https://clarionproject.org/docs/islamic-state-dabiq-magazine-issue-7-from-hypocrisy-to-apostasy.pdf

Dabiq, Issue 8, Jumada Al-Akhirah 1436 (March, 2015), CLARION PROJECT,

https://clarionproject.org/docs/isis-ISIL/DAESH-islamic-state-magazine-issue+8-sharia-alone-will-rule-africa.pdf

Dabiq, Issue 9, Sha'ban 1436 (May, 2015), CLARION PROJECT,

https://clarionproject.org/docs/isis-ISIL/DAESH-islamic-state-magazine-issue+9-they-plot-and-allah-plots-sex-slavery.pdf

Dabiq, Issue 10, Ramadan 1436 (July, 2015), CLARION PROJECT,

http://clarionproject.org/wp-content/uploads/Issue%2010%20-%20The%20Laws%20of%20Allah%20or%20the%20Laws%20of%20Men.pdf

Dabiq, Issue 11, Dhul-Qa'dah 1436 (September, 2015), CLARION PROJECT, http://clarionproject.org/wp-content/uploads/Issue%2011%20-%20From%20the%20battle%20of%20Al-Ahzab%20to%20the%20war%20of%20coalitions.pdf

Dabiq, Issue 12, Safar 1437 (November, 2015), CLARION PROJECT,

http://clarionproject.org/wp-content/uploads/islamic-state-isis-ISIL/DAESH-dabiq-magazine-issue-12-just-terror.pdf

Dabiq, Issue 13, Rabi' Al-Akhir 1437 (January, 2016), CLARION PROJECT,

http://clarionproject.org/wp-content/uploads/Issue-13-the-rafidah.pdf

Dabiq, Issue 14, Rajab 1437 (April, 2016), CLARION PROJECT,

http://clarionproject.org/wp-content/uploads/Dabiq-Issue-14.pdf

Rumiyah, Issue 1, Dhul Hijah 1437 (September 2016), CLARION PROJECT,

http://clarionproject.org/wp-content/uploads/Rumiyah-ISIS-Magazine-1st-issue.pdf

Rumiyah, Issue 2, Muharram 1438 (October 2016), CLARION PROJECT,

http://clarionproject.org/wp-content/uploads/Rumiyh-ISIS-Magazine-2nd-issue.pdf

Rumiyah, Issue 3, Safar 1438 (November 2016), CLARION PROJECT, http://clarionprojstg.wpengine.com/wp-content/uploads/2014/09/Rumiyah-ISIS-Magazine-3rd-issue.pdf

Rumiyah, Issue 4, Rabi' al-Awwal 1438 (December 2016), CLARION PROJECT, http://clarionprojstg.wpengine.com/wp-content/uploads/2014/09/Rumiyah-ISIS-Magazine-4th-issue.pdf

Rumiyah, Issue 5, Rabi' al-Akhir 1438 (January 2017), CLARION PROJECT, http://clarionprojstg.wpengine.com/wp-content/uploads/2014/09/Rumiyah-ISIS-Magazine-5th-issue.pdf

Rumiyah, Issue 6, Jumada al-Ula 1438 (February 2017), CLARION PROJECT, http://clarionprojstg.wpengine.com/wp-content/uploads/2014/09/Rumiyah-ISIS-Magazine-6th-issue.pdf

Rumiyah, Issue 7, Jumada al-Akhirah 1438 (March 2017), CLARION PROJECT, http://clarionprojstg.wpengine.com/wp-content/uploads/2014/09/Rumiyah-issue-seven.pdf

Rumiyah, Issue 8, Rajab 1438 (April 2017), CLARION PROJECT, https://qb5cc3pam3y2ad0tm1zxuhho-wpengine.netdna-ssl.com/wp-content/uploads/2017/05/rome-magazine-8.pdf

Rumiyah, Issue 9, Sha'ban 1438 (May 2017), CLARION PROJECT, https://qb5cc3pam3y2ad0tm1zxuhho-wpengine.netdna-ssl.com/wp-content/uploads/2017/05/Rumiyah-9.pdf

Rumiyah, Issue 10, Ramadan 1438 (June 2017), CLARION PROJECT, CLARION PROJECT, https://qb5cc3pam3y2ad0tm1zxuhho-wpengine.netdna-ssl.com/wp-content/uploads/2017/08/Rumiyah-ISIS-magazine-10-issue.pdf